JEAN RENOIR:

Essays, Conversations,
Reviews

by

PENELOPE GILLIATT

McGraw-Hill Book Company
New York • St. Louis • San Francisco • Düsseldorf • Mexico • Montreal •
Panama • São Paulo • Toronto • New Delhi • Kuala Lumpur • London •
Rio de Janeiro • Sydney • Singapore • Johannesburg

Library of Congress Catalog Card Number:

75-6905

First McGraw-Hill Paperback Edition, 1975

0-07-023224-5

1 2 3 4 5 6 7 8 9 MU MU 7 9 8 7 6 5

Some of this material has been published in different form
in the *New Yorker* and *The Observer* (London)
and is reprinted here with their courteous permission.
"Le Meneur de Jeu" reprinted from *The New Yorker* and
Unholy Fools copyright © 1969, 1973, by Penelope Gilliatt.
All rights reserved. Reprinted by permission of *The New Yorker* and The
Viking Press, Inc.

Book design: *Hiag Akmakjian*
Cover design: *Robert L. Mitchell*

For Jean Renoir and Nolan

CONTENTS

*Le Grand Monsieur de
Deux Guerres,
Libéré par Lui-même*

JEAN RENOIR WAS BORN on September 15, 1894, in Paris. He was brought up there and at the old Renoir home, Les Colettes, in Cagnes, Provence. The great filmmaker has made and largely written 44 pictures, besides acting, doing an opera libretto, writing plays and a novel (*Les Cahiers du Capitaine Georges*), a biography of his father (*Renoir, My Father*) and a typically simple late biography of himself (*My Life and My Films*).

The genius of this most dear man, who takes part in the world with the wisdom, sense, and humor that reigns in his films, lies perhaps in his gift of intense concentration. His power of focus on the topic at hand is total. Of hobbies, for instance, he once said to me in Paris, "They are very charming, but if you are at work they are like physical training or gardening or brushing the teeth. One does the merest necessary when one is working, don't you think? If I worry about two things together I die in a week." On the other hand, there is the very opposite of ferocity in his absorption. He adores any arrangement of life, work, talk, sociability that has a just sense of balance. He said, again in Paris, "I spend my time reestablishing balance in a film but I have never had the idea that it should be established simply by means of elements in the plot. One can do it with an object on a table, with a color if it is a color film, with a sentence which means nothing at all but which has less weight or more weight than the sentence before it."

Renoir's friendship and conviviality first came into my life through revivals of his early films and premières of his later ones that I saw in London as a child, and then when I began to go often to the Paris Cinémathèque and to the National Film Theatre by the Thames to write about them: always, I hope, in his sense of an "amateur" (Renoir sheers away from "professionalism" as he defines it). His presence, which cheers any day even now that he is ill in Los Angeles and unable to travel, was something that I first encountered when I was in Paris and writing a profile of him for *The New Yorker*. This book is by no means a comprehensive book about his films, although I have seen them many times. Nor is it distantly analytic: his work forbids distance, since it invites you into his company, like great music or Chekhov. His work is eloquent enough to talk for itself, and so is he. I hoped more to transcribe some of the taste and purity of his conversation, and the mood and technique of the movies that I particularly love. As to the lack of analysis proper, I can only think of something Renoir once said to me on the subject, with his usual absence of asperity: "There is a certain type of person who wonders if it is the eggs on the muffin that make eggs Benedict."

What a man this is. What a span of work. Think of *La Chienne*, his first true sound movie after the tests he made in directing *On Purge Bébé*, with Michel Simon as a middleaged Sunday painter innocently in love with a whore and a bitch. Apart from its technical originality, which is still as striking and necessary as true originality always is, the news-clipping story is raised into something poetic, just as moments are in his much later *Le Déjeuner sur l'Herbe*, where a film that could be a mere satiric idyll of modernity becomes an idyll of the Freezer Age. Like his great father, he also has the Impressionists' love of the physical. When he photographs a pillow that has just had someone lying on it, the shot has the insight and beauty of a Bonnard painting of a girl in a bath.

Somebody once wisely said that it is very easy to make art of evil but very hard to make art of good and evil. Renoir does it. He sees everyone, good and bad, with a mixture of sweetness and irony that some wrong-headed people have called amoral. Renoir is not disingenuous. No one who has been such an innovator could be. The bans and butcherings of his two prescient anti-Fascist masterpieces—*La Grande Illusion* and *La Règle du Jeu*—prove that all too well. Perhaps his born pacifism and his loathing of all divisions between people make him seem misleadingly mild now to a few arid members of the politically engaged. But just before the Second World War, when he was making *La Grande Illusion*, the antiwar nature of the film and its affectionate respect for the German commandant played by Erich von Stroheim were strongly unpopular attitudes in France. Renoir said in 1938, in an interview in *The New York Times* of October 23, that Hitler "in no way modifies my opinion of the Germans." He described the film to me as a "reenacted documentary, like *La Règle du Jeu*," and went on to say, "They are documentaries on the condition of society at a given moment. I made *La Grande Illusion* because I was a pacifist, I suppose. And am. At the time, the usual idea of a pacifist was of a coward with long hair yelling from a soapbox and getting hysterical at the sight of a uniform. So I made a pacifist film that is full of admiration for uniforms and escapes. The idea came to me in the thirties when an old friend of mine, named Pinsard, turned up in command of some nearby airfield when I was shooting a scene—for another film—that was driving me mad. This old friend had saved my life in 1915. A German flew so near to us that I could see his impressive whiskers."

La Grande Illusion was being shown in Vienna the day the Nazis entered the city. It was stopped in mid-reel. The history gives Renoir a certain amount of satisfaction. "We had wanted to make the film for three years but no one would put up the money," he said. "French, Italian, American, British producers saw nothing in the project. They wanted a villain. They said the German to be played by von Stroheim was not sufficiently a villain. I said the villain was the war. 'The public won't understand that,' they said. Well, finally a group of businessmen risked forty thousand dollars, and at the end of the first year I believe the profit was ten times the investment. You know, years and years before that, in his *Foolish Wives*, von Stroheim pointed out something to me that I hadn't known at all. I saw that film twelve times. It changed things. Something very simple I hadn't known—only that a Frenchman who drinks red wine, and eats Brie, with Paris roofs in front of him, can't do anything worthwhile except by drawing on the tradition of people who have lived like him. After *Foolish Wives* I began to look. I mean, the movements of a woman washing her hair that we might see through this window, or of that man with the broom—I found that they were terrifically valuable plastically."

The prologue of *La Grande Illusion* happens in a bar near the French Front where Lieutenant Maréchal (Jean Gabin), a former mechanic, is asked to escort a smooth man with a monocle, called Captain de Boïeldieu (Pierre Fresnay), on a mission behind enemy lines. The plane is shot down by von Rauffenstein, played by von Stroheim, whom Hollywood had dismissed as a wild-eyed esthete. Like de Boïeldieu, he is an aristocrat and a career officer: he invites the two Frenchmen to luncheon. Their prison camp roommates include a schoolteacher, a surveyor, an actor guilty of terrible puns, and a garment maker called Rosenthal (the great, delicate-gestured Marcel Dalio). There is no sense of class here. Everyone is hellbent on digging the escape tunnel that has already been started. There is a talent show: the effort of the prisoners to evoke the women they miss by putting on women's clothing is pathetic, though never sentimental and often funny. It is typical of Renoir's sense of absurd, bitter, passing catastrophe that, just as the tunnel is finished, the prisoners are moved on and replaced by Englishmen who speak not a word of French and can therefore make no use of the tunnel.

With a series of quick dissolves showing repeated attempts to escape—no one is more succinct about narrative than Renoir is, just as no one spends more time on irresistible irrelevancies—we see that Maréchal and Boïeldieu are now being hauled off to a disciplinary camp in a castle-fortress for their pains. They are greeted cordially by their enemy: von Rauffenstein again, stiff-backed from chin to waist in a leather corset that has to be worn because of a war wound. He is delighted to remeet de Boïeldieu, though he regards Maréchal as a rather unfortunate product of the French Revolution. De Boïeldieu is alone in realizing that his noble class is doomed. Rosenthal, Maréchal, and de Boïeldieu plan yet another escape by a plaited length of cloth. The escape is to be covered up by de Boïeldieu tootling a French folk-song from the ramparts. Von Rauffenstein, stricken that he should have to do his duty by killing his ally in caste, shoots him in the stomach. Maréchal and Rosenthal, beginning to quarrel, sprint for Switzerland on foot, Rosenthal with a sprained ankle. They take refuge in a farm where Maréchal falls hopelessly in love with a German:

again, Renoir's view of frontiers. They have to leave,
though. Struggling on in the snow, they are spied by a
German soldier. He starts to shoot. "Forget it," says a com-
rade, "they're in Switzerland."

The film swiftly states Renoir's view of a man's life as a
state of being rather than an undertaking. It also perfectly
expresses his view of the nonsensicality of divisions between
people. No wonder Goebbels banned the film—remember
that it was made in 1937, obeying Renoir's unfailing, urgent
sense of malaise, a signal that he believes artists have to
follow even if it means being dangerously in the lead ("In
running faster than the others, the artist fulfils a function,"
he said to me)—and that the Nazi head of propaganda put
pressure on Mussolini to prevent its being given a prize at
the Venice Film Festival. Though the film is about the First
World War, the ideas in it were to be perilously appropriate
to the next. Wars, it says, are run for dictators and
ideologists safely at their desks, an idea Renoir was to repeat
in *Le Caporal Épinglé*. They will never be conducted in the
interests of the men who fight them. The flag here is a
remote symbol, and military honor is vapid; it is the fineness
of grain shared by an aristocratic Frenchman, an aristocratic
German, and a Jewish garment maker, not any empty idea
of courage or belief in boundaries, that unites the characters. Renoir was to suffer for his warning of the sickness
perturbing his contemporaries. The film was banned and
the negative seized by the Germans (it was found much later
by the Americans in Munich). A 1946 reissue was criticized
for being kind to the Germans and for anti-Semitism, which
is entirely to miss the spirit of this great tribute to tolerance.
Like Luther, Renoir says politically, "Here I stand." For
instance, he made *This Land Is Mine* during the war, in exile

in Hollywood, as a retort to the prevailing idea in America that the European resistance movement was a legend and that everyone in an occupied country was a collaborationist.

But, he said recently, "I believe now I see a state of benevolence, of well-wishing. If I am wrong, people can always laugh at me. I take that risk." About what he spoke of as "the Czech affair," with sorrow, when the Russian tanks had rolled in, he said, "It happened perhaps to save this wild world, the miniskirts, the crazy singing in London, the marijuana. I am trying to understand the Russians and what is behind them in spite of themselves." His habit is to take in the whole spectacle of paraphernalia and then to sort out the essentials, just as he does in a minor way when he is working on a set. He said, "I leave the propman to do what he wants, but I ask him to do too much and then I take out almost everything. I find it handy to have the choice. To crowd the set and then to empty it." Everything interests him. In Paris, watching a newsreel with me once, he was touched and tenderly amused by a sequence showing the back view of a plump Olympic girl solemnly running with a torch. "I am against great themes and great subjects," said this maker of two of the world's greatest films. "To me, a theme is exactly like a landscape for a painter. It is just an excuse. You can't film an idea. The camera is an instrument for recording physical impact." The impact, for him, can lie in very small details. In *La Chienne*, it lies in a small girl practicing her piano on the far side of one of his favorite courtyards, in the sound of a couple quarrelling somewhere, in the burble of a lady talking. The impact is one of great weight, for the observation is dense and exact. "I had a good friend who owned a theater in Biarritz," he told me. "A very interesting man. A Russian who had been a sailor in the Turkish navy. He could put a coin somewhere, swing a blacksmith's hammer and stop exactly half an inch from the coin. With such a man you can be confident." The words might have been said to commemorate the confidence one feels about Renoir himself, just as *La Grande Illusion* is an unwitting tribute to the nobility of his own heart.

LONDON, NEW YORK, 1974

Le Meneur de Jeu

"LOOK AT THIS," SAID JEAN RENOIR in his Paris apartment, bending over an art book. "It is the Annunciation to the Virgin Mary, and the angel is just shaking hands. It is an interesting way to tell someone she is pregnant." He had been speaking French, but now he switched to English and repeated the last sentence, with characteristic absorption, substituting for "interesting" the word "funny," which he pronounces "fonny." The ideas of what is comic and what is interesting truly overlap for him. He looked out of the window and said that the roofs of Paris houses go at angles that always remind him of theater wings. A child was playing somewhere below in this offstage life, and a wife was shouting while her husband strolled away from her, pulling on his cap at a nonlistening slant and then putting his hands in his pockets. "The first films I made were very rotten," Renoir said. "Then I started to make a sort of study of French gesture, and maybe they improved, with the help of my accomplices." The sight of his own gestures as he was talking made me remember one of those fugitive shots which can break through his films so piercingly—a shot in his 1939 picture *La Règle du Jeu* of the plump character played by Renoir himself, the fortunate, poignant stooge, who has just idly let loose the fact that he would have loved to be a conductor. In a shot late at night, on the terrace steps of a grand country house, he can be seen for a second from the back in an image of the clown sobered, conducting the

invisible house party inside to the beat of some imagined
musical triumph. His big shoulders droop like the withers of
a black pig rooting in the dark. Recently, after I had spent
some time with Renoir, it struck me that the character
perhaps embodies a little of the way he thinks of himself,
and that this great, great master of the cinema, who has an
amplitude of spirit beyond our thanks, actually sees himself
as a buffoon.

Renoir walks with a limp bequeathed by a wound from
the First World War. He has a blanched, large face, very
attentive, which turns pink as if he were in bracing air when
he is interested or having a good time. At the beginning of
the 1914 war, he was twenty. Nothing in our benighted
century seems to have undercut his sense that life is sweet.
He makes films full of feeling for picnics, cafés, rivers,
barges, friends, tramps, daily noises from the other side of a
courtyard. It is singular and moving that a man whose talent
imparts such idyllic congeniality should also have such a tart
and sophisticated understanding of caste. In his 1935 film
Le Crime de Monsieur Lange, for instance, the hero's world of
the badly off and hungrily gregarious is pitted against a boss
class of steely, swindling fops. The heroic Lange, who murders with our sympathy, is a young man who writes thrillers
in the time left over from a dull job in a printing plant.
Renoir's murderers are always strange to crime: an unhappy clerk, a down-at-heel, derided lover, a gamekeeper—people near the bottom of the heap who take desperate action because they have been driven beyond their
limits. The limits usually have to do with what a man will take
in punishment to his dignity and his seriousness about how
to live, and his gestures state everything. There is the essence of ache and hesitancy in Dalio's double turn, near the

end of *La Grande Illusion,* at the door of a woman who has sheltered him while he was on the run from a prisoner-of-war camp and whom he cannot quite declare his feelings for. Renoir's own way of standing reminded me sometimes of a shot of Michel Simon in *La Chienne,* his big head bent in watch over a murdered woman. The tonic passion and lightness of the dissolving shot would be recognizable as Renoir's in a thousand miles of film. So would a special kind of cheerful misrule that sometimes runs amok in a scene, like the time his tramp Boudu, in *Boudu Sauvé des Eaux,* lustily wrecks a room in the process of merely cleaning his boots, carousing around the world with an abstracted serenity in the midst of riot.

When Renoir is in France—he spends a lot of time in America, at a house he and his wife, Dido, have in Beverly Hills—he lives in an apartment close to the Place Pigalle, in a *rue privée* with a black iron gate that is guarded, not very vigilantly, by a caretaker. The little curved street inside is lined with plane trees, and moss grows through cracks in the pavement. There are elegant iron lampstands, and gray shutters on the beautiful, run-down old houses. His apartment is on the second floor of a house with ivy spilling over the front door. The stairwell is painted in a peeling burnt sienna with a turquoise design. It is all very dilapidated and very nice. "I think it's better when things aren't brand-new," Renoir said. "It's less tiring for the eyes." He sometimes speaks of the apartment as if it were an obstreperous old friend with long-familiar attributes, many of them a bit grating but all indispensable. "I like the proportions," he said one day, looking around at the place. "It's not entirely convenient. When it rains, it rains in here." He showed me drip trails at various points, accusingly. "But I like the proportions. If you want to make me happy, you should feel absolutely at home."

In the drawing room, where he works, there is an old-fashioned telephone, paintings by child relatives, comfortable armchairs with springs gone haywire, ancient white-and-gray plasterwork on the walls, records of Mozart and Vivaldi and Offenbach. During the days we spent together talking, Renoir usually wore a tweed jacket and old leather moccasins—with a tweed cap when we went out—and he always had a pen clipped in his jacket pocket. We seemed to spend a lot of time in the kitchen. It has two tall windows, and between them a splendid freehand drawing in brown paint of a window with curtains looped back and a bowl on the sill. He did it himself. He said, "A mirror fell down and broke, and it left a patch, so I put up that piece of paper." I said that it wasn't a piece of paper: that it was a drawing, and looked rather like a Matisse. This so embarrassed him that I had to say quickly, "Matisse on an off day, with a headache." The drawing made a third window to look through, so to speak, when we were having lunch opposite it every day at his scrubbed kitchen table. Renoir's doctor recently gave him a choice of whiskey or wine, and he chose wine. We drank rather a lot of it, and cooked gigot. I mentioned Céline at one point, and he lowered his head and looked pleased. "Greater than Camus," he said. "He was entirely hidden for twenty years. He was not the fashion." Renoir was genuinely unable to think it right that I should have come all the way from New York to see him, and in the end I had to put it as if I were using him as a way station on a journey to my house in England. "I rather hate airplanes," he said. "We should be able to part the Atlantic like the Red Sea and drive across it in a bus. I'm fond of buses." We swapped bus stories.

We caught ourselves in a mirror one day as we were coming into the apartment, talking mostly about actors, whom he distinguishes from stars as though a star were to be removed from the matter with a long-handled pair of tongs. He made a face at our reflections and said, "To be a star and play yourself all the time—a beautiful doll imitating yourself . . ." Ingratiation is one of the few flaws that really seem to scrape on his nerves. He picks up any hint of it fast. He once remarked to a filmmaker whom we both know that there is something that bothers him in Chaplin's films, which in general he admires. He called it "an anxiety to displease nobody." Though Renoir's own films seem expansively charitable, they are altogether uncompromising. "I believe in the Tower of Babel, I suppose," said Renoir. "Not in the story, exactly, but in the meaning. The tendency of human beings to come together. My first attempts at filmmaking probably didn't find this point. But one gets into practice. When things go badly on a film, I think I will go and raise dogs, and then the crisis blows over. At one moment I feel that a story is terrible and at the next that it's wonderful, and in rare flashes of lucidity I feel that it's neither good nor bad. And so, indeed, quite like everything else. I am very much in favor of intelligence, but when you are at work on a film or a story or a painting I think you have to go on instinct. In *La Règle du Jeu*, for instance, I knew only very roughly where I was going. I knew mostly the ailment of the time we were living in. That isn't to say that I had any notion of how to show evil in the film. But perhaps the pure terror of the danger around us gave me a compass. The compass of disquiet. You know, there is a sense in which artists have to be sorcerers twenty years ahead of their period. I don't mean that they are wiser than anyone else

—only that they have more time. And, well, though it is much harder for an artist to do this in the cinema, because the cinema insists on being an industry twenty years behind the public, it can sometimes be done."

He turned out to be thinking now of many young film-makers whom he admires, and to have left altogether the topics of his own pictures and of his own shocking and lifelong difficulties in raising money. At this moment, in 1968, he has virtually had to give up the prospect of making a movie from a very funny script, written by him, which Jeanne Moreau wants to play in. No financing can be found for it. The situation seems commercially unintelligent. It is also an offense, as if Mozart were to be deprived of music paper. A short while ago,'another script—a comedy about revolt, which Simone Signoret wanted to do—similarly fell through. In the meantime, Renoir remains not at all bilious and works on other things. He is writing his second novel —his first was called *Les Cahiers du Capitaine Georges*, and was published in 1966—and directing a series of sketches, also by him, for French and Italian television. He always declines to fuss. I had the impression that he doesn't like weightiness of any sort. In 1938, when he was abused by some people for making a film of *La Bête Humaine* that wasn't slavishly true to Zola, he stoutly said that he hadn't particularly wanted to serve Zola, he'd wanted to play trains. "You have to remain an amateur," he said to me one day about directing. "The big problem is not to stop at being a voyeur. Not to look on at people's predicaments as if you were a tourist on a balcony. You have to take part. With any luck, this saves you from being a professional. You know, there are a thousand ways of being a creator. One can grow apples or discover a planet. What makes it easier is that one isn't alone. One doesn't change or evolve alone. However great the distance between them, civilizations move a little toward one another. And the worlds we know, the directions to which interest bends us in our knowledge or our affection, incline to be one in the same way."

A French television unit came one day to direct Renoir in part of the shooting for a long program about him and his father, the painter Auguste Renoir. He needed a companion for a walking scene in Montmartre, and I was the obvious person, although I told him that the only acting I had ever done had been on account of having red hair.

"Lady Macbeth," he said.

"Yes," I said.

He told me what it had been like at school for him because he had had red hair, as his father painted him in the famous childhood portrait. "And who else did they make of you?" he asked, stroking his head unconsciously. "The Pre-Raphaelites?"

"Agave in *The Bacchae*," I said. "For the same reason."

The French sound man said politely, after a long time, that he was getting only a moan from me on his earphones, and could I talk more loudly.

"Her diction in English is excellent," said Renoir.

"Now a new setup," the TV director said, after another long time.

"Which side do you prefer?" Renoir asked me.

I said that the next part might go better from the other side, because of my nose. Renoir took me by the shoulders and had a look at me.

"A girl ran into me in a corridor at school and bent it," I said.

"It's true," he said, nicely, and put me on his other side, and we moved around a lamppost. He held my wrist, perhaps to help himself travel a slope, and then slipped his hand up to my elbow to support me through the prospect of having a seven-word line to say, while he improvized a monologue of incomparable invention and warmth.

Some time later, I asked him about an actor I liked very much in *Monsieur Lange*. Renoir beamed, and said something incidental about his own way of working. "I'm pleased you pick him out. He was excellent, exciting, subdued. However—not that it mattered—it happened that he couldn't remember his lines easily. So the thing was to give him a situation where he had to say what he had to say. Where he couldn't say anything else."

And the same day—"He is the most French director," said the actress Sylvia Bataille, who worked with him on the 1936 film *Une Partie de Campagne* and on *Monsieur Lange*. "The most cultured. He has a sense of history like no one else's. He was the precursor of everything in French cinema now. You know, when he is directing you, he has a trick. Well, not a trick, because that sounds like something deliberate. A way of doing it—a habit, the result of his nature. He will say, 'That's very good, but don't you think it's perhaps a bit boring to do the next take exactly the same way?' He will never say that the next take is to be totally different because in the first one you were terrible. I think the reason he is a great director is that he knows all there is to know of the resolves that people keep to themselves. He knows the human reaction to anything. I'm not very good, but he made me magnificent."

There exists an affectionate French documentary of Renoir directing some actors. He listens to them as if through a stethoscope. Then he may talk of other times, the times of "Monsieur" Shakespeare, "Monsieur" Molière—speaking without sarcasm. Again and again he says, *"Trop d'expression."* He tries to get a highly charged actress to speak "like a telephone operator." There is a big moment, and he tells her not to be sweet. *"Soyons pas mignons."* It is always "us." *"Soyons secs."*

"If actors look for feeling at the beginning of a reading, the chances are it will be a cliché," he said to me. "When they learn the lines alone or when we learn them together—the second being the better—in either case I beg them to read as if they were reading the telephone directory. What we do is to read a few lines that can help the actors to find the part. Pick a few lines that are symptomatic. Now, what happens then is that, in spite of himself, the actor begins to find a little sparkle, provided he forbids it. Whereas if you begin to play with feeling, it will always be a generality. For instance, suppose an actress playing a mother has to speak of 'my son' when he is dead. For most actresses, it is the devil's job for this not to be a cliché if they begin with the sadness of it. And if you start with an idea of how to say it, then it is very difficult to remove it. You should start with the lines quite bare. You see, even in our day everyone is different from her neighbor, or his. We must help an actress to find a 'my son' that will be hers and only hers."

This strong feeling that people are different is obviously part of Renoir's great gift for friendship. I said something about disbelieving and fearing the cool comfort that everyone is replaceable and no one indispensable. He said securely, *"Everyone* is indispensable." We talked about Brecht, whom he was very fond of. They had fun together, loping along the streets by the Seine with some friends, in a

gang. "He was a very modest man, you know," Renoir said.
"Well, perhaps he was, like many modest men, proud inside.
He was a child. It's not so easy to remain a child. And he was
also sarcastic, which people never understand. He was
romantic but also sharp, and sharp people are not well
understood. We had many adventures. We wanted to make
films. I remember once we went for money to Berlin, to the
king of German cinema. We suggested a subject. He said no.
He said, 'You don't belong to the movies.' You see, he was
right. On the way home, Brecht said, 'Look, Jean, don't let's
make movies. We should call what we want to do something
else. Let's call it *pilm*.'"

When we were back in Renoir's living room after the
television shooting, he said to me, "In directing, I don't
follow a script very closely. And I think it works best to
choose a camera angle only after the actors have rehearsed.
I suppose that between my way of working and the one of
following a script closely there is possibly the same difference as between Indian music and Western music since the
tempered scale. In Indian music, there is a general melody,
and this general melody is ancient and must be held to, and
then there is also a general note played on a particular
instrument, and this note is repeated all the time and keeps
the other instruments up to pitch. And so there is a melody
and a pitch, and the musicians are free to move around these
fixed points. I think it is a magnificent method, and I try to
imitate it with actors and filmmaking, up to a point."

We drifted into talking about Stanislavsky. Renoir said
that he had learned endlessly from Stanislavsky but that
Stanislavsky had "a big problem." He explained, "Often the
Moscow Arts Theatre had to speak in front of an audience
that didn't know Russian at all—or, if so, not good Russian.

It forced the company to make too many clear signals. To shout inner things, so to speak."

We sat in the drawing room on another day. "Excuse me," said Renoir. "My maid is here today and I want to know how she feels. She has a bad eye." He went out and stood talking with her, his head hanging down as he listened, like a fisherman's watching a river. She was insisting that she was all right and could work, making gestures with a dustpan: a short, alert woman, one eye covered with a patch of bright-pink sticking plaster. They stood there for a time, visible through two doorways and faintly audible, like people photographed in the unemphatic style of his films.

"She won't go home," said Renoir, coming back into the room. "She's very strong. She doesn't look it. She's built like a French soldier. Frederick the Great was amazed by how small we were. Just before a battle, he said, 'How can they fight?' " Renoir limped around and got some wine and said, "We lost, I believe." And then he sat down again and went on watching the woman for a while through the doorways. I looked at a photograph pinned up over his desk. It showed a cluster of men in cloth caps sitting on the ground and laughing. The scene looked rather like a factory picnic, but not quite. Renoir said that the picture was by his friend Henri Cartier-Bresson and that the men were convicts. "When their sentences were over, they didn't want to leave the labor camp, so they just stayed. They had their friends, et cetera, et cetera. And also, you see"—he spoke seriously—"I think they'd come to like the work."

We talked about a London prison where I had once lectured and shown *La Règle du Jeu*. He asked a lot of questions, often using the words "interesting" and "interested," which sprinkle his talk, like "et cetera." "I quite

enjoy lecturing when I'm doing it," he said. "Not so much
when it's over. Doing it is generally the only thing, isn't it?
One sees that even with banking, which God knows is a
stupid occupation. But when a banker is actually making the
money he thinks he needs to retire with, then he is happy,
and with luck the retirement never arrives. I suppose I really
believe work and life are one, as the Hindus do. When I'm
making a film, for instance, I don't know where the divisions
are in the job. When I'm writing, I'm cutting the film in my
head. And when I'm cutting I'm doing more of the screenplay. You understand, this isn't to say that there aren't terrible
days before we start, when nothing is possible." He paused,
then went on, "But Hollywood, because it has this genius for
departments, has found the perfect way to make pictures
that have no sense. A producer has a wonderful screenplay,
by wonderful authors—plural—and he puts wonderful actors in it, and then he hires a wonderful director, who says
'That's a little slow,' or 'Please be more warm.' And so—well,
it is most efficient, and what it reminds me of is a perfect
express train racing along perfect steel tracks without having any idea that one of its compartments contains a beautiful girl leaning against beautiful red plush with a most
interesting story to tell. A lot of people who are quite sincerely critical of Hollywood say that the trouble is that the
people there worship money, but I believe them to be wor-
shipping something much worse, and that is the ideal of
physical perfection. They double-check the sound, so that
you get perfect sound, which is good. Then they double-
check the lighting, so that you get perfect lighting, which is
also fairly good. But they also double-check the director's
idea, which is not so good. It brings us straight to another
god—or perhaps I should say devil—that is very dangerous

in the movies, and that is the fear that the public won't understand. This fear of 'I don't understand' is terrible. I don't see how you can ever understand something you love. You would not say that you understood a woman you love. You feel her and like her. It has to do with contact. Something many people ignore is that there is no such thing as interesting work without the contact of the public—the collaboration, perhaps. When you are listening to great music, what you are really doing is enjoying a good conversation with a great man, and this is bound to be fascinating. We watch a film to know the filmmaker. It's his company we're after, not his skill. And in the case of the physically perfect—the perfectly intelligible—the public has nothing to add and there is no collaboration. Now I am going to be very trite and say that it is easier to make a silent film than a talkie, because there is something missing. In the talkies, therefore, we have to reproduce this missing something in another way. We have to ask the actors not to be like an open book. To keep some inner feeling, some secret."

Renoir's feeling for ambiguity is powerful. He clings to doubt as if it were a raft. I told him about a playwright friend of mine called N. F. Simpson, the author of *One-Way Pendulum* and *A Resounding Tinkle*: wonderfully funny plays that some humorless drama expert in London once lammed into for having no form, though this is a great part of their funniness. After a particularly fierce battery, I remember Simpson—a schoolmaster, to boot, who could have run rings of logic around the drama expert if he had been moved to—sitting on the floor with his back against my hi-fi and saying, his long face no more melancholy than usual, that the man was perfectly right, that the plays had no shape at all. "It struck me at the time that I could have given them a shape," he said. "But it seemed like breaking faith with chaos."

"This question of perfection," said Renoir. "Bogus symmetry. It is one of the reasons modern objects are so ugly. Plates, dresses, colors. If you take the blue of faïence, the blue of delft, it is never absolutely pure, you see. There is nothing quite pure in nature. In the Army, with the cavalry, I learned that there are no white horses and no black horses. They always have a number of hairs that are another color. If the horses were plastic, that would be an unforgivable fault. My father used to talk about this idea. Not about plastic, of course. . . . He had, for example, a small piece of advice for young architects. He said to them that they might think of destroying their perfect tools and replacing the symmetry produced by their instruments with the symmetry produced by their own eye. When he was asked about a school for artists, he said he would like to see inns—inns with the temperament of English pubs—where people would be fed and where they would live and where nobody would teach them a single thing. He said that he didn't want the spirits of young artists to be tidied up. His talk was terribly interesting. Toward the end of his life he would think deeply, perhaps because he couldn't walk. I believe sitting in a wheelchair helped him to think as he did. Often I would suppose he was working, and then just find him sitting, and we would have a conversation much like the one I am having with you. A certain spectrum of life would interest him."

Renoir's cast of mind often seems very like his father's. "As the years went by, I found he was becoming rather a marble bust instead of a man," Renoir recalled. "I wanted to stop that. It was why I wrote a book about him, I think." He spoke about Auguste Renoir's attitude toward prowess, and it defined his own. He said that his father "didn't care for *tours de force*"—that "to his way of thinking, the beauty of, say, a weightlifter was at its greatest when the young man was lifting only something very light." The filmmaker son does that. The world he created in *La Règle du Jeu* spins on his forefinger. We talked about the biography. It is called *Renoir, My Father*, and he published it in 1958. I had the impression that he misses his father daily. We also talked about his books. "I like writing," he said. "Because it doesn't matter."

Another day, we went to see a film. The screenplay of the film—Truffaut's *Stolen Kisses*—he found "very interesting." He said, "It has no suspense. I hate the sanctity of suspense. It's left over from nineteenth-century romanticism. The film is to the point and comic. It is a sort of synopsis of the times, this humor. It is not so much something to laugh at as an attitude toward life that you can share. At least, in *this* film you are permitted to share it. So the film must be good, I think. I like it very much."

We walked out into the cool sun. Renoir inspected the streets and said, "It seems to me that the people of Paris are gayer than usual. Perhaps it's the weather? ["*Il a une telle correspondance avec la nature*," Sylvia Bataille had said a few days before.] Or perhaps it's still the effect of the events of May in 1968." He looked closely at everything, as if he were going to draw it from memory later.

The taxi we took had a postcard of a Picasso stuck in the dashboard: inevitably, in Renoir's company, it seemed. He instantly leaned forward and started to talk about it. The driver, who chatted with hair-raising responsiveness in the Paris traffic, turned out to be a spare-time painter. "Only to amuse myself, you understand," he said.

"Why not?" said Renoir. "Everything interesting is only to amuse yourself."

The driver, making the taxi lurch horribly, produced a magazine called *Science & Art*. We nearly hit something because he was finding a page to show Renoir and then stabbing a forefinger at the place, leaning over to the back seat with his eyes on the magazine. "Paintings by madmen," the driver explained during a feat with the clutch and the accelerator.

Renoir looked at the page and exclaimed. It showed a schizophrenic's painting, a gilded dream of a Madonna and Child that also had something carnal and pagan about it, like a Bonnard, and something quite free, as things tend to be in Renoir's presence.

The two men talk with passionate absorption about, in turn, madmen, the Madonna, and paintbrushes. As we get out, the driver gives Renoir the magazine, shakes his hand, and offers his name.

"Renoir," responds Renoir, and he thanks the driver for the present as he climbs out, his bad leg slowing him a little.

"You are of the family Renoir?" says the driver, amazed, moved, something dawning on him, looking at Renoir's face.

"Yes."

"Of the painter Renoir?"

"Yes. He was my father."

The driver goes on looking. "You are yourself, then . . . There was a famous man of the theater and the cinema . . ."

"That's my nephew Claude. A cameraman. Or my brother Pierre, perhaps. The actor."

"No, someone some time ago, a most famous man of the theater and the cinema, I believe."

"Yes, I think you are right, I believe there was once another Renoir who worked in the theater. Not related."

When we were pottering about the kitchen one day at lunchtime, Renoir said severely, "We will not have much. You don't eat, and now I don't eat, either. You must have been easy to ration," and he started talking about the Second World War. He was very kind to the English, even to the food. "Without the English, we should now all be under the jackboot. Yorkshire pudding, Lancashire hot pot. Exactly how is shepherd's pie made?" Just before the fall of Paris, Renoir and Dido joined the flight to the Midi. He took with him some of the most treasured paintings in the world. His own car was in the country, far away. "I didn't know what to do," he said. "At last, it occurred to me: perhaps one can still hire a car. Perhaps the Peugeot people are still working. So we went to the Peugeot factory, and there is every clerk at work as usual, still filling out forms, with the Germans ten miles away. I have to fill out all these forms, and then we have a car, and we drive to the Midi, very slowly, with the canvases of Monsieur Cézanne, et cetera, in the back. A big trek to the south. Everyone who could find a cart or a wheelbarrow. It was a very bad sight."

Renoir has his father's strong respect for touch, and for a kind of conviviality that is unmistakable and moving when he creates it in any of his films. He is a fine friend to spend time with. "One of the things I like about Shakespeare, very much, is that the characters have a great variety of intimacy," he said to me. "They are different according to whom they are speaking to. Of course, Shakespeare had a great advantage over cinema directors. It is one that in-

terests me a lot. He shares it with, you could say, Simenon.
You could call it the advantage of a harness. Elizabethan
plays and also thrillers are constricted, and that is very
liberating. In the cinema, you can do all too much. For
example, when the hero of a modern film has a phobia, you
are obliged to explain it by flashbacks: I mean, to go back to
the time when he was beaten by his father, or whatever thing
is supposed to have had such a result. This freedom can be
quite enfeebling. It makes one very literal, very anxious to
make everything clear, get everything taped. You know, I
believe one has to have only a rough idea when one is
making a film or writing a story, or whatever. A rough
scheme, like a salmon going upstream. No more than that.
It's no true help—is it?—to know already where one is going
to arrive. In fact, I think targets have done a great deal of
harm. This nineteenth-century idea in Europe, and now in
America—this idea of targets—has caused terrible damage.
Rewards in the future, and so on. Those never come. Pen-
sions. I thought about this a good deal in India when I was
making *The River*, in 1949 and 1950. India was a revelation. I
suppose I'd been looking for such a place and thinking it was
all past, and there it was. Suppose you are interested in
Aristophanes, and suppose you go down the street and
suddenly see people who are exactly his contemporaries,
who know the same things, have the same view. That's what
India was like for me. I had been starting to fall off to sleep.
In India, you could make a full-length picture just by following someone through the day. A grandmother, say, getting
up in the morning, cooking, washing clothes. Everything
noble. Among poor people in India, you're surrounded by
an aristocracy and a nobility. The trouble now is that the
advanced countries are trying desperately to grow better by

the mistake of removing the ordinary. We're trying to reach greatness by reading classics in houses that have no cold in the winter and no heat in the summer, and where everything can be done without the natural waste of time. One of the things I liked about India is that the people have the secret of loitering." This brought up Los Angeles, the city famous for picking up as a vagrant anyone who is merely strolling along a street. Renoir was very firm. "All great civilizations have been based on loitering," he said.

Much later, coming back to this point after a loop of talk about food and operetta, Renoir said, "Think of the Greeks, for instance. One of the most interesting adventures in our history. What were the Greeks doing in the agora? Loitering. Not getting agoraphobia. The result is Plato. My film *Boudu* is the story of a man who is just loitering."

Renoir spoke of Satyajit Ray, his helper on *The River*, whose Indian films are much like the ones that Renoir had just envisioned for me, and who feels Renoir and *The River* to be vital inspirations of his own work. "He is quite alone, of course. Most other Indian films are—well, I suppose they would be called uninteresting, though I have to say that they often interest me very much. There is sometimes a wonderful mixture of fairy tales and daily life and the religious, and no one thinks of it as at all comic, because no one is conscious of incongruity. I saw this in an Italian theater once. A little theater, not much bigger than this room. At the front of the stage, a man threatening to kill his mother. In the back, by some trick, a locomotive rushing. It was very fine. Hamlet and railway stations. Genuinely popular. You know what I mean. Every now and then, one gets this in Indian films. In the middle of a story about Siva and a film star and dancing and so on, there will suddenly be a god with a mustache who looks like a cop. It is practically the only question of the age, this question of primitivism and how it can be sustained in the face of sophistication. It is the question of Vietnam."

This question is much on his mind, and he came back to it another day by another route. "You know, I have a theory about the decay of art in advanced civilizations," he said. "Perhaps it's a joke, but I believe it may be serious. It is that people *want* to make ugly things, but at the beginning their tools don't allow them to. When you find figures or vases in Mycenae or Guatemala or Peru, every one is a masterpiece. But when the perfection of technique allows men to do what they want, it is bad. Perfection of technique —sophistication—has nearly destroyed the movies. In the beginning, every movie was good. When we see the old silents at the Cinémathèque, they are all good. This isn't nostalgia. They are. And, believe me, I know some of the directors who made them and they aren't geniuses. It also has something to do with puritanism. I'm in favor of puritanism, I think. Not for me. But for a nation it can be very good, and for art. Those early movies in Hollywood reflected the decorum of the people, a kind of thinking that I could not abide for myself. We would demonstrate against it now, I daresay, including me. You know what I think about all this? I believe that Creation has a considerable sense of humor. Of farce. The closer we are to perfection, the farther away from it we are. This makes me think about Hollywood, of course. The interesting thing about Hollywood, Beverly Hills, Los Angeles is that it isn't really materialist at all—not in the true sense, because it obviously doesn't care for the material in the slightest. In fact, that's the big advantage of Hollywood: the fact that the buildings don't count. It is therefore a place in the abstract. You are there—no, I should say that *one* is there, and I suppose I must mean myself—only for one's friends. When Clifford Odets died, I thought I wanted to leave Hollywood. He was a prince. Every gesture, every way of thinking was noble. Although I love Hollywood, I have to say that it is without nobility. But I stayed, of course. You know what I like about America? Among other things, the obvious. The generosity. There is a great desire to share. To share feelings, to share friends. Of course, this can be a travesty and ridiculous. It can be reduced to 'togetherness' and the vocabulary that could find such a word for such a thing. But it also has to be said that there exists in America a stout attempt to do in language exactly the opposite, to make things noble. For instance, calling tea a beverage, calling a barber a hairdresser. It doesn't work, but the attempt, in the face of the obstacles—well, it's interesting and nice, isn't it? It is very much harder to live nobly in America than in India. One of the things that are helpful to Indians is the concept of privacy. It is so strong there that to have spiritual privacy they do not even need physical privacy. In America, this concept is not so easy to have, partly because of the ethic of sharing, perhaps, and partly because of the ethic of proselytizing and persuading other people, which Hinduism is entirely free of, and which has arrived so dreadully at Vietnam for America. The problem of caste—of Western caste, of paternalism, et cetera—has led us into this proselytizing. I suppose caste is what all my films are about. Still, any big society is a melting pot, as they say. Take Rome. And the banal melting pot of America that is so much in question at the moment really works pretty well except at one point. The point of the Negro. One forgets that the slaves weren't originally brought by the Americans. They were brought by the French, the Spanish, the Portuguese. The really difficult thing to explain is that the slave owners pretended to be Christians. All men are brothers, and in the meantime the brothers on your estate are slaves. I suppose it has to be recognized that much of the truth about Christianity is about money, and most of the truth about subjection and propaganda is about money. Outside Paris now, there are Arabs living in shacks built out of gasoline cans who make a great deal of money for Paris businessmen. Americans make money out of Negroes, and Frenchmen make money out of Arabs. Every country has a worm in the apple, and the worm in the apple of America is a very tough one."

We went out into the Place Pigalle. "Much changed since the days of my father and Monsieur Cézanne," Renoir said, perfectly cheerfully. There was a night club on the corner which had the present special tattiness of the recently new. "Sensass!" a placard said of a stripper. The whole place was plastered with the words of some arid new Esperanto. "Chinese," Renoir said firmly. "A Chinese dialect that is understood only on this side of the square."

He talked about his new novel. It is about a murder, and based on a real crime that he heard of as a small child from Gabrielle, his father's famous model. It happened in a village between Burgundy and Champagne. "Two murderers," he said. "One with a big nose, the leader, and the other the weak one. At the time of the murder, which was very terrible, the villagers heard the sound of the ax blows on the earth to bury the corpse. The earth was very cold. The sounds seemed to them to be coming from under the earth. That was the way Gabrielle remembered them. They came from the private cemetery. Somebody seemed to be trying to escape from the ground, everyone thought. The cemetery

had been made for a man in the French Revolution who
didn't want to be buried in a religious place." A while later,
considering what the story might be like as a film, he said,
"Too violent. I'm an admirer of violent films, but I can't
make them. Also, I am scared of them." He was about to
spend five days or a week in the country where the murder
happened. The name of the village—very near his own
family region—is Gloire-Dieu. Someone had sent him a
browned clipping of a local song about the crime, which he
said had deeply wounded the villagers' sense of blessedness
in their name:

COMPLAINTE SUR LE CRIME DE LA GLOIRE-DIEU

> *Écoutez la triste histoire*
> *Désolant notre pays.*
> *En faisant le récit,*
> *Vraiment on ne peut y croire,*
> *Car le pays bourguignon*
> *N'a pas un mauvais roman . . .*

Renoir talked about a lot of other plans. Some that had
been scotched seemed no particular cue for regret. The
ideas continued to interest him, and it was sometimes quite
hard to be sure whether he was describing a plan of his own
or the plot of some favorite already achieved: the "Satyri-
con" of Petronius, for one. He recited the stories of classics
in the present tense, and they acquired his own tang. "There
is this matron who lost her husband, and she is so much in
love she can't bear the thought of being alone," he said,
limping along the cobbles and helping me. "She stays in the
cemetery near the corpse of her husband. There is a soldier
nearby who is watching thieves. The crucified bodies of
thieves. The authorities have to have a soldier there, because

one thief's family wants to steal the body. The soldier says to the woman, 'Don't cry so loud,' and he comforts her so well that after two or three days he makes love, and the family can steal the corpse, and so everyone is happier, except that the soldier has failed in his official task and what on earth can he do?"

Without changing his tone, Renoir went on from Petronius to describe his unmade film about revolt. He had written it in two parts. At no time did he speak of it in the past. "One is a revolt against an electric waxing machine. The other is about war. Two corporals from two armies hide between enemy lines beneath the roof of a kind of cellar. We start with a very polite fight about who will be the prisoner of the other one. In the end, they decide there is only one decent position in the modern world and that is to be a prisoner. But each doesn't like the enemy food. Oh, and now I have suddenly found the ending, in talking to you. I think this is the ending. They change uniforms, and then each can be the prisoner of the other and have the food he likes."

The television show he is doing is "like a revue." He continues, "Some of the sketches are very short—no more than a sentence. There is one sketch of the Armistice, and a burglar breaks a vein in his neck and wakes a sleepwalker and they are the first victims of the peace. Before this, there is a soldier who is told by a sergeant that if he dies before the Armistice he will be right and if he dies after the Armistice he will be wrong. You know what has happened? Patriotism is really quite a new idea to the ordinary citizen. It happens to be useful in politics to pretend that it is a powerful emotion, but it isn't. Not widely. Most people have never thought first of their country; they've thought first of their family.

You know, I adore England. I have English relatives. I'd like
to live there. People live there very agreeably." (Though I
should think he could live anywhere, given friends, just as
he can make enjoyable work for himself in strange countries
or in atrocious circumstances.)

"The trouble is that techniques change and the actors'
style of playing changes," he said. "Just as fashions vanish, so
our films go into oblivion to join others that once moved us."

The greatest of Renoir's will never do this, but he
doesn't seem to know it. It makes you pause to see a man
with such a powerful sense of the continuity of the general
life engaged with the form that most deals in quick deaths.
He eludes that blow by understanding filmmaking another
way, as play. He will sometimes describe a director as *"le
meneur de jeu,"* and he calls his friends and collaborators his
accomplices. "The cinema uses things up very fast. That's
the point," he says. "It uses up ideas and people and kinds of
stories, and all the time it thinks it wants to be new. It has no
idea that film people themselves change and are new all the
time. Producers want me to make the pictures I made twenty
years ago. Now I am someone else. I have gone away from
where they think I am."

PARIS, 1968

Concerning 11 Films

Salute to Mayhem:
Boudu Sauvé des Eaux (1932)

BOUDU SAUVÉ DES EAUX, shows disruption triumphant. Michel Simon in the part of Boudu, the haywire tramp whose vision of the way life should be anticipates the hippies' by nearly forty years, gives it a curious benediction through Renoir's filmmaking genius. At the beginning of the film, Boudu has lost his dog. A policeman brushes aside his request for help. Boudu is not a lovable tramp. He is nothing like Chaplin. When he attempts to commit suicide by drowning, a bookseller saves him and tries to rehabilitate him in his own house, but there is nothing doing. The bookseller's kindly aim is to turn the unruly man into a good bourgeois like himself, but Boudu prefers to be left alone. He doesn't want to be saved. There is no place in society that he covets. If this is the world, he would rather be out of it. He does his best to impel the move, by saying with a chortle that he doesn't absolutely *need* an offered necktie, by pursuing the bookseller's mistress (who is the housemaid), by seducing his wife, by saying that the sheets make him sweat ("I get sick"), and by taking firmly to the bookseller's floor.

The film, written by Renoir and Albert Valentin from a minor play of the time, is a lyric and riotous account of a dissident who escapes by a system of mayhem. He wants none of the things that respectability wants him to want. While the wife grows petulant in the kitchen, he lies down on his shoulder blades and props up a doorjamb with his carpet slippers, says he suspects that the bookseller fished him out of the drink because he needed a servant, and spits genially onto a first edition of Balzac. The wife, dusting herself with talcum powder, mutters distractedly that her nerves are going to crack. It is obvious to her that one should rescue only people of one's own class. Michel Simon's loose, doggy face, visible in typical Renoir shots through a spiral staircase and in distant rooms as he concocts worrying schemes, incites the wife to spite: "I can only shun the man who spat on Balzac." To her horror, he not only makes love to her, which stays well within the bounds of what she finds socially acceptable, but goes as far as to call her by her first name. Her husband is slightly mollified by getting a medal for the rescue. Meanwhile, Boudu intones *Les Fleurs du Mal* in the doorway and smokes an obviously smelly cigar. The film comes full circle when he marries the maid and sets out in a bowler hat with his bride in a boat. Nearly trapped in a social act, he throws himself into the river. Not suicide. Not despair. An escape from what is expected of him. Barking and rolling like a sea lion, he floats slowly down the river and eventually hauls himself up onto a bank, staggering drunkenly and embracing a scarecrow as though it were a colleague. There is a three-hundred-and-sixty-degree shot of the free world regained, and then the camera sinks down to the grass and the white dust raised by a breeze in the summer heat. You can have seen the film fifteen years ago and still remember that grass, that dust, that freedom.

Locked Out of a Golden Circle: *Toni (1935)*

VIEWED IN HISTORICAL context or not, *Toni* is still one of the most remarkable achievements of realism in the cinema. Renoir never beats the drum. His method of shooting and of directing actors is always to leave air around them. He is interested in people's actions less than in their reactions, interested in scenes less than in the actors moving about in them, interested in whole scenarios less than in scenes.

He shot this film in the Midi, without makeup, studio sets, or stars. The cameraman was his nephew Claude. The film, which is transformed by Renoir's characteristic beneficence, began with his equally characteristic simplicity as a dossier on a *crime passionnel*. The story is about Toni, an Italian immigrant who comes to France to find work (your country is where you can eat), and about the two women who love him. He has a long-lasting affair with his landlady, Marie, and a thwarted one with a Spanish girl called Josepha, who marries a Belgian farmer from the quarry where Toni works. The composition of the shots of men working the quarry looks very like Bruegel's "Tower of Babel." The film is full of wonderfully exact observations: the sense of a dying relationship in bedroom scenes between Toni and Marie, a baby howling during a quarrel about money in a poor kitchen, the sounds of motorbike engines, and a funeral bell and a guitar intervening disconnectedly on the track.

Toni is a monument to Renoir's undying preoccupation
with meetings and intruders. How to enter, how to belong.
Again and again, in many different films, he has asked the
same question: what happens to strangers in milieus that are
not theirs? And alongside this question, which must lead
always to explosions (in *La Règle du Jeu*, for instance, and
even in *Diary of a Chambermaid*, the finest film of his Hollywood exile during the war, though it is constrained by the
presence of stars, the then alien language, and the even
more alien studio sets)—alongside this there is the pacifying
effect of the details of side-life, which have the balm of the
manifold and prodigious.

Boon Nights:
Le Crime de Monsieur Lange
(1935)

RENOIR WAS BORN in 1894, so he was twenty in 1914, but it seems that the stop that was then put to the world's sense of *douceur de vivre* never happened to him. He has survived every derangement and bleakness of the century. I don't believe one enjoys Mozart because of the arrangements of the notes; as Renoir once said of someone else, you enjoy yourself because you have a good conversation with Mozart. After seeing other and mediocre films, *Le Crime de Monsieur Lange* is like friendship after days of trivia on the telephone. Renoir has a particular view of life—some plenitude of spirit—that is vivacious and reviving, particularly at moments in the history of this planet when ground seems sorely lost. Without sacrificing shrewdness, he really does believe that people have a tendency to move on. His characters are always peculiarly alert, as if he never failed to sense in others a wish to find out more. The atmosphere in *Monsieur Lange* made me remember something he said when he was on location in India after Independence, directing *The River*. He looked at the fighting then going on between Hindus and Muslims and said only that they had not yet caught up with the times.

I suppose *Le Crime de Monsieur Lange* couldn't be called his most important film, if that means much. It isn't as shapely or powerful a masterpiece as *La Grande Illusion* or *La Règle du Jeu*, but the same man made it, and this very man would forgo such tape measuring. It is suffused with light and the possibility of happiness and a sense that life is simultaneously serious, absurd, impossible, and inescapably interesting. He made the film in the Depression. It has a simple plot. It amounts to a fable about capitalism, to a caustic revenge farce, to an idyll, and to a stingingly undeceived tale about being near the bottom of the heap. Renoir has created a Brechtian narrative that is also pastoral and bitten with fugacity, and filled every shot with flickering notations of living.

The picture begins with a flash-forward of lovers on the run. The man, Monsieur Lange, is technically guilty of murder, though the murder was poetically justified, and it can't be long before he is captured; but he still has left to him a pause to love his girl, and the grace of reprieve flows back from this scene over the rest of the picture. He is played by René Lefèvre, the star of René Clair's *Le Million*. At the beginning of the story proper, we see him spending as much time as possible in bed, writing Wild West stories that nobody reads. His employer, Batala (Jules Berry), is a foppishly dressed embezzler who publishes junk magazines, starves his employees, and farcically deceives his backers. There is one scene that has a vivacity very like the temperament of Restoration comedy, with Batala sidestepping the inquiries of an equally courtly backer who has been under the impression that the firm would be publishing wholesome books called "Hymn to Work" and "Whither Are We Drifting?"—the backer's idea being that these holy bromides for the underfed should include a few plugs for some pills called Ranimax.

Batala diverts the furious but dapper enemy with questions about the man's inappropriately amiable little dog.

"It's called Daisy," the investor says impatiently.

"That's an English name, isn't it?" asks the embezzler.

"*Belgian*," snaps the investor, trying to edge nearer to a mannerly suggestion that the word "swindle" is applicable.

Batala suddenly has an idea involving the neglected Lange. It is his stroke of impresario's genius. He says, grabbing air, that the Wild West Stories are in a class with *Les Misérables*. His mind races. He can adapt Lange's hero in *Arizona Jim* to push the pills. "Just imagine, Don Quixote taking Ranimax pills. . . ." The author raptly signs his rights away.

Batala is capable of exploiting anyone. He sends off his own mistress to content a creditor. Toward sceptical employees in the printing office he behaves like a patronizing kindergarten teacher. He tells them how to draw. The corpse should show, he feels. And there should be more detail. "Remember, a crime is full of small details," he says, patting the neck of a man who would like his blood, or at least a living wage. (All the dialogue scenes go very swiftly. Every now and then, the camera moves down to a yard below the office, where children play and dogs look for food, and an unseen church bell rings. It is characteristic of Renoir, this way of giving you the sense of time passing in a place at the margin of incident.) Batala eventually goes too far, and the creditors nearly nab him. Having committed every crime of the soul, he climbs onto a train where he talks indignantly with a priest about the immorality of the age and disappears. *Arizona Jim* turns into a hit, the publishing office becomes a cooperative, and Lange's flower-faced girl friend loves him. There is a rhapsodic feast. "Every time I'm drunk, I think it's Christmas," a nearly unconscious worker shouts cheerfully. Then Batala reappears, alive and kicking and disguised in the priest's vestments, after the train accident that was supposed to have killed him. It is too much to be borne. It means the end of the co-op, and a plumper Batala than ever. Lange takes his revenge, and the end of the film links back to the beginning. He and his girl still have a little freedom left. The last long shot of them, pushing their luck in some plundered interlude, has a kind of piercing beauty that mysteriously belongs more to comedy than to tragedy, like the racking supposition of Falstaff that his boon nights with Hal are going to go on forever.

Renoir wrote the story with Jean Castanier—"a spherical Catalan friend . . . who spent most of his time getting drunk on the air of the Paris suburbs," as the director described him in 1961. (Jacques Prévert wrote the screenplay.) Renoir had another crony at the time, Carl Koch, who was the husband of the animator Lotte Reiniger and became his collaborator on *La Grande Illusion*. Koch had nothing directly to do with *Monsieur Lange*, but Renoir drew him into the description of things to me, all the same: "Our strolls on the banks of the Seine were favorable to the birth of a story. Sometimes Bert Brecht got off the boat with one or two friends. A young woman would unwrap a concertina from its newspaper . . ."

Renoir's talk is very like his films. Things happen, people come and go, all belong. No wonder he responded to Hinduism when he made *The River*. "The great word of the Hindu . . . is that the world is one," he said in an interview with Jacques Rivette and François Truffaut soon after-

wards. "This does not mean an acceptance in the Moham-
medan manner, a kind of fatalism. The single man can act.
Nevertheless, you cannot undo what has been done. . . . It is
a sort of comprehension by the senses of everything that has
happened." This is the morality that pours out of his films. It
is a morality of bearing witness.

Flophouse:
Les Bas-Fonds (1936)

THERE EXISTS a rare old Russian screen record of Gorky's *The Lower Depths* as it was played long ago by the Moscow Arts Theatre, with the great Kachalov, now dead, as the Baron. Renoir's marvellous *Les Bas-Fonds* of years later is interestingly different. The Moscow Arts picture is entirely Russian in the wit, the buffoonery, the richness of idiosyncrasy, the profusion of swollen, hallucinated faces, dreaming and condemned. Renoir's version has Louis Jouvet in the Kachalov part and remains entirely French, where any other director would have tried to confect Russianness. "Bresson has said that originality is when you try to do the same as everybody else but don't quite make it," Renoir once remarked to me, apropos of something quite different. The flophouse in his *Les Bas-Fonds*—built around one of the courtyards he loves—is unconsciously just as much Renoir's original issue as Gorky's. Renoir's character is all there in the film: in the response to a story about a dandy who has been stripped by the bailiffs and fallen among guttersnipes who recognize and fear his class; in the minute social sense; in the bitter tenderness; and in the breath of temperament and curiosity that fills the frames of any Renoir film with unmistakable liveliness. He begins with a long shot on Jouvet, the debonair Baron in military uniform, hearing out a voice-

over lecture from a superior officer about debts. The shot is
held daringly, as Godard often holds one now. In the
Baron's palatial home, run by a sadly grateful, class-
conscious servant who is never going to get his back wages, a
burglar played by Jean Gabin comes in to pinch the valu-
ables and sits down with the Baron to a comradely glass of
champagne on tick. The Baron knows what is going to
happen to his life, like everyone else in his circle. He has
squandered a fortune. In the gambling rooms, his unami-
able friends can always tell when he has lost: he walks out
calmly enough with a cigarette, but it is unlit, whereas he
unconsciously lights it if he has won. The slope now leads
only downward, and he already knows himself to be in
Gabin's shoes. When he gets to the flophouse, after leaving
his empty mansion and his unpaid servant with an air, he
finds himself at an irreparable distance from everyone else
there. Gabin leans on an elbow in a field and talks to him, in a
way that he can't quite recognize, about being fed up. "The
mattresses . . . saucepans . . . every word that is spoken is
rotten to the core," Gabin says, talking beside a river with a
grass-blade in his mouth, in one of the interludes that Renoir directs as no one else can. The Baron and the burglar
have escaped for the moment from the flophouse: from the
girls desperate to get married as a way out, from the
jammy-mouthed government inspector promising to make
a princess of one of the down-and-outs if she will have
dinner with him, from the crazed alcoholic actor who sees
visions of a cure. The Baron has disabused the drunk of
those visions, and the drunk has hit back: "You're a real
baron. Even with holes in your shoes, you're destructive."
Lying with Gabin on the bank, the Baron says that everything in his life has seemed like a dream, consisting mostly of

changing clothes—beginning with being a schoolboy, then being married, then a government official—and he looks down at his tramp's coat, the sleeves ending four inches above his wrists.

Les Bas-Fonds is unmistakably Renoir's. He shot in deep focus long before Orson Welles and Gregg Toland, because he wants to see everything in motion at the same time and because he prefers not to commandeer your eye. He always likes to see what is going on in the next room, through half-open doors, or across a courtyard, so his compositions often have the tunnelling perspectives of the great Flemish interior paintings. The scenario of the film was presented to him by Jacques Companeez and Eugène Zamiatin, and he responded to it at once. The adaptation and the dialogue are by Renoir himself, with Charles Spaak, who later collaborated with him on *La Grande Illusion*. He seems always to have been interested by the idea of a beggars' kingdom, like Gay, Brecht, and Weill before him. More than this, his version of the Gorky play becomes, through his temperament and intellect, a heartrending poem about the loss of caste. The delicate comprehension it proffers to the resolves and wounds of class that are often made light of now by progressive film directors puts it thematically with *La Règle du Jeu* and *La Grande Illusion*, his two masterpieces. (And, indeed, with practically every other film he has ever made. He said to me recently, about another director, "Probably everyone makes only one film in his life, and then smashes it into pieces and makes it again.") Renoir's feeling in *Les Bas-Fonds* for the fop deposed, for the grandee who has lost his birthright in high style and will always be mistrusted by his new familiars for that very stylishness, expresses the ideas and the love that led him to his greatest works.

Plight of a King:
La Marseillaise (1938)

IN LA MARSEILLAISE Louis XVI is played by Pierre Renoir, Jean's brother. He is a monarch much moved by culinary thoughts. Far from being asleep after what are referred to as the Herculean labors of his hunt the day before, he
is first seen busy with a colossal breakfast in bed, with chicken
fat running up the sleeves of his nightshirt as he eats
what looks to be a whole chicken and swigs wine as if it were
soda water for a headache. He is told by La
Rochefoucauld-Liancourt that the Parisians have taken the
Bastille. "Ah," he says intelligently, the royal mouth full.
"Is it a revolt?" "No, Sire, it is a revolution," says La
Rochefoucauld-Liancourt. Outside, the peasants scent
freedom. They kill blackbirds with a sling. Someone laughs
hoarsely about the burning of the rich, making a dissenter
say gravely, almost to himself, that the nobles have taught
bad habits and that they have created their slaves in their
own image. Renoir finds it inapt of us to try to make things
stay in place when everything is always naturally in motion.
The films of this born innovator dart with life on the move.
In any frame, there always seems to be something happening apart from the major point of dramatic attention.
Renoir's characteristic deep-focus lens uses doorways almost as proscenium arches for stages filled with activity. In
La Marseillaise he brings his usual native affection to bear on

the plight of the rigid. There is a fine scene showing homesick nobles in Koblenz, daydreaming of the common people still kneeling back in France. One patrician sings at the spinet, two play cards, another fiddles with a yo-yo like a lunatic dauphin. "Now we are the allies of Prussia. I once met His Majesty the King of Prussia," says a beauty who looks like a crinoline-lady cover to be put over a teapot. "An Agamemnon . . . two hundred and eighty pounds." Meanwhile, a nobleman named Saint-Laurent remembers the new concept of nationhood which was given him by Arnaud, the man who deprived him of his noble position. "And yet he was a gentleman," Saint-Laurent goes on to recall. "Yet he was a patriot. If there are many like him, we shall not have an easy time." Politically speaking, we are watching men struggling to discover the wheel. Only Renoir could make the struggle graceful, comic, and courageous: a documentary of crass primitivism and muddle which somehow, paradoxically, expresses divine sensibility and equilibrium. He treats peasants and emigrant courtiers with equal dignity and respect and a deal of humor. There is a very funny exchange between the King and Marie Antoinette about the brushing of teeth. Louis approves of the novelty: "I will gladly attempt this toothbrushing."

Mishaps and irrelevancies appeal to Renoir. On the road from Marseilles, the volunteers exchange irritable theories about what to do for sore feet. "A pair of roomy boots packed out with straw," says one to his insteps tenderly. Another says, "Paper." Another says, "Tallow rubbed between the toes." There are complaints that the song "La Marseillaise" is full of unpronounceable words. An exhausted enthusiast says quietly that he "likes the lines that a schoolteacher wrote: 'We'll replace our parents on the battlefield.' " The terse, slangy talk is all of a piece with Louis's compliments to the lately introduced tomato. Where Saint-Laurent sees the passing of an élite, Louis says the tragedy is that unfortunately the members of the court are the actors in this drama, "which is obviously less convenient than being the spectators." It is inconvenient, too, for the passionate speaker at the meeting of the Tribunes in *La Marseillaise* that she is a woman. "Your place is in the galley!" a heckler shouts.

Heredity:
La Bête Humaine (1938)

TRUFFAUT ONCE SAID to me that Renoir has a sort of "trade secret." He meant the trade secret of sympathy. Renoir degrades no one. His vein of affection makes one think of Octave, the character played by Renoir himself in *La Règle du Jeu*, who says, "You see, in this world there is one awful thing, and that is that everyone has his reasons." Renoir would accord reasons even to the accepted kind of heroism, though he reacts against it almost as strongly as he does against the Renaissance, which he identifies—in his beautiful introduction to André Bazin's book about him—as the movement that "laid the foundations of industrial society" and was "ultimately responsible for the atomic bomb."

Bazin records that, after a few years of what Renoir cheerfully pronounced to me to be utterly rotten pictures, the director resolved to study French gesture as it is reflected in his father's paintings. "I was beginning to realize that the movement of a scrubwoman, of a vegetable vender, or of a girl combing her hair before a mirror frequently had superb plastic value." His films from then on have always been full of shots of frozen action which seem to come from Impressionist paintings. In *Le Caporal Epinglé*, a small, shy child in a silent German crowd raises a hand muffled in a woolen mitten to ranks of passing French prisoners. In *La Bête Humaine*, one of the very best Renoir films, adapted from Zola without the novel's rhetoric and, ironically, without its falsely "cinematic" scheme, Jean Gabin plays a locomotive engineer. (The story is that the film got started because Gabin had always wanted to drive a train.) There is an abundance of gesture between him and his fireman, signifying unity in a clamor that no words can be heard in. The Gabin character comes from a long line of drunkards. Himself a teetotaller, he is gripped by moments of sadness that move him to an intolerable self-hatred. He begins to think he is paying for all his ancestors who drank, and gives himself pathological fits far worse than alcoholism. In a calm between storms, he throws two quick glances at his reflection in a looking glass. The contempt in his eyes is like the gaze of a basilisk. No one is better at this sort of grim, drained detail than Gabin, a Renoir actor if there ever was one. Renoir likes everything—even in his comedies and deliberately theatrical pieces—to be quick, dry: *sec*. Gabin's two glances are like stones hurled at a prison wall to bounce back and wound the prisoner.

Renoir has always been struck and stirred by the closed worlds that some people think they have to live in: a little series of glass cubes and spheres from which they can see other people, wave to them, copy them. The glass boxes devised by the technocrats who have so constrained liberty are prisons too low to stand in and too small to lie down in. They are torture chambers as minute as the primitive kind of prison called little-ease, but not so small as to prevent the inhabitants from grandiloquent posturing. Heredity can be wondrous, as it is for Renoir himself, who speaks again and again of his father as though the famous painter were still alive; in *La Bête Humaine*, though, heredity is another little-ease. Natural enough that the Gabin character should work on trains. They are a metaphor for his life, which runs on tracks and is sometimes catastrophically derailed. And the heroine pushes him to kill in a way that destroys his owner-ship of his soul. The prison in *La Grande Illusion* is made spacious by the two main characters' equality of calling. The German von Rauffenstein and the French de Boïeldieu are both aristocrats of the heart, enemies allied in sensibility. Renoir extends his devotion to those lords of inner liberty, though in his films they are more generally to be found among the populace than among the nobility. In *La Bête Humaine*, the one free man is Cabuche, the poacher—played by Renoir himself—who foreshadows the poacher in *La Règle du Jeu*. Poachers leap walls; owners hang back for form's sake, so that the rest of their party can catch up. The poacher has a sense of himself; the owners have a sense only of how they look to others. For Renoir, the master of acting movement as well as camera movement, gait expresses the difference between freedom and slavery in a second. In *La Marseillaise*, for instance, the volunteers marching from Marseilles to Paris walk like tired Boy Scouts; the palace guards move like chorus girls.

Game Without Umpire:
La Règle du Jeu (1939)

RENOIR'S LA RÈGLE DU JEU is one of the few sophisticated films about love that achieve irony without the stain of malignity. It is a work to be put with *Così Fan Tutte* and *The Marriage of Figaro*. Society is satirized with Mozart's own mixture of biting good sense and blithe, transforming acceptance. Like the operas, the film has a prodigality that is moving in itself. Fugitive moments of genius pass unstressed, because there is always infinitely more to draw upon, in the way of those Mozart melodies that disappear after one statement instead of spinning themselves out into the classic a-b-a aria form. The serene amplitude of Renoir's view floods the plot and turns it into something else. He thought at the time, in 1939, that he was making an anti-Fascist warning film in the guise of a story about a contemporary houseparty. Mozart probably had an equivalent feeling when he was setting da Ponte's librettos. The script of the film, by Renoir himself, with Carl Koch, was written with actual memories of eighteenth-century plays in mind, and it opens with a quotation from Beaumarchais.

Even for a masterpiece (masterpieces generally have savage voyages), the film has had a hard and strange history. It was made in the conditions following Munich. The opening in Paris, during the summer of 1939, was received with fury. Renoir saw one man in the audience start to burn a

newspaper in the hope of setting fire to the cinema. Because
of the presence in the cast of the Jewish actor Marcel Dalio
and the Austrian refugee Nora Grégor, the film was attacked by both the anti-Semitic and the chauvinist press.
Butcher cuts were made. In October of 1939, it was banned
by the government as demoralizing. Both the Vichy and the
German Occupation authorities upheld the ban throughout
the war. Until 1956, it seemed that only the mutilated version of the film was extant. Then two young French cinema
enthusiasts who had acquired the rights to the film found
hundreds of boxes of untouched footage in a warehouse.
After two years of editing, under Renoir's supervision, they
were able to reconstruct his original film. When it was first
shown again publicly, I saw someone who had worked on it
originally sitting there with tears running down his cheeks at
the sight of it restored.

The plot is a pattern of three triangles—two of them
above stairs, one below—seen mostly at a chateau during a
big houseparty for the shooting season. The Marquis de la
Chesnaye, played by Dalio, is a dapper man who collects
eighteenth-century clockwork toys. He has Jewish blood, as
his male servants point out behind the baize door to demonstrate that he can't be relied upon always to know the rules of
being an aristocrat. His wife, Christine, played by Nora
Grégor, is a high-bred Austrian woman, frightened to find
herself fond of an aviator who has just flown solo across the
Atlantic and let out an angry declaration of love to her at Le
Bourget during a radio interview. This is one of the triangles.
The second is made up of the Marquis, his wife, and his
mistress, a dark, overanimated society girl whose most sober
thought is that she wants to be happy; she says it sadly two or
three times during the film, between spasms of social chat-

ter. "How are your factories?" she gabbles brightly, blotting out pain to greet a moneyed woman at the chateau. The third triangle is formed by Schumacher, the Marquis's gamekeeper; his wife, Lisette, the Marquise's maid, who is based in Paris away from her husband and living a surrogate life because of her loyalty to her mistress; and a poacher who crosses the lines to respectability and becomes a bootboy, because the Marquis has been tepidly attracted by the fact that the man is more efficient than the gamekeeper at trapping the rabbits that lower the tone of the shoot. With Lisette's adored mistress in town so much, Schumacher feels he might as well be a widower. He tries to get the Marquis to pay heed to the problem, in a desolately comic scene on the chateau doorstep while they move between car and front door, but the Marquis has guests and rococo and rabbits on his mind. This ignored third triangle is to intersect fatally with the others when Schumacher, run amok with loss and jealousy, mistakenly kills the aviator because he thinks it is Lisette rather than the Marquise who is with him. And through it all—through the bright welcomes and the glances and the melancholy accommodations to loveless social rules, through the shooting party and the amateur theatricals and the good-night scenes in long corridors where nobly born men horse around with hunting horns while a lordlier-looking servant walks impassively past them—through the whole intricate gavotte of the film wanders the solicitous figure of Octave, played by Renoir. Octave is the external extra man, the buffoon who really has both more sense and more passion than the others of his class, the one who best loves the Marquise and pines to look after her in memory of her father, who taught him music in Austria long ago. He would have liked to be a conductor. The man whom

everyone idly holds dear for being the perfect guest suddenly speaks of himself with hatred for living the life of a
sponger. How would he eat if it were not for his friends?
The thing is to forget it and get drunk. Though then, after
feeling better, he feels worse—that's the nasty part. But he
will grow accustomed, as necessary. He used to dream of
having something to offer. Of having contact with an audience. It would have been overwhelming. . . .

The houseparty's formal shooting scene has its double
later on, in the desperately actual one when Schumacher
runs among the guests and tries to kill the poacher. The
amateur theatricals that everyone treats so seriously have
their mirror image also in this drama, which the houseparty
takes for play. The intrusion of the aviator into an alien
society—the romantic hero thrust among sceptics trained in
old rules, the pure among the impure—has its counterpart
in the poacher, catapulted into a world of snobbery-by-
proxy and of a chef's adopted airs about making potato
salad with white wine. He accepted the Marquis's offer
gratefully, because he had always dreamed of being a servant. Limited hopes, delusory debts. He had always liked the
clothes. Julien Carette plays him wonderfully. When he is
seen in the servants' hall for the first time, a vagrant corral-
led within the laws of the housebound, his right arm wheels
with embarrassment as he introduces himself. There is a
shot of him in front of a palm tree with the Marquis during
the evening fête, straightening the master's tie. "Did you
ever want to be an Arab?" asks the Marquis. They are both
thinking about women. The Marquis, with two women on
his mind, envies Arabs for not having to throw out one for
another. "I hate hurting people," he says, and he means it, in
his fashion. "Ah, but a harem takes money," says the

poacher. "If I want to have a woman, or to get rid of her, I try to make her laugh. Why don't you try it?" "That takes talent," says the Marquis.

La Règle du Jeu is delicately good to every character in it, even to the most spoiled or stilted. For its characters, driven to their limits, it has the special eye that Renoir always reserves for people nearly beyond what they can manage. There is a wonderful shot of Schumacher, the violent, rigid gamekeeper, now sacked from his job because of the shooting affair, and thus separated completely from the lady's-maid wife he was trying to save for himself. She chose to stay with Madame. He stands with his forehead against a tree, stiffly, finished, like a propped scarecrow. The game has gone wrong. The rules—for him as for the aviator —were so much dead wood, but he was deceived in hoping to hack his way back to life by violent action. For the others the game still holds, although the idea of honor has petered out into the advisability of avoiding open indiscretion, and the idea of happiness into being amused. The *crime passionnel* of the plot, terrible for all three triangles, is given the labelling of his class by the Marquis. It is called "an unfortunate accident." He tells his guests that the gamekeeper, who was actually egged on by the poacher to shoot the aviator because they thought he was poaching Lisette from them both, "fired in the course of duty" on an intruder suspected of the only kind of poaching that gamekeepers are supposed to deal with.

Like the script, the editing is everywhere immaculate. The shooting-party scene, with smocked beaters thwacking the undergrowth and a sound-track like a panicky cuckoo clock, is one of the best set pieces in the French cinema; the cuts between the preoccupied lovers and their animal victims, alike jerking with damage, are brutally apropos. Renoir's formal command of his film is beautiful. During the last part of the picture, the camera moves about almost like another guest. It must be some quality of Renoir's that makes his camera lens seem always a witness and never a voyeur. The witness here communicates a powerful mixture of amusement and dismay. *La Règle du Jeu* was made in 1939, after all; it is not only a masterpiece of film-making, not only a great work of humanism and social comedy in a perfect rococo frame, but also an act of historical testimony.

Acting:
Eléna et les Hommes (1956)

IN ELÉNA ET LES HOMMES, one of Renoir's clearest expressions of his feeling for the theater, Ingrid Bergman plays a politically infatuated Polish princess of the nineteenth century who has fallen on poorer days. Her idea of fending off poverty is to sell a pearl. The film is like a late-Shakespearean comedy of gesture and romance about a woman who believes herself dedicated to causes. She is buoyed up by a dilettante (Mel Ferrer), for whom lounge-lizardry is an art, and a general (Jean Marais), founded on the real-life Boulanger, whom the French people want to make into their presiding genius. The populace is eager to grow excited about its own dreams. Love's exhibition at the end, when Eléna is forced to appease a crowd by appearing at a balcony window with Mel Ferrer—substituting Ferrer in order to save the general from the mob—is the final stroke of theatricality, with the balcony almost playing the dividing theatrical role of footlights. The spectacle of romantic love meets a receptive audience. The crowd roars its approval of this slave of the heart, this outsider who echoes the regional Venus of Balzac's *Eugénie Grandet*. She is an emblem of real love submerged in farcically pompous and maladroit disguises. All through the film, starting with the moment when she mingles with the crowd on Bastille Day, there is a sense of movement and light irony which is pure Renoir.

The film is about the intrigues of the early years of the Third Republic. *Eléna* is a big movie in the guise of a breakable and fine-tuned little gem, with a diamond watch movement that the people in the film take to be the same tick-tock that the dropsical Fielding, laughed at for his size by the watermen at Rotherhithe, thought the activity of his own great heart to be. Impromptu, Eléna sings gloriously in a café scene, yet with the Renoir hint that there is something faintly ridiculous in bel canto: the same suspicion is embodied in the marvellous warbling of Jeanne Moreau in *Le Petit Théâtre de Jean Renoir* (1969). *Eléna et les Hommes* is the ultimate extension of Renoir's feeling for the theater. Politics are reducible to shadow plays, to romances, to crowd appearances of beauties in hats burdened with flowers; it is love and art that supply the real values. One thinks of the dramatic sense in *La Règle du Jeu*, and of the comedy about romanticism implicit in the way Mel Ferrer deals with Ingrid Bergman's difficult clothes in *Eléna et les Hommes*; for instance, avoiding the darts of the white ostrich feathers that sprout from the evening dress on her perfect shoulders, because he hopes not to be tickled into sneezing in their box at the opera. One thinks, too, of the cruel, audacious theatricality of *Le Crime de Monsieur Lange*, which is a step away from mere theater, and beyond the theater in its icily deliberate use of the stage's furthest devices of alienation, like *Les Bas-Fonds*, the fiercely melodramatic version of Gorky's *The Lower Depths*. Drama is seen by Renoir as more truthful than politics, which he depicts as a misleadingly lifelike form of staging, with the voters playing the part of an extension of the audience; a Brechtian weight of unreal emphasis on art's techniques, he feels, can embody perceptions more truly than verisimilitude. In an equally startling way, he celebrates a certain kind of very attentive sloth, as it must have been known by the brillant spectators dawdling in the Greek agora. Renoir understands this sort of inertia as the most productive form of energy: unrestless and alert, like him. In the cinema of Renoir, when style rules, content will be there to an almost religious degree.

Not that anything in acting should be self-conscious or cute, he believes. It should be all strong and quick. The style accommodates works as superficially different as *Boudu Sauvé des Eaux* (with Michel Simon), *The River* (1950), *Le Carrosse d'Or* (1952), *Le Testament du Dr. Cordelier* (1959), a Jekyll-and-Hyde story with Jean-Louis Barrault, and *Le Déjeuner sur l'Herbe*. In other words, it accommodates neorealism, romantic dialogues with nature, dramas of high and sometimes self-mocking artifice, melodrama, and those peculiarly Renoir moments when comedy dissolves into emotion. He rehearses his actors so that they can quit mannerism and use force instead. We watch them having something unknown to them drawn from their inner resources, as if Renoir had found ideas in their heads which first appeared as little pieces of thread, and then as lengths of string, and then as ropes. Renoir's films are so gentle-spirited that it is easy to miss his innately theatrical instinct for finding the moment when a character is at the end of his tether.

Pagan:
Le Déjeuner sur l'Herbe (1959)

IN LE DÉJEUNER SUR L'HERBE Renoir makes use of an
earnestness about topics which is to be found in TV specials.
The topics here are artificial insemination and the Common
Market. A Professor Alexis is solemnly researching artificial
insemination. He is candidate for the Presidency of a united
Europe, and related, luckily, to the major chemical fortunes
of both France and Germany. At the same time, he is in the
middle of announcing his engagement to a beautiful German cousin who loves Scouting. A stuffy engagement ceremony for the press takes place in Renoir's loved Provence
and would despoil the countryside except for nature's protest, in the form of a windstorm that sows confusion. Things
begin to become bacchanalian in the drowsy heat. The se-
date professor is entranced by the sight of a girl bathing
naked. Theories about artificial insemination will have to
wait till tomorrow. We are once more in the midst of a way of
life that flows like a tide.

Renoir is drawn again and again to the polytheistic and
materialist conception of nature which has been so ravaged
by Christian rationalism. In a pinch, Renoir would trust the
pagan view every time; and this great experimenter and ally
of novelty is forever looking for the pagan virtues in new
forms, believing that it is better to make bad films, always
attempting fresh things, than to keep to the tried and al-

ready successful. His people expose their spirits to us. Just as his great father loved women for baring their bodies, Jean Renoir loves his characters for the immodesty of baring their souls.

Pax:
Le Caporal Épinglé (1962)

WHERE THE CONVENTIONAL antiwar film piously says that killing people is wrong, Renoir's *Le Caporal Épinglé* gently makes the incontrovertible remark that killing *me* is wrong. The picture is rather like Joseph Heller's savage satirical novel *Catch 22*, in which all the hero's rage and cunning are directed against the people who are trying to prevent his staying alive, most of whom are on his own side. War-film makers are often behind the mood of their period: it has taken a long time for anyone to see the heroic comic possibilities of this kind of softly stated and entirely congenial self-interest.

Like *La Grande Illusion*, *Le Caporal Épinglé* is set in a prison camp. The hero's driving force is simply that he wants to get out of it. Now and again there are scraps of newsreel about the atrocities that are happening in the world beyond, but they haven't very much to do with the reality of his own life. All that he knows is that he is young, and intent on existing if possible; and the enemy guards seem to be in much the same mood. The most obvious advantage possessed by the Germans in this film is that they have first call on the *pissoir*. The prisoners spend a lot of time emptying the cesspool, and the impulse that makes one of them disappear to add to it in the interests of making the job more his own is a comically dignified comment on the pride of working for oneself. This is a sage and touching film. There is a moment of typical compassion when the corporal, beautifully played by Jean-Pierre Cassel, is given a bowl of beans by a friend after his umpteenth escape and a spell in solitary: all he can say, weeping, is that the beans are too hot. Renoir somehow communicates that his comic hero is a man of great virtue, by which he means nothing at all to do with the qualities taught by War Offices or Pentagons.

The soldier's code, he implies, is a counterfeit; togetherness under the flag cannot console anyone for killing or being killed. *Le Caporal Épinglé* takes for granted the fundamental truth, ignored by most people who make battle films, that the catastrophes of war do not happen to men in platoons, they happen to a man in isolation. Renoir's films always express the belief that people's endeavors are admirable whether they come to nought, as they do in *Le Caporal Épinglé*, in which the heroes do the most low-down jobs ("To think we set out to liberate Poland!" says one P.O.W. on sewage duty to another as they clean out cisterns while maintaining an air of unquenched lyric patriotism, overlaid with considerable affront), or whether the characters are engaged in the French Revolution, as in *La Marseillaise*, and changing the whole course of human affairs.

Renoir has always been exhilarated by keen-eyed, strolling characters who are not overbusy with acquitting themselves well. He thinks the Garden of Eden must have had a population of nonheroes and loiterers. For him, heroism lies in having new ideas and in pursuing them alone. Ballochet (Claude Rich), in *Le Caporal Épinglé*, an ex-employee of a gas company who is appointed an interpreter for his fellow prisoners, though he doesn't speak a word of German, disappoints his friend the Corporal—who is never

even allowed the dignity of a Christian name—by refusing
to go on taking part in the Corporal's continuing attempts at
escape, which are all failures until the sixth. Ballochet ac-
cepts the confines of prison camp almost in a mood of
idealism. This is at least better than his old job, which was a
nullity in the prewar order of Christian and chivalrous
tenets: nothing very Christian or chivalrous about the gas
company. To the Corporal's disgust, Ballochet enjoys his
retreat into a liberty of the mind, though he says mildly that
it's annoying to be a loser, and that it plays hell with one's
habits. He seems at first a cowering soul. But not to Renoir,
who shows him at last slowly inspired to walk out of their
prison hut toward the barbed wire, armed with a pair of
pliers from his old days with the gas company. He dies. The
Corporal, the discouraged friend who felt a whiff of contempt that Ballochet had given up trying to escape with him,
is suddenly Ballochet's intimate again, in a shot on Jean-
Pierre Cassel in which he visibly walks every step with the
loner and jumps like a pheasant during a shoot when the
machine guns burst out. Others wanted to take the impossible risk, too, but Ballochet said, "My kind has to go it alone,"
walking away from the others and adjusting his spectacles.
Dignity makes caste disappear. The Corporal is
pinned—*épinglé*—into a system of automatized heroism,
whereas Ballochet was able to see that the prisoners hardly
knew any longer why they were attempting to escape. Still,
the Corporal keeps trying. For Renoir's Corporal, as for an
E. M. Forster character, heroism rests in behaving a little
better in crisis than one normally would.

Eventually the Corporal succeeds in escaping, and
makes his way to Paris with his second-best friend, Pater
(Claude Brasseur). There are meaningless swift goodbyes

and empty promises to meet again at the front: awful to hear
social fibs at this stage between two close members of a
group that once said gaily, in the early days, that Roosevelt
was writing to Hitler, "Dear Adolf, Release French prisoners
or we'll declare war," and that made undying promises to
have dinner together in Paris when it was all over. Life is full
of brief shafts of disappointment. We know that Pater's and
the Corporal's vows will never be kept. This is not where
their heroism lies. With the completed escape, the Corporal
has laid himself open to the arrows of real life's distress, and
can find encouragement only in the memory of a German
girl, a dentist's assistant, who said, "I like a man who's not a
slave."

But the film says at the end that "this is only a
beginning"—the idea that was to become the slogan of the
student rebels during the uprising of May, 1968. Renoir is
the youngest of us, the most gently rebellious, the most
studious. Things are never more than a beginning for him.
How like him not to have hesitated to make a picture about
prisoners of war a quarter of a century after he directed *La
Grande Illusion* on the same theme. The later film is not a
masterwork, but it moves on the same hawser of sociability
in impossible circumstances. An aged and very drunk German whom the escapers meet on a train says to the Corporal
and Pater that he likes the French, and he tries to stop Nazi
soldiers from catching them. Then he is killed by the Allies
in an air attack. As the Corporal and Pater get near the
border, they meet an amiable French farmer who turns out
to be a First World War prisoner who later married the
German woman with whom he had been billeted. A sense of
the general flux of things suffuses Renoir's work. There are
scenes in *Le Caporal Épinglé* in which the camera abruptly

pulls back, as if to "resituate the characters in a better life," as Renoir once put it. The movie is made in revolt against the ruling absurdity of existence, what with the drunk on the train, and the chaotic air attack. The meditative film is watching, with cool eyes, a case of delirium taking place before a softer morning. The delirium is entirely recognizable but entirely unfamiliar, as Renoir would want. His passion for novelty and his breadth of spirit are at the root of his vivacity. He is our perpetual revolutionary and our perpetual beginner.

The Compere of the Game:
Le Petit Théâtre de Jean Renoir
(1969)

LE PETIT THÉÂTRE DE JEAN RENOIR, directed when he was seventy-five, has the vigor of a first work. It has a modest appearance, like everything else he has ever done. In form, it is a series of three sketches that begin on a red-swagged toy stage. The great director, looking pale but always himself, behaves as a sort of compere. The picture written by him was made for television, but it suits the movie screen much better. The convivial, saddened, magically revived temperament of the last story has some of the nature of *La Règle du Jeu*.

Henri Langlois, the archivist who is world film history's sage, Cerberus, spy, Foreign Legionnaire, and acknowledged king—the scholar of silent movies who calls the talkies "the babble-toy"; the big witty man whose arms fall forward as if he would prefer to be on all fours when he is speaking—opened a season in America of great films from the Cinémathèque Française archives with Renoir's *Le Petit Théâtre*. Otherwise it is a season of brilliance, quixotry, love, and disorder. ("Disorder is the Greek thing. . . . Disorder is the energy," Langlois said in a hurry at the opening, offhandedly defending a lifetime.) It is his witness in America of an aim realized after ages of scholars' squabbles; his conspiratorial gift to the movie land that has precious little concrete recall of world movies. Typically, the Dionysian antiquarian began the season with this Apollonian film of Renoir's. The picture was made for French and Italian television. That should put no one off, least of all distributors. At seventy-five, the master does things in this film that are as funny, convivial, and moving as anything in his career.

In the middle of the picture, at the end of the second of three sketches, Renoir makes one of his appearances and says, "I invite you now to an evocation of what it is convenient to call the *'belle époque.'* " He looks rather serious. "I know very well," he says, "that the *belle époque* wasn't as beautiful as all that, that it had its injustices, its cruelties, but I like it, because it furnished us with touching elements for the mounting of spectacles." Your head hums a bit with boredom, but this is Renoir, after all. You make room. He goes on, "I asked Jeanne Moreau to be our guide on this excursion into the past. With infinite grace, she agreed to lend her beauty and her talent." It is rather stuffy, like the opening of a fête. Then Jeanne Moreau comes on in a wasp-waisted dress and sings a terrific piece of nineteenth-century sentiment composed by Octave Crémieux and called "When Love Dies." (Marlene Dietrich sang it in *Morocco*.) The solemnity is immense. Love dies splendiferously. The camera moves slowly in and out with heavy respect, like an intimidated member of the chorus tiptoeing around the stage deathbed of a soprano who is elocuting some very long and effulgent last words. So this isn't nostalgia at all. It is high, stone-faced, crackup spoof. The magnetic thing is that Jeanne Moreau's expressions are completely out of sync with the stuff she is singing. In full flood, she looks obscurely distracted. As she belts out a particularly hefty line of lament, a wisp of anxiety will cross her face. Something is bothering her. The song, presumably. Then she will muster herself and carry straight on, gazing at a point that exquisitely just misses the camera, her beautiful eyes sometimes slightly crossed. The famous mouth drags down in misery, and the upper lip gets very long, like someone suppressing a yawn.

The number is simple and mysteriously hilarious. Jeanne Moreau must be very bright. Perhaps funniness often occurs when everything is in good order except for one small thing that has slipped. In this two-minute set piece, it is the visibly skeptical cast of the singer's mind that throws everything out. In the sketch that this squib of a song follows, called "The Electric Waxing Machine," it is something else. Renoir introduces the sketch as an opera: "Well, at least, there are songs, choruses commenting on the action, et cetera, et cetera. It is also very topical, because it is about the struggle between mankind and the machine." A prim and pretty housewife (Marguérite Cassan, superb), a Dresden-faced chirper who is obsessed with cleaning, comes back to her apartment one day and slips dreamily into snowshoe-size carpet slippers before breasting around her living-room floor so as to polish the parquet. Her passion to own an electric floor-waxer easily dwarfs any passion she has ever had for her husband (Pierre Olaf), a benign, decorous man who looks much in need of exhilaration. He has just been upped to second clerk, but his wife pays him no heed at all, apart from saying that the promotion will pay for a polisher. When the man tries to be master in his own house, it is an act that he can sustain only by stalking away from her and delivering experimental pieces of firmness from hidden positions in other rooms. He is beaten, of course. The electric polisher comes to stay. The husband soon dies of a blow on the head, flat on his back after slipping on the glassy floor. Sorrowing but practical, the widow quickly gets married again and goes on adoring her floor. "A spot!" she hisses, on hands and knees, thrilled, while her new man is trying in his turn to be forceful about getting her not to use the noisy machine when he is at home. She turns girlish. "I'm going back to my mother," she whines. The comic bit of displacement here is that the actress really looks twenty years too old for the line. The little fable is always perfectly acted, with funny spurts of fury and some moments of Tati automation behavior. It also has the unusual and transforming provision that it is cryptically interrupted now and then by singers, who elbow their way to the camera and wail rather bossy comments on the action. Joseph Kosma's witty music—he wrote the score for Renoir's *La Grande Illusion*—is in the style of, say, the Nadia Boulanger school. It is advanced. The singers look concentrated and forbidding. A fierce egotism visibly operates among them: a man and a woman will bawl nastily in counterpoint at each other, for instance, while a taller man in the middle, irritably holding another nontune, cranes over them and fixes the camera with a chill stare. Sometimes a lot of the singers will be clumped together, desperately pretending to be ordinary people in the middle of their recondite yelling. There is one difficult song when they mill, trying vainly to look as if they were chatting, each of them equipped, for no credible reason, with a long loaf of bread. Like a Greek chorus, they have reactions that are a mixture of the high-flown and the fusspot, and they exclaim a great deal about rapture and delicious excess in a rather nagging, petit-bourgeois tone of voice. The little story is gracefully characterized in the performances and very funny about twentieth-century music and ancient Greeks.

The film begins low, with a tale called "The Last Christmas Eve," derived from Hans Christian Andersen. A navy-blue-cheeked tramp has been hired to look hungry outside the window of a restaurant so as to sharpen the Christmas appetites of the gossipy celebrators within, who have the attention span of gnats. The sentimentality of the tramp's last Christmas Eve, spent with an old beggar-woman friend and going to sleep hungry in a snowfall, is not Renoir's, but the talk of the well-heeled, scatty people inside the restaurant is his own and funnily inane. Fighting off thickets of paper streamers, they utter the blithe bird cries of a holiday without a context. ("I *adore* convention," says one man, drumming up enthusiasm for the boring with no visible luck, while everybody else in the room ignores him anyway.) Someone idly recommends whiskey and cayenne for toothache to a wretched beauty who looks as if she has been forced into her tight dress with a monkey wrench. She says little and nurses a painful wisdom tooth. Apart from poverty, though, and the conceits of fairy tales, why does the tramp take on the fanciful job? To assassinate boredom, he seems to suggest. "Hunger, cold, I can manage all those. But boredom . . ." he says faintly. This is a slight piece, made charming and idiosyncratic by Renoir.

The third piece, "The King of Yvetot," is fine enough and characteristic enough to remind you often of Renoir's *La Règle du Jeu*. ("I enjoy repeating myself," Renoir said happily a while ago. "One gets interested.") A character called Duvallier (Fernand Sardou), a heavy, poetic, shambling figure a little like the Octave whom Renoir himself

played in *La Règle du Jeu*, is married to a pretty girl much
younger than he is. They live in the country, in a small town
where the men play bowls and Duvallier always wins. This
nourishes the old French superstition that winners at games
must be in the midst of being cuckolded. He laughs amiably
at that, and continues to dote on his wife. He also deals
sweetly with their maid, who wants to quit service and become a high-class concubine, like Camille or Messalina—"a
hetaera." (She wants to do a lot of things. Later on, she
aspires desperately to own a butcher's shop. "It's perfectly
possible to be a hetaera *and* a butcher," her master says
encouragingly.)

"I'm nervous," says his wife, out of the blue. Why? She
doesn't know. Her skin is tingling and she looks ready to
run. His big head hangs. He's old and she's young, and that's
the root of it—they should separate, he says lugubriously.
No, she says, believing she means it; she is married to a big
bear at loose and alone in the world, and she loves him, and
life without him would be insupportable. In the middle of
this—events in Renoir's best films flow in and out of one
another like water, with unrelated small mishaps interrupting moments when the people talking are trying to confront
their lives—their dachshund is hurt. The vet comes, in a
very small white car, heralded by the ceremonial but clipped
entrance music of four bars from Beethoven's Fifth. The
crisis passes, the couple and the vet have lunch, the distraught maid produces an uncooked fish, and the vet and
Duvallier strike up an alliance because they discover that
they both believe in loafing. (Duvallier sings a scrap of a
nineteenth-century jingle about the endearing king of
Yvetot, "little known in history," who lay about in bed most
of the time "and slept wonderfully, though without glory.")

The vet falls for the wife, of course. There is a moment when he kisses first the dachshund's head and then the girl's mouth. She looks mildly dissident. Duvallier finds out about the affair very soon. You see his back view going down a lane: an ambling creature, quizzical, much wounded, with a jacket that hangs loose behind. What would the other men in the village do if their wives took lovers? He asks a sailor. "I wouldn't bother myself about it much," says the sailor, and then, with an unmarked turn in the line that is typical of Renoir's dialogue style, "I haven't got a wife." Another adviser says, "I'd kill her, and him, too." "You love her that much?" says Duvallier. "It's not how much I love her," the adviser, who deals in rabbit skins, says loftily, "but I wouldn't want to be taken for a fool." The wife blooms in love; the aging husband, hanging his heavy head like a cart horse put out to grass and stumbling away into the world beyond his once idyllic garden to think, is smartly saluted by a tramp. The locals admire his luck at bowls but take it for granted that it means he is unlucky in love. On the way to join them, he picks a straw of grass, wipes the tears from his papery cheeks, and gives some money to the saluting bum, whose experience of love and sex turns out to be slight when Duvallier asks for advice. "Your orders are to get plastered," Duvallier says gently. "Aye, aye, sir," says the tramp, this unmarried innocent, touched for no reason he can put his finger on. "What would you do if your wife cheated?" Duvallier asks another man near the village. "She's too old" is the reply.

Duvallier himself is irretrievably pacific, but he comports himself like no fool. The vet, in an immolatory mood masked as belligerence, offers pistols. No taker. "You don't wish to duel with me?" says the vet piteously. I don't think so,

Duvallier holds. A possible course, and better, would be to live out the triangle as it is. "But there are conventions," says the vet, scandalized. None of this is Duvallier's style, which is the style of reconciling. He is old, if hurt. His wife is young, if casual; she's fond of him. And the vet can't imagine life without either of them, he says, telling the patent truth. Duvallier typically regards it as his task to cheer everyone up. The distraught vet talks of going to China. Think of my wife, says Duvallier with his usual *douceur* of spirit. But it would be a revolution to stay together, all of us, says the vet. On the contrary, says Duvallier, it is the small revolutions that make life bearable. The vet beams. Duvallier goes on: about revolutions in the kitchen, the bedroom, the village square, which he considerably dreads because he is going to be laughed at. "You're an extraordinary man," says the vet.

And then, at this rather sad moment in praise of accommodation, Renoir suddenly seizes the last few seconds of the picture and throws them into the air like a kite, turning a shot of people playing bowls and laughing at the cuckolded Duvallier into an image of the husband, wife, and lover laughing together, and then, pulling back in a continuous shot, into the sight of them still laughing together but now as actors taking their curtain call. The speed is beautiful. This is a little work by a great master, and it is little partly because he can do what he wants in the breath of a second. That may have something to do with the succinctness of age, but it also has something to do with his lifelong genius for throwing great things away very fast. The last part of the film, which is spiked with marvellous funniness and spirit, embodies some rather serious ideas about the tolerance of contradictions—a notion that runs through

THE COMPERE OF THE GAME: LE PETIT THÉÂTRE DE JEAN RENOIR 83

Renoir's work—but he gives us the whole piece as a toy, for the fun of it. He would never have enjoyed being a general, which is the way a good many directors see their role. He is a born corporal, teaching a platoon how to hang on to a horse, because that's the entertaining part. There are a lot of moments in the picture that one wishes would go on longer, but he cuts them short out of a sure instinct that there are plenty more where these came from. The prodigality makes your eyes sting, and not because of his age.

BOUDU SAUVÉ DES EAUX (1932)
(The Museum of Modern Art
Film Still Archive)

TONI (1934)
(Contemporary Films/
McGraw-Hill)

LE CRIME DE MONSIEUR LANGE (1935)
(The Museum of Modern Art
Film Still Archive)

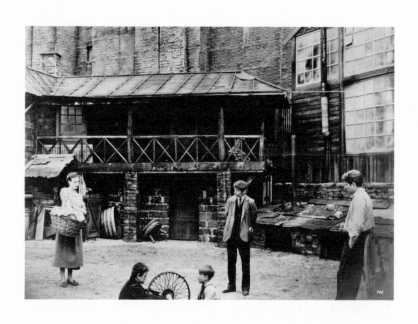

LES BAS-FONDS (1936)
(The Museum of Modern Art
Film Still Archive)

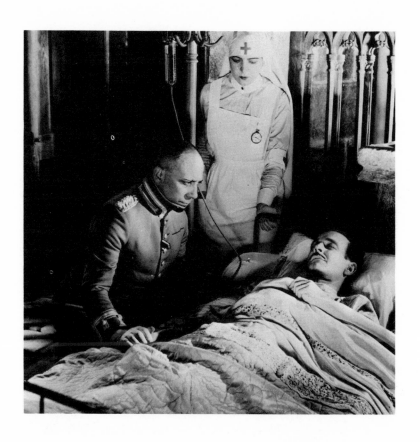

LA GRANDE ILLUSION
(1936-37)
(Janus)

LA GRANDE ILLUSION
(1936-37)
(Janus)

LA GRANDE ILLUSION
(1936-37)
(Janus)

LA MARSEILLAISE (1937)
(Contemporary Films/
McGraw-Hill)

LA RÈGLE DU JEU
(1939)
(Janus)

LA RÈGLE DU JEU
(1939)
(Janus)

LA RÈGLE DU JEU
(1939)
(Janus)

LA RÈGLE DU JEU
(1939)
(Janus)

ELÉNA ET LES HOMMES (1956)
(The Museum of Modern Art
Film Still Archive)

LE DÉJEUNER SUR L'HERBE (1959)
(Contemporary Films/
McGraw-Hill)

LE CAPORAL ÉPINGLÉ (1961-62)
(Contemporary Films/
McGraw-Hill)

LE PETIT THÉÂTRE DE JEAN RENOIR
(1969)
(Phoenix Films)

Filmography

UNE VIE SANS JOIE, made in 1924 (reedited in 1927 and
    released as *CATHERINE*).

80 minutes

Directed by Albert Dieudonné
Screenplay by Jean Renoir from a story by Jean Renoir and
    Pierre Lestringuez
Produced by Jean Renoir
Photographed by Jean Bachelet and Gibory

CAST:

Catherine Hessling *as Catherine Ferand*
Albert Dieudonné *as M. Mallet, the owner*
Pierre Philippe *as Adolph, the pimp*
Pierre Champagne *as the younger Mallet*
Oléo *as a prostitute*
Georges Térof *as Gédéon Grané*
Eugénie Naud *as Madame Laisné*
Jean Renoir *as the subprefect*
Louis Gauthier *as Georges Mallet*

LA FILLE DE L'EAU, made in 1924 (English-language title
    THE WHIRLPOOL OF FATE).

70 minutes

Directed by Jean Renoir
Screenplay by Pierre Lestringuez

Produced by Jean Renoir
Photographed by Jean Bachelet and Gibory
Assistant director Pierre Champagne
Sets conceived by Jean Renoir

CAST:

Catherine Hessling *as Virginia Rosaert*
Pierre Phillippe *as Uncle Jef*
Pierre Champagne *as Justin Crepoix*
Harold Lewingston *as Georges Raynal*
Maurice Touzé *as the little vagabond*
Georges Térof *as M. Raynal*
Henriette Moret *as La Roussette*
Charlotte Clasis *as Mme. Raynal*
Pierre Renoir *as a peasant·*
André Derain *as the owner of "Au Bon Coin"*
Van Doren *as the leading man*

NANA, made in 1925-26.
98 minutes

Directed by Jean Renoir
Screenplay by Pierre Lestringuez (based on Émile Zola's
    novel), adapted by Jean Renoir; titles by Denise
    Leblond-Zola
Produced by Jean Renoir
Photographed by Jean Bachelet and Edmund Corwin
Assistant director André Cerf
Edited by Jean Renoir

CAST:

Catherine Hessling *as Nana*
Werner Krauss *as Count Muffat*

Jacqueline Forzane *as Countess Sabine Muffat*
Jean Angelo *as Count de Vandeuvres*
Raymond Guérin-Catelain *as Georges Hugon*
Pierre Champagne *as La Falaise*
Pierre Philippe *as Bordenave*
Valeska Gert *as Zoé, Nana's maid*
Harbacher *as Francis, Nana's hairdresser*
André Cerf *as Le Tigre, Nana's groom*
Claude Moore *as Fauchery*
Jacqueline Ford *as Rose Mignon*
Nita Romani *as Satin*
Marie Prévost *as Gago*
René Koval *as Fontan*
Pierre Braunberger ⎱ *spectators at Le Théâtre des*
R. Turgy ⎰ *Variétés*

SUR UN AIR DE CHARLESTON, made in 1926 (alternate
    title *CHARLESTON-PARADE*).

22 minutes

Directed by Jean Renoir
Screenplay by Pierre Lestringuez from an idea by André
    Cerf
Assistant director André Cerf
Photographed by Jean Bachelet
Music by Clément Doucet

CAST:

Catherine Hessling *as the dancer*
Johnny Hugging *as the explorer*
Pierre Braunberger ⎱ *as angels*
Pierre Lestringuez ⎰

LA P'TITE LILI, made in 1926.

11 minutes

Directed by Alberto Cavalcanti
Screenplay by Alberto Cavalcanti from a song by Louis
    Benech
Produced by Pierre Braunburger
Photography by Rogers
Edited by Marguerite Renoir
Music by Max de La Sasinière
Sets by Eric Aës

CAST:

Catherine Hessling *as La P'tite Lili*
Jean Renoir *as the pimp*
Guy Ferrand *as the singer*
Roland Caillaux *as the concierge*
Eric Aës ⎫
Rogers   ⎬ *silhouettes*
Dido Freire ⎭

MARQUITA, made in 1926-27 (originally titled
     MARCHETA, from a song by Saint Granier).

87 minutes

Directed by Jean Renoir
Screenplay by Pierre Lestringuez from an adaption by Jean
    Renoir
Produced by Artistes Réunis
Photographed by Jean Bachelet and Raymond Agnel

Assistant director M. Gargour
Sets by Robert-Jules Garnier

CAST:

Jean Angelo *as Prince Vlasco*
Marie-Louise Iribe *as Marquita*
Henri Debain *as Count Dimitrieff*
Lucien Mancini *as the stepfather*
Pierre Philippe *as the casino owner*
Pierre Champagne *as a taxi driver*

LA PETITE MARCHANDE D'ALLUMETTES, made in 1926
(English-language title *THE LITTLE MATCH GIRL*).

29 minutes

Directed by Jean Renoir collaborating with Jean Tedesco
Screenplay by Jean Renoir from the Hans Christian Andersen story
Produced by Jean Renoir and Jean Tedesco
Photographed by Jean Bachelet
Assistant directors Claude Heyman and Simone Hamiguet
Music from Mendelssohn, Strauss, Wagner, and others

CAST:

Catherine Hessling *as the little match girl*
Jean Storm *as the young man and the soldier*
Manuel Raaby *as the policeman and the emissary of death*
Amy Wells *as the dancing doll*

TIRE AU FLANC, made in 1928 (*THE SLACKER*).

80 minutes

Directed by Jean Renoir
Screenplay by Jean Renoir, Claude Heymenn, and André
    Cerf from a play by A. Mouézy-Eon and A. Sylvane
Produced by Pierre Braunberger
Photographed by Jean Bachelet
Assistant directors André Cerf and Lola Markovitch
Titles and drawings by André Rigaud
Sets by Eric Aës

CAST:

Georges Pomiès *as Jean Dubois d'Ombelles*
Michel Simon *as Joseph*
Felix Oudart *as Colonel Brochard*
Jeanne Hibling *as Solange Standin*
Jean Storm *as Lieutenant Daumel*
Paul Velsa *as Corporal Bourrache*
Manuel Raaby *as the adjutant*
Fridette Fatton *as Georgette*
Maryanne *as Mme. Blandin*
Zellas *as Muflot*
Kinny Dorlay *as Lily, Solange's sister*
Esther Kiss *as Mme. Flechais*
André Cerf ⎫
Max Dalban ⎭ *soldiers*

LE TOURNOI DANS LA CITÉ, made in 1928.

72 minutes

Directed by Jean Renoir
Screenplay by Henri Dupuy-Mazuel and André Jaeger-
    Schmidt; adapted by Jean Renoir

Produced by Maroussem and François Harispuru
Photographed by Marcel Lucien and Maurice Desfassiaux
Assistant director André Cerf
Edited by André Cerf
Sets by Robert Mallet-Stevens

CAST:

Aldo Nadi *as François de Baynes*
Jackie Monnier *as Isabelle Ginori*
Enrique Rivero *as Henri de Rogier*
Manuel Raaby *as Catherine de Médicis*
Suzanne Despres *as Countess Baynes*
Gérard Mock *as Charles IX*
Vivian Clarens *as Lucrèce Pazzi*
Narval *as Antonio*
Janvier *as the King's Guard officer*
William Aguet *as Master of the Horse*
Max Dalban *as Captain of the Watch*

LE BLED, made in 1929 (*THE BACK OF BEYOND*).
87 minutes

Directed by Jean Renoir
Screenplay by Henri Dupuy-Mazuel and André Jaeger-
    Schmidt; adapted by Jean Renoir; titles by André
    Giraud
Produced by Henri Dupuy-Mazuel
Photographed by Marcel Lucien and Morizet
Assistant directors André Cerf and René Arcy-Hennery
Edited by Marguerite Renoir
Sets by William Aguet

CAST:

Jackie Monnier *as Claude Duvernet*
Enrique Rivero *as Pierre Hoffer*
Arquillière *as Christian Hoffer*
Diana Hart *as Diane Duvernet*
Manuel Raaby *as Manuel Duvernet*
Bérardi Aissa *as Zoubir*
Jacques Becker *as a farm laborer*
Hadj Ben Yasmina *as the chauffeur*
M. Martin *as the falconer Ahmed*
Mme. Rozier *as Marie-Jeanne*

LE PETIT CHAPERON ROUGE, made in 1929.
Short film

Directed by Alberto Cavalcanti and Jean Renoir
Screenplay by Alberto Cavalcanti and Jean Renoir; adapted
      from a story by Charles Perrault
Produced by M. Guillaume
Photographed by Marcel Lucien
Edited by Marguerite Renoir
Music by Maurice Jaubert

CAST:

Catherine Hessling *as Little Red Riding Hood*
Jean Renoir *as the wolf*
André Cerf *as the notary*
Pierre Prévert *as a girl*
Pablo Quevedo *as the young man*
La Montagne *as a farmer*
William Aguet *as an old Englishwoman*

LA CHASSE À LA FORTUNE, made in 1929-30 (alternate
     title *LA CHASSE AU BONHEUR*).

Short film

Directed by Rochus Gliese
Screenplay by Lotte Reiniger and Carl Koch, from an idea
     by Alex Trasser
Produced by Comenius Films
Photographed by Fritz Arno Wagner
Music by Theo Mackenben

CAST:

Jean Renoir *as a businessman*
Catherine Hessling *as Fortune*
Bertold Bartosche *as the pedlar*
Jean Tedesco ⎫
Alexander Murski ⎬ *silhouettes*
Amy Wells ⎭

ON PURGE BÉBÉ, made in 1931.

62 minutes

Directed by Jean Renoir; this was Renoir's first 100% talking
     film
Screenplay by Jean Renoir from the Georges Feydeau play
Produced by Charles David
Photographed by Théodore Sparkuhl and Roger Hubert
Assistant directors Claude Heymann and Pierre Schwab
Edited by Jean Mamy
Sets by Gabriel Scongnamillo

CAST:

Michel Simon *as Chouilloux*
Marguerita Pierry *as Julie Follavoine*
Olga Valery *as Clémence Chouilloux*
Louvigny *as Follavoine*
Sacha Tarride *as Toto*
Nicole Fernandez *as Rose*
Fernandel *as Truchet*

LA CHIENNE, made in 1931.

100 minutes

Directed by Jean Renoir
Screenplay by Jean Renoir and André Girard from the
    Georges de la Fouchardière novel
Produced by Charles David and Roger Woog
Photographed by Théodore Sparkuhl and Roger Hubert
Assistant directors Claude Heymann and Pierre Prévert
Edited by Denise Batcheff-Tual, Marguerite Renoir, and
    Jean Renoir
Music by Eugénie Buffet
Sets by Gabriel Scongnamillo

CAST:

Michel Simon *as Maurice Legrand*
Madeline Bérubet *as Adèle Legrand*
Janie Marèze *as Lulu Pelletier*
Georges Flammand *as André Jauguin, called Dédé*
Gaillard *as Sergeant Alexis Godard*
Jean Gehret *as Dagòdet*

Lucien Mancini *as Wallstein, the gallery owner*
Sylvain Itkine *as the lawyer*
Alexandre Rignault *as Langelard, the art critic*
Max Dalban *as Bonnard*
Colette Borelli *as Lily, Lulu's friend*
Romain Bouquet *as M. Henriot, store owner*
Pierre Destys *as Gustave*
Jane Pierson *as the concierge*
Henri Guisol *as Amédée, a waiter*
Argentin *as the magistrate*
Mlle. Doryans *as Yvonne*

LA NUIT DU CARREFOUR, made in 1932.

80 minutes

Directed by Jean Renoir
Screenplay by Jean Renoir and Georges Simenon from a
    Georges Simenon novel
Produced by Jacques Becker
Photographed by Marcel Lucien and Asselin
Assistant directors Jacques Becker and Maurice Blondeau
Edited by Marguerite Renoir, assisted by Suzanne Troye
    and Walter Ruttmann
Sets by William Aguet, assisted by Jean Castanier

CAST:

Pierre Renoir *as Inspector Maigret*
Georges Térof *as Lucas*
Winna Winifred *as Elsa Andersen*
Georges Koudria *as Carl Andersen*
Dignimont *as Oscar*

Lucie Vallat *as Oscar's wife*
G. A. Martin *as Grandjean*
Jean Gehret *as Emile Michonnet*
Michel Duran *as Jojo, the garage attendant*
Jean Mitray *as Arsène*
Max Dalban *as the doctor*
Gaillard *as the butcher*
Jeanne Pierson *as Mme. Michonnet*
Boulicot *as a policeman*
Manuel Raaby *as Guido*

CHOTARD & CIE, made in 1932.
113 minutes

Directed by Jean Renoir
Screenplay by Jean Renoir and Roger Ferdinand from the
    play by Roger Ferdinand
Produced by Roger Ferdinand
Photographed by Mundwiller
Assistant director Jacques Becker
Edited by Marguerite Renoir and Suzanne de Troye
Sets by Jean Castanier

CAST:

Fernand Charpin *as François Chotard*
Jeanne Lory *as Marie, his wife*
Georges Pomiès *as Julien Collinet*
Jeanne Boitel *as Reine, his wife*
Malou Treki *as Augustine*
Louis Tunk *as the subprefect*

Dignimont *as Parpaillon, Julien's friend*
Max Dalban *as a grocery shop assistant*
Robert Seller *as the police chief*
Fabien Loris *as a guest at the ball*

BOUDU SAUVÉ DES EAUX, made in 1932.
83 minutes

Directed by Jean Renoir
Screenplay by Jean Renoir and Albert Valentin from the
    René Fauchois play
Produced by Michel Simon and Jean Gehret
Photographed by Marcel Lucien and Asselin
Assistant directors Jacques Becker and Georges Darnoux
Edited by Marguerite Renoir and Suzanne de Troye
Music by Raphael and Johann Strauss
Sets by Jean Castanier and Laurent

CAST:

Michel Simon *as Boudu*
Charles Granval *as Lestingois*
Marcel Haina *as his wife*
Sévérine Lerczinska *as Anne-Marie*
Jean Dasté *as the student*
Max Dalban *as Godin*
Jean Gehret *as Vigour*
Jacques Becker *as the poet*
Jane Pierson *as Rose, a maid*
Georges Darnoux *as a guest*

MADAME BOVARY, made in 1933.
102 minutes (210-minute version never shown)

Directed by Jean Renoir
Screenplay by Jean Renoir from Gustave Flaubert's novel
Produced by Gaston Gallimard
Photographed by Jean Bachelet and Gibory
Assistant directors Jacques Becker and Pierre Desouches
Edited by Marguerite Renoir
Music by Darius Milhaud and Donizetti
Sets by Robert Gys
Costumes by Medgyes

CAST:

Valentine Tessier *as Emma, Madame Bovary*
Pierre Renoir *as Charles Bovary*
Daniel Lecourtois *as Léon*
Fernand Fabre *as Rodolphe*
Alice Tissot *as Charles Bovary's mother*
Helena Manson *as the first Mme. Bovary*
Pierre Larquey *as Hippolyte*
Max Dearly *as Homais, the pharmacist*
Robert le Vigan *as Lheureux*
Maryanne *as Mme. Homais*
Léon Larive *as the prefect*
Florencie *as Abbe Bournisien*
Romain Bouquet *as Guillaumin, the notary*
Georges Cahuzac *as Rouault*
Allain Dhurtal *as the surgeon*
Henry Vilbert *as Canivet*
Robert Moore *as the footman*
Georges Denebourg *as the Marquis de Vaubyessard*
Edmond Beauchamp *as Binet*

André Fouchet *as Justin, the chemist*
Jean Gehret *as the prefect*
René Bloch *as the coachman*
Marthe Mellot *as the old Nicaise*
Monet Dinay *as Félicité*
Christiane d'Or *as Mme. Lefrançois*

TONI, made in 1934.

90 minutes

Directed by Jean Renoir
Screenplay by Jean Renoir and Carl Einstein, suggested by a
    newspaper article
Produced by Pierre Gaut
Assistant directors Georges Darnoux and Antonio Can
Assistant Luchino Visconti
Edited by Marguerite Renoir and Suzanne de Troye
Music by Paul Bozzi
Sets by Léon Bourelly and Marius Brauquier

CAST:

Charles Blavette *as Toni (Antonio Canova)*
Celian Montalvan *as Josefa*
Jenny Hélia *as Maria*
Max Dalban *as Albert*
Edouard Delmont *as Fernand*
Andrex *as Gaby*
André Kovatchevitch *as Sebastien*
Paul Bozzi *as guitarist Jacques Bozzi*

LE CRIME DE MONSIEUR LANGE, made in 1935.
90 minutes

Directed by Jean Renoir
Screenplay by Jacques Prévert from a story by Jean Renoir
    and Jean Castanier
Produced by André Halley des Fontaines
Photographed by Jean Bachelet
Assistant directors Jacques Prévert and Georges Darnoux
Edited by Marguerite Renoir
Music by Jean Wiener and Joseph Kosma
Sets by Jean Castanier and Robert Gys, assisted by Roger
    Blin

CAST:

René Lefèvre *as Amédé Lange*
Jules Berry *as Batala*
Florelle *as Valentine*
Nadia Sibirskaïa *as Estelle*
Sylvia Bataille *as Edith*
Henri Guisol *as Meunier*
Marcel Levesque *as Bessard, the concierge*
Odette Talazac *as his wife*
Maurice Baquet *as Charles, his son*
Jacques Brunius *as Daigneur*
Sylvain *as Batala's cousin, a retired police inspector*
Edmond Beauchamp *as a priest on the train*
René Genin *as a cafe customer*
Marcel Duhamel ⎫
Jean Dasté   ⎬ *printers*
Guy Decomble   ⎪
Paul Grimault ⎭

Paul Demange *as a creditor*
Claire Gérard *as the prostitute*

LA VIE EST À NOUS, made in 1936 (English-language title
    PEOPLE OF FRANCE).

66 minutes

Directed by Jean Renoir with the help of Jacques Becker,
    Jean-Paul Le Chanois, Henri Cartier-Bresson, Pierre
    Unik, B. Brunius, and André Vaillant-Coutourier
Screenplay by Jean Renoir and André Zwoboda
Produced by the Parti Communiste Français
Photographed by Jean Isnard, Jean-Serge Bourgoin,
    Claude Renoir, and Alain Douarinou
Edited by Marguerite Renoir
Music the "Internationale," other songs of the Popular
    Front, Shostakovich
Banned by censors in France and not shown publicly there
    until 1969

CAST:

Jean Dast *as the schoolmaster*
Jacques Brunius *as the president of the Conseil d'Administration*
Max Dalban *as Brochard*
Madeline Solange *as a worker*
Charles Blavette *as Tonin*
Jean Renoir *as the bistro owner*
Edy Debray *as the usher*
Henri Pons *as M. Lecocq*
Gabrielle Fontant *as Mme. Lecocq*

Gaston Modot *as Philippe*
Léon Larive *as a customer at the auction*
Nadia Sibirskaïa *as Ninette*
Marcel Duhamel *as the National Volunteer*
O'Brady *as the car washer*
Julien Bertheau ⎫
Guy Favières ⎪
Jacques Becker ⎬ *unemployed workers*
Tristan Sevère ⎭
Jean-Paul Le Chanois *as P'tit Louis*
Emile Drain *as Gustave Bertin*
Sylvain Itkine *as the accountant*
Simone Guisin *as a woman at the casino*
Teddy Michaux *as a fascist*
Pierre Unik ⎫
Madeline Dox ⎬ *secretaries*
Fernand Bercher ⎭
Claire Gérard *as a woman in the street*
Roger Blin *as a sailor*
Georges Spanelly *as the factory manager*
Marcel Lesieur *as a garage owner*
Charles Charras ⎫
Francis Lemarque ⎬ *singers*

AS THEMSELVES

Marcel Cachin
André Marty
Paul Vaillant-Coutourier
Jean Renaud
Martha Desrumeaux
Marcel Gitton
Jacques Duclos

Maurice Thorez
and the involuntary participation of Colonel de la Rocque

UNE PARTIE DE CAMPAGNE, made in 1936.

37 minutes

Directed by Jean Renoir

Screenplay by Jean Renoir, based on the short story by Guy
de Maupassant

Produced by Pierre Braunberger

Assistant directors Yves Allegret, Jacques Becker, Jacques
Brunius, Henri Cartier-Bresson, Luchino Visconti,
Claude Heymann

Edited by Marguerite Renoir and Marinette Cadix

Music by Joseph Kosma

Sets by Robert Gys

CAST:

Sylvia Bataille *as Henriette Dufour*

Georges Darnoux *as Henri*

Jacques Borel *as Rodolphe*

Jeanne Marken *as Mme. Juliette Dufour*

André Gabriello *as M. Cyprien Dufour*

Paul Temps *as Anatole*

Gabrielle Fontan *as Grandmother Dufour*

Jean Renoir *as Poulain, the innkeeper*

Marguerite Renoir *as the servant*

Pierre Lestringuez *as the curé*

Jacques Becker *as a seminary student*

Alain Renoir *as a little boy*

LES BAS-FONDS, made in 1936.

91 minutes

Directed by Jean Renoir
Screenplay by Jacques Companeez, Eugène Zamatin;
    adapted from the Maxim Gorky play by Charles Spaak,
    Jean Renoir
Produced by Vladimir Zederbaum
Photographed by Jean Bachelet
Assistant directors Jacques Becker, Joseph Soiffer
Edited by Marguerite Renoir
Music by Jean Wiener
Sets by Eugène Lourié, Hughes Laurent
Costumes by Alexander Kamenka

CAST:

Louis Jouvet *as the Baron*
Jean Gabin *as Pepel*
Suzy Prim *as Vasilissa*
Vladamir Sokoloff *as Kostilev*
Junie Astor *as Natacha*
Robert Le Vigan *as the actor*
André Gabriello *as the Inspector*
Camille Bert *as the Count*
Léon Larive *as Felix*
René Génin *as Luka, the drunkard*
Jany Holt *as Nastia, the prostitute*
Maurice Baquet *as Aliochka, the accordionist*
Lucien Mancini *as the restaurant owner*
Paul Temps *as Satine*
Henri Saint-Isles *as Kletsch*
Robert Ozanne *as Jabot*
Nathalie Alexeieff *as Anna*
Jacques Becker *as a silhouette*

LA GRANDE ILLUSION, made in 1936-37.

114 minutes

Directed by Jean Renoir
Screenplay by Charles Spaak, Jean Renoir
Produced by Frank Rollmer, Albert Pinkovitch
Photographed by Christian Matras, with Claude Renoir,
    Bourreud, Jean Bourgoin
Assistant director Jacques Becker
Edited by Marguerite Renoir
Music by Joseph Kosma
Sets by Eugène Lourié

CAST:

Jean Gabin *as Maréchal*
Pierre Fresnay *as de Boïeldieu*
Erich von Stroheim *as von Rauffenstein*
Marcel Dalio *as Rosenthal*
Dita Parlo *as Elsa*
Julien Carette *as the actor*
Gaston Modot *as the engineer*
Jean Dasté *as the teacher*
Georges Paclet *as a French soldier*
Jacques Becker *as an English officer*
Sylvain Itkine *as Demolder*

LA MARSEILLAISE, made in 1937.

135 minutes

Directed by Jean Renoir
Screenplay by Jean Renoir with the help of Carl Koch, and
    M. and Mme. N. Martel-Dreyfus for the historical de-
    tails

Produced for Confédération Générale de Travail

Photographed by Jean Bourgoin, Alain Douarinou, Jean-Marie Maillols, Jean-Paul Alphen, Jean Louis

Assistant directors Jacques Becker, Claude Renoir (nephew of Jean Renoir), Jean-Paul Le Chanois, Claude Renoir (brother of Jean Renoir)

Edited by Marguerite Renoir, Marthe Huguet

Music by Joseph Cosma, Sauveplane, Lalande, Grétry, Rameau, Mozart, Bach, Rouget de Lisle

Sets by Léon Barsacq, Georges Wakhevitch, Jean Perrier

Shadow theater Lotte Reininger

CAST:

The Court
Pierre Renoir *as Louis XVI*
Lise Delamare *as Marie Antoinette*
Léon Larive *as Picard, Louis XVI's valet*
William Aguet *as La Rochefoucauld*
Elisa Ruis *as Mme. de Lamballe*
G. Lefébvre *as Mme. Elizabeth*

The Civil and Military Authorities
Louis Jouvet *as Roederer*
Jean Aquistapace *as the mayor of the village*
Georges Spanally *as La Chesnaye*
Jacque Catelain *as Langlade*
Pierre Nay *as Dubouchange*
Edmond Castel *as Leroux*

The Aristocrats
Aimé Clariond *as Saint-Laurent*
Maurice Escande *as the lord of the village*
André Zibrol *as M. de Saint-Méry*
Jean Aymé *as M. de Fougerolles*

Irène Joachim *as Mme. de Saint-Laurent*

The Inhabitants of Marseille
Andrex *as Arnaud*
Edmond Ardisson *as Bonnier*
Jean-Louis Allibert *as Moissant*
Jenny Hélia *as the questioner*
Paul Dulac *as Javel*
Ferdinand Flament *as Ardisson*
Georges Péclet *as Lieutenant Pignatel*
Géo Dorlys *as a Marseille Leader*
Géo Lastry *as Captaine Massugue*
Adolphe Autran *as the drummer*
Alex Truchy *as Cuculière*

The People
Nadia Sibirskaïa *as Louison*
Edouard Delmont *as Cabri*
Sévérine Lerczinska *as a peasant woman*
Edmond Beauchamp *as the curé*
Gaston Modot ⎫
             ⎬ *volunteers*
Julien Carette ⎭
Marthe Marty *as Bonnier's mother*

LA BÊTE HUMAINE, made in 1938.
105 minutes

Directed by Jean Renoir
Screenplay by Jean Renoir, assisted by Denise Leblond-Zola
    from the Émile Zola novel
Produced by Robert Hakim and Roland Tual
Photographed by Curt Courant and Claude Renoir
Assistant directors Claude Renoir (sen.) and Suzanne de
    Troye

Edited by Marguerite Renoir
Music by Joseph Kosma
Sets by Eugène Lourié

CAST:

Jean Gabin *as Jacques Lantier*
Simone Simon *as Séverine Roubaud*
Fernand Ledoux *as Roubaud*
Julien Carette *as Pecqueux*
Blanchette Brunoy *as Flore*
Gérard Landry *as Dauvergne's son*
Jacques Berlioz *as Grandmorin*
Jean Renoir *as Cabûche*
Marcel Perez *as a railway employee*
Jenny Hélia *as Philomène*
Marceau *as a mechanic*
Tony Corteggiani *as the section boss*
André Tavernier *as the magistrate*
Colette Régis *as Mme. Victoire*
Claire Gérard *as a traveller*
Charlotte Classis *as Phasie Misard*
Georges Spanelly *as Grandmorin's secretary*
Guy Deconble *as a railway crossing guard*
Georges Péclet *as a railway employee*
Émile Gènevois ⎫
⎬ *farmhands*
Jacques Brunius ⎭

LA RÈGLE DU JEU, made in 1939.

113 minutes

Directed by Jean Renoir
Screenplay by Jean Renoir, with the collaboration of Carl
    Koch

Produced by Jean Renoir, Claude Renoir
Photographed by Jean Bachelet
Assistant directors André Zwoboda, Henri Cartier-Bresson
Edited by Marguerite Renoir, assisted by Marthe Huguet
Music by Mozart, Monsigny, Saint-Saëns, Johann Strauss,
    arranged by Robert Desormières and Joseph Kosma
Sets by Eugène Lourié, Max Douy
Costumes by Coco Chanel

CAST:

Marcel Dalio *as Robert de la Chesnaye*
Nora Grégor *as Christine de la Chesnaye*
Roland Toutain as *André Jurieu*
Jean Renoir *as Octave*
Mila Parely *as Geneviève de Marrast*
Paulette Dubost *as Lisette*
Gaston Modot *as Schumacher*
Julien Carette *as Marceau*
Pierre Magnier *as the General*
Pierre Nay *as Saint-Aubin*
Richard Francoeur *as La Bruyère*
Eddy Debray *as Corneille, the majordomo*
Léon Larive *as the cook*
Claire Gérard *as Mme. La Bruyère*
Anne Mayan *as Jackie, Christine's niece*
Lise Elina *as the radio reporter*
Tony Corteggiani *as the huntsman*
Camille François *as the radio speaker*
André Zwobada *as the engineer*
Henri Cartier-Bresson *as the English servant*

LA TOSCA, made in 1939.

96 minutes

Directed by Carl Koch, started by Jean Renoir
Screenplay adapted by Jean Renoir, Carl Koch, and
     Luchino Visconti from the play by Victorien Sardou
Produced by Arturo A. Ambrogio
Photographed by Ubaldo Arata
Edited by Gino Bretone
Music by Puccini

CAST:

Imperio Argentina *as Tosca*
Michel Simon *as Scarpia*
Rossano Brazzi *as Mario Cavaradossi*
Massimo Girotti *as Angeloti*

SWAMP WATER, made in 1941.

86 minutes

Directed by Jean Renoir
Screenplay by Dudley Nichols, from the novel by Vereen
     Bell
Produced by Irving Pichel
Photography by Peverell Marley and Lucien Ballard
Edited by Walter Thompson
Music by David Buttolph
Sets by Thomas Little
Costumes by Gwen Wakeling

CAST:

Dana Andrews *as Ben Ragan*
Walter Huston *as Thursday Ragan*

John Carradine *as Jesse Wick*
Eugene Pallette *as Sheriff Jeb MacKane*
Anne Baxter *as Julie Keefer*
Walter Brennan *as Tom Keefer*
Mary Howard *as Hannah Ragan*
Virginia Gilmore *as Mabel McKenzie*
Ward Bond *as Jim Dorson*
Guinn Williams *as Bud Dorson*
Russell Simpson *as Marty McCord*
Joseph Sawyer *as Hardy Ragan*
Paul Burns *as Tulle McKenzie*
Dave Morris *as the barber*
Frank Austin *as Fred Ulm*
Matt Willis *as Miles Tonkin*

THIS LAND IS MINE, made in 1943.
103 minutes

Directed by Jean Renoir
Screenplay by Dudley Nichols and Jean Renoir
Produced by Dudley Nichols and Jean Renoir
Photographed by Frank Redman
Assistant director Edward Donohue
Edited by Frederick Knudston
Music by Lothar Perl
Sets by Darrel Silvera and Al Felds

CAST:

Charles Laughton *as Albert Mory*
George Sanders *as Georges Lambert*
Maureen O'Hara *as Louise Martin*
Kent Smith *as Paul Martin*

Walter Slezak *as Major von Keller*
Una O'Conner *as Albert Mory's mother*
Phillip Merivale *as Professor Sorel*
Thurston Hall *as Major Henry Manville*
Georges Coulouris *as the prosecutor*
Nancy Gates *as Julie Grant*
Ivan Simpson *as the presiding Judge*
John Donat *as Edmond Lorraine*
Frank Alton *as Lieutenant Schwartz*
Leo Bulgakov *as the little man*
Wheaton Chambors *as Lorraine*
Cecile Weston *as Mrs. Lorraine*

SALUTE TO FRANCE, made in 1944.

20 minutes

Directed by Jean Renoir in collaboration with Garson Kanin
Screenplay by Philippe Dunne, Jean Renoir, and Burgess
    Meredith
Produced by the Office of War Information, New York
Photographed by the Army Pictorial Service
Edited by Helen van Dongen

CAST:

Claude Dauphin *as Jacques, narrator, soldier, and other multiple
    roles*
Burgess Meredith *as Tommy*
Garson Kanin *as Joe*

THE SOUTHERNER, made in 1945 (alternate title *HOLD AUTUMN IN YOUR HAND*).

91 minutes

Directed by Jean Renoir
Screenplay by Jean Renoir from the George Sessions Perry novel *Hold Autumn in Your Hand*; adapted by Hugo Butler
Produced by David L. Loew and Robert Hakim
Photographed by Lucien Andriot
Assistant director Robert Aldrich
Edited by Gregg Tallas
Music by Werner Jannsen
Sets by Eugène Lourié

CAST:

Zachary Scott *as Sam Tucker*
Betty Field *as Nona Tucker*
J. Carrol Naish *as Henry Devers*
Beulah Bondi *as Grandma*
Percy Kilbride *as Harmie Jenkins*
Blanche Yurka *as Mom*
Charles Kemper *as Tim*
Norman Lloyd *as Finley Hewitt*
Estelle Taylor *as Lizzie*
Noreen Nash *as Becky*
Jack Norworth *as the doctor*
Paul Harvey *as Ruston*
Jay Gilpin *as Jot*
Jean Vanderbilt *as Daisy*
Nestor Piva *as the bartender*
Paul Burns *as Uncle Pete*
Dorothy Granger *as a girl at the dance*

Earl Hodgkins *as a wedding guest*
Almira Sessions *as a customer in the store*
Rex *as Zoonie*
Florence Bates *as Rose*

THE DIARY OF A CHAMBERMAID, made in 1946.
86 minutes

Directed by Jean Renoir
Screenplay adapted by Jean Renoir and Burgess Meredith
    from the novel by Octave Mirbeau and the play by
    André Leuse, André de Lorde, and Thielly Nores
Produced by Benedict Bogeaus, Burgess Meredith
Photographed by Lucien Andriot
Assistant director Joseph Landew
Edited by James Smith
Music by Michel Michelet
Sets by Eugène Lourié
Costumes by Barbara Karinska

CAST:

Paulette Godard *as Célestine*
Burgess Meredith *as Captain Mauger*
Francis Lederer *as Joseph*
Hurd Hatfield *as Georges*
Reginald Owen *as Lanlaire*
Judith Anderson *as Mrs. Lanlaire*
Irene Ryan *as Louise*
Florence Bates *as Rose*
Almira Sessions *as Marianne*

THE WOMAN ON THE BEACH, made in 1946.

71 minutes

Directed by Jean Renoir

Screenplay by Jean Renoir, Frank Davis, J. R. Michael
    Hogan, adapted from the Mitchell Wilson novel *None
    So Blind*

Produced by Jack Gross and Will Price

Photographed by Harry Wild and Leo Tover

Assistant director James Casey

Edited by Ronald Gross

Music by Hanns Eisler

Sets by Darrell Silvera

CAST:

Joan Bennett *as Peggy Butler*

Robert Ryan *as Lieutenant Scott Burnett*

Charles Bickford *as Ted Butler*

Nan Leslie *as Eve Geddes*

Walter Sande *as Otto Wernecke*

Irene Ryan *as Mrs. Wernecke*

Frank Darien *as Lars*

Jay Norris *as Jimmy*

Glenn Vernon *as Kirk*

THE RIVER, made in 1949-50 (Technicolor).

99 minutes

Directed by Jean Renoir

Screenplay by Rumer Godden and Jean Renoir from the
    Rumer Godden novel

Produced by Kenneth McEldowney, Kalyan Gupta, and
    Jean Renoir

Photographed by Claude Renoir and Ramananda Sen Gupta

Assistant directors J. Das Gupta, Sukhano y Sen, and Bansi Ashe

Edited by George Gale

Music by M. A. Partha Sarathy

Sets by Bansi Chandra Gupta

CAST:

Nora Swinburne *as the mother*
Esmond Knight *as the father*
Patricia Walters *as Harriet*
Radha *as Melanie*
Adrienne Corri *as Valerie*
Thomas E. Breen *as Captain John*
Arthur Shields *as Mr. John*
Richard Foster *as Bogey*
Suprova Mukerjee *as Nan*
Penelope Wilkinson *as Elizabeth*
Jane Harris *as Muffie*
Sahjan Singh *as Ram Prasad Singh*
Nimai Barik *as Kanu*
Trilak Jetley *as Anil*
June Hillman *as the narrator*
Jennifer Harris *as Mouse*
Cecilia Wood *as Victoria*

LE CARROSSE D'OR, made in 1953 (Technicolor).
100 minutes

Directed by Jean Renoir
Screenplay by Jean Renoir, Jack Kirkland, Renzo Avanzo,

Giulio Macchi, and Ginette Doynel; adapted from the
Prosper Mérimée play *Le Carrosse du Saint-Sacrement*
Produced by Francesco Alliata
Photographed by Claude Renoir
Assistant directors Marc Maurette and Giulio Macchi
Edited by Mario Serandrei and David Hawkins
Music by Vivaldi; adapted by Gino Marinozzi
Sets by Mario Chiari assisted by Gianni Poldori
Costumes by Mario de Matteis

CAST:

Anna Magnani *as Camilla*
Duncan Lamont *as the Viceroy*
Odoardo Spadaro *as Don Antonio*
Ricardo Rioli *as Ramon*
Paul Campbell *as Felipe*
Nada Fiorelli *as Isabelle*
George Higgins *as Martinez*
Dante *as Arlequin*
Rino *as the doctor*
Gisella Matthews *as Marquise Altamirano*
Ralph Truman *as the Duke of Castro*
Elena Altieri *as the Duchess of Castro*
Renato Chiantoni *as Captain Fracesse*
Giulio Tedeschi *as Baldassare*
Alfredo Kolner *as Florindo*
Alfredo Medini *as Ploichinelle*
Medini Brothers *as the four child acrobats*
John Pasetti *as the Captain of the Guards*
William Tubbs *as the innkeeper*
Cecil Matthews *as the Baron*
Fedo Keeling *as the Viscount*

Jean Debucourt *as the Bishop*
Lina Marengo *as the old comedienne*
Raf de la Terre *as the magistrate*

FRENCH CANCAN, made in 1954 (Technicolor).

97 minutes

Directed by Jean Renoir
Screenplay by Jean Renoir from an idea by André-Paul
    Antoine
Produced by Louis Wipf
Photographed by Michel Kelber with Henri Tiquet
Assistant directors Serge Vallin, Pierre Kast, and Jacques
    Rivette
Choreography by G. Grandgean
Edited by Boris Lewin
Music by Georges Van Parys and an assortment of tunes
    from the cafés-concert of the turn of the century; lyrics
    by Jean Renoir
Sets by Max Douy
Costumes by Rosine Delamare

CAST:

Jean Gabin *as Danglard*
Françoise Arnoul *as Nini*
Maria Félix *as the Abbess*
Jean-Roger Caussimon *as Baron Walter*
Max Dalban *as the owner of "Reine Blanche"*
Dora Doll *as La Génisse*
Gaston Modot *as Danglard's servant*

Gianni Esposito *as Prince Alexandre*
Valentine Tessier *as Mme. Olympe*
Michèle Philippe *as Eléonore*
Jean Parédès *as Coudrier*
Lydia Johnson *as Guibole*
Anna Amendola *as Esther Georges*
Philippe Clay *as Casimir*
France Roche *as Béatrix*
Annik Morice *as Thérèse*
Jacques Jouanneau *as Bidon*
Michèle Nadal *as Bigoudi*
Sylvine Delannoy *as Titine*
Anne-Marie Merson *as Paquita*
Albert Rémy *as Barjolin*
Michel Piccoli *as Valorgueil*
Patachou *as Yvette Guilbert*
André Claveau *as Paul Delmet*
Edith Piaf *as Eugénie Buffet*
Jean Raymond *as Paulus*
Jean-Marc Tennberg *as Savatte*
Pierre Olaf *as the heckler*
Leo Campion *as the Commandant*
Jacque Catelain *as the minister*
Hubert Beauchamps *as Isidore*
Mme. Pacquerette *as Mimi Prunelle*
Gaston Gabarouche *as Oscar, the pianist*
Pierre Moncorbier *as the bailiff*
Jean Mortier *as the hotel manager*
Robert Auboyneau *as the elevator operator*
Laurence Bataille *as the pygmy*
Jacques Ciron ⎫
Claude Arnay ⎭ *dandies*

Chauffard *as the police inspector*
Jacques Hilling *as the surgeon*
Jedlinska *as la gigolette*
Jean Sylvère *as the groom*
Palmyre Levasseur *as a laundress*

ELÉNA ET LES HOMMES, made in 1956 (English-language title *PARIS DOES STRANGE THINGS*) (Eastman-color).
95 minutes

Directed by Jean Renoir
Screenplay by Jean Renoir with Jean Serge
Produced by Louis Wipf
Photographed by Claude Renoir
Assistant director Serge Vallin
Edited by Boris Lewin
Music by Joseph Kosma; songs by Juliette Greco and Leo Marjane, with other songs of the period
Sets by Jean André
Costumes by Rosine Delamare and Monique Plotin

CAST:

Ingrid Bergman *as Eléna*
Jean Marais *as General Rollan*
Mel Ferrer *as Henri de Chevincourt*
Jean Richard *as Hector, Rollan's servant*
Magali Noël *as Lolotte, Eléna's maid*
Juliette Greco *as Miarka*
Pierre Bertin *as Martin Michaud*

Jacques Jouanneau *as Eugène Godin*
Jacques Morel *as Duchêne*
Jean Claudio *as Lionel*
Renaud Mary *as Fleury*
Elina Labourdette *as Paulette*
Jean Castanier *as Isnard*
Mirko Ellis *as Marbeau*
Gaston Modot *as Romani, the leader of the gypsies*
Gregori Chmara *as Eléna's servant*
Paul Demange *as a spectator*
Jim Gerald *as a cafe owner*
Dora Doll *as Rosa la Rose*
Leó Marjane *as the street singer*
Michèle Nadal *as Denise Gaudin*
Claire Gérard *as a woman in the street*
Robert LeBéal *as the doctor*
Albert Remy *as Buchez*
Olga Valéry *as Olga*
Frédérik Duvallès *as Godin*

L'ALBUM DE FAMILLE DE JEAN RENOIR, made in
     1956.
27 minutes

Directed by Roland Gritti
Screenplay by Pierre Desgraupes
Produced for Paris Télévision
Photographed by Jean Tournier

CAST:

Jean Renoir
Pierre Desgraupes

LE TESTAMENT DU DOCTEUR CORDELIER, made in
          1959 (English title *EXPERIMENT IN EVIL*).
95 minutes

Directed by Jean Renoir
Screenplay by Jean Renoir; freely adapted from Robert
          Louis Stevenson's *Dr. Jekyll and Mr. Hyde*
Produced by Albert Hollebecke, and Cie Jean Renoir
Photographed by Georges Leclerc
Assistant director Maurice Beuchey
Edited by Renée Lichtig
Music by Joseph Kosma
Sets by Marcel-Louis Dieulot
Costumes by Monique Durand

CAST:

Jean-Louis Barrault *as Dr. Cordelier and Opale*
Michel Vitold *as Dr. Séverin*
Teddy Bilis *as Joly*
Micheline Gary *as Marguérite*
Jean Topart *as Désiré*
Gaston Modot *as the gardener, Blaise*
Jacque Catelain *as the ambassador*
Régine Blaess *as his wife*
Jacqueline Morane *as Alberte*
André Certes *as Inspector Salabris*
Jacques Dannoville *as Commissaire Lardout*
Jean Renoir *as the narrator*
Jean-Pierre Granval *as the hotel manager*
Jean Bertho *as a passerby*
Didier d'Yd *as Georges*
Raymond Jourdan *as the cripple*
Raymone *as Mme. des Essarts*

Madeleine Marion *as Juliette*
Primerose Perret *as Mary*
Sylviane Margolle *as the little girl*
Dominique Dangan *as the mother*
Ghislaine Dumont *as Suzy*
Claudie Bourlon *as Lise*
Jacqueline Frot *as Isabelle*
Françoise Boyer *as Françoise*
Annick Allières *as a neighbor*

LE DÉJEUNER SUR L'HERBE, made in 1959 (Eastman-
   color).
92 minutes

Directed by Jean Renoir
Screenplay by Jean Renoir
Produced by Ginette Courtois-Doynel
Photographed by Georges Leclerc
Assistant directors Maurice Beuchey, Francis Morane,
   Jean-Pierre Spiero, Hedy Naka, and Jean de Nesles
Edited by Renée Lichtig under the direction of Maurice
   Beuchey
Music by Joseph Kosma
Sets by Marcel-Louis Dieulot
Costumes by Monique Dunan

CAST:

Paul Meurisse *as Étienne Alexis*
Catérine Rouvel *as Nénette*
Jacqueline Morane *as Titine, her eldest sister*

Fernand Sardou *as Nino, Étienne's father*
Jean-Pierre Granval *as Titine's husband*
Robert Chandeau *as Laurent*
Micheline Gary *as Madeline, his wife*
Frédéric O'Brady *as Rudolf*
Ingrid Nordine *as Marie-Charlotte*
Charles Blavette *as Gaspard, the shepherd*
Jean Claudio *as Rousseau, the steward*
Ghislaine Dumont *as Magda, Rudolf's wife*
Hélène Duc *as Isabelle*
Jacques Dannoville *as M. Paignant*
Marguerite Cassan *as his wife*
Raymond Jourdan *as Eustache, the cook*
François Miege *as Barthélmy, the chauffeur*
Régine Blaess *as Claire, the maid*
Pierre Leproux *as Bailly*
Michel Herbault *as Montet*
Jacqueline Fontel *as Miss Michelet, the secretary*
Paulette Dubost *as Miss Forestier, the telephonist*
Andre Brunot *as the curé*
M. You *as the foreman, Chapuis*
Dupraz, Lucas, Thierry, and Péricart *as announcers*

LE CAPORAL ÉPINGLÉ, made in 1961-62 (English title
          THE VANISHING CORPORAL; American title
          THE ELUSIVE CORPORAL).

105 minutes

Directed by Jean Renoir
Screenplay by Jean Renoir and Guy Lefranc from a Jacques
          Perret novel

Produced by Réne G. Vuattuox
Photographed by Georges Leclerc
Codirector Guy Lefranc
Assistant director Marc Maurette
Edited by Renée Lichtig assisted by Madeleine Lacompère
Music by Joseph Kosma
Sets by Eugène Herrly

CAST:

Jean-Pierre Cassel *as the Corporal*
Claude Brasseur *as Pater*
Claude Rich *as Ballochet*
Jean Carmet *as Émile*
Jacques Jouanneau *as Penchagauche*
Mario David *as Caruso*
O. E. Hasse *as the drunk on the train*
Philippe Castelli *as the electrician*
Guy Bédos *as the stutterer*
Raymond Jourdan *as Dupieu*
Gérard Darrieu *as the squinter*
Sacha Briquet *as the prisoner escaping dressed as a woman*
François Darbon *as the French soldier married to a German woman*
Lucien Raimbourg *as the station guard*

LA DIRECTION D'ACTEUR PAR JEAN RENOIR, made in 1968.

27 minutes

Directed by Jean Renoir
Produced by Roger Fleytoux

Photographed by Edmond Richard
Edited by Mireille Mauberna

CAST:

Jean Renoir
Gisèle Braunberger } *as themselves*

THE CHRISTIAN LIQUORICE STORE, made in 1969.
90 minutes

Directed by James Frawley

Jean Renoir *as himself*

LE PETIT THÉÂTRE DE JEAN RENOIR, made in 1969.
100 minutes

Directed by Jean Renoir
Screenplay by Jean Renoir
Produced by Pierre Long and Jean Renoir for television
Photographed by Georges Leclerc
Assistant director Denis Epstein
Edited by Geneviève Winding, assisted by Gisèle Chezeau
Music for "Le Dernier Reveillon" by Jean Weiner
        for "La Cireuse Électrique" by Joseph Kosma
        for "La Belle Époque" song by Octave Crémieux
            and G. Millandy
        for "Le Roi d'Yvetôt" by Jean Weiner
Sets by Gilbert Margerie

CAST:

Introductions by Jean Renoir

"Le Dernier Reveillon" (*"The Last Christmas Eve"*)
Nino Formicola *as le Clochard*
Milly Monti *as la Clocharde*
Roland Bertin *as Gontran*
André Dumas *as the manager*
Robert Lombard *as the maître d'hôtel*
Roger Trapp *as Max Vialle*

"La Cireuse Électrique" (*"The Electric Waxing Machine"*)
Marguerite Cassan *as Émilie*
Pierre Olaf *as Gustave*
Jacques Dynam *as Jules*
Jean-Louis Tristan *as electric waxing machine salesman*
Denis Gunzburg ⎫
Claude Guillame ⎬ *the lovers*

"La Belle Époque"
Jeanne Moreau *as the singer*

"Le Roi d'Yvetôt" (*"The King of Yvetot"*)
Fernand Sardou *as Duvallier, Roi d'Yvetôt*
Françoise Arnoul *as Isabelle, his wife*
Jean Carmet *as Ferand*
Andrex *as M. Blanc*
Roger Prégor *as Maître Joly*
Edmond Ardisson *as César*
Dominique Labourier *as Paulette*

AND

1954 Debut as a theater director, when he staged a Grisha
and Mitsou Dabet adaptation of William
Shakespeare's *Julius Caesar*

CAST:

Henri Vidal *as Julius Caesar*
Jean-Pierre Aumont *as Mark Anthony*
Loleh Bellon *as Portia*
Yves Robert *as Cassius*
Françoise Christophe *as Calpurnia*
Paul Meurisse *as Brutus*
Jean Parédès *as Casca*
Jean Topart *as Octavius Caesar*
And others

1955 Second theater direction when Jean Renoir staged
           Orvet, a comedy in three acts written by him for
           Leslie Caron in 1953
Music by Joseph Kosma
Sets by Georges Wakhevitch
Costumes by Karinska and Givenchy

CAST:

Leslie Caron *as Orvet*
Paul Meurisse *as Georges*
Michel Herbault *as Olivier*
Catherine Le Couey *as Mme. Camus*
Raymond Bussières *as Coutant*
Jacques Jouanneau *as William*
Marguerite Cassan *as Clotilde*
Yorick Royan *as Berthe*
Suzanne Courtal *as Mother Viper*
Pierre Olaf *as Philippe*
Georges Saillard *as the doctor*
Georges Hubert ⎱
Henry Charrett ⎰ *huntsmen*

1956 Renoir wrote a play, *Carola,* and adapted Clifford
        Odets' play *The Big Knife*

1957 Renoir wrote the story for a short ballet on the war,
        "Le Feu aux Poudres," which was performed by
        Ludmilla Tcherina as the first part of a dance
        program named "Les Amants de Teruel"

1958 Renoir wrote a biographical study of Auguste
        Renoir titled *Renoir, My Father*

1968 Renoir wrote a novel called *Les Cahiers du Capitaine
        Georges*

1974 Renoir wrote *My Life and My Films*

Index

(Italicized numbers indicate listing in filmography)

A TALE ENDLESSLY RETOLD,
A VISION ETERNALLY BORN ANEW

Since its original appearance over 2000 years ago, *Ramayana* has served as the model for poems, stories, folktales, plays, and films in India, Burma, Cambodia, Thailand, Indonesia, and the Philippines. In each of these lands, writers modified and built upon the original epic to enhance its impact and meaning for their own cultures.

With this English version, *Ramayana* may truly be said to have reached the West. As B. A. van Nooten says in his fascinating introduction, this is "an extraordinary accomplishment. . . . In the minds of many people who hear the *Ramayana* a mystery is being presented, and slowly, erratically, parts of the mystery unfold. . . . We get glimpses of a higher, purer reality that holds out hope for those enmeshed in the sorry state of mundane existence. Again and again [we] experience this joy of discovery. The struggle between good and evil is on our behalf, and Rama is our hero."

"A fascinating tale of adventure, heroism, exciting plots, and frightful monsters."
—BERKELEY GAZETTE

"Mythology can be beautiful literature; the Ramayana, and this particular edition, which I like, are good examples."
—LOS ANGELES TIMES

WILLIAM BUCK devoted his life to translating the great classics of India into colloquial English. He died at the age of 37, leaving as his legacy the *Ramayana* and *Mahabharata*.

MENTOR Books of Special Interest

RAMAYANA
KING RAMA'S WAY

Valmiki's *Ramayana*
told in English prose by
William Buck

WITH AN INTRODUCTION BY
B. A. van Nooten

FOREWORD BY
Ram Dass

A MENTOR BOOK
NEW AMERICAN LIBRARY

For Paul, my son

Contents

CONTENTS

Foreword

In the winter of 1967 I found myself living in a tiny temple in the foothills of the Himalayas. This was the culmination of a path which had taken me through western psychology, then psychedelic chemicals, and finally to the East in pursuit of methods of awakening and stabilizing expanded awareness. I had finally found my Guru, a man who I was certain knew what I needed to know, and he had placed me in this temple.

At the time I spoke no Hindi, and so I understood little of what was happening around me. Each day many people would visit the temple to ring bells, make offerings and do obeisance before various statues, and receive gifts of food and red marks on their foreheads, placed there by the priest. Having grown up in a culture where idolatry was considered profane, I felt a discomfort bordering on aversion toward these alien practices.

However, there was one statue of a monkey called Hanuman that attracted me. The statue was over eight feet tall, made of cement, painted an orangey-red, and was crude in detail. Hanuman was depicted tearing open his chest, and in the middle of his heart were two tiny figures depicting Ram (God) and Sita (Ram's wife). Often I would meditate upon Hanuman and ask him to explain himself to me. Of course, interspersed with this one-sided dialogue were thoughts about the humor of the situation. I could imagine my former colleagues from the Harvard faculty finding me sitting before this huge monkey. Obviously, they would think, old Dick Alpert had gone over the edge.

Though my sophisticated western mind held back on the periphery and watched all of this strangeness with some disdain, something within me felt that I must be missing some crucial link in the chain of understanding. For my Guru was clearly no fool. In fact he was the wisest being I had ever met. And yet he allowed the statue of Hanuman to be present and even encouraged people to do *puja* (prayers) to it. And one day a further incentive to understand was presented: my Guru named me "Ram Dass." The meaning of the name was "servant of God"; specifically, it was another name for Hanuman.

At times, as I looked at my big cement namesake, he seemed to look back at me in a certain way or to move ever so slightly. But of course that was all my imagination, or the result of my keeping my attention focused so steadfastly on a specific object. Certainly such an inanimate object could not really move. But when I mentioned these occurrences to Indian friends, they smiled indulgently at my rationalizations. To them, this was not a statue, but a *murti*. A *murti* is a statue that has been consecrated: it has been invested with living spirit. And so it stood to reason that a *murti* could manifest its life force in movement, and might indeed move for someone who looked upon it purely. At this time they related the following incident.

In a small village there was a tiny Hanuman temple to which the local people would come. It is a practice for devotees to bring some sweets and offer them to the *murti*. The priest takes the sweets and goes into the room that contains the *murti* and draws the curtain. Then he offers the sweets to the *murti* with appropriate mantras (invocations). After this, the priest usually takes a few of the sweets and sets them aside to be given later to the poor neighborhood children. The remainder he brings back to the devotee-donor as *prasad* (i.e., consecrated or offered food), which the devotee then eats as a blessing from Hanuman.

It so happened that the old priest in this village was called away by illness in his family, and he left a young neighborhood boy, who always loved to be around the temple, to take care of it while he was away. Soon some devotees came and brought sweets. The boy took them as he had seen the priest do, and went behind the curtain. Now he had never been with Hanuman when the curtain was closed, but he offered the sweets to Hanuman. Hanuman didn't take them. The boy became upset and pleaded and then demanded that Hanuman accept some of the sweets. Finally in exasperation he picked up a stick and began to beat the *murti*. Suddenly all the sweets disappeared from the dish. The boy returned to the devotees, joyfully explaining that Hanuman had accepted their offering. However, the devotees, who were used to receiving a portion of their gift back, concluded that the boy had decided to keep all of their gift for himself and so they beat the boy and sent him away. Later the old priest returned and was told about this incident. He said, "All my life I had hoped to become pure enough so that my offerings would be accepted by Hanuman. But I have not been thus far. This young boy had such purity and was so blessed."

The web of my involvement with Hanuman was deepening. I read and reread the *Ramayana*, and more and more my heart opened to it. The hill people with whom I lived treated this book the same way the Bible is treated by Judaeo-Christians, or the Koran by the peoples of Islam. For them it is more than a fantasy; even more than a historical event. It is a sacred message written upon the walls of time, a message by God, about God. It is grace given form to guide and strengthen faith.

These hill people were good people whose compassion I trusted. And in the course of sitting with them around their braziers or fires, night after night, during which the exploits depicted in the *Ramayana* were sung with purity and love, I found their deep reverence for Ram and Sita, Lakshmana and Hanuman, being transmitted to me. Slowly I came to the realization that in this story lay the blueprint or map for my own spiritual journey.

For those of us who have received the grace to touch living spirit within our lifetime, the challenge that confronts us is how to translate this spirit into worldly action. Or, looked at in another way, how to live our lives in such a way as to deepen our spiritual connection. To this end there are many paths: paths of prayer, of study, of redirecting bodily energies, of devotional song. But for many of us the path that draws us is the path of service; service that is designed to alleviate suffering of our fellow beings, service that is in harmony with the deepest way of things (what the Chinese call the Tao). Such service when guided by the heart feels like making love with God.

It is such service about which the *Bhagavadgita* is concerned. And this too is what the *Ramayana* is about. Each of the characters within the *Ramayana* represents a different aspect of service, but it is Hanuman who is a perfect embodiment of all of the qualities of selfless service. For his service is done with purity, with one-pointed love of God, free of greed or self-aggrandizement, with the perfect bravery and courage that comes from knowing that one's acts are in harmony with the deepest pulse of the universe, and with the vast powers that are reflected in Christ's statement "Had ye but faith ye could move mountains." In fact, at one point in order to save Ram's brother Lakshmana, Hanuman actually does indeed lift and carry aloft a mountain. But then are not all holy books speaking ultimately to the same truth?

> Who is this monkey Hanuman? Rama has let him loose in the world. He knows Rama and Rama knows him. Hanuman can break in or break out of anywhere. He cannot be stopped like the free wind in flight. Hanuman can spot a tyrant, he looks at deeds not words and he'll go and pull his beard. Disguises and words of talk cannot confuse a-mere wild animal. . . . Hanuman will take your sad tune and use it to make a happy dance.

> Rama said, "As long as men shall speak of you, you will live on earth. No one can equal you. Your heart is true; your arms are strong; you have the energy to do anything. You have served me faithfully and done things for me that couldn't be done."
> "It's nothing," said Hanuman, "I am your friend, that's all."

> Hanuman, the work of the world, however difficult, is made easy by your grace.
> —from the *Ramayana*

When Einstein was questioned about his work, he said, "I didn't arrive at my understanding of the fundamental laws through my rational mind." Here he was honoring a deeper or higher or more intuitive mind. Again and again scientists, great composers such as Beethoven and Bach, great artists and inventors and writers such as Dante, Blake, Emerson, and Whitman, have described how they received the grace to enter into nonconceptual realms where they experienced a oneness with the way of all things. Later, when they returned to what William James referred to as "normal waking consciousness," they described a tiny bit of what they had seen or felt through whatever concepts, skills, and tools were available to them. Some wrote a great work, others created a building such as the Taj Mahal, and still others, great religions. These manifestations, when coming through pure instruments, have the ability to take you into these higher realms. It is as if they point, not to themselves, not to the words or brushstrokes or formulas, but to the awe and grandeur that lies beyond. The *Ramayana* is one such work.

There are so many levels at which a book such as this may be read. And a subtle and compassionate teller of stories such as William Buck happily leaves the reader free to take it at whatever level is most comfortable. It is a romantic tale of the battle between good and evil. It is perhaps a veiled account, distorted through oral transmission over time, of an actual historical event. It is a symbolic metaphor for the battle of sacred and secular forces that rage within each of us. It is a sacred book of living spirit.

Perhaps as you read this delightful version of the *Ramayana* you will allow Hanuman and his friends to come into your heart and be your friends. And just perhaps, such friends may refurbish faith where before there may have been cynicism, may awaken love where previously there was dryness, may deepen hope where there was doubt and despair. Of course, you may think, this is just another book. That too. But it is also an incredible statement of living spirit . . . for those who have the eye to see and the ear to hear.

RAM DASS

Santa Cruz, California
April 1978

Publisher's Preface

In 1955 William Buck discovered an elaborate nineteenth-century edition of *The Sacred Song of the Lord, the Bhaga-vad-Gita of Lord Krishna* in a state library in Carson City, Nevada. Captivated by this find, he plunged into a study of Indian literature which has resulted in this rendering of *Ramayana*, a retelling of *Mahabharata*, and an unfinished manuscript of *Harivamsa*—unfinished because of his death in 1970 at the age of 37.

His discovery of the *Bhagavad-Gita* moved Mr. Buck to read the *Mahabharata*, and he would be satisfied with nothing less than a full translation. An 11-volume set was then being reprinted in India, and in his determination he subsidized the reprinting when it became apparent that the publisher had insufficient funds to complete the task.

Midway through his reading, Mr. Buck decided the *Ramayana* and *Mahabharata* should be rewritten for a modern English-speaking audience. In his own words, "*Mahabharata* was about 5,000 pages, and *Ramayana* much shorter. When I read these translations I thought how nice to tell the story so it wouldn't be so hard to read. We talk about all the repetition and digression of the originals, but as you read all that endless impossible prose a very definite character comes to each actor in the story, and the land and times are most clearly shown. I wanted to transfer this story to a readable book."

To this end, William Buck began years of reading and rereading the translations, studying Sanskrit, planning, and writing. One of his approaches was to decipher and list all the elaborate appellatives used in place of names for heroes and gods and kings and princesses in the original text. He then used the qualities of these appellatives to describe the characters in his own renderings and thus preserve their mood and meanings. He read all available English versions of the two great epics, but said of them, "I have never seen any

versions of either story in English that were not mere out-
lines, or incomplete, except for the two literal translations."
He always kept in mind that the epics were originally sung,
and reading aloud from both the original translations and
Buck's own work became part of the Buck family life.

William Buck's vision of his task was firm, and he had the
balanced form of each epic clearly in his mind as he worked.
In his words, "It is always apparent just what is the thread of
the story and what are later interpolations. It is stuffed with
preachments, treatises of special interests, doctrines of later
caste systems, long passages of theological dogma, but these
are in chunks, and only slow the story." His goal was to tell
the tales in such a way that the modern reader would not be
discouraged from knowing and loving them as he did. He
wanted to convey the spirit, the truth, of the epics.

In answer to a critic of his manuscripts he replied, "I've
made many changes and combinations in both books, but I
wish to have them considered as stories which they are,
rather than as examples of technically accurate scholarship,
which I told you they weren't. One thing however is true.
Read the stories and you get the real spirit of the original
once you're done, and if they're entertaining that's all I ask."
And in another letter: "*Ramayana* is one of the world's most
popular stories, and it is part of its own tradition to be re-told
in different times and places, as I have done."

That was his aim—to make it possible for contemporary
readers to know the *Ramayana* in terms meaningful for modern times, as well as in terms of its origins. Of the finished
manuscripts he wrote, "My method in writing both *Mahabharata* and *Ramayana* was to begin with a literal translation from which to extract the story, and then to tell that
story in an interesting way that would preserve the spirit and
flavor of the original. My motive is therefore that of the storyteller. I'm not trying to prove anything and I have made
my own changes to tell the story better. Here are two great
stories just waiting for people to read them. Based on the
words of ancient songs, I have written books. I tried to make
them interesting to read. I don't think you will find many
other books like them."

Introduction

by B. A. van Nooten

Few authors in world literature can lay claim to having inspired as many poets and dramatists, and to having transmitted moral and ethical values to as vast and receptive an audience in nations living thousands of miles apart and with radically different languages and cultures, as the obscure, almost legendary composer of the Sanskrit *Ramayana*, a poet known to us as Valmiki.

Valmiki probably lived somewhere in northeast India, where much of the action of the story takes place. Legends make him a reformed robber converted to a virtuous life by a saint, but from the one and only literary work that remains of him we recognize him as a poetic genius, a man of refined and aesthetic sense and a pure instinct for moral living. The *Ramayana* (literally "Rama's Way") is one of the two great epics of India, the other being the *Mahabharata*. It is a long epic, some 25,000 verses in extent, and tells a story of courtly intrigue, heroic renunciation, fierce battles, and the triumph of good over evil. Prince Rama of Ayodhya is the hero. He is born into a noble family of rulers, but treacherous machinations of his stepmother force him to abdicate his claim to the throne of Ayodhya in favor of his half-brother, Bharata. Rama himself withdraws into the forest for thirteen years accompanied by his faithful wife Sita and his devoted half-brother, Lakshmana. Here they move in a strange world, part mythical, part spiritual, populated by gentle, God-seeking sages, but also by grim ogres and vicious demons who try to disturb Rama's tranquil life and thwart his noble intentions. In that world, a conflict develops between on the one hand the righteous Rama, a scion of the illustrious ancient solar dynasty, and on the other hand the legions of the dark, the Rakshasas or demons with ugly, menacing, repulsive forms who stalk the forest in search of mischief. Thanks to Rama's gallantry, he, Sita, and Lakshmana overcome the demonic powers until a great calamity befalls them: faithful Sita is abducted by the monstrous demon king Ravana. He flies with her to Lanka, his capital, but she never yields to him, reminding him steadfastly of her vow to Rama, her one and only lord.

Meanwhile Rama and Lakshmana search frantically for signs of life from Sita, going from one witness to another to learn of her whereabouts. Finally, they ally themselves with an army of talking monkeys and bears under the generalship of the mighty monkey Hanuman. The animals discover the place where Sita is kept prisoner, an island not far from India, probably prosperous Lanka, now known as Ceylon, or Sri Lanka. Hanuman with a tremendous bound leaps across and visits Sita. After setting fire to the city he returns to Rama who decides to rescue his wife by force. Thousands upon thousands of monkeys help to build a causeway across to the island, the remains of which are still visible—or so tradition goes. A frightful battle ensues. Hosts of monkeys and demons are slaughtered, the heroes use not only conventional weapons, but also divinely inspired arms and magic tricks. The demons can change shape at will by virtue of their maya, or magical power, and often succeed in deceiving the heroes. Rama and his allies perform feats of incredible fortitude, lifting up huge rocks and even mountains and suffering injuries beyond comprehension. In the end, as can be expected, the good are victorious and it is at this point that Rama discovers his divine antecedents. He is an incarnation of the great god Vishnu who has come on earth to save mankind from oppression by demonic forces.

Rama and Sita return to the capital of their country, Ayodhya, where Rama is crowned king. For many years their rule is glorious but then evil tongues spread rumors about Sita's abduction by Ravana long ago. Was she really as pure as she professed to be? Had the handsome Ravana really never touched her? In deep sorrow Rama asks Sita to leave for the forest and never to come back. No just ruler can live under a cloud of immoral conduct, even if it is no more than suspected misbehavior. Sita goes to the forest and gives birth to Rama's two children, Kusa and Lava. The great poet-sage Valmiki takes care of them and in time teaches them the great story of Rama's exploits, the *Ramayana*.

About the *Ramayana*'s date little can be said with certainty. It is a major work in the Hindu tradition but this tradition concerned itself very little with exact historical chronology. Roughly, and mainly by virtue of external and linguistic evidence, we accept a period of a few hundred years between 200 B.C. and A.D. 200 as a likely date for its composition. It probably grew fairly gradually, with the beginning and the end of the story being added on at the end of that period. So the story of Sita's second rejection by Rama as well as the incident of her being swallowed up by the earth are later additions. It is safe to say that Valmiki (if he really was the composer) drew upon a number of popular Rama folk tales for his epic which he wove together into a great frame story, together with numerous exotic and fabulous incidents. The conventional techniques of Sanskrit narrative are found here also: the use of narrators at various stages, the descriptions of nature to suggest the mood of the action, occasional divine interventions, and so on. It is, therefore, a traditional Indian literary work, but its impact on the people of India has been no less than phenomenal. It has inspired the themes for hundreds of major and minor literary works and plays. For two thousand years, down to the present day, Rama's exploits are celebrated in religious festivals, temple ceremonies, public holidays, and private ceremonies. Places where Rama walked are now famous as places of pilgrimage where thousands of Hindus flock every year. People in the villages tell their children the story of Rama, as we tell our children fairy tales. People in the cities can watch cinematic adaptations of Rama episodes and read abbreviated forms of its narrative in pocketbook editions. Rama has been transformed into an object of devotion and Rama worship is still a powerful religious force. The last words of the famous statesman Mohandas Gandhi were "Ram-ram," before he died from an assassin's bullet.

What can the popularity be attributed to? Among several factors, perhaps the most important is the characterization of the *Ramayana*. It is a work of exemplars, of models of good behavior which people in distress and frustration, when doubts assail them, can follow and imitate with beneficial results. We have Rama, the noble and virtuous prince whose supreme heroism lies not so much in the fact that he conquers his enemies, but in the fact that he stoically and dispassionately endures the greatest hardships, including rejection and calumny on the part of his nearest family. Sita too is a non-heroine: she is the constant victim of fate but all through her tribulations she remains faithful to her husband and does what he wants. She has become a model that pious Hindu women attempt to copy down to the present day. In these days of female emancipation these are unpopular sentiments in the West, but there is a perspective on life in which this model of behavior is as certain a way to liberation as the staunchest rebellion—and many Hindus have that perspective.

For many Indians, especially those who worship God as Vishnu, the *Ramayana* is mainly a religious poem describing the *avatara* (incarnation) of God on earth, his struggles with the powers of evil and his victory. The incarnation is often unaware of his divine role, but his actions are always noble, his regard of his fellowmen gracious and kind, his patience and forbearance of other people's slights exemplary—until he is faced with the embodiment of real wickedness, the devil incarnate. Then his righteous ire is aroused and his determination to eradicate and kill the evil powers cannot be stopped. For many in the audience listening to *Rama's Way*, that constitutes the essential story. But even those who are not particularly religiously oriented appreciate the *Ramayana* as a fascinating tale of adventure, heroism, exciting plots, and frightful monsters. It lends itself to bombastic portrayals in art and sculpture. For instance, the scene of thousands upon thousands of frantic monkeys clashing in combat with hordes of sinister-looking demons was portrayed on the wall reliefs of the Cambodian temple of Angkor Wat and in the Ketjak dance in Bali. There are romantic and emotional scenes, too, such as Rama's pathetic departure for the forest with Sita and his brother. The sorrow Rama feels when faithful Sita has been abducted is hard to forget. The scene of Sita's suffering in Ravana's palace in Lanka, in the midst of his spiteful, haughty wives who constantly pressure her to yield to their lord, is a touching example of her unswerving conjugal faith.

The question may be raised whether the great battle in the *Ramayana* represents an historic event. It is hard to answer. We can only speculate, as others have done, that the poem is based on a battle of great antiquity. The oldest Aryans, the ancestors of the Nordic people in India today, descended from the Iranian plateau into India some time in the middle of the second millennium B.C. They met speakers of Dravidian languages who now mainly live in South India. That meeting ultimately led to a fusion of the Dravidian and Aryan cultures in North India which at present has a largely homogeneous population. But the Aryan influence came into the south at a much later date, perhaps around the time that the Rama stories appeared. So speculation goes that the

Ramayana represents a glorified account of this excursion of the Aryans into southern India with Rama as the Aryan cultural hero, and the Rakshasas of Lanka, as well as the monkeys and bears, the less developed races encountered by the Aryans.

This theory is highly speculative and probably false. As more archaeological evidence is uncovered we find that there have been flourishing civilizations in southern India for almost as long as in northern India. It is, therefore, not correct to believe that the *Ramayana* is a poeticized account of the Aryan inroads into South India. It is similarly incorrect to think of the figures of the bears and the monkeys somehow as contemptuous designations of uncivilized tribesmen. On the contrary, they are respected and even venerated creatures who embody qualities of strength, persistence, and enthusiasm, with a characteristic trust in their human leaders, which is often moving to observe. Without resentment and with blind faith they hurl themselves into battle and almost certain death because they believe the superior human creatures know what they are doing. To see in them portrayals of human beings is a matter of interpretation, not of fact. They are monkeys and bears capable of communicating with people; they are not caricatures of human beings.

As was stated earlier, the *Ramayana* has had a vast distribution over the countries of Southeast Asia bordering on the Indian Ocean and the Pacific. Burma, Cambodia, Thailand, Indonesia, and even the Philippines, to name only a few, are places where the Rama story was introduced and where it was accepted by the people and incorporated into their own cultures. In the course of this assimilation changes were oftentimes made, some deliberate, some unconscious. Sometimes the court poet of a local raja would celebrate his patron's greatness by picturing him as Rama, the hero, the conqueror of the world. He would fabricate a few scenes, omit a few others, and so compose a new Rama story. The geographical names were often changed to agree with the features of the locale, but the reverse also happened. In Indonesia, for instance, mountains like Brama, Sumeru, and rivers like Serayu still attest to the ancient influence of the Hindu epics. But the literary works, in addition, often had a popular version that was passed down by word of mouth, by professional storytellers, or just by merchants and travelers. In these popular versions the influence of local customs is often much more evident, and it is sometimes even difficult to discern the original Rama-Sita plot in amongst the incidental local stories. Such is the case, for instance, with the recently discovered Philippine Rama story.

Against the background of this cultural adaptation of the *Ramayana* we should view William Buck's translation. It is not really a translation but more of a rewriting of the *Ramayana,* using as source material the published English translations. For translations of the *Ramayana* into English do exist, but none so far is very satisfactory, either from a scholarly, or from a literary point of view. William Buck's adaptation is an extraordinary accomplishment. He was neither a scholar nor a well-known author, and though he retells the Rama story with many variations of detail, he has succeeded in capturing the most important characteristics of the *Ramayana*: the simple religious tone that pervades the Indian original. We find in this rendering of the work the same awe of divine creation, the same wonder and unquestioning belief in the interrelation of natural and supernatural events that have appealed to millions of people who in the past two thousand years have listened to the recitation and reenactment of the Rama story. In the minds of many people who hear the *Ramayana* a mystery is being presented, and slowly, erratically, parts of the mystery unfold. If we are fortunate, we get occasional glimpses of a higher, purer reality that holds out hope for those enmeshed in the sorry state of mundane existence. Again and again this revelation causes us to read and rethink the epic in order to experience again this joy of discovery. The struggle between good and evil is on our behalf and Rama is our hero.

It is pointless to enumerate all the places where Buck's *Ramayana* differs from the original, but a few of the more important differences should be mentioned. One of the most striking concerns Sita's reunion with Rama at the end of the battle, when she is brought before him in the crowning moment of triumph after a nightmarish war. One expects Rama to receive her graciously and tenderly back into his royal household and so, indeed, he acts in the story recounted by Buck. But in the Indian *Ramayana* there is no such happy episode. Here Rama haughtily rebuffs Sita when she appears before him led by Lakshmana. He believes that her honor has been compromised in Lanka and that she is unfit to become a queen. In despair Sita threatens to immolate herself in a fire that Lakshmana has lit at her request, but as if by magic, the God of Fire rises out of the pyre and refuses to burn her. He chides Rama and then the two are reunited. Buck has omitted this controversial episode and instead, has the Fire God lead Sita to Rama. Also, at that time Buck produces a stone letter sent by Ravana posthumously to Rama announcing his reconciliation. The Sanskrit *Ramayana* has no such incident.

The *Ramayana* epitomizes the spirit of ancient India with its vague but grand concepts of moral rectitude and its consequences for a person's fate. Both Rama and Sita are portrayed as following their *dharma,* a term meaning "personal duty," as well as "law, eternal law" and personified as the God of Justice. Adherence to *dharma* secures for oneself a more agreeable position in the next life one is to lead. The concepts of reincarnation and *karma,* the inexorable law of retribution for evil deeds and reward for unselfish behavior, dominate the lives of the people and semi-divine creatures that roam the earth. As in the *Mahabharata,* another Indian epic, gods sometimes interact with human beings. They are powerful, immortal, but not omnipotent. Vishnu who is usually represented in sculpture with a discus, mace, conchshell and lotus in his four hands, a mighty god who wields great power over the fate of mankind, is nevertheless compelled by the magic energy of a sage like Narada to yield his emblems of divinity. Likewise, the great god Indra was defeated by the demonic Ravana and his son. By performing ascetic practices (Sanskrit *tapas* which also means "heat"), a human being can cause Indra's throne to heat up, forcing him to grant a wish. In this way men and women can assert their will over gods.

Rama's Way tacitly assumes that we are aware of some of the conventions of Sanskrit mythology and literature. The world as we see it is the product of a long evolutionary cycle, subdivided into four world ages (*yugas*). In the first, mankind is perfect and *dharma* "righteous behavior" goes on four feet. In the second *yuga* it loses a quarter of its power and mankind becomes less perfect. In the third, another quarter is lost and in the present fourth *yuga,* or Kali-yuga, misfortune, calamity and moral degradation are rampant. The world ages are named after the four throws recognized in the Indian dice game: Krita, Dvapara, Treta, Kali. The *Ramayana* takes place in the Treta-yuga. In each yuga the Brahmans constitute the upper caste of four classes of society. The three upper castes are regarded as the "twice-born" in the society they live in, once naturally and once when they receive the sacred thread. The sacred thread is given by a priest to the young boy of the family at a solemn ceremony which takes place before puberty. It is worn next to the skin over the right shoulder. Girls do not receive a sacred thread.

In other places in this work we meet up with literary clichés and conventions. Ascetics, for instance, usually wear their hair flattened down without ornamentations, in contrast to city people and royalty who groom and style their hair. Rama before entering the forest also adopts the matted hairdo of the wandering mendicant, but when he leads the army into Lanka he gives up the wanderer's life and lets his hair flow free, again. Another convention is that mountains used to fly around freely until Indra shot their wings off. Hence Mainaka Hill is said to have possessed wings. Also certain practices are sometimes mentioned which have no correspondence in our literature. Smelling somebody's hair, for instance, is a common manifestation of affection.

At times Buck has inserted some Sanskrit terms by way of *mantras*, "magical spells" endowed with supernatural power. They are not really meaningful expressions so their translation has been omitted. For instance, the terms *rakshama* and *yakshama* (Sanskrit *rakshyaamah* 'we shall protect,' *yakshyaamah* 'we shall sacrifice' p. 20) are simplified etymologies for the words *raksasa-* and *yaksa-*, semi-divine beings. The word *yaman* (p. 40) means something like 'may I restrain, control' and is a convenient etymology for the name of the God of Death, Yama.

The main sequence of events in the Indian original and in Buck's rendition is the same, except that in Buck's version the story begins ten thousand years after the war, when Rama's children Kusa and Lava, unbeknownst to their father, have learnt the story of his battle from Valmiki and are reciting it in the Naimisha forest. The original *Ramayana* begins in the city of Ayodhya with the events leading up to Rama's birth. Valmiki was called the Adikavi, or "first poet" of Sanskrit literature and some of his remarkable talent shines forth in this English rendering. The reader will find pleasure in reading it aloud to himself or to others. In that way he may experience the fascination the epic has held for so many people for such a long time.

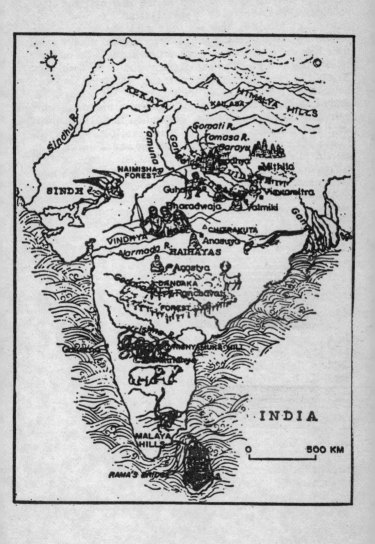

List of Characters

AGASTYA. The forest saint who gave Rama a bow and arrow.

AGNI. The fire god.

AHALYA. The most beautiful woman ever created.

AIRAVATA. Indra's elephant.

ANUSUYA. Atri's wife, who gave Sita ornaments in the forest.

ANGADA. The monkey prince.

ANJANA. Hanuman's mother.

ARJUNA OF A THOUSAND ARMS. The Haihaya king.

ARUNA. Charioteer of the sun.

ASWAPATI. Kaikeyi's father, the Kekaya king.

ATRI. A saint dwelling near the Vindhya mountains.

BHARADWAJA. A hermit of the woods who received Rama; he lived on to become the father of Drona.

BHARATA. Dasaratha's son and Rama's brother; no relation to the namesake of the Kurus.

BRAHMA. Grandfather and Creator of the worlds.

CHANDRA. The Moon.

CHITRARATHA. The Gandharva king, lord of heaven's musicians.

DADHICA. An ancient warrior, revived by Indra.

DADHIMUKHA. A monkey, keeper of Sugriva's Honey Park.

DASARATHA. Rama's father.

DEVI. Shiva's consort.

DUNDHUVI. A giant buffalo.

DURVASAS. A grim ascetic.

GARUDA. King of Birds, ridden by Narayana.

GAUTAMA. A sage, Ahalya's husband.

GUHA. The hunter king.

HANUMAN. The monkey, Son of the Wind.

HEMA. An Apsarasa, Queen Mandodari's mother.

HIMAVAN. The Lord of the Himalya, Devi's father.

ILVALA. A cannibal.

INDRA. The Rain God, King of heaven.

INDRAJIT. Ravana's son.

INDRANI. Indra's wife.

JAMBAVAN. King of the Bears.

JAMBUMALI. Prahasta's son.

JANAKA. The Videha King, Sita's father.

JATAYU. The Dandaka vulture King.

KADRU. One of Kashyapa's wives, mother of the snakes.

KAIKASI. Sumali's daughter and wife of Nishrava.

KAIKEYI. Bharata's mother.

KALA. Time.

KAMA. The god of love. He is bodiless.

KASHYAPA. An ancient sage.

KAUSALYA. Rama's mother.

KHARA. Demon commander of Dandaka Forest.

KUMBHAKARNA. Ravana's giant brother.

KUSA. Rama's elder son.

LAKSHMANA. Rama's brother, Sumitra's son.

LAKSHMI. The goddess of good fortune and Narayana's consort.

LAVA. Rama's younger son.

MAINAKA. A live, golden submarine mountain.

MALI. One of the three demons for whom Lanka was built.

MALYAVAN. Mali's brother.

MANDAKARNI. A sage dwelling in a lake.

MANDODARI. Queen of Lanka.

MANIBHADRA. The Yaksha king.

MANTHARA. Kaikeyi's old nurse.

MARICHA. The demon who became a golden deer.

MATALI. Indra's charioteer.

MATANGA. The saint who lived by Rishyamukha Hill.

MAYA THE ASURA. The divine artist of illusion, a magician.

MAYAVI. Dundhuvi's son.

MEGHANADA. Indrajit's birth name.

NALA. The monkey who built Rama's bridge to Lanka.

NALAKUBARA. Son of the god of wealth.

NANDIN. Shiva's white bull.

NARADA. A heavenly sage born from Brahma's mind.

NARAYANA. The great god Vishnu who preserves the three worlds.

PARVATI. A name of Devi.

PRAHASTA. Ravana's general.

PULASTYA. One of Brahma's sons. He impregnates Trinavindu's daughter.

PULOMA. Indrani's father.

PUSHPAKA. A huge aerial chariot.

RAHU. The Asura whose living head, cut off at the neck, causes the eclipse of sun and moon by swallowing them in the sky.

RAMA.

RAMBHA. A lovely nymph.

RAVANA. The demon king.

RIKSHARAJA. The first monkey. He changes sex.

RUMA. Sugriva's wife, queen of Kishkindha.

SAMPATI. Jatayu's brother.

SAMUDRA. Ocean.

SARANA. Demon spy of Ravana.

SARASWATI. Goddess of speech.

SARDULA. Demon spy of Ravana.

SATRUGHNA. Rama's brother, Sumitra's son.

SAUNAKA. Who hears the story.

SAUTI. The storyteller.

SAVARI. A female hermit, friendly to Rama.

SHIVA. The great god whose third eye will burn the universe.

SINHIKA. A female monster.

SITA. Rama's wife.

SUBAHU. A demon killed by Lakshmana.

SUGRIVA. The monkey king.

SUKA. Ravana's minister.

SUKESA. Father of Mali, Sumali and Malyavan.

SUKRA. Indrajit's preceptor.

SUMALI. The third of the three Rakshasas who first lived in Lanka.

SUMANTRA. The royal charioteer of Ayodhya.

SUMITRA. Mother of Satrughna and Lakshmana.

SURABHI. The cow of plenty.

SURPANAKHA. Ravana's sister.

SURYA. The Sun.

SWAYAMPRABHA. An enchantress.

TARA. Wife of the monkey king Vali.

TRIJATA. The Rakshasi who befriended Sita.

TRINAVINDU. Father of a nymph.

TUMBURU. A Gandharva.

UCCHAIHSRAVAS. A famous horse.

VAISHRAVANA. The treasure king.

VAJRA-DANSHTRA. Thunder-Tooth.

VALAKHILYAS. Benign little deities floating in the air.

VALI. Sugriva's brother.

VALMIKI. Who invented poetry.

VARUNA. God of the waters and guardian of the west and of the worlds undersea.

VASISHTHA. Dasaratha's priest.

VASUKI. King of Serpents.

VATAPI. A cannibal in the Vindhya mountains.

VAYU. The wind god.

VIBHISHANA. Ravana's brother.

VIDYUJ-JIHVA. Lightning-Tongue.

VINATA. One of Kashyapa's wives, mother of Garuda.

VIRADHA. A long-armed monster.

VISHNU. The great god Narayana, pervading the universe, moving in the waters, preserving and restoring life.

VISWAKARMAN. Heavenly architect and lord of the arts.

VISWAMITRA. Who took Rama to protect him in the forest.

YAMA. God of death.

YUDHAJIT. Bharata's uncle, prince of Kekaya and Kaikeyi's brother.

Oh Man, I am the demon warrior Indrajit, hard to see. I fight invisibly, hidden by enchantment from your sight. I attack behind the wild winds of evil thought; I put out many lights left unguarded. I know you, and good deeds done in life are your only shield when you must die and go alone past me to another world. You may hide at night from the Sun, but never from your own heart—where lives Lord Narayana. The entire worlds are watching your deeds, and therefore forgiveness is Dharma.

Valmiki the Poet looked down into water held cupped in his hand and saw into the past. Before he looked, he thought the world was sweet poison. Men seemed to be living in lies, not knowing where their ways went. The days seemed made of ignorance and doubt, and cast from deception and illusion. But in the water he saw—a dream, a chance, and a great adventure. Valmiki trusted the True and forgot the rest; he found the whole universe like a bright jewel set firm in forgiving and held fast by love.

Widen your heart. Abandon anger. Believe me, your few days are numbered; make one fast choice now and no second!

Come, clear your heart and quickly walk with me into Brahma, while there is time.

PART ONE

THE PRINCE OF
AYODHYA

Om!
I bow to Lord Narayana,
To Lady Lakshmi of Good Fortune,
To Hanuman the best of monkeys,
And to Saraswati,
The Goddess of words and stories:
JAYA!
Victory!

Born as a Man

Sauti the storyteller told this tale to his friend Saunaka in Naimisha Forest. Bending with humility he finished the wonderful *Mahabharata* in the evening, and the next morning Saunaka asked, "Lotus-eyed Sauti, who was that monkey Hanuman who met Bhima in the Hills, and who stayed in Arjuna's war-flag while he fought? What is that story of Rama, which keeps Hanuman alive so long as it is told by men on Earth?"

Sauti answered, "That story is *Ramayana*, a tale of romance and love and of wild adventure, the very crest-jewel of poetry and a legend of the times and worlds of old. Arjuna the Pandava is gone, and Fire took away his bow, but somewhere Time waits to rearm him. So Time is beyond Fire, but *Ramayana* is beyond Time. Rama's days have long gone past; I do not believe there ever existed before, or will ever exist again such days in the world we know. . . ."

Saunaka said, "Tell me again an old story."

Sauti said, "Rama ruled the Earth for eleven thousand years. He gave a year-long festival in this very Naimisha Forest. All of this land was in his kingdom then; one age of the world ago; long, long ago; long before now, and far in the past. Rama was King from the center of the world to the four Oceans' shores."

Saunaka said, "I never tire of listening, I am never satisfied. If you know more stories tell them to me."

"Yes," answered Sauti. "If you would hear it, listen to *Ramayana* as it happened."

Listen, my friend—

I love this *Ramayana*. We live now in the third age of Time, and Rama lived in the second age of the world. *Ramayana* has long been standing above other stories; you must look up to find it. Valmiki the Poet put the deeds of

3

Rama into musical verses; he clothed them in the sound of singing. Before *Ramayana* there was no poetry on Earth.

As a young man, Valmiki searched through the world seeking open friendship and happiness and hope, and finding none of these he went alone into the empty forest where no man lived, to a spot near where the Tamasa river flows into Ganga. There he sat for years without moving, so still that white ants built an anthill over him. There Valmiki sat inside that anthill for thousands of years with only his eyes showing out, trying to find the True, his hands folded and his mind lost in contemplation.

Then one cloudy winter's day, at noon, the heavenly sage Narada, the inventor of music, born from Brahma's mind, flew from heaven to Valmiki and said, "Come out! Help me!"

"It's too cold," answered Valmiki. "Away with the worlds, where a little pleasure costs a lot of pain. Don't make trouble."

"Would I ever? See how Life goes by, with every creature doing what follows his nature." Narada knelt and looked in Valmiki's eyes. "Master, what can I say to you?"

Valmiki said, "Just name me one honest man and I'll move."

"Rama!" said Narada. "Come out of there!"

"Who is Rama?"

"Rama rules as King in Ayodhya. He is born in the Solar race and a descendant of the Sun; he is brave and gentle and firm in fight. By Rama's command his adorable Queen Sita is being brought here into the forest on a chariot, and though she suspects nothing yet, here she will be left abandoned. Unless you comfort her she will drown herself in Ganga and kill as well her unborn sons by Rama."

"What did she do wrong?" asked Valmiki.

"Nothing," said Narada. "Sita is innocent and blameless. She has lived as Rama's Queen for nearly ten thousand years; before that, Rama saved her from great danger by wondrous and incredible deeds. And now behold one of the terrors of kingship, that Rama must let her go because his people talk against her. Get up, save her life, and let her live here with you and your companions; and make in measured words the song of Rama, and teach it to Rama's two sons."

"I have no companions here," said Valmiki.

"You have now. Coming here, I sang a friend-gathering song. Valmiki, I've seen other skies than these, other worlds, and other friends. People are counting on you . . . and I can hear the chariot from Ayodhya approaching across Ganga."

Valmiki said, "I have no skill in any craft, even in words."

"There stops the chariot! Right now—here they come across Ganga in a boat, or will you also give way and forsake Sita too from fear of other people? *See!* She has discovered she is lost, and the boat is launched back without her. Oh hurry—there the sunlight comes from behind the dark clouds—there Ganga the River Goddess begins unseen to whisper spells over Sita and makes her swift-flowing waters seem a warm safe home. *Act now, Valmiki; call out and the rest must follow."*

Valmiki stood up and broke free out of that hard anthill. Suddenly he saw all around him many houses of hermits and their families, young trees carefully watered, a retreat cleared from the forest. Four boys ran up to him from the river and cried "The wife of some great warrior weeps by Ganga. She is fair as a Goddess fallen from heaven all bewildered, all alone, never seen before, with child, and with small gifts from the city tied within a silk cloth beside her. Go to her, welcome her, protect her. . . ."

Valmiki ran to Sita on the riverbank. "Sita, stay here in my hermitage, you have found here your father's house in a foreign land, we will care for you as our daughter." And seeing Sita he thought, "What a fine fair woman, how beautiful!"

Quickly the hermit wives surrounded Sita and took her to their homes. Narada had gone. Valmiki went alone to the clear Ganga waterside and bathed. He washed away the anthill dust and peeled grey bark from a tree and made new fresh clothes.

Then he sat back resting against a stone. He watched two small white waterbirds in a tree nearby. The male bird was singing to his mate when before Valmiki's eyes an arrow hit him, and the little bird fell from the limb. He thrashed on the ground an instant and then lay dead, and blood drops stained his feathers.

Heartbroken the dead bird's mate cried—*Your long feathers! Your tuneful songs!*

A bird-hunter came from the forest holding a bow. Valmiki's heart was pounding and he cursed the killer—

> *You will find no rest for the long years of Eternity,*
> *For you killed a bird in love and unsuspecting.*

One look at Valmiki and the hunter ran for his life, but fever already burned in his blood; he died that day. Valmiki turned back to his hermitage thinking, "This is truly how I remember the ways of the world." Then he thought, "Those words I cursed him with make a verse, and that verse could be sung to music."

For days the words ran through Valmiki's mind. Whatever he seemed to be doing he was really thinking of his verse. On the fourth day after Sita's rescue, Lord Brahma the creator of the worlds appeared in Valmiki's new retreat. He looked like an old man with red skin and white hair, with four arms, with four faces around one head, holding in his hands a ladle and a rosary, a waterpot and a holy book.

Valmiki greeted Brahma, "Sit by me," and taking water from a pitcher he washed Brahma's feet, and gave him other water to drink. But after that, even sitting there with the Grandfather of all the Universe watching him, still Valmiki remembered only the two waterbirds and thought to himself, "What a crime! There was not one bite of meat on that little bird! What use is a world run all wrong without a grain of mercy in it?"

Those thoughts were as clear to Brahma as if Valmiki had been shouting in his ear. Brahma said, "So, by a river, the world's first verse has been born from pity, and love and compassion for a tiny bird has made you a poet. Use your discovery to tell Rama's story, and your verses will defeat Time. As you make your poem, Rama's life will be revealed to you, and no word of yours will be untrue."

Lord Brahma returned to his heaven, far above the changing heavens of Indra and the gods, riding on his chariot drawn by white swans and snow geese. Valmiki sat every day facing East on a grass mat. He held a little water cupped in his hands, and looking down into it he clearly saw Rama and Sita. He saw them move, he heard them talk and laugh. He saw all Rama's life happen within the water; he held the past world in his palm; and part by part he made *Ramayana* delightful to the ear, pleasing to the mind, and a true happiness to the heart.

Not many months after Valmiki began his poetry, Sita's twin sons were born. Valmiki named them Kusa and Lava. They grew up resembling their father Rama as the Moon's reflection resembles the Moon himself. Kusa and Lava were handsome as Kama the Love God disarmed by pleasure. All the hermit women loved them, and watched those two boys instead of offering worship to the gods.

As Valmiki composed *Ramayana*, and as Kusa and Lava grew old enough to learn, he taught it to them by memory. When they were twelve years old Valmiki had brought his story nearly up to the present, and Kusa and Lava knew every foot of it, and sang *Ramayana* to a lute and a drum, like Gandharvas, the heavenly musicians.

That year King Rama held a year's celebration in Naimisha Forest along the river Gomati. At home, Kusa and Lava rehearsed their song. Deer listened from the wood and birds from the trees. They practiced long, and many forest men came to listen. After each day they brought Kusa and Lava gifts and presents—a waterjar, a bark-cloth shirt, a deerskin, some thread, a grass belt, red cloth, an axe, a cord to tie firewood, a cooking pot, and wild food they had gathered.

Then they all went to Rama's festival. People had come there from all over the world. Valmiki kept Sita hidden, but he sent Kusa and Lava to sing *Ramayana* in a clearing. When they started to sing the other business of the festival stopped. They held their hearers motionless. For a year they sang some of *Ramayana* every morning, and never told their names. Everyone gathered round them. Every day King Rama came to listen. He looked long at his two sons he had never seen and wondered who they were, and beside Rama stood a golden statue of Sita, for Rama loved her though he had sent her away.

Kusa and Lava began, "We sing a song of kingly fame—Oh Listen. . . ."

Rama, free your mind from malice and ill will; this is Valmiki's song.

On the banks of the Sarayu river is Fair Ayodhya, the royal capital of Kosala. She is a fabled city, famed among men, twelve leagues long and ten wide, with Sala trees, filled with grain and gold. Heaven is fair, Ayodhya is fairer; Heaven is cool in summer, but the Kosala hills are better.

Majesty, when your father Dasaratha was alive he ruled from the tall white Ayodhya palace built atop a rising hill; he was Lord of the Earth and the Lord of Men: he was a solar King bright as the noonday Sun. In those bright days now gone by forever, the gods from the air saw Kosala to be clear

as a mirror, with no least touch of evil to make any black
shadow over the land. The Kosalas were well-fed and
healthy, the Sarayu was filled with boats, every cow's horns
were covered with rings of silver and bands of gold. Every
man could keep what he had in peace and gain what more he
wanted.

The young people wore elegant clothes, and life was joyful
among the gardens and in the pleasure-parks. Three- and
seven-storied mansions lined the wide straight streets. The
Kosalas had no enemies and Ayodhya was unconquerable.
Flowers grew all over. Long-tusked elephants walked the
streets wearing bells on their necks. There were rows of full
shops with open doors, pale white palaces, and lordly trees;
rattling chariots drove by and there was music; foreign cara-
vans came bringing merchants and rich tribute from lesser
kings.

Fair Ayodhya was filled with warriors, like a mountain
cave filled with lions; her warriors were impatient and deadly
to foes. Each man of them could alone defeat ten thousand
chariots, but no one came against them. They kept the city
safe and tried to right whatever wrongs they could discover.
Dasaratha's ministers were loyal and wise, able to find hidden
motives and fight with words, cautious, never binding themselves to a lie, acting by their word. and sending out spies to
report what took place in all the world.

Fair Ayodhya was a matchlessly brilliant city with lots of
food and wood and water. But though Dasaratha was an old
man, sixty thousand years old, he had no son to inherit his
kingdom. He called his priest Vasishtha and said, "Brahmana,
I always long for a son. I can find no happiness without him,
therefore make a sacrifice with fire, to please the gods."

Vasishtha said, "Excellent. Well done. You will have sons
after your own heart."

Dasaratha told his charioteer Sumantra *Arrange for this.*
He went to his three Queens and said, "We will have sons,"
and hearing those sweet words their faces shone like lotus
flowers opening out after the long cold winter's end.

Sumantra piled provisions by the Sarayu and Vasishtha
chose a day whose ruling stars were fortunate. After his
morning bath King Dasaratha on that day watched Vasishtha
light the holy fires by the river. Vasishtha began then to sing
spellbinding mantras, he reached out for a flat wooden ladle
and dipped it into clear liquid butter, and he started to pour

the offering into the sacrificial fire—*Indra King of heaven, Come.*

In heaven above, Indra turned and sighed and hissed like an angry snake. His fine robes were burnt and torn, his face and chest were covered with dried blood. He was angry; he heard Vasishtha's call and it made him still angrier.

Indra looked about his heaven. It was a hopeless ruin. The once beautiful heavenly garden Nandana was uprooted, crushed and buried beneath soot and cinders. Heaven's long golden street was littered with slain Gandharvas, with Apsarasas, the dancing women of heaven, lying killed, and with the corpses of Rakshasa demons. The high stately pleasure-palaces were razed to broken stones and tiles. The heavenly stream of Ganga ran red with blood. Exhausted thunders and broken lightnings lay underfoot, drawn Rakshasa swords were already rusting in the river, lingering fires and smoke ate smoldering holes in heaven's high walls, the charred Gate of the Gods lay split and wrenched from its heavy posts.

Indra had just fought the Battle of Heaven. He had proudly stood up against the Demon King Ravana. He alone had not submitted with his people to the Rakshasas. He had fought back hard and lost, he had been captured and released and now stood again in heaven.

Now Indra's eyes filled with tears. He ground his teeth and clenched his fists; then reaching down he seized a chunk of shattered adamant and flew with it up to Brahma's high heaven beyond change. He stood there before Brahma's palace, and with tremendous force threw the stone right through the beautiful gold and jade bars of the biggest window. Guards ran out with spears and swords. But when they saw Indra they hung down their heads in shame and motioned him to enter.

Brahma sat on a lotus throne of sandalwood in a room at the end of a long hall and through a doorway set three steps beyond the end of the Universe.

Indra entered. "You are to blame! It's your fault, all of it!"

"Alas," said Brahma, "it is *my* loss that ever I created any of you."

"Ravana the Ten-headed Rakshasa King has wantonly slain my people!" said Indra. "His son Indrajit captured me fighting invisibly, then soon freed me for some reason."

"I arranged that."

Indra frowned. "And you have also arranged it so that no one in heaven can kill Ravana! You set him over us all. He asked and you granted it—*look what you've done, you old* —" But the last word couldn't come out of Indra's throat. Whatever word he thought of, none was strong enough to tell his feelings, so he couldn't speak.

"An old fool!" he said at last. "Why? Why? Just tell me *why* you grant boons to demons?"

"O Indra, it was but an elusive impulse."

"This time you've made a monster invulnerable. Ravana is the disgrace of all Creation and a reproach to the worlds. How can we withstand him when even the gods cannot kill him? Are we to live under evil?"

Though he already knew, Brahma asked, "Where are the other gods?"

Indra replied, "Agni the Fire God heats the stoves in Ravana's kitchens; the rains do his washing; Vayu the Wind sweeps the yards of Lanka; Varuna Lord of Waters supplies the wines for Ravana's court; the Sun lights Ravana's halls and the Moon his gardens . . . so great is the power of fear!"

"Oh Indra, look again."

Indra looked down at Earth and Lanka. "Why, those forms are false! The others have escaped. . . ."

Brahma held out a silver bowl of Soma wine and Indra swiftly drank it down. Then he sighed again, but smiling. Brahma too drank, and looked carefully at Indra.

"God of Rain," said Brahma, "let the pain go. Where is Viswakarman the Architect of heaven?"

"He is always by himself somewhere." said Indra.

"Put him back to work. Rebuild heaven."

Indra squeezed his arms. "Besides all the rest, Ravana himself enjoys the food men sacrifice to us gods, and basks in all our smoke. Destroyed are the gardens in heaven that once made my eyes happy and my heart sing. Now there is no song heard, and I fear even to go down to the sacrifice of the Ayodhya King Dasaratha."

Brahma said, "Remember how to speak the old language with me . . . Ravana is careless . . . he has long been careless. *Stop your suffering and raise your head.* Dasaratha will reach his desire. Four sons will be his. Take the Kosala King's offerings and no one will stop you. Keep out of Ravana's sight and be patient. Do not fight him again and how can you be defeated? Think before and not after you act."

Indra's weariness was gone. He said, "Like the poor Earth,

my heavens themselves are now proved flawed and fleeting, fast-dying and stricken by devilish demons. Have a care for my world! I am Lord of the Gods. I am not weak like a mere man, I am Indra of a Hundred Sacrifices, Destroyer of Cities, Indra of the Thunder-Hand, Lord of Paradise, Lord of Lightnings! And a demon beast overcame *me*—"

"Indra, be ashamed! Be silent!" Brahma refilled their Soma bowls. "What can I do? I can never lie, and I do not know every answer."

Indra asked, "Who knows then?"

"Go to Narayana," said Brahma. "Only Narayana knows, or maybe he doesn't. But for myself, where can I find the end, where the beginning, where the middle of all this? Ask Narayana—*How was Ravana careless?*—then obey the mantras of Vasishtha."

Indra went to Narayana, the Lord Vishnu, the Soul of the Universe. Narayana sat watching Indra approach. Indra pressed together his hands, touched his brow, and bent his head low to Narayana's feet. "Searcher of Hearts, I bow to you, *namas*. I have still faith in the Good Law of Dharma." Indra looked up past Narayana's wide dark chest crossed by a neckchain of sapphires, up into the great god's joyful black eyes wide as lotus petals.

Narayana in his yellow saffron summer robes smiled down at Indra. "Yes, a good enough fight," said Narayana. "No fear, Lord of Gods."

"How shall we bring down Ravana?" asked Indra. "Because of Brahma's boon is the Demon King strong, and for no other cause of his own. Help me, you are my only refuge, there is no other for me. *I will gather my storms again and attack Lanka, give me your permission to fight Ravana once more!*"

"Never!" said Narayana. "Don't you understand that Brahma's words are always true? Do not falsify the three spheres of life. I would not have let you fight in the first place, though you were right to resist and Ravana was wrong. Ravana asked Brahma—*Let me be unslayable by every creature of Heaven and of the underworlds.* And Brahma promised—*So be it.* That boon is unbreakable, yet will I cause Ravana's death. That is the truth. Only ask me. . . ."

"Ah," said Indra, "from disdain Ravana did not mention men or animals, and took no safeguard against them. He eats

men; they are his food and why should he fear them? Lord,
on Earth life resembles Hell again. We need you again. Look
at us, see us, and bless us. For the good of all the worlds,
Lord Narayana, accept birth as a man."

"I already have."

Waves of happiness washed over Indra. "Dark blue Narayana clad in yellow, become four. Put aside the shell trumpet,
the razor-edged chakra, the lotus and mace you hold in your
four hands. Empty your dark hands; descend into the bor-
rowed and fanciful world of men, desperate and glittering.
Become Dasaratha's four sons born of blood and seed. Take
your Goddess Lakshmi and let her be your mortal wife."

"We will go down," said Narayana.

"Lord, kill him, kill Ravana forever. I hate that proud and
pampered Rakshasa. Favor me and curse him; give to Death
his faces torn apart; dry away our fear as the Sun dries
morning dew."

"I will," said Narayana. "Listen, Vasishtha begins to call
you to Earth with songs, to Ayodhya by the sleepy Sarayu."

The melted butter from Vasishtha's ladle fell into the
flames. Vasishtha sang—*Indra be my bridge from high to
low, do my bidding, obey me. . . .*

The tongues of fire danced, and Indra came unseen in the
sky, free again and feasting on smoke. Vasishtha sang—
*Narayana, we take your protection. Leave your home a mo-
ment, draw near, come to us. . . .*

Vasishtha threw flowers in the fire and quickly stepped
back to stand beside King Dasaratha. They heard a ringing
loud noise, a fierce clang of metal; but saw nothing.

"What was that?" asked the old King.

"The sharp discus drops," said Vasishtha.

They heard a crash like a falling tree and Vasishtha said,
"The huge mace is fallen." There was a hollow rolling sound.
"The shell is down." They caught the sudden scent of lotuses.

Then a giant black man rose from the flames in a stream
of smoke and a burning shower of sparks. He stepped out
from the fire and frowned and glared with menace at the
King, but Dasaratha faced him unmoved. The giant wore
crimson, his whole body was covered with dark lion's hair,
his belt was a bowstring, his palms were marked with thun-
der-signs and the soles of his feet with wheels. He had a thick
glossy beard and long black hair on his head. He had the yel-

low eyes of a tiger and held out a steaming golden bowl like the Sun with a silver cover.

Dasaratha took the bowl in his hands. The black giant said, "Feed this to your wives, it will bring you sons." The fire crackled and the black man vanished.

Inside the bowl was rice cooked with milk and sweetened with sugar. Vasishtha walked three times round the fire in right-turning circles. Dasaratha felt like a poor man who has found a treasure undreamt of, like a man rich in happiness, like a lost voyager finding the way home.

Dasaratha went to the inner rooms of his palace. All the servants of his three Queens were smiling; their faces lighted the rooms as the sky is flooded with the lovely beams and rays of the autumn Moon.

Dasaratha gave the gleaming bowl to his first wife, Kausalya, and said, "Eat half of it." When Kausalya had eaten half the rice he gave his second wife Sumitra half of what remained. He gave his youngest wife Kaikeyi half of what Sumitra had left. He thought a moment, and gave all the rest to Sumitra again.

A year later on the ninth day of spring Rama was first born to Kausalya. Later that same day Bharata was born to Kaikeyi; then still later Sumitra bore two sons, Lakshmana and Satrughna. Their father lit their birth-fires in jars of Earth; he named them on the eleventh day of their lives, and the Kosalas danced in the streets and rang all the temple bells.

Rama grew to be his father's favorite son. Rama was not tall and not short. He had more energy than the Sun and a deep voice. He had colorful green eyes; his skin was cool soft green and so smooth even dust would not cling to him; his wavy hair was dark green; he walked like a lion; the soles of his feet were flat and marked with royal Dharma-wheels. There was no hollow between his shoulder blades on his back; his arms were long and reached to his knees; he had forty identical white teeth all shaped like pomegranate seeds; his thumbs bore the four lines of knowledge where they joined his hands. He had high shoulders like a lion, and a graceful brow, a broad chest, three folds in his neck at the base of his throat like the spirals on a shell. He had deep collarbones and a long tongue, a sharp nose, heavy jaws and the eyelashes of a bull. His breath was lotus-scented. Of all men only Rama was born knowing his own heart.

Lakshmana was Rama's second self; he was Rama's own life walking beside him. He always kept Rama company, and served him in everything before himself. Lakshmana was of golden skin and measureless strength, his eyes were blue as wildflowers and his straight hair was golden-brown. Lakshmana would not sleep without Rama near him nor eat unless Rama shared his food. When Rama went riding on horseback, there rode Lakshmana behind him holding a bow.

Prince Bharata was born with red skin, rosy eyes and scarlet lips and fiery hair red as flame. His brother Satrughna had dark blue skin and black eyes and black hair. And in the same way that his twin Lakshmana was drawn to Rama, Satrughna accompanied Bharata everywhere and thought Bharata dearer than his own life itself.

When the four princes were sixteen years old the recluse Viswamitra came to Kosala in the spring. The frontier guards sent word to Ayodhya and King Dasaratha met him there on foot outside the city. The King held flowers and water, grass and rice, and said, "Welcome to you, brahmana. I hope your journey to me went well."

Viswamitra answered, "I hope your land here is peaceful and your kingdom rich. Are all your friends well? Are your warriors obedient to you and defiant to your enemies? I hope your foes are dead and that you keep well the duties of a King."

They walked together into Ayodhya. The priest Vasishtha met them and said, "Viswamitra, you arrive here like summer rain, like the recovery of something lost, like bright dawn after night. By our good fortune we have gained your company. Today our births have borne fruit and our lives gained their goals."

When they were seated in the palace Dasaratha said to Viswamitra, "Why have you come? Whatever you want I will gladly give you."

"Promise me," said Viswamitra.

"I promise."

Viswamitra said, "Majesty, that promise becomes you alone. No one else would make it. The pathless forest where I live has become a courtyard of evil and no longer is there any safety from the Rakshasas of the monstrous Demon King Ravana."

The Thorn in the World's Side

Where I have been there is no light
From any Sun; we have no Moon nor Stars,
No lightnings like these, much less any of this Fire.

There I must light up all around me.
By my sight all is illumined.

Here I am born again to kill the Evil,
And like a black she-leopard going with me in my shadow
Never does Victory leave my side:
One; one only and no second!

Viswamitra said, "King, for years I have tried to complete a sacrifice in the solitary forest. I do nothing wrong and leave nothing out. I never daydream, and my work is absolutely without lapses or holes. The most learned Rakshasa could surely detect no entrance, yet when I speak a blessing I hear the heavy tread of countless running feet in the air above me and see no one. Just when I am to make the offering and end the rites, flesh and gore fall on my altar. My waterjars break untouched, my figwood ladles warp and groan and my fires go out."

Dasaratha said, "How have Rakshasas overcome Brahma power? Where are the gods who should protect you?"

Viswamitra replied, "Majesty, we are living in the second age of the world, and the quarter part of Virtue has now died among men. These are faded days and Dharma declines. In the first age food came by wishing and grew from Earth without tending. No one wept, nor was cruel, nor hurt another; and there were not many gods then among different men but only one.

"This age began with the first slaughter and sacrifice of an innocent animal to some lower god; men started to take action to gain objects and rewards; they gave no more gifts free just for the giving, except rarely, more and more rarely as years pass. This is a time of scene-shifting and contrivance; men no longer live as long; there are all about us arguments and objections and ambushes and devious cunning, deceitful sorcery and craft and fraud and guile and trickery and lies and many devices. King, against Ravana's Rakshasas there is no help in the forest and no help from the gods."

"I pity those living after us," said Dasaratha. "Who is Ravana?"

"He is King of Lanka," said Viswamitra, "a piece of grit in the world's eye to make her weep. Ravana has conquered Heaven and Hell. His brutal helpers hunger for me. They fly fast and change shapes at will; they love eating hermits; they feed on harmless men and consume creatures like Death himself."

Listen, Majesty—

By the light of very ancient history you will learn how the three worlds have fallen prey to the inhuman race of the Night-Wanderers. You will hear what the hateful demon Ravana has done.

At the last beginning of Time as at every beginning, Brahma the Creator of the Worlds was reborn from a lotus. That flower grew from the navel of Lord Narayana as he slept afloat on the waters, lying on the white coils of the endless serpent Sesha. Brahma saw water everywhere and he grew anxious lest it be stolen. So out of water he made four guardians; two mated couples male and female.

Those four people said, "We are hungry and thirsty."

Brahma told them, "Watch this water, don't let a drop of it get lost."

One couple answered him, "*Rakshama*, we will protect it."

The other pair said, "*Yakshama*, we shall worship it."

Those couples were the first Rakshasas and the first Yakshas. Narayana then carefully rescued the Earth from under water. Brahma somehow made the five elements; he fashioned the worlds and made food and other races.

The Rakshasa couple lived on Earth. That Rakshasi was pregnant; she was filled with child as a raincloud is filled with water by the sea. Majesty, Rakshasis conceived and give birth all in one day. She went alone to a deserted hillside and bore a son, then she left the baby demon there abandoned.

She forgot him and hurried back to her husband, and her newborn child put his fist in his mouth and cried slowly.

Just then above that hill in the sky Lord Shiva was riding with Devi on the back of Nandin the white brahma bull. Devi heard the faint little cries; she looked down and saw the helpless baby, and she sent the great god Shiva down onto the hill.

The terrible Lord Shiva bent over that child, picked him up and held him gently. Shiva Lord of the destruction preceding creation wore a tiger's skin still dripping blood, the holy thread over his shoulder was a mottled serpent; he had in his hair the crescent Moon; he was in form a pale white man with white ashes in his hair and his throat was blue, and on his brow was his deadly third eye closed. He gave that baby his mother's age and to please Devi gave him the power of flight; and these gifts stayed with the Rakshasa race, and their children grow to their mother's age the day they're born.

That Rakshasa was Sukesa. He was charming and polite, and welcome everywhere. He married the daughter of a Gandharva, and her company made him happy. He had three sons and named them Mali, Sumali and Malyavan.

Those three young Rakshasas wanted a better place to live. They wanted their earthly homes to be beautiful. They flew to heaven to Viswakarman the heavenly architect. They found him forging an iron axe with a steel hammer, pounding away while sparks flew burning holes in his leather clothes.

Viswakarman was surrounded by tall clay jars of waters and oils for tempering blades. His anvils and firepits and bellows and dirty charcoal bags cluttered the room; long leather belts and running wheels and whining wooden gears went rattling overhead in confusion; round the rafters hung thunderbolts to be sharpened and spare axles and chariot chains; underfoot were metal cuttings and pointed scrap and curly shavings; the light was bad; acid fumes and coal dust filled the hot air; and clamor and din never ceased in his workshop.

Malyavan drew near and said in a loud voice, "Dear Lord of Arts. . . ."

Viswakarman stopped hammering, but his furnaces still roared and the gears ground on. He yelled back—*Is it made of metal?*

Malyavan shouted, "A home . . . beauty . . . for us . . . somewhere quiet. . . ."

Viswakarman ran his grimy hand over his sweaty brow and brushed some filings out of his hair. He gestured toward a back door—*Come follow me*.

He led the three Rakshasa brothers through that door into a quiet room, light and clean, ideal for an artist. The goddesses and wives of heaven came to welcome Viswakarman warm glad smiles and cool drinks. And Viswakarman no longer looked like a metalsmith. Just by going through the door he had changed into a beautiful sensitive workman wearing airy clothes and remote from care.

Now Malyavan could speak. "Prince of Artists, you have made the gods' flying chariots; you have put speed into the legs of horses; you have given the strong their strength; you have made husband and wife the one for the other from before their birth, and those who love the gods got that love from you. When your daughter married the Sun and found him too bright you put him on your lathe and shaved him down a bit. What is there you cannot create or model?"

The goddesses gave Viswakarman garlands and loving looks, and he asked Malyavan, "What shall I build for you?"

"Build us a home grand as the Halls of Shiva, with high painted ceilings, rich in ornaments and flowered gardens."

Viswakarman smiled. "I hear that Shiva lives in a drafty hut that every moment threatens to collapse on him."

Malyavan fell at Viswakarman's feet. "Oh, we are truly ignorant and poor. Make us a fine city, a fortress where we may live."

Viswakarman answered, "On Earth the Isle of Lanka in the southern sea is vacant. I will build Lanka City there for you, on the brow of Trikuta Hill rising to the clouds, somewhere not far below the highest of his three summits."

Before their eyes Viswakarman changed again. He became all-seeing and had on every side eyes and faces and arms. From his back came the two great wide wings by which he fashions all forms and shapes, fanning the air and blowing them into life.

Viswakarman took a staff, went outside and struck the ground of heaven hard. A golden city arose; there was Beautiful Lanka of golden walls. "Can you live there?" asked Viswakarman.

"We will live in her as the gods live in heaven," said Malyavan. "How skillful, what an admirable artist you are!"

The city vanished. Viswakarman said, "If you like the plan

of it I will make it real. First I must cut the trees and mine the gold and shape the stones."

"Have you no helpers for that?"

Viswakarman turned on him. "Of course not, are you mad? When the master carpenter no longer goes out into the forests to choose his own tree, when he no longer cuts it down himself and saws his own boards then say farewell to the arts!"

So Beautiful Lanka was built. The race of Rakshasas flourished under Sukesa's three sons. Sukesa himself lived with his wife in a Gandharva house on the slopes of Himalya until he died, a courtly old demon kind to all.

But as they increased in number there was not room for every Rakshasa to live in Lanka. Some left the others and prowled roaming through the forests across the sea to the north, and there began to eat the raw flesh of men, as they do now, striking by night. They would murder the gentle teachers in their retreats and avoid the well-armed tribes of hunters as though picking only the easy ripe fruit from a tree.

In those days the heavenly sage Narada sat in the sky trying to play a song of music on his lute of tortoise-shell and yellow wood. When he was in a good mood he was unreasonable, irritable and cross and wondrously disagreeable; and interruptions infuriated him. He could not even tune the lute-strings, for horrible cries rising from Earth's forests filled his ears. Narada set aside his lute and soared down, and in Dandaka Forest he stood angrily before the first demon he saw and said, "Be quiet or else!"

The Rakshasa said, "Oh Man you are my dinner now."

"I am no man, I live in heaven and. . . ." The Rakshasa had swallowed him whole. But Narada was hot as a barrel of embers. The demon spat him out and still his stomach burned.

Narada glared at him. "Your peaceful days are gone! *I will sing such a song. . . .*"

Narada flew back to his lute.

> *For I will play in your despite,*
> *And I will make the wrongs all right.*
> *For I will do, what pleases me. . . .*

He perfectly tuned his lute with shaking hands, and sitting inside a cloud high above Dandaka Forest he sang—*Dark blue Narayana and black Rakshasas!*

The awful dark shadow of the giant shell-trumpet Panchajanya fell over Lanka; the water-born king of shells roared. Narayana came on the bird Garuda in armor bright as a thousand suns!

Sentries ran to Malyavan and the brave Night-Wanderers rose into the sky. Their chariots and elephants came racing through the air; their fast-flying graceful war-horses, red and white and pale blue, milled and pawed the sky. Garuda flew to the attack. Narayana was hidden by swarms of demon arrows hard-hitting, true-flying and thirsty.

> *He has disappeared; listen, he is lost.*
> *He is lost, but do I hear*
> *A crying bowstring! Do I hear*
> *Fear to the demons!*

The demon horses stumbled. The noise of Narayana's bow turned their elephants to stone; they fell from the sky and broke. Wildly swung the war-flags, blood poured in rivers, Lanka was measured by corpse-lengths. Narayana beheaded Mali. Sumali and Malyavan fled wounded and burning in grief down to safety in the underworlds beneath the sea, through a door under Ocean.

Garuda shrieked and screamed and turned in the air like a hurricane. Narayana'a arrows flew, white-hot flights of arrows humming, piercing Dandaka Forest, raining down into Lanka. The Rakshasa pride was fallen; their heroes were dead; the southern sea was stained; the Forest ran red with Rakshasa blood. The demons fled like the clouds of doom driven before the black wind of the End of the Worlds. Their jeweled necklaces and earrings fell over Lanka Island, their dark bodies covered the waves.

Narada set down his lute. No living Rakshasa remained on Earth. Lanka City was empty.

So, Majesty, were the demons driven away once long ago, but they hoarded their possessions and hopes far underground in the Naga Kingdoms and watched for some chance to return.

Pulastya was one of Brahma's Mind-born sons, one of the inspired forefathers of life. He lived on a lonely hill of the Himalyas, alone, looking out over the lowlands. He felt no need to be busy; he watched the world go by; he was in love with the quiet of the high hills, with the pines and the deodars, with Himalya rising to heaven.

That same hill was a favorite playground for Apsarasas and Naga girls, who ran about singing and laughing together with the daughters of the local hermits. When they disturbed him for the hundred-and-eighth time Pulastya told them, "If I ever see any girl playing around here any more she will become pregnant!"

Fearing that they stayed away. But the daughter of the hermit Trinavindu had not heard this curse. The very next day she came looking round Pulastya's home for her friends. She came into his sight as he was singing; he only glanced at her but she turned pale and ran to her father.

Trinavindu said, "Why are you no longer a maid?"

She wrung her hands. "Nothing happened, I was walking alone."

Trinavindu centered his mind and in an instant he knew the answer. He led her back to Pulastya and said, "Take this girl as alms from me, for your happiness."

Pulastya accepted her. Their son was Vishrava. Vishrava married a brahmana's daughter and when his son was born he called him Vaishravana.

Vaishravana was a happy child, good-spirited and friendly. He stayed on his grandfather's hillside smiling away, greeting the days like new friends. So happily did he live that he forgot to eat or drink, and for a thousand years he even forgot to breathe.

When he did that, in heaven Indra's marble throne grew hot. Lord Brahma had to come down and ask Vaishravana what he would like to have or to be.

"I want to be always generous," answered Vaishravana, and Brahma made him Lord of Treasures and Riches and Wealth. The Treasure Lord took the Yakshas of the hill-lakes who loved water for his treasure-keepers and made their king Manibhadra his friend. And from Brahma he also received the huge aerial mind-driven chariot Pushpaka made by Viswakarman in heaven, that could fly with horses or without them and was big as a small city, and all covered with flow-

ers. And further, Vaishravana got immortality and all the
wealth of the three worlds and kingdom over kings.

But Brahma gave him nowhere to live. Vaishravana asked
his father what to do, and Vishrava sent him to deserted
Lanka. The Yakshas carried the treasures of the worlds
across the southern sea or rode over the waters in Pushpaka
chariot. Vaishravana made Beautiful Lanka his home, and
from time to time he would return to Himalya to visit his
parents, floating along by himself on rays of light.

In the netherworlds of the Nagas Malyavan and Sumali
were still alive. Looking up through the saltwater of the
southern sea, from beneath a crevice in the ocean floor they
saw Vaishravana taking his riches to Lanka. Malyavan didn't
mind, but when Sumali saw Vaishravana's wealth gleaming
and casting brilliant lights even on the floor of the sea he was
hit by envy. Unhappiness fell on him and he asked questions
and learned all about the birth of the Treasure King.

Sumali told his daughter Kaikasi, "Go to Vishrava and get
sons like that!" She cast down her eyes, but fearing to disobey her father she went to the Hills.

She stood before Vishrava scuffing the ground with her toe.
He looked at her and she said, "I am Kaikasi, read the rest
for yourself."

Vishrava took her for his second wife, and when she gave
birth it was to four Rakshasas, three sons and a daughter.
First-born was Ravana. Ravana had ten hideous heads and
twenty arms; he was blacker than a heap of soot and fit to
horrify the Universe; he had two fangs curving up from each
mouth and coppery lips and twenty red eyes. When he was
born every dog in the world howled as loud as he could and
chased his tail madly turning left in circles.

Next was born the giant Kumbhakarna with ears shaped
like the big earthen waterjars that stand higher than a man's
waist, and he grew up in one day to stand taller than a high
house. Then the frightful girl Surpanakha was born, and last
of all was born Vibhishana the good demon.

Not long after their birth, Ravana and Vibhishana saw the
Treasure Lord come home on one of his visits. Ravana became sad that he had no such brilliance himself. Then Ravana made the colossal Kumbhakarna stay home and not

wander over Earth eating saints, and in that wide mountain forest the three brothers sat contemplating the absolute immensity of Life. In contemplation they entered Eternity.

And at the end of every thousand years, Ravana cut off one of his heads and threw it into fire as a sacrifice, until nine of his heads were gone and but one day remained before he would cut the last one. That day was passing. Ten thousand years and Ravana's life were about to end together.

Ravana held the knife to his throat, when Brahma appeared and said, "Stop! Ask me a boon at once!"

"I am glad that I please you," said Ravana.

"Please me!" said Brahma. "Your will is dreadful, too strong to be neglected: like a bad disease I must treat it. Your pains make me hurt. Ask!"

"May I be unslayable and never defeated by the gods or any one from any heaven, by Hell's devils or Asuras or demon spirits, by underworld serpents or Yakshas or Rakshasas."

"Granted!" said Brahma quickly. He gave Ravana back his burnt heads better looking than before. They rose living from the ashes and settled on Ravana's necks. Ravana smiled and smoothed down his black moustaches.

Brahma told Vibhishana, "Ask."

"May I never forget Dharma in peril or in pleasure, in comfort or in distraction."

Brahma said, "Yes; and you will be immortal on Earth and exempt from death or oblivion; and my truth knows no turning."

Lord Brahma turned to Kumbhakarna, but the Wind came to him invisibly and whispered, "Grandfather, give him nothing. He has already eaten seven Apsarasas and ten Gandharvas and many saints; he blunders about ruining peace and happiness. Consider what he did with no boons, and with them he will eat everyone."

Brahma thought, "Saraswati white Goddess of Speech, for a moment capture the words of Kumbhakarna." She entered the giant's throat and Brahma said aloud, "Kumbhakarna, quickly ask and quick be given."

Kumbhakarna answered, "What I really want is to sleep for half a year after every day I have to spend awake in this stupid world." He no sooner spoke than he fell over into a deep sleep.

Then did Sumali come from under Earth. He embraced Ravana and said, "Now why fear? No god, not even Narayana can hurt us. Lead us back to Lanka as before!"

Ravana sent Sumali to Lanka, and the old Rakshasa told Vaishravana, "Go, this is our city."

Again the Treasure Lord asked his father what to do. Vishrava said, "Don't fight your own brother. Leave Lanka as you found her, move your treasure, live on Kailasa Hill north of these Himalyas, live on Silver Mountain." So Vaisravana became the Guardian God of the North, one of the four Guardians of the world's four directions.

Ravana moved into Lanka, and the millions of Rakshasas who had multiplied in exile underground came there with their families and animals. Old Malyavan stood blinking and smiling on Lanka's sunny beach, happy and proud of Ravana. Rakshasas went over the lands again, dark as thunderclouds, with earrings of bright gleams of gold.

One day Ravana was walking alone through the forests on the side of Trikuta Hill by his city. There he met the Asura Maya standing under the trees, holding hands with a beautiful fair-skinned girl. The Asuras are the former gods of old; they are from before.

Ravana asked, "Who are you and whose is this fawn-eyed girl?"

Maya smiled. "I am Maya, a poor artist struggling to survive. She is my daughter Mandodari; Hema the Apsarasa is her mother. I lived happily in love with Hema for a thousand years, but then just after Mandodari's birth her mother left us on some affair of the gods. Now in the sorrow of separation we live in grief in our humble home; we wander sadly in our golden palace; through tearful eyes we watch the stars at night; we languish long on diamond stairways; we sigh by silver curtains and fountains of nectar; and in our ten thousand empty rooms we hear from the trees outside the moaning of our singing wind-harps strung with glass and there we cry."

"I am Ravana and your servant," said the Demon King.

"You must be a warrior." Maya sounded more cheerful. "In all truth, my boy, a daughter's father must choose between misery and dishonor. I spend all my time watching her. She has got to be given away. I have to get rid of her. Long is the way, for someone must marry Mandodari, but no one comes to ask for her. Her youth is passing. She is artless and innocent, but who knows *who* may ask for her? Unmarried she puts all our ancestors in uncertainty. Ravana, you are a handsome fellow, your faces quite striking, your arms very original, your faults surely not worth mentioning . . . we go out walking, but always I must bring her back home again, like carrying my own illusion home with me. . . ."

Ravana said, "Brahma himself is my great-grandfather and I am King of Lanka."

"Fascinating!" said Maya. "Charming! Take her, My Lord, take the daughter of Maya the Master of all Arts and Skill."

So Ravana wed the golden-skinned Daughter of Illusion. He lit a fire and married her. And days later, there stood before Ravana his full-grown son Meghanada, like fire released from hiding in fuel, set free to burn. Meghanada had a voice like a cloud full of thunder. He changed his form and appearance at will; if he had a true form only his mother Mandodari knew what it was.

Then from the Himalyan hillside Ravana and Vibhishana carried Kumbhakarna to Lanka as he slept, and Ravana had built over him a huge mansion of one big room like a shed. He chose the demon Prahasta as his General, and Prahasta gathered soldiers into an army. Then the Demon King threw ten arms around his son and the other ten round his General, and they began to fly off with countless soldiers to rape the worlds for days at a time.

They would make many raids into the Himalya hills and there like the Wind they broke down trees and tore the orchards and pavilions set along the paths to heaven. Gandharvas and Apsarasas visiting on Earth were captured and eaten, men were devoured. Ravana stole fair maidens of every race for his warriors in Lanka; and then refugees ran to Vaishravana on Mount Kailasa.

Vaishravana sent a Yaksha to see Ravana in Lanka. The Yaksha said, "The noble Treasure King hears of your bestial attacks on the innocent and asks you to remember right and wrong and not to dishonor your family. He tells you—*Stop, brother, for I live near heaven and I hear the gods wish for your destruction and seek ways to kill you.*"

Ravana smiled. "My jewel-bellied brother!" He drew a sword and killed the Yaksha. He sent him to the kitchen to be roasted and served, and his bones made into broth.

And when they had eaten, Ravana and Prahasta rose into the sky. They darted north over the sea and flew over cities and streams and plains, racing to silver Kailasa.

Manibhadra the Yaksha King saw them come and ran to stand in the gate of the Treasure Palace. Ravana yelled at him, "Surrender or die!"

"Where's our messenger?" asked Manibhadra.

"He's dead. In the soup!" cried General Prahasta.

Vaishravana heard that from inside his palace and called out a window, "That does it! Kill my brother!"

Yakshas poured out the palace windows. Manibhadra flew over the walls like a hawk, followed by whirling flame-crested Yakshas spinning in the air, filled with the energy they had stolen from careless treasure-lovers in the big cities of men, and crying their war-cries—Yes. No. I don't want. Let me have. More!

Prahasta killed a thousand of them and Ravana got the rest. But Manibhadra remained under the gateway arch of gold. His green eyes were shining; his blue hair was tied with strings of white blossoms; his lavender skin was steaming. He was very strong; he frowned and stamped his feet; he waved his powerful arms and glanced from his eye-corners. He pulled the palace gate from its stout hinges and flattened Prahasta with it. He grinned and sailed through the air at Ravana, and hit him with his fist from above so hard the mountain shook. Manibhadra drove Ravana right down into the ground like a post, turned and saw Prahasta trying to get free, and with a magic wave of his hand put fear of loss and hope of gain into Prahasta's heart in exactly equal parts and so paralyzed him.

But where is the straight fair fighting of the Yakshas and where are the tricks of illusion that Rakshasas use? Ravana blinded Manibhadra with darkness and hit the Yaksha King on the head with a steel mace, so hard that ever after Manibhadra's skull was dented in on the side.

Manibhadra fell unconscious. The nine invisible treasures sent their spirits to carry him to safety. Vaishravana came sadly out from his palace and told Ravana, "We surrender. You have conquered our world and destroyed our friendship. Take what you want, for nothing now will ever more be freely given you. I won't fight you any more . . . you may take me for a coward, afraid to do wrong."

Ravana pried Prahasta out from under the gate-leaf and from his brother he took the giant aerial chariot Pushpaka. All by itself the chariot rose into the sky, and riding there with Prahasta Ravana left for Lanka thinking himself master of all and everyone.

Indra came down from his Heaven and said to Vaishravana, "Your slain Yakshas are flying through my sky. Ravana is your brother, but now I turn my face from him, I curse him forever."

Vaishravana shook his head in wonder. "He will not stop!"

"If not, he will *be* stopped," said Indra. "He'll be *crushed!*"

Vaishravana sighed. "In ignorance he drinks poison, in confusion he refuses the antidote. He plans in detail his own ruin and wastes all his strength. Straight-speaking people cannot even talk at all with one so outrageous and treacherous. I could not even talk with him here. . . ."

As they flew south in Pushpaka, Ravana and Prahasta saw a golden reed forest held in nets of sunlight on a mountainside, a woodland of bamboos and canes. They were taken by the sight and turned the chariot for a closer look, when all at once Pushpaka came to a jarring halt and stuck there immovable in the sky.

Prahasta groaned, "This thing won't work, there's always something wrong with everything."

But then they saw Nandin, Shiva's white bull, grazing below them. Nandin looked up and changed his shape. He became a yellowy-brown dwarf and rose to stand in the air near them, his ugly head shaven, his limbs too short for his body, his chest like a barrel. First he just looked. Then he sniffed, then he growled under his breath, then in a lordly tone he said, "Turn and go, turn and go, Ravana. Shiva sports here with Devi, no one can approach the Wood of Reeds, no one can ever pass me."

When Ravana saw that badly dressed midget looking down his nose at him he yelled—*Who is this Shiva?* Ravana jumped down onto the foot of the mountain, but there before him was that same little Nandin. This time he was leaning on a stick and wearing the red face of a monkey.

Ravana had to laugh. He threw back his heads and laughed as loud as all the thunders ever made rolling together over heaven. But Nandin spoke quietly, "Demon King. you may frolic and mock my face, but animals looking like me will destroy you. I could finish you off right now, easy as talking, but your own deeds will kill you, not me."

Ravana snorted, "Little cow, I'll uproot this bump of dirt! How dares Shiva play here like some special king with no fear of me?" Ravana grabbed the hill and shook it like a rag.

All Shiva's twisted goblins and speckled imps and tiny
gnomes and ghosts rolled tumbling down from above. On the
hilltop Parvati the Himalya's daughter trembled and caught
hold of her Lord Shiva.

Shiva pressed his big toe gently on the ground, and that
mountain struck his stony roots right through the Earth
round Ravana, and bars of stone held the Demon King a
prisoner. Ravana pushed and fought to get free but the
strength of his twenty arms was nothing.

Then Ravana began to sing from his prison under the
mountain's foot, and on the summit Shiva listened from afar
with Devi on his lap. The great Lord Shiva smiled; those
were good songs. Shiva sat on a bench, one leg bent under
him and the other touching Earth, holding Devi, holding a
trident, wearing rags and snakes, drinking wine and eating
ganja, his hair adorned with the streak of the Moon. Ravana
kept singing and years passed by as though they were moments.

For the beauty of his songs Shiva set Ravana free. By that
time Prahasta had recovered somewhat, and they returned to
Lanka in the immense stolen chariot. But Ravana could not
remain content. As soon as he had rested a little he again set
out with Prahasta on Pushpaka, this time to overthrow the
kingdoms of men.

Ravana stood on the chariot with his General under a
royal white umbrella of a hundred ribs of gold and went
from city to city, seeking war. But all the kings had heard of
him and thought Ravana invincible. They all said—*We are
conquered*—until working his way north Ravana reached the
capital of the Haihaya people.

That was the city of King Arjuna of the Thousand Arms.
King Arjuna had ruled there for eighty-four thousand years
when Ravana landed by the city walls and sent in the
message—*Surrender or die!*

Four of the gods were in the city. When they heard Ravana had arrived they took the disguises of animals. Indra became a peacock, Yama the Death Lord turned into a crow,
Vaishravana became a lizard and Varuna the King Under
Waves chose a swan.

King Arjuna was out, but his old war minister came to the
gate. He spit out some red betel juice, leaned back on his

heels, looked way up at Ravana and said, "Ah how fine it is
to rule the world just by saying you do! Great Hero, we blink
our eyes in flattery and worship; we praise you for defeating
your own brother. But we don't know what to do. We have
never heard words of challenge like yours except when we
say them to others in conquest. Our King is not here, but he
bathes in the Narmada River with his wives."

Ravana went after King Arjuna. The gods within the city
dropped out of their disguises, but still those four living animals were standing there.

Indra said, "Peacock, you will never have to fear snakes.
Your tail will no longer be plain blue, but will have a
hundred iridescent eyes, and when the rain falls you will
dance with joy remembering our friendship."

Yama said, "Crow, you will never die unless you're killed.
In famine you will eat before the hungry men. The only person to watch out for is someone walking alone down the road
past your tree, who bends over and picks up a throwing
stone."

In those days swans had blue wingtips and their breasts
were green as tender grass. Varuna said, "Swan, become the
happiest of birds, swim white and peaceful on the water near
me."

Vaishravana the Treasure Lord said, "Lizard, I am pleased
with you, you will be golden-gleaming, your head will shine
with gold."

In the Vindhya Hills Ravana brought his chariot down to
Earth by the Narmada river racing gladly to the western sea.
He decided to worship Shiva before he fought, and broke
flowery boughs from the white and gold blossom trees and
carefully set them out by the water. Ravana then bathed and
splashed in the river like an elephant, then put on a clean
white robe and got ready to sing. He held his twenty hands
pressed together two by two. His ten heads fanned out, his
heavy earrings swayed, he bent his weight over and stood on
one foot in the sand.

Downstream aways, King Arjuna was showing off for his
wives. With his thousand arms he dammed up the Narmada.
The water rose in waves and flowed backwards; it came up to
Ravana's knee and washed away his every flower.

"That must be Arjuna," said Ravana. "I'll handle this man
alone." He walked downriver, and saw the Haihaya King, an
immovable hill of a man with arms outstretched, red-eyed
with wines, his long hair afloat on the water. Two soldiers

came and saluted Ravana. "Your Majesty, our King is drunk and plays with his women. Be our welcome guest until morning and then fight him."

But Prahasta came running up, barging through the trees bringing Ravana his steel war-mace, and then King Arjuna cocked his ears. King Arjuna stepped out of the river and the waters surged away. He didn't waste any time. He picked up a golden club five hundred hands long and hit Ravana. The club broke against Ravana's chest, bits of burning gold went shooting through the air; and Ravana wept, and backed away four steps and sat down.

Arjuna put down his club and picked up Ravana. He held the Demon King squirming in a fifty-arm grip, and roared like a tiger clawing down a deer, so loud that Ravana's grandfather Pulastya could hear it in the Himalya Hills.

Pulastya went to save Ravana. King Arjuna welcomed him, "Now my poor river is better than heaven, for here and not there do I meet you."

Pulastya said, "Majesty, Ravana is hard to bind as the Wind but you have done it. Now his glories are yours. Be satisfied, free him for me."

King Arjuna said not a word but set Ravana free at once. Ravana went shamefully back to his chariot and drove aimlessly away in disgrace.

As he and Prahasta passed over a deserted forest somewhere, they happened to see the heavenly sage Narada riding by on a cloud. Narada came close to them and said in midair, "Ravana, you are unslayable even by gods, and men are mortal; they are already dead, so fight a worthy enemy."

"Who?"

"Men are made of straw," said Narada. "They are worthless and frail and contemptible, their brief lives are loans that must be soon repaid. They are Death's subjects, Yama the Death Lord rules them; therefore conquer Yama."

Ravana's faces brightened. He forgot his defeat and felt as good as ever. Narada said, "But how could even you go while living to the Land of Death?"

Ravana said, "Consider it done!" He pointed Pushpaka to the south. That flowery chariot picked up speed and shot past the southern horizon and dipped down into Yama's kingdom like a rain of jewels.

There was the Vaitarani River running with blood; down

there were steep black barren hills, the death-wind moaning, hot sands and shrieks from the darkness. Prahasta flew away in fear and Ravana was alone. And in the ghastly flaring light of Hell Ravana saw a corpse shrouded in brown sitting on the wasted ground and looking at him, grinning at him like a skull, his yellow skin streaked with cremation ashes and cemetery dust, skin like leather stretched taut, bones all showing. There were red fires in his dried and sunken eyes, and when he breathed it sounded like the death-rattle of the dying.

That person looked at Ravana and said, "Do not enter here like a dog, Rakshasa King!"

The sword-bladed trees of Hell rang in the wind. Ravana narrowed his eyes and said, "Where is Yama the God of Death?"

"What do you want with him?"

Ravana said, "I have taken him for my lasting enemy and I take you for the same whoever you are."

The seeming corpse replied, "Demon King, seek for Death among the living and not here. These black hills are the frontiers of Hell, Hell that burns with the fire of deeds done wrong. With the fire of acts, Ravana, is Heaven brilliant and Hell aflame. Do you believe in Hell, or will you play the fool in my presence, until it is too late, until you begin to learn but it is all too late . . . cringing and whimpering and all too late. . . ."

"Who are you then?"

The corpse laughed a dusty laugh. He pointed with his wrinkled bony hand. "Yama is that way. Oh Ravana, be gone, I am Kala . . . I am Time . . . I am Time. . . ." And there he changed, and became a fair young man, wearing fresh flowers and smiling with all his life before him; and the sights and sounds of Hell became those of a love-park on the fair countryside of Earth.

While Ravana was talking to Time, Narada flew to Yama, who was sitting at home. The Death King turned his head to see him with his immovable eyes and said, "Narada, who do I see you here? You are too fond of strife and trouble."

"Listen," said Narada, "Ravana comes to vanquish you."

"Does he?"

Suddenly before Yama stood Death, Death who wears many faces, Death who makes nothing of all this world, standing with many rods and maces in his arms. Narada shivered and Death watched him.

"Sad it is," said Yama gently, "to have an enemy like this Death. Therefore try to make him your friend; you have met before, and come to you he must, once more at least. I have partly veiled him. Do right, Narada, tune your lutes and cease to meddle in the wonderful universe."

Death spoke to Yama, "Let me go. Great warriors in strong armor fail and fall before me like bridges of beautiful sand. I can dissolve anything; it takes no strength of mine."

Yama said quietly, "Stay still, Oh Death. The very Sun, my father, does not boast of his power; in fact, he manages to be silent."

"My dear Master, release me. . . ."

"Hide them, my friend, hide those scepters and rods."

"My patient Lord . . . ."

"Not yet. I walk to meetings slowly and on foot, I do not run."

"Let me but touch him. . . ."

"*Yamam!* I restrain you!" Yama raised his green hand, and Death vanished.

Then Ravana came and bowed to Yama. "Death Lord, surrender to me."

"I surrender to you," said Yama kindly, "until you call for me some day."

Yama also disappeared. Ravana turned to Narada. "See, I rule over the Death Lord. Who dares deny I am the Emperor of every wide world?"

"Who dares deny it?" said Narada. "If you have the time, sit down, I'll tell you their names."

"What need?" smiled Ravana. "I will visit my devoted subjects for myself."

Ravana found General Prahasta hiding somewhere and the two of them returned to Lanka. This time, there Ravana collected a small Rakshasa army of three million demons, put them all on Pushpaka chariot, and with his son Meghanada beside him drove to the Naga worlds of the underground serpents, the luxurious underworlds far more delightful to every sense than heaven. They stopped by a palace of columns and pillars lit up by brilliant gems, brighter than if it stood in sunlight.

That was the home of Vasuki the King of the Serpent Tribes. By the doorway hung a plow for delving Earth and a pestle for grinding ores. Vasuki came out to see who was there, in form a man from the waist up, a snake below, dressed in purple, wearing a white shell necklace and a tall tapering crown of white waxy flowers. He hated to see strangers in his home; he scowled and looked around as though he had entered another's cave by mistake.

Oh Dasaratha, the hooded serpents of the underground are hard to frighten; they do not threaten very easily, never knowing when to fear. Vasuki advanced to within striking distance, joined his hands together and said, "Why Ravana, you didn't bring enough demons here with you, go get some more, you can hardly even trouble my sleep with these toy devils!"

"Surrender to me," said Ravana.

Vasuki answered him, "I rule the Nagas, but we are all the people of the Water King Varuna, our Lord Undersea. See him. I hope this is bad news to you!"

"Little worm, where is he?"

Then Vasuki turned himself entirely into a venomous snake. He spread flat his hood and swayed slowly from side to side. *Weaknessss to you, Ravana, ssspare me your sneersss.* . . . Vasuki's flat glittery head was weaving back and forth; his glassy round eyes were fixed on Ravana and never blinking, first one eye and then the other, their irises yellowy and their pupils round and black, round black circles, eyes that held. . . .

"We will burn you like fire," said Vasuki, "we will burn you to the bones, here your life is worthless to ussss . . . our Lord Varuna has left his white palace running with streams. He is in Brahma's highest heaven hearing songs."

"Tell him to give up and I won't harm him."

"Oh I will tell *that* to Varuna!" Vasuki straightened himself out and flew away like an arrow. When he returned he was riding with Brahma, calmly coiled in the corner of Brahma's swan-chariot, no longer angry.

Brahma said, "Varuna who embraces Earth with his seas and oceans must surrender to you every kingdom below the lands and under waves. Ravana, how have you lost all the goodwill, all the love and kindness that is the heart's release?"

Ravana bowed his ten heads and sighed. Brahma was gone; Vasuki was gone; everyone was dying; no deed was worth doing; old age was dry and brittle.

Behind him Ravana heard a dry cough. He turned. There

was Time, standing behind him, letting his shriveled shadow fall over the Demon King.

Ravana drove Pushpaka back into daylight, and still with his army he rose up into the sky to the home of the Sun. Fast as the chariot flew it was a long trip. It was twilight when Ravana arrived. He could see the rays of Surya the Sun shining out from cracks between the stones of his palace. He could smell heat, hot iron and baking stone; he saw the one-wheeled golden chariot just returned, the seven white horses harnessed still with serpents; he saw a sky-road with no support, a long road and no turning, a going forward with no help.

When Ravana stopped his car there was a great silence. Then a gatekeeper came from the palace, crossed the fields of air with his hair burning and his fingers covered with hot copper gloves. He said, "As you wish, Ravana, as you wish."

Ravana took that for a surrender. He set a new course for the lovely bright mansions of the Moon, eighty thousand leagues above Earth in outer space. It was truly cold there, cold as winter's Moon in the clear frosty night high in the hills. Cold mists turned slowly over dark lakes in the distance; stark black trees broke leafless from the barren ground. There were white freezing glaciers creeping closer. Ravana saw only cold desolation, cold ice, cold stars; and felt a brittleness like glass in the air.

A star spirit appeared, casting a thin shadow behind him from the bright glory of his beaming face. "Lord of Lanka, what lunacy is this? Do not oppress my Lord Chandra the Moon, the silver King of Stars, for he wishes well to all. Consider this your home . . . stay here with us forever. . . ."

Ravana saw General Prahasta already looking over his shoulder for the way home, and said quickly, "I accept your surrender." Pushpaka chariot went back down toward Earth and the air was warmer. Ravana smiled at his son Meghanada, "Nothing to it!" They turned again, rose in a different way, and came to the gate of Indra's heaven. Ravana looked in at the immortal celestial city of Amaravati built along the heavenly Ganga river. He said, "This won't take a moment," and got out of the car.

A five-crested Gandharva, some musician of heaven, stood leaning by the Gate of the Gods. Ravana went up to him and said, "Summon your Master Indra to admit his defeat."

"Who?"

"Your Master Indra."

"Do *what?*" smiled the Gandharva.

Ravana drew his curving sword. "Who do you think you are?"

"I am Chitraratha the Gandharva King, the Lord of Music, and I don't run errands for dirty black spiders!"

Ravana swung at him with his sword and missed. Suddenly in Chitraratha's hand was a long Gandharva wand shimmering and waving. Ravana had a terrible sword; but Chitraratha's wand was tough and supple and springy like a riding whip, gay and colored, cut from the edge of a rainbow, so slender that twenty hands were no guard against it, and it sang and whistled when it cut the air.

"Get out of our sky!" Chitraratha jabbed Ravana in the stomach and struck him across the fingers so hard that he dropped his sword. Chitraratha flew away and the massive Gates of Heaven slammed closed behind him. The latch shot home, the bar fell, the bolt was drawn through and the lock snapped shut. Ravana heard Chitraratha singing a war-song, he heard thunders mutter and the iron wheels of war-chariots turning and heavenly horses running in armor. From behind heaven's pale adamant walls Ravana could see the flashes of lightnings, and flying sparks of fire tossed in the winds. The ground quaked as heavy thunderstones rolled into place, and shook beneath the feet of elephants. Storms were gathering in the air.

Ravana yelled, "I will plunge my arms into these dishwater gods!" And inside the walls Chitraratha flew to Indra and said, "I hope you know what you're doing."

"Never fear at any time!" Indra drew his silver sword and the day grew brighter. He drank some of his Soma. "I shade the sun himself with rain! Find some shelter for the dancing girls and the quiet spirits."

"They won't leave you," said Chitraratha. "Give me some of that juice." He drank Indra's Soma bowl dry in one swallow. "The beautiful Apsarasas, those gems of women, refuse to go, but stand armed with bows and brazen knives. The silent writers will not run and hide now; they prepare to tell their tales in someone else's blood for a change."

"Well done!" said Indra. "I don't care what *anybody* says, never will I take orders from that overbearing monster Ravana, that evil fraud—look out!"

The old Rakshasa Sumali came charging headlong at them

over the wall, throwing out maces and arrows like flagstaffs, chopping down the Gandharvas in his path and heading straight for Indra. Indra took a diamond thunder, made in six points like two tridents set one at each end of a short rod; he gripped it at the middle, took aim and threw it. No person but Indra may bear the touch of a thrown thunderbolt. It hit Sumali and left no trace of him; he was blasted into blazing light.

Dasaratha, so began the Battle of Heaven, a year before your four sons' births. Fatal weapons of every virtue clashed in the air; the walls fell; the warriors of heaven gave way, sinking, embracing each other, falling like a river cliff undercut.

Ravana knew they had won already, and he raised the flag of Lanka, pure cloth-of-gold. But too soon. The storm gods tore it away. They hit the demons with power like a tidal wave, like the summer rains beating down, like the lightnings streaming from the clouds, like herds of elephants stampeding downhill. They hit the demons hard as the death of a friend. The Rakshasas were a mountain of dark blue ore crumbling and the wild winds sang through their spears.

Then Meghanada brought black darkness by illusion and blinded gods and demons all but himself. In that bewilderment the old Asura chief Puloma came to save his daughter Indrani the Queen of Heaven. Puloma came darkly dressed, darkly adorned, darkly glancing. He plowed untouched through the demons and took Indrani down to his home under sea, and he also took brave Chitraratha with him to sing to comfort her.

Still the storm gods searched blindly for Ravana. Airavata, Indra's white elephant, swung his trunk and flapped out his ears, he stuck out his tail and charged at a terrible speed trumpeting and tossing his head and guided by scent. He collided with Ravana and with his four tusks threw him down on his back. Ravana lay with armor torn and drenched with rains, bruised by thunders and burnt by snapping lightnings, battered by the whirlwinds filled with the fragments of war; and across Ravana's breast ran four deep bleeding wounds and Airavata stood over him calling in rage and challenging all Hell to War.

Meghanada thought—*Father's dead!* He bound Indra in illusion, then invisibly he approached Ravana and shouted, "Are you alive? I have Indra captive!"

Those words ended Ravana's pain. Every might and power went out of the storms. Then followed by Ravana and all the demons still alive, Meghanada carried Indra still bound to Lanka, threw him prisoner into a dungeon, locked him in and kept the key.

Brahma came to Lanka. He said to Ravana's son, "Now call yourself Indrajit, Indra's Conqueror. Free him and take something from me in return."

Indrajit answered, "Immortality."

"Prince, I cannot give that gift to you, if you have asked for it."

Indrajit said, "Grandfather of the Worlds, when Ravana is in danger may I call up with offerings from the fire altar a war chariot drawn by four tigers that moves at will; while I ride on it may I be charmed to win any battle against any creature; and may no one but other Rakshasas see me when I wish to fight invisible."

"I give all that," said Brahma. Indrajit held out the dungeon key but Lord Brahma will never touch a weapon. By thought Brahma first removed from Indra's mind all despair and fear. He sent the idea—*I am free*—and so annihilated the jail walls.

"Now throughout the forests Rakshasas cruelly torment us like men in Hell," said Viswamitra. "You have heard what evil has befallen Earth and all the worlds. At night the demons yell to one another—*I am Narayana! I am the Moon! I am Everything!* These are their more meek and modest boasts, what can I say of their serious praise and sincere drunken flatteries? The Night-Wanderers strut and swagger and pull apart Dharma. Out there, Dasaratha, beyond these walls of Ayodhya demons range over the worlds like the winds. Two of them especially cross me. So I have come to Fair Ayodhya. I must have a warrior. I need Rama to kill them."

"My child!" said the King.

"I will not use up any of my hard-won merit to curse demons," said Viswamitra. "I have come for Rama. It must be Rama. I will cover him with blessings and fame, though he wears still a boy's long side-locks, though he is but sixteen."

Dasaratha said, "After living through sixty thousand long years, in my old age have I at last gained a son. How can you take a tender child, my firstborn son, and lead him to Death?"

"Very well," said Viswamitra, "break your promise. And if you are doing right may you be happy!"

Vasishtha said, "Brahmana keep your temper; King, keep your word. Observe the defects of this world and do not add to them."

Taste This Water

Mother Earth laughed—

I quake; the Cities of Men downfall.
Yet these Kings, these mortal puppets
Are willing to admit they own me!

Viswamitra said, "Majesty, when I am tired in the evening, Desire and Wrath whom the gods cannot tame come bowing to me and gladly rub my feet. When I ask anything, that command is valuable. Whoever finds the chance to obey me is in my debt."

"Take Rama and his brother Lakshmana," said Dasaratha. He called for Rama and Lakshmana and told them, "Arm yourselves and serve this brahmana."

"Do not fear for your sons," said Viswamitra. "I have not run from demons in fear; but the retreat of a strong man is like the silent drawing back of a fist to strike a blow!"

The old King held his two sons. He embraced them, and smelled the hair on the crowns of their heads. They were still round-faced children and so young. But Rama and Lakshmana expertly put on their bows and quivers, donned their swords and archer's gloves like men; the King smiled then, and felt no more grief for their going.

Viswamitra led the two boys from the city. Just outside the white walls of Fair Ayodhya they stopped by the Sarayu River. There Viswamitra sat by the water and said, "Princes of Ayodhya, because Ravana overlooked men I have things to teach you; I have places to guide you, therefore become my students."

Rama and Lakshmana shed their weapons, and they each gathered and brought to Viswamitra a bundle of firewood sticks, as one does when first meeting his preceptor. Then in a hermit's cup made from half a coconut shell Viswamitra dipped up some water and told Rama, "Take this cup and drink it down. Drink it all at once or you will never finish it, and it will do no good." Rama drank it. Viswamitra taught him two mantras, one for strength and one for more strength. He refilled his cup and did the same for Lakshmana. He taught them both how to rightly time and correctly speak the words.

"These are two spells of Power: they are the daughters of Brahma." said Viswamitra. "Say them and you gain wisdom and good fortune; even when you are asleep or distracted, no enemy can surprise you: tiredness or thirst or illness or hunger cannot get to you; you can easily find the answer to any uncertainty, solve any secret, end any argument, reach the True. These are great words. they are Brahma's own."

They went on: they all three slept the night on leaves and grass. In the morning Viswamitra sang to the Sun and bathed: they followed Saravu downstream and that afternoon approached the deep roar and thunder of the meeting of the waters of Saravu and Ganga. in Angadesha Forest, where every tree was thousands of years old.

That night Viswamitra taught heavenly weapons to Rama, beginning with the dread Brahma weapon and working down. They sat in the dark. Rama said the controlling mantras and one by one the weapons appeared before him. He touched each one and said. "Return when I remember you." Some weapons had celestial shapes. some were like live coals. some were smoke. some looked like great suns and moons. They went turning round Rama and vanished.

The next morning some hermits took Rama and Lakshmana and Viswamitra across the holy River Ganga on a raft, and before noon they were at Viswamitra's retreat, a lonely hut of canes and branches. The brahmana unpacked his traveling fire and put a bowl of flames from it onto his sloping altar.

"Now I will begin," said Viswamitra. "Stand here. Protect me for six days and nights, then on the seventh day be more alert, especially toward night as the sacrifice draws to an end, and once I begin I will not speak." He fell silent. Mentally he called Agni the Fire Lord; mentally he presented him a place to sit, asked about his journey, mentally offered him water on which flowers floated.

On the seventh evening Viswamitra put a handful of jewels and colored rice all mixed together onto his altar, and a few flowers. He lit some incense and laid out green and white grass stalks and a bowl of liquid butter.

Then out of nowhere, like two black clouds the Rakshasas Maricha and Subahu swept in over the treetops, and on Viswamitra's altar the fire flickered in terror. Rama took three aiming steps backwards, for about the distance of a staff, and he shot three arrows at Maricha. The three arrows came together and struck Maricha's heart all as one. But they did not kill him; their force carried him through the air for hundreds of leagues and dumped him unconscious into the far western sea.

Lakshmana killed Sabahu with one shot. At full dark the sacrifice was finished, and Viswamitra said, "This wood is clear of demons, that was my desire." He looked at Rama. "Prince, they were off guard. This time it was light and easy for you, but many hard things are easy to begin . . . If ever again you meet Rakshasas, do not move your mark, do not spare them from kindness again."

Viswamitra said, "I dislike lowlands. I was here only to do this rite, now come with me part way back to my home in the Hills, where my sister is a river. For in the Videha kingdom of King Janaka, the Husband of Earth, there is a bow no one can bend. They say it's Shiva's bow. It hangs within a box in the smoke of aloeswood, decked with flowers. Rama, you must see that bow."

When they reached the Videha land, walking by easy stages, the tigers and serpents of Angadesha who had escorted Viswamitra turned back as an army will disperse when the King enters his palace from a journey, knowing their friend was safe in Janaka's country. The hills were rising and the rivers ran swift and cold. Not far from Mithila, the capital of Videha, Viswamitra stopped a little way off the road, and there in a grove of trees Rama saw an ancient crumbling stone wall overgrown with vines. The wall trembled when the dust from Rama's feet touched it, and it seemed to be almost alive.

"Where are we?" asked Rama.

"This is the empty retreat of Gautama," answered Viswamitra, "and for long it lies under his wrathful curse."

Listen, my Prince—

Using his mind, Brahma created some creatures called Men, all the same in color and speech, all absolutely identical. Then he created the same number of females for them, but this time he gave all of the beauty to just one woman and named her Ahalya.

Indra saw her, but before he could speak to her the hermit Gautama married Ahalya and lived with her here, while Indra waited and watched for his chance. Finally he took Gautama's form while he was away from home bathing one day, and made love to Ahalya. She was not fooled by his disguise, but she consented out of curiosity.

And after, Indra hurried to leave. He was almost out of sight when Gautama appeared in wet clothes and saw him.

> To man and woman,
> Forbearance is a becoming ornament;
> Very hard to do—
> Hardest of all, to forgive a god.

Indra lost his male sex; and since that curse of Gautama the rule of no Indra is secure, the role of Indra is impermanent. Indra fled to Agni. He hid inside a firepit that was within a forge that was inside a furnace. In the presence of Fire Indra said, "Oh I took from Gautama the power that threatened heaven, his merit is gone by my stirring his anger to cursing. All for the work of the gods, for *your* sake am I cursed!"

Agni replied, "Barely escaped alive, and already the bad is changing to good in your story! I restore your male sex."

Agni went to the dead Fathers and said, "I am Fire; only Fire can eat anything pure or impure; I am Fire burning."

The shadowy souls replied, "Take the impurity. Burn away from the sacrificial rams those fleshly parts. We take the rest; we will take pure watery offerings clean as a new life, tranquil as a lake deep and cool."

And so today in black smoke those male parts of rams are lifted by Agni to heaven when we offer burnt food to our Fathers, and Indra feeds on them and they restore him. Here on this spot Gautama told his wife, "Beauty alone caused this. No longer will you be the one fair woman in the universe." He took her beauty and scattered it to others, he took so much beauty from Ahalya that she became invisible, and her spirit lives concealed by boughs and leaves somewhere by that stone wall.

Ahalya said, "We have no neighbors. He looked just like you." Gautama could not retract his words but he could limit them. He made an end for his curse in the future, "When Rama comes to this grove you are free."

"His curse expires as I speak," continued Viswamitra, "so enter there this ruined hermitage, and deliver the divinely beautiful Ahalya."

Rama went in. There was a shower of marigolds out of the blue sky and they heard Gandharva music. Ahalya came gradually again into sight by the old wall, as beautiful then as ever, like the Sun rising reflected in rippling water, and like the Sun she could not be looked at too closely or too long. Rama saw Viswamitra waving—*Come away;* and at the same time Ahalya the Beautiful swept her arm gracefully to one side—*Sit as my guest.*

Rama went and sat by her a moment. Ahalya pressed her right hand over his heart and smiled—*From the Ancient World.* Then Rama rose and rejoined Viswamitra and Lakshmana. They all walked three times around Ahalya, keeping her on their right, and they left her there behind them, sitting among golden flowers. When they had gone on aways they looked back and saw a beautiful halo of all colors brilliant and shining through the trees, and saw Gautama in a flying chariot return for her.

Soon they saw Mithila, a city of castles and spires, and they found King Janaka coming to meet them. He brought cool water to Viswamitra. "Blessed are we, brahmana. Obliged and well-favored are we with your visit. But why have you led young warriors by this back trail to my city?"

"These are the Ayodhya princes Rama and Lakshmana," said Viswamitra. "They are eager to see your bow."

"Long since did Shiva give me that heavenly bow," said the King. "To bend Shiva's Bow is the dowry of my daughter Sita, whose mother is Prithivi, the goddess Earth."

Rama asked, "How could that be, Majesty?"

Janaka answered, "Rama, this land, this kingdom, all this wide world under the curving blue sky belongs to Mother Earth and to no one else. Only in a flight of the mind, only in a dream is all this worldly land called a kingdom. Fourteen years ago I was plowing in a clearing beyond the city, when turning back I found her lying in the furrow I had just made; I found Sita. As a golden-skinned baby she rose from her mother Earth and sat throwing handfuls of dust over her feet. I consider her a treasure well-found, well-revealed. She is a delight for my fields and hills. And Sita is beautiful, a girl more lovely than any garden, half divine and unmarried."

Rama said, "We are curious to see the strength of your bow."

King Janaka called an order, and five strong men with great difficulty brought Shiva's Bow out from its own house in Mithila, drawing it along on an eight-wheeled cart, that held the bow protected within a long iron case covered with flowers.

"You must understand," said Janaka, "that Sita has the final consent. Others have come; none could even lift this bow. I passed them by, I have used this jewel of a bow as my raft to cross the sea of fourteen years. Now you have come. It is sad for me, but it is time for her to marry, and I am a poor man about to spend his last coin."

Janaka's minister came and said, "Here it is, Majesty, show it if you think it worth showing."

Janaka said, "Rama, open the box."

Rama raised the lid. Sandalwood dust and incense ash fell off from it in a powdery cloud. Rama looked and thought, "This bow is beyond men. But playfully first let me just touch it." He touched it. "Perhaps I can try to hold it. . . ."

All the Videha men had come out of the city and were watching. Rama balanced the bow and lifted it. He strung it. Then he drew it so strongly that it broke in two above the grip, with a noise so loud that everyone watching fell down, except Rama and Lakshmana, Viswamitra and King Janaka.

Janaka shook his head. "Who would have believed?" He helped his minister to rise. "Ask Sita."

The minister rubbed his ears. "She has seen him from her high window and touched him with her eyes and fallen in love with him already."

Janaka sent a fast-riding herald to invite King Dasaratha to the wedding. The herald came to Fair Ayodhya and said, "Let the Videha King free himself from his promise. Strength is Sita's dowry, so let Rama marry her, and come with me to Mithila, and bring your priest Vasishtha."

Dasaratha replied, "Justly is Janaka King. A gift from a superior must be accepted."

"Janaka's brother has also three daughters. If you are willing let Lakshmana marry, bring Satrughna and Bharata and let them marry."

Dasaratha said, "Excellent, take gold, take silver."

The charioteer Sumantra arrayed the army and loaded fat pack elephants with presents. King Dasaratha carried the four birth-fires of his sons onto his chariot, and seven days after Rama had broken Shiva's Bow he reached Mithila. A plowed royal field of furrows cut across the road, and King and soldiers stopped, and Vasishtha went ahead alone, stepping carefully through the new-plowed land.

Vasishtha found Janaka and said, "The Ayodhya king has come, we await your commands."

Janaka asked, "I wonder, who is the warder there who makes you wait? Who follows rules when entering his own house?"

"Earth herself cuts across our way," said Vasishtha.

"So it begins. We will marry them outdoors, in that field, good fortune to you."

Viswamitra joined Vasishtha. The two brahmanas built up with shovels a wide altar of Earth. Over that they strung from poles an awning thatched of grass. They built a fire of buttered sticks in a clay bowl, lit it and set it on the altar; they set out flowers and golden spoons, waterpots painted with colors and trays spread with ripe grain, shells and incense burners, cups and vases, and saucers spread with colored parched wheat, and a bronze bell-metal milking jar filled with milk and honey for the gods, and put down carpets to stand on.

Rama and Lakshmana came out from Mithila; Dasaratha and his four sons stood by the altar. Then Janaka came striding over his field, smiling, leading four maidens like flames of fire. Three of them were lovely. But the most beautiful was Sita, Sita the Star of Beauty born from Earth.

Sita was a fair young girl. Her dark eyes were like the eyes of a doe, her lips were full, her long dark hair was falling down her back clear to her ankles and it was fragrant from being scented over incense smoke. She had a red brow-mark and lines of red and white sandalwood paste on her arms; the soles of her feet were dyed red with lac; she wore crimson robes and silver veils light as air, belts of embroidery and fine chains swaying as she walked, jeweled diadems and bell anklets, new barley shoots behind her ear, bridal garlands of jasmine, and seven strands of pearls around her neck and falling over her full round breasts. But who describes Sita?

All this was forgotten when she looked at you. When she smiled, what else existed?

As his wedding gift, King Janaka tied into Sita's hair over her forehead a round pearl on a leaf of gold. He had brought out her birth-fire and now poured it into one earthen bowl with Rama's. He led Rama and Sita to the altar under the awning and stood them near the mingled fire.

There were no pretentious brahmana priests in Videha. Long before had Janaka got rid of them. First they told him he needed them to make offerings to the little gods, so Janaka broke all the statues of the lesser gods. Then the priests said that anything a man did for himself trying to find the True was wrong and useless and only they knew all the answers. Janaka didn't argue. He put a hearty curse on them, their heads fell off and their brittle bones were stolen by thieves.

So King Janaka himself married Rama to Sita. He said, *Ramachandra, Rama like the Moon, take Sita as your companion in the living of your life. Look at her, never see enough of her, cherish her with the eyes of love. Sita, love him well forever, walk with him as his wife and follow him like his own shadow forever. I marry you.*

Janaka brought together Rama's hand and Sita's, green and gold touching. He poured water over them—*So overflows my happiness.* Then Rama led Sita away, a new-married man.

Sita knew that she and Rama were destined lovers for all time past, will be so for all future to come. She rejoiced to meet him again after long separation. She saw Rama closely for the first time and thought. "He is surely Kama the Love God . . . yet Kama has no body . . . he can't be seen and Rama can. . . ."

Before Fire for a witness Rama's three brothers were also married, taking their brides' hands. Round the field the Videhas blew shells and rang bells with loud hard mallets and beat their drums and sang.

The next day Dasaratha said, "Janaka, best of men, let my sons' wives come home with them to Ayodhya."

"Farewell," said the Videha King.

Viswamitra was also leaving. He said to Janaka, "I will go on uphill."

"Keep climbing higher," said Janaka. "Do you have a shield?"

"I'm not a soldier," said Viswamitra.

"No matter," said Janaka. "Take Dharma for your shield, brahmana. Have you a sword?"

"What sword?"

"Take Truth."

To each of the four brides Janaka gave two great Videha wolf-dogs, an elephant and sixteen horses, a basket of gold beads and four deerskins, two fine yellow woolen blankets and an entire chariot full of turquoise from the Hills. Janaka told Sita, "Her father protects a maid, but once she is wed, she must ever take the safety of her Lord. You leave me now, but never your mother Earth." He embraced his only child; he held her gently in his hard strong hands that were rough from a long lifetime of plowing and planting and reaping. Then Sita got on an elephant with Rama and they rode off to Kosala. Janaka followed walking behind for a short way and turned back to Mithila.

The Kosalas met Dasaratha and his sons a day's journey from Ayodhya. Along the city streets people waited, eager to see the brides. And in the high white royal palace overlooking Fair Ayodhya the three Queens welcomed the brides with every enjoyable object; happiest of all to see them was the youngest Queen, the joyful slender-waisted Kaikeyi. The four princesses first put flowers at the Ayodhya shrine, then they bowed to those who deserved it, then they went away alone with their husbands.

Rama and Sita lived in Rama's black stone Palace of the Moon, and twelve years went by in Ayodhya. Little by little Dasaratha turned over the work of the kingdom to Rama.

Rama's nature was quiet and free. He didn't give good advice and tell others what he thought best and show them their mistakes. He knew when to save and when to spend. He could judge men finely and keep his own counsel. He could read hearts. He knew his own faults better than the failings of others. He could speak well and reason in a chain of eloquent words. Half a benefit was more to him than a hundred injuries. Bad accidents never happened near him. He could speak every language and was an expert archer who shot golden arrows; and he didn't believe that what he preferred from himself was always best for everyone else.

Rama was kind and courteous and never ill. To harsh words he returned no blame. He was warmhearted and generous and a real friend to all. He tried living right and found it easier than he'd thought. He collected the King's taxes so that over half the people didn't really mind paying him. He was a remarkable prince and every Kosala loved him except for five or six fools. He was hospitable and he spoke first to every guest in welcome words. He was a quiet strong man; he could bend iron in his hands or fix a bird's broken wing. He would not scold the whole world nor take to task the universe, and so his pleasure and his anger never went for nothing.

Rama would not work very long without a holiday; he wouldn't walk far without stopping to greet a friend, nor speak long without smiling. His entertainments and dances were the best in the world. He loved Sita well; he lived his life for the sake of her being a part of it. He would often find a new gift for his friends. He did not fear to pass a whole day without work. Whatever he did, he ennobled it by how he did it. Rama's way was noble.

HERE ENDS THE
BOOK OF THE BOYHOOD OF RAMA.
HIS YOUTH IS PAST.
THE AYODHYA BOOK BEGINS.

The Two Wishes

You saved my life;
I love you;
Ask me twice for anything!

Wide grey mountain eyes flecked with gold,
Lined with black and innocent—
And now tears!
Oh King, be careful!

After Rama and Sita had been married for twelve years, in
the spring Queen Kaikeyi's brother Yudhajit, Bharata's uncle,
came riding to Fair Ayodhya from the hill kingdom of
Kekaya and told Prince Bharata, "Your grandfather King
Aswapati, the Lord of Horses, wants to see you, for he is
now an old man who has never seen his grandson."

Dasaratha gave permission, and Bharata with his brother
Satrughna left on a chariot for the Hills with Yudhajit. While
they were gone Dasaratha all at once felt he had enough of
kingdom, and more than anything wanted to see Rama rule.
He thought, "Why die first? Let me see him on my throne
from here on Earth, not looking down from heaven."

He called the Kosala Council—the lesser Kings and the
governors, provincial noblemen and the brave heroes, the
wise and the learned and the Kosala judges whose just and
certain eyesight was reason. They assembled and sat in a
half-circle looking up at Dasaratha on his throne.

Dasaratha said, "I have grown very old, I have reached
great age. The one thing remaining for me to do on Earth in
this life is to make my son Rama a King, if you will approve
that. I give you gifts, I welcome you. Tell me what you think
of my son Rama. The opinions of disinterested men are dif-

ferent from the beliefs of a father, and the Truth may sometimes come out like Fire from friction between the two."

The assembly cheered; they gave the full-throated Kosala lion-roar and shook the palace. They said, "Make the coronation ceremonies! Of all the princes among men Rama is best! Make him our King in the morning!"

But Dasaratha said in anger, "Be still! You wish for Rama as soon as you hear my desire. While I still rule why do you wish for another King?"

For the briefest moment the chiefs and warriors talked together, then Sumantra the charioteer rose to speak for all of them. "We say this, Majesty—let your son Rama ride the huge white elephant; let us see his face beneath the white umbrella. Some men rule themselves; we Kosalas are ruled by excellent kings. Dasaratha, you follow the Dharma-path walked by your ancestors, and thoughtless of your own happiness you protect us. We know you, we have seen you teach to Rama all royal skill, we want you to see your son made King. Give away your duties and rest without burdens now, for old age has fallen on your mortal body and Time approaches you. If we deserve happiness give us Rama wearing the crown of many good talents. We love to see Rama. When he looks at us our doubts vanish and our debts are paid. I have seen Rama riding by the fields and as a father enquiring after his well-loved sons, he will ask the teachers—*Do your students obey you?* He will ask the preceptors of arms—*Do your students never walk without their weapons?*"

Dasaratha said, "Do not let a father's fondness deceive an entire kingdom."

"We won't!" said Sumantra. "Follow your own heart's true feelings, Majesty. Those true feelings are one with right Dharma. No one ever born can govern Kosala better than Rama, or better care for Fair Ayodhya and look after her. Our women young and old pray to their gods morning and night for good fortune to Rama. Why ask for anything else? While Rama lives here what can go wrong? He knows all our names. He would gladly spare us all his time if we would take it. He asks of our shops, and wishes well to our sons, to our fires, to our wives and animals. I, Sumantra the Charioteer, have seen him weep at our sorrows; I saw him laugh with us at our festivals."

"Are these your reasons?" asked Dasaratha.

"The one reason," replied Sumantra, "is that if Rama says something to me I can believe it." Sumantra sat down. All the

men in that court audience raised their hands palms touching
to their heads, and King Dasaratha looked out on those joined
hands as though looking at a pond covered with unopened
lotus buds.

Vasishtha then rose and said, "Majesty, though Bharata
and Satrughna are still in Kekaya, yet tonight begins a rare
and fortunate meeting of the Moon and stars that lasts but
one day. Let me install Rama as our King tomorrow for the
happiness of all the world."

Dasaratha sat upon his throne, very old, his hair white, his
beard white, his robes white, resembling some father-god, his
life nearly parted and gone. He blinked his eyes and tears fell
down his face. "My people, I am very happy. My influence
with you is very great."

Dasaratha dismissed the assembly and told Sumantra,
"Give this twice-born Vasishtha whatever he needs and bring
Rama to me in my private rooms."

From his window Dasaratha saw Rama quickly climbing
the palace steps, Rama his son, like his own image in a mirror seen rightly adorned with youth. Rama entered and knelt
and bowed low to his father. "I am Rama, Majesty."

Dasaratha reached down, held Rama's hands and raised
him up. "Oh Rama, no longer bow to me. You are now *my*
King. Listen—for many nights have I dreamt of stars falling
to the ground in daylight with terror and noise. The region
round my star of life is invaded by fatal planets and my
Death, I think, rushes swiftly at me. So my thoughts have
changed and left this world, for ever-changing is the mind of
man. Rama, to me the sight of you on the Ayodhya throne
will be cool rain coming after summer's life-draining heat.
Tomorrow while our groves blossom take this Kosala as your
inheritance. I have in my lifetime given to the gods hundreds
of offerings and sacrifices and so paid my debt to them; I
have studied and passed on what I learned that was not secret
and so satisfied my teachers; I have fathered sons and so paid
off my ancestors; I have given gifts to brahmanas and to other
men and made them happy, and they have no claim on me;
and by enjoying a good life I have pleased and paid my debts
to myself. All are paid. I will rule no longer."

Rama said, "But sir, warriors can't take gifts, rule on,
Majesty."

Dasaratha smiled. "My son, I command you, tonight keep

fast and silent watch till dawn, and let your friends guard you well—many things can go wrong, in the dark night before a King is made." The old King sighed, and rubbed his hand over his eyes. "Rama, I have had . . . strange, many strange visions. . . . I don't know, I cannot be sure, but beyond Ayodhya people await you; they will offer you things that are really yours already. These things . . . take them, no fear of breaking Dharma to you!"

Rama went to his mother Kausalya. She was at her altar, wearing new white silk and bright bracelets, offering water to the gods. The other Queens were there with her. Kausalya said, "Rama, Rama, I am so happy! Always I wanted to see this day."

Sumitra said, "You will be the Best of Kings."

Kaikeyi kissed him. "Now your father will not have to work so hard; he will have more time for just living and finding joy with me, with all of us." She smiled. "I would like to see the King as free as any of his common people, able to lie in the parks when he will, free to come and go and let the busy world just pass him by."

Vasishtha then came for Rama. Rama's three mothers blessed him, and Vasishtha led him to his own palace. When Rama and Sita had bathed that evening, and said their twilight prayers, Vasishtha threw strong mantras over them, and left them seated on grass on the bare floor and sworn to stay wakeful, not to speak, not to eat. Then Vasishtha made his way out of Rama's black palace past the warriors, past the old men softly singing spells to the stars, past the guard of tribesmen, out into the noisy crowded streets of Ayodhya.

So it was that Fair Ayodhya seen from the rooftops became a blossom of colors unfolding, a stream of lights swimming, a lake of stars in motion. The Royal Master of the Revels smiled and put on his vests and medals, his key and chain and furry hat, and unlocked the doorway to the palace wines, and gave out drinks of kindly kingly cheer. The streets were sprinkled with flowers and water. The taverns were full. The beautiful courtesans threw their great houses open to all. Grand officers in steel armor and helmets and silver shoes, wearing silks alive with colors, wearing leather gauntlet gloves and black belts and long swords were in the royal palace and the courtyards of the King helping Sumantra make everything ready. The Ayodhya marketplace was impassable. Music and cheerful noise poured out into all the streets from all the houses. The lame broke their crutches and danced; sick people got up out of bed; misers gave away gold; the King's kitchen served out free food, butter and roasts and steaming rice; and the young women came out walking by the flower stalls in their best clothes, armed with Love's arrows shot from the glances of their eyes and impatient for the next night when the celebration would really begin.

As evening came, as the lamps set on branching crystal trees lighted the roads and crossings of Ayodhya, Manthara the hunchback, Kaikeyi's old serving woman, climbed limping up the outside stairs of the royal palace white as another Moon and tall as Himalya. Manthara herself came from Kekaya; she was Queen Kaikeyi's old family nurse, a sin-seeking hag, sour and malicious and cruel, bent and twisted in her heart.

Like an old furtive turtle she blinked and peered down through the hanging gardens at the festive city. She entered the palace and saw a passing serving girl wearing a new bangle. Manthara grabbed and punched her and screeched, "Where did you steal those diamonds?"

The girl backed against the wall. "Kaikeyi made us presents, dear Manthara."

"Eh? What? Never!"

"Oh happy Manthara, tomorrow Rama will be our King!"

Manthara's face crumpled and collapsed like a hill of poor worthless stone knocked apart in an earthquake. She ran to Kaikeyi and yelled, "Get up! Get up! Here comes the high tide of misfortune!"

Kaikeyi was lying on her back eating mangoes. Her eyes had dark outer corners that nearly touched her ears. She laughed like a girl and threw a sack of rubies at Manthara. "Don't spoil our night with gloom."

Manthara caught the rubies and threw them down. "Oh Queen," she whined, "the brighter the light the blacker the shadows! Here comes enduring destruction! Danger, evil, loss and grief . . . Rama will be King!"

"I know." Kaikeyi tossed her a bigger bunch of gems. "Take them for your reward for welcome news, and if you can't be happy be quiet."

Manthara frowned, her brow was like a cliff of folded stones. "Tell your son Bharata never to return. Think of him now as an orphan in hiding."

Kaikeyi leaned upon her elbow. "You're still angry. After twenty years you cannot forgive gentle Rama for once shooting a play-arrow at your hump."

"Don't you know your lazy days are over?" said Manthara. "Rama's mother will be almight around here. How do you think she really feels about you?"

"All I know is I like her fine," said Kaikeyi. "Just what do you mean anyway?"

"Kausalya will soon have you as her slave. All will look down on you. And with your fall I will fall as well, because I am so loyal."

Kaikeyi said, "Rama is just as dear to me as my own son Bharata. Ever since Rama was a child you have tried to lay on him your own vices, which are indeed truly large enough for more than two."

"Take the measure of your enemies and destroy them while you can," said Manthara. "You can be Mistress of the World. Or a slave, take your choice."

"What can I do even if I wanted?"

"Make Dasaratha install Bharata as King. Use your two wishes. Or do you still remember, how once as a young man Dasaratha entered as the gods' ally into their war against the Asuras of drought?"

"That's when I drove his sky-chariot and saved his life," said Kaikeyi.

"It was you who told me all I know of this," said Manthara, "and from friendship to you I have not forgotten it. He promised you two wishes and you answered—*My joy is great enough that you still live. What do I want but your love from you My Lord? Keep the two gifts till I ask.*"

Kaikeyi looked at an old white scar across the heel of her right hand, the sign of a deep cut, just missing her wrist. "Oh, he was badly wounded, Manthara, and the wheel came nearly off the chariot way up in the sky, and he was badly bleeding . . . I had his blood all over me. . . ." Kaikeyi sighed and her eyes were far away, she was seeing again the past. "Alright, I'll ask him to give Ayodhya to Bharata."

Manthara said, "You must banish Rama to the forest with the second wish. Send him away for fourteen years, then he will no longer be the people's favorite, or otherwise he will kill Bharata to recover the throne!"

"My son, Oh my Bharata!" Kaikeyi burst into tears, seeing in her mind Bharata's corpse, his skin blanched by poison, on his face a frozen dead smile; her son killed by treachery.

Oh King Rama, our Master Valmiki looking down into the
past world held in his hand, looking into the water saw Time
cast his shadow over Kaikeyi's heart, a sight hard to watch.
The dancing feet of Ayodhya stopped dead.

Kaikeyi the youngest Queen of Ayodhya! Her breathing
tightened and her palms perspired; her soul was all dark; her
heart pounded and Anger pressed his mask over her beautiful
face. She hastened to take wrong for right, turned the wrong
way like a doe running to the trap where her fawn is tied. "I
had not understood, Manthara, the plot against me. You are
bent but beautiful, you are curved as a flower bowing to the
wind. Take ornaments and your beauty will challenge the
Moon's."

Kaikeyi ran to the palace anger-room, slammed the door
and locked it behind her. She broke off her strands of pearls.
She lay in the dark thrashing her arms on the bare stone
floor, tearing her clothes and screaming—*I want to die!*

It was a little before dawn. Servants awoke Dasaratha. The
King came quickly down the halls, into the women's rooms,
to the anger-room door. That chamber had but one brass-
bound iron door, no windows, little air, no light unless one
were brought in—and inside Kaikeyi lay amid her broken
pearls and flowers and jewels, feeding her evil, panting and
weeping from her puffy eyes, turning down the corners of her
mouth, an Apsarasa fallen for the sake of love from heaven
and abandoned to despair on the Himalya hillside by her
lover.

Dasaratha was old, but he easily shattered that door by one
stroke of one hand. He looked around for some enemy, his
face flaming in wrath, his breath hot like a Naga's. Taking a
lantern he entered the room, he saw Kaikeyi lying like one illusion spread out to capture another, and pain crossed his
face, and the jewelry broken on the floor glittered like stars in
the sky.

"Who does you hurt? Who shall mourn?" said Dasaratha.
"Arise, I am the King of Kings in this world, all the land that
lies in sunlight is mine."

Kaikeyi sobbed, "No, this is way beyond you."

Dasaratha said, "I can do anything. I have physicians
well-paid to wait for times like these; let them see you. I tell
you, I am the King! I can fearlessly please or displease anyone. I can disgrace my friends, reward the undeserving, pun-

ish the innocent or promote fools to high rank. I can raise up
a poor man or lower a rich one to poverty. I can seize wealth
and contribute it to charity and pay for priests to pray for
me!"

"But this is too high a price to ask of you, Majesty," said
Kaikeyi. "It was wrong of me to do this, forgive me and
think no more of it. I fear, I am shamed I came here."

Dasaratha grew very proud. *"My Lady, what is it? What do
you want?"*

"I want my two wishes."

"Take them, whatever you want."

"Make Bharata King and not Rama. Send Rama to the
forest for fourteen years."

"Change your mind, Kaikeyi."

"Do both these things for me now. Grant me my two
wishes."

"I give what you ask," said Dasaratha. He looked at
Kaikeyi as though she were a stranger to him. "I will honor
your wishes. Why are you uneasy as if you had done some
wrong in taking what is yours? You have asked me to redeem
your promises from a Solar King, you will not be cheated by
me, promises must be true. Yet you have put me and all
Earth in ill-humor. I am a stag facing a tigress, a snake held
within a charmed circle."

"Then you'll do it?" asked Kaikeyi.

"My one thought," said the King, "is but to see Rama once
more before he goes away, for his departure will kill me.
Kaikeyi, if you somehow married Death himself you would
soon be his widow, I think you would kill anyone!"

Then the charioteer Sumantra came and approached the
anger-room. "Majesty, Night has fled before the morning's
light, and the wakening Earth filled with life awaits you."

Dasaratha turned on Sumantra in rage. *"Charioteer, this
hound from Hell, this bitch betrays me!"* Sumantra stepped
back in fear of his life. "Sumantra, from happiness I slept but
lightly till I was summoned here. But this Kaikeyi changes
her love as often as lightning changes her path, she severs af-
fections like a sharp knife, and in doing wrong she is swifter
than an arrow. *I curse her!* Let this carnal Queen fall to dam-
nation; let her spend the rest of her life in dread of the next
world!"

"What?"

Dasaratha could not at first speak more, he was choked by

the mist of grief in his throat, by the fumes of wrath. Then he said, "At once bring Rama here."

Rama came with Lakshmana, stood at the anger-doorway and said, "Victory to you, Father."

Dasaratha faintly said, "Oh Rama."

Rama waited but the King said no more. Kaikeyi spoke, "Gentle Rama, let Bharata become our King, and instead of the throne of Ayodhya, take a hermit's life in the vast forests for fourteen years."

Rama said, "Bharata or myself, we are much the same. But without the King's command I cannot come or go a single step."

"But these are my two promises!" said Kaikeyi.

"That is between you two," said Rama. "You had no need to use them, I would have gone at your wish. But why does Dasaratha breathe so slowly, and stand silently weeping, staring at the floor?"

"Rama, have I done right?" asked Kaikeyi.

"If you say you have, you have; I will believe you. But Mother, I cannot leave the King in sorrow."

"He will soon recover. Hurry and go."

Rama bowed to his father. "Sir, I am Rama."

Dasaratha whispered, "Child, I am insane; therefore confine me and become the King."

"I would never make you lose your faith and honesty," said Rama. "I will go today out from Ayodhya for fourteen years. I will return to say farewell before I leave." Rama rose to his feet and said to Kaikeyi, "Dasaratha never takes back, never fails to carry out what he has once spoken. Mother, I am like my father, trust me, have no fear."

Rama walked away. He looked just the same as ever, but Lakshmana was stunned and followed him in a daze. They went through the palace and Rama greeted his friends as always, he did not look wishfully at the throne nor did he turn his eyes from it. The clear Moon is handsome, and slipping behind a cloud or waning he is still good to see.

Rama went to his mother's rooms. Kausalya was in tears, she saw him and said, "Were you never born I would have but the one sorrow of barrenness. Do what you want, you don't have to obey him. Stay with me, hide here in my room for fourteen years."

Lakshmana then spoke, "Even the King hopes Rama will

refuse! But a wrong thrown at Rama seems to bring out no anger in him; it is like a seed thrown on stone."

Kausalya sat on a golden couch and said, "Sit by me, Rama."

Rama only touched the gold frame and stayed standing. "I need a seat of grass, I'm a hermit of the forest now, I want no softness."

"I sinned greatly in another life," said Kausalya. "Surely I kept children from their mothers. My son, my heart is iron for it does not tear; there is no room for me in the Land of Death, for Yama will not lead me from life though I desire to go."

Lakshmana looked round the room and said, "Queen, the King is a slimy old fish who eats his own brood. Why allow him to put us all in another's power? Wait, I will just go kill my father, I will not stand this." Lakshmana waved his golden arms.

Rama looked at him. "Oh Lakshmana."

Lakshmana went on. "Brother, leave everything to me. Go on with your business, when I unleash my strength the entire population of the three worlds cannot obstruct you." He started for the door. "My hands are for killing, how has he ruled so long?"

Rama held him back and turned him around. "Be still, or you may yet see seeds sprout on stones, Lakshmana!"

"I am also your parent," said Kausalya. "Rama, I command you to stay. Or else I will die, for you are dear to me, and the King makes war on me as well. Do what you want, Rama!"

"I'll go, Mother."

"Do that," she said, "and Kosala is ruined, I am dead, your father's life and fame are gone, and out of all of us only Kaikeyi and Bharata will be happy. You will fall into Hell for killing your mother!"

"Have you seen Death's face," said Rama, "have you seen Hell that you will talk of it so lightly and use it for your blame? Kaikeyi was always carefree; this deed is nothing like her, and it is truly not her doing to sadden the King. I wait patiently for you to open your eyes and see. No man is always the same. Worry and care waylay us all. Kings will misrule one day and bring justice to all the next. Singers will fall into the pit of helpless misery for no cause, and then may sing their happiest songs. Men may take anger against all in the world and from that rage do great kindness and fashion wonders of beauty. People who think they care for nothing at all have saved more lives than they ever knew, yet believe themselves alone, and unloved."

Lakshmana said, "I must go with you."

Rama said, "Lakshmana, I bind you with an oath of the cruel Kshatriya Dharma, as with chains, to go with me and protect me."

"I promise."

"Queen Kausalya, I bind you with an oath of Love's Dharma, as with happiness, to remain by your husband as a warrior's wife among your enemies."

"I promise," said the Queen. "I bless you for your journey, both of you, and whoever shall go with you, and whoever shall help you and welcome you."

Rama said, "Wait for my return. Wait for me, everything will be all right."

Rama went alone to Sita and said, "The time will quickly pass, you will soon see me return."

She answered softly, "It is very strange, My Lord, that you alone among all men in the world have not heard that a wife and her husband are one."

"There is no happiness in the forest," said Rama. "There is danger. Lions roar and keep pitiless watch from the mouths of their hill-caves, waterfalls crash and pain the ears, and so the wood is full of misery."

"Surely your fortune is also mine," said Sita.

"Enraged elephants in their fury trample men to death."

"Kings in cities execute their faithful friends at any hour, day or night."

"There is little to eat but windfallen fruit and white roots."

"I will eat after you have taken your share of them."

"There is no water, vines shut out the Sun, at night there are but hard beds of leaves."

"I will gather flowers."

"Creeping serpents slither across the trails and swim crookedly in the rivers awaiting prey."

"The wayfarer will see flocks of colored birds fly and disappear into shady trees."

"There is always hunger and darkness and great fear," said Rama. "Scorpions sting and poison the blood; there is fever in the air, fires rage uncontrolled; there are no dear friends nearby, and so the wood is full of misery."

"It is Ayodhya that would be the wilderness for me without you," said Sita. "Your bow is no decoration, your knife is not for wood-chopping, your arrows are not toys, but keep me from your arguments. We will be together. The water will be nectar, the thistles silk, the raw hides many-colored blankets. I'll be no burden. Rama, I depend on you. I cannot be cast away like water left in a cup. Dear Rama, I am the humble dust at your feet, perfectly happy. How will you avoid me?"

"Then come," smiled Rama. "You love me and I love you, what more is there? Without delay give away all our possessions that we won't take with us, and get ready to go."

Sumantra the charioteer found the priest Vasishtha in the silent street and said, "Brahmana, the world is without support, it is gone to Hell. The old Kshatriya Dharma is vanished forever. Sorrow will kill the King, shackled by lust to a vile prostitute posing as our Queen."

Vasishtha said, "Truly I find the world much the same as ever."

"Hear Ayodhya, silent with blame!"

"Let go anger, abandon violence," said Vasishtha. "Don't you know anything? Rama is the Sun of the Sun, the fame of fame. He goes with Sita, he goes with Lakshmi, he goes with victory."

"Ah no," said Sumantra. "Clever speakers feign piety to deceive and tell others of Dharma in rich tones, but there was a time. . . ."

"Clever profiteers also feign foreign wars to deceive the simple and all paid liars are not priests," said Vasishtha. "Traitors make a show of righteousness and holding knives behind their backs they plead for peace. But my place is to calm, to avoid, to soften, to look before walking and take thought before speaking. Men must have laws, sometimes hard to follow, but harder to find once lost. Dasaratha will die, so let him die in peace, for your life too must end one day. Give up war's desires. Throw out fear of fearful things. An hour of separation cannot be avoided. Let the King die alone in a room as an elephant badly wounded by a lion goes to die in peace."

"The gods are blind. Brahmana, how will Rama who never knew misfortune live in bark rags and eat bad food?"

"Sita will cherish him. He will eat well and live well. Cease to judge men by their outsides. Store the coronation supplies for Bharata, as you gathered them for Rama. Time alone causes change. Kaikeyi loved Rama. She never cared for government but only for Dasaratha. With her he would relax, she never forced him into anything, but gave him love and let him forget that he was different from any other man. Time makes her press relentlessly for Rama's exile with harsh words. She was easy-going. And why has she never used these wishes before? What is beyond understanding—that is Destiny."

"Destiny?" said Sumantra. "That is a poor frail thing, where all is lost because a good hour passes and the stars who care nothing for us are not in their right places. Who is Time to turn his back on *us*? And we not *men*? But now soon Earth will be a widow, the King will die."

"Time is hidden from you, charioteer. You can only see his work, not him."

"I'll not believe that, brahmana. When I meet a roadblock I break it!"

"Destiny is unthinkable, how can you regret it?" asked Vasishtha.

The Kosalas came pushing through the streets again, crowding their way to Rama's palace—*Throw down your inventions and your plows, go see Sita, she gives away riches. End your hard work to feed your little children!*

Vasishtha and Sumantra followed the crowd, but when they arrived all the clothes and jewels and horses and elephants and chariots were gone, and Sita had given the palace itself to her servants, to live in on full salary till their return.

Rama was there and Vasishtha asked him, "What do I get? I am idle but I love good things, that's the mark of my high birth."

Rama pointed to a long pasture filled with grazing cows that ran from the side of his house to the river. "Sita has emptied every room here," he said. He gave Vasishtha a short heavy staff. "Those cows are all I have left, and they are yours as far as you can throw over them."

Vasishtha took the rod, stood in the yard, quickly tightened his robe round his waist and hurled the staff. It went sailing far over every cow and fell clear on the other side of the Sarayu.

Then Vasishtha smiling held up his two hands palms outwards and let his arms fall in circles to his sides. All fell silent. Rama and Sita and Lakshmana drew near. Vasishtha knelt in the sunlight with the others kneeling round him and said—*Life is short.*

"Truly it is! Rama, now no one sings your praises to wake you, no chariot will clear a way before you, no servants will run ahead to build a resting place, and also no one any longer plots against you.

"Rama, Sita, Lakshmana. For your safety I give the gods flowers and smoke and praise. I place you as travelers in the care of the holy mountains and the sacred trees large and small, in care of the birds and the Sun and Moon, the air, the day and the night, the lakes and islands; and let them all lend you their strength. I throw seeds into the fires for the Guardians of the world's directions and ask them to stop the breath of all who are hostile to you. I throw flowers up into the air and make my blessings fall—*No fear, no grief, and follow me.*

"Depart from us encircled and protected by the heavens and the sky, and served by creatures moving or immobile, by the planets and stars and by Mother Earth. Return when the trees blossom again for the fourteenth time. As much as I can, I turn aside from you all hurt and harm from horned beasts and every injury from flesh-eating animals. . . . May the every prayer said in the forests by the holy men crown your way with good fortune."

"Rama, Sita, Lakshmana!" Vasishtha dropped over their heads grains of colored rice. *Sorrow flees from you.*

Vasishtha stood over them. "Go wherever you like. I will see you return. And on that day, when Rama is in royal robes I will gaze at you, my face will shine with joy!"

Then Rama went to the King's palace to say goodbye to his father and Sumantra fell into stride beside him. They went down the palace halls. There the weeping Revel Master took off his finery. He shut the wine-vault doors and locked them closed and barred them; he sat there dressed in forest clothes, like an old hermit. He threw away the key and could see no joy; he sat not in a palace but in a death-waiting house, he was a pilgrim come to die at some holy place in one of the little stone-built rooms.

Sumantra sighed and shook his head. "So! See revealed the poverty of gentleness, that cannot help you who always use it. Rama, be forgiving while it's peacetime, but when people come against you, you'll only win by force. Reason must at last resort to power, and compassion is feeble, it is weak, it trembles."

Rama stopped walking. "Did you then want me very much for your King?"

"You know I'm right!" said Sumantra.

"No, only truly angry," said Rama.

"I will kill Kaikeyi cleanly, a warrior's way, for she has murdered my King!"

Rama said, "I thought you were a real fighter, not just an edgy old man who kills women, boasting beforehand of his sins to come."

"Has that bleating ass Vasishtha stolen your manhood?" asked Sumantra. "Why listen to his pretended talk of Time and Fate? What real man meekly bows to Destiny?"

"Rama does."

"Then you have a man's form and a woman's deeds! You've spent all your courage. Prince, pay Fate no regard, do not believe in good and evil!"

Rama said, "Rust will come to bright things, fire will burn our homes, blight will consume our grain, all these are sendings from Fate."

Sumantra caught Rama and banged him up against the wall. "Little green Rama, how dare you adore Time while your King still lives? I will go see Dasaratha now, and you will wait, and you will not tell me any more talk!" Then instantly he released Rama and fell to his knees. "I take you for my King, Rama."

"Must you see him? Rise, my charioteer. With more abuse must you burn him, though I forbid it?"

"I can't take wrong orders from anyone," said Sumantra. "Majesty, listen. You have little anger now, but if you ever have don't hide it in your own heart; let it fall on your foes lest your heart burst! I won't hurt that whore. I prefer your company for one moment to the wealth of all creation. But in my mind burns a summer wildfire of grief inflamed by the hot gale winds of your departure, fed by my inflammable tears, kindled by my remembrance, and smoking black."

"Never match strength with me," said Rama. "You do not have to drive over your friends and injure them. Go ahead, I permit you."

Rama looked away, and Sumantra went to the anger-room, where Dasaratha paced back and forth, and Kaikeyi sat frozen in a corner. Sumantra said, "Desire bites hard, Dasaratha! Break your shameful fetters, let this hour never pass, let Rama never leave. Don't obey this woman, she has no whit of decency."

Dasaratha only said, "Those were my promises, Sumantra."

Sumantra said, "You're far astray; my hurt is that you call it Dharma that you follow. I've known you all my life—and *now* I must regret it, for I am of honest ways and I am yours."

"I have nearly finished my life," said Dasaratha. "Will you not stand as my friend for only a few days more? Better I died yesterday, for I must drive Lakshmi of good fortune out from my city. Do not take away from me the closest friendship that I ever had, and the best regard in which I was ever held. I deserve from you a better end to life than that."

"I will not take them away," said Sumantra, "That I will never do. Give me your leave; may I be the one to drive Rama to the forest if he must go. I had great anger against you, but it's gone."

Dasaratha said, "You may take him. You are Sumantra the best charioteer, the best driver ever born in all this world, this world where there is but one right road, where the directions and the ways are hard to see, hard to find, hard to remember."

Sumantra went to get his chariot ready, and Rama went in to see his father. Dasaratha stood pressing his hands together, sighing, shaking his head in dismay. Dasaratha said, "My son, Sumantra is really a peaceful, sober man, happy to sit with me and remember our past wars and our ancient battles for the gods. He is right, I am degraded. By a petty promise I have broken a greater law in a fit of madness. I have violated fair combat and chosen lingering murder. Am I not a cowardly assassin, Rama?"

"Not to me," said Rama, "never to me. I can tell an enemy in the form of a friend—you are my father and no foe of mine. Will I disobey you and judge your commands because your motive may be desire? As though it were on a wheel, whatever we see of happiness and sorrow all turns round Fate. Fear and bravery, freedom and bondage, birth and death, love and anger all pivot on Time's wheel-hub. Wise men may give up long hard training all in an instant, things well-begun may be hindered by unthought-of accidents, all from Time. The Father is the Master. You gave me my life.

So end Kaikeyi's alarm and find peace. Drive out bad feelings as you banish me, I will see you free from debt when I return. One must keep promises or not make them."

"I think that is no longer true," said Dasaratha.

Rama said, "If I disobey you, no other good deed, no wealth, no power will restore my good name. Keep your word and preserve the three worlds, keep us safe. For every broken promise breaks away a little Dharma, and every break of Dharma brings closer the day the worlds too must break apart. When Dharma is altogether gone the three worlds will end; they will be destroyed once more. If man breaks his word, why should the stars above keep their promises not to fall? Why should Fire not burn us all or Ocean not leap his shores and drown us?"

"That is all true," said Dasaratha. "Oh Rama, if you doubt something be careful, for when you once speak you are bound! Never threaten harm to an enemy; just hit him hard!"

Rama said, "I ask you something."

"Ask anything."

"Earth Lord, it is only noble to be good. Do right, while you can. Change your curse on Kaikeyi."

"Then let her spend but the wink of an eye damned in Hell, for I cannot withdraw my words completely, or I would, Rama, I would do anything for you."

"Never curse her again."

"For now, for all the future I'll speak no bad to her."

"Love Bharata."

"I love."

"Let Sita go with me."

"Once given as your wife, she is yours even after death. The shade of your feet is better for her than a palace roof alone or a home in heaven. You are Lord to her, I will not sin more by preventing her."

"Let Lakshmana protect us."

"I let him."

"Goodbye, my father."

"But do not go today; stay with me tonight and leave tomorrow."

"I said I would go today. I will hold your feet after fourteen years. Farewell, father."

"Farewell, Rama."

Lakshmana came in. "Great King, Maharaja, rule for a thousand years, and farewell."

"Farewell, Lakshmana."

Sita entered. "My house is now the forest. Farewell my Father."

"Farewell, Sita. *All is lost! All is lost!*"

Rama and Lakshmana and Sita met Vasishtha by a small back door to the palace. Rama and Lakshmana first put on their impenetrable armor all of gold, and Lakshmana put on a black hide belt with a gold-handled belt-knife. Then over that they put on the two pieces of soft dyed barkcloth worn by ascetics, tied on belts of grass, put on forest sandals. And Vasishtha said, "Rama, never forget the weapons you learned from Viswamitra."

Sita held some bark clothes, cast down her eyes and asked Vasishtha, "Brahmana, how do hermits dress in these?"

"A knot by the waist," said Vasishtha, "but throw those down. Wear your silks and ornaments, Kaikeyi had not her eye on you, and the wishes say nothing of this."

Then Sumantra drove up on the royal chariot, a four-horse war-car rattling with noise. He said, "Prince Rama, I feel better now. I will drive you from the city, but the streets seem near impassable. Ornaments clash as the women strike their breasts, and the men cry—*Who ever exiles his own son?* Rama, they consider empty the life of anyone who will not see you leave, at whom you will not look as you go. They consider banishment the reward of virtue for every man now; they set at nothing the world's comforts and the highest joys of heaven if they can but see you. The Kosalas cannot withdraw their minds from you, they will rush after you like thirsty travelers sighting water in the desert. All the forest guides prepare to lead; your wrestling partners, all your friends, all the merchants and their women, all the little children and the dreadful warriors of Ayodhya—now all of us will follow you!"

"But why?" asked Rama. "What have I to do with a following? I'm leaving Ayodhya, how can I take her people? Who keeps attached to an elephant rope once the animal himself is free?"

Sumantra smiled. "But this will be a great departure indeed, more than was bargained for! Your people, they call themselves. They leave garden and field, they carry everything out from their homes and now dig up their buried treasures, and load all onto carts, and go out the gates, and line the roads."

"Not now," said Rama. "Can't you tell them? Charioteer, there may some day be a time, when all may follow me—ask them to wait."

"But you depart!"

"No, not now, later I may truly depart."

"They say it must be today. From this day forth will Ayodhya be vacant, her dusty yards unswept, her cattle gone, her flags torn down, her wells dry, her fires dead. Broken things abandoned will clutter her streets, and these broad ways will be the paths where wild cats and owls roam. Rats will crawl and cunning snakes will slither from hole to hole. Nevermore will any offerings be made from here to heaven; the temples of Fair Ayodhya will be without their garlands, without their images, abandoned by the gods, and ominous. So they say, Rama, so they say."

"What can I do? I give them all to Bharata, he won't harm them."

"No King ever yet gave the free Kosala men to anyone," said Sumantra.

"How can they think to live?"

"All our stores of food have been loaded onto wagons. In the forest the Kosalas will kill deer and elephants; they will drink wild honey, and see many rivers, and drive the lions back here into Ayodhya's ruins. They will forget this city, and again forget her, and at last never speak, never dream of her. The Kosalas will make new fields, cut the grass and plant grain. They will leave behind the golden coins and silver bars in the treasury, let Bharata have them; we have better; we have all our hopes . . . there can be no kingdom where you are not King . . . you'll see the forest flourish into a city, or we will wander homeless with you!"

Rama looked at Vasishtha. "Brahmana, help me! Fair Ayodhya is my city, don't let me hear in the forest that she has died of shame. You must somehow prevent them."

Vasishtha said, "Let them do what they want today and they will be tired tomorrow. Rama, the people's outcries last seven days, no longer. If I have ever said anything wrong to you from familiarity, or given you offense through ignorance, forgive me. Rama, I salute you, I bless you."

Vasishtha turned to Sita and said, "You do not forsake your Lord in misfortune, I salute you, I bless you!"

He told Lakshmana, "Prince, this design of yours to serve Rama is already a great blessing to you, a great good fortune, your high wide way to heaven. You follow him, I salute you, I bless you."

Then the brahmana Vasishtha embraced Sumantra the Charioteer. *So there is still one good heart in the Kosala Kingdom! I see honor, I see again that proud warriors' Dharma of kindliness and bravery and gladly casting off the body on the battlefield of war. I see fairness and skill and courage once more! That is the Kshatriya Dharma that I remember. It is good to see, old man, good to see!*

Lakshmana put Rama's fire inside a bowl in a corner of the chariot. Sumantra put bows and arrows on board, and under the driver's seat in front he put a hoe and a root-gathering basket bound in goathide. Vasishtha helped Sita get on the car; the two princes climbed up; Sumantra got on and the exile began.

Sumantra held the reins. The four horses raised their heads, the chariot trembled, it seemed to come alive. Sumantra said, "Go."

The red horses ran. They were out of the back palace courtyard, through the palace gates, and racing wildly down the street to the southern gate of Ayodhya. Then Dasaratha cried down from a palace balcony behind them—*Stop! Stay!*

"Go faster," said Rama. "Later say you did not hear him."

Too late, Dasaratha rushed from the palace. Too late he repented. He covered his face with his hands; he could not endure the sight of that fleeing chariot. *Stop them!*

Sumantra told his horses, in a voice not loud, "Go on, run, go on."

The gate guards heard the King. Sumantra came too fast at them; there was no time to close the gate but they swiftly formed ranks to block the car.

Sumantra bent over and took up a war-whip, a whip for striking men not horses. "Hang on, Sita!" His white hair streamed out straight back from his head in the wind of flight. Again Sumantra drove with his warrior behind him, alone against a hostile army, ready to fight anyone. Sumantra was never easy to stop. The red horses never slowed, never broke stride. There came the gate, the hooves and wheels thundered, the gateway rattled like dice.

Sumantra flailed his whip to this side and that. He hit back the Kosalas from the street, then with blows and lashes, holding his breath in anger he struck down forty rows of guards, and in terrible confusion broke free through the gate. The chariot dashed away from Fair Ayodhya over the narrow Kosala road going south in the evening.

Wind-driven black clouds swept the vault of heaven like ocean waves and covered the sky. Along the road the tall trees sounded in the wind, and in the trees the still birds did not fly to seek their food, but sang piteously begging some help against disaster.

Suddenly the rapid raging river Tamasa threw her dark waves across the road to forbid Sumantra. By the riverside the charioteer uncoupled the tired horses, and when they had rolled in the dust he bathed them and made them drink. He fed them grass while Lakshmana built a fire in the high wind, and while the many people following from Ayodhya drew near in the night.

Lord of the Wild Trees

*It is not strange to me nor wonderful that
Indra should downpour rain, or the thousand-
rayed Sun banish darkness from heaven, or the
Moon bathe the clear Night in his rays, or that
a good friend like you should bring me delight,
or that whatever is graceful should be harbored
within you.*

In the windy night the old men of Ayodhya first arrived
where Rama was and said, "We so commanded the dark Tamasa River and she obeyed us. Like her, we throw ourselves
at your feet. Friend Rama, we beg you to return. We put
down in the dust our shaking heads, our hair white as
cranes."

Rama replied, "You are old in years and honored in wisdom, and the merits of your good deeds are great. But you
must take all this water away from my path. I uphold the
King's word, and you cannot use the streams of Earth against
Earth's own Lord."

"Oh Rama, we told the fleet horses not to go on. They
have ears and know our prayer." The old men reached out
and touched Rama, and gazed at him in the firelight, drinking him in with their sight. "In all justice you must be carried
into Ayodhya and not away from her."

"What cause for sorrow here?" asked Rama. "Bharata will
be a strong and gentle King. You will do me good if you return and cheer my father."

The old men said, "Oh Rama, look back, see the fires that
walk following you on the shoulders of loyal Kosala men, see
by their glare those umbrellas still open, tossed by the wind,
that will give you shade when it is day once more."

Rama sighed and said no more to them. He went to Lakshmana and said, "With you by my side near me I am easy about Sita's protection. My brother, tonight I will fast and drink only water. From now on, do not let your mind dwell long on our past happiness."

Lakshmana made a bed of branches and leaves, and there Rama and Sita slept that night. Lakshmana and Sumantra sat by Tamasa's shore among the trees growing from the water, talking softly together about Rama until just before the first hint of dawn.

Then Rama in his sleep felt the air change, he felt Night depart and awoke. He saw the Kosalas who had followed him still asleep all around. He quietly awakened Sita and told Sumantra, "I must deliver these men from their own misfortune. If we can escape they will have to go home where they will recover, I cannot drag them after me into my exile."

Sumantra went to his chariot and without a sound pulled it by hand out from the sleepers. By a small noise he summoned the four horses and harnessed them. He drove his three passengers down the midstream of the river, and after awhile let them out across the river to wait near a forest track, and filled the chariot with stones. Then returning through the water to the Tamasa camp he drove ashore right near where he had entered the river and went back toward Ayodhya. And finally as he went, he threw out the stones one by one, and the lightened chariot gradually left no path on the hard earth.

Then he told the horses, "Run." There was not one little branch broken where he passed; those red horses had years before pulled a flying chariot through the air, and leaving no hoof-marks was not difficult for them. They stirred no fallen leaf and made no sound, and swiftly Sumantra circled back through the forest, again crossed Tamasa, and met Rama before any Kosala had awakened.

For a moment Sumantra faced the chariot north to invoke good fortune and a successful journey. And Rama stood facing Ayodhya and touching his hands together he said, "Best of cities, I will see you again, the gods guard you well."

Sumantra said, "Quickly get on." They drove away from Fair Ayodhya to the lands of the southwest. The forest track soon joined the south road. The countryside of Kosala stretched out away in the distance; far as the eye could see the round trees rose from the flat plains. All day they rode through the kingdom of Kosala stopping only for noonday prayers. The villages and the fields grew fewer and farther between, then in the late afternoon there were no more settlements. They saw no more white cattle and no houses or ponds—only the forest closing in on them. Their road began to fail. It turned into a cowpath and then vanished. They were crossing the southern boundary of Kosala. At dusk Sumantra stopped the chariot by the Ganga River flowing from heaven through Shiva's hair; Rama got down with the others, and they walked a little way and stood under a huge ancient spreading nut tree.

That tree marked the Kingdom of the Far Forest and the realm of Guha the Hunter King. Rama and Sita, Lakshmana and Sumantra all bathed in the beautiful Ganges, where bathing a man may wash off the sins from his heart as he takes the dirt from his skin, and both come out clean.

Then as they stood in wet clothes under the trees of the Secret Forest, they heard whistles from the wood and looked in their direction. They saw nothing and when they looked back they saw Guha come to welcome them.

Guha was a little thin brown man, short, with soft brown eyes, with a beard of a few hairs and a pure white grin. He was painted and tattooed with red and blue lines and wore a short black bearskin skirt for his only clothes. He had on a necklace of tiger teeth and a belt of deer hooves laced on a thong, musical anklets of claws and pieces of ivory and black wood tied together, bone earrings, armbands of braided grass and bright spotted beans and stone beads cut with corners. In his curly hair were feathers, red and yellow and green and white and black. Hung from his belt were a magic rattle of bone rings and shells, a horn of honey, a bird noose of vine and a worn bamboo case that held tiny poisoned wooden darts. He was Rama's friend.

Guha ran to Rama, and Rama embraced him in a hug hard enough to crush a bear, and the savage King pounded Rama's back with friendly stunning blows, and laughed like a child.

"Oh Rama, Rama! Now you are an outcast like me!"

"You! You look more outlandish than I remembered you!" laughed Rama. Guha whistled and hunter-men came out of the trees bearing wooden trays of hot steaming food.

"Eat!" cried Guha. He threw himself on Lakshmana and thumped Sumantra. He smiled at Sita and spread down a blanket for her and his men put down the food and drink. "Princess," he said, "I know your mother well and I have known Rama since he was a boy."

"How glad I am to find a friend at last," said Sita. She smiled. "We meet you here!"

"That smile is all my payment," said Guha. "Queen, take food. Tell me what I can give you. Listen—demons fear me, men fear me, dear friends dare not come near me when I am out of sorts, and here on my own ground, in my own forest I can defeat any army ever created."

Sita said, "Oh Guha, we have had such a bad time!"

"Eat! Eat! Today is over. In Ayodhya men are driven raving mad by too many laws and rules. Freedom for me! I am a man of action, I heard what happened and never mind." -

"How did you meet Rama before today?"

"A chase led me once to Ayodhya, and there I met Rama and Lakshmana, and though they were city boys I cared for their friendship. While they grew into men I met them again many times among the trees outside the city. I taught them forest lore and hunting. Lakshmana learned well." Guha smiled. "But Rama I could never teach to hunt."

Now the silent dark men of the greenwood came and made a fire under the great nut tree. They all sat around it and ate from banana leaves and drank from horns. There was meat and fish and sugar-bread, small sweet wild fruit and eggs and strong blossom-wines. Rama had fasted one night looking forward to happiness; he had fasted a second night looking back on a sad day. Now he ate thinking of nothing; he breathed in the clean air and the firelight lit up his face with golden light.

When they finished Guha put a necklace of pink seashells over Sita's head. "I adopt you into my people," he said. "You are in my family, for your heart is free."

Sita laid her head on Rama's shoulder. One of Guha's men said something in the whistling bird-language, and Rama carried her to the bed they had made for him. Sumantra relaxed and lay on his back looking up at all the stars of heaven through the trees; then he was asleep and Guha's people covered him with many thin blankets.

Guha lit up a fat cigar of sandalwood dust and nutmeg powder all rolled in long leaves and held together with goat butter. He leaned back against the tree and puffed smoke and looked at Lakshmana. Guha said, "Bows in hand we will watch over them through the dark night by Ganga. Oh child, we have made a soft bed for you also, lie down and rest. I am used to being awake at all hours but you deserve comfort."

Lakshmana closed his eyes and crunched a candied apple in his teeth. "King of the Wilderness, with Rama asleep on the ground and in misfortune what use would be my comfort?" He sighed. "I remember when you would come near to Ayodhya in happy days. . . ."

"Then I challenge you to a drinking contest," said Guha.

Lakshmana threw his bark back off his shoulder. "I accept." Lakshmana chose two horns and tried to make sure that each held the same amount. They seemed to, and he filled them with wine.

Guha carefully lined up five full wine jugs in a row and took one horn from Lakshmana. His men left more wood for the fire and retired into the shadows of the night as if into nowhere. "Prince, do not worry over the future," said Guha, "or try to outguess fortune, for it is hard enough to know what one is doing at the moment right now. I will tell you a story."

Listen, Lakshmana—

A busybody cannot sleep in peace if he knows of one man free to do as he will; he cannot tolerate someone who likes to live alone, in his own way. Did you never wonder how I got to Ayodhya, the one time I've ever been inside a city?

Your father's priest Vasishtha decided to reform me and my people. He sent some brahmanas over the border into my forest, and by Ganga they set up a stone image of Shiva, under the branches of this very nut tree twenty years ago.

Many men are all talk and no deeds, all words and no wisdom, and what they don't know of they think does not exist. Those pious brahmanas lived in fancy tents not far from here. Morning and evening they brought flowers and offered food to that stone Shiva and praised him. I met them and gave them a good welcome and some little presents of gold birds and nine-headed snakes of lead. But I told them—*I worship only God, and God is a tree*. And every night when I returned from hunting I would go and give that statue a good kick.

Then the rains came. The forest floor was an ocean of mud, and Ganga rose in flood and forced those brahmanas away to high ground. They left Shiva all alone half underwater for days at a time. Yet every night, even when I had to wade over logs, when I was exhausted, when I was hungry or sick, every night I went happily up to that senseless block of stone and kicked it.

Shortly after the rains, one night when I was going home very late I arrived here at the time of the animals' drinking. A lean wolf-pack greeted me. Their shiny eyes were hungry, the rains had starved them. My arrows were all gone. I had no fire to frighten them. They kept me from the statue, but though I could have outrun them and gone home I climbed this old tree. I held onto a limb and thought, "One way or another, before this night is over I must kick that rock."

So I waited in the tree above Shiva. I had not eaten all day, so I tried to eat the green nuts on the tree, but they were so bitter I could not even swallow one bite but spit it out. That annoyed me a little bit, and the wolves round Shiva's statue snapped up at me with sharp white teeth trying in vain to reach me, but I waited for my chance to kick Shiva.

I had no food, there was no place to sleep, the night turned cold and the dew fell. The wolves would not go, and I shivered in the moonlight so hard that leaves and dewdrops and bitter green nuts fell all over the statue. Finally at dawn the wolves ran when my people came tracking me, but the night had passed. I had failed to greet Shiva as he deserved, and I was so passionately angry that I chased the brahmanas back to Ayodhya where they hid behind Vasishtha's skirts.

Dasaratha met me there. I told him, "I will adore only the holy trees!" He took my hand and made me a King. I already ruled this whole forest, but until then I was but a common man!

When I got back here, Lakshmana, Shiva's image was gone somewhere else and I forgot about it. I went on hunting and eating and drinking until one afternoon I felt ill. A little green bird sat near me unafraid, and I died in my hut after a short attack of fatal fever.

Yama's messengers came to get me, four ruffians holding snarling dogs on chains. With contempt they tore my soul from my dead body, bound me in a noose and started south with me to Yama's world, all done in an instant. I could imagine my reception. As a soul I was no bigger than a thumb, but still I struggled violently. But that death-noose could not slip loose even in a dream.

Then as we came round a narrow turn in the forest path, a small mean-looking dwarf stood in the way. He fixed his round brown eyes on Yama's bullies. He snorted and said,

"Unknot that noose! Give over Guha's soul to me, he is not to die yet."

The death-spirits laughed. "He is *already* dead! Stand aside, we will leave you now!"

"Try it and I'll block you. I am Nandin the peaceful guardian of the wild. By Shiva's order release him."

"This is his *death*, you little runt!"

"Liars," said Nandin. "You are but thieves, it is not time for him to die."

"What did you call us?"

"Have a kindness to the small and the weak," said Nandin. "I beg you to let him go—"

Well, that did it. Yama's guards released their dogs and advanced on Nandin. I saw that surly little animal scatter the dogs and give the first death-guard a stupendous blow that broke his head in. There was a great commotion but I fell face down into a pile of old leaves and could see nothing more.

"Torment a poor defenseless animal will you?" I heard bones breaking and dogs yelping and running feet and chains coming apart. Then Nandin gently picked up the end of my noose and flew with me to the high Himalya.

There he came to Earth and changed into his true form, into a sleek white humpy bull. He serenely carried me hanging still bound from his soft wet mouth. We entered a flimsy cottage. Nandin's breath smelled of sweet grass in the sun. Nandin stopped and I saw Shiva sitting tall and fair, his two eyes like honey looking in my soul, his third eye closed on his brow, his hair unkempt and wild, wearing an old worn deerskin and rags, and looking at me and looking, with Parvati the mountain's daughter on his lap.

Then Nandin the bull and Shiva both faced the door. In a moment a quiet green man in a red robe entered and stood turning his head to see this way and that and looked at us with his dark unmoving eyes.

Yama joined his hands with fingers touching and said to the great Lord Shiva, "In my scribe's dusty record book this Guha is a killer charged with crimes. He has sinned; his life has been shortened; his time is up; his days are over. Why did you take his soul away from me, and leave us with an empty place in Hell?"

The wind began to blow through Yama's long black hair. Shiva said, "Death Lord, Guha was the one person faithful in saluting me when I came to his forest. Before he died he once fasted and kept sleepless watch for my sake in a tree all night, and offered me food he needed for himself, and showered me with water, and gave me ornaments of leaves. And he took such rage against men pretending to love me that he threatened their lives and drove them out. Therefore, Oh Yama, I overreach you, his soul is mine and not yours to take."

"Yama smiled and left us without a word," continued Guha. "Nandin took my soul back to my body and I returned to life. So when even the Court of Death cannot tell right from wrong, it is surely very hard for us to judge things."

Lakshmana answered, "But certainly our father did wrong."

"Who told you that? This banishment will kill your father; it is simply time for him to die."

"It is the fault of those promises."

"No," said Guha, "those wishes are but the blind instruments of Fate. King Dasaratha was not such a foolish man. Once before, in my presence Kaikeyi asked him for one of those wishes."

"What did he say? What did he do?"

"That was years ago, before you were born," said Guha. "The Ayodhya King came on a hunting trip, and Kaikeyi was with him, and he stopped to see me and ask permission to use my forest."

Listen, Prince—

I gave him the freedom of my wood, and that evening I sat with Dasaratha in his camp near by my house, and with us were Sumantra the charioteer and Queen Kaikeyi. The forest was noisy. The day-animals were speaking before they slept, the night-prowlers were talking and arising, and a full Moon beamed down on us. We were surrounded by screeching and singing and howls of warning.

Your father knew the animal tongues. Suddenly a stag barked loudly, another stag answered, the first one called again, and your father was overcome with laughter. Kaikeyi was very curious and asked, "Majesty, what are you laughing at?"

"It would not be funny in translation," laughed Dasaratha.

"You can tell *me*," Kaikeyi pleaded. "If you love me what secrets are between us?"

"There must be this one, for you cannot understand the animal languages."

She said, "Teach me."

But Sumantra replied, "The King cannot. If he reveals even half a word he will die. That is the agreement, the price of his friend Jatayu the Vulture King, who rules Dandaka Forest and who taught him this speech."

So Kaikeyi was still and said no more right then. Awhile later she again asked for that secret learning and was again refused. And after another while in passing she mentioned her two wishes but never pursued the subject, and I would have said all was forgotten when the King and Queen retired to sleep.

No one knows what she said to him in bed that night, but in the morning Dasaratha came from his tent looking deplorable, and walked by me in sad distress saying to himself, "All is lost, all is lost. . . .

He said that over and over. He ordered his own funeral pyre to be built. He planned that day to tell Kaikeyi animal speech while sitting on the pyre. By the terms of his contract as Jatayu's student his heart would then burst, and we were to burn his body.

I didn't know what to do. I had not yet died myself and so had little wisdom. I refused to help make the pyre, but Sumantra did it anyway. Kaikeyi eagerly took her seat near that stack of wood and I saw Dasaratha come out of his tent in white funeral clothes and walk slowly toward her.

But he had to pass my house and my yard where I kept many wild hens and a red and green and gold bantam fighting rooster, and also several ewes with an old short-tempered ram. And as Dasaratha went by the ram said to my rooster, "How can this pitiful bungler be called King of the World?" And the rooster replied, "Why, if I even thought of spoiling my hens like he does that woman I'd be out of business here in the flash of an eye, teacher's curse or not!"

"When your father heard that," said Guha, "he went back to his tent shaking his head, biting his tongue and smiling to himself. He got dressed right and told me what my animals had said. He refused Kaikeyi and she was glad of it. Do you think for any reason that he has changed now, other than his

approaching death? Lakshmana, if we live long enough, it is
Time that wears out our bodies. Old men grow tired at last,
their hearts remember the past more than the present. Death
comes nearer, then they feel they must rest; they are about to
fall asleep after a hard day. Death stands behind a man's
shoulder, he touches him and there is no more will to live,
and the man welcomes him. Try what he will, Lakshmana,
through no fault of his own your father's life fails at last."

Lakshmana said, "But then the King asks Rama to do
what will kill him."

"I think so. He sees what he does but does not care."

"Why does Rama go along with this?"

Guha said, "I later learned bird and animal talk for myself, and listening to them I have heard that once the Ocean
talked with his beloved rivers. They described for him the
land and what grew there. Big strong trees he had seen, carried down to him on the flood waters. But he had never
glimpsed a bending cane nor seen a blade of grass. No river
had ever washed down such a yielding plant to him, not since
the world began."

Guha's winejars were all empty, and Lakshmana's eyes
were clear and bright as his own. The drinking contest was a
draw. The sky started to get light. It was near sunrise, the
glorious Sun was burning hot low behind the eastern hills,
and day was breaking, and our blessed mother Night was departing.

Rama woke. Sita slept with her arm across his chest and
he gently moved it aside. He sat up and stretched. He looked
around at the forest and up at the sky, with eyes like someone newborn, unafraid and accepting.

Rama smiled; he stroked Sita's hair and woke her. He
walked over to Guha and said, "Hunter Chief, we will cross
Ganga fast washing to the sea, my friend."

Sumantra came and said, "I'll leave the chariot and come
with you, and I will carry you home after the fourteen years.
All that time will be an instant with you or a hundred gener-
ations if we are separated."

Rama touched his right hand lightly on Sumantra's shoulder. "Turn back to Dasaratha, we will continue on walking."

"Shall I go back with an empty chariot having lost a life
that was in my keeping, as though driving alone away from a
battlefield, my warrior killed and fallen? What can I say
when people ask me of you? Rama, as a stingy man cannot

enter heaven with no good deeds beside him, so I cannot enter Fair Ayodhya alone!"

"Go," said Rama, "so that Kaikeyi will believe that I am in the forest and not mistrust our father. And Life willing ... if you and I still live we will meet again someday."

Sumantra said, "You must never cast aside a faithful servant who lives by your way and serves you well."

Rama said, "Charioteer, do not be sad, for pain and pleasure must come in their turns to all men and mortal gods. Cheer my father. Guard him and keep him. He is very old, he must be protected from harm like a child. Tell him— *Lakshmana and Rama and Sita are well. They have no grief. After these fourteen short years you will soon see them return, and may that time quickly pass for you as if in sleep.*"

Then as hermits do, Rama and Lakshmana matted their hair up over their heads with the sticky paste made from banyan bark. Guha gave both of them a deerskin, and to Sita he gave a fine feather cloak all of green and gold. Guha's men brought out from hiding a raft of logs with seats of fresh-broken leafy roseapple boughs, and took the three across Ganga. In midstream Sita made a silent prayer to the beautiful River Queen. "Ganga, protect my Rama. Beautiful bride of the Sea, let him return safely to his own Ayodhya. Let it be so, and I will bow to you. I will sing songs in the holy shrines along your river beaches. . . ."

Then they were all alone in the forest, far away from the smiling fields and gardens of men. There they felt the sadness of no one being near to care what happened to them. They walked in single file. First went Lakshmana holding his bow and carrying their fire and few possessions. Two quivers were on his back and he kept watch for animals and pitfalls and trod down the thorns and sharp grass. Sita followed him and Rama came last, looking down, his bow not even strung, just a few arrows tied carelessly at his belt and in his mind the mantras that could make those arrows countless.

They went still to the south, walking all day along the river Ganga. From inexperience of the forest they could not go fast nor get very far that day. They wasted their strength in many ways. When evening caught them Lakshmana shot a wild sow and cooked her, and they could eat very little.

That night Rama said, "Lakshmana, you've got to go back in the morning or else Kaikeyi will poison our mothers. Even

Kausalya's pet parrot would try his best to defend her and bite her enemies, but I'm of less use to her than a gaudy bird. I am sent away just when her pains of motherhood should be rewarded, and my mother of slender fortune must lie weeping in the dust."

"Forget it," said Lakshmana. "You're tired, go to sleep with Sita. Don't tell me about inevitable things that displease me."

"You are right, despair is a bad enemy," said Rama. "Alone or with me, Lakshmana, in our exile always guard Sita."

"I'll stay with you right through the gates of blazing Hell as long as you want me!"

Rama and Sita fell asleep, a lion couple on a desolate summit. Lakshmana stood guard at that lone place in the wide forest. His blue eyes looked into the black night. Truly, he stood guard naturally; he had no fear and no violence in his heart; he had no envy and once he had sworn by Dharma he obeyed Rama. He never doubted Rama was right, or that he was right to obey him.

The next morning was sunny. They followed an uneven trail and soon they could hear the meeting of the waters of Ganga and the Yamuna river rushing together. On the land between the rivers there was a clearing surrounded by deep green banyan trees with red fruit like heaps of emeralds mixed with rubies. Set in the clearing was a hermitage, the home of the saint Bharadwaja.

They entered and bowed to that old ascetic sitting on the grass, and Bharadwaja said, "I have heard. I see you after you have walked long. My place here is yours, stay close by me and I will care for you."

Bharadwaja, a great man, washed Rama's feet, and Rama said, "We cannot stay so close to Ayodhya, but tell us somewhere good to live."

Bharadwaja slaughtered a bull for their dinner. When they had eaten he said, "Go to the hill Chitrakuta ten ear-shots distant from here. Chitrakuta's peaks are clear and bright-colored. There deep rivers run, there live birds fair to view. From there many saints with hair white as skulls have gone to heaven, but now that hill is deserted by men."

In the morning Rama and Sita and Lakshmana crossed the Yamuna studded with islands. First going south a way, they then turned and went west along a little stream flowing toward them.

Two days later they reached Chitrakuta Hill, standing alone and towering above them, engarlanded by his own flowering woods thick with flowers of red and gold and blue and white and every color. He had crags and ridges, round stones and giant boulders. Through his stone ran veins of black and yellow and silver-colored ore. He was alive with singing birds. He was like the garden of the gods, like the Gandharva groves in the Himalya. Clear rivers and little streams flowed down from him like graceful braids; they ran over glittering sands and dashed their loud-laughing waves against blue rocks of lapis. The forest floor by Chitrakuta was wholly covered with flowers, the paths were overarched by joyful blossoms and by branches bending low with ripe fruit, and no man there to taste them.

It was all-colored spring in the forest. The bees hung their huge honeycombs on the high limbs. The forest trail where Rama walked seemed to be the eternal peaceful pathway of the saints. The fine trees up the steep-sloping hillsides above were a gathering of clouds, the wind played through them and they bowed and waved their leaves, catching gleams of the sun on them and smiling as clouds smile by their lightnings. The trees grew way up the hill; they crowned the heights.

The round chakravaka birds who cry plaintively in the night if separated bobbed on the water in the river ponds and swam in mated pairs. Ducks were afloat in the streams and herons stood among the waving lotus flowers near the banks. Blackbirds sang to the Sun. Timid deer grazed in meadows, and tigers and lions who had never seen men watched the newcomers through the leaves.

Sita, that beautiful young woman blameless and beloved, looked on the perfumed trees and shrubs never seen before. Rama told her their names, and Lakshmana brought her flower-shedding boughs and bushy branches of tender green and rosy leaves. They found a homesite on a tableland of rills, above a gentle rise on Chitrakuta, overlooking the level plain below.

Near a cave, by a clear sweet mountain spring Lakshmana built on pillars a strong house framed with long bamboos and floored with grass, whose walls were of woven wood tightly lashed by cords to keep out wind, whose roof was leaves. It had one door and many rooms and fair windows, and seeing it Rama said, "Surely we shall live here. How did you learn to build so well and do all this for us?"

As soon as he finished the house Lakshmana killed a black deer and dressed it and threw it into a fire. When it was hot and well-done Rama took the meat and set it out along with grass and water for an offering to the hill spirits. Then a household god came to live in their home filling it with gladness and warding away wrong. Only then did Rama and Sita enter the house.

Having like Rama gone a long way, the glorious Sun was sloping down and ready to depart from the sky. The light-giving Lord of the Day carried away with him all Rama's red-dyed grief at leaving Fair Ayodhya. The loving embrace of blue evening made even the Sun renounce heaven and leave the sky.

It was twilight and the trees stood motionless. From all sides came the enveloping dark veils of our Lady Night, forgetful and restful. Rama and Sita beside him were asleep in their house, they had no farther to go. The sky slowly turned above with stars for her bright open eyes, and the splendid mild-beaming Moon rose to dispel the darkness and touch all hearts with his glad rays, and Lakshmana watched the midnight gradually pass away.

When the Kosalas awoke at daybreak by the Tamasa River they found that Rama had eluded them. They saw that Sumantra's chariot was gone and made a great outcry— *Shame to sleep! How could he? Our lives are over! Here is deadwood ready for our funeral pyres. Alas, all is Destiny!*

Then they cheered and rejoiced. They had found Sumantra's false trail and they stubbornly followed it, tracking and looking, undaunted and obstinate, talking and waving and swinging their arms in the air, trying to listen for noises and telling each other to be quiet. They lost the fading wheelmarks within sight of Ayodhya. They entered the city. They were tired. They spoke quietly—*What else? How can we men defeat the supernatural?* They went home again.

The great grey elephants of Ayodhya wept as wild elephants weep when one of their Kings is captured in the forest. The Kosalas' faces were washed by warm tears, their hearts subdued. Everyone thought only of Rama, Rama they had lost. That night the lamps and lanterns burned dim, strange foreign stars clustered overhead and no one could sleep. In Fair Ayodhya the warriors ceaselessly burned and sighed.

So passed the day after Rama was banished, and the night after that, and the next day. Then that evening Sumantra drove up to Ayodhya's walls at dusk, his face muffled by the end of his upper robe. He drove to the palace and walked still masked through the halls. He found King Dasaratha lying in Queen Kausalya's unlit bedroom, fanned by Kausalya and tended by Queen Sumitra, kneeling beside him.

Sumitra rose and looked at Sumantra. Her eyes were wet with tears and she said, "The King is blind."

"Lord!"

Sumitra said in a low voice, "Charioteer, listen. As your chariot sped away, grief struck down strong men. The King went to the city gate and watched unmoving in the direction you had taken, and Kausalya and I stood on either side to support him. Again he cried for you to wait, if but for an instant. He rose up on his toes to see the distant dust of your car, and when that dust was gone from sight and the south road was empty of you four, he fell and pressed his ear to the ground. When he could no longer hear the running horses we helped him to rise and led him slowly back. The people came out past us to follow you. We told Dasaratha, 'Do not follow far one who will come back to you,' but he heard nothing. He repented as though after burning his hand in a fire. He looked down at the straight wheel tracks as we followed them returning, and they beginning to be blown away by a doleful wind, and the sky darkening and all light failing. Stopping again and again, he said—*The last trace, the last trace of my son that I will ever see!*

"Sumantra, his tears soaked the ground; they bathed him as though he were already dead and being washed before the burning of his body, and our grieving people were his mourners. We came to this room, he stumbled and fell onto that bed, and though he was not asleep he lay not moving for half the night with his eyes shut. And when he opened them at midnight he could not see. He blindly reached out to Queen Kausalya and when she took his hand he said, 'Mother of Rama, touch me for my sight follows your son and does not yet return. Oh Rama, they are very happy men who will see you return and embrace you. They are not men, but blessed gods.'

"So, old warrior, long have I stood here never leaving him, well pleased by my sweet son Lakshmana whom I love, in my mind praising his wisdom, bearing my hope shining within myself as the only flame of warmth left in all Ayodhya."

Sumantra advanced to the King. "I am Sumantra, covered with road-dust and hiding my face. I touch together my hands and salute you, Majesty. Will you not speak to Rama's envoy? Arise, Kaikeyi is not here!"

Dasaratha whispered, "What did he do? Where is he?"

Sumantra uncovered his face. He answered, "I left them in the solitude, walking alone in the forest. This morning he sent me back to you and crossed Ganga. He bows to your feet, for you are his father. He claims to be well. What I was first going to say about Kaikeyi on sudden impulse I have forgotten. I stood there speechless, and so Rama went away, and so Lakshmana left me behind, and so Sita disappeared into the trees.

"Hoping Rama might yet summon me I stayed awhile with Guha, but then turned back. Your favorite red horses were slow and spiritless. As I crossed back through Kosala, I saw that in all your kingdom the trees let fall their leaves and have no flowers, no scented fruit, no new buds. In your land the ponds are desolate, the streams are dry, the wells are bitter and silted. Groves wither, no creature moves or speaks, beasts of prey will not wander. The empty woods are stricken dumb; they have no nobility; they stand in gloom on all sides. Food has no flavor and no one wants to eat it anyway. Stones are burnt black. Grass is faded and dead. Crops and waterplants perish. Fish and gardens die. I drove a cheerless dreary road, my Lord. Where there had been gardens lean birds were drooping in the leafless trees, their bright plumes stained. No fires burn. Cattle give no milk. The air has no freshness. All sounds are faint and the world is indistinct. No one moves from where he is or opens his eyes once closing them. There is no difference between a dear friend or an enemy or an uncaring man. People are not dead yet they do not live, all vitality is now lost and gone away. . . ."

The old King tried to rise. He trembled. "Charioteer, if I have ever done any good thing, drive me to Rama!"

"I cannot," said Sumantra. "I don't look back. I don't know where he is."

They left Dasaratha alone with Queen Kausalya close by him. He slept uneasily for a short time but soon awakened. Kausalya still held his hand and said, "I am here."

Dasaratha said, "In my sleep I have remembered what I did long ago to cause all this misfortune. Gentle woman, as a man's deeds are good or evil so are the events which follow them, and which the man must face in their time. I have cut down sweet fruit trees for being slow-growing. In their place I've faithfully watered the rampant gay-colored trees bitter of fruit. Excited, mindlessly lured by pretty flowers on the branches, I came to expect a good yield. I looked forward to happiness but all the while I coveted delusion."

Kausalya said, "You lived a good life. You were a good man. Why do you blame yourself so? If you can't change what you've done wrong don't dwell on it."

"But the season has come," said Dasaratha. "Even when I was a young prince I leaned on a staff though I did not need it—and now I am old and have never stood alone. Asleep just now I have met Truth, I tremble."

Listen, Kausalya—

When you were a maid unwed and I was young, my Love, I ever lived as I pleased, I never denied myself a thing, I knew not any sorrow. I was a great marksman. I could shoot with bow and arrow aiming by sound alone and I was proud of my skill. Then once in the rainy season I rode out hunting. It was the evening twilight and the water had stopped falling for awhile. I rode along the Sarayu and the river twisted by in torrents red and black, dyed with ores and sands from the mountains and foaming in flood.

I stopped and waited by the river, planning to kill any game that came to drink. It grew dark. I could see but not very far. Then to one side I heard the sound of an elephant drinking and I sent an arrow flying at the sound. The arrow hit and I heard a cry—*Night, who has killed me?*

I felt cold fear. I had heard not an elephant but the sound of a filling waterjar. I ran to the voice and found my arrow piercing through a young man's heart. He knelt by the river. My bow fell from my hand and he fell over partly into the river. Blood poured from his breast and water poured from his waterjar lying overturned.

I held him in my arms and he looked at me. "Prince Dasaratha, what have I ever done to you? You have also killed my old blind parents who are lame and cannot move. They await my return with water. Never in their long lives have they injured another even for a good cause . . . take out your sharp arrow. . . ."

I said, "If the arrow is left alone it pains, but if it is withdrawn Death will come. I will go for a physician—"

But he sank in my grasp. His eyes fluttered upwards and with terrible difficulty he said, "No, I endure Death. I calm and clear my mind. Do not hesitate, it was but an accident . . . boldly release my life. . . ."

So I gently bit off the arrowhead where it came out his back and withdrew the shaft. He drew in his limbs, sighed once and died watching me with no fear in his eyes, a peaceful man dying in victory. I straightened his deerskin robe and laid him along the river shore.

I thought long how to mend my sin and at last very frightened I filled the waterjar and carried it along a narrow way that bore his footprints, leading to his parents' home. I thought that it could not be right that he should die and they know nothing of it. As I approached the end of the path I heard an old couple talking about their son, feeding on the hopes I had destroyed. Then I saw them sitting like birds with broken wings, and no one to help them move about.

The old man turned his blind face to me. "Your mother feared you had gone swimming at night, my son. Answer us, do not be angry with old people who worry."

My footsteps faltered. In a voice of fear I spoke the hardest words I ever said. "I am Dasaratha, no son of yours but a warrior, a butcher. Without knowing, I have killed your son with an arrow, thinking him from sound to be an elephant drinking. Burn me with your wrath like fire, for he has died from my ignorance and from my sudden wound."

They were silent and I said, "Command me, Oh Ascetic."

He said, "We were unable to help our only son. We are like trees, who cannot rescue one another from the attacks of the winds. Had you not come to tell us this your head would have burst into a thousand pieces. Had you given him even a slight wound intentionally you would by now have fallen alive and screaming into Hell. Not to mention warriors, I can pull down Indra himself if he knowingly hurts a harmless forest man. Carry us to our boy."

I carried them. The old man and his wife fell over their son and their blind hands went tenderly touching his corpse. The old man said, "Ah, it is hard to get a son like you in this world, and you are dead!" He turned to me. "Where is he?"

I looked up. At first I could not see what path his soul had taken. I searched heaven with my eyes. I answered, "He is waiting by the door to the heaven of warriors slain in battle."

The old man said, "Prince, by your permission."

I said, "Yes." Indra opened the door and let him in.

"Go, my son," said the old man. "Born in our race you cannot come by evil." The parents poured the death-water for their son and the man drew me aside. "Kill us. Burn us three on one pyre."

"Yes, I will."

He said, "I do not curse you, nor does my wife. But I fear for you. Be careful in the future, be on your guard if you should have a son. The giver receives back the things he gives away. Will you not one day find your own death over your own lost son? Will you come by this same fate?"

I found some dry wood under a great tree where no rain had gone, and I killed them as they asked me to, and I burned them in fire that burned fiercely powered by their sacrifices, and the heat and flames of their generosity drove me backwards.

"Queen," said Dasaratha, "that whole crime now comes home to me. If Rama could touch me I might live, but I have no other help. I cannot hear my own voice. My hand grows numb. I can hardly feel your hand, I barely speak. My death fast approaches. I have wronged my son, but he has done well toward me . . . Rama. . . . Where are you? . . . Rama. . . ."

Yama the Death Lord softly touched the locked doors of the Ayodhya palace and they flew open for him. Death holding his maces and bars in his hands entered unseen. Yama walked quietly beside him along the well-guarded halls, going gently to the King, casting sleep over Kausalya. Lord Yama reached into Dasaratha's breast and took out his mortal soul. Round the soul he put the diamond-wire silver noose of death and slipped tight the knot, then he took him away.

Two fires of grief past and present had dried away the life of the Ayodhya king. When that night was sometime passed he all unnoticed breathed no more, and departed this life. So did he die, the far-famed King Dasaratha, a warrior with no enemies alive.

Dasaratha dies

Bharata Returns

*An orphan lion cub with his eyes still closed
shut from birth was given milk by a wild ewe
who found him in her meadow. He grew to call
a ram "Father." He grazed with a herd of
sheep, knowing no other animals.*

*Then one day a jungle lion roared on a hill.
Every lamb and sheep fled, but the little lion
looked up. He thought,*

"How could I have run with sheep so long?"

Lord Rama—at daybreak in the Ayodhya palace the royal
singers clapped their hands and sang the praises of Dasaratha
and his ancestors to awaken the old King, and all the birds in
the gardens sang outside. Serving maids threw sandal powder
into warm water for Dasaratha's bath. Menservants came to
the doorway of Kausalya's bedroom, and there they set out a
golden jar of Ganga water for the King to sip. They laid out
new-woven cloth and new bright metal mirrors and fresh-cast
ornaments and many new things of good fortune and excellent virtue, so that the King would see them first thing on
awakening. So long as the Sun did not yet rise they awaited
Dasaratha.

Then golden sunbeams poured light in through the windows and the King did not appear. The serving maids entered
Kausalya's room. The Queen slept beside Dasaratha, her
hand had slipped from his. They first spoke quiet words, and
when Dasaratha did not awake they touched him, and he was
cold, and they shook like water grass in the waves.

Kausalya awoke. Queen Sumitra came running. Kaikeyi
stood at Dasaratha's feet all forlorn and crying—*Oh Love!*
The sounds of lamenting for King Dasaratha filled every cav-

ern on Earth with sorrow, and carried through the sky to the end of every direction.

The charioteer Sumantra put the King's body in an iron vat of oil. He sent out three swift horsemen to ride to the Kekaya land, to summon Bharata and Satrughna home to make the funeral.

The three horsemen rode fast. They overtook the winds. Their horses' hooves drove dents in the stones, they broke down the trees they passed near; where they crossed rivers they left them dry. They rode three black horses running abreast, running with head and neck and flying tail all in a line. They pounded through the forests haunted by bird-ghosts, they raced past brahmanas cupping their hands to drink water from Narayana's footprints at dawn. They went northwest and leapt the river whose waters turn to stone what they touch. They darted across Panchala and by Hastinapura the Elephant City, never stopping day or night. After four days a wall of dust appeared at Kekaya City, covering the mountain lakes and shrouding the sky. The sunset burned the dust red. Night came, and midnight. And the Ayodhya riders came from the dust and entered the city like thunder over a bridge in the dark.

Bharata had been asleep, but an evil dream had awakened him. In that dream he saw the ocean dry, saw the Moon fall to Earth, he saw the tusks of Dasaratha's elephants shatter, and the fires of Ayodhya go out, and saw smoke come from the hills of Kosala.

Bharata awoke in the night shaking and frightened. His grandfather Aswapati the Kekaya King was still awake. He tried to cheer Bharata with light happy music and comic plays, but the prince could not smile. Bharata's red skin was pale, his red hair was dark and damp with sweat. His throat was dry, his eyes were red as blood and he couldn't sit still.

Satrughna came to his brother and stood by him blacker than Night, and the gold bracelets on his dark arms flamed in the torchlight. Bharata said to him, "I feel terrible. Suddenly for no reason I hate life."

Satrughna said, "Someone has died but I don't know who."

Then the Ayodhya riders entered, showing no sign of sorrow. King Aswapati and his son Yudhajit rose to meet them. The riders told Bharata, "Hurry to Ayodhya."

"Rest a moment," answered Bharata. "How is my father?"

The riders said, "We cannot linger."

"How is my mother?"

"We cannot rest."

"How is Rama?"

"Do not delay. Restless fate and fortune call you home."

Bharata said, "Grandfather, give us Kekaya horses for our chariot."

"I give." The aged King Aswapati embraced Bharata and Satrughna; he smelled their heads and pressed his hands down through their hair. "Go, my children, I permit you. Tell my daughter Kaikeyi that we are all well here, give her my love, and return to me when I remember you."

Bharata's uncle Yudhajit said, "We send no gifts. We are your friends in any threat or danger. Call us if you have the smallest need. Do not waste time on the polite ceremonies of leavetaking."

Driving their chariot garnished with gold, by the fiery light of sunrise Bharata and Satrughna saw Ayodhya, and slowed their mountain horses. They looked down on her from the soft-rising hills to the north. They stopped. There was not a sound from the still city. The countryside was strangely quiet, as though Lord Shiva were walking abroad in the dawn, among the trees somewhere near.

Satrughna frowned. "The streets are empty. The doors are closed and shutters drawn against the windows. This is a sad view."

"Do you remember?" said Bharata. "In the early morning standing here we could always smell the scent of wines, and the wind would carry faint perfumes."

Satrughna said, "Our Great Father the Sun now rises and no one sings."

Bharata said, "Our homes are burnt out. Those are but their shells remaining."

They drove into Ayodhya. Their chariot wheels growled low and moaned as they passed through the Victory Gate, once guarded like the gateway into heaven. No guard stood there. No young couples drunk with Love's honey-wine came walking home from the parks at dawn.

They didn't see a living soul. Satrughna was brooding. He said, "If anyone still lives here, they ought to leave or they'll be dead by tonight."

They came up to the Ayodhya palace once flooded with

light. Bharata said, "Dread of what awaits me hides in my heart and will not go!"

They entered the palace. The doors were half open. There was rust on the hinges and nothing was seen as it had been during the King's life. Satrughna went to find Rama. Bending his head, Bharata walked slowly to his mother Kaikeyi.

Kaikeyi rose from her window seat and Bharata knelt and held her feet, then he stood and asked her, "But where is my father? Why is your golden bed empty?"

Kaikeyi said, "My son, every marriage must end in sorrow unless both man and wife die together. He has gone to the next world under the law of Time. He lives no longer, he has died."

Bharata tore off his headband and let his long hair fall. He took ashes from an incense dish and rubbed them on his brow. He said, "I take Rama for my refuge, I take Rama for my protection. But how hard to bear! What did Dasaratha say when you last saw him?"

"He said—*Who will see Rama again?*"

Bharata stood grave as the ocean and still as the sky. Smoke rose from his body. His eyes burned like red gleams of Hell's light. "Where is Rama whose soft hands brush the dust from me when I fall?"

"Your father disinherited Rama so that you could take this kingdom without a rival, and he banished him and died from the grief of parting."

"Why? Whose wife did Rama take?"

"He took no other's woman. This was done to please you."

"Whom did Rama wrong, rich or poor?"

"No one. Why are you not delighted?"

"What did Rama steal?"

"Nothing, for no crime was he banished," said Kaikeyi. "I used my two wishes. The Kosalas are yours, Ayodhya is yours. You are the King!"

"How hateful!" Bharata ran from the room.

He ran to Queen Kausalya's room. There were his friends. Kausalya and Sumitra were there; Vasishtha and Sumantra the charioteer and his brother Satrughna stood by them.

Bharata knelt before Kausalya. "Mother, we return from the Hills . . . I did not know! I'll never take it. I don't want to rule others, I don't want possessions. I know nothing. . . ."

"Enough, you are innocent." Kausalya laid her hand on his

head. "You are the one injured. No one blames you." She held him.

Sumantra said, "I left Rama in the forest. This is a bad world."

Bharata said, "The whim of a whore."

"She's your own mother," said Vasishtha.

"Not any more," said Bharata. "What good is anything without Rama?"

Satrughna said, "Lakshmana did right to go beside him."

Bharata said, "True enough."

Satrughna said, "How will father look the gods of heaven in the eye?"

Bharata said, "Death will be small comfort to him."

"Be still a moment," said Vasishtha.

Bharata asked him, "Brahmana, why did she darken our fame? We all loved her and she always said she loved us. Why does she hate us now?"

Satrughna said, "And what has she gained anyway?"

"Crushing sorrow," answered Vasishtha.

Bharata said, "Surely desire easily outruns honor."

Sumitra said, "Everything will be all right, Bharata. My son Lakshmana is with Rama; my son Satrughna is with you, we are friends."

Bharata smiled at her. "Do you think so?" He looked away. "She trapped him and killed him like a deer lured into a snare by a sweet song."

Sumantra the charioteer said, "Rama—"

"What about Rama?" asked Bharata.

"He commands you to obey your father and not to take away his authority in his old age. He is covered by the blessings of Queen Kausalya. Vasishtha blessed him; he blessed them all."

Bharata said, "Did he promise?"

Vasishtha said, "Prince Bharata, listen to me. Rama said he would go away for fourteen years. He will never break his word. We need a King."

"What for?" asked Bharata.

Vasishtha said, "In a kingless land there is no rain. Families break apart in shame. Charity cannot be kept. Kindness goes. There is no law. Then who sleeps with an open door, or finds a safe road? Bandits will invade Kosala. Disputes will arise and not be solved. There will be no justice. Our ancient stories will never more be heard."

"What is there to do?" asked Bharata.

"Take my advice," said Vasishtha. "Rule us."

"No," said Bharata. "For my part I will go to the forest and bring Rama back."

Sumantra smiled. "I'll find him for you."

Bharata said, "The King did not consult with old friends like you."

Vasishtha said again, "Be our King until Rama returns."

"Watch it!" said Bharata. "Do not sell treasures with one hand and hold back happiness with your other. Or I will move out against you."

"There is a great ocean of grief to cross," said Vasishtha. "Regret and remorse are his whirlpools and tears are his tides. Kaikeyi's wishes are his near shore, and fourteen years is his expanse, and the shrill words of the hunchback Manthara are his ravenous sharks."

Satrughna said, *"Whose words?"* He started for the door.

"Wait," said Bharata. "If Rama hears we have killed Manthara he will never look on us again."

Shrieks of crazy laughter rang through the palace, but Satrughna sat down and ignored them. Vasishtha said, "By the heavens, multitudes have censured Manthara and found no peace of mind from it! Burn the body of the King, Bharata. Do this much. Free the people; let their sorrow come out. One may fall and bear being kicked by another, but one cannot fall and bear ever so little sorrow. Sorrow deforms our thoughts and our reflections; it grows within and smothers our hearts. Sorrow has made Ayodhya unbeautiful to see; it has dishonored her. Who can live here? What is life without joy? Don't let sorrow beat down the Kosalas. Make the King's funeral and let us be done with it!"

"I don't want any part of it."

"You rightly despise the clutter of this world."

"But here I am," said Bharata. "I'll burn the dead King in Rama's name."

Over the burning ground by the Sarayu black funeral smoke hung in the air. Bharata wept like a hurt boy and Vasishtha put his arm around him. Atop the pyre Dasaratha's face still showed as if he slept, a little pale. The rest of his body was buried under flowers and under solid perfumes that began to melt. The flames kindled from the firechamber of Ayodhya then reached up and hid the King's corpse.

That burning freed Dasaratha's spirit. It let him come out

from Yama's shadowy land and get from the Moon his heavenly body, and in celestial robes take his rightful place in heaven.

Bharata said, "In my youth, Time's true nature was hidden from me, but now I see all his harmful ways. I'll never forgive, I'll never forget what my mother has done. I want to go away and never hear her name. Vasishtha, how will she be born in future lives?"

"She will never understand, never know the True," said Vasishtha. "She will doubt life while facing the Sun. She will be a mad beggar eating dirt from a skull. She will be a miser living alone then robbed by thieves. She will be a poor man with a large family in a land ruled in fear by a bad King. She will be a great teacher who forgets all his learning and shameless turns to dice and women and puts his old servants out to starve in the streets."

"What else?"

"She will not do one good deed. She will betray friends and hand them over to the King's soldiers. She will give wealth to unworthy liars and dash the hopes of poor men who look up to her trustingly. She will refuse water to thirsty travelers by lying that she has none. She will poison wells. She will be an unwelcome philosopher who quarrels painfully over points of view and she will be born again as one who listens to such talk."

"What else?"

"In this very life she will not live to see Rama return."

"Is that all?" Bharata sighed.

Vasishtha said, "I have added nothing and left out nothing. All this will be her lot—unless you forgive her, Bharata."

Bharata said, "I forgive."

Vasishtha said, "Compassion is great enough where it can have no effect. Used to accomplish something it is supreme!"

"A son comes to life from the blood of his mother's heart," said Bharata, "therefore he is dear to her."

Listen, King Rama, our Master Valmiki knows. Once tears fell on Indra as he flew in the sky, and looking up he saw Surabhi the white wishing-cow of heaven gazing past him down at the Earth and crying. Indra flew to her and asked, "What is wrong? It must be a great injustice." She replied, "Lord of Gods, I mourn my sons fallen on evil days. See the two of them below, lean and sunburned and tired from plowing." And Indra stood amazed and speechless, thinking how Surabhi's children number in millions and fill the worlds, how

though she lived in heaven and was herself the very essence
of good fortune she cried over two of them as though her
heart would break. . . .

The three widowed Queens of Ayodhya said watery prayers and bathed at the riverside. For eleven nights they slept
on the bare ground. Then they gave away gifts in Dasaratha's
name—food and drink and salt and homes, goats and cows,
cloth and gold, silver and servants. After that, Bharata
gathered his father's bones from the cold white ashes of the
funeral pyre, raised them over his head and threw them into
the Sarayu River.

That ended the mourning. At sunrise the next day the Kosalas awakened Bharata with loud shell trumpets and he went
to them and said, "Never do that again, I am not the King."

Bharata told the charioteer Sumantra, "Only the son
first-born may be King in our Solar race. I will take Rama's
place in the forest."

Sumantra first asked the elephant-god Ganesha—*Remove
the obstacles, widen the road, smooth our way.* Then he
drove Bharata out of the city, passing under the groves of the
Sarayu, under the flowers violet and gold.

Satrughna came next driving the three Queens in a chariot.
After them came nine thousand war-mounted elephants, then
six thousand chariots carrying light-handed bowmen, then
many horsemen and footsoldiers running by the roadsides
bearing shields like suns, then the wives and families of the
soldiers came last leading mule-carts and pack-animals.

The wide road to Rama! The swift-rising Sun set alight the
spear-points like a curving line of stars. The road gained
loveliness as they proceeded. It was tree-lined. There were
fair wells with resting places. There were fruit trees and orchards. The country people put flags by the roadside. They
moved on, the people came all following Bharata, like the
swelling high tide of the sea rolling on, like the entire Earth in
human form.

They halted in grand tent-cities, and after three easy days
they came to the first Sala trees of Guha's forest and stood
on the far border of Kosala. The Sun hung aslant and low; it
was the hour of evening.

Hidden within the Secret Forest, Guha looked out at them.
From Sumantra's chariot flew the flag of the Kosalas, a green

ebony tree shining on silver. Guha could see no end to all
those people.

He sat down and cleared a flat space with the edge of his
hand. He took nine bird bones from a leather bag and shook
them in his hands three times saying, "Rama is my friend,
who is Bharata?"

He threw his fortune. The bones said, "Don't hinder him."

While the Kosalas made their camp, Bharata and Satrughna came to the ocean-going Ganga and offered her clear
cool water to their father, so that in heaven Dasaratha's spirit
was bright-shining with pleasure. Bharata bathed in Ganga
and was no longer tired. He drank her holy water and glad-
dened his heart. Then he sat thinking how to make Rama
come back, sitting under the same wide-spreading tree where
Rama had been. That old tree threw out his heavy arms in
joy to the sunset starry sky above, and Bharata said quietly,
"From here, I bow to Rama in the forest."

There Guha met him bringing bread and butter and honey.
Bharata asked, "Where is Rama? Do you know where he
went?"

"All those people," said Guha.

"We want him back," said Bharata.

Satrughna said, "Dasaratha had died, now Rama is our
king."

Little whistles and barks sounded from the dark forest
around them. Guha grinned. "They've heard you. The bird
people are singing of your fame, the deer praise you. They
say you are an unclouded sky, beautiful in the daytime, beautiful at night. They call you a true man, a real friend, they
wonder if there is anyone else like you on Earth, who would
give back a kingdom. . . ."

Guha clapped his hands and torches gleamed into light and
came carried by Guha's men, out from the trees. "I have
hundreds of fisher-boats hidden along the river," said Guha.
"Leave your chariots here, tomorrow I will take you and
your animals all downstream to Bharadwaja." Guha took a
torch. "See, under this great and ancient tree the hard rough
grass still shows where it was pressed by Rama's limbs. Look,
here are silk threads pulled from Sita's robe. Here slept
Sumantra, here Lakshmana sat."

"It seems incredible to me," said Bharata. "Oh, had I not
gone to Kekaya. . . ."

"No, no," said Guha. "Time does what he must, powered
by the past. When Time does us wrong, we are lucky just to

live on and get another chance at him, and what harm did you intend?"

"Then," said Bharata, "surely if Time will help me, Rama cannot long refuse to return."

The Sun had gambled away all his splendor, and Night spread over Earth. Then as a smoldering tree already burned by forest fire will show only by night that it still burns, so Bharata sighed in the dark.

The Sandals

I see two birds on the same branch;
One eats the sweet fruit,
One looks on sadly.

The first bird wonders—
In what prison does he live?

The second marvels—
How can he rejoice?

With noise and shouting Guha's men ferried the Kosalas down the River Ganga, showing off with their boats in fancy formations, and the Kosalas who could not wait their turn floated among the boats hanging onto pitchers that were upside down in the water and full of air, and the elephants swam along like islands come to life. Guha himself took Bharata and Satrughna and the three Queens on board a serpent-prowed boat trimmed in gold and hung with bells, and steered them down to where Ganga's white waters met the deep dark Yamuna with a roar.

When all the Kosalas had been landed, the hunter-men and Guha swept back upstream in their boats and left them there. Bharata kept the Kosalas back and went alone on foot into Bharadwaja's hermitage, plainly dressed in a single robe and unarmed.

Bharadwaja met him with water to drink and water for foot-washing. They sat together and Bharadwaja asked, "How is the city of Fair Ayodhya?"

Bharata said, "Brahmana, are you well? I hope your fires burn as you want them to. You do not ask about my father."

Bharadwaja replied, "I know the King is dead."

"The King is alive," said Bharata. "The King is Rama. I want to get him and bring him home."

99

Bharadwaja smiled. "Do I not know you, young prince? But why have you left your people behind you at the riverside?"

"They are thousands," answered Bharata. "I have soldiers and women and children. They would make holes in the ground here, and hurt your trees, and put mud in your water."

"Have them unpack and bring them here for dinner."

Bharata looked around, and saw only the woodlands around the little clearing, and Bharadwaja's small hut standing alone by a trickling stream. "I have been entertained by water and the sight of you. By your words have you well received us all."

"But you are too easily pleased," said Bharadwaja. "Tell them to come. I invite you all."

Bharata walked back to the river and Bharadwaja went into his house and sat by his fire. There nodding his head he sipped water from his hand three times, and rubbed it on his lips and said—*I will entertain my guests.*

Down from heaven came the architect Viswakarman. He stood in the center of Bharadwaja's clearing and unfurled his great wings and swept them through the air. He turned; he moved his hands, and the trees moved back, the clearing grew. He built a dream, he made a garden where new wonders grew. Viswakarman knows all worlds. His arms shaped the air; he spoke names.

The south winds blew scented with sandalwood. The rivers of the world came there and ran with water and wines and milk and sugar syrup, ran through blue grass, among the coral trees brought from the wishing-forests of the Treasure-Lord. Heavenly Gandharvas played music and Apsarasas danced. Flowers fell from the air. Tree spirits were tumblers and dwarves, and the vines of the forest were beautiful women all dressed in flowers. Food appeared and buildings arose.

Viswakarman folded his arms and closed his wings and was gone, and the Kosalas entered what had been Bharadwaja's poor hermitage. Nagas in human forms met them and led aside their horses and elephants. The Kosala grooms forgot their animals and the animals forgot them sooner. Only Sumantra the charioteer would let no one else comb his red horses.

A Naga girl waited for each soldier, took his bow, untied his armor and fed him. The spirits of the air materialized and poured out drinks; the Gandharvas played dances; the Ayodhya warriors laughed and talked.

That was Bharadwaja's welcome. The Kosalas said—*Peace be to Bharata. Great happiness to the recluse Bharadwaja. We are within a vision of heaven. Why retreat, why advance, why move?*

So entertained like gods the Kosalas passed the night in good cheer. They ate and drank all they could wish for. They fell asleep smiling in dreams.

Then, while they slept, the beings and spirits who had worked for their banquet went back to where they had come from. The stray fruits half-eaten, the heavenly flowers scattered and crushed underfoot, the goblets and bright dishes all vanished, and Bharadwaja's grove became again as it was before.

Bharata awoke early while the others were still sound asleep and went to the door of Bharadwaja's hut. Bharadwaja came out and asked, "Were you pleased?"

Bharata answered, "How wonderful it was! I salute you. I think . . . I begin to learn." Bharata looked around at the Kosalas, some of them just beginning to stir, the rest stretched out sleeping like the dead. "I bow to you. We will go on. Look after us with a friendly eye."

Bharadwaja said, "Set alone like a colorful jewel in the empty forest is Chitrakuta Hill beautiful to behold. Rama lives there, my child. A river flowing in waves bends around that hill, and part way up the high forest slopes above the river is Rama's house . . . but introduce me to your mothers, let me meet them before you go, I would like that."

Bharata went to where his brother slept. "Get up, Satrughna, why do you sleep?"

Satrughna instantly arose and Bharata said, "Bring Queen Kausalya, and Sumitra and Kaikeyi."

Satrughna and Bharata and the three Queens stood before the hermit Bharadwaja. Bharata said, "This is Kausalya, she is Rama's mother."

Kausalya knelt and touched Bharadwaja's feet. He said to her, "Rama is very strong; he is the desired guest of the hills and woods, and the reasons for many things are lost in Time."

Bharata said, "This is Queen Sumitra."

"She is ever a kind friend," said Bharadwaja. He smiled and took Sumitra's hands in his. "Friendliness and love and protection, my Lady, I call that good, very good!"

Kaikeyi hesitated. Then looking down at the ground she walked once round Bharadwaja, and stopped, and at last looked up into his eyes.

Bharadwaja said, "No one must blame you, those are my words. Sending Rama to the forest will truly be for the great good of all the worlds, and what you have done will bring happiness to every man and joy to heaven. I bless you, Kaikeyi, you have done no wrong."

Kaikeyi smiled, and her son Bharata put his red arm around her shoulders and drew her close to him. Then Bharadwaja turned and bent his head to enter his small house again.

The Kosalas departed from Bharadwaja's retreat and left behind them Ganga the Queen of Rivers, and moved slowly toward Chitrakuta.

The springtime trees of Chitra were perfect as a scene imagined from a storybook. They grew short and tall, thin and spreading, leafy and open. Their leaves were grass-green, blue-green, yellow-green, dark green, light green, crimson and brown and yellow, glossy and dull, smooth and sticky, round and pointed like fingers, fluttering and still. The barks of the trees were rough and smooth and furry, grey and white and green and black, cool and warm. The flowers grew in bunches or grew apart; they were red, yellow, white, pink and honey-colored; they were green and blue and purple and orange and silver and gold and lavender; they were large and small. All among the trees were tapering vines and slender creepers, rushes and canes and reeds, ferns and shrubs and grasses and orchids and bamboo and moss.

There grew the climbers whose leaves close in the rain, and the trees that burst into blossom at a woman's touch, and the water lilies that open when deep thunder rolls through the blue rainclouds across heaven above. And to Lakshmana all these plants surrendered the supplies of a rich caravan. He got from them needles and thread and cloth, food and cords and soap, cups and jars and medicine.

> *These trees in flower*
> *Have been engarlanded by the gods.*
> *This forest is a Garden,*
> *This Hill an ornament of Earth.*

Rama loved the deep forest. One early morning he and Sita went for a walk above their house, by wild rose trees and shady lilac. Hill flowers carpeted the meadows. Sparrows who lived only on rainwater sang. From the soil the trees had drawn ores and minerals up through their roots, so that on their trunks and branches there were gleaming streaks of gold and quicksilver, and bands of blood-red ruby dust glinting from right within the bark.

Sita walked holding Rama's hard arm that was her pillow at night. With her walk Sita rebuked the wavy gait of swans. Wherever she went, Sita of slender waist was always at home in Rama's heart, sheltered by his love, as the path they followed was sheltered over by the trees.

They walked along a stream, past waterfalls and little islands. The water ran through the feet of herons and through the drinking pools of deer, and water tumbled over the rapids spilling like pearls and rolling away.

Rama and Sita swam in the river, then they climbed onto the breast of Chitrakuta. There Rama fell asleep, his head on Sita's lap while she sat back against a tree and stroked his hair.

While Rama slept, a black crow flew at Sita. She frightened him off with a stone. Rama awoke, looked up and saw her angry, trying to push back the robe that had slipped from her shoulder, her face glowing and her lips trembling. Rama smiled at her and sighed, and went back to sleep. But the crow returned. He attacked Sita, beat his wings against her breast and tore her flesh with his sharp claws.

Her blood fell on Rama and she cried out for him. Rama instantly awoke and saw the crow with red claws swiftly dart down inside the Earth. Rama put the Brahma Weapon on a grassblade and threw it after the crow. The blade burned with fire round its tip, and it pursued the crow wherever he flew. It chased him through all the heavens and under all the worlds and back to Earth. The gods shut heaven's doors against the crow and the saints looked away when he asked their protection. Even Hell was locked.

So the crow flew to Rama and said, "I find no other refuge against him," and bowed at Rama's feet.

"Surrender a part of your body for the weapon to hit," said Rama, "and I will protect your life."

The crow surrendered his right eye, and that eye broke from his face like shattered glass and he saved himself. The crow flew away and Rama comforted Sita.

Returning home they stopped to rest on a ledge by the mouth of a red-stone cave. Sita embraced Rama like a vine twined round a tree. Rama reached down and touched the red dust, and put a mark on Sita's brow with his fingertip.

Then they walked on downhill together. A monkey suddenly ran up a tree right beside Sita, and she jumped into Rama's arms in fright. He held her and her red brow-mark was printed on Rama's broad green chest. Sita was very happy and would not let Rama wipe it off.

When they came near their house they met Lakshmana bringing a black deer home from the hunt. Sita made wild wheat bread and Rama gathered honey. They ate under a golden vine by a clear silvery spring, and the woodpeckers tapped in the trees.

The Kosalas caught sight of lovely Chitra Hill arising out of the Earth. They all had flowers in their hair like men from the south. They waited by a stream while Bharata went on alone up the hill.

Bharata found a trail that had been marked. He saw white smoke in the air ahead of him. Bark garments were hanging out to dry on the branches of a tree. By the path were stacks of firewood. Bharata walked out into a clearing on the mountainside and saw Rama standing by his house.

Rama stood very still, with matted hair and dressed in black deerskin. Bharata approached and knelt before Rama. He looked up and said, "Oh Arya . . . noble Rama. . . ."

Rama bent over and raised Bharata. "What is it? Why have you come here?"

"Our father who enjoyed all the world is dead."

When they heard that, Rama and Lakshmana and Sita took some cakes down to the river, threw some of them into the water and put the rest on the grass. Rama held water in his hands—*May this reach you, may it be so.*

Then they returned, and Rama sat with Bharata near their house. All the Kosalas quietly approached and watched them sitting together and wondered, "What will Bharata say to him?"

Bharata raised his hand and spoke. "Rama, peace to you: I decline the ownership and possession of the Kosala kingdom. We have no King. Return to Ayodhya with these people, I will replace you here."

Rama said, "I think a father may divide his inheritance as he pleases, and surely his sons will obey him. Bharata, a man's unbroken word is like a bowl of clear glass; once shattered, no one can put it back as it was by any art. I must do what I said I would do, stay here for fourteen years."

Bharata said, "Your absence already seems unbearably long. Father died soon after you left. Now I come seeking you. A wife ought to love her husband more than even a thousand fine sons. Gentle Sita deserves to live in a palace. What unbeautiful thing has she ever done? The eldest son must be King. Father died desiring you to be happy, remembering you."

Rama said, "Keeping a given word, Bharata . . . that is more important than Kosala customs. I have no time for kingdom, Bharata. I have no time for any useless thing. It is not for me to do the work of others. Our father Dasaratha was a wall of Dharma like a mountain. Death is at last found to be a part of all life, and never can we escape it, and Death does not change a promise made. At the end of life, when this body is burned, a man takes Brahma's way if he has lived well; he takes a good way well-wrought by men of the past, and looking back at his family let him not see foolish sons set aside his last wishes."

Bharata said, "Come home. Men lose their sense as their Death approaches. Rama, why must men suffer ignorance? Ignorance will surely destroy a father's many kindnesses and a mother's pains. Why do we waste our food to set out offerings for the dead? Do the dead eat? Who do we feed? Small animals eat it all. Such blind rules are wrong, Rama. Engage your soul in happiness. Men are born for joy. Do not make ease your guide and do not follow discomfort. Do right deeds, forget to always say the right words. In land after land, one may find wives and meet friends. But I can now never get another brother."

Rama said, "The first betrayal may be easy or it may be hard, but after the first betrayal then the others soon follow. The heart, Bharata . . . keep note of your heart and don't stifle it. There lives the soul, clear, never stained, watching all we do or think to do, so let a man be still and find his heart. That is the only safe rescue. What use is a castle or a palace or a great stone fortress that is no defense against Time? Since we have come together, our separation some day is certain. While we are together as two men during this lifetime, let us keep the truth."

Bharata said, "It is true, that nights gone by do not return, and every day shortens our lives. But I think some things endure. Surely love endures beyond our brief lives. All the Ayodhya Kings have loved their City. Our fathers have left Ayodhya shining pure white in her fame and glory. Now our City is miserable; she is an unhappy lake without a guardian serpent, unprotected, ruined, drifting and lost as an abandoned ship on the seas."

Rama said, "Death keeps a man company and after going with him a long way as his dear friend, Death returns with his soul. Man suffers scars and wounds, his hair turns grey, his strength departs and his memory flees; he seems not to know even his own children. Life is passing as a river ever flowing away, never still, never returning. Life is changeable as the flashing lightning, a pattern of as little meaning, and impermanent. Where can one live long? Life is bright and colored for a passing moment like the sunset. Then it is gone and who can prevent it going? Therefore, Bharata, once in this perilous body deplore your own condition. Mourn your own self and do not lament anything else."

Bharata said, "Oh Rama, kingdoms wash over you, but you are calm. You know the mysterious soul and the life where he swims. The Sun of our father's life first grew milder and then set, its journey done, and Night begins her course. Night is starless then, and then is water frozen to ice, and our City is like a fair woman forsaken. I came to see you, ask of me whatever will please you."

Rama said, "You say you love me, will you not wait?"

"Yes."

"That will make me very happy, Bharata."

When the Kosalas knew that Rama would stay in the forest, they were proud and sad. They sat on the Earth and said—*Well said! Well spoken! We call that excellent, well done, well done!*

Bharata said, "Give me your sandals."

Rama took off his wooden-soled sandals that had colored flowers painted on them.

Bharata took them. "Rama, you are the true King. I will

go back, I will rule Kosala in trust for you for fourteen years, and your sandals will be on the throne. If I do not see you on the first day after those fourteen years I'll walk into a fire and die."

Bharata retraced his steps. In Kosala he put the sandals on the head of the King's own lucky elephant. Satrughna brought the royal throne out from Ayodhya and put it in the little village of Nandigrama nearby. Vasishtha brought all the signs of royalty to Nandigrama, and there Bharata led the elephant.

Bharata put Rama's shoes on the red and gold Ayodhya throne. Over them spread the gold-ribbed white silk umbrella and the white yak-tail fan of silver and emerald. Bharata and Satrughna put on barkcloth and sat at the foot of the throne.

Every day the ministers and noblemen of Kosala came out from Ayodhya all in bark like hermits. They would bow to Rama's shoes as to a King. The warriors were dressed like holy wanderers seeking for the Lord somewhere, begging their way. Rama's sandals lay quiet if justice was done before the throne, but if any case was wrongly judged the sandals swiftly beat together their loud wooden soles.

In Ayodhya heralds furled the bright silk flags. For fourteen years there was silence in Fair Ayodhya and no sound of mirth or learning. Many days the Sun was clouded because of heaven's dark-hearted sorrow. Musicians unstrung their lutes and played no music, because there was no music in the forest where Rama was. The Kosalas took the wheels off their chariots and walked where they had to go, because Rama had no chariot and had to walk in the woods. The Ayodhya women alone still wore flowers and fine clothes and ornaments, because Sita went to the forest dressed in fashion. The gardeners kept their gardens of Ayodhya alive and watered the flowers in the hanging gardens on the hillside leading to the empty royal palace.

Ayodhya was like the pools by the seashore when the tide is withdrawn. Where once the waves had foamed and thundered on the stones, now in the little ponds were only tiny silent ripples born from a gentle wind from the sea. She was like a mare slain in war; now dead, yet an instant before alive and strong and in motion and attacking.

The mate of a young bull will not eat grass without him beside her. In summer a stream will dry away. Her water will turn warm, her animals will be lean and her fish will die. In winter her floods will drown small creatures. After many years a bamboo will flower once and then die.

We may be the playthings of Fate. We cannot breathe without taking life. As we talk here, we are ourselves the cause of the deaths of countless little lives. We have surely let old bodies go many times, as though changing from old clothes into new ones. We may have died more times in the past than all the times we have fallen asleep since being born twelve years ago.

Await the time. What use is impatience?

Rama went barefoot for the rest of his exile. He thought Chitrakuta still too close to Ayodhya. One morning soon after Bharata had come and gone, Rama and Sita and Lakshmana set out towards the Vindhya Hills, south into the forests. Late in the day they came to a large lake fed by springs, with shores of soft white sands shaded by trees.

There were water-flowers, red and yellow and blue, and green water-leaves, and plump silver fish swimming, all spread out like an elephant blanket of many colors. There were cranes and fisherbirds and floating tortoises, and swans and frogs and pink geese. Rama and Sita and Lakshmana stopped and they could hear from within the water the sound of singing and of music. They heard laughter and drums, the ringing of ankle-bells and the pouring of wines, but the lake looked clear and they saw no one.

They entered a glade of green grass, and saw a house and an old couple sitting by it, and in the late sunlight the glow of Brahma power stood out as a halo around the old people. That was the home of Atri, one of the seven oldest saints in the three worlds, and his wife Anasuya. That is their earthly home; in heaven Atri lives in one of the seven lights of the Bear in the sky.

Atri welcomed Rama and Lakshmana, and Anasuya smiled and rose and took Sita aside. Rama asked, "What is that wonderful lake we passed?"

Atri replied, "That is Five-Apsarasa-Lake. Long ago the

hermit Mandakarni stood there beside a little rain puddle and lived only on air. The longer he did that, the larger the water grew. He stood on the edge of a lake. Indra looked down from Heaven and saw that Mandakarni would soon drown the Earth. Indra sent five beautiful Apsarasas to stop him. Mandakarni saw the five dancing girls all lively as lightning and he changed his life. He married them all and made an invisible home within the lakewater. He had won enough merit to keep himself young forever. Mandakarni lives happily there and his five wives do everything to please him. When they drink and feast and dance we may hear their dancing-bells and sweet songs, and sometimes their fair-winged words, and even catch the scent of their five celestial perfumes."

Anasuya sat apart with Sita. Anasuya was very old; her hair was wispy white and her body shook with age like a leaf in the wind. She said, "Sita, with you Rama may have some pleasure in the forest."

Sita said, "He is my man."

"What shall I do for you?" asked Anasuya, whose name means Kindness. "Take a gift to please me." Anasuya opened a box and from it she gave Sita a never-fading garland of rare loveliness, and put it over Sita's head next to Guha's pink shell necklace. Then Anasuya gave Sita gold and silver ornaments that never tarnished and a jar of sandalwood cream that never emptied.

Sita took the ornaments and put aside some of her former ones she had worn from Ayodhya, and said, "These are very beautiful." Sita was surprised and smiling.

Anasuya said, "They will keep you beautiful forever. Oh Sita, look, the Sun has set. By the last rays of daylight the smoke rising from our fire is colored red. Open trees appear dense with leaves, nothing can be seen at a distance, and the hermitage deer lie by the altars. Night crested by stars and robed in moonlight has come, and day has gone from the sky and the Earth. Stay with us tonight, dear Sita."

The next day Rama and Lakshmana, and Sita wearing those friendly presents, went on their way. They went west and a little south, walking the length of the Vindhya Hills after climbing their northern slopes. There Lakshmana found many places to build a home. They would live in one place for three months or eight months or a year, and then would move on to another place. They did this until thirteen years of Rama's exile had passed away, and it was late in the fourteenth and last springtime.

THIS ENDS THE
SECOND BOOK OF AYODHYA
HERE BEGINS THE FOREST BOOK

PART TWO

SITA'S RESCUE

OM!
I bow to Lord Rama,
To Sita of beautiful fortune;
I salute Hanuman the monkey,
And the Goddess Saraswati:
JAYA!
Victory!

Dandaka Forest

It was almost the fourteenth summer when Rama and Sita
and Lakshmana crossed over the Vindhya Hills and began to
walk down the southern slopes. One evening after walking far
they entered a large grove of trees, and many clear streams
crossed the path with their branches of water. There was
woodsmoke on the air, and Rama said, "We are coming to
the home of Agastya, the brahmana who lowered the
Vindhya Hills, destroyed two demons and settled here."

Sita asked, "How did he do that?"

Rama answered, "Agastya is a small man, but what is impossible for even the gods he can do easily."

Listen, Sita—

Long ago, the Vindhya Hills were jealous of the Himalya,
and in envy Vindhya began to grow higher and higher.
Vindhya told the Sun and Moon, "Circle around me now, for
I am the new center of the world!"

Sun and Moon would not do that. They kept going around
the golden hill Meru in the Himalya. But Vindhya rose until
his peaks blocked the skies. Surya the Sun could not pass to
the south. The stars and Moon were blocked and rainclouds
and Wind could not go where they wanted.

Agastya came walking from the north. He got to the
Vindhya foothills and saw how Vindhya had grown impassable. There were no trails and the hills were lost in cold
clouds. Agastya asked Vindhya, "Best of mountains, I must
go south for awhile. Let me go by and come back again."

Vindhya said, "Pass, brahmana." Vindhya bowed low to
Agastya, and these hills decreased to their present height, well
below the sky-paths.

Agastya said, "Don't rise again till I cross you coming
back." Then he settled here, south of the hilltops, and he has

never yet gone back north, and Vindhya obeys him. Vindhya still waits for Agastya faithfully, with his head bent low.

Then men could cross these hills and travel here, but they were hunted by two demon brothers named Vatapi and Ilwala. Ilwala took the form of a brahmana, and speaking refined language he invited anyone he met to eat with him, and led his guest up to a little cottage by the edge of a wood.

Inside in the kitchen Vatapi took the form of a ram and Ilwala cooked his brother and served him outside, and when the guest had eaten the ram Ilwala would say—*Come out shouting!* Then Vatapi bellowing like a ram would tear his way out from the traveler's body and kill him, and Vatapi and Ilwala would drain and drink the corpse's blood.

In that way they destroyed nine thousand men. Then one evening Ilwala met Agastya and brought him home and served him dinner. Small as he was, Agastya ate up every shred of the roast mutton, and sat back smacking his lips and smiling.

Ilwala facing him took a deep breath and said—*Come out. Come out shouting!*

Nothing happened. Agastya washed his hands in a bowl of water and looked at Ilwala. "Beware of the Dharma-appetite," said Agastya. "I have digested your brother. I have sent him to Death as my delicious well-cooked dinner."

Ilwala's fingernails grew into blue poisoned claws. He leapt at Agastya. But with one fiery look from his eyes Agastya burned him dead as he jumped. He burned him with a glance that flashed real fire and real flames.

"We have met woods-dwellers before," said Rama, "but there is no one else like Agastya. North lives Lord Shiva, north are the Himalya hills, and Mount Meru the center of the world, and Kailasa Hill of silver, and all manner of weight, and Agastya alone by living here in the south keeps Earth from tipping over. He is very powerful, and the heaviest person alive."

Rama said, "Lakshmana, go ahead alone and greet Agastya and tell him we are here."

Lakshmana found Agastya clad in bark sheets tied with a belt of vines, sitting on cut holy grass that was blue as lapis stone, his feet crossed and tucked up over his knees as though he were warding away some evil. Lakshmana said, "Command Rama and Sita what to do next."

"I have been thinking of Rama in my mind," Agastya looked keenly at Lakshmana. "After a long time, by good fortune Rama has come to see me. Where is he? Let him enter my home, why have you not brought him?"

Rama and Sita walked past the flat stones where Naga Kings of the underworlds and gods of heaven would come to sit and talk with Agastya. Agastya rose and greeted them and said, "Sit and eat supper with me. The host who won't feed his friends will eat his own flesh in the next world, just like a false witness." He served Rama and Lakshmana and Sita a supper of edible flowers and bulbs that left them with no slightest thought of hunger.

When they had eaten, Agastya said, "Rama, let me see your bow."

Rama held out to him the bow he had brought from Ayodhya to use in the forest. Agastya glanced at it and set it aside. He said, "It is flawed, because the man who made it was at that time engaged in an affair with another man's wife and his mind was ill at ease."

Agastya's house was nearby. From within it Agastya brought out a long bow and a covered quiver, and gave Rama the bow. That bow was backed with diamonds and curving golden plates. Its belly was smooth and painted with colors like Indra's Bow of Rain. It was covered with gold on its tips and its bowstring was unbreakable.

Then Agastya opened the quiver and took out from it all that it held: two arrows made from long grass stalks, and vaned with vulture feathers, one bladed with brass, and the other with silver. He gave the silver one to Lakshmana and the brass one to Rama.

Agastya said, "Rama of the war-chariots, take from me this sweet-sounding bow in exchange for your old one, and take this arrow. One day I found these things in the forest. I think they have fallen from heaven, perhaps during the confusion of Ravana's attack many years ago. This bow will better bear the weight of those weapons Viswamitra taught you. The blades of these arrows have never needed to be polished or sharpened, and so I think they may be infallible, shot by the right person. . . ."

The evening deepened into night and Lakshmana made a fire. Agastya said, "Rama, round my home on every side all the waters are clear. Live here with me. Harmless deer haunt this forest, bewitching people by their beauty. Aside from that, there is no menace here."

Rama, said, "Lakshmana would hunt those trusting deer for us to eat. That would pain you, we cannot stay."

In the morning Agastya led Rama out onto a spur of the mountains, high on the hillside looking south. Below them the Vindhya Hills ended and the thirsty dry jungles of Dandaka Forest reached out to the south as far as they could see over the land.

"We are far from Lanka," said Agastya, "but the edge of Dandaka is the frontier of the Rakshasa kingdom on Earth. For the most part Dandaka is a huge wasteland. It knows no master but Ravana. Whoever goes down there must be himself his own protection. Oh Rama, Ravana the Demon King believes he owns the universe; what are men to him? Pleasures distract him and he scorns men as but his food, weak and worthless. Men live surrounded by chance and danger and they cannot tell right from wrong. Their lives are short and miserable. They are prey to hunger and thirst, disease and old age. Unending evils overwhelm them. Behold Man, ignorant of his own ways in the world—now merrily drinking and dancing, now blindly weeping all in tears.

"Fourteen thousand Rakshasa veterans garrison Dandaka, commanded by the demon general Khara. Away to the south they have an army station in a thistle grove, and watchtowers of stone around it. And in the jungle Gandharva sentinels sent by the gods watch in the trees. Serpents arch and bend up from underground holes, guards for the Water Lord Varuna. And whirling and sparkling in the night are the Yakshas, placed as sentries by the Treasure King Vaishravana. Every god fears that Ravana may yet move farther against him, and send demons to enforce his evil empire."

Rama said, "I did not know that there was anywhere on this Earth that Rama and Lakshmana could not freely go."

Agastya said, "Strike back at him."

Rama smiled. "I still have a year to wander." He turned and looked behind him at Agastya's hermitage. That grove of trees and little house could remove any weariness of body or heart. No Rakshasa could enter there.

Agastya said, "There are still a few pleasant spots here and there in Dandaka, but for the rest it is infested by blood-drinking demons. Be careful, especially at night. Don't let the Rakshasas surprise you and they will not win. If you meet them, prevent them as you go." Agastya embraced Rama.

"That is the path. I use it sometimes, for a little way, to gather sticks. <u>Rama, demons do not love men, therefore men must love each other</u>."

Rama and Sita and Lakshmana, with their one new bow and two new arrows given by Agastya and with their arrows from Ayodhya, went downhill into Dandaka. The morning Sun, like a man newly rich, shone too proud over the forest. They left behind Vindhya of a thousand summits with his caves of lions and falling fountains, and his crystal rivers laughing aloud as they flowed down his sides.

The trees of Dandaka were like columns of wood and their branches were twisted like the crooked hearts of evil men. Their leaves were brittle and dry. The air was wavy and hot; there was a hot wind, and huge hot boulders threw back the heat, and curled shreds of bark fallen to the forest floor rustled as the Sun got hotter.

All Dandaka was creaking in the heat, warning away men. The ground was uneven, trackless and deserted, overgrown with hard red burr-bushes and brush that cried out underfoot. Every pond that Rama and Lakshmana and Sita saw was encircled with wavy lines and blackened grasses that showed how the water had receded. The wind blew in gusts and they heard screams from the lines of dead whistling canes bent down in the wind. Dandaka stretched before them, fearsome and wild and wide.

Past stumps and trunks Lakshmana led them on into that hair-raising wilderness, and Dandaka grew deeper and denser and filled with noisy chiming crickets, and vultures sat on bare branches. Then at noon they saw the eighty-four thousand little Valakhilya saints of the wood. They were people smaller than a thumbnail, floating in the air, drinking in sunbeams, looking like motes of dust in the Sun.

They spoke to Rama and said, "Oh child, we are meek and unassuming. Here it is dreadful and lonely. It is a sadness to live here. Rakshasas prowl for flesh by night. They overshadow the darkness as though they would crush the mountains down. We must endure demons and submit to them. We have seen mountains of bones from the victims they have slaughtered, white bones, Rama, white bones. . . ."

Rama said, "Let me just walk on, through this forest. Give me your permission to see who will stop me."

"We see your strength," said the Valakhilyas. "Free this ancient forest, deliver us from the Night-Wanderers."

Rama answered the little saints. "I have strayed from the

Dharma of warriors if this has happened while I was near you."

The Valas said, "We hide from Rakshasas of Lanka walking abroad through Dandaka, in form like hideous charred corpses from some cremation ground. They'll rush at you, Rama. They will hit you from behind with unfair weapons."

Lakshmana said, "If they attack us by day or by night we will hunt them down and kill them all."

The Valas said, "Oh Lakshmana and Rama like the Moon, they cannot bear you. More than anyone they will resent you; go on your way and be on your guard." The Valakhilyas clustered in the air. "Oh Rama, we are peaceful. We don't know . . . we think . . . we think war is better than fear, if you will fight it for us. . . ."

Rama and Sita and Lakshmana left the Valakhilyas and went along south for awhile, and Sita said, "We are not forest people. Do not carry war with you; in Ayodhya once again become a warrior. Don't let desire make you do wrong, do not kill demons without cause for war. I have heard that Lord Indra, when he envies the merit won by an ascetic, will take on the guise of a warrior, and go into the forest, and leave his fine sword with the hermit for safekeeping, and go away. So the ascetic will keep by him a sword sharpened only to kill men. Then he will begin to carry it with him when going from home. Then he will one day draw it. He will kill."

Rama said, "I won't start any war."

"How can you tell?" asked Sita. "Discard Agastya's arrows. After all these years we do not need them to hunt our food, and they are meant only for killing demons. Do not carry war with you, or by small degrees your mind will alter."

Rama said, "Princess, war is within us, it's nothing outside. No warrior neglects his weapons. He never gives them up. It is a shame to me that those saints must seek my protection that should be theirs without asking. Sita, while he may a warrior like other men enjoys peace, but misfortune and peril make him flame up in anger and resist."

"How can you tell what is right?" asked Sita. "You are only doing what you like."

Rama said, "Dharma leads to happiness, but happiness cannot lead to Dharma. There is some reason for all this. The Valakhilyas have great power, yet they have done nothing against Ravana. The Demon King must surely have some strong defense that can't be broken by their merit, or they could all by themselves easily destroy all Khara's soldiers and suffer no loss doing it."

"Who are those tiny people?" asked Sita.

"No one remembers when they were born," said Rama. "They float through the air all together, like a cloud formed from streaks of light, and once by just a little of their power they created the King of Birds Garuda."

Sita asked, "How was Garuda born?"

Rama said, "Garuda is the mount of Narayana, and he lives with Narayana in a great heaven far above the realm of Indra and the lesser gods. He carries Lord Narayana on his back and never tires."

Listen—

Kashyapa is like Atri. He is another of the seven sages of old who live in the constellation of the Bear. The first Indra and six of the gods were his children. Their mother Aditi then retreated into the infinite heavens, she is the goddess of the unbounded Universe that goes on and on, free forever.

Kashyapa took two other wives and planned a sacrifice so they would bear him sons. Indra helped him prepare and offered to bring firewood, and the Valakhilya saints said they would do the same.

So Indra was flying in the air carrying great loads of wood. He looked down and saw all the thousands of Valakhilyas walking on the ground and staggering under the weight of one dry leaf, dragging it around the water pooled in a cow's hoofprint. Lord Indra laughed at them and flew by. The little Valas saw his shadow and looked up and said to one another—*He won't help. He wouldn't help us!*

The Valas pulled their leaf aside and crumbled it and lit it afire right where they were, and sang—*Let him come. Let a better Indra come!*

Indra could hear them chanting. He fled to Kashyapa and said, "The Valakhilyas will replace me with another King of Heaven. I take your protection."

"No fear," said Kashyapa. Kashyapa found the Valas humming songs over their smoking leaf. He told them, "Success."

They glittered with pleasure—*As you say, as you say.*

Kashyapa said, "Do not make another Indra, but make someone else instead."

Very well Sir. The leaf was all burned. From its ashes the

Valakhilyas took two seeds. *For your wives. Sons for you then.*

Kashyapa went home. He told Indra, "Do not mock humble people." He gave a seed to his wife Vinata and a seed to his wife Kadru, and they swallowed them. Then Kashyapa left home and went away to be alone by himself in the hills.

A year later Vinata gave birth to two eggs and Kadru gave birth to a thousand eggs. They put each egg into its own jar of warm butter. They put the jars outside in the sunshine and rain, in the day and night. Time went by. After five hundred years all of Kadru's thousand eggs hatched into baby Nagas, but Vinata's two sons were still in their shells.

Vinata could not bear to wait any longer. She opened one of her jars and took out the egg inside and cracked its shell. Inside she found her son Aruna, alive but not fully formed. He had no legs and his whole body was translucent. Aruna told his mother not to disturb her other son for another five hundred years. Then he flew away up into the sky. He became the charioteer of Surya the Sun. The light of dawn shines right through Aruna's skin and bones, and so the dawn is red, as he first drives the Sun's chariot each morning on its way.

Vinata left her second child alone to hatch. But Kadru thought that she was better than Vinata because she had so many more sons, and they were already born. So Kadru made a bet and cheated to win it. Long ago the Ocean was churned, and changed from milk into saltwater. Many things were created from that churning, and one was the King of Horses named Uchchaih-sravas, an all-white stallion. He belonged to Indra but during those years he could come to graze on the Earth, and Kadru and Vinata often saw him standing on a hill.

Kadru bet Vinata that the horse was not all-white, and each one agreed to become the slave of the other if she lost the bet. Kadru then made her thousand babies change into black hairs and hide in that horse's tail, and Vinata lost her freedom.

Garuda was born from that second egg. He struggled out of his shell and began soaking up the sunshine. He grew into a giant within a few moments of his birth. Garuda was a huge eagle, with golden feathers on his body and brilliant red ones on his wings. He had the head and wings and talons of an eagle, but he also had the arms and hands of a man, and his torso was a man's though covered with gold feathers.

Garuda looked around with his round yellow eyes. He saw that his mother Vinata did all the drudgery and housework and wore ragged sleeves and got only leftover snake food to eat, while Kadru lolled around in ease and idleness.

Garuda asked his mother why she was poor, and when he heard about the bet he went to Kadru and offered to ransom Vinata at any price.

The thousand Nagas were long since grown up. They all took counsel together, then Kadru said, "There is in Indra's Heaven a cup of amrita, the nectar of immortality, churned from the milk sea long long ago. Bring it to us and we free your mother."

The wondrous fair-feathered Garuda opened his wings. They spread over the sky like a wind. Garuda flew to the hills for advice from his father Kashyapa.

Kashyapa was happy to see his son. He said, "My boy, eat a little something before you try to fly to heaven and steal amrita from Indra. But never eat a man. Remember that."

"Yes, Father."

Kashyapa continued, "There's a big lake behind this hill. There live two big animals always fighting one another—a tortoise whose shell is ten leagues around, and an elephant who stands six leagues tall. They are two men reborn. They are two brothers drawing out in lowly animal forms their senseless quarrel over an inheritance that began when they were men."

"What did they inherit?" asked Garuda.

"Money I think. Go eat them, son."

"Father, what's money?"

"Money. . . ." Kashyapa smiled at his son. "Money is . . . it's . . . it's really nothing."

"Yes, Father. Father, what's a league?"

"A day's travel with one yoking of animals. Remember now, never eat a man. Man is Master of all animals. If you swallow one he'll turn into fire or poison or a razor. Go now with my blessing, and seek your fortune."

Garuda blinked his eyes. "Goodbye." He flew up, then dove down at that lake. The animals were fighting as usual. The elephant was trying to pull the turtle onshore and the turtle was trying to drag the elephant underwater and drown him. They had been trying to do that same thing for ages, annoying all the hills with their yells and wails.

Garuda caught one beast in each claw and flew up high with them, looking for somewhere to alight to eat them. By the western seashore he saw a very old banyan tree, one of whose limbs went way out over the water. That limb was so stout it would take ten thousand ox hides tied end to end to go round it, and it went out over the ocean for one hundred leagues.

The old tree looked up and called out to Garuda, "Sit on my great magnificent branch."

Garuda landed there, but his weight broke the branch. It cracked off right near the trunk and started to fall into the sea. As it fell Garuda saw the Valakhilya saints hanging from it upside down all clustered together. He didn't know what to do, but he thought they might be men and he ought to save them, so he caught the falling limb in his beak and flew up again still holding the two squirming animals as well.

Kashyapa had kept his eye on his son's first adventure. Now he approached Garuda in the air and yelled in his ear, "Fly easy, don't vibrate." He dropped down and talked to the Valas. "Victory to light. Forgive my son, he didn't see you."

Oh yes Sir, we know him, we know Garuda. The Valakhilyas left their perch and flew off someplace. Kashyapa showed Garuda a barren hill where he could drop the branch. The great high forest trees bent and waved and swayed like a field of wheat from the downwind of Garuda's wings. He dropped the branch with a universal crash, and then he sat on the hill summit and ate his breakfast, and his strength was doubled.

Garuda flew up toward heaven, slowly flapping his wings. In heaven, Indra's yellow marble throne got too hot to sit on. His thunders sizzled and rattled, his arrows attacked each other, and a dry wind arose full of dust and grit.

Indra and Agni the Fire God went to heaven's gate and looked out. Indra asked, "What's that golden gleaming fire down there? Are you trying to burn us all?"

"That's no fire of mine," said Agni. "That is Garuda, King of the Birds, created by those little Valas you made fun of."

"Some unearthly *bird?*" smiled Indra. "Oh, that's hard to believe . . . go see what he wants, will you?"

Garuda was floating like a hawk, on the wings of the wind from beyond, wondering where to go. Agni put on a cape of fire and a hood of flames to keep himself cool as he approached Garuda. Below were the Sun and Moon and all the heavens were above.

Agni sang a song to Garuda—*You are the elements of form, you are the light of life; Garuda moving in the sky, we take your protection.* He said, "Garuda; you are making the ether boil and warping the precise circles of the Universe. Diminish your energy and speak to me."

"Before I do that," said Garuda, "I need some amrita."

"Wait, just a moment." Agni went back to Indra. "Give him a little Nectar of Life."

"Never," said Indra.

"He'll take it then," said Agni. "He's too hot for you."

"What! Let me see!" Indra looked down again. "He doesn't look so great. Summon all my fighters!"

The amrita was kept inside Indra's palace. Indra set rows of heavenly guards around the building. They stood fearless in their golden breastplates that shone like suns. The spears they held started to smoke and their axes shed sparks.

Garuda came flying up over heaven's horizon. His wings blew up too much dust from the ground of heaven for the guards to see anything, and the winds he made sucked the air out of their lungs and they fainted. Behind the guards Garuda found fires fed by hurricanes. Garuda changed his form and grew eighty-one hundred mouths. He fled back to Earth and drank up eighty-one hundred rivers, and came back to Heaven and quenched all the fires.

Then Garuda took a tiny form, with just one head as before. He went inside Indra's house, and broke through a fine-mesh net of steel links. Behind that was a block of adamant and a round passage bored through it leading to the amrita. A fan of sword blades whirled in the passage with no room to go around it, but Garuda went right through the fan too quick for it to cut him at all.

At the end of the passage was a room with the cup of amrita in it, and by the cup were two angry serpents to guard it. Those snakes had poisonous breath, the glance of their eyes would turn you to stone, and their tongues were electric pieces of lightning slickering in and out.

But Garuda was going too fast to be seen. He brushed between them like a ghost and took the cup of amrita and was going back out the passage before the serpents knew he had even come in. Going out he hit the sword-fan dead center and smashed it. He flew outside, grew large again, and took away the only cup of amrita in all the worlds held in one claw.

Garuda hurried along back to the Earth, not drinking a

drop of amrita himself. Narayana met him as he went, and speeding on fast as Time they talked together as though they stood still on solid ground.

Narayana the One Lord said, "I make you immortal and forever healthy without taking any of that drink. I'll put you above me, on my flag on my chariot."

Garuda answered, "Lord, I will carry you on my back when you want to ride me, wherever you wish to go."

"Excellent, I make you King of all the birds of all the worlds for all Time." Vishnu left him then.

Near Earth Indra was hiding. He threw a thunderbolt and hit Garuda's breast. With that strike, all knowledge came to Garuda. He knew everything that ever had been or was or will ever be, knew it all in an instant.

Sita, listen. Indra's thunders are made from the bones of the giant Dadhicha. Dadhicha was an ancient warrior, the strongest person who ever lived, tall as a mountain. All men were that size in the days when Dadhicha was born.

Dadhicha went apart once from the others, and sitting like a sage he fell into a trance in the hills, and there as though asleep he outlived his time. His body grew weathered and had the look of stone. He never moved and seemed himself to be another mountain.

Then after Dadhicha had been that way for countless years, the Asuras made war against Indra. They were winning. Indra went to the hills and kicked the ground on a hillside in anger. But Indra was not standing on a hill, he was standing on Dadhicha.

The giant opened his eyes and looked out over the fields of Earth, and saw the men and animals there. Dadhicha asked Indra—*How have men grown so small? Where is my King?*

That was a voice from the beginning of the world. Indra knew nothing, he had never known such men, or such a King. He said, "I don't know."

Dadhicha asked, "Who are you?"

"I am Indra. I rule heaven. Nowhere in any world have I seen a man large as you, nor heard of any."

"My King has died to you," said Dadhicha. "I am Dadhicha. My people have gone over, they have left and I shall follow behind. Why have you come to me, Indra?"

"I thought you were a hill."

Dadhicha laughed. "The worse for you then!" Indra smiled back. "I have overslept," continued Dadhicha. "I should have died long ago. I miss my King. So farewell, but since you have come to me, even by mistake, do not go without some gift, or you will anger me. What do you need?"

"A miracle," said Indra. "I am at war."

"And losing," said Dadhicha. "When I die, take my bones; they will be ready at once, for I will call down the ages past to me. My servant Time will age me to your eyes and you may fashion my bones into bolts of thunder. . . ."

Dadhicha began to age, and Indra watched amazed from the air. The giant called out—*I'm coming, here I am! Oh, for the Blessed Land. . . .*

Then there was nothing left of Dadhicha but his bones. Indra summoned Viswakarman, and the heavenly architect made thunderbolts out of the bones, shaping one bone with another, for they were the hardest things he'd ever met. Indra won his war and brought his rain down.

Now from respect for days gone past, when that unbearable thunderbolt hit him Garuda dropped one feather. The golden feather turned over in the air, the size of a war-shield. Garuda looked to see who had hit him.

Indra put down his thunders and came from hiding. "Let us be friends," said the Lord of the Gods. "Surely you can do anything . . . but if you won't drink that amrita why not return it to me?"

Garuda told Indra why he needed the amrita and said, "My bargain is to bring the amrita but I didn't promise anyone a drink of it." He went on down to Earth and Indra followed him invisibly.

At home once more, Garuda said to Kadru, "Here it is." The thousand Nagas all came up and crowded around. "Now free my mother forever."

"She's free, she's free!" The Nagas brought a grass mat. Garuda put the Cup of Life down on it. He gave the Nagas a strange look.

"What's wrong, what's wrong?" they asked him.

"It's just . . . oh, it's nothing I suppose," answered Garuda.

"What, what?"

"Well," said Garuda, "*I* wouldn't drink this down like a bowl of soup without washing first. After all, this is a treasure."

"Right! Quite right!" Then the Nagas and Kadru went to wash before tasting immortality. Instantly Indra took back the cup, and when the snakes returned the grass mat was bare. Still, they licked the sharp-edged grass hoping that some amrita had spilled over, and ever since then Nagas have had slit tongues.

"And the touch of the cup holding amrita also gave its power to our sacred grass that was used for the mat," said Rama. "And this story is true."

Sita smiled. "But—" Suddenly before she could say any more a long hairy red arm reached out from the trees to one side, grabbed her round her waist, and withdrew holding her fast.

Rama and Lakshmana ran after her. The arm that held her was so long, that they couldn't see where it came from, and as they ran it just kept pulling Sita away before them. Rama and Lakshmana followed on and on through a thick stand of dark spiny trees laced with dead vines.

Then they came out of the trees and saw a red Rakshasa standing holding Sita. He was very tall and held her at his waist. His body was covered with up-pointing bristly red hair. He had ears like javelins and hollow green eyes. His mouth went from ear to ear. He began to howl. In his other hand he held an iron spit that had impaled on it three dead lions, four deer and the bloody head of an elephant that stared at Rama and Lakshmana with dead eyes wide open.

"Scum!" sid the Rakshasa. He stretched out his arm again and put Sita up in a tree. "I am Viradha! No weapon can kill me! You travel here with a common wife, you dirty men, I'll drink your blood! Then I marry the girl!" He advanced.

Lakshmana shot Viradha full of arrows. They were sticking out all over him. But Viradha yawned and all the arrows fell off him. He snorted and caught Rama in one arm and Lakshmana in the other and walked away with them. Soon they were out of sight of Sita.

Then Rama broke the arm holding him, and Lakshmana broke the other, and they beat Viradha down to the ground with blows. Viradha roared and yowled until Rama held him down and quiet by his foot on the demon's throat. Lakshmana dug a deep hole, and they threw Viradha in it and buried him under rocks and stones and killed him.

A Gandharva of heaven arose out of that burial mound, a handsome drummer dressed in silks and silver. He said, "Oh Rama, I am Tumburu the musician, Lord." Tumburu smiled. "The Treasure Lord Vaishravana cursed me. I was gone from my post with an Apsarasa, and so love put me into a demon's body, and violence freed me."

Music was in the air. A darkly beautiful dancing girl came out of somewhere in the sky, and floating above Tumburu, and let fall from her hands a long drum with a head at each end. She looked at Rama and gave him a happy smile. Tumburu took the drum, slung it round his neck by a strap and let his fingers run on it. Chitraratha the Gandharva King became visible in the sky, sitting holding a lute with lots of strings, playing dreamy tunes, and Tumburu stopped drumming.

The Gandharva said, "I was doomed to a demon's life till you should kill me, Rama, and then bury me the way the forest Rakshasas bury their corpses . . . I have reached out my arms for every moving thing in Dandaka, hoping to find you. Remember, any violent death in this Dandaka forest leads to heaven. . . ."

Chitraratha changed his music, it was time for the drums and Tumburu tossed his head and flew up to join his King and his girl, and they went higher and higher until they were gone.

Rama and Lakshmana went back and helped Sita down out of her tree. Rama said, "He wanted to die, and so he told us our weapons were useless."

Rama and Sita and Lakshmana kept going south through Dandaka Forest and reached the Godavari River. Lakshmana built them another house, near the river in a place called Panchavati where five whispering trees banked the stream, not far from a hillside cave.

One morning soon after they arrived they were all sitting out in the open by the house. Rama was telling some story to Sita and Lakshmana, when out from the forest surrounding them came the Rakshasi Surpanakha. She was Ravana's sister.

She saw Rama and desired him. Surpanakha was misshapen and mean. Her yellowy skin was rutted like a bad road. She had a pot belly and ears like flat baskets, claws on her fingers and toes, squinty eyes and messy hair.

She was gnawing a raw bone but she threw it away and leered at Rama. She pointed at Sita and said, "My dear, why keep that skinny girl?"

Rama stood up and said, "I am Rama."

"And I am Surpanakha! I have chosen you for my husband."

Lakshmana said, "A great gain."

Surpanakha said, "I'll take you to the broad city of Lanka by magic, dear Rama. My brother's wealth will let us live like a King and Queen."

Rama smiled at her. "You see—I am already married. To a proud woman like yourself, a co-wife is misery. Don't think more about it."

Surpanakha looked at Lakshmana. Lakshmana quickly said, "Don't take second best."

"Why make shy excuses?" Surpanakha cracked her knuckles. "It's natural to marry."

"Bless you, maiden," said Lakshmana, "but leave us alone. May all creatures be happy. A good wife is hard to find, may you soon be wed."

Rama said, "My brother Lakshmana is also married."

Surpanakha cried, "I see the trouble!" She rushed at Sita, and held out before her her claws curved like elephant hooks. But Lakshmana caught her. He took the gold-handled knife from his belt, and swiftly cut off Surpanakha's ears and threw her down. "Were you not a woman you'd be dead!"

Surpanakha ran away bleeding and fled to the Rakshasa garrison commanded by General Khara. She flung up her arms and fell at Khara's feet like a stone falling from the blue sky.

Khara caught his breath in boundless wrath. In a voice deep and low as thunderclouds he said, *"Arise!"* The Earth trembled as he spoke. Landslides fell down from the hills around the Rakshasa camp.

"I've been attacked!"

"Don't roll on the ground! Who did it?"

"Two men and a woman. As if I had no protection!"

"Sound the alarm!" A Rakshasa soldier smashed a big hanging brass plate with a metal mace and kept on smashing it for a hundred and eight times. Khara yelled at Surpanakha, "Where are they?"

She yelled back, "Panchavati!"

The alarm stopped and the Rakshasa garrison assembled, fourteen thousand strong. Khara stood before them and said, "Like Death, let us kill the three humans at Panchavati and please this lady!"

In Panchavati, Rama's Ayodhya arrows started to smoke. His new bow hummed. Rama strung it and said, "Lak-

shmana, we have sharply angered them! For a moment hide
with Sita in that cave, and cover the mouth with trees."

Rama stood alone, glancing up into the sky, in the direction Surpanakha had gone. His green hand drew back his
bow. His lips shook with anger and his eyes were red with
blood.

The Rakshasas came, flying low just above the trees and
led by Khara. When they saw just one man facing them they
hesitated. Rama called out. "Stop! If you value your lives!"

Khara replied, "Surrender yourself then."

Rama said, "I live here quietly. Why seek to injure me?"

"You are destroyed!" answered the demons. Rama spoke a
mantra and he took three steps backwards to get his aim.
Khara looked around, saw no one else but Rama, and waved
his arm. The Invincible Legion of Dandaka attacked.

Rama killed them all, fourteen thousand Rakshasa warriors
and General Khara. He used what he needed of the mantras
and weapons Viswamitra had taught him. Rama's golden arrows swept the sky like yellow lightnings. There was no escape.

Surpanakha was watching at a safe distance. She dove into
the Earth and flew by Rakshasa power through the solid
stone, right under the southern ocean. She surfaced in Lanka
just outside Ravana's palace and ran inside to her brother.

Ravana was on his throne holding court. Surpanakha came
in wailing—*Rama! Rama! Rama!*

She ran up the stairs to the throne and grabbed Ravana's
legs in a grip like an iron vise. Her ears were gone. The court
of the Demon King fell silent from shock and Ravana rose
and cried—*Who dares?*

Surpanakha said, "Khara is dead."

"What?" cried Ravana.

"And all his soldiers."

Ravana beckoned with his ten left hands and Rakshasa
physicians hurried forward. They snapped their fingers and
restored Surpanakha's ears and gave her something to drink,
and let her see herself in an unbreakable mirror. Ravana had
her sit down and came down from the throne to sit beside
her and said, "Now tell me."

"I am the only one still alive," said Surpanakha. "Like Hell itself, Dandaka is bathed in blood. In half a moment Rama killed Khara and his legion with whistling screaming arrows of dazzling gold, and the harmless men that we have killed for food in the woods watched from heaven as your army died. The kindly saints and hermits now may mock you and walk safely through dreadful Dandaka."

Ravana cleared his ten throats. All his eyes were looking all around. They danced in his heads like fiery coals. "Who did it?"

"Rama!"

"Who is Rama?"

"A prince."

A man? Ravana looked closely at his sister. "How many millions were in his army?"

"He had no army."

"What gods helped him?"

"No gods. Rama fought alone, and I take your protection for bringing bad news."

"Bad news? Why . . . a man? He's drunk poison. He's poked his finger in a black snake's eye! He is pulling lions' teeth inside a burning house!"

"The Wanderers of the Wood are dead and broken on the Earth," said Surpanakha. "Rama looks like a hermit, but it is only to destroy you that he has come."

"Me?" Ravana looked tenderly into his sister's face. "If they did me wrong, I would kill that tyrant Death, I would burn Fire and smother the Wind. Have no fear."

Surpanakha said, "Brother, you're a disgrace. You're all muscle and brawn, you rule by brute force and ignorance! Here you are lost in pleasure, idle and greedy and useless. You're not going to do anything, are you?"

"Enough!" roared Ravana. "By all the demons, Surpanakha, the Earth is wide and who cares what mere men do on every bit of her? Dandaka is a worse wasteland than the back of the Moon. There's nothing worth having there anyway."

"You don't know Rama," said Surpanakha, "but you are merciful. You will let the best bowman in the world live on your land with his brother and his fair wife Sita."

"Sita?"

"Whomever she warmly embraces will outgain the gods in happiness. It was Rama's brother who cut off my ears, but when Khara tried to avenge me only Rama fought us. The three of them can't do much harm there. At this very moment Sita must be holding Rama lovingly, and healing his wound by her caress."

"Then he was wounded!" said Ravana.

"He hurt his heel as he backed away barefoot."

"Then he retreated!"

"He was aiming, to shoot down your army."

"Go on, tell me about her."

"She is more beautiful than any of your wives, but all she thinks of is Rama."

"Indeed?"

"Her skin is gold; her eyes are dark. Her fingernails are round and red, her breasts are full, and her waist is slender as an ant's."

Ravana said, "Sita."

The Demon King dismissed his court and retired alone to his rooms. Surpanakha left Lanka and went to the Asura underworlds beneath the sea, and there she married.

Early the next morning Ravana went alone to his stables, armed with a bow and arrows and a sharp sword. He got in a small gold chariot that was pulled by asses with the faces of fiends. The chariot rose into the air and Ravana flew north, across the vast ocean and then across our continent to Gokarna. There in a hermitage lived his uncle Maricha, whom Rama had shot as a boy but had not killed. Ravana's twenty hands rested on the chariot rail. From the center of the rail hung ten ornamental golden arrows tied together with golden string. They were Ravana's only sign of Empire and Conquest: ten arrows for the ten directions; South and the other three, and the four in between those four, and up and down, all was Ravana's.

The Golden Deer

Sita of great beauty,
You are a woman.
To a woman everything is becoming,
Every one is her own,
May I be yours.

Maricha the Rakshasa sat alone in a clearing, clad in black deerskin. Ravana's chariot came soaring down and landed, and the Demon King walked over to his uncle. Ravana sat beside Maricha and said, "How good to see you, my old friend."

"Why are you here?" asked Maricha.

Ravana said, "The Dandaka demons have all been killed by—"

"Stop!" Maricha looked around. "Ravana, if you wish me to live, do not speak that name in my hearing! Fear of him has made me a hermit."

"Then you know about it," said Ravana.

"I saw Khara's legion die by magic sight."

"Magic," said Ravana. "That's what I want to talk to you about."

"Ow!" Maricha rubbed his knee and looked painfully at Ravana.

"What's wrong?" asked Ravana.

"Go away! Don't bother me. This talk pains me."

"You're making that up, Uncle!"

"He did not at first strike to kill me," said Maricha. "And now forever will I see him, wherever I look, dressed like the trees in bark, watching me where he cannot be."

"I won't let him get away with it," said Ravana. "His dear loving Sita is in the very bloom of her passionate youth!"

Maricha looked at Ravana as though he saw him already

dead. "Innocent Sita? I have abandoned war, Ravana."
Maricha sighed. "Happily, here I see so few fools any more.
What enemy disguised as your friend mentioned Sita's name
to you?"

"Surpanakha. They attacked her unprovoked."

"No," said Maricha. "Her heart envies you your fortune.
She will ruin you by your own hand. She has spoken the one
word of your doom, and there may be some use for dust
from the trodden roadside, but useless is a fallen King."

"I will steal Sita by deception and he will die of shame!"

Maricha's eyes did not blink and his dry mouth hung open.
"Give this idea away. Let the Sun and Moon stand in fear of
you but let Sita be! Your army went down like a grainfield
under a hailstorm. You will be nothing against him!"

Ravana said, "That was an accident."

"The whole world may well be an accident," said Maricha.
"Forget it; let it go. His name is danger to me and to you as
well. As a clever man hits on a secret and solves it, so did he
eliminate your army. He hit them and they do not exist! And
his brother Lakshmana is just as strong; he is his own second
self."

"No matter," said Ravana.

"You have everything to lose and absolutely nothing to
gain."

"You've got that backwards," smiled Ravana.

Maricha said, "This is the severing of the summit of the
Rakshasa race. It is for your death that the forest hermits
have so long poured butter on their fires. For your death and
not Khara's did they direct that man to Dandaka. Wherever
your soldiers looked they saw him before them, and for all
their wrath and rage he easily killed them all. He can bring
down the stars with his arrows, or break apart the continents
and let in the sea, or raise Earth once drowned and create all
Creation anew."

Ravana said, "He meekly submitted to an exile in the
woods when his father banished him."

"Many quiet men are strong," said Maricha. "Just pray to
your favorite gods that he never notices you."

"He has been disgraced once," said Ravana, "and is now a
delicate failure, a false hermit with a holy hairdo yet schem-
ing and desiring and bearing arms and tied to a woman, a
laughable weakling. May such a life befall all my enemies."

"Do not scorn men!" Maricha shuddered. "Ravana, rare
and unpleasant is the truth to an idiot King, but this greed

will draw you swiftly to your doom. Ravana, be peaceful and
content yourself with the wives you have. They love you, go
home to them. Think of our people. Do not destroy them by
the whims and envies, the vanities and glories of their King.
You see things wrong. You imagine that man as someone
small and weak. You think of Sita as harmless and inviting, a
delightful woman whom you may play with safely and come
to no harm."

"Uncle, do not always measure things and count them."

"Ravana, listen. Once I flew where I wanted over the
Earth. I was swift and roaring, cold and heartless and huge
as a hill. I wore a golden crown and was strong as a thousand
elephants. Viswamitra kept trying to make a sacrifice, and his
hymns were faint and scratchy, and I would let no god answer him. I bullied everybody and no one could stop me.
Then Viswamitra brought that man, but he was still a boy.
He had no sign of manhood on his face and he wore his hair
as a child, but he protected the sacrifice. He was the soul of
all the worlds, but I passed him by and went for the altar. . . ."

"Maybe so, maybe not."

"You are still thirsty for poison. Try doing right and
people will be your friends; many of us care for you. Or else
you will delight all your victims by destroying yourself."

Ravana said, "Cheer up. Pull yourself together. I've done
all right so far, haven't I?"

Maricha said, "If it is not your Time, again and again
snares of all kinds may be set for you in vain, but when your
death's moment comes you will not see the trap that catches
you until too late. You won't listen to me, but I am your
friend. However strong and great you once were, you are a
straw figure now, falling into poverty."

Ravana smiled. "I don't listen to criticisms any more, just
tell me the good parts. Come, delay defeats any deed. Change
yourself into a golden deer and help me." He embraced Maricha and went on, "Let us plan this kidnapping with more delight. Let us be generous to each other; let us help each other
through this life, happy and carefree as Kings." Ravana
waved one of his hands over the ground and a jug appeared
with two coconut halfshells. "Now, a taste of wine?"

"Well, I don't know."

"You lure him away, out of earshot, then escape." They
drank. "Separate Rama and Sita, that's all I ask. I'll do the

rest. I can handle Lakshmana. When he discovers what has happened, Rama will die of heartbreak."

"Rama. Rama!" Maricha rolled his tongue around his lips. "I can say it!" Ravana refilled their winecups.

The Demon King took a sip of wine with each head, one after another, and wiped his moustaches. "Kings must be adored!" he said loudly.

"Soft welcome words!" cried Maricha. "Just say how much you like the idea . . . whenever possible. Look for faults and you'll find them!"

"Precisely! I will give you half my kingdom. Half my World Empire."

"No." Maricha put down his cup. "It is Death that's paid me a visit today. Keep your kingdom if you've got one."

Ravana yelled at him. "Then I'll kill you!"

"You?"

"Yes, don't you fear Death?"

"What for? Why should I?"

"But—"

"But still, Ravana, it is better to be killed by the better person. I won't escape him but I will lead him away and let him kill me." Maricha stood up. "I will go if you will promise not to brag to me along the way."

"Of course, anything you say." Ravana started to get up.

"Just one moment," said Maricha. He sadly tidied up his few old possessions and quickly performed his own funeral.

Then they were on Ravana's chariot, going through the sky to Panchavati. Maricha drew in the fresh air in deep breaths and stretched his arms and legs.

"There's always just a chance," said Maricha.

Ravana said, "That man isn't worth a finger-flick."

Ravana landed the chariot some distance from Rama's house. Ravana crept up close to the house, leading Maricha by the hand. Ravana said, "There they are."

Maricha became a deer. His face was of living blue sapphire like a moving mask made of a blue mirror. His antlers were ivory tipped with moonstone points and his hooves were glassy black flint. His lighted eyes were violet amethyst. His golden hair grew this way and that, and there were silver spots on his sides, and when he danced like a deer the golden hair ran the light in rays over his body. His underbelly was pale pink and his tongue bright red. He held his tail straight up and arched his neck a little and ran off.

The other deer scented a Rakshasa and fled from Maricha as he approached Rama's house. The tigers drew back and did not dare to roar. Maricha ate grass in a green meadow by the Godavari river, then ran past Rama's house, then stopped and turned, and lay down nibbling leaves.

Rama and Sita and Lakshmana were all at home, and Sita saw the deer. She called, "Rama, come quickly. Can you catch him?"

Rama said, "How beautiful."

Lakshmana came up and said, "There is no such deer on Earth. That is an illusion."

Rama strung his bow and took one arrow. "Wait here with Sita. I'll try to get him alive, or else I'll shoot him."

Lakshmana said, "See how his shape seems to shift and change around the edges."

"I'll be careful," said Rama. "If that is a Rakshasa illusion I will destroy it."

Maricha got up. He started to walk right for Rama. Then he noticed a man there. He backed and jumped and walked away into the trees just out of bowshot. He stopped and turned and gazed at Rama with his ears out.

Then Maricha went away running and jumping, taking long leaps with his forefeet drawn up to his chest and his back legs straight out. Rama went after him. Maricha didn't seem to see Rama pursuing him and so Rama didn't shoot him for a long time, hoping to follow the deer home and capture him alive later. But though Maricha now and then seemed to tire, or sometimes lose his way, he tempted Rama farther and farther from home, and Rama began to lose sight of him.

The golden deer reappeared and Rama saw him through the stark trees of Dandaka, and decided to kill him. Rama shot a gold arrow and hit the lovely deer through his heart. Maricha leapt up high as a palm tree, then fell on his back, and at the point of death resumed his true form.

A black demon lay there dying. Rama ran up holding his diamond and rainbow bow. With his last breath Maricha shouted in Rama's voice—*Help me!* He threw back his head and died.

Maricha's cry was much louder than any man could shout. Rama knew they would hear it at Panchavati, and could not hear him from where he stood. Every hair on Rama's body was on end. He made sure Maricha was dead and ran for home as fast as he could.

Sita heard Rama's voice cry help and said, "Lakshmana, he is hurt!"

"That is not truly his voice," said Lakshmana.

"How much has Bharata paid you to betray us?"

"He is not in danger," said Lakshmana. "He told me to wait and stay with you. That deer was a demon, don't you understand?"

Sita wept. "Would you let him die? Oh, you don't care, you don't care!" She looked wildly around then started to go after Rama herself. Lakshmana held her back. She pleaded, "Let me go ... Rama. ..."

Lakshmana held her and looked her right in the eye. He sighed and frowned. She was breathing fast, she said, "Then is it me you want? Take me but save Rama!"

Lakshmana covered his ears. Real anger was on his face. He saw red. Red Sita, red trees, red sky. "First you have sent Rama away to fetch you an illusion," he said. "And now you order me to obey a false voice. Do not move!"

Lakshmana looked out into the forest. He said, "Wrong words are nothing new for a woman." He drew a circle around Sita on the ground, with the tip of his bow.

"Do not step out of this circle and do not cross this line," said Lakshmana. "Let these trees witness that I have done right!"

Sita was paying no attention. Lakshmana thrust out his lower lip in anger. He took his quiver and entered the edge of the forest, bent low a bit, went under a branch and was out of sight.

The Rakshasa King Ravana watched him go. Then Ravana came boldly across the clearing toward Rama's house covered with the disguise of an old holy man, like a treacherous deep well covered and hidden by tall grass. Sita saw him coming and dried her eyes.

Ravana looked like a man. He wore soft red silk. There was one lock of white hair left long on his shaven head. He held a parasol and wore sandals, and he carried resting over his left shoulder a long triple bamboo staff with a waterjar slung on it. Ravana came and stood silently by Sita's house, as holy men do when begging their daily food. There was no sign of Lakshmana or Rama. All around them there was only the forest land of green and brown.

Sita stepped over Lakshmana's line and said, "Worshipful brahmana, be our guest. Sit, take some water, wash and I will bring food."

Ravana hummed—*I walk the sweet Earth, Lord; I see you have made beautiful creatures, Lord; how fine and true, Oh Lord of Love.*

He spoke very fair. "How do you come to live here alone, my girl, in perilous Dandaka land?" He stood looking at her. "By the Book, fair are your jewels."

"I am Sita. These jewels were presents. Don't fear demons, for my husband Rama will be back soon."

"Ah," said Ravana, "his name can't be Rama, he must be Kama! You are Rati the wife of Love, wantonly hiding in the forest." He smiled like a father. "Oh, you timid girl, of slender waist and tapering thighs! You've had a lovers' quarrel with Kama. You belong in a palace. I can see you like jewels and luxury!"

"Brahmana, sit down and what can I give you? I am Sita, a mortal woman and my husband is the Ayodhya King. These jewels were gifts from Anasuya and this necklace came from Guha. Tell me your name and family."

"Beautiful," said Ravana. "I am the Rakshasa King Ravana. I rule the universe. Come to me, Sita. I will take you to Lanka with her engines and weapons, and I will put you over all my other Queens."

Sita laughed. "Garuda mating with a goose? A firefly courting the Sun?"

"Seek me! Cross the ocean with me!"

"A gnat trying to suck up a bowl of butter! Can you swim?"

"Don't play around with *me!*"

"I won't, don't worry," said Sita.

"You will have five thousand serving maids."

"Never." Sita looked again at the quiet forest and could see no one.

Woman, I am Ravana feared by the Gods! Ravana clapped his hands and his disguise fell away. He was tall as a tree. He had ten dark faces and twenty dark arms, and twenty red eyes red-rimmed like fire. He had yellow up-pointing fangs. He licked his lips with sharp tongues. He wore golden armor, long heavy gold earrings swaying, gold bracelets, gold armbands, ten golden crowns set with golden pearls, gold belt-chains crashing and gold rings all over his fingers. Fragrant white flower-garlands went over his shoulders and around his ten necks.

Ravana had a long ivory bow hanging down along one shoulder, its back rich with pearls, and by his hip he had a supple sword, of blue steel in a blue case. And on his back he had a long quiver formed of human skins stretched over a frame of men's bones, and the outside of that quiver was painted with demon faces drawn in blood, and those spectral faces moved of themselves; they were grim or laughing at will, changing as though alive, following with their eyes. The quiver held fifty tall blue-black arrows of solid iron, vaned with thin iron blades.

Ravana shook his heads and rattled his crowns and looked down at Sita. Seeing that evil one revealed, the leaves did not flutter. The trees of Dandaka did not move. No breath of wind dared stir about in the woods. The fast-streaming Godavari river slackened her speed from fright. The glorious Sun, who every day looks down upon our world, this time dimmed his light from the sadness of what he saw.

"I will have you!" said Ravana. "Princess Sita, you are half divine, why mingle more with men? Rule every world with me. Sita, I stand in space and I pick up Earth in my hand. I close the Moon within my fingers and put the Sun in my pocket, and arrest the aimless planets. You will forget Rama with me!"

Ravana bent down, a black mountain come to life. Sita knelt near his feet hiding her face, clinging to a tree. Sita wore a clear yellow robe and Anasuya's ornaments and Guha's necklace. Her skin was golden, she was like sunlight in among the trees, and Ravana reached for her. In one left hand he held her long dark hair. He caught her legs in two of his right arms and lifted her, and his demon chariot came to meet him through the air.

> Oh Rama,
> After the theft of Sita who can escape Death from you?
> That damned Demon might walk and breathe
> But be dead.
> He might win immortality, drink dry the Cup of Life in
> heaven, win every god's blessing
> And be dead.

Sita cried—*Rama! Rama!* many times and struggled to get free but it was useless. Ravana was on the chariot, holding Sita like a fireball in his bare arms, and the chariot began to move south.

In her mind Sita called the river Godavari, called the trees of Dandaka and saluted their tree-gods, took her refuge with the deer—*Tell Rama. Tell him.*

Then Sita saw a great huge vulture asleep high in a treetop and cried aloud to him—*Tell Rama!*

The vulture awoke. He raised his neck and looked hard after Ravana's passing chariot with round green eyes. His breast was yellow and black and his wings were grey. Swiftly he spread his wings and went gliding in the air.

Instantly he overtook the demon car and stayed above it balancing on his still, open wings, with their tip feathers spread like fingers. He softly spoke to Ravana, "Brother Ten-Necks, I am Jatayu the Vulture King. I rule the birds of Dandaka. While he lived I was Dasaratha's old friend, we were born on the same day. Fear to do evil in my sight, Ravana, for I know the right ways of life."

"Go back to sleep!" said Ravana.

"I am King of the Air," said Jatayu. "Do not harm Sita. Free her or die, for not in safety will you carry her from my land, as if she had no husband. Demon King, I am sixty thousand years old, in my age peacefully ruling here and I forbid you." Ravana kept on going.

Jatayu said, "I am too old and tired to talk any more!" He hooked a talon through Ravana's chariot rail, a claw as long and curved as an elephant's tusk, and sharp, and hard as an iron gate-bar. Jatayu easily tore the rail away and on the wind of his wings he gently lifted Sita out of Ravana's hands and set her down unharmed beneath a tree.

Ravana cried out in shock and rage. He shouted, "I care nothing for you!" He turned the chariot to attack and flew at the Vulture King, holding his ivory bow and aiming an arrow.

Jatayu snapped that bow with one bite. He clawed the armor from Ravana's back, and with his beak tore out the hair from the Demon King's heads. With his wings he struck Ravana down and sent him falling. In blind fury Jatayu ripped the asses that drew the chariot to shreds, he shattered the car with one wing stroke and the golden chariot wheels spun through the sky like two suns, the iron axle smashed down on end into the forest, and everywhere fell bits of gold and crushed wood, and a rain of torn flesh.

The old war king Jatayu screeched in triumph. Ravana lay on the Earth faint and bewildered, streaming blood and only armed with the sword still at his waist. But Jatayu was exhausted. His vision faded and blurred and he could not see. From above he looked for the Demon King. Ravana saw his blindness and rose to attack.

Jatayu struck him by sound. Jatayu hooked his talons again into Ravana's back, and hung on, and with his mouth wrenched off Ravana's ten left arms one by one and let them fall. All Ravana's faces trembled in pain. His bones shook in agony, but those ten arms grew right back, and Jatayu could not see them but thought they were destroyed for good.

Ravana drew his sword with one left hand, and he cut off Jatayu's wings with it. The Vulture King fell dying, and Sita ran to him where he lay and held his head and wept over him.

Ravana roughly tore her away with bloody hands. He flew south with her, very fast, as though driven through the sky before an evil wind. Ravana was dark and Sita was golden. As Ravana went past he seemed a dark violent cloud holding lightning, smoke hiding a fire, a dark hill catching a sunbeam.

The loss of Sita outraged the worlds. Ravana flew over the Earth. He passed over hills and the hills saw him: they recited charms aloud with the sounds of their falling waters: they uplifted their waving arms of green trees: in anger they yawned, opening their valleys to the sky. Lakes looked up and whirled their waters: white open lilies were their fearful eyes, and watery foam and mists their robes thrown off in grief. The waterfalls wept.

Ravana's shadow raced over the ground, and where it passed lions and tigers ran after it, and clawed at the shadow to kill it. Ravana held Sita round her waist by one arm, and he ran flying, and fled for home. That was all he thought of then, to win home to Lanka. Ravana carried Sita south across a dark river and looking down she saw two monkeys standing on a hill by a lake watching them, shading their eyes, one gold monkey and one white one.

Sita reached down her hands and broke the anklets off from her legs and let them fall down on that plain-looking hill. She took off her earrings and dropped them. Sita let all the ornaments of Anasuya fall, and she tied Guha's necklace in her yellow scarf edged with gold and dropped it also. Ra-

vana did not notice. He sped away, and Sita's hair streamed
out on the wind, and they left behind the two monkeys.

The two monkeys watched with their yellow-brown eyes
never blinking, while Sita's gold and silver bells and bracelets
fell ringing down and crying. The yellow scarf flashed down
like lightning; the silver ornaments were the Moon and white
stars dropping.

Hanuman!

A real deer made of precious stones and gold
Never yet lived in this world.
Such a thing cannot be;
But Rama followed a golden deer
And lost Sita.

She is his Sita.
That girl born again and again
Like a flame from the furrow,
In the King's fields.

Ravana looked at Sita and he thought—*Mine*. He brought her to the back of his palace in the city of Lanka. Ravana smiled at her. His faces were all smiles and he said, "You will not see Rama again. Here you are safe, you have no more husband, and so there can be nothing wrong in our love."

"To Hell with you," said Sita. "You took me like a thief. And barely made it past an old vulture—."

"Quiet!" Ravana screamed at her. Then at once he composed himself. "My dear . . . capture is a good way to get a wife . . . I want your love. I will wait for you to love me."

"Do what you will with me," said Sita, "I will feel nothing."

"When you get to know me, perhaps . . . we shall see, my dear. Come inside with me now, change your clothes and eat and rest."

"I won't enter your kennel."

"Damn you! Hey, Rakshasis!" Female Rakshasas ran up. "Take her and imprison her in the grove of tall Asoka trees back behind my room and guard her day and night."

A demoness took each of Sita's arms and led her away to the Asoka grove. Ravana told the rest of the Rakshasis, "Use hard words and soft, threats and gifts and temptations. Break her to my will and give her at any time whatever she may ask for."

Then the Demon King called after Sita, "When winter begins and the Sun turns north, if you haven't come into my bed I'll eat you minced for breakfast!" He went in the building.

In his high heaven Lord Brahma summoned Indra and said, "Sita must not die or end her life in Lanka."

Indra asked, "Why me?"

Brahma looked at him. Indra said, "I'll see to it, Sir."

Lord Indra waited until night. Then taking the Goddess Sleep for his companion he approached Lanka carrying a bowl of heavenly wheat and butter.

Sleep spread out her arms over Lanka. *For the good of the gods. For the downfall of the Night Demons.*

The Rakshasis guarding Sita fell asleep. Indra entered the scarlet Asoka grove and touched Sita lightly so she awoke. She was not afraid.

"I am Indra, the Lord of Heaven, good fortune to you. My Lady, the demons sleep. I bring you food. Eat this and never will you hunger nor thirst for a year."

"How do I know who you are?" asked Sita.

"I am Indra, and you know me."

Sita took a little wheat and dropped it to Earth. "Whether Rama lives or has died let this nourish him." Then she ate.

Indra said, "Don't fear Ravana. He cannot force you, for he is under a strong curse, and he'll die if he does."

"Who cursed him?" asked Sita.

"While Evil lies borne down by Sleep I will tell you what happened," said Indra. "Anyone who desires an unwilling woman burns himself, and he who loves a willing one will find delight."

Listen, Sita—

Viswamitra the hermit, who led Rama to your father's land, used to be only a King. He spent a long time winning merit by austerities in the Hills. He was gaining on me, and I sent the divinely beautiful Apsarasa Rambha down to Earth to tempt him. She approached him on Kailasa Hill but Viswamitra turned her to stone for ten thousand years.

Viswamitra never stayed long in one place and soon he left Kailasa. The Yakshas of the Treasure Lord Vaishravana found Rambha. They thought she was a statue and took her into their palace gardens.

Years passed, and the spell wore off one day. It was spring. Rambha became flesh and blood again. She blinked her eyes, and sighed, and turned around. She saw Vaishravana's son Nalakubara walking in the gardens and fell in love with him then and there. They met, and after that Rambha came back to Heaven. She told me how tired she was. But at night she would go down the path leading from Heaven to Kailasa, to visit Nalakubara.

When Ravana's son Indrajit had defeated me in Heaven, and when Ravana had taken all creation into his supposed Empire, the King of the Rakshasas became dissatisfied with having only one wife. So he made Mandodari his chief Queen, but he started to ride all over on Pushpaka chariot, capturing women. Ravana took whom he pleased, caring only for beauty and for nothing else. He had hundreds of wives kept guarded on the huge chariot—Naga girls, hermits' daughters, mermaids of the seas, bird-maidens of the northern lakes, daughters of gods, woodland spirits, the wives of Kings and common men.

Ravana killed any one who tried to stop him. Hot women's tears streamed from Pushpaka, and their complaints were very sad. Ravana looked them over. He decided he had to have at least one Apasarasa, and he steered Pushpaka to the Himalya Hills and landed near the silver mountain Kailasa.

That night the clear rising Moon shone brilliant on the hill, and from the Treasure Castle of Vaishravana came song and music. A cool night breeze brought the scent of flowers, and stirred the trees, and made them let fall a silent shower of petals soft over the ground.

Ravana waited near the summit, hidden in the black shadow of a tree that grew beside the narrow way that leads up to heaven, and down to the Hills of Earth. He heard someone descending, and heard ankle bells and waist-chains ringing and swinging in step.

Rambha came picking her way downhill. Her body swayed; she was barefoot and trying not to step on stones, and flowers from the five wishing-trees of heaven were in her hair. Rambha the Apsarasa had all of a woman's artful graces and all of her natural beauties.

Rambha's summer robe was light as air, her eyebrows were arched like bows, her thighs and hands were soft to touch. Ravana stepped out in front of her and slightly bent near to her, and he said, "Where do you go? Whose time for ecstasy and bliss has come? What favored lover will drink the nectar of your mouth? Whose hard chest will touch your soft breasts?"

Rambha brushed back a lock of hair off her forehead. "You're Ravana, aren't you?"

"Rest here on this fine grass," said Ravana.

"You rule even over heaven," said Rambha. "And so if you are my King, I am a young girl to be protected and you are my father and my guardian." She stood looking down.

"Love me," said Ravana, "love me now!"

"But I am married, in my heart," said Rambha.

"Apsarasas don't marry!" Ravana threw her down and raped her. Then he went away and left her there, and Rambha went on to her meeting with Nalakubara.

Rambha wept when she saw Nalakubara and cried, "You are my husband, forgive me that a woman's strength is less than a man's."

Nalakubara called servants; he sent her with them and all alone he stood on a bare rock and he cursed Ravana. First he looked as far as he could see in every way, but the Demon King was gone. Then he let fall from his eye a tear, onto the stone where he stood, and that boulder shattered, cracks ran through it.

Nalakubara the son of the Treasure King looked south. He got a branch of a pine tree and held it, and it burst into fire and burned, dropping tears of fire itself, and Nalakubara said—*Ravana, when you next attack a woman who won't have you, your ten heads will burst!*

Oh Sita, had I been watching Kailasa that night! Those cursing words went right into Ravana's ears in Lanka where he had gone with his chariot full of captives. They heard the curse too. Up till then those captive women had lamented, but now that they knew they were safe, that only made them love Ravana. They felt sorry for him.

Rambha and you are the only women who have refused themselves to Ravana since that time. Such is Ravana's charm and appeal that some of these queens helped Ravana to steal them, and one lady killed her brothers who would have stopped her, and drank their blood, and turned to Ravana with a red mouth. I think women are more cruel than demons. Very often they are, when they may be so.

Yet, Princess, since Nalakubara's curse many times a madness has possessed the Demon King, and proof of this is

his taking you although his wives love him. He has again hurt
someone weaker than he. The tears that Rambha wept that
night will burn him down.

"For there is nothing worse than the tears of the innocent,"
said Indra. "Sita, you haven't on your body any sign of
widowhood. Rama will rescue you; you won't dwell here
long. Those monkeys will tell him that they saw you."

"And Jatayu?"

"By the Gods," said Indra, "Jatayu has had a place in
heaven for a thousand lifetimes, but he won't use it; he won't
be born anything but a bird, and he loves Earth. Over and
over, again and again he gives his life for what's right, never
once wondering should he do it or not, nor reflecting will it
do any good, nor would it be better to live to fight another
time! Ah Sita, I think Jatayu is very wise."

Sita smiled at Indra. The food he had brought her had
taken away her rising hunger and sorrow. The Lord of the
Gods touched his hands, knelt before Sita, and returned to
heaven, taking the Goddess Sleep with him.

In Dandaka Forest, Rama running for home met Lakshmana running towards him and shouted—*Go back!*

They ran home together. They found their house empty
and looked everywhere for Sita. Rama asked the river
Godavari, "Where is Sita?" But although Sita had told the
river to speak to Rama, Godavari did not dare answer,
remembering still the terrible form of Ravana.

Rama spoke to the trees, "Show me my Sita slender as a
bough." He saw a glimpse of yellow and ran toward it. But it
was a cluster of yellow flowers and not Sita's dress. Rama
looked all around. He called, "I see you there! Come on out,
I can see you!"

Lakshmana carefully examined all around their home. He
went where Sita would go to bathe, or to draw water, or to
pick flowers. He found the forest gods were gone. Wildflowers were faded, and the Earth herself looked worn and very
old. He found a huge footprint. The highest branches of
many trees were broken. Some deer came, and looked at
Lakshmana, then jumped and ran south looking up at the
sky, and back at the house, and at the Earth, and they were
making little sounds.

Lakshmana went to Rama and said, "She was taken in an aerial car to some place on Earth south from here."

Lakshmana gathered their possessions, took the weapons and left the rest, and led Rama south by the hand. Lakshmana kept down his eyes, and soon he knelt. "Rama, a strange white flower lies here fallen, holding a drop of blood, still threaded with silk from a garland."

Slowly they continued on. First Lakshmana found broken bits of ivory inset with pearls. Then he discovered a sharp torn piece of gold armor; then a belt; then a sharp bladeless iron arrow, feathered with iron, eight paces long and stout as a mace; a long quiver packed full of such arrows, the whole thing crushed and all the arrows broken inside; then a huge vulture wing-feather crushing to death beneath it two asses who wore the faces of demons; an axle standing on end; yokes and tresses hanging in the trees; the wreckage of a war-chariot overturned from the sky and fallen in many pieces; the ground blooksoaked and raked with hooves and claws and marks not human.

Then Lakshmana found ten great bleeding dark arms torn off at the shoulders. Rama looked at all this and said, "Here the Rakshasas fought each other over Sita, and they tore her apart and this is her blood all over. They pulled her head off. . . ."

Lakshmana said, "These are all left arms. The hands wear costly gold rings. They are marked on their palms by the royal birth-wheels of an Emperor."

"What does that mean?" asked Rama.

"The Rakshasa King himself was here—look there!"

They saw Jatayu. The Vulture King lay on his back, barely alive. Lakshmana and Rama ran to him, and slowly Jatayu said, "Lord Rama, it was my age . . . my old age alone kept me from killing Ravana to save your wife!"

Rama said, "The plain truth is that there is no end to my bad fortune. You have given away your life for me, and despite that my life herself has been taken from me, and they killed her. . . ."

"She is alive. Sita lives!" Jatayu coughed. "But not without cost did Ravana go past me, strong though he was, well-armored and on a sky-chariot—." Blood ran from Jatayu's beak and he died.

Rama said, "See how in every race of creatures live the brave!" Rama and Lakshmana performed Jatayu's funeral. They burned his body, and Lakshmana put out food for the birds of Dandaka, strips of meat from the killed asses. To Rama, the fire that burned Jatayu was cool.

Rama and Lakshmana went south, and all the happiness and life had been worn out of the land they walked on. That was the ground beneath the flight-paths used by the Rakshasas going between Lanka and the garrison that had been north in Dandaka. The Rakshasas had ruined it by flying overhead.

Empty houses sheltered jackals, and their yards were littered with broken things. There were no deer, only dogs gone wild. They found no more signs of Sita or Ravana until at last they came to the southern limit of Dandaka Forest, crossed a dark-flowing river and saw a lake, and a hill nearby covered with green.

That was Lake Pampa. In that place had lived a hermit named Matanga. Once when he was too tired to search for water, Matanga had brought rising from the Earth the waters of every ocean. His touch took away the salt and he made a freshwater lake and lived on its shore with an old woman named Savari.

In the year that Rama was first exiled, Matanga had died. But his virtue lingered and the waters of Lake Pampa kept the country green and fair, and Savari still stayed in their hermitage. Rama and Lakshmana walked by the lakeside and saw her house in a clearing, in a wood of coral trees.

Savari was very old, all dressed in white with long grey hair, and she had become very thin and short with age. She was sitting beside a newly made funeral pyre.

Savari rose to welcome guests, and Rama and Lakshmana sat down by her, and Rama said, "I am Rama. Are you well? Do you use little food and little anger?"

"I am Savari." She smiled. "Favored now is my birth and favored my long service to Matanga since you have come, my Lord Rama."

Rama asked, "Where are we?"

Savari said, "Ayodhya Prince, I stayed behind to receive you when my Master died; we knew you would come to Matanga's wood. He told me. Those little fires burning there by the edge of the trees were kindled by Matanga and he would tend them, but since he died they have burned on all by themselves, and those lowly blue flowers growing by them are from drops of sweat that fell from my Master as he bent to put on wood. Those clothes of bark hanging there have not dried in thirteen years. Everything waits. That hill is Rishyamuka. It is guarded by little snakes, and over it Ravana carried Sita away through the sky."

"You saw them!"

"Rama, in misfortune seek for friendship."

"Where?" asked Rama.

Savari replied, "On Rishyamuka live the two monkeys Sugriva and Hanuman. We are not far from the hidden cave city of Kishkindhya, the capital of the monkey people, and the monkey King Vali has driven out Sugriva from there and banished him. Only Hanuman remained Sugriva's friend. Vali tried to kill them but they came here. Vali is Sugriva's brother, yet he has separated him from his loving wife."

"Done what?" said Rama.

"Hanuman doesn't know his strength. He and Sugriva fled in fear. Here they are safe, because Matanga cursed Vali once. Neither Vali nor any of his people can enter this wood that goes over the hill."

"Hanuman." Rama looked at the hill. "Who is this monkey Hanuman?"

"That white monkey?" Savari laughed. "Oh, no one can equal him. He is Sugriva's one loyal friend. He is brave and kind. He is the child of the Wind. What do you want to hear about him?"

"A friend," said Rama. "Tell me everything."

"Then," said Savari, "I will tell you the best story I know."

Listen, Rama—

Mount Meru is at the center of the surface of Earth, no man knows where. On Meru the Sun will appear to travel around you. Bright sunlight has turned that mountain's soil into gold. The whole mountain is solid gold, but because the sunlight changed the ground so gradually none of the plants were harmed, and from the gold still grow grasses and trees. Birds and animals live there as on a common hill, and there is water.

Lord Brahma comes down to our world of Earth when it pleases him. Once he rested on Mount Meru. He shed a tear from his eye, and where it touched the golden ground, right then and there the first monkey was born.

Brahma named him Riksharaja and stayed on Meru to keep him company. Riksharaja played on the hill. He wandered around and explored by day and ate all the fruit he wanted. Every evening Riksharaja returned to the Grandfather of the Worlds and put some flowers at Brahma's feet.

Early one morning Riksharaja saw his own reflection when he bent over to drink from a lake. He thought it was the face of an enemy trying to take his water. Riksharaja attacked. He jumped in the lake, went completely underwater, and found no one there. When that monkey came back out onto the shore again, he had been changed into a female.

She was a monkey girl so beautiful, that as she stood on the hillside of Meru both Indra and Surya the Sun fell in love with her. That same morning, first Indra and then Surya came down and made love to her.

The gods' children are quickly born. That monkey girl had two gold-colored babies, and that afternoon she washed them in the lake. They splashed water all over her and by the time they were clean Riksharaja found that he was again a male.

Riksharaja took his sons to Brahma. They named Indra's son Vali and called his younger brother Sugriva. Brahma gave Vali the city of Kishkindhya. Brahma made more monkeys and populated the woods, and gave them the friendship of the bear people. Vali became the monkey King, and Indra gave his son a victory-garland of little lotus flowers cut from gold.

Riksharaja stayed with Brahma as his friend. They lived in Brahma's heaven and Riksharaja could see whatever happened to his sons. Vali seemed to get everything, and so Riksharaja asked Vayu the Wind to father a son, a monkey who would always be Sugriva's true friend.

Vayu the restless Wind went to Kishkindhya and looked around. The best-looking monkey girl he saw was Anjana. If Anjana took human form she could have the love of any man. She was walking atop a green mountain near here, when Vayu came to her. He gently stole away her clothes and embraced her in his long arms.

That same day, Hanuman was born. He was a little monkey with white fur and a red face and brownish-yellow eyes. Anjana was married to another monkey. She left Hanuman all alone by the mouth of a small cave on that hill and went home.

Little baby Hanuman was hungry. Night came, and went by, and dawn approached. No one came to feed him. He lay on his back by his cave looking at his toes, and the sky grew

lighter and lighter. In the east there was first a pale grey
light, then there was a silver, then gold and rose.

Hanuman saw the glorious Sun rise into the air like a big
ripe mango fruit. Newborn though he was, he knew what
fruit was. He licked his sharp bright little teeth, crouched
down and jumped with a leap and a bound up into the sky
and went flying straight at the Sun.

His father the Wind came blowing over Hanuman from
out of the north, cool and fresh from the snows. He saved
Hanuman from being burned up. Hanuman drew near to
Surya and the Sun beamed at him. Hanuman smiled back at
the Sun. The fire of daylight was burning all around the Sun's
chariot, and the flames sucked up the air and pulled Hanuman into the crackling white fire.

There Hanuman tumbled and spun unhurt inside the Sun's
fire. It was time for a solar eclipse. The immortal disem-
bodied head of the Asura Rahu advanced to swallow the Sun
alive. He came close and opened wide his black mouth.

Hanuman bobbed and swirled in the updraft of the Sun.
He was trying to get out of the fire and fighting against the
currents of air and flames. Then he came sailing out and ac-
cidently put his foot right in Rahu's eye.

Rahu went to Indra. "Another Rahu is eating the Sun!"

Indra said, "Look, are you sure?"

"He hit me in the eye!"

"More trouble!" said Indra. He got on his great white elephant Airavata, who was wearing fancy hangings and was
painted with leaves and flowers all over his skin.

Rahu led the way. This time Hanuman got a good look at
him. Rahu was just a round head. He looked like a bigger
mango than the Sun did, and Hanuman jumped him and bit
his ear.

Indra cried—*Stop that!* Hanuman turned. He saw Airavata.
The biggest fruit of all!

Hanuman attacked Airavata and Indra. He came at them
waving his arms and swinging his legs, all out of control.
Airavata stepped aside and Indra pushed Hanuman away
with the flat side of his thunderbolt.

Hanuman fell back to Earth. He broke his jaw falling on a
stone by the mouth of his own cave. Vayu the lord of the
Winds saw this and was angry. He went to his son Hanuman
and took him inside the little cave, and held him.

The Wind hid himself. The bodies of living creatures became hard as wood and their joints stiffened into knots. Like

a banner lowered and put on the ground, the ever-moving air moved no more and lay still. Vayu looked out in anger at all the worlds and stayed with his child, and that was the vanishing of the Winds.

Lord Brahma came to Hanuman's cave and with a touch healed his jaw. Brahma said, "Wind, you are breath. Having no heavy body you pass through all beings." Still Vayu silently held his son. Brahma said, "I made you for life and for life's happiness."

Vayu said, "Who can go where the Wind waits?"

Brahma said, "Hanuman on the lap of the Wind, shining white, you will live as long as you wish to live; you cannot be killed."

Vayu stirred. Then Surya the Sun entered the cave, dressed in gold and jewel-crested clothes, wearing earrings and armbands shining in colors. He smiled at Hanuman. He blinked his eyes and there were blinks of black in the cave, and his lighted jewels went out and came back alight. Then Hanuman slept, as deeply as Night sleeps, and Surya the Sun set three mangos down beside him.

That pleased the Wind. He came out and the worlds could breathe. Hanuman awoke the next day, ate his breakfast, and met his father the Wind outside his cave.

Vayu carried Hanuman to Lord Shiva. Shiva taught Hanuman to change form at pleasure. Nandin the bull taught him languages. Hanuman learned poetry as well, and as he increased his skill at poems Hanuman discovered that he had been wearing golden earrings all his life without knowing it. No one else can see those little gold rings except some person as yet unknown to Hanuman, who will meet him and be his friend and master, so said the bull Nandin.

Hanuman grew up and lived with Sugriva in Kishkindhya. Vali was the King. At first Vali was well-liked, but he soon became petty and mean, and the bears withdrew their friendship.

Vali would go out of Kishkindhya looking for fights. He would stand on top of hills and throw their peaks into the air and catch them. By the entrance of Kishkindhya cave there was a pile of the white bones of those who had accepted Vali's challenges.

Dundhuvi was a giant buffalo, and he was the only other animal as ill-mannered as Vali. Dundhuvi lived in the underworlds, and whatever anyone said to him he took offence at it. Dundhuvi was born angry and impatient and all set to do anyone wrong, and as he got older he got worse, and he left his home to seek new enemies.

Dundhuvi arose from the underworlds through the ocean, swam ashore, and stood on the seashore swearing and cursing and pawing the sand. He looked at the waves. They just kept on coming, they didn't seem to care if he was there or not.

Dundhuvi hooked his horns in the surf and bellowed— *Fight me!*

Waves swept the shore. The long watery arms of the Ocean hissed and pulled and swirled around Dundhuvi's feet—*Go back. Go back. Go back or drown.*

Dundhuvi retreated two steps. "Afraid to show yourself!" he yelled. A great wave arose, foaming and rumbling, coming closer. Dundhuvi walked quickly away on stiff legs with his head in the air.

Then he saw from the distance the snowy Himalya, a low-seeming row of hills white as Shiva's smile, a lotus white. Dundhuvi climbed up into the Hills and battered them with his horns. He broke the rocks and yelled—*Coward! You coward!*

The Mountain King Himavan appeared above Dundhuvi, and he turned his rocky face to look down at the buffalo. Himavan stood on bare metals that struck out from the mountain. He was clothed in a white robe of snow and falling water, with a belt of ice locked fast. He resembled an old man with grey eyes and long white hair, but he was very tall.

With slow gestures Himavan touched together his deeply lined hands. He said, "Do not bring war over the world's edge." The Himalya summits towered away into heaven. An avalanche cracked and fell. "Would you harm my men of Peace . . . ?"

A storm came blowing and the black pines moaned, the dark deodars cried and ice broke like glass from their boughs. It began to sleet.

Himavan spoke. "The strong are not angered . . . we know, and you do not know. . . ." Cloud closed out the world. The Hills and Himavan disappeared. They were standing, hard to move, lost in the blasting white wind.

The frozen snow and ice tore down at Dundhuvi, biting and whirling along on the screaming wind that cut over the blades of the sharp ridges above. Dundhuvi ran.

He ran until he got to Kishkindhya. There he stuck his

head inside the cave city and roared like a drum. Vali came
out on a balcony of his palace. He had his arm around his
Queen Tara, and he gave her his wineglass and said, "Don't
stay while you can still go, you dumb ox!"

Dundhuvi said, "I'll return when you are sober. Don't
worry, enjoy yourself!" He roared again just to hear the echo.

Vali said, "But I am only drunk at the sip of a fight!" He
put on his golden garland and jumped down. Dundhuvi
backed off outside the cave, and Vali came out and faced
him like a fire placed on the Earth.

They fought for a long time, but in the end Vali caught
Dundhuvi's horns and broke his neck. He let the body fall.
Then he swung the dead buffalo around by the tail, and let
him go.

Dundhuvi's corpse fell right there on Rishyamuka hill, and
as it flew overhead through the air blood poured from its
mouth and touched our altar here. Matanga cursed Vali to
die if he ever came here. He gave the monkeys who lived
here one day to leave, and then he put the curse of death on
any of Vali's people who would enter Matanga's Wood.
Matanga thought of this forest as his son, and the monkeys
would tear the trees.

Dundhuvi's son was the Asura Mayavi. Mayavi came to
Kishkindhya for revenge. At midnight he challenged Vali.

Sugriva and Vali both came out. They chased Mayavi and
saw him enter a cave hidden by grass. Vali ordered Sugriva
to wait outside and entered alone. "I don't need any help to
win!"

Sugriva waited there for a year, then blood came out of
the cave. Sugriva heard the cries of Asuras. He went just inside and called Vali, over and over. There was never any answer, and Sugriva could hear the Asuras of the underworld
coming up and their noise got nearer.

To keep them from attacking Kishkindhya Sugriva left the
cave and sealed it with a stone. Sugriva became King of the
monkeys and bears. But Vali was not killed. He spent a year
down in that cave searching for Mayavi, and then Mayavi
and many other Asuras attacked Vali. Vali killed them. He
came up the cave passage to Earth and found it closed, and
kicked apart the stone Sugriva had put there, and like a ghost
he returned.

Sugriva willingly surrendered the crown-diadem of Kishkindhya. But Vali wrongly exiled Sugriva for treason. Vali holds Sugriva's wife Ruma a prisoner. Only Hanuman has stayed with Sugriva. They remembered Matanga's curse and came to live on this hill, after many wanderings.

"Whoever hears this story of the monkey Hanuman," said Savari, "gains his every desire. Rama, the King of the Monkeys and Bears cannot be a thief. He can't take the wives of others. The true Monkey King is on this nearby Rishyamuka Hill, and the quest for Sita is in his hands. Oh Rama, Vali is strong, but Sugriva has sunlight in his soul, though Vali has darkened his happiness."

Lakshmana said, "We will go to Hanuman and Sugriva at once, with your permission."

"Be Sugriva's friend," said Savari, "for he knows all the worlds in fine detail. He can find her wherever she is. Now I wish to die. . . ."

Rama said, "We will leave you now." They left Savari and walked on along the lakeside.

> *I greet my Death.*
> *Yama, come my Friend*
> *And take me home.*

Savari lit her pyre. She bowed her head and walked into the burning flames. Her old body fell from her in ashes.

Rama and Lakshmana looked back. They saw the golden flames rise and saw a chariot coming, armored in silver and drawn by ten grey horses running on air.

That was Indra's chariot flying gold and silvery flags. Indra came to Savari's fire. Under a white umbrella hung with flowers Indra leaned over the chariot rail not far above the ground, and spoke to Savari.

All around the marvelous chariot were the Gandharvas of heaven, wearing crimson cloth and holding drawn swords. Across their chests were blazing chains, and they were all twenty-five years old, the eternal age of heaven.

Savari became a young woman in a golden robe standing in the fire. She rose up and Indra took her on the chariot, and like a streak of light they went away up through the many skies of the world.

Matali the heavenly charioteer drove through the stars, turned through those fields of far lights. He passed above Indra's heaven, and went by the sky-homes of the saints. Above it all, they stopped at Brahma's realm. Lord Brahma saw Savari and said—*Welcome home.*

Rama and Lakshmana bathed then, in the waters of the seven seas in Lake Pampa. Rama said, "How shall I live without my Sita?" They climbed onto Rishyamuka Hill covered with trees. Sugriva and Hanuman stayed hidden near the summit and watched them coming closer.

THE BOOK OF THE FOREST ENDS.
THREE PARTS ARE PAST, AND FOUR REMAIN.
HERE THE BOOK OF KISHKINDHYA BEGINS.

On Rishyamuka Hill when a man falls asleep, if he has bad in him he is beaten by Asuras in a dream, and wakes up sore and bruised all over. But if a totally good person sleeps there he dreams of gold and wakes up really rich.

Rama and Lakshmana were climbing when a poor woodcutter appeared from the woods. He bowed and smiled at them. He put down his bundle of sticks and sat on it.

"What whim has led the Sun and Moon to visit me here?" The woodcutter wiped his hands. He smiled and nodded his head. "Are you truly gods walking on foot through the world? Oh, you two, you look at me like lions, my boys!"

Rama smiled. He looked around the hill, as though he had stepped fresh from the world's beginning to look around and see what had been done. He looked at the woodcutter. "Oh Hanuman of golden earrings."

"Rama, I remember you now." Hanuman shook himself. There he was, white with glossy fur, a long tail curved gracefully, long thin arms, feet like hands, a red face and white teeth and light eyes almost all yellow. "Why do you want Hanuman?"

"Ravana took Sita."

"We looked long after her," said Hanuman. He grew bigger. "Get on my shoulders," he said, and took them on uphill to meet Sugriva.

Sugriva had gold fur, and his throat looked like a piece of

shiny gold. Rama embraced Sugriva. There was a small fire and Rama and Sugriva walked around it for a pledge of friendship, and each of them promised to take the other's joy and sorrow as his own.

Then Sugriva and Rama and Hanuman and Lakshmana sat down, and Sugriva the Monkey King said, "See what fell on our hill." He brought out Sita's scarf, untied it, and all Sita's ornaments were there. "A young goddess whose eyes curved back round to her ears was carried away by Ravana."

Rama asked, "Are these hers, Lakshmana?"

"Yes."

Sugriva said, "I know every place beneath the Sun's many rays."

Hanuman said, "Wherever he took her we can find her. Yet we have to hide on this hill, and Sugriva must suffer for the separation from his wife."

Rama said, "Let this meeting be the turning point of your fortune."

Lakshmana said, "Truly, a friend is protection against injury and a help for sorrow."

Hanuman smiled. "We'll keep these till we may give them back to Sita."

At that moment elsewhere in the world Sita felt her left eye wink by itself, and the same thing happened to Vali in Kishkindhya, and Ravana's ten left eyes also winked. That is a good sign for females and a bad one for males. Hanuman served roast fish from the lake and water in lotus-leaf cups shaped like boats.

After they had eaten, Sugriva said, "All Vali's other enemies are dead and their wives are widows. I don't know what we can do. Look, over there is the immense corpse of the buffalo Dundhuvi, and Vali threw him here all the way from our city."

Rama got up, and went over to the corpse and pushed it with one toe. The tough dry skin and all those bones went far over the horizon.

"Ah, now it's light as grass, but Dundhuvi was heavy when he was killed," said Sugriva.

Rama opened his quiver. He took out a war arrow. The arrow was gold plated, thicker than a finger, half as long as a staff, marked with Rama's name and vaned with the feathers of the fastest birds and steel tipped.

Rama strung his bow and said, "It is wrong for people in love to be separated!" He shot and his arrow went through seven old ironwood trees stout as turrets.

The next day Rama and Lakshmana and Hanuman and Sugriva went to the mouth of Kishkindhya cave and hid in the forest. Sugriva said, "I've run in fear from Vali for a long time!" He tightened his belt and stepped out in the open, and called for Vali to come out of Kishkindhya and fight.

Inside, in the monkey palace in the cave city, Queen Tara said, "Listen, that is Sugriva. Something is wrong. Take warning, there is danger."

Vali replied, "From him?"

"Our people have seen Rama and his brother nearby."

"My brother's a coward, why would anyone help him?" Sugriva called again.

"Don't go out," said Tara. "Be kind to your brother, and return him his wife, she is so sad here."

Vali said, "He is the one starting the fight." He sent for a sentry. "Who is with Sugriva?"

The guard said he had seen no one. Vali said to Tara, "Rama would not hide to harm me; he would never break the fair rules of war."

Tara laughed. "Rules?"

Vali gave her a pat. "My dear, the only reason to consult a woman is to find out what not to do!"

"No woman advises any man she does not love, even among monkeys. Be his friend."

"Oh, I won't hurt him," said Vali, "I'll chase him off, that's all. And it is actually wrong for wives to command their husbands."

Lovely Tara tied Indra's golden garland over Vali's shoulders. Vali ran out of Kishkindhya like the golden Sun popping up over a hill. He saw Sugriva and grabbed him, and the two monkeys were wrestling all over the clearing in front of Kishkindhya.

They were moving so fast they both looked the same. At first Rama could not aim. Then one of them was winning, and he wore gold flowers and Rama shot at him from the trees.

The bowstring twanged. There was the arrowy sound of air

being torn like cloth, and the sound of a blow. The arrow hit
Vali and went right through his heart.

Vali lay fallen on his back and only his golden garland
kept him alive. Rama and Lakshmana stepped out of
concealment and Queen Tara ran out from Kishkindhya with
her son Angada. Weeping softly, she told Angada, "That is
Death there in the form of an archer leaning on his bow, and
from a distance he has killed your father the King."

Sugriva and Rama and Hanuman and Lakshmana stood
near Vali. They were pale and stared aimlessly at the ground.
Sugriva was crying and his tears were mixed with blood from
a cut under one eye. The Kishkindhya monkeys gathered
whispering, sad whispers like the night wind heard by a
lonely man.

Tara fell like a star and embraced Vali. "My Lord, send
away these people and turn to me."

Vali looked at them all. He smiled at Tara, and he said to
Angada—*My son, for anger I die. Help Rama.*

Vali the shelter of hundreds was dead. Time, you have no
friend and no kinsman and no family. The long-leaping monkeys trembled.

Hanuman picked up the golden war arrow that had pierced
through Vali's heart, and turned the shaft in his hands and
watched its mark—*Rama . . . Rama . . . Rama. . . .*

Tara touched the corpse. "Why won't you reach out to me?
If you are angry, at least speak to your son . . . Oh. . . !"
She looked at Rama. "Will you eat your kill, noble man?"

Hanuman spoke to Tara. "Vali has left us on a long journey. The affairs of life are now our task. We live on, but in
heaven Vali will win the hearts of the dancing women in
their bright robes and their coronets and red flowers. Look
on what was his body for the last time, Queen."

"Give me that arrow," said Tara. "Vali was my mate. I
loved him, he was a good King."

"Here, take it."

"Hanuman, I am myself but a part of Vali."

"Oh Queen," said Hanuman, "a mate is this world's best
gift to anyone."

"They say that Death has met us all."

"Many times, I have heard."

"When a weakling has been abused and has at last a
chance to get even, he is allowed to leave the True."

"My Lady, your King kept my King separated from his mate."

Tara said, "Surely that is wrong, to part two people in love."

Hanuman said, "As wrong as war, my Queen. That was not right."

Queen Tara answered, "Oh Hanuman, tell Rama I forgive him, I forgive his murder—" Tara drove the arrow through her own heart and died.

The Monkey Prince Angada looked at his mother and father and looked at Rama. Angada said, "I'll help you. Grief does the dead no good, and the wives and sons of our warriors never lament, not by day nor in the night."

That evening the monkeys brought out their royal hearse, like a war-chariot without wheels. Monkeys carried it on their shoulders, and other monkeys dressed the dead King in jeweled clothes.

They took Vali away on the bier covered with flowers, only his face showing. The monkeys went away from Kishkindhya, up toward the banks of a hill stream. Some walked before the hearse breaking apart jewel ornaments in their hands, and letting the pieces fall to Earth, and others cast down broken pieces of shiny silver. Then behind the corpse came singers—*Glory! Glory to the Moon. Glory to Water. We burn Vali. Vali slain by one arrow!*

When they had gone Hanuman said to Rama, "Come into the unconquerable cave city of Kishkindhya. Tomorrow we will make Sugriva our King."

"No," said Rama. "The rain is coming."

Sugriva said, "Rama, it is after midsummer, but still we have a few days. . . ."

Rama said, "King, go into your city. Lakshmana and I will live in the woods somewhere by here. You've been a long time away from home."

There was a faraway thunder. Sugriva said, "People can't travel in the rainy season, that's true enough, Rama. When the rain ends, I promise you, we will find Sita and obey you."

"I'll take you to a good place to stay," said Hanuman. "Follow me, my Lords."

Hanuman went bending low through the trees, up the slopes of Prasravana Hill, the hill of Springs, and led them to an airy wide cave, well lit, with water near, and he touched his hands. "I could have saved Sita by now more than once," said Hanuman.

Rama started to speak, but the wailing of grief from Vali's funeral came to their ears just then. Rama said, "Leave us alone, Hanuman."

The Search

*The Truth upholds the fragrant Earth and
makes the living water wet. Truth makes fire
burn and the air move, makes the sun shine
and all life grow.*

*A hidden truth supports everything. Find it
and win.*

As Hanuman turned back down the hill the rains began.
First, Lord Indra opened Heaven's gate and threw a thun-
der-stone tearing and crashing through the dark clouds in the
still and heavy air. Then another thunder came, sloping on a
shallow path, rolling and rolling nearer. Hanuman ran for
home, thunders fell crashing closer and striking down, and
round black clouds grew like pavilions in the sky and covered
over all the world.

The ever-moving wind half-blew past the hills; then he
swept impatiently down on Earth, snapping the flags of the
cities, pressing through the forests and over the hills, driving
the dust along the hot fields, throwing himself headlong
against the world. Peacocks unfurled their tails like colored
fans dancing on the mountain in the trees. The sky rumbled,
and over Prasravana Hill a golden lash cut into the sky and
the lightning fell and the rains were born. The Earth shook
and the mad wind sang. The sky broke open, the rain down-
poured, and all the world's water fell in an endless torrent.

The cold heavy rain fell on and on in big drops from Indra's dark blue clouds. Lightnings blazed and thunders exploded; the violent wind whirled and rattled the bamboos;
and the racing air sent the rain streaming up and around and
sideways in every way. The rays and lights of the Sun and
Moon were gone. The dust was slain, and Earth with all her
trees was soaking wet, in the night and in the storm. All light

163

faded, the long dark night began, and the wind broke down the bamboos so their pearls fell out and rolled in the water.

Soon after the rain begins, the sound of the water changes. Very soon the brittle dryness of a year has gone, and all is wet through, and day after day the lasting rain falls into mud and beats down on wet stones and breaks the leaves. The hill seems made of water. Then all things reveal that they are but made of water.

The swift hill-rivers rushed brimful and laughing down the hill, dark brown in flood, roaring and foaming with white-crested waves. Water ran down the stony trails and the land below disappeared underwater. The world was an overflowing lake and the hills were islands. The heavy dark clouds had to rest on the high mountain peaks and seemed to take root there, and rows of white herons flying in the wet wind were a white garland for heaven.

In the dripping forests the brahmanas sang the holy Veda, and around them the rivers ran like sacred threads over the shoulders of mountains, ceaselessly murmuring with water. Elephant kings, those enemies of trees, walked themselves like mountains wrapped in dark clouds, and turned back in anger at the lightning storms and the cloudbanks of thunder, tossing their white tusks, waving their ears and trumpeting, thinking that some other elephant hung with a golden chain had challenged them in a deep voice.

Then the rains relented and the wind withdrew; you could catch the fresh breeze like cold water in the hollow of your hands. The wild plane trees flowered dark red, and Autumn came and smiled at the world. In the evenings the sunbeams came pale and yellow through the clouds. Hills and trees were fast asleep shrouded in white mist. The woods steamed. The pouring red rivers that had washed down the metals of the mountain became clear, and there were birds again upon their waters. By Rama's home, the lovely rivers fell downhill, and the weeping boughs of trees trailed in the water and tried to hold them back, but though the rivers were pleased, though they turned back a little, still glittering and sparkling bright, adorned in silver, they excitedly approached their lord the Sea.

The sky would open and show the stars for a moment in the nights. By day new shoots unfurled and the buds opened on the trees, and from water-soaked meadows grew green moss and green grass and green fern. Full waterfalls cascaded and plunged with noise. Lions again walked through the morning dew and purred softly in their new coats of fur, and in the pines the birds sang to shake the water from their paled wings, and flew out from their homes and back again.

Then the Sun! All the watery drops shone like rainbow jewels fallen on the grass and leaves from an Apsarasa's necklace broken in love. At noon the Sun felt good, he was steadily fleeing far to the south, leaving the far Himalyas covered with snow. Fire was comfortable in the cold west wind, and the night hours grew freezing and long. Roseapples ripened and then fell, waterflowers opened and blackberries blossomed. Then the lotuses died from the frost and left only their dry stalks above the water that was so cold thirsty elephants like cowards withdrew their trunks when first touching it.

The mild yellow Sun took the cold Moon's good fortune, and the Moon was veiled as a glass breathed upon, and dim. On Prasravana Hill Rama watched the white moonrise and thought—*Earth is in tears.*

Then for many days heaven was clear over all the world, and the river banks emerged from under water. In the north snow came at night on fast dark winds. On the warm plains the golden grain slightly bent its heads. The peacocks furled their tails and gave up love and games. Many-colored snakes came from their pits, and wide-winged swans returned to the lands around Kishkindhya. Elephants rolled in the dust, birds rose in flights from the grainfields, silver fish swam in the slow rivers, and it was almost Winter.

From within Kishkindhya cave Rama and Lakshmana could hear the monkeys singing and dancing to drums, and still they waited for Sugriva to come to them. Monkeys kill no game, and all round their city the small and harmless deer were unafraid. Rama felt Sita's loss the more when he saw them so secure in their woody homes. New flowers began to reappear. Rama saw a new open lotus and said, "These petals are shaped like Sita's eyes. . . . When Ravana eats her, she will cry out to me in fear, and her round breast once colored with red sandal-paste will be bathed in bright scarlet blood."

"Better to act than wonder and dream," said Lakshmana. "I'll have a word with Sugriva."

Lakshmana took his bow and set out for Kishkindhya, thinking over what he would say and knocking trees aside with his leg, thinking how Sugriva would answer and breaking rocks to bits with his feet. He entered the cave and saw Kishkindhya city's bright towers rising; he jumped over the monkey barricades, leapt their moat and approached the wall. The monkey guards looked down and Lakshmana stared back at them and sighed, and at that sight the sentries ran away.

Angada the monkey prince opened the main gate. Lakshmana said, "My child, announce me—*Lakshmana waits for your promise at the gate.*"

Angada ran for Hanuman, and Hanuman ran to the king. He found Sugriva sprawled out asleep in his drinking room and grabbed his feet and shook him. Sugriva awoke with a start and blinked his bleary red eyes. "What are you doing?"

Hanuman said, "Get up, you fool!"

Sugriva sat up. "Who has been telling you tales about my imaginary shortcomings?"

"You've been drinking for over three months," said Hanuman, "and now Lakshmana is at the gate."

"Oh gods of heaven give us a little peace and quiet around here, can't you?"

"Are you still drunk?" asked Hanuman. "Get up, go to him, kneel, fold your paws together like a family man, and bow down that he may abuse you and spare your life. A promise-breaker is so vile no beast will eat his body when he dies, and an angry friend is worse than an enemy."

Sugriva said, "Cold water, Hanuman, not talk. . . ."

At the gateway Lakshmana grew tired of waiting and entered the caverns of Kishkindhya city, walking down the sloping outer halls where beside the path fresh water flowed down stone channels to the city within. He went through rooms and past flowery gardens, and saw many monkeys in their robes and garlands, and they greeted him silently with touching hands, raised to their brows. He came to a wide road watered with perfume and lined with sandalwood trees. At the road's end he crossed over a clear river on a footbridge, and went through a golden-arched gate in the crystal walls of Sugriva's palace.

The tall white and silver roof spires rose up into the cave above, and one long tower pierced through the top and disappeared. Lakshmana walked through a grove of blue-flowering trees, stepping his way over low flowers colored like gold melting in the cool shade. He entered a doorway and crossed seven rooms where women on gold and silver couches were stringing flowers. Then he came into the heart of the monkey women's quarters—a dancing hall of marble and jewels, with soft seats round the walls and tables for banquets—and stood guiltily in a corner.

Lakshmana thought—*I don't belong here, where shall I go?* From within some unseen secret inner apartment came happy women's voices and music and the jingling of bells and jewel belts. Lakshmana couldn't remember how he had come in. There were fine-cut window screens everywhere in the walls and too many doors. Then Lakshmana pulled his bow, let go the string, and the bowstring rang out like the snap of a whip. Lakshmana looked for some escape.

Nearby, Hanuman heard the bow-cry and he jumped. *He's really here!*

"Relax," said King Surgriva. "He can't get out. A job for the Queen."

Sugriva called Queen Ruma. "Dear, good men like Lakshmana out there will not usually hit a woman. Go to him, read his heart and console him."

The good-looking Queen Ruma went before Lakshmana with many downcast looks, her feet unsteady, her eyes red with wine, her golden belts flowing about her hips. She said in a husky voice, "Oh Lakshmana, why are you angry with your loving friends?"

Lakshmana said, "It's your husband, my Lady."

"After long fear and shame," smiled Ruma, "he is lost again in the early springtime countryside of happiness, and led astray by summery love. Carefree, even a man in love forgets who he is, what of a monkey? Forgive us our pleasure, be not angry against us. And he is still true to you, come."

She led Lakshmana to Sugriva. The golden monkey King now sat on a rich carpet, and rose to join his hands together, wearing a gaudy garland round the ruff of gold fur that was his neck. "Welcome, Lakshmana, welcome."

"Best of monkeys," said Lakshmana, "Vali's path is not so narrow that no one else can follow him, also killed by Rama's arrows. Remember past kindnesses and beware; there's nothing that can't be accomplished by a little work."

Sugriva smiled. "But we care! Climb the watchtower with me."

They went up a long winding stairway of silver, out through the cave roof and onto a balcony high above a hilltop. Lakshmana looked out at the valleys he had just left. Everywhere, hordes of monkeys and apes and big shaggy bears covered the land.

Sugriva said, "Thirteen days ago, I laid my commands on my people, and I asked for help from the bears. We are all aware of illusion; we are versed in arts and the law; we are strong and we come from all over the world. Oh Lakshmana, when we fight we hurl entire hills and rock faces, we stamp down the forests like grass underfoot and splash the water from the sea. If we trip, the Earth cracks, if we want rain we capture the clouds and just wring them out, if we give a small celebration the noise knocks the birds stunned right out of the sky, and we number in millions. . . ."

Hanuman went to tell Rama the animals had come. Sugriva and Lakshmana went back downstairs from the tower, and in the throne room of Kishkindhya they met Jambavan the King of the Bears, an old dark bear with a crown and earrings of gold, with smoky grey eyes, huge paws and long arms, who stood on two feet or on four, just as he wished.

"Who came?" asked Sugriva.

"I will tell you," growled Jambavan. "Outside your cave are the white tree-dwelling monkeys who change their forms at will; the tall blue coconut monkeys strong as elephants; the yellow honey-wine monkeys with sharp teeth; the charcoal monkeys, born to the daughters of Gandharvas, who worship the Sun; the grey apes from the woods skirting the Edge of the World, who are handsome from eating only berries; the black ones with snaky tails, from the caves and hidden passes of Ganga, who never praise themselves; the red ones with lion-manes; and all the great bears of Earth have come here dark as gloom, brown and black and terrible to meet."

"Leave your families here with ours in Kishkindhya," said Sugriva, "and go out to find Earth's daughter who has been stolen. Because for her Rama laments, and the dark-eyed forest people weep to hear him."

Sugriva told Lakshmana, "Fleeing from Vali I have come to know every place in the world." He sat on his throne and sent for the General of the East. An old grey monkey entered, moving slowly, his eyes bright and round, dressed in hides tied fast with a bowstring, a red cloth tied round his forehead, white bow scars all over his arms. He looked sharply at Lakshmana and then at Sugriva, and said nothing.

"Search the Eastern quarter of the world for Sita," said Sugriva. "Go through the silver mines and the mulberry

groves where silkworms feed; search the mounta[...]
rich cities embraced by the Eastern Sea; search the [...]
houses of the barbarians whose ears fold across their [...]
like scarves, those curious men of red hair and yellow bodi[...]
and hard round faces black as iron, who eat men, who have
but one foot and yet outrun the deer. Search those islands
where bristly hunters live on raw fish and mermen swim undersea, where the hillmen run on four legs and strange fisher-
men never leave their boats all their lives. Search the Gold
and Silver Islands whose sharp hills pierce heaven, where live
the swans and the gods. Go through the wilderness and the
deep woods of stony rills, the mountain crags, the hermitages
and sweet gardens and bowers, the farms and villages and
sandy deserts, the bare ocean islands cut off by dark waves
and storms howling at sea. By the Eastern Sea of salt beware
of the huge hungry demons hanging head-down like misshapen rocks on the cliffs over the surf, who die every day
when struck by the sunrise, but fall into the sea and revive,
and return to hang again on the cliffs. Go beyond, to the
limit of the world's land, to the shore of the primeval milk
sea, whose breast ripples with white milk waves like strands
of pearls, where silver lotuses shine with filaments of gold.
Stop by the tall golden palm tree that Indra planted on the
last shore to mark the end of the East. There through a crevice cleft in the Earth you can look down and see far below
you the serpent Sesha white like the Moon, who upholds
Earth on his coils, who has a thousand heads with wide lotus
eyes, who is clad in blue. Farther east, far out to sea is the
submarine fire burning, coming out from the mouth of a
horse, changing the milk to salt seawater again, from under
water boiling up steam to make the rains, waiting for when
the world ends the next time to consume for food all this
wondrous universe of life that moves and of creatures immobile. You may hear from afar the cries of feeble ocean-beasts
in fear of those flames, and across that lonely sea you will
dimly see the beginnings of the impassable Mountains of A
World and No World, the boundary hills surrounding the
Universe, their far sides in perpetual darkness, so high that
all other mountain peaks would lie at their feet, and our
noble summits would but form their base. On their flanks
trees and high abodes rise up beyond our vision, nor can we
ever approach them. Over the milk sea, across the barrier
Hills of A World and of No World, no creature can go. They
encircle the universe. Past them in every direction is eternal

acherous, without Sun and Moon and
it darkness itself and all the cosmos is
shell of an egg.

wn first appears bright with brilliant glory
an the sunrise gates of gold, and people living
nile also become golden colored. Search everywhere
I have said to look, and wherever I have not named. Stay
away no longer than one month from today."

The Monkey General of the East bowed to his king, turned
on his heel and walked stiffly outside the cave city. One quarter of the monkey soldiers set out following him. Their
weapons blazed, their supply wagons rumbled along, the dust
from their march trapped the sunbeams in the sky and hid
the day. There was a bewildering noise, the floor trembled in
Sugriva's throne room, and they were gone.

Then the red-haired monkey General of the West entered
before Sugriva, muttering to himself. He came to a halt,
smashed his brass sandals against the stone floor, swept off his
iron helmet that trailed long green plumes and parrot
feathers, swirled his red cape, fell to his knees with a crash of
bronze armor and cried—*Victory to the King! Jaya! Jaya!*

Sugriva said, "Explore the West for Sita. Search her out by
force and by skill; discover what has happened to her; learn
if she is waiting somewhere on the way West."

"Majesty!"

"Listen to me," said Sugriva. "In the West the Sun's light
ends and there the kind Lady Night has her home. Follow
west the cool forest streams that flow from the high cold
lakes; search the wide western kingdoms and empires, the hot
plateaus and tablelands, the natural arbors of entangled
creepers and vines so hard to penetrate. Where the Sindhu
river falls into the Western Sea is the Hill of the Moon, with
a hundred crests and ten thousand ridges lost in the sky,
where live those giant wild birds who carry up to their nests
whales from the sea and elephants from the land, and keep
them there for little pets. Their nests are so large that the elephants happily roam and wander within them eating their fill
in the shade of huge trees, and round the edges where the
rain collects the whales swim and dive. Search this place.
And near here as well, do the hermit Gandharvas store food
for the rains and keep orchards. Take no fruit from them, let
none of these creatures see you. Past that place is Diamond
Thunder Mountain, a steep hill of blue adamant. Cascades
run all through channels deep within it, and along those dark

swift waters boars and lions roar, forever excited ?
and echo of their own voices. Westward of that hill beg
golden flower trees that lead up sixty thousand low hills
gold which surround Sunset Hill. The Sun dispels the
darkness of the world up to this point. You can go this far.
Do not go beyond, where the Sun and Moon are put out, and
nothing can ever be seen. Look wherever you might expect to
find Sita, and wherever you would think that she could never
be. Return here to me within a month."

"Jaya Sugriva Raja Maharaja Jaya!" The General of the
West battered his way to his feet, touched his hands together
in a salute and left the room.

The white-furred Bear General of the North quietly removed his satin shoes at the door and gracefully entered unbidden, and knelt to the monkey king. "May you be pleased
to command me, Lord."

"Survey for me the northern quarter of the world," said
Sugriva. "Carefully search the Bharata and Kuru kingdoms.
Go on into the bordering deodar forests of the bird tribes in
the foothills, and cross the hair-raising lifeless desert beyond,
and enter the enchanted lands of the Northern Kurus. Keep
your wits about you. As wild animals who are free to come
and go, search Kailasa Hill pale and silver as the moon, and
got through the palace of the Treasure Lord Vaishravana,
who is bowed down to by all creatures who can bend. North
of that, cross the Stone river where Apsarasas swim and play.
Don't let the water touch you, but lean across by using the
tall bamboo stalks lining the banks. Look among the magic
Wishing Trees, and the trees that bear drinks and pearls for
fruit, and the ground vines bearing couches and blankets like
melons on stems. Examine the passes and the sloping sides of
the icy Himalaya, and listen there closely for the sound of
music and the voice of sweet song and happy laughter; because what may seem to the eye to be but a bare mountainside at first, will often be an illusion, that hides the
playgrounds of the Naga serpents beneath a spell of invisibil-
ity. Discover these hideaways and search them. Those
Himalyan Naga people are blessed and fortunate, they are
never sad nor want any beautiful thing, and every day they
gain marvelous abilities and skills. And among the Hills is
Mount Meru the center of the world, invisible to doubting
people, round which revolve the Sun and Moon; indeed, in
half an instant the Sun swiftly passes over Meru at noon.
Farther north are treeless hills that hold the homes of horse-

...men. It should be dark beyond there, for ...aches, yet in many vales and caves live ..., and the Northern Kuru land is visible by ... night. On and on to the Far North stretches that ...nally silent, shining with all the loveliness and reality ...y ground warmed by the Sun, though there are few ways for moving creatures and the wide sky is empty of stars or clouds or light from heaven. Go on if you can, and you will reach the North Sea whose waters are black. Look at it from a distance but do not touch the surf and do not lose sight of Mount Meru behind you. Those North Sea shores are made of grey stone and black slate and shrouded in fog. There the cold wet wind blows onshore forever and the sea-spray freezes to salted ice in the air. Waves break like glass on the shore, darkness blots the air, fire will not burn, each day and night become a year and time is lost in eternity. Turn back quickly from this fearful northern border of the world, and let not more than a full month pass before you return."

The Bear General of the North touched his sword-hilt and said—*Yes*. He rose and left the room, and so out from Kishkindhya had gone three-fourths of the animal warriors, gone to search in three of the four directions, when Sugriva said, "Summon Hanuman, bring me Hanuman."

Hanuman came in with Rama, padded over barefoot to the middle of the floor and sat down. The golden monkey prince Angada brought some rugs and also sat, and Sugriva left his throne to join them, and there also sat Rama and Lakshmana and the towering old Bear King Jambavan.

"Now the thing is," said Sugriva, "we saw Ravana fly South. Lanka is South. I make Prince Angada leader. Oh Rama, Hanuman the Son of the Wind will surely find Sita; if you will, stay here with me until they return, and let Lakshmana stay, and let Jambavan go, and let them return in a month." Sugriva stood up. He withdrew a scroll from his robes and gave it to Hanuman and said, "You know what to do and how to do it . . . here is a little message for the Demon King if you should chance to meet . . . don't lose it before you memorize it. . . ." Sugriva smiled and returned to his inner rooms and fell asleep.

Hanuman joined his hands. "Rama, we'll come back soon. Lanka is hard to reach and far away, but I know every province and city and puddle and footprint and demon stronghold in the world. When Vali would chase me and Sugriva we would fly so high that we saw below us all the world like a picture, clear as your face in a mirror. We saw Earth herself turning in space with a strange whirring noise like a firebrand swept quickly through the air. She was like a wheel, and her cities were like small golden coins and her rivers were crossing like threads. Her forests and meadows were tiny patches; the Vindhya and Himalya Hills all covered with rocks looked like elephants in a pond as they rose from the flat Earth."

Jambavan the bear smiled. "Sugriva trusts this Hanuman, and Hanuman relies with even more confidence on himself, and I will also accompany him."

Rama gave Hanuman a wide gold ring. "This is mine and she will know it, for her father Janaka gave it to me after our wedding, and on it is written my name three times—*Rama, Rama, Rama!*"

So with only one thought in their minds, the monkeys and bears fanned out from Kishkindhya into the four quarters of the world. They gave orders and ignored them, passed impassable torrents and climbed unclimbable crags, sifted the sands of the deserts and combed the meadows. They drove the yellow tigers yowling from the glens and the butterflies flapping from the gardens and the village cats running from the fields so that they all fled together. The monkeys and bears rushed along and shouted in high voices and low—*Step Aside! Move over! Let me by, it won't take me long!*

The animals of Kishkindhya ran up along the narrow ways that lead from certain holy temples to the hidden side-doors of heaven. They looked into sealed royal vaults and pawed through secret treasure-rooms forgotten from the past. Disguised as men, they bumped into people and picked their pockets; posing as bandits they shook out the tents of travelers as if they were cleaning rugs, and rattled the caravan wagons like dice to see what would fall out from them.

The monkeys and bears asked the birds a thousand searching questions. They peeked inside closed flowers, talked to the wild beasts and spoke to the tame buffalo. They listened to leopards in the quiet jungle and to men in the city bazaars. They followed streams to their sources in the hills to be sure they were not the water from Sita's tears. And at night they slept on the ground under fruit trees, making their beds beneath their breakfast.

Hanuman and Jambavan and Angada and a quarter of the animal warriors went South. After half a month they were not far from the Malaya Hills where sandalwood forests grow, when they entered a dead forest. Once in that wood, a hermit's son had died when he was but ten years old. His life had run out then, and for that his father cursed all the land to lose its life. There was no food to be found, not even a bee lived there.

Angada led them on through valleys choked with thorns, through twined thickets and dense underbrush and clumps of thistles. They crossed chasms and ravines, and the Monkey Prince made them every one stay in the sight of another, until at last, tired and exhausted, the monkeys and bears collapsed under the dead trees to rest, lying on the dry grass curved over the hills, far to the south.

Then round a hillside flew two swans. His voice faint from thirst, Angada said to Hanuman, "Let's look around there." The birds flew by dripping water from their wings. Around the hill they saw the rocky mouth of a cave. A long narrow lightning scar seared the stones just outside it, and by the entrance grew water-loving trees, and they could feel a cool wet breeze when they looked inside.

But they could see nothing. It was dark as a black night pouring rain. First Hanuman went on in; Angada grabbed his tail, someone else held Angada's tail, and so forming a chain all the animals followed. The floor led down, then the slope steepened and the stones underfoot were wet. Hanuman slipped and started to slide. Angada stumbled and couldn't hold him back; then all the animals began to fall after Hanuman, still holding onto each other, unable to stop, falling faster and faster. The floor become the wall of a tunnel leading down. There were no handholds and nothing to stand on.

They fell for a hundred leagues. Finally they saw a light below, coming up to meet them, and then they dropped down into the bright lighted underworld. They fell all in a heap somehow unhurt, beside a wide splashing river running with cool white wine, with goblets growing from silvery rushes alongside, flowing in a channel lined with delicious little oysters.

It was a large cavern lit up by magic mirrors and chunks of gleaming gold set in the walls and ceiling high above. They all had a drink. Then Hanuman looked around and saw

a white palace with gold balconies and windows screened by
nets of pearls. There were pools and ponds of water and
wines set out in a park, and playing fountains, and petals on
the paths. And in that park the living fish were real gold and
the turtles were chased silver.

The monkeys and bears started to celebrate their rescue.
But by accident Jambavan the bear broke off a branch from
a lovely red rosebush. Blood ran out from the break; the
roses lost their color and were drained white. Then Hanuman
made everyone be still, and with Jambavan cautiously approached the enchanted palace.

A beautiful young girl dressed in a soft black antelope
robe was sitting in the shade of a bell tree, on a bench of
purple lapis, by the jewel stairs that led into the house behind
her. One by one, all the monkeys and bears came and sat
down quietly around her.

And though they did not know it, that marked the end of
the month's time. From wherever they had gone, all the rest
of the animals came again to Kishkindhya, from East and
North and West. The General of the East covered his face;
the General of the West sighed; the General of the North returned covered with ashes. Sugriva said, "Oh Rama, now it is
only Hanuman the Son of the Wind who will succeed in finding Sita . . . but the time is past and where is he?"

In the cave where they had fallen, Hanuman asked that
girl, "Who are you and whose home is this?"

She said, "I am Swayamprabha, a mortal woman, though
here things are not always what they seem. This is Maya's
Cave of Trees. The Asura Maya of masterful art and illusion
built all this."

"How did you get here?" asked Hanuman.

"Little monkey, I am a dancer. I dance, and I dance so well
that Apsarasas from heaven come to watch me, and in this
way I became self-luminous and a dear friend of Hema the
Apsarasa." Swayamprabha smiled. "I'll give you mangoes and
bananas and honey, and will you not tell me why you were
going through the desolate forest on Earth above us?"

"I am Hanuman. We are looking for Sita."

"Oh," said Swayamprabha, "I am pleased, I am well-
pleased with meeting the quick-footed monkeys and the furry
bears!"

While the animals ate, Hanuman asked, "Where is Maya?"

"He could be here right now," smiled that winsome girl.
"Maya the Asura is a true artist, a magician of marvelous
power. Whatever Maya creates is perfect and complete, while
it lasts, before it changes. All is illusion, Hanuman . . . he
would often say—*believe it and make it true*. . . ." Swayamprabha's dark eyes filled with tears, ". . . before he
died. . . ."

Hanuman was all ears. "What happened?"

"Indra killed him," she said, "by the mouth of this very
cave. Hema the Apsarasa inherited this place, and I take care
of it for her. She was Maya's consort, and that angered Indra."

Hanuman said, "Hema's daughter is Queen of Lanka."

"Yes, it was soon after her marriage to Ravana; it was in a
storm on Earth above . . . you can still see the path the
lightning made blasted into the stones!"

"Still—" said Hanuman.

"You're right," said Swayamprabha. "Indras come and go.
Maya is a true genius, the Master of Time. He could escape
that down-lighting thunderbolt."

Hanuman grinned. "And Indra saw it hit?"

"Absolutely! He saw Maya blasted to bits by thunder, right
below his very eyes!"

"All one thousand of them!" said Hanuman.

"Indra had kept Hema closely guarded after her daughter
was born, and Maya got the child somehow, and only the two
of them, father and daughter, stayed all alone in empty
rooms."

"But now Indra is off guard, I think, and in some beautiful
home—"

Swayamprabha laughed. "The Asura Maya is a consum-
mate actor; they never found his body. Who knows? He
might return, he might be very angry to find thousands of
monkeys and bears in his cave. . . ."

Hanuman saluted Swayamprabha. "How may we go?"

She answered, "So you will go to Lanka? But once anyone
enters this captivating cave of illusions, especially by mistake,
he can never return alive to Earth by his own power. But I
will help you, call the others." She put on her dancing bells.

The monkeys and bears assembled. Swayamprabha said,
"Fair fortune to you. Stand still, close your eyes and cover
them. You must not look until I tell you."

The monkeys and bears covered their eyes with their soft
paws and hid their faces in their hands. They heard Swayam-

prabha's dancing bells chime, and it seemed they could smell the ocean.

You can look. They looked around and found themselves facing South, standing by the shore of the Southern Sea, with the coastal Malaya Hills close at their backs. They smelled the sandalwood trees, and from within those hillside forests the southern Nagas watched, coiled in their serpent forms, hidden in the branches behind the pointed leaves.

The blue sea, far and wide, vast as the blue sky! A light breeze lifted spray from the wave-caps, and the waves fell lightly ashore, and slipped back sighing into the deep. A delightful river crossed the beach, lined by trees that hid her waters and islands, and veiled her, like some young girl going to meet her secret lover.

Prince Angada shaded his eyes and stared toward the Sun. Then he slumped to the ground and cried—*Hanuman!*

"What?" Hanuman ran up fast.

"Look where the Sun is! We've lost our other half a month! How long were we inside there?"

Hanuman stared at his shadow. "The month is up alright . . . I thought we had more time. Through ignorance we entered Maya's treeful cave underground and lost all the time. . . ."

Angada got up and stamped his feet. "We were tricked by illusion! Rama's work isn't done, the King's orders aren't obeyed—oh, happy are the dead!" He turned to the others and shouted, "I won't straggle home a failure, I'll starve myself to death right here!"

The monkeys and bears swung their arms and yelled, "We will die with you!" Except for Hanuman and Jambavan the bear, they all sat facing the south, all over the seashore. They fell silent and entered meditation and resolved to die.

Hanuman and Jambavan turned away. They walked on down the beach and left the others there behind them. It was a beautiful day, in the early afternoon. It was quiet. The waves were low and long between. The river ran over round rocks and spoke in whispers, and the gentle wind blew in off the sea.

The old bear Jambavan shuffled slowly along, and the sunlight made his dark fur seem to glow, tipped with reddish lights. He stretched out in the spotted shade beneath an ancient honey tree, and Hanuman lay back against Jambavan's soft flank, and yawned, and began to daydream.

Jambavan snorted and blew some sand away from his nose, and said in a rumbly voice, "Monkey, how was Sita lost? Tell me Rama's story."

Hanuman closed his eyes and put his hands in his lap. "This tale is full of peril and safety," he began. "It will armor noble souls with courage, and bring heart failure to cowards. It will perplex the wise and baffle the foolish, and make them both follow their hearts. It gives reasons for acting in every way; its chapters haunt the mind; its verses make heroes hunger for glory. Its lines shed warm love, its words bring smiles of rage and tears of joy. Oh King of the Bears, this story is not for worried ears and weak nerves, for it holds dread and rash chivalry, sweet honor and elegant danger, and graceful bravery and bountiful generosity beyond knowing."

Hanuman's Jump

Look!
The Son of the Wind leaps into the air,
And flies through the clouds with a roar,
While the enemy waves on the green salt sea
Splash and foam below!

Oh, gold and silver found wild
Are better than coins tamely won;
Treasures found on a hunt are as good
As the pleasures of fancy in heaven.

The little wind carried every word down past the other animals and up into the Malaya foothills. Hanuman said, "Listen well, Oh Jambavan. Once in Fair Ayodhya there was an old King who had no children. . . ."

Hanuman told of Rama's birth and marriage, of his exile and his father's death, of how he killed the demons of Dandaka Forest, and of how Ravana made a golden deer, and of the theft of Sita. The monkeys and bears around Angada began to fuss and squirm. They strained to hear the story, and began to wring their hands and sigh and exclaim things under their breaths.

Then suddenly a flying shadow fell over the beach. Down from the blue Malaya hills swooped a huge vulture. But his flight feathers were burned. He couldn't slow his fall; he waved his wings at the air and landed heavily on the shore. His wings threw up a cloud of sand that buried Angada and all the suicidal monkeys and bears up to their ears in grit.

Hanuman and Jambavan were out of the draft, and Hanuman went right on with his story. The vulture picked himself up. He turned his head and looked at the monkeys and bears he'd buried, first with one big round orange eye, then with the other.

179

"It's true," said the vulture. "People are really rewarded for past good deeds, for here are fat little animals all set out in rows for me by the kindly gods. They've lived all their lives just for my dinner!"

Then down the wind came Hanuman's words, and the vulture heard him say, "Great was the deed of Jatayu. Old though he was, for Sita's sake he nearly killed Ravana before the Demon King tore his soul from this life."

The hulking vulture turned and peered under the honey tree and said—*Who speaks of my little brother Jatayu, King of the Air?*

Hanuman replied, "I am Hanuman. This is Jambavan the Lord of Bears. The animals of Kishkindhya are searching for Sita. Ravana took her from her husband Rama, and he killed your brother when Jatayu tried to stop him in Dandaka Forest."

"My name is Sampati," said the vulture. "If I could still fly I'd go to Lanka and kill Ravana for that!" Towering over the beach he rubbed one leg against the other, like scraping a thousand scythes over pieces of slate.

Prince Angada jumped up out of the sand. Courteously he introduced himself, and said, "Please let us die in peace. All is vain. We can't find Sita, and now whatever I have not seen and heard and done must wait for my next lowly life."

"But monkey prince," said Sampati, "I thought you knew; she is in Lanka, if she lives at all."

"How do you know?"

"My eyesight is as clear as the good Dharma law," said Sampati. "The vulture race can see movement from afar, for a hundred leagues. We have magic golden eyes."

"Are you sure?" asked Angada.

"Prince, I am Sampati, swift as the wind. Eight thousand years ago Jatayu and I went flying together. We went over wood and forest, streams and kingdoms, and higher, and over clouded lakes where snow-geese swam, and over hills of grey stone, and always higher, until we went so high, we saw the Sun shining near and large as the Earth! Then the heat struck us down, and I fell, shadowing Jatayu with my open wings. I fell in a glare of light that made all the worlds seem burning, with no shadow, and no way to know where I was. Then all at once I lost the wind. My brother and I fell apart from each other. I found myself here on these southern hills and slowly my memory returned.

"My wings were useless, and after all these years I have

only today recovered enough to rise from my back. And this year, this summer as I lay helpless I saw Ravana fly overhead with Sita. I kept him in sight all the way to Lanka, and he has not left the island with her since then. She is somewhere behind the city walls, over the sea.

"None of my people knew where I was, until one of my sons found me yesterday night. He was very sad that he could offer me no food, and said he would bring me some later today. He said, 'Father, I caught nothing today. It's the first time I have failed on a hunt since once before the rains, when I prepared to attack a dark demon with ten necks as he flew in the air over a mountain pass, going south, not far from here. He carried a fair woman and peacefully begged me—*I admit my defeat and take your protection.* I could not attack someone who had surrendered to me and I let him go on. And then I heard the sky-voices saying—*That was the doomed Rakshasa King Ravana. By good fortune Sita still lives, and passed you safely by.* But I will bring you food to-morrow.' So it was her, Prince Angada, and there are two of us who saw her carried away. Age has not weakened my mind and eye, though my life now hangs loosely upon me, for I have not eaten since I fell from heaven."

The animals who were still buried in the beach looked worried. Angada told them, "Stop thinking. Bring us some vulture food."

"Say no more!" they cried, and ran to the mountain woods.

Hanuman said, "Sampati, Rama himself burned Jatayu's body, and now your brother lives in heaven. We may live for thousands of years and never hear of a braver deed than his. Had Jatayu been even one day younger he would have won. All noble creatures love Rama, and in his kind service will live their lives for him, and do gentle good to each other, and bad to Rama's foes."

The food arrived, and as Sampati ate, young new feathers began to grow from his wings like golden down. Then Sampati said, "Ignore your time limit, for truly Ravana took Sita at a time when what is lost is soon regained, at a moment most unfortunate to a thief."

Angada asked, "How far is Lanka?"

"Just about a hundred leagues, no more," answered Sampati.

Angada looked out at the sea. One place his still water reflected the image of all this world and all the sky; elsewhere, blown by the wind, he rose in playful waves as high as hills. Angada felt waves of doubt run through the monkeys and bears.

"Who will leap the ocean and bring back news of Sita?" asked Angada.

The monkeys and bears answered, "I can jump ten leagues . . . I can go thirty . . . seventy . . . I can jump a hundred but I can't get back."

Angada said, "I'll try myself."

"You can't,' said Jambavan, "you're our commander. You're the root of our search, it's we who must resort to you and serve you."

"Then there's not a hope."

"No hope!" said the old bear. "Oh, there was a time—" He turned to Hanuman who stood beside him. "Listen, little monkey, are you going to stand there looking at us like an idiot?"

Hanuman said, "What?"

"You're young and strong, what have you done to help us?" said Jambavan. "I didn't hear you say anything just now about how far you can jump."

Hanuman said, "I'll do it."

Oh King Rama, Wind is Fire's best friend. Wind shatters the hills and moves across the eye of heaven. He cannot be seen, but only the heavy things he moves are visible. Hanuman is the son of the fast-racing generous Wind. He equals his father in flight. To enhance the sorrow of the Rakshasas he wants to leap into Lanka. There was dismay and faint sorrow, and it was time to be strong. Then like a storm Hanuman drove away low spirits, like a light he brought courage.

> THIS IS THE END OF THE
> BOOK OF KISHKINDHYA.
> HERE FOLLOWS THE SUNDARA KANDA,
> THE BOOK BEAUTIFUL.

In his mind Hanuman had already crossed the sea and entered the demon city. He climbed one of the Malaya hills to get firm ground under his feet. He began to fill up with power. He grew very large and heavy, and his tread pressed down the hill and crushed the caves of serpents. Out from underworld came the richly dressed Nagas, bruised and hiss-

ing, their hoods spread wide. In their anger they rolled on the
ground with tongues flaming; they spat fire and bit the rocks
in passion. Their venom cracked the hill, and gleams of red
metal and stone showed from within the Earth.

Hanuman climbed higher. With smiles of amazement, the
heavenly Gandharvas and their Apsarasas rose half-dressed
from the hill into the sky and looked down to watch. Hanuman climbed up through their hillside parks, where Gandharva swords and bright-colored robes were hung on the
trees, and golden winecups and silver dishes were on the
ground in fair shady gardens hiding lovers' beds of lotus
petals.

Hanuman neared the summit. His feet squeezed water
from the hill. Rivers tumbled down, rockslides rolled, bright
fresh-broken veins of gold sparkled, tigers ran off and birds
flew away. The tree spirits fled, and in their dens the wildcats
yelled in a frightful chorus, like the cry of the mountain himself through the voice of all his animals.

Hanuman stood on the hilltop. He held his breath and
sucked in his stomach. He frisked his tail and raised it a little
at the end. He bent his knees and swung back his arms, and
on one finger gleamed Rama's gold ring. Then without
pausing to think he drew in his neck, laid back his ears and
jumped.

It was grand! It was the greatest leap ever taken. The
speed of Hanuman's jump pulled blossoms and flowers into
the air after him and they fell like little stars on the waving
treetops. The animals on the beach had never seen such a
thing; they cheered Hanuman, then the air burned from his
passage, and red clouds flamed over the sky and Hanuman
was far out of sight of land.

That white monkey was like a comet, pushing the sky from
his way and bumping clouds aside. The wind roared under
his arms and was pushed down from his breast as he passed,
and made the ocean pitch and roll. Sea spray rose and
steamed up the Sun. Beneath Hanuman as he went, the green
salt water parted, and he could see the whales and fishes like
people surprised at home. The air around Hanuman became
electric, and sheets of light gathered and crackled—blue, and
pale melon green, and flickering orange and red.

Halfway across to Lanka, the golden mountain Mainaka
lived on the ocean floor, and from under sea he saw Hanuman coming and thought he would be tired. Mainaka spread
his glistening golden wings, rose from his watery bed and sur-

faced on the sea. Water poured from his shining sides and looming up against the blue sky he spoke to Hanuman.

"Rest awhile," said Mainaka. "Let me repay my ancient debt to your father the Wind."

Hanuman stopped and leaned on the air. "Who are you?"

"I am Mainaka, the son of Himavan the Mountain King, the brother of Ganga the beautiful river Goddess. I have long hidden deep in the ocean from fear of Indra. In return for the sea's faithful protection, I have stayed as an outer gate against the Asuras from under Earth, who dare not approach me. Come down onto me, land and rest."

Hanuman asked, "What did my father do for you?"

Mainaka said, "In the olden days, long ago, all the large mountains of Earth had wings like I do. We flew where we wanted, but when we landed we were sometimes a little careless. We bowled over the little hills and flattened kingdoms flat as a floor. We got a bad name with the forest men, and they complained to Indra. Then with furious thunderbolts the Lord of Heaven cut off our wings, till out of all the hills only I could still fly. When Indra chased me the Wind carried me away, and here I took refuge of the sea. The wings of the broken mountains have now become clouds. So blessed be you, gentle Hanuman, rest and continue refreshed."

"Forgive me, but I must not break my flight," said Hanuman. He only touched that golden hill with his fingertip and sped away to the South.

When he had gone, Indra came from heaven and told Mainaka, "Keep your wings if you will, for you welcomed Hanuman and you have cared to keep him from danger," and Mainaka went back below the waves.

In the strong sea-currents that lay twenty leagues off Lanka lived the old Rakshasi Sinhika. She saw Hanuman flying and said, "This is the strangest bird I've seen in eight hundred years!" She swam to the surface and seized his shadow, and in the air Hanuman felt himself being dragged down and held back.

Sinhika stood on the water holding Hanuman's shadow in her claws and looking at him with tiny red eyes. She opened her ugly mouth and bared her yellow scaly teeth, and started to pull at his shadow.

"Watch out!" said Hanuman. "Beware, I am on Rama's service, and his kingdom is all the world. . . ."

She pulled him closer. "You can never escape me!"

"Oh yes, I will if I want to!"

She saw how large Hanuman was and opened her mouth
wide as a cave with a long tongue. But Hanuman became
quickly small as a thumb and flew down her throat like a tiny
hurricane. He crushed her heart with his sharp fingernails,
turned, and darted up out from her ear. Sinhika threw her
arms about and collapsed on the sea. Her blood burst and
spread through the water, and the fish came quickly to eat
her.

Then Hanuman regained his jumping size and flew on in
the sky, where birds fly and rainbows gleam, where heroes
ride in bright chariots drawn by miraculous lions, where the
smoke of fires rises and the rains and winds live. He went on
through the pure sky embellished by planets and stars and
luminous saints and by the holy Sun and Moon, the support
and glorious canopy of this live world, the sky made and well
made by Lord Brahma long ago.

The green hills of Lanka Island rose from the horizon.
Hanuman saw the shoreline of warm white sand and scattered stones and water pools, and behind that many tall swaying palms, and plane trees, and forests of aloes. He saw rivers
meet the sea, and saw where pearls and cowrie shells and fine
corals had been spread to dry. He flew inland, over stacks of
gold and silver from the demon mines that lay blazing in the
sunlight, and then he saw the City.

Beautiful Lanka was built on a level place just below the
highest summit of the three-peaked hill Trikuta, as though
built on clouds. She had four gates facing in the four directions and her strong golden walls were the color of sunshine.
Preceded by a little breeze, Hanuman landed under an over-
hanging cliff on the hill not far below the city, amid fruit
trees in full flower and bearing fruit as well, in a soft scene
like heaven. Blue rivers laughing with flowers fell running
down channels and stairs of ruby, and trees of every color
growing uphill reached out to catch the faint pink clouds.
The warm sea-wind smelled like pepper and cloves and fragrant spices.

Hanuman ate some dates and thought, "Not a hair out of
place, I'm ready to do it again! I call that little ocean a
puddle . . . not like other people . . . I'm better than any
bird. . . ."

Carefully Hanuman crept out from hiding, just enough to
see the main highway to Lanka's north wall. Around the

walls ran a deep moat fed by a mountain river, shark-filled, running in a bed of iron and wearing pale floating lotuses and lilies. The tall red-golden gateway panels were painted with green plants and twining vines, with fish and trees and flowers, flights of birds and clouds and stars. Elephants stood under the stone gate arch, and Rakshasa bowmen looked out from the crowning roofs and turrets. Seen from below, Lanka was a lofty city moving in the sky and built on air, embraced by clouds and held by sunbeams.

"We'll have to kill them all," thought Hanuman. "We can't be friends, they are too proud to approach. They would never betray Ravana. They can't be bought off, they are too bold and strong."

Beautiful Lanka was decked out like a maiden. Waters and woods were her clothes, bristling spears and darts on the wall were the ends of her long hair; the many-colored waving banners and the cloth-of-gold war-flags nearby them were her jewels and earrings; the high stone missile towers were her breasts cleaving the sky. She was Beautiful Lanka of the Waves, well-defended, built in time long past by Viswakarman the architect of heaven. She seemed a city woven from beauty, made by the mind from a wonderful dream half-remembered.

The late afternoon shadows lengthened, and Hanuman thought, "I will first meet Sita somewhere in there, and she will tell me what to do."

Then as the twilight of evening came and Night fell black over the dark world, Hanuman diminished his size, and took the form of a small long-haired silver tabby cat. He tied Rama's ring round his neck and it was lost in fur. He hid in a ditch and said, "If they see me, a cat roams free at night, and may explore wherever he is curious to go. Three times I take refuge in Rama, who is the safe shelter of all who flee for help from any thing."

In the dark Hanuman sprang over the moat and walked away from the road, down along the base of the wall to where there was no gate, prancing like a cat on four feet, going a little sideways, his legs stiff and his tail like a plume straight up in the air. Suddenly a dark-skinned woman appeared from nowhere before him, her face crooked in an unlovely smile, flames for her hair and a bleeding tigerskin for her dress, standing there in a halo of glowing lights and moving colors that looked like the burning clouds at the destruction of all the three worlds.

She looked down at Hanuman and said in a despicable voice, "Now be careful, be on your guard! Advance half a hair's point farther and I will kill you!"

"Who are you?" asked Hanuman.

"I am Lanka herself, surrounded by protections, ruled by the hand of Ravana. You cannot enter me, little cat!"

Hanuman said, "Gentle goddess, I am curious to see your hidden charms and attractions. I am a mere monkey, just let me take a quiet look around—"

"Never till the end of Time!" She hissed and kicked Hanuman hard, but he didn't move at all. He sat, and fastened his left forefingers into a fist. Then he jumped up and hit her right between the eyes. Lanka fell on her back. Hanuman helped her to rise, and she put her foot in his way, and drew it back, and stood aside.

"When a monkey knocks you down, know that a fear and a curse have come to the Rakshasas . . . so have I heard," said the goddess. "You have vanquished the realm of Lanka with one blow; enter if you will."

Hanuman leapt over the high wall, where there was no door, by night, and landing within he first touched the ground with his left foot, putting that foot on his enemies' heads.

Hanuman went to the shadow of a tree, and knelt and joined together his hands. "I trust in Rama," he said. "World-famous Lanka is inconceivable and lovely, a fortress city whose moat is the sea. She shines in her glory. No one can subdue her by force. She is guarded by Rakshasas standing with their weapons uplifted in their upraised hands, yet I have entered. I remember the ancient saints, and call to mind the warriors of the past. I trust in Rama, I trust in Rama . . . he is very strong—and alas, that for their one king's wrong this noble race of demons must perish!"

Then to help Hanuman, the small clouds withdrew from the sky. The bright round Moon was revealed, the friend of the sea, reaching his long silver rays over all, making the shadows blacker, afloat like a white swan in the clear starry sky, in the bottomless lake of heaven. The Moon was full, it was the last full Moon before winter. Watching Hanuman that night over Lanka was our Lady Lakshmi of good fortune, who sometimes wanders on Earth's high hills or walks at evening by the seas, standing in the sky beside the Moon.

Hanuman waited, and Heaven turned above him. The

Moon gleamed like a mirror, like the face of a king gaining a
kingdom. Midnight came, when among humans couples end
their quarrels with love and sleep together; and among
Rakshasas, in the forests the hideous Night-Wanderers, aston-
ishing and terrible, go out to eat flesh and drink the blood of
carnage. In Lanka began the night-life of every enjoyment;
and at midnight Hanuman began his search for Sita.

The brick streets of Lanka were lined by tall adjoining
houses set behind trees and built of white stones marked with
a thunderbolt and hook by Viswakarman the architect. Behind the main streets were gardens and alleys, and there
prowled Hanuman, looking in the lattice windows and running over the roofs. He heard the sounds of every indul-
gence—lutes and horns and two-headed drums and
late-at-night laughter; chattering parrots and demons clapping
time; running feet, and here and there droning sing-song
chants from the holy Veda.

He saw many a fair demoness, and some of the Rakshasas
also appeared much like men of good height and form. But
other demons were black, or a ghastly pink, or pale and
nearly transparent. Some were unbelievably handsome, others
were maimed and deformed, repulsive and frightful even in
their splendid clothes. On the streets carrying torches Hanuman saw the night patrols of Rakshasa warriors from every
demon nation, clad in rich and regal heraldry, or in feathers
and quills, or wearing rotting raw skins, or walking naked
with shaven heads. They were armed with studded bludgeons
or knives or blow-pipes or handfuls of holy grass enchanted
into spears and javelins. These were the warriors who had conquered heaven and received the surrender of the seven
netherworlds.

Hanuman saw many things, shamelessly looking in windows and doors. He saw the royal spies with matted hair like
holy beggars. Their plain-looking hermit's staves and rods
were secretly loaded with heavy metal cores, and they
concealed blades and razors in their hair, and wore mantras
tied on their arms with strings, and death-spells were hidden
in their traveling fire jars that they would carry innocently
slung over their arms.

Hanuman saw demons who looked wise and powerful even
when drunk and asleep with wine, with women, or with their
arms round their beloved bags of gold. He saw army officers
with coppery lines of sandalpaste on their bodies, talking and
waving their strong arms, stretching tough bows and looking

disdainfully at maps and beating their chests and sending out orders—*Hurry up! Wait!* He saw violent, swift demons who never slept, lying in the dark rolling their dismal staring eyes and wearing earrings of charred bone, all alone in the dead of night. He saw courtesans entertaining the rich; by joyous smiles and long slow side-glances of their eyes they trapped all hearts in loveliness and glamor and made all life a pleasure. He saw young new-married wives with their husbands, held by bashfulness and bliss both at once; and girls sad for separation from lovers dear to their souls, weeping heartbroken. And over all the wind chimes and little temple bells, the hum of mantras being chanted grew louder as the night went on, the very sound of the power of Lanka, filling the air.

Hanuman worked his way to the center of the city. There a lesser wall ran in a great circle, made of sixteen colors of rose gold, enclosing the palaces of King Ravana. Hanuman jumped over it and landed in a garden. Bright-flaring lamps burned on golden posts and standards of silver, and the gravel on the garden paths was made from jewels. All around him were garden temples where black incense burned, secluded libraries and detached pavilions and arbors and retreats. And rising above them all, in the center of the great park was a spired palace with royal golden domes, a building clad in costly gems and starred with diamonds, a mansion only different from the best one in heaven in that it touched the Earth of Lanka.

Hanuman slipped past hooded watchmen who sighed impatiently into the night, expecting an attack, looking forward to stopping some invasion. He went unnoticed past fanatical birds set out in crimson amaranth trees and trained to scream an alarm if they were disturbed. Hanuman searched one side of the castle grounds, and then the front of the garden, and then he entered a great courtyard on the third side of Ravana's palace, running the whole way from front to back.

That courtyard was as large as half a city, and there filling it entirely was the huge aerial chariot Pushpaka that Ravana had stolen from his brother Vaishravana the Treasure Lord. That colossal chariot was transcendently beautiful, a car made everywhere of flowers, made by Viswakarman in Heaven, the chariot of Spring, driven by the mind, and lightly resting in Lanka two fingers off the ground. Pushpaka the Car of Flowers is a field of treasures; he is a joyful way to travel, a vehicle of swift vision and soaring fancy; he rides as smooth as the transport of a man by a dear wish come true.

Hanuman got on that car and searched it. By the light of the full Moon he could see a forest of flagpoles like rows of tall trees against the night sky, and from them flew a skyful of flags and silken streamers and pennons bright and colored. Pushpaka had hills and green lawns, sweet-smelling rosebeds and ivory benches covered with brocade. There were figures carved out of gold of wolves and horses placed by houses made of vines. There were ornate and curious iron railings and far-looking balconies, little silver doors set with rubies that led somewhere under the green grass, wind-nets of tiny silver bells, crystal windows and secret passages, a gallery showing pictures of elephants bathing, silk tents and a theater, fishponds and moss gardens, overgrown paths and glades of ferns, and a swimming pool with a splashing fountain whose water fell over a stone image of Lakshmi standing on a big open blue lotus of turquoise, holding in her hand a little red lotus bud cut from coral.

Viswakarman the Architect of Heaven always considered Pushpaka chariot his masterpiece. When Pushpaka flies at night with his running fires and lights on, it seems that all the sky moves with its starbeams and planets; bells ringing and flags flying, by day he is a marker for the Sun's path, and one may look up and see how all his chariot hull is built of rainbows tied together.

Pushpaka can fly behind a thousand horses or without them. The materials used to build him have come from all the Universe, from these worlds and from other worlds. In some places the rays of his yellow topaz garden walls will keep day-lilies open at night; and elsewhere even by day the night-lotus is ever open, held in the rays of dark emeralds that stop the daylight and cast beneath them a deep shade and an illusion of Night, like being somehow within a lightness heavy raincloud.

Pushpaka chariot is Earth's ornament embodied to view, and a gathering of all wonderful things. He goes through the air in infinite motions. On him, you go where you will. You can look out the windows, or ride out in the open air under the Sun, standing on carpets, among jewels all around you that wink when the great chariot turns in the sky and the sunlight moves overhead.

Hanuman searched all through that vast and beautiful chariot as he would have explored an old climbing tree with

many holes and branches. There was no one aboard. Nothing
moved. Hanuman stood at the forward rail sniffing the air.
At first he could still smell the carved sandalwood of Pushpaka and all his flowers, but then the wind turned just a bit,
and brought from somewhere the scents of foods fit for a
King and of well-mixed iced drinks, and the smell of the
costly perfumes palace women use at night after bathing.

Hanuman left Pushpaka and followed his nose to the side
of the royal palace set in the very center of Lanka and surrounded by its own gardens, and he caught a glimpse of
many lights as he approached. Hanuman thought—*Find the
pleasures of the senses, and there find the Demon King.*

Hanuman went into the palace. He went bounding and
sniffing past a thousand enduring pillars and columns,
through stately chambers and long rambling halls lit by hanging war-shields and the gleam of magic bows stacked close together. The corridor walls were made of deep blue tiles and
bands of bricks glazed crimson, and set high above were large
windows covered by networks of gold and crystal, or of soft
ivories and silver, or curtained over with silks. There were
rooms of precious stones and serving dishes and full metal
winejars, and of these many rooms none had been built by
conquest, all were made for the asking.

The scent of food and wine and women grew stronger.
Hanuman went on over alabaster floors and up a stairway of
cool lapis and burnished gold, until he reached the end of a
silver-paved hall and opened a tall jade door with a cut amethyst handle big as a coconut. Behind that the doorway was
closed by a hanging woolen curtain colored in stripes, a
drawn veil shaped like the Earth—four-cornered, and flat,
and as wide as the world with all her lands and people and
homes.

That was the entrance to Ravana's bedroom. Hanuman
ducked under the left corner of the draw-curtain and stood
just inside with his back to the wall, looking out at a huge
floor lit by flaming lamps of gold and covered with sleeping
women so tumbled together that Hanuman could not tell
where one lady left off and the next began.

There was hardly space to step anywhere. Those were the
countless wives of the Demon King asleep in disarray, lying
all over each other, women beautiful and bright as flashes of
lightning now locked fast in Sleep's embrace. Hanuman

thought, "When even the form of a heavenly star is less than enough, virtue's divine reward for a good life must be to receive such fair shapes and lovely limbs as these!"

Once arriving in that room of women, it would be harder for any man to remember who he was or where he stood or why, than to fly across the sea in the first place. And though Hanuman was not a man, still when he looked at each one he thought no other woman could be fairer, and when he saw the next sleeper she was in turn the best and most beautiful as he looked at her. Truly, among those magnificent women the rays of the one's beauty showed off the charms of another; they slept deeply after an evening of drinking and dancing and playing music. Their fragrant hair was loosened and their bracelets scattered; their beauty marks of sandal paste were smudged and their colored robes unclasped and their waist-chains ran loosely straying to the side; their hazy garlands were disbanded and their pearls had gone and their earrings were lost.

Hanuman feared to do wrong and never broke a good law unless he had to. "It is surely wrong," he thought, "to gaze even by accident at another's wife lying unclothed or defenseless or asleep. But I take refuge in Rama, I take shelter with him. The mind commands the eye and sends out sight in good or evil fashion. By Rama's help, my mind will not change by this looking. I am saving Rama's life by seeking for Sita, and surely a woman may be found among other women."

Even the bedroom lamps looked openly out at all those women while they had the chance, as Ravana slept. Hanuman picked his way among the love-skilled Queens of Lanka who were draped over the floor and looked at their faces. They smiled or frowned or sighed in their sleep; their pillows were others' arms and legs and laps; they pulled each other's robes and wrapped themselves in them. With their eyes lashed shut in sleep they were desirable as closed flowers; when they touched each other they smiled and drew closer, believing they pressed Ravana with their breasts. Even asleep the dancers moved enticingly; the girl musicians slept embracing drums and hugging lutes like their long-absent lovers.

The golden lamps on the walls watched over them unblinking, and in their light the gold and jewels of those Queens made a river of lights and colors and shimmering waves of gold and silver. Their pearl necklaces were white water-birds asleep between their breasts, rising and falling; their strings of turquoise were families of blue teal and their hips were the

waves and the riverbanks; their faces of golden or white or
deep blue skin were the lotuses; when they stirred sleepily,
the small bells sewn on their silken clothes were the ripples
moving with little sounds; and the bruises and scratches of
love on their tender breasts were signs of where the lion and
tiger had come to drink.

Then across the room, in a corner Hanuman saw a crystal
bed raised above a short flight of jeweled steps, under a white
umbrella of seven tiers fringed with colors. Flame-red Asoka
flowers hung from the four ivory bedposts, and at the head
and foot mechanical men, silently driven by falling water in
some hidden way, gently fanned the air with yak-tail
chowries.

Hanuman drew near and looked up onto the bed. The pale
yellow silk sheets were trimmed in diamonds and the many
soft pillows were covered with fleecy ram skins. And on that
bed lay the Demon King Ravana fast asleep—heroic and
dark, wearing white, with twenty arms like gate pillars
marked with cool blood-red sandal paste, with ten devilishly
handsome heads, with his faces aglow from long heavy gold
earrings, sleeping like a deep-breathing hill. Ravana slept unsuspecting, all worn out from love and wine. He was the dear
desire of every Rakshasa daughter, and the happiness of every Lanka warrior.

Hanuman shrank back in awe. The back of Ravana's bedroom opened onto an outdoor drinking terrace. Hanuman
quietly went out there, and climbed onto a long table heaped
with savory leftover roasts and perfumed rice and good cooking made to thrill the seven thousand nerves of taste. Delicately, still in the form of a cat, Hanuman padded between
the plates, and there he sat entranced, looking over at Ravana
from a little distance. Hanuman was a monkey of the woods,
he did not desire fair women and he ate no cooked food . . .
but he could not take his eyes off Ravana lying asleep there
in the majestic lamplight.

Ravana lay like a collection of wrongs, a mass of harm
and injury and brutality and darkness of heart. On the
Demon King's broad breast were the old curving white scars
from the tusks of Indra's elephant Airavata; on his strong
dark arms were the burns of thunderbolts and lightnings and
scars from the bowstring; around nine of his necks ran thin
lines to show where he had once cut off nine heads and
burned them as an offering to the gods.

At last Hanuman looked away for an instant, then back at

Ravana. *As long as he stays there*—he thought. He looked over the foods on his table and poured himself a drink. Then Hanuman ate some melons and peaches, and lapped up some cream, and began to purr and wash himself, just like a cat. He licked his paw till it was wet, and washed down through the whiskers by his mouth, and up over his ear. He wasn't thinking about anything special and his cat's eyes roamed idly here and there.

All at once he stopped washing and squeezed his arms like a monkey. He saw Mandodari the Queen of Lanka sleeping apart on her own bed, very beautiful, the mistress of all the palace. He thought, "Rich with youth and so beautiful, she is Sita! It's her!" He kissed his tail, jumped off the dining table and ran in gleeful circles. He sat and slapped his hands on his knees and smiled and hummed a joyful tune, acting just like a monkey. He ran over and up and sat perched atop one of Ravana's bedposts.

"Oh no!" Hanuman had another thought. He sighed and stopped still. "That's not her. What a shameful apish idea— *Where would Sita have any place in this bedroom?* That's the Queen of Lanka, the daughter of illusion . . . though Ravana may well wish that she were Sita. First taking a false form, the Demon King was barely able to steal her at all. Sita will drink no Lanka wine or ever love another husband . . . when do elephants mate with hogs, and who finishes a good meal with a glass of vinegar?"

Hanuman jumped from Ravana's bedpost to the bedroom terrace, and from there he leapt into the yard behind the palace. Only behind Ravana's mansion had he not yet looked.

With a little snap, Hanuman discarded his cat disguise. He was again a white monkey, and Rama's ring was on his finger once more. A low stone wall enclosed a grove of Asoka trees behind the palace, and Hanuman sat on that wall slumped over, staring blankly ahead at nothing, scuffing his heels against the stones. The little leaves of all the trees around began to stir in the faint wind of the end of night.

Hanuman was tired out. It seemed he had opened and closed half the doors and windows on Earth; he had looked in rooms and burrows and holes, and even under water along the bottoms of Lanka's lakes and ponds, and he could not find Sita.

Hanuman held his breath a long moment, and then sighed.

He talked to himself and addressed the empty gardens. "She is surely dead, for the vulture Sampati blinked his tired eyes, and missed seeing her fall from Ravana's grasp somewhere into the sea. Or Ravana delighting in evil has killed her. He flew so fast she could not breathe, or he crushed her—Sita is dead, she lives no more, and sadly she cried out for her Lord Rama with her last breath!"

Tears dripped from Hanuman's yellowy eyes and ran down his red face. His words grew all choking wet. He wrung his hands and shook his head and switched his tail. "Ah, how unhappy! What heartbreak, what a failure! I can't return with nothing to answer Rama, never again will I laugh and play with my friends of the forests . . . or run through the trees . . . I have lost all my skill in searching, my fine garland of fame has expired—*Oh I can't stand it, I'll die*—"

Every word of all this empty talk went down the air to the long ears of Vayu the Wind Lord, the rain's lover who clears the air. Vayu stood behind the winds of the worlds and sighed, and stirred, and started to whisper at his son Hanuman. That miserable monkey lay draped on his stomach across the low wall, sobbing and rubbing his eyes, and in from the ocean, over the shore a little wind swirled up the flanks of Trikuta Hill and into Lanka.

Hanuman still complained. He held his paws over his face and gave a last gasp. "It's suicide, and my body may then at least bring meager happiness to some poor bug. . . ." He went limp.

Then from afar came the Winds, nearer and nearer. The million flat leaves of the mountainside trees trembled, they rustled and tried to speak and waved like dancers' hands. That was the first time since Ravana had come to Lanka that the Wind had dared to blow hard, but now he came in wild and free again over the walls of Lanka with all of his great might; he came flat out like an ocean gale with nothing to stop him, daring Ravana. He threw down the rows of flags and sang through the catapult wires; he banged the palace shutters and broke off branches like cannon-shots.

Hanuman heard the running wild Wind speaking—*How long? How long?* He opened his eyes and peeked out through his furry fingers. A whirlwind was headed straight on at him, pressing down his hair. Leaves and flowers sailed past him, twigs were snapping, trees were waving, and from Ravana's garden paths loose jewels whipped from the walks and flew singing past his ears. Vayu the Wind took a deep breath and

blew his son right over the wall—*Away with you, Oh Child
how long, how long will you seek to annoy me? Follow the
winds, follow the winds. . . .*

Hanuman tumbled and rolled under an Asoka tree. He
picked himself up and brushed the dust from his fur. The
wind died down. Hanuman was in Ravana's Asoka Grove. It
looked like a wood, but was too neatly kept; it resembled a
garden, but it had grown too wild. The beautiful asoka trees
had round crests and clusters of long red flowers, and with
many other trees and plants they were in a long inward park
behind Ravana's sleeping rooms.

Dawn swiftly approached. After a hush, the awakening
birds and deer began to talk, but their voices were strangely
unhappy. Hanuman wondered, "What grief can there be
here?" He looked around. "Where is Sita? She is somewhere
faint and forlorn as the misty Moon, hard to see as a streak
of gold covered by dust, hard to find as a bright yellow reed
broken grey in the frosty wind and lost when winter comes,
fading away as the red scar from a new arrow wound, from
the fresh cut of some sharp heavenly weapon."

In the center of the grove Hanuman saw a tall overgrown
Sinsapa tree of golden leaves and small white flowers standing by a pond, with torches flickering round it but no one
there. And as Night departed and the Sun rose from the sea,
he climbed that tree and hid in the leaves, lying along a stout
limb and thinking, "Sita always loved to walk the woodlands
and bathe in ponds like this among wild creatures; soon she
may come here at sunrise."

Here I Am

All Heaven's stars may fall
And Earth may break apart,
Fire may burn cold,
And waters run uphill—

But Sita never turns from Rama.

Oh Rama, the pond below Hanuman clearly reflected the
world in the calm at sunrise, and the sunlight traveled swiftly
into Lanka, down from the top of Trikuta Hill, and gleamed
on the golden city walls. In the still morning Hanuman heard
Rakshasa priests within their temples singing to welcome light
to the sky. Then in Ravana's bedroom the drums started to
go off and the lutes tuned up, and the bards of Lanka sang
praiseful songs to awaken their King.

Then some Rakshasis, female demons acting like guards,
came from among the asokas and put out the torches burning
round Hanuman's tree. They were a gruesome ugly group of
hideous horrors; they bore the faces of rabbits or dogs or
owls, swine or tigers or fish; they had the legs of cows or elephants or horses; and the ears of buffalo or goats' beards or
fangs like snakes. They were a small host of furies and glut-
tons and scolds and fiends. Some carried sticks, some had
three squinty eyes, some were bald and some had ratty stiff
hair like a mangy camel. They wore misfitting clothes. They
had hanging bellies and blotchy flapping lips, voices like rasps
working away on sheet metal, and flat crooked noses set
askew or upside down on puffy faces. They were leering or
grim, dwarfish or tall, and most still drunk from the night before. Hanuman saw his fill of low brows and broken nails
and bloated faces. And it seemed not one of them had ever
bathed in all her life, unless she had been caught outside in
the rain or fallen into a river, and the bloody gore of past

197

dinners and murders stretching back for years on end covered
them like a cloak of garbage. They made Hanuman's eyes
sore.

The first thing when he woke up every morning, Ravana
the Demon King thought of Sita held captive. He got out of
bed smiling and straightened his robe. He slicked down his
hair and his ten moustaches and went out a back door and
through a gate in the wall around the Asoka Grove, blinking
his glaring red-shot eyes in the sun. After Ravana, came
about a hundred of his wives, sleepy and stumbling. And
Queen Mandodari walked beside Ravana giving him sips of
wine from a bowl, one head at a time.

Hanuman saw that Ravana was heading his way, and as
the Rakshasis below him formed perspiring ranks and foul
rows, Hanuman shook himself and diminished his size till he
was no bigger than a hand, and fled up the Sinsapa tree to a
higher branch. There like a hidden bird he watched from far
within the dark shadows of the leaves.

Then he saw her. Hanuman saw a fair woman of the human race arise from sleeping in the dirt under another nearby
tree. She came over and sat with her back against the Sinsapa
tree, her legs drawn up and her worn dusty yellow robe covering all her body, her glossy black hair tied in a long braid
that fell down her back to her hip.

Hanuman thought, "It is Sita, much changed since I saw
her carried away." But he wasn't sure. She seemed bewildered, lost and fallen. Hanuman kept staring at her and looking, puzzling as one will do when trying with learning long
unused to read another tongue. Here was a woman imprisoned as a Naga girl held on her way by staying charms
and spells. She was a river dried away, a torn leaf from a
doubtful book, a muddied lake; she was dead love and disappointed hopes. Beneath him Hanuman saw an inspiration
thwarted by distractions, a reputation lost, a just and royal
law disobeyed and a prayer unfinished.

But it was truly her, it was Sita of fortunate looks, thin
from grief and fasting, lean and trembling. That was the robe
she had worn, and there below him Hanuman could still find
her fair brows and white throat, her round breast and red
lips, her lustrous black eyes with curling lashes, large and
wide. It was Sita born from a furrow in the Earth. Even in
captivity her every limb was lovely; she was still beautiful to
all eyes, as is crisp Autumn's sky after the rain's end.

Hanuman thought, "Oh Ravana, we'll get you for this!

Here is Rama's joyful Queen fast plunged into grief! My master Rama is truly strong, for he yet breathes without her and has not entirely consumed himself with sad thirst and longings."

Ravana came to the Sinsapa tree and without speaking knelt and bowed his heads at Sita's feet. He rose and smiled, "My dear, how can you fear me? I am helpless in the bonds of Love. Don't be shy . . . how does it become you to lie on the bare ground when you can be Mistress of my kingdom? Desire me, be kind; reward my love, for youth is uncertain and passing, and beauty will not last forever."

Sita put a grassblade between herself and Ravana. "For your own death you touched me," she said. "Ravana, even in a picture have you never seen black Kalee dance, and the horrid skulls of her necklace laugh, and the darkness of Death come down like Night?"

"But every god serves me these days!" said Ravana. "There are three hundred and twenty million warriors here; if I need the help of one, a hundred come forward. Rule over my other wives and my city as you rule in my heart. Why hold yourself back? If you command it, I will do good to all the world. Favor me, dear Sita."

Sita said, "You see everything reversed, because you are so near to your own death. If you are really strong, follow Dharma and take me back, no one will harm you."

"Forget him!" yelled Ravana.

"Why, you are but his prey," said Sita. "Can you not feel the noose of Death?"

"Oh timid girl of slender waist, enjoy yourself. Look at this wealth around you; open your eyes, it will all be yours."

"You are a magician selling sunlight as if you owned it," said Sita. "Are you mad to tempt me with wealth, when all the treasures of Earth belong to my one Lord? I am his alone. After the Lord of Men has held me I can never seek another. For you, I am a red-hot iron image awaiting your embrace!"

"The *nicer* I am," said Ravana, "the worse you treat me!"

Sita answered, "Then know me for the daughter of a *real* King and a true man's wife!"

RRRrraarrR! Ravana gave her a terrible look, he roared and shook his heads and hands. His twenty red eyes went spinning and rolling in different-turning circles and opposite ways. He ground his grim teeth. His robes swirled like the

stormy sea. He seemed to be having a fit and up in his tree
Hanuman nearly jumped out of his skin.

But Queen Mandodari took Ravana's arm and said, "My
Love, pass her by and come with me. She's not better than I.
She still loves Rama, for one insect will only love another of
its kind. Sita's thin destiny will not let her enjoy your grand
company. . . ."

Then Mandodari full of love turned Ravana around and
led him back to their bedroom, speaking softly—*Whatever
you will, my dear Lord, whatever you say.* And as they left,
behind Ravana's back his other wives, daughters of gods and
of great kings, consoled Sita with their eyes. Then they left
Sita alone with her guards and followed the Demon King.

Hanuman tightly held his tree and thought, "Does that fool
go through this every day?" He looked at Sita and bared his
teeth. "For this Lady were the demons of Dandaka Forest
slain, for her was King Vali killed from ambush, for her I
flew the ocean—it would be entirely right had Rama for her
sake overturned the Universe. Like the waters of a river flowing by, Time cannot be called back, and so Earth's daughter
of golden skin finds herself a poor prisoner here; yet she and
Rama are never parted from each other's thoughts or they
would die."

The Rakshasis told Sita, "Our unconquerable King stands
in a regal halo of white glory, and for your good luck he has
fallen in love with you. He pays you court politely and acts
so charming. Why cling to Rama who lives with animals?"

Sita replied rudely in the voice of a lioness who talks to a
little dog. "Don't be too bold with me. I would never even
spit upon your unwashed king. Fall in love? No, but he will
truly fall! Asking and answering, Rama will find the way and
come to get me."

"Look," they said, "we're satisfied. You've acted well. But
there's no need to go on any longer." Their eyes could see no
more there than a prisoner unarmed, alone and powerless.

Sita looked at them. "Shut your mouths, don't menace
me!"

"*What?*" they cried. "We're just too kind and soft-hearted
and easy going!" Some of them had knives, now they drew
them and shook them at Sita gleefully. "We've put up with
you so far just to help you! Our words to you are always
well-meant, it's for your own good, face reality!"

Sita laughed.

They screamed, "Be happy! Or else!" One demoness drew closer and cried, "Or else we'll eat you up. Liver for me!"

Bones to crunch and snap, blood and froth to lap! The Rakshasis started pushing and shoving each other, all yelling at once. "Ravana will be happy again, why quarrel, divide her into equal servings. Get the axe and kettle! Lots of sauce! Let's dance! Torn ribbons of soft flesh for the crows!"

Hanuman crouched into the shadow of the tree trunk. He clicked his tongue against his sharp teeth and hissed in his breath; he curled his tail and darted his fiery eyes about; he flexed his fingernails and got ready to jump down fighting from the yellow Sinsapa leaves.

But just then the old Rakshasi Trijata hastened forward and stepped beside Sita. At first glance she looked like any nice old woman wearing her hair in three white braids, but her eyes were upside down, set in her face with their outer corners touching her nose. She was the only one who treated Sita well.

"Shut up!" Trijata faced the others. They stopped shrieking and shouting at once. "Be still," she said, "for last night in a dream I saw terror and the overthrow and conquest of Lanka." She raised her two hands before her breast, her palms outwards, saying without words—*Peace to you*.

Trijata turned to Sita. "Princess, I will tell you all my dream, so you may save us from death—

"You stood wearing white atop a snow-white hill beaten by white sea-waves round its base. On that hill I saw Lakshmana sitting on a pile of white bones, drinking milk and eating rice. Then Rama came to you riding a white elephant with four ivory tusks bound in white silver. He wore white flowers and white clothes on his green limbs, and he sat on the elephant's back on an ivory throne.

"Then like light meeting the Sun you were beside him. You embraced Rama and were on the elephant with him. You raised your arms and held fast in your hands were the Sun and Moon.

"Then I saw Ravana dressed in red clothes and red flowers riding a hog, drinking oil, the hair shaved off all his heads, fleeing Lanka. As he rode to the South our city sank into the ocean behind him. Ravana was demented; he shouted insane words and laughed and wept like a maniac. He rode into a dry lake-bed, and there a dark woman wearing a red shroud and a necklace of skulls twined her dusty arms through his

necks. She pulled him to the Earth and dragged him away,
always South, to the Land of Death.

"Sita, I saw our Good Fortune running North like a
frightened girl weeping, bleeding from many cuts, and a tiger
fell in running beside her to protect her, and guide her to
safety. They ran to Fair Ayodhya. . . ."

Trijata shook her head and looked at the other guards. She
said, "Like a field of grain, evil ripens slowly in time. When a
fruit is ripe, then may it fear the fall. Console Sita and ask
her forgiveness. There is no unlucky mark on her body. She'll
never be a widow. This captivity is not her true fate, it just
seems like it, and I have seen her rescue while I slept. Even
at this moment, danger comes at us here from Rama's sending, so ask her pardon."

Sita smiled at them and said, "When this becomes true, I
will save you all."

The Rakshasis disbanded and went to guardposts away by
the Asoka gates and along the walls, and Sita sat alone under
Hanuman's tree. Hanuman thought, "Demons can take any
form; how can I speak to her so she will trust me? If I talk in
Sanskrit like a brahmana she'll think I'm the Rakshasa
King. . . ."

So in a quiet voice no one else could hear, Hanuman said
in the animal language, "Rama—Rama—"

Sita raised her head and listened.

Hanuman went on softly speaking. "—Rama killed that
false golden deer. He spoke to the dying Vulture King Jatayu.
Rama is Sugriva's friend, and all the animals of Kishkindhya
have searched for you. I found you, I alone leapt over the
sea. I am Hanuman, the Son of the Wind . . . here I am
above you."

Sita looked up into the Sinsapa tree and saw a white monkey like a tiny bunch of little lightnings, his red face smiling
down at her, his light yellow-brown eyes shining with fires
and lights. She rose and held a low branch and said, "Who
are you? Now I have let my mind slip into illusion."

Hanuman came down to that branch. "Mother, it's me,
Hanuman. I serve Rama. But who are you? Are you a bright
star-spirit hiding from her Lord in jealous anger, or are you
Sita?"

"I am Sita." Silently she began to cry and tears poured
from her eyes. "What star-spirit sheds tears on hearing the

name of a mortal King? Oh Hanuman, every sight speaks to me of him, and I fear you are also only a phantom in my mind."

"Ah no, I am not!" Hanuman came closer. "Listen, too much crying's bad for your eyes! Everything's going to be all right . . . very soon, Sita. . . ."

Sita looked down at her feet on the Earth, and every detail was clear and distinct. It was no dream; and when she looked back, by her own heart Sita read Hanuman's inmost thoughts and feelings.

Hanuman said, "You're welcome! I've already put my foot on Ravana's ugly heads!"

"Oh my *pretty* monkey!" She squeezed him and ruffled his fur. "You've come like medicine to a dying man, at the last painful moment. Where did you find Rama? How have monkeys and men met as brothers?"

"Remember when you dropped your ornaments from the sky onto a hill by a lake?"

"Oh yes!"

"That was me and my King Sugriva. We were in hiding. We saw you and gathered up your things. Then Rama and Lakshmana came to our hill of Rishyamukha, wandering in a beautiful forest, and we showed them your jewelry. Sugriva and Rama became friends, and Rama restored Sugriva to his wife and made him King of Kishkindhya, and for his part Sugriva will rescue you, the monkeys and bears will come to Lanka. . . ."

So they talked confidingly together, Sita standing with her head near the golden sinsapa leaves and her sweet voice soft and low, and Hanuman stretched on a branch that began to bend a little from his weight, as he started to grow bigger again from the happiness of his success.

"This is his ring," said Hanuman. "Take it." Sita read the name on the wide gold band—*Rama, Rama, Rama*—and Rama seemed to be there touching her.

"If one can keep on living somehow," said Sita, "real true happiness comes to each of us once in a hundred years! I remember all the good times I'd forgotten!"

"Everyone was looking for you," said Hanuman. "We only waited out the rains. Take heart. I am famous all over the three worlds. I'm hard for enemies to look at and impossible to stop."

Sita's face was beautiful. She looked at Hanuman and smiled a luminous slow smile bright as the day-star. Her dress slipped from her left shoulder a little, and Hanuman could see part of her arm revealed, he saw her slim muscles under the golden skin strong as steel within silk. Hanuman grinned at her. Then he fell into a short animal trance and said half to himself—*A huge black woman strikes her belly with her many hands, driven to anger until she shall devour the Rakshasas, impatient to reach out and draw them into her terrible mouth. . . .*

Sita pulled up her robe and caught her breath. "What are you saying?"

Hanuman blinked. "You mean about the rains?"

Sita smiled a sad sweet smile. "Hanuman, has Rama lost his love for me through long separation?"

"He hardly eats or sleeps. To him the cold nights are like flame and the gentle moonbeams burn him. Get on my back and I'll take you home."

She laughed, "Here again I see your monkey nature!"

Hanuman said, "My first womanly insult." He jumped from the tree and became as a white hill eighty spans high. He was crouched ready to leap, with a coppery face, nails and teeth like thunders, yellow lantern eyes like dazzling brass plates. Then before anyone else saw him he was small again. He ran back to Sita and up into the tree.

"I believe you!" smiled Sita.

Hanuman beamed. "I could take back all Lanka with her stupid King and her walls, and no one could catch me."

"No, let Rama recover me if he will—but now that beautiful man is freed from a wife like me."

"Princess, if Rama sees a flower you once liked he falls into a fever. If he hears your name, it will sometimes comfort him, or else will worsen his pain. Now he is distracted, but once he knows for sure that you are here, I swear by all the delicious fruits of the forest, he will come with a large army to save you."

Sita was both sad and happy, like rain in the sunshine. She said, "Blessed are the gods who can steal a look at Rama where he hides, and blessed are the holy men who never love or hate. People cannot thwart Time; behold all of us so sad."

Hanuman replied, "When Rama's hot anger breaks over the world the seas may well boil away. Dear Sita, before Love's eyes Time does not lay on year by year the little heart-blinding spells of age. Before true Love, the maces of Death are frail stage-weapons, fragile and useless for combat.

Death gives way to Love and has never dared to war with him."

Sita sighed, and her breath burnt a few sinsapa leaves that hung down near her face. "Soon you must leave me and return, my Hanuman. People will fancy what they see and forget those who have gone. Shamefully I loved a jeweled deer and sent my man away. Here there is no cliff to jump over. I haven't any knife or poison, and only my own braid to hang myself. How is one better than a slave to this life that will not end when it is over and done? Often I weep longing to die. . . ."

"Destroy your sorrow," said Hanuman. "You're the most beautiful woman I've ever seen."

"Oh Hanuman."

"But you are, you are supremely fair. Oh Sita, Rama is like a fire-temple, burning from his own fires within. Love's shadows and his darkness are really lights. Tell me what to do for you."

"Does Rama remember the crow that clawed me when we lived on Chitra Hill? Take him this message—*For me you sent the dread Brahmastra weapon to kill a little crow, so why do I appear to have no protector now? Am I helpless? Have you enough love left for me to set weapons against the demons? On that day far from care, on Chitraukuta Hill my red brow-mark was printed on your green chest and near your heart.*"

"I'll tell him, I promise," said Hanuman.

Sita said, "Stay nearby awhile, rest here with me today. I have no one. When you leave I will miss you, and who knows if you will ever return? It is very hard to enter Lanka, and I fear no one but you can cross the sea. Complete good fortune, and a friend to share it with, is very rare and unlasting. My monkey, spend this night with me and go tomorrow."

Hanuman smiled a sunny smile. "Why would King Sugriva send any of his best monkeys out on an errand like this? I am a common animal, the poor child of the homeless Wind. Nothing can stop the monkeys and bears, nothing can stop Rama and Lakshmana. We can go anywhere as fast as we want to. We fight on the ground or up in the air; our weapons are uprooted trees and blocks of stone broken out of the mountains. Let me go back and bring them here to you, here and now, this very day."

Sita looked at that remarkable and amazing monkey again and again. Her sadness had come and gone, as clouds will draw across the clear night sky, and cover the moonlight, and go again. "Faithful Hanuman, at the year's end Ravana will kill me. Speak so Rama will save me, let him do it, and farewell."

"Farewell, it won't be long."

Hanuman ran unseen to the wall of that Asoka Grove farthest from Ravana's palace. He got all set to jump back across the ocean when an instant monkey thought crossed his mind.

He looked back at Sita. Her face was fair as the Moon. His eyes brightened and he thought, "Will I leave her once more in danger with no sign of good cheer?"

He popped over the low wall and out of Sita's sight. He got bigger again. He said to himself, "I won't hurt Sita's grove and I won't touch the good chariot Pushpaka . . . but all the rest . . . right or wrong!"

A great idea! Hanuman was off like a bolt from a bow-string. He plowed through Ravana's lawns and flowerbeds and pushed over his pavilions. He threw benches and bricks through the palace windows and splattered the sentries with wet muddy lotuses. Horses shied and elephants stampeded, and the deer stared roundeyed and frozen in panic. Dust and leaves fell all in a wind over Lanka; and standing amid the wreckage of Ravana's gardens, Sita's Rakshasi guards saw an infernal monkey crackling with energy, growing bigger and bigger.

That was a wondrously harmful sight, a true regret to their eye. They ran to Sita and asked, "Lotus-eyes, who is that?"

"What do I know of your terrible Rakshasa magic?" answered Sita.

Ravana heard the racket in his courtroom. The palace bodyguard of eighty thousand fighters did not wait for any orders. They served together always, and knew and loved each other; in full armor they flew out the tall windows and saw Hanuman sitting on top of the big main gate in the circular outer wall around Ravana's home.

Hanuman cried out—*Victory to Sugriva the King!*

What King?—shouted the regiment.

Hanuman grabbed an iron gate-bar and stood in the air. *My King!* He beat them all to death with it and the ground shook.

On his throne Ravana could hear that Hanuman was winning. His ten heads turned here and there and his eyes roved over his court. Then commanded by a royal glance, the goodlooking young warrior Jambumali arose, the son of the demon General Prahasta. He bowed and left the court, and once outside the door he broke into a run.

During those moments, after he had hammered to death the royal bodyguard, Hanuman pounced from his gate onto the goldplated Rakshasa city temple across the street. In back of that building priests were talking senselessly or rolling in the dirt or just smiling like religious idiots. Inside there was an image of the goddess Lanka made of sapphire. Hanuman stuffed her down a drain and slapped his armpits so loudly that big pieces of the golden ceiling fell blackened by ages of incense smoke.

Hanuman fled outside, broke off a marble column, and flew to the top of the temple roof. *Let me bless my beloved demons one by one, are you ready?* He spun the pillar around so fast that it caught fire, and coals and flares and sparks whirled up in the air, and the priests ran for their lives, the temple burst into flame and exploded.

Jambumali heard it blow up. A piece of flying stone just missed his head, with a sound like a hummingbird flying by his ear. The noise awakened everyone in the world who was still asleep that morning.

Jambumali got on his light two-wheeled chariot. It was brightly colored and drawn by three white mountain ponies, as curved and fanciful as the toy car of a princess, but made of adamant and armored in death-spells. He drove to where the temple had been. Two pillars still stood there; on one of them a loose plank was balanced, and on that plank Jambumali saw a monkey picking cinders from his coat. And though his anger grew like a fire fed with butter, Jambumali looked calmly at Hanuman with the gaze of a young lion; and Hanuman looked back, thinking, "How young he is!"

Jambumali got down from his pretty car and walked nearer to the ruined temple. He held a red bow curved in two curves with the straight grip between, decorated with solid gold flowers. He had a soft quiver slung over his shoulder, covered outside with embroidered silk showing colored birds and dancing girls, heads of ripe grain and flowers; inside his arrows scraped and swore, and their tips danced with light.

Then very quickly Jambumali shot an arrow straight up in the sky and cast his mantras, whispering—*Come down falling!* Hanuman's plank tilted and started to slip.

It was a perfect quiet morning. Hanuman's board stuck there on that column at an impossible angle and did not fall. Hanuman yawned and stretched out and closed his eyes. Jambumali stared.

A tremendous piece of stone fell tumbling down out of nowhere just missing Jambumali. Another boulder fell, they were falling all over. Jambumali cursed. Those were grains of dust! Something else was falling, a huge long tree-trunk. The arrow returning! A giant long shadow growing, too fast, a whistling and a wind—

Jambumali was crushed and killed, there was no more sign of his body or bow. Hanuman himself knew some small magic also. He saw Ravana watching from the palace, and he howled like a metal drum so that the windows rattled. *Rama!*

Ravana instantly turned and walked down a narrow stair and through a tunnel under the city wall. He came out a secret door into a grove of the hillside woods that was hidden from view by magic. There under a downgrowing banyan tree sat his son Indrajit. Indrajit had once taken the god Indra prisoner in war, now he sat pale and thin beside a hermit's waterbowl, with a butterjar for feeding a little fire, wearing deerskin with a grass belt, in a field filled with the slaughtering posts and altars of many sacrifices.

Ravana went to approach Indrajit but the preceptor Sukra stopped him. Sukra had come from the Asuras undersea to teach Indrajit. He said, "Majesty, do not speak to him just now or make him break the vow of silence. He has been fasting to center himself in the spirit. . . ."

Ravana said, "What identity does he seek? Is it well done to worship my enemies the gods?—I do not understand my son!"

"King, don't speak of what you can't understand," said Sukra. "Do not say 'I won't believe,' for this is real. This is the final hour and moment of the five-day rites called the Gift of Gold. Every power that Indrajit has just won by meditation and endurance and devotion, he now offers back to Lord Shiva."

"Why do that?"

"A small gift for your good fortune," answered Sukra, "for against you will come Ramachandra, Rama like the Moon, and you will—"

"Silence, brahmana. I need him now! Let him study war, not mysteries, and return to my side here in this world of passing sights and nets of pleasures and of pain."

Then Indrajit arose. "Father, the gift to Shiva is done and I am ready. Or else, why would I part from Shiva the Lord?"

Ravana said, "My son, bring me that animal. Beguile him by unreality and take him by force. Use things that begin one way and end in another."

Smiling, Indrajit said in a gentle voice, "This life is an echo in the air and a wave on the sea. That is Hanuman. I'll take him if you want him; war or peace, it's all the same to me."

Then Indrajit's fairseeming form changed. Gone was the friendly lean ascetic. There was Indrajit the raven-haired warrior, dressed in blue and yellow silk, his skin dark red like spilled blood, a yellow flower in his long hair, his eyes sharp green with cat's pupils, a golden chain wound nine times round his waist, a white spot of sandalwood on his brow, a great round blue steel shield in one hand, a bow backed with gold serpents in the other, a full quiver slung over his back and a sword at his belt in a silver sheath.

"Long life to you, my Father." Indrajit went to the burnt temple in Lanka. Hanuman was waiting for Ravana's next champion to come against him, lying there on his unbalanced board.

Indrajit knew Hanuman could not be killed. So on an arrow he put a mantra that can be sent but once at anyone, and never sent again. He shot the spell of Shiva's noose, and Hanuman fell to the ground tied invisibly hand and foot and unable to move.

But before Indrajit could reach him or speak, other Rakshasas ran from hiding and in the blink of an eye they had tightly locked Hanuman in chains. Indrajit bit his lip and sighed. For the binding force of Shiva's noose will never hold nor return, when there is any other bond laid over it.

"Boundless ignorance again takes command," thought Indrajit. Cursing and kicking Hanuman, the demons dragged him off to the palace. Indrajit saw that by no sign did Hanuman show that he was free. "Those fools—*I bow to Shiva who places us all in true danger now*. Oh, let lust and anger keep their distance, let all this unreal world be far from me!" And Indrajit went back to his grove of meditation without speaking a single word aloud.

The New Moon

The footrest on your high throne
Is worn smooth from the crest jewels
of lesser kings,
Bowing their crowned heads in surrender.

But good fortune is a wanton harlot,
Going where she will—
Oh Majesty, is she still yours?

The Rakshasas pulled Hanuman into Ravana's court. There on his red and gold throne, in a better hall than any room in heaven, the Demon King sat like threats of darkness. Ravana had earned all his wealth and power by his own strength. He was fortunate and splendid and rich. Ravana had the patience and strength to protect all Creation from harm, but he did just the opposite and took the worlds for his possessions.

Ravana's throne was covered with doeskin and was set in the center of a long indoor altar, made of a golden frame filled with Earth, a low-banked hill running on each side away from Ravana to the corners of the room. At each end Rakshasa priests tended fires and hummed songs, and when they made their offerings they could choose from among the spoils of the Universe and the treasures of the three worlds.

The entire Majesty and Glory of the Rakshasa King! The demons carried Hanuman close. Ravana was very tall. He wore ten crowns of flaming red flowers and gleaming gold. A gold breast-chain hung from one ten-armed dark shoulder to the other, forged of flat heavy links from which were hanging golden devil-faces with amethyst eyes and open ruby lips and long shiny ivory teeth.

Ravana looked at Hanuman with twenty eyes, and from the smooth emerald floor Hanuman in chains looked steadily back. And the Rakshasa King remembered what the bull

Nandin, wearing the face of a monkey, had told him on Shiva's Hill of Reeds long before—*Animals with faces like mine will destroy you.*

Ravana's younger brother Vibhishana came from the ranks of courtiers and bent over Hanuman. His face was black and his eyes dark blue. He said, "This is Lanka, long built here, long prospering. You have killed our people and broken our holy temple. But good fortune to you. Do not fear, but tell us the truth. Who are you and where did you come from? Why are you disguised as a monkey?"

Hanuman replied, "I *am* a monkey! I've a message for Ravana."

The Demon King leaned forward on his throne. "Insensate animal! What message?"

"Majesty," said Hanuman, "I am Hanuman, I am Rama's slave. I came to find Sita. Hear the words—*In the cave city of Kishkindhya your brother Sugriva, king of the monkeys and bears, asks after your welfare. Listen to his desire: in Dandaka Forest Sita was harmed, and I have promised Rama to find her; therefore do not confine another's wife but return her.*"

"How did you get here?" asked Ravana.

"I jumped."

"Don't make me laugh!"

Hanuman grinned. "Don't worry, I won't!"

Ravana opened wide his eyes in anger. "Unlucky beast, you've lost your weak wits from seeing the beauties of my city."

"Lord of Lanka, I am the son of the Wind, fast or slow, irresistible in my course. I'm an animal; what you call beauty won't turn my head. I crossed the ocean, as a person without attachment to worldly desires easily crosses the ocean of existence. Withdraw your heart from Sita, or that will be a costly theft, for it's by her energy that I jumped over the sea."

"Impossible. Vibhishana, cut off his head!"

"No," said Ravana's brother. "You can brand or shave a messenger but not kill him."

Ravana said, "What good are you as a demon? I've killed them before!"

Vibhishana said, "But I wasn't here before."

"All your life you've been timid and weak as a woman."

"Just the same," smiled Vibhishana, "here I am standing up and telling you no."

Then the Rakshasa General Prahasta rose from the audience and said, "Have a heart, Ravana! Give us a chance. In the army we've eaten your food and spent your money, and all we have to show for it is peace! You must release Hanuman. It is sweet to make a real war and win! Set free this monkey who killed my son, because if he does not return no one else can ever find Sita, and we will never fight against Rama."

Hanuman lying in chains said to Ravana, "Are you bored with your great-seeming wealth and do you wish to end your life? Whatever happens to me, how can you believe that Rama will abandon his beautiful wife and let Sita be taken from him and not recover her? Actually, your conquests are uncertain and your treasures unnecessary. Past merit still protects you, but somehow I think you strangely desire death."

"No, you tiresome little monkey, I do not desire death!" Ravana swirled to his feet. "You have now seen us both. Tell me truly, how Rama compares to me."

"Truly," said Hanuman, "you are the bright Full Moon, the light of the night world; and my Rama is the New Moon, a thin shred of light, no more."

"Excellent," said Ravana. He summoned a band of grim demons. "Monkeys take pride in their tails. Set his tail aflame, carry him around through Lanka and then throw him out."

They slung Hanuman on a couple of carrying poles and took him outside. They started to wrap his tail in oily rags. They wrapped and wrapped, and it seemed the whole length of Hanuman's tail wouldn't be covered by all the cloth in Lanka. So the demons just bundled up the end of his white tail. They set the rags afire, lifted the poles to their shoulders and carried him around the streets yelling—*Look what happens if!*

In the Asoka Grove Trijata told Sita what was happening. Sita gave her a cool smile and went to a little shed where the guards kept a tiny flame always burning in a clay cup filled with butter, to light their nighttime torches.

Sita looked into the little flame and said—*If I've kept faith, be cool to Hanuman.*

The fire flamed and bent to the right—*Yes, I am good to him.*

So Fire let the Wind be cool right next to his son's tail and Hanuman felt no heat, though flames played in the air and burnt the oil in the rags. The demons carried him bouncing along, and Hanuman thought, "I've seen their incredible King, why stay in chains?" He broke loose, lashed out with his fiery tail, and sprang into the sky like a lightning streak.

Hanuman flew, setting fire to rows of mansions and houses with his burning tail. Flames devoured Lanka like a cremation yard; smoke blocked her roads and vultures settled on her golden walls. Burnt were sweet sandalwood and diamonds, corals and fine silks, golden vessels and piles of weapons, furniture and ornaments, ropes and elephant cords, beds and perfumes and hides and armor, all burnt.

The carved windows blazed and bricks melted into glass. Down fell roofs and towers and burning beams. The waterborn pink and blue pearls shattered in the walls; the golden moons and silver crescents melted away. Along whole streets the houses collapsed outwards and fell over aglow with fires. Gates and grills snapped and smoked, and living flames blossomed alive in the air. The demons cried alarms and jumped into their lakes and ponds, fire brigades tore past, and thin rivers of hot iron and molten bronze ran down the streets like quicksilver.

Hanuman flew to the very top of Trikuta Hill and looked at what he'd done. He had to shade his eyes from the heat; it seemed Lanka was flaring brightest, before she would die. Even the restless waves of the sea were red from the burning.

Indrajit had been brooding in his grove outside the walls. He said, "I will destroy the six senses. Eye, I will pierce you; mind, I will cut you. . . ." And his senses answered, "You will pierce only yourself, you will cut only yourself. . . ."

Then Indrajit forever wearing different forms heard the wails of woe and saw the fire. The Prince of Lanka swiftly bathed in a stream and put water in a bowl. He threw aloes thorns on his altar and lit them, and sat down on scattered grassblades. He spoke to Fire, "The grass isn't even woven into a mat. The time is long ago and we have no skills. You are not the fire of Lord Shiva's third eye spreading wide your tongues. You are not Shiva's wish."

Indrajit dipped three fingers into his waterbowl. Agni the Fire God rushed out of Lanka and a cone of sparks and fire came over Indrajit's altar.

"Heat and thirst!" cried Agni.

Indrajit said, "Ashes!"

"Smoke and anger!"

Ashes! Indrajit sprinkled water on his aloes fire, and Agni the Fire Lord backed off a little.

Indrajit said, "I hold you."

"Fear me," answered Agni.

"No, my Lord. Never are you patient, but always you burn. Never are you filled by burning, hard are you to stop once grown. Oh evil companion, I am a storyteller myself, I am an actor too. Now I send you away and I watch the doors for your flames' return."

Then a finger's depth of water appeared and covered all of Lanka, clinging to walls and ceilings and floors, and the fires had to go out. Hanuman sitting above the city quenched his tail in a mountain spring and thought, "Never again! What have I done? I've burned Sita!"

Hanuman held his head in his hands. "A fool will try anything. It's never too late for him to ruin a successful affair. Any kind of evil can be easily done in thoughtless anger." Back he jumped into Lanka, through the clouds of smoke and steam. He landed on a hot street, ran to the back of Ravana's palace, and headed for the Asoka Grove.

Nothing was harmed there. Sita was safe by the sinsapa tree. How could Fire have burned Sita? It is she who can burn Fire if she will.

That amiable woman smiled and said, "Oh Son of the Wind, have you returned for your honors and decorations? We praise your wit and wisdom, your brave courage and fine knowledge of politics."

Hanuman knelt before her and touched his palms together. "My mother, I salute you in the dust. A fool's excuses are worse than his crimes. Blessed are people with good sense."

"By good fortune I see you unhurt," said Sita. "My Child, if you are tired after all this, rest by me."

"Let me leave while I still can," said Hanuman, "give me your permission. Jumping the sea is easy. It's all this running from guards and watchmen that tires me. I will come back with Rama. Ravana has truly already been slain by your anger, and yet awaits only Rama's strength as the means of his death."

Sita said, "Monkey, in one reckless moment one can kill the innocent and boast wrong words, forget friends or lose all the harvest of pleasure, profit and dharma. You did none of this. They set your tail afire and you burned them back! So throw off your care as a snake abandons his old worn skin and leaves it behind him. Hanuman, when you stop to think you are strong, you are intelligent and good, you know time and place."

"I feel better already."

"Listen, Lanka will be soon rebuilt. If you so heedlessly destroy these demons you will cloud Rama's fame. Take this to Rama, get him to act." Sita untied the corner of her robe and took out the pearl mounted on a gold leaf that her father Janaka had tied into her hair on her wedding day.

"How did you keep that all this time?" asked Hanuman.

"Head pearls are common," smiled Sita. "Say this—*I seem to have no husband. Rama best of men, seeing this gift was like seeing you. Now I part from it and keep your ring. I will live on here for a month and not longer. Do you still think of me at all? I send this pearl so you may know—you are loved by me, you are loved by me.*" Sita smiled her warm white smile that had never an equal then in all the worlds, nor ever shall.

Hanuman hid Sita's jewel in his belt. He walked round her in three right-turning circles, bristled up his fur and flew off to the north.

Hanuman left Lanka behind him. He flew booming along through the air like the wind through a canyon, and the monkeys and bears waiting on the seashore heard him coming. They ran up a grassy hillside and made a circle holding hands, and Hanuman landed in the middle.

"I talked to her; she's alive!" Animals encircled Hanuman; they brought him fruit and water and fresh boughs to sit on; they came up smiling to touch him; they sang and cheered.

With gold bracelets on his arms and wrists, Prince Angada embraced Hanuman. "No one is like you. Can we go get her?"

"Don't do that," said Jambavan the Bear. "We were only to find her."

"Just leave her there?" asked Angada.

Hanuman said, "You usually do the right thing, Prince."

Then all at once came Angada's order—*Return*—and the miraculous monkeys and bears leapt from that hillside and flew home to Kishkindhya, supporting Hanuman's flight by their admiring looks and glances. Near Kishkindhya they saw

King Sugriva's Honey Park. There the Monkey King kept his finest forest honey wines under guard.

The animals smelled ripe warm fruit and nectar in the sun. They looked at Angada for permission, but before Angada could answer Hanuman shouted, "Let's go! Follow me!" and landed in that Wine Forest.

The yellow monkeys and the sable bears said, "All the world honors Hanuman. We'll follow him even into wrong; what to speak of perfectly correct things like this?"

The animals descended from the air. Down from the trees they pulled the rare and ancient honeycombs, fermented and dusty and venerable, and broke them open. In a moment they were all fearlessly drunk, staggering and lurching along, all talking at once. The monkeys were swinging in the trees and waving their tails, and the bears were nodding and dancing.

That Honey Park was guarded by the elderly peace-loving monkey Dadhimukha, who lived in a small cottage in a secluded corner. He heard people breaking his trees and splashing in his streams. White-faced, he went swinging down through the trees to see what was going on, and came to a mob of bears all bristly with glee, who were singing and imitating birds and thumping their feet on the ground.

Dadhimukha dropped from the trees and told the bears, "Stop it!"

They laughed. "We'll drink to that!"

"Get out!"

"We just got here!"

Dadhimukha sucked his teeth dry. *Oh yes?* He furiously pulled up a tree and swept the bears away. More bears came. Dadhimukha struck them down with his fists before they could speak. He threw them here and there, pulled handfuls of fur from their coats and showered them with insults and blame. But they just laughed and kept on eating great gobs of wild honey. Some of them said, "Catch me first!" and ran; others sat there and said, "Leave us alone, help!"

"Why ask?" yelled Dadhimukha. He slapped the bears, and they didn't seem to feel it. Belligerent drunken bears began side-arguments among themselves. Still more bears came. Some of them started to weep over life, and others with stern authority rebuked them for crying and then wept themselves. Others laughed and bumped into trees, and old Dadhimukha was swallowed up in bears and chaos.

Hanuman whizzed out of the bushes. He had orange-petaled flowers and red berries, vines and blue-green leaves and buds stuck all over his white fur. He looked like Spring running lightly over the world. "Father, let's not fight over nothing—"

Dadhimukha snorted. "Repent, world-famous Hanuman!" He kicked Hanuman and sent him rolling like a ball into an orchard. Hanuman banged into a tree and juicy fruits fell down all over him. "Respect your betters," called Dadhimukha.

Prince Angada came running up, but that swift old monkey bent down, caught the prince's knees and threw him over. "Stop right there, all of you!"

But it was pretty hopeless. Nothing could stop the pushing and shoving, so Dadhimukha flew to King Sugriva. Sugriva was sitting outside Kishkindhya cave, with Rama and Lakshmana on their hill, awaiting some word of Hanuman. Dadhimukha's clothes were all torn; he bowed before the Monkey King and said, *"Lord of the Forest!"*

"Speak."

"Hanuman's army has fallen on your favorite ancestral forest from above. I tried to gently reason with them—"

Sugriva coughed. "They're drinking my honey-wine?"

"It's all gone."

"I forgive them." Sugriva's tail stuck straight up with joy. He turned to Rama. "He's found her! This is a wonderful return." He told Dadhimukha, "Why make such a fuss over the small faults of my children? Arise, calm yourself and send them all here to us."

Dadhimukha found Prince Angada dozing and starting to float on the air in the Honey Park. "The King awaits. He's with Rama on the hill; go to him."

A rumbly sound spread through the wine park and the bears were stirring. A wind came up. Animals ran from Kishkindhya Cave to get a sight of the southern search-party returning; they climbed the rock-rooted trees and amid blossoms and leaves they waved the tag ends of their robes and cheered.

There was Hanuman, flying to Rama's hill. Whatever the obstacle, Hanuman likes strong love leaps over it and goes on. The high forest hill danced in the wind, his treetops swayed. Wind tossed the flowering branches together in collision as though he were stringing them touching on a garland-thread.

Hanuman landed before Rama and touched his hands to his head. *"She lives!"*

Yellow trees like lions' manes and golden crowns;
Mangos white as fame like dancers on the hills:
Love has weakened you, here comes the swaying wind.
You've run out of fighting Dharma;
You've slighted your warriors:
What will you reply when people ask of Sita?

Hanuman and Rama and Lakshmana and Angada and Sugriva sat on a wide flat stone, in a smooth meadow high on Prasravana Hill. The other animals gathered round to listen, and with a glad heart Hanuman said, "My Lord, Sita is held prisoner in Lanka, on an island beyond the end of the sea. She is within the city walls of Lanka, behind locked yards and garden gates, in an Asoka Grove behind the lordly palace of the Demon King, guarded by Rakshasis.

"Ravana has threatened her death if she will not submit to him. But her heart carries her love to you; her thoughts are the well-bred chariot horses, driven by her spirit—*Here we will go, and this will be true.* She's true to you, but she is all alone, like a tuneful lute without a player.

"She is gifted with beauty. I saw Ravana's bedroom, and Sita's loveliness makes all those sleeping consorts seem vile and monstrous, of lurid hue and form. Her dark eyes are as wide as lotus petals, her skin is golden, her breasts are close-touching and firm, and her posture bent slightly forward by their weight.

"Her waist is thin as a swordblade, her brows just meet and then go back to touch her ears, her hips are round and smooth . . . and her soft smile . . . though she is there without any ornament at all, what is mostly missing for her is the ornament of a husband, her ornament of you."

Hanuman looked to the South and thought of Sita. "I gave her your ring and she sent you this." He gave Rama the wedding pearl.

"Emptiness," said Rama. "Echoes and emptiness . . . that's all I have."

"Don't let your loss make you lose heart," said Hanuman. "You can't give up after all we've done for you; you must bring her back to life and music!" He told Rama all he had seen and done in Lanka. "Sita herself will live but one month more imprisoned. She says—*I love you*—and tells you of the time you sent the Brahma weapon against a crow, and of when her brow-mark was imprinted upon your chest. She kept that pearl by her with great care, and I took it for you in my hands."

"I begin to remember our love and happiness," said Rama. "Tell me what else she said."

"She said, 'Hanuman, blessed are you, for you will soon see Rama the best of warriors. Speak to him so he will act. Demons cannot withstand Rama. Let his life return, let his heart regard me again. Speak so he will act. Inspire him to kill Ravana; he can do it.' " Hanuman fell silent.

"What else?" asked Rama.

Hanuman twitched his tail. He stretched his fingers and toes and his white fur rose on end. Then he said to Rama in silent mental speech, "Oh Lord, if men from ignorance still praise you—sad for them, it is a lie. If your spirit's broken it was weak to start with. Sita was fooled when she wed you, and Shiva's long bow would have broken anyway just sitting in its box. Where are your wits that you're not suspicious of despair? Sita's never thought of a second husband. She has no one else but you, and in fear you left her. Like a coward, like a common ordinary stage-actor you traded her over to another. You told her to go to him though you'd long loved her. Why do you serve Ravana as best you may, and give him Sita for his pleasure? You forsake her. She is encircled by evil. You've let Ravana throw you away for his own good. Rama, do not be a meek little man, fawning and unclean, unholy and afraid. . . ."

Only Rama heard those silent words and his face darkened. "What did you say?"

"I said never fear to love well," said Hanuman. "If you can't bear it who will?"

Rama wept. He embraced Hanuman and then held his shoulders at arm's length. "It's alright."

Hanuman said, "Now make me a promise, Rama, an unfailing promise."

"What?"

"Kill Ravana!"

THIS CLOSES THE
BOOK OF BEAUTY.
HERE THE WAR BOOK BEGINS.

"Let your arrows pierce him through," said Hanuman. "Ravana is mighty strong, but he is poor, for it has been very long since he stood out in the open grass under a green tree he did not own."

Sugriva the Monkey King said, "Rama, open-hearted people like you suffer more in sympathy than the selfish do. Your heart is undefended. Grief undoes good fortune. Good things are ready to happen, do not prevent them." He swept his hand round in a circle. "Look, here we all are! Make a plan, do something great!"

Lakshmana said, "Who approaches close-guarded Lanka of the Waves and returns from the demons? Who even approaches? We cannot cross the sea. . . ." He looked at Jambavan. "What do you think?"

"Get out of my way!" answered the old Bear King. He looked at Rama with a deadly gaze. "Attack! Don't think and listen. Act! Call out our animal rage, Rama, release our violence. We are senseless wild animals—blood all over, their blood, our blood—who knows, who cares? We fight, that's all, and if we're at bay we fight worse than ever, we fight till we die! We feel no pain then, and when have you ever seen us surrender?"

"That's right," said Sugriva. "We never reason and think if things are hopeless or not. Rama-chandra you are the King. You are the Moon; does the Moon go out because dogs bark and howl at him? Where can Ravana hide from you? Be brave, do what you think best."

"I will stand straight," said Rama. "I will never bow down before sorrow again. Warriors who won't get angry can't win."

Jambavan the bear smiled and growled low. "Anger is madness, that's what you need in war. I've dealt death—I smell fear, I close in . . . I've felt the blood spill and tasted it, all my life. . . ."

King Sugriva said, "Release us from your hold and let us go. Order us. We will gladly enter fires for you."

Rama replied, "We will cross the ocean, and once beyond that, Lord of Rivers and Streams, we will lay siege to Lanka."

Rama said, "Let Hanuman tell us again about the defenses of Lanka, for he has seen her armies and walls."

Hanuman answered, "Beautiful Lanka's wall is like sunshine. There are four heavy wide gates facing in the four directions. Lanka is on the steep brow of a hill, but outside

the walls there is enough level ground to fight. All the
Rakshasa soldiers are loyal. There is a moat, and at three gates
drawbridges, but where the main road enters at the North the
gate-bridge is immovable, lined with a railing and benches of
gold. Set on the walls are many hostile machines and engines
to repel attack. There are catapults that will not reveal their
aim from their positions, loaded with secret weapons bound
in cords and hooped in iron that when fired break apart into
spikes and maces and kill by the hundreds. There are cannon
that spew out red hot nails and knives, and swords strung together on barbed chains, and burning arrows which pursue
their target though he twist and turn to flee. There are patrols
in the forests and many ways are mined with traps and pitfalls. Lanka is a celestial fortress, a joyful city of heavenly
beauty taken by demons. She is artificial but looks natural;
her sentries never sheathe their swords; she is the jewel mirror of arts and inventions and the home of happiness and
comfort.

"Against us are Ravana, and his son Indrajit who is invisible in battle, and his brother the sleeping giant
Kumbhakarna. General Prahasta desires war against you; his
armies are calm and mindful and alert. But for all that,
consider Ravana already dead. Rakshasas can overflow the
world, the Sun can go backwards across heaven, but no army
can frighten old Jambavan and his bear tribes, or resist Angada and our people, or stop Lakshmana, if you will yourself
lead us to save Sita."

Rama said, "Tomorrow Sita's birthstar is ascendant; the
planet of Death will be in conjunction with the Moon; we
will leave for the South at midday, at the fortunate moment
when the Sun is highest."

The next day the animal armies said farewell again and
left their families behind in Kishkindhya. They began to
march. The brown and yellow monkeys went first, covering
Earth like a far-reaching field of grain. Angada carried
Lakshmana on his shoulders and Hanuman carried Rama.
Behind them came Jambavan with his dark bears and white
ones, whose faces now bore war-marks of vermillion. More
and more apes and monkeys followed them. King Sugriva
went from side to side and front to back, urging them on,
and the welcome wind blew from the north as cool as the
Moon to touch, and the days were clear and bright.

Advance parties made a roadway, they drained swamps
and brought water to dry camps; leveled hills and filled hol-

lows; broke boulders into gravel and cut away brush; and did all their work under lucky signs, at good hours on prosperous days. In three days they first began to smell the sea, and then sandalwood, and then they started to arrive at the Malaya Hills. Monkeys and apes and bears crowded onto the mountains by straight roads and side paths. They went down to the seashore between the cliffs overlooking the waves, raising fine clouds of colored dusts from the slopes of bright metal ores, waving their arms as they talked and knocking over trees with their gestures.

Rama saw the deep-sounding brimful Ocean. At dusk he took his bow and went down to the surf with Sugriva. The crested racing waves fell over the rocky coast, and broke on the round white stones and beaches of sand. The wind blew onshore and carried the salt foam of the sea onto the land, and the daylight failed. The sea became like the sky and the sky like the sea, there was no difference between them. The stars of heaven appeared above, and from far within the sea sparks of light showed gleaming out from the Naga castles under water, guarding the sea-doors to their underworlds. Dim grey clouds moved under one corner of the sky, and grey waves ran over one side of the seawaters, stirred by the winds. Night came, and the Moon rose reflected on the Ocean's silver breast. Waves caught the moonlight and laughed; they rose and fell and came forward endlessly, one after another forever.

Rama told Sugriva, "Camp nearby and keep a watch for strangers, and leave me here alone."

Then in a while the animal talk died down and the watches of Night began. Rama heard the silvery waves—*Who? Who? Who shall cross us?* He thought, "I am richly gifted with misfortune. When will I ever again slightly tilt up Sita's face and when will we embrace? What can I do? I am a lovesick stranger, a poor man all alone, wronged and begging help." His hands trembled—then he caught himself, he remembered what he'd said—*Dismay and sad thoughts I'll never feel. I reject you; I banish you!*

Then not speaking, Rama touched a wave of the Ocean with his hand and lay down with his right arm for a pillow, not eating, not sleeping, not moving. *Ocean, speak to me.*

The Night went by, the light of dawn appeared and the stars were going. The wind diminished, and there was no answer. Rama stood and strung his long bow; he put an arrow on the bowstring and held it drawn back to his ear and said to Ocean, "Fools mistake patience for weakness. Honor's for those who boast and victory serves great heroes who bribe the strong and attack those too weak to fight! You would disregard anyone, were he unarmed and quiet!" The arrow flew hissing and tearing into the waters. Smoking seashells and underwater stones flew up in the air.

"Damn you!" Rama brought down the winds. Loud waves of hesitation rose straight up; the water whirled. Samudra the wide-souled Ocean rose from his dark bed below and sat on the waves looking at Rama.

Samudra was mild and peaceful to see. His dark skin was wet like a cool lapis stone. The Water King wore bright gold bracelets and bands, and a green robe. Seawater poured from his long white hair and beard, foaming in torrents down his smooth chest, carrying a flood of rolling pearls down over his shoulders.

Sea-mists and clouds were behind Samudra, and the beautiful rivers of the world swam near him in the shapes of fair women. The Sea Lord touched his hands and bowed his head a little toward Rama. "I am the sea. This is another world. . . ."

"Don't try to net me with illusion," said Rama. "One glass of wine has a lot more pleasure than all your tasteless waves."

"Oh Rama," said the Ocean, "the worlds are made of water; it is my eternal nature to be fathomless and uncrossable."

"You are very large and know not my power. Let us by, or dry towers of dust will blow through your bed and choke you."

"Oh man, I drink down all the worlds and sigh."

The sea became silent. The waves died and the air was still and waiting. There almost seemed to be no air to breathe. The tides stopped.

But only for a moment. Samudra smiled. "Blessed be you, Rama, blessed be! I am immeasurably old, my soul is wide as my waters. What is wrong, Rama? Never was I your enemy but only your friend. Why use fear on a friend? The Goddess Earth and myself, Wind and Light—forever do we four keep our nature and never do we change. Why would you pass me by?"

"For Love."

"Indeed," said the Ocean Lord, "my heart is as large as the sky who is over me. I will help you. The monkey Nala who is with you is a son of Viswakarman, and he was born with the imperfection that whatever he throws onto water will float and not sink." The Ocean King smiled. "I will support on my surface any foundation Nala lays down. Oh Rama, as long as you wish, for you I will be bound by a bridge. . . ." Samudra of the Seas vanished back into his own depths.

Rama found Nala the monkey, and Nala said, "Did he say that? I used to just float stones for fun! Why then I'll throw out a bridge. . . .

"Get everybody to help me." Nala set to work. He looked to the South. He looked back at the Malaya Hills. Then he sat in the sand drawing lines for a long time, glancing up and out at Ocean, looking back down at the sand, absorbed in his work and seeing no one else as all the animals gathered around him.

Nala gave his orders. First the animals made stakes and lines and measuring rods; then they made the other tools; then they collected the materials from the hills. Then they began to build a bridge that would be a hundred leagues long and ten wide on a foundation of stones and boulders. Over the rocks they laid down a roadbed of poles, then Nala paved the road with grass and wood.

When they heard of that bridge-building the little people of the squirrel tribes came to help Rama. They wet their fur in the surf and rolled in the sand. They quickly ran out onto Rama's bridge and shook themselves, and the sand fell into all the tiny spaces left in the paving and made it firm.

But they were forever underfoot. Hanuman scooped them out of his way while he carried big stones along. The squirrels ran to Rama and said, "Master, brutal Hanuman kicks us and hits us and shames us."

Rama ran three of his fingers down their backs to cheer them, and from that time until now every squirrel in the south has on his back the marks from the fingers of Rama. The squirrels went back to work and Hanuman told everyone else, "Watch your step; don't harm the little tree people!"

The Building of the Bridge

Do not let the ways of the world
Dismay your heart,
Being a warrior.

Lord Rama, on the day after Nala began that bridge, in Lanka Ravana called his council of noblemen and said, "Bring your minds with you for once."

When they had assembled Ravana said, "We have repaired the damage he did, but yet Hanuman all by himself invaded my unreachable city and will return with Rama. What must I do? What must you do? The superior person will gladly take good advice before acting."

Those empty-headed Rakshasa elders replied, "Yes, we agree!" They said, "Majesty, you rightly rule the Universe. Everything's been just fine so far. We will free the world from monkeys."

Then Vibhishana stood and spoke. "Rama will pardon us if we return Sita. She has not been harmed."

"I'll have no more of that!" Ravana was as angry as a liar whose word is questioned.

Vibhishana said, "All the gods' animals are running loose! They are building a bridge and plan to cross the sea and surround Lanka. You want war, but what do you know of their strength? What protection do you take against them?"

"Are you trying to anger me?" snarled Ravana.

"Well," said Vibhishana, "to tell the truth I don't have to; it's an angry mind that won't understand all this."

"They will never go back over that bridge!" said the Demon King. "I find nothing to fear from simple animals. Have you no shame to suggest surrender?"

"King, no one else dares tell you the truth; you have no real friends left but me. You could hide in the veil of the

winds, and use the Sun for a shield, and the sky for a wall,
and still lose to Rama. He will kill you; there's no escape."

Ravana said, "What do I care? I do what I please!" He
motioned with his hands—*Sit down, you have finished.*

"No," said Vibhishana. Four strong armored Rakshasas
loyal to him came forward and stood to guard Vibhishana,
cradling maces in their arms, facing the four directions.
Vibhishana looked around the royal court of Lanka. He saw
General Prahasta and his captains of the demon war-bands.
Still as always, priests tended the palace altar to each side of
Ravana's high throne, setting out their jars of curds or fire or
butter or rice, gossiping uselessly in the corners.

Vibhishana said, "I blame you for a coward long loving
evil. You're a sneak-thief—"

"Silence!"

"What will you hold against me? How can you stop me?
For these hard words I deserve your praise. Are you incapable of reason? Do you want to live on congratulations
and embraces and elegant flattery? For the second time I warn
you to give back Sita, and send gifts with her."

"Do you think I'll stop and change my ways though the
whole world says I'm wrong?" asked Ravana. "Kings have
nobility, cows have milk, and kinsmen have envy in their
hearts! My brother, blind with selfishness, would betray me!
You would unfold the way of defeat. It truly must not please
you that I am Emperor of Creation, and for myself I would
rather live among open enemies than with you in my family."

"Open your eyes and mend your ways," said Vibhishana.
"Wake up and do right! I don't speak just to talk; I have for
my heart's purpose the rescue of the Rakshasa race, but I'll
not go on repeating myself forever. You are a slave and
wrath your Master. We have surely been through this all before in other lives. Consider right and wrong. For the third
and last time, give her back."

"Get out!" said Ravana.

Vibhishana answered, "Good fortune to you, now I go far
away."

Vibhishana left the palace with his four knights. They put
on their helmets and flew across the sea, north to Rama's
bridgehead. Already the beginnings of the bridge struck out
like a line parting the sea, aimed curving at Lanka, pointing
like an accusation before all the world.

I'm not an actor or a singer,
Not a fair woman nor a clown;
Then what have I to do
With the palaces of Kings?

Sugriva saw Vibhishana and his bodyguard and told Rama, "We'll end their short lives today." But Rama said, "Wait."

Vibhishana stood in the sky and looked here and there with his dark-blue crystal eyes. He saw Hanuman and beckoned to him. Hanuman came close and Vibhishana said, "Rama! I take Rama's protection, I take the true King's shelter!"

"Why are you here?" asked Hanuman.

"Ravana rejects my words. Except for that I could save him. It would be the easiest thing in the world to give Sita back. But now, white monkey, I must try myself to save even a part of our race on Earth."

"Come on down, I'll be your friend as you were mine." Hanuman led Vibhishana by the hand to Rama, and as they went the monkeys and bears drew back from them. But Vibhishana smiled at the animals, showing his handsome fangs, and swept off his helmet when they reached Rama.

Vibhishana said, "The protection of Rama! I am yours, may you be my safe refuge for all time."

Rama said, "No fear to you from fearful things."

Hanuman said, "Rama, in Lanka this Prince Vibhishana saved my life from his elder brother Ravana."

Vibhishana said, "I will help you when I can, but I cannot fight against our people."

Sugriva the Monkey King was there. He said, "He came to spy and kill us in our sleep."

"I want to do right, that's all," said Vibhishana.

Hanuman said, "His true nature will show."

"I don't believe him," said Sugriva.

Hanuman replied, "King, you're trying to make me mad again! Withdrawing from Lanka proves his wisdom. Stop forbidding things and saying *No* like a King. Be more cheerful; like an animal . . . must every Rakshasa choose evil just to please you?"

"He's Ravana's brother isn't he?"

"Sugriva," said Hanuman, "this is only because *you* have not met Ravana. You were home drunk in bed. Therefore in ignorance you can talk a long time about this when there's really nothing to say. I take this Vibhishana for my own friend, and if you don't like it. . . ."

Rama said very evenly, "I will fight Ravana but not the innocent. Vibhishana's face and gestures and words are open. He has done no wrong. He is not clever or busy. One must blame the blameworthy and favor the good wherever they appear. Lowly people who know everything may follow their suspicions, but when someone seeks my refuge he cannot be slain, he will be saved though it will cost my life."

Vibhishana said, "I'll be a powerful friend, Rama, I'll pay you back some day. . . ."

Never murder one who is not fighting,
Nor a warrior who hides or flees bewildered,
Nor any one wounded.
Though he has just now stopped war,
Though his cunning hands touch over a proud heart,
His betrayal blocks your Dharma like a frontier barrier,
A wall of stones.

The monkey King said, "Without Dharma there is no strength nor power. This is no wonder for you, Rama. *Jaya,* victory to you. I also welcome Vibhishana as an equal friend."

On the first day Nala built his bridge out for fourteen leagues over the sea. The second day he built twenty leagues more, on the third day he added twenty-one leagues, on the fourth day twenty-two, and the fifth day he built twenty-three leagues more onto all he had done already and the bridge touched Lanka Island. Then Rama and Lakshmana discarded their deerskins and unmatted their hair.

It was a slightly curving bridge finished in grey stone and supported by arches that rested steady on the sea. That fifth evening Vibhishana and his four knights guarded the southern end but no other Rakshasas appeared. Early the next morning the animals began to cross the wooden pavement from the north, running so swiftly that the first of them began to arrive on Lanka that same afternoon. Sugriva was standing on the north shore ready to go across when a hawk flew in from the ocean and sat on the branch of a nearby tree.

That hawk was Suka, the most trusted minister of the Demon King. Suka said, "Lord of the Monkeys, I am sent here to speak with you. Listen to Ravana's words—*Dear brother, I have only friendship for you. Best of Monkeys, why build a bridge like a rail of anger over the sea? Do me no harm; return to Kishkindhya and rule the forests forever.*"

Sugriva saw Angada stalking that hawk from behind and answered, "Why tell Ravana about our little bridge and disturb him? Just don't pay us any attention and we'll go away ... after all. . . ."

Prince Angada grabbed Suka out of the tree and squeezed him tight in his paws. Suka gave him an angry look. "Take care, you are at chance, you are in danger! Kill me at your own peril—for if you do, the fruit of the countless evil deeds I've done from the night of my birth till now—all will be yours!"

"What'll I do?" asked Angada.

"Drop him quick!" said Sugriva. Suka flew back up in the tree. Sugriva told him, "Say to Ravana—*You have killed one old vulture. You do not see me this day; you do not know I am stronger than you. Rama rules Earth forever.*"

Suka flew home. That day Hanuman and Angada carried Rama and Lakshmana over the bridge. By evening Jambavan and Sugriva and most of the animal armies had all crossed over, and on the Lanka beachhead they sang of fame and victory in their camps along the cool wooded streams, and the aloeswood crackled in their fires.

The next morning the animals climbed Trikuta Hill and began to assemble outside Beautiful Lanka, on the western side of her walls. By the time they had almost all arrived it was past midday and those golden walls were sunlit. Then from the battlements the Rakshasas blew blaring shells and glaring horns and beat their drums. The animals then for the first time knew that many of them would die there, and fell silent a moment. Then they yelled back twice as loud; they roared a lion's roar of victory.

Ravana in his palace spoke to Suka. "Nobody could believe in a bridge across the sea! And all those animals unbelievable! . . . but send someone out to count them."

"I'll send two," replied Suka. He called the faithful spies Sardula and Sarana. "Go outside the walls, count the enemy; find out their plans and dreams, and return."

They said, "Victory to Ravana!" Outside Lanka they took monkey shapes and mingled with Sugriva's army, until Vibhishana happened to glance at them. Vibhishana's crystal blue eyes were sharp-sighted, and he kept them illumined with black kohl dust round his lashes. He could see clear in shadowy light; he could see a still black ant in the black shadow of a black rock on a moonless night. He could have found a lost hair in the darkest corner of a lightless basement vault.

Vibhishana saw Sardula and Sarana for the demons they were. He snapped his right fingers three times and broke their disguises, caught one under each arm and dragged them to Rama.

Sarana was so afraid that he shrank away to nothing; he vanished completely and was never seen again by anyone anywhere. Sardula stood alone before Rama, despairing of life and barely able to breathe.

But Rama only said, "If you have discovered all you came to find out, go safely home. If you have missed anything see it now, Vibhishana will escort you."

"No thank you," said Sardula.

Rama said, "Now your King Ravana may use against me that great force he used to steal my wife!"

"And farewell," said Sardula.

Sardula found Ravana on a high balcony overlooking the ramparts of Lanka's wall, facing west. The Demon King said, "Why are you pale, did they catch you?"

"Alas, I am covered with shame," said Sardula. "I can't count them. Some are still at the bridge, some are still climbing the hill. Sir, Vibhishana sees through us."

"And you call yourself a spy!"

"No longer. I resign, with your permission."

"Are you afraid?"

"Well no, but my stomach hurts!"

"Yes, you may go, you are no warrior," said Ravana.

Sardula looked at the King. "I will point out and name their best fighters for you, before I go to live with my wife and family in the Naga lands under the world."

"Never mind," said Ravana, "be still. This goes beyond the making of a report and the declaration of this and that. Peace be to you, Sardula; this is real. What you can see from here and what I see are different things, and I am master of what must next be done."

Then Ravana was alone. He saw the broadshouldered monkeys and scowling bears climbing uphill, carrying huge rocks and uprooted trees. He looked out at his moat and thick walls. He saw his loaded slings and firebombs. And he saw the animals all looking up at him with their ancient eyes; the ancient eyes of the animals, the first friends of man in ages past. . . .

In his bedroom, standing by the back door to the Asoka Wood, Ravana summoned his two magicians, Lightning-Tongue and Thunder-Tooth, and said, "By spells of deception and illusion make for me by magic the severed head of Rama, and his bow with an arrow set on its string."

Thunder-Tooth said "Yes." Out from beneath his robes he drew a bow with diamond and gold on its back and many colors on its belly, strung and holding a golden arrow which was marked—*Rama*.

Lightning-Tongue took his wand from his belt and turned aside. He bent down, straightened up, and held out in his hand a gory green head, bruised and dusty and stained with dried blood. Ravana rewarded them with pearls. He took the bow and told Lightning-Tongue, "Await my call."

Ravana went over to Sita in the Asoka Grove and said, "This is your Lord's honored bow still strung." He snapped it in two.

"Dear Sita," said the Demon King, "Rama arrived on this island last night with his armies. At midnight General Prahasta fell upon them as they slept. He beheaded Rama with a curving broadsword; he turned aside a little and fatally stabbed King Sugriva; he crushed Hanuman to death beneath an elephant; with a bloodwashed axe he cut off Jambavan's legs and broke his neck. Prahasta's warriors used a net of flying chariots to pull the traitor Vibhishana from the sky; they left Angada rolling in the dirt and torn by agony and arrows. Now animal corpses cover our shores and litter the wooded hills by the sea and float drowned on the red tide. They lie hewn and mangled in caves where they ran to hide and then to die; their bones are broken, their sinews severed, their tendons torn and their blood spilled out. Dumb and speechless, stricken and badly wounded, Lakshmana alone ran away and fled to safety. And if any others still live they are dying now."

Ravana told one of the Rakshasi guards, "Call out from the palace that cruel Lightning-Tongue who brought me Rama's head!"

Ravana said to Sita, "Here, I'll show you." Lightning-Tongue approached holding that head of illusion by the hair. He looked at Sita and slithered his long forked tongue over his thin lips. He threw Rama's head down right at her feet, bowed to Ravana and swiftly departed. "Prahasta killed that mere man and sent these relics to me. See for yourself the final sad death of Rama and marry me!"

Rama's head stared up at Sita with dead green eyes. She saw the familiar brow, the long dark-green hair tied back with a war-cloth, the kind mouth, the broken emerald war-earrings. She wept piteously and said, "You foolish man, I was really your death and never your wife."

Sita sat and held the head in her lap, and her shining tears fell down upon it—*You died to save me, what could be worse?* Sita began to let go of her life. She quietly opened her hand, and let life slip and fall away through her fingers.

"Hey Ravana!" The back door to the palace banged open, and in full armor General Prahasta came swiftly striding through the Asoka trees towards the Demon King. His bronze armor clanged, his sword slammed and rattled against his iron-clad legs, he waved and smashed his metal arms against his sides—and from without the palace wall, from the city Sita heard the deep white-faced drums of Lanka pounding, and the beating of the brazen gongs, joining in one after another from every direction.

"Victory! Victory! Excellent success!" shouted Prahasta. "Aha, it's *War!*" He cracked the fingers of his steel gloves and smiled. Elephants were trumpeting in the city. Lines of lance-points tied with colored sashes went by just visible beyond the palace walls. The gates of Lanka swung shut on diamond pivots and closed with a jarring noise, then the brass bolts falling, and the latch-guards of steel. Chariots clattered through the streets, the arsenals and armories opened their doors, and by heavy chains the three drawbridges of Lanka were raised into the outer walls.

"Forgive my interruption," yelled Prahasta. "Did you see them? The sea is a hundred leagues across and rough with huge breaking waves, yet Rama has crossed it like a village cow-trail. Rama has come!"

The ground of Lanka shook. Ravana smiled at Sita the best he could. "You must excuse me, Princess, there seems to be something. . . ." Ravana and the long-handed General Prahasta turned and left the Asoka park, and when Ravana

had gone Rama's head and bow melted and disappeared. On
the big city walls the fire-machines were ignited. Shooting
over the sky appeared the gleaming reflections of many colors
thrown from squadrons of polished Rakshasa shields and
golden chariots, a dire luster like the raging wildfires of summer.

Sita was still bent over weeping, so blinded by tears she
could not see that the false bow and head were gone. The old
Rakshasi Trijata came beside her and said, "Daughter of
Earth you are no widow. What you hear is our call to arms.
Now the warriors will gather to discover why they are
called—Rama is right now in a field outside Lanka. He is
alive!"

Sita could not understand. "Kill me, let me fall by my husband."

Trijata reached down and lifted Sita's head, so quickly that
her teeth snapped together. Trijata was angry; her bare toes
made the grass curl and smoke. *Disbelieve it! Disbelieve it!
Disbelieve it!*

When Trijata said those words three times her speech
broke through and reached Sita's heart, like welcome rain
falling on the hard dry fields of Earth. "Listen—" said Trijata. "—are you listening?"

"Yes. . . ."

"My every word is true—Rama knows himself and cannot
be surprised asleep, nor can Prahasta so easily kill those animals as Ravana pretends. Look, that head and bow are gone.
They are wrong and untrue, they were an illusion spread
about you, a momentary glamor and a passing spell."

"What?" Sita was bewildered.

"Rama advances on our city with a great army of woodland animals. They may well deny it! Ravana has gone to a
war council. I take refuge with the Sun who makes our days
and gives our joys and grief; I swear by the Sun who goes
round the world like a dancing horse round a circle—*this is
Truth!*"

Trijata continued, "Out in the streets everyone is armed.
Weapons are a sign of fear made visible, and we are afraid.
Hear the horses neigh while their hair stands on end, hear the
archers calling. Our bloodthirsty soldiers flourish their
weapons and shake them at the sky, to bully the heavens and
terrify the serene planets and stars and frighten the clouds.
But this time they don't fight gods! The creaking high saddles

are tied upon the elephants' backs, the horsemen mount, the jangling chariots are harnessed. Like water that pours into the sea, the Rakshasa warriors rush here from all sides, mailed demons of wondrous forms, all doomed to die. . . ."

A Rakshasa patrol swept by overhead armed with swords and triple spears, their cowls and capes crackling and snapping like whips in the air behind them, their shadows tearing through the Asoka leaves. Trijata smiled and said again, "Lakshmi embraces you. Your sorrow will be demolished. Dark-eyed Sita, I can take any message to Rama."

> *Rama and Lakshmana are your help,*
> *Not long will you dwell in this*
> *Dreadful demon city.*
>
> *I'll wait for my beloved,*
> *He is not far away.*
> *My Rama is not far from me,*
> *I'll wait out the time.*

"Find out instead what Ravana plans to do with me," said Sita.

Trijata became a wasp and flew to the windows of Ravana's courtroom. She returned, took back her real form and said, "He won't free you, Rama must first kill him."

In Ravana's war-meeting was the old Rakshasa Malyavan, who with his two brothers had asked the heavenly architect Viswakarman to build Beautiful Lanka long ages before. He sat there, and he thought he had some warning to give Ravana.

As Malyavan had grown older and older he had come to look more and more like a man. He had lost his fangs and teeth, and he trimmed the claws on his slender fingers till they looked like nails. His short hair was white; he was very thin and dark; he dressed simply in a white cloth, with no ornament and no colored borders. Malyavan had eaten but one bowl of rice a day for many years; he had seen his brothers killed; he slept very little. He sat against walls and trees outside and smiled with his eyes open and his head leaning back in the sun. He told ancient stories to children and awake at night he watched the streets of Lanka.

And as the world grew dark in the evenings, Malyavan had many times lately seen a withered man with his head shaven going along the streets, wearing a brown worn shroud, covered with dust and ashes, coughing a dry cough, peering into the doorways of the demon mansions with his hollow eyes and grinning like a skull. Beautiful Lanka had been built for the asking, once she had been young and now Time walked her streets. How had those dirty monkeys and bears come so far to hurt her?

Malyavan slowly got to his feet in Ravana's courtroom. He stood and saw all the assembled officers and warriors sitting silent, staring straight ahead and awaiting orders. Then for a moment a memory of war's blind anger changed Malyavan's face, and as though he were young still, he looked at them all with a proud and evil look that faded right away again. Ravana watched him as he looked around.

Malyavan tried to remember what he ought to say. In one of the open windows behind Ravana's throne was a wasp that was really Trijata. Beside the wasp stood a blue-and-green bird eavesdropping who was really a Rakshasa, one of Vibhishana's four warriors, staring Malyavan right in the eye with his head tilted to one side. There was something important to say but Malyavan had forgotten what. It seemed to him, all this had happened once before. He smiled a wrinkly smile at the king and raised his open hands before him—*Blessings upon you, I will go*. Malyavan shuffled away and left the room without speaking.

When the war-meeting had ended that afternoon, Vibhishana's courtier returned to him and said, "Ravana believes himself already victorious. When we attacked heaven we had altogether fewer warriors than now attend each gate of Lanka. The least of Ravana's soldiers is as strong as ten elephants, and every warrior now paces behind the wall of Beautiful Lanka saying—*I will go first*."

Vibhishana went to Rama and said, "Even if he knows the difference, Ravana will still rather do wrong than good. He will fight. There stand the Rakshasas, golden in their armor on the walls, like a second wall on top of the first one."

Rama said, "When we fight let no animal change shape, and with your four knights be with us in Rakshasa forms."

Then Rama told Prince Angada, "Go as my messenger and ask Ravana once more."

Angada flew into Lanka. He saw Ravana walking the walls and like a fiery golden ball with the sunlight in his golden fur, Angada dropped from the sky beside Ravana and was surrounded by dark demons pushing forward like heavy clouds.

"Who are you?" asked Ravana.

"I am Vali's son," said Angada, "and these are Rama's words—*Too long, Ravana! Give back Sita, or bid farewell to your friends and come out to me, I am waiting to kill you.*"

"Ah," said Ravana, "I will not blow out like a light from windy words. When I win this battle I will at last finally impress Sita and she will love me back." Ravana smiled ten wide smiles and his twenty eyes laughed. "Angada, you are a good messenger, you added nothing and you left nothing out. Won't you stay to dinner?"

"Ravana, all your wealth is wasted, what's the use of being rich if you won't spend your gold to do good for other people?"

"Someone said that already," replied the Demon King. "Come, make yourself at home, I will protect you here."

Angada said, "Majesty, I hope you don't think I believe that for one moment, do you? You think it's so superior to be evil! You think it makes you *better!*"

"You are yet only a rash child, a meal time visitor, a pleasing presence; but keep it up and one of these days. . . ."

Angada tossed his head. "Shall we all put out our eyes? Is the Sun dark, because some men are blind?"

Ravana frowned. "You are speaking like a fool! We could all die at any time—" He bent down and thrust his ten faces suddenly snarling close before Angada. His lips were drawn back and his moustaches quivered; his wide-rimmed red eyes were aflame and veins were throbbing on his brows crowned by diadems. A deep low growl came from his ten throats.

Angada was faint with fear. His heart froze. The blood drained from his face and he couldn't breathe. Ravana said, "Now you are caught in the meshes of war; there's no way out of this for you! Fools have sharp eyesight and they stay forever on the good Dharma-Wheel, but the wise do not see so well." He reached out for Angada. *Who the dark Demon King seizes in his grip, who he holds in anger dies crushed and cursed, he never lives!*

Then Ravana just touched Angada. He brushed him away like a little piece of cloud, and off Angada floated. . . .

Ravana called after him, "Tell Rama—*Grief to you! Men are vile, may this war increase your pain and bring joy to the demons!*"

Angada recovered his strength and backed away into the air. He returned to Rama. And in Lanka, Ravana rang all the brass and iron bells, the great bells of Lanka rung with swinging logs. From the ringing mouths of bells came . . . daring . . . defiance. . . .

The crimson Sun set behind Sunset Hill at the western edge of the Earth, beyond the sea horizon. The sky grew pale lavender while still holding light, like the color of old silver. Then it was dark and the stars came out.

Angada said, "Ravana will not listen; he cannot clear his mind."

Rama answered, "Then where will he escape while I live?"

The Siege of Lanka

This perilous Life is a drop of water,
A hanging raindrop on a lotus leaf;
Soon it falls back in the pond below
And is lost.

Indrajit,
In war or peace
You are falling away.

Early the next morning Ravana was leaning on the wall over the northern gate looking out, leaning on his twenty arms spread side by side by side along the ramparts, under the shadow of a royal white umbrella. He patiently watched Rama and his army while two demons fanned him with white chowry fans made from yak-tails and trimmed with peacock feathers. He wore white robes like fame and glory, adorned with rubies red as blood; and for a long time he quietly watched the animals.

Ravana saw the golden-haired Sugriva fathered by the Sun; the black-and-brown bear Jambavan; Angada with his long fine yellow hair, pacing with his arms folded, yawning in anger and slapping his tail on the ground; the white monkey Hanuman, come back again to Lanka, strong and gracious; and beside him Rama of tangled hair and dark green skin, holding a bow whose arrows can slice the Earth or pierce the sky—Rama King of the World whose anger is Death, surrounded by animals all willing to die for him.

Sugriva told Rama to stay behind the army with Hanuman. Lakshmana walked back and forth in front of the animals, his skin like pure gold, his lips swollen with wrath, not easy to pacify. *Aaah* . . . the Rakshasas on the Lanka walls sighed like the long-traveling wind storming in from off the sea. They flaunted their glorious war-banners on shiny golden

239

flatstaffs. And back from the monkeys and bears came another deeper sigh, deep and loud as weights of water pouring
through a broken sea-wall. *Aaaaa.* . . .

Then at the same instant Lakshmana pointed at Lanka
with his bow and Ravana raised a mace over his head. In
Lanka the Royal Artillery Commander waved his sword. Bat-
teries of Rakshasa artillery roared fringed with fire; the monkeys and bears closed ranks; the big north gate of Lanka
opened; and the youngest third of the Demon Army came
out to attack, led by Prahasta on a war-chariot.

But the demons could not win in daylight. Bears broke
their cars and killed them with their own axles and flagpoles;
long-armed apes caught them and pressed them to death;
monkeys flattened them with uptorn trees and cliffs and
chopped them up with captured axes like firewood. At noon
Prahasta ordered a retreat, and the Rakshasas poured back
into Lanka, and the huge northern gate snapped shut like a
trap. They waited for darkness.

Then Night fell, increasing the strength of the demons. At
dusk the War Chief Prahasta and King Ravana were on the
wall again, and the darkness grew. Pale silk flags and standards crowned Beautiful Lanka with all their colors fast-fad-
ing and moving in the twilight wind. Up on the wall the air
from the city below carried the scents of incense and the
murmur of Rakshasa prayers to welcome Night. Demon soldiers were everywhere kneeling before fires built in the
streets, stringing their bows, tying on their armor, and then
putting on over that many garlands of flowers blessed with
mantras of safety. And on the battlefield outside the animals
built many fires to light the ground.

Ravana said, "Let the young warriors rest. Arm the
veterans."

"That's what we're doing."

From a stone flask Ravana poured out a glass of soma
juice somehow stolen from heaven and gave it to Prahasta.
General Prahasta drank it down and ate up the glass along
with a dried string of red-hot peppers. He crunched the glass
and chewed on the pepper seeds and smacked his lips. Ravana backed away from him a little.

Prahasta said, "I'll go with them. I'll drive way the
animals and isolate Rama. I'll entertain my friends with his

flesh!" Little flames began to come from Prahasta's mouth, licking over his lips.

He touched his hands together and bowed his head and saluted Ravana. Ravana said, "Be careful." Prahasta came down from the wall and tied back his flowing hair and got on his chariot.

General Prahasta's chariot had two wheels covered by sheets of gold, that turned like rolling suns and rumbled like the clouds. Steel scythes were mounted on the axle hubs, and a long iron spike pointed forward from the harness pole that was all painted with crescent moons. Sixty-four mottled green serpents drew that car, harnessed by unsolvable knots; the chariot bristled with racks of swords and harpoons; it was armored with bullhide warshields and metal plates.

Things were loaded all over Prahasta's chariot. He had slaughter-sledges, butcher knives and meat-hooks, chains and claws and clamps; he carried bombs and rockets and poisons and appalling jealousies; delusions and bad dreams, diseases and ambitions, many crises and confusions. Wrong-way road signs and false maps of mirages were tied on with broken promises. Small iron wheels spun in the air, their rims striking sparks against flint-stones and whirling in flames in the Night. There were lights and shadows and lying smiles, prisms and colored lenses and crooked brass mirrors and baleful green cats'-eyes. There were puzzles with essential parts missing and loaded dice and heartbreak and many first loves lost.

It was quite a sight to see! From a high flagstaff in the center of the car flew Prahasta's flag showing a serpent of emeralds and a clawing lion of topaz stones sewn onto blood-red silk. From that central flagpole a defensive net covered the chariot like a tent, made of glowing diamonds closely tied on blue steel threads, woven tightly with spun strands of adamant, guarding Prahasta as he fought and leaving small hidden ways for him to shoot his arrows.

It was fantastic. Still, Prahasta was a great archer; he had never turned back from a fight on Earth. Prahasta flexed his twisty bow and rolled his eyes. He leaned forward and told his charioteer—*Take me to War!* The chariot leapt forward protected by hatchetmen in winged demon helmets. Again the north gate opened, and General Prahasta led out from Lanka the elite veterans, and Grand Army of the Rakshasas. The teeming soldiers followed, riding and shouting, bells tied on their arms and legs, mounted on chariots drawn by running scorpions and toads, riding on the backs of porpoises and camels and giant goldfish, on lizards and pigs and huge blue rats.

The Rakshasas laughed in anger and blew ten thousand out-of-tune shells. They came onto the battlefield and charged at the monkeys and bears. The animals fled back between their fires and the demons cried—*Easy! Easily done!*

But it was a trick. In one motion, all of them together, the animals threw great stones out from behind their own lines, over their own warriors, over Prahasta, and aimed them to fall in front of the following Rakshasas. They made a road-block, a strong stone wall that cut off Prahasta, and when demons tried to fly over it the animals beat them back with trees, and closed in behind the General's chariot.

Arrows long as chariot axles flew from Prahasta's bow. None missed. He struck five or seven animals with one single arrow, or hit one monkey with seventeen arrows, or pierced a bear with twenty-seven or with ninety. The monkeys and apes and bears gave way and drew back from Prahasta, all but Nala the bridge-builder.

Nala alone faced Prahasta's chariot. He dodged a thousand flights of arrows and rockets that flew at him. Then he just stood still and let Prahasta shoot. A big brass club bounced off Nala's head, but it only killed a mosquito who was about to bite him. Nala stood among the falling missiles and arrows with his eyes closed like a proud bull standing in a rainstorm.

Then Nala opened his eyes, narrow in rage. He watched every move Prahasta made. The heavy Rakshasa chariot turned and bore down on him. There was noise like peals of thunder; the ground shook; Nala could see every armor plate, every diamond, every stone in the war-flag, every mirror flashing lights. He almost felt the serpents' breath.

Then quicker than the twinkling of an eye Nala threw his weight onto one foot and Trikuta Hill lurched off-center and Prahasta's chariot overturned. The serpents who had drawn the car slipped their harness and dove into the Earth. The chariot splintered to bits, Prahasta's bow broke, his protective net fell down, and suddenly the Demon General was standing free from the wreckage, holding a mace under his arm, spitting fire from his mouth and rubbing his hands together in a bath of flame.

Prahasta swung his mace in both hands and struck Nala twice; swinging out he hit his shoulder and on the back-swing gave a glancing blow on Nala's hip. Nala pulled one of the golden wheels off the broken chariot. When Prahasta raised his arms to strike again with a downwards blow, Nala threw the wheel in under his guard. He struck Prahasta over the heart. He knocked the mace from his hands and drove the life out from his body.

When they saw Prahasta killed that midnight, the Rakshasas bent back like tall trees in a windstorm; they tore loose their hair in shame, and returned leaderless to Lanka, looking down and not speaking. On the war-field west of Lanka Prahasta's chariot was smashed; it lay bent and smoking like a dead bolt of thunder fallen from heaven. The charioteer was dead. Prahasta lay on his back, terrible to see. His remorseless eyes were open and from his mouth little flames still darted out between his teeth that were burned black by his fury.

Nala stood wounded over Prahasta, one arm hanging broken and blood on his leg. Rama approached him carrying a torch. As Rama came near, Nala knelt and bowed to him. Once kneeling he was too exhausted to rise, but looking up at Rama's face his eyes still glittered and glowed like the eyes of a cobra just struck a blow with a rod, spreading wide his hood.

The monkeys and bears carried their dead up the hillside of Trikuta and laid them in a forest. All the demon arrows, stone-sharpened and hardened in fires, were removed from the dead and wounded, and broken and burned.

The demons also left many dead behind them killed by the claws and teeth of animals, but to conceal his losses Ravana from within Lanka spirited those corpses away into the sea. Prahasta's body was gone without a trace.

In the city Ravana called his minister Suka and said, "One must make his own good fortune wherever he goes. Six months have passed—awaken my brother Kumbhakarna!"

The giant Kumbhakarna slept for six months after every day he was awake. He lay stretched out on his back inside a huge one-room mansion, the largest building in Lanka. Suka told the demons in the kitchen to start Kumbhakarna's breakfast, and with many servants holding torches and lanterns he went to the long giant house. Cooks arrived driving carts full of steaming rice and vats of wine and crisp roast buffalo, and Suka opened the great doors to let the scent of food inside.

Kumbhakarna didn't stir. Suka entered. He fought the

windy push and pull of Kumbhakarna's breathing and drew near his ear. Kumbhakarna's hair and beard were six months wild; his hairs were like young forest trees, and when he was awake and felt like hunting, that giant would tie a boulder to each hair and go stand among his prey and shake himself, and crush his victims under stones.

Suka reached in his robe, pulled out two big brass cymbals and smashed them together by Kumbhakarna's ear. Kumbhakarna yawned, and his monstrous throat looked like a red mine-shaft leading down to Hell. A team of eighteen trained elephants ran in through the door, up Kumbhakarna's side and across his chest; there they made a line and sprayed his face with cold water.

Suka kept battering and banging his cymbals, and Kumbhakarna awoke. Trainers called the elephants back just in time. Kumbhakarna sat up, opened his eyes, reached outside for a vat of wine, and drank it down and sighed, "Ah, it is full Night!"

The food-wagons drove in, and Suka stood quietly at a safe distance until Kumbhakarna had eaten. Then he approached and said, "Prince, General Prahasta has been killed in war. Lanka is surrounded by Rama and his armies."

"Rama, Rama?" asked Kumbhakarna. "What god is Rama? . . . never mind, I'll help you."

Suka replied, "Here in Lanka you alone sleep happily, knowing nothing of our fate. Rama is a man, and his warriors are monkeys and bears from across the sea. Our soldiers have been twice driven from the field, and Ravana wants you at the palace."

"No fear," said Kumbhakarna, "be calm. Behold the magnified evils of being awake and subject to reason. My only law is dreams. . . ." He bent his head, went out the tall doorway and washed his face in a lake.

As Kumbhakarna fully awoke, he became so dark and menacing that he seemed to soak up all the light from Suka's torches and from the stars of heaven, and by a sudden fancied dimness in his courtroom Ravana knew his brother was coming. Rakshasas lined the streets to the royal palace and called up to Kumbhakarna—*Don't step on these fragile temples. Houses are there, here stand soldiers.*

After a few steps Kumbhakarna was near the palace. He sat outside near Pushpaka chariot, where he would have room to talk with Ravana. The Demon King came outdoors and saw his little brother blotting out the sky, and ran to meet him with ten happy smiles.

Ravana said, "Scatter my enemies like a strong wind!"

Kumbhakarna asked, "What have you done wrong while I slept peacefully?"

"I'm at war with Rama because I took his wife Sita," answered Ravana. "His animals have killed our warriors who were never before defeated."

"Give her back," said Kumbhakarna.

"But I am in love with her," said Ravana.

"A tremendous mistake. Stop yourself."

"But cast the blame where it belongs, it's not my fault she's so good-looking and easy to see! No one in any world is like Sita, but she won't get into my bed."

"Best of Kings," said Kumbhakarna, "here you are speaking of the waking world of impermanence, of suffering and unreality. Those are the animals of Lord Narayana, and this is the death of the Rakshasas."

"I won't believe it," said Ravana. "What I don't like I don't hear!"

"Oh, let alone the animals, Rama can himself defeat you all alone. Do some good before you die. They are eager to kill you; why won't you make peace with them?"

"Not for fear of all the worlds!"

"Majesty," said Kumbhakarna, "after you've done this thoughtless deed full of flaws and holes, then you call on me. You've begun at the end and ignored the beginning."

"What do you know about it anyway?" asked Ravana.

"I know forgetfulness, and sleep . . . as a child falling asleep . . . what I knew then years ago, as I fell asleep, I still know. Forget. Sleep and forget her. . . ."

Ravana rubbed his eyes. "Yes, I am tired and spent—" But then he shook his heads, took a deep breath of the night air and sighed. "But I have lost myself in longing."

"Your entire education was a waste," said Kumbhakarna. "For nothing did you read the holy Veda and throw your heads into the fire when we lived in the high Himalya Hills."

"Well, it's done, isn't it! Why must you tell me about the aftermath of evil? If I'm wrong I need you to save me all the more. Ah, if you could only see her, like an idol of gold, the very handwork of Maya himself. . . ."

"There's no greater wrong than stealing another's wife," said Kumbhakarna. "Lord of Night, what else but a harvest of misfortune could follow? You have many ladies in your own house; be happy with them. Enjoy in peace your honors and kingdoms. Keep for a long time your wealth; preserve your life. Return her to Rama and get more sleep. A King is the root of his people's happiness, and if he is wrong their lives are in danger and their nation will die. Your ministers cannot take this to heart, they do not serve you well. They plot to kill you. They do not fear your anger. Majesty, those two men Rama and Lakshmana are the flame and the wind meeting—will no one tell you this except me? I will kill Vibhishana for not caring to prevent you doing this."

"Vibhishana did try to stop me," said Ravana, "and when he failed he went over to Rama. He's out there on the field right now."

"Now he was right to do that, and surely it was wrong of you to force him to go. Give back Sita. You have no gift of protection against men and animals. . . ."

"She is my beloved. . . ."

"And I am your friend," said Kumbhakarna. "Listen, I have an idea. Take Rama's form by magic, go to Sita, and she will willingly love you."

"No, I can't," said Ravana. "The transformation would have to be complete; I'd have to take on all Rama's virtues as well to fool her, and then I could do no wrong, I couldn't lie to her and say I was someone I wasn't. Help me to cure my sorrow. In my mind I am sure of your victory!"

Kumbhakarna smiled. "Then they must first kill me to get at you! Dear brother, have a good time, do as you please. Be merciful while you may and think no more of Rama."

Ravana was very happy; he beckoned for his warriors and told Kumbhakarna, "Consider well your own strength and theirs, do not go out alone."

But Kumbhakarna said, "I want no helpers. Everyone here who has been awake and kept silent about your careless love is your fawning enemy. The simple truth is that Rama and the animals have outwitted you all; they've built a bridge while you sat around saying it couldn't be done! Let these others help you feather your conceits, but I alone will kill Rama tonight and drink his blood!"

Ravana felt reborn. Kumbhakarna smiled at him again and went back the way he came to put on his war-clothes. But though he seemed in good humor Kumbhakarna thought to himself, "Dharma is the root of all good fortune, and you have uprooted Dharma; the happiness of others is light for the spirit but you have darkened the worlds."

Then Kumbhakarna put sympathy aside; he put his heart into the stone age. He donned his armor of bronze and his helmet of gold. The chains of his belts were heavier than the chains that raised the drawbridges of Lanka; his bracelets were like the metal tires on chariot-wheels; his garlands of flowers were as long as a day's journey.

When Kumbhakarna had dressed he drank down two thousand vats of war-wine, and from his long house he took out his black iron spear decorated with animals inlaid in gold. When Kumbhakarna touched it, deadly blue fires burned round the spear-point like the fires at the birth of Time, blazing for a moment large as a funeral pyre. Kumbhakarna walked to Lanka's wall and over the western gate the Rakshasas raised his flag, a black banner hung with crimson flowers, showing the Death-Wheel of oblivion, a giant wheel sewn on it in golden thread.

On the battlefield that Night Rama could see the bearded Kumbhakarna, dark and startling, visible behind the high walls like walking Death. He asked Vibhishana, "Who is that?"

"My brother Kumbhakarna has awakened," answered Vibhishana. "He'll make one mouthful out of our whole army. He is the very crown of our cruelty and the banner of our strength. Did he not sleep so long he would by now have eaten up all Life on Earth. If he can reach them, he will scrape up your animals and swallow them like little grains of rice. . . . But tell the monkeys and bears that this is an uplifted war-engine, a huge machine; for if they know he is a living being they will die of fright at the thought, whether he touches them or not, and we will swiftly lose this war."

"I'll send them to the back." Rama summoned Sugriva and told him, "Withdraw from the field."

"No," said the Monkey King. "They say that the gateway arch to Kumbhakarna's house rises so high that every noonday the Sun must pass under it on his way around the Earth. They say that giant is so heavy that he draws in the flood tides when he walks near the sea. But people talk too much! Why should we move aside? Why give way, leaving you behind us?"

Kumbhakarna stepped over the wall, swinging his mon-

strous arms in anger. Like a pillar of light, his spear-shaft
caught the torch-beams of Lanka on its golden ornaments. Kumbhakarna saw the monkeys and bears and
thought, "Animals like these were always the innocent ornaments of our gardens. Rama is the cause of this war; I will kill
Rama and end it!" He turned in Rama's direction and cried
out his horrible, unnatural war-cry, a shuddering sound, so
low and deep it could be felt through the ground, and yet
shrill and piercing, and getting louder—

And that cry alone broke the formations of the animals.
They fell unconscious, or lay trembling and unable to move,
or ran to hide in quiet places, not looking back, and a curtain
of dust rose from their feet running in panic.

Kumbhakarna took a long step towards Rama, and
beneath his foot Earth lurched and swayed like a swing. The
animals' war-fires spilled and rolled burning over the land.
Prince Angada tried to stop the fleeing monkeys and bears.
"Think of the King, think of your good name and fame!
Your wives will scorn you—"

Still they ran past him—*Life is dear!*

"Sound an alert! Return!"

But each animal thought, "He is after me!" In an instant
the army had fled. But Hanuman came from somewhere and
stood quietly beside Angada, and they saw Sugriva not far
away, and Jambavan the sullen Bear King had stood his
ground. But between Rama and Kumbhakarna there was
only Lakshmana.

Then from where he stood Hanuman jumped hard and
high at Kumbhakarna and bit a piece out of his ear.
Kumbhakarna whirled, very fast, and struck Hanuman down
with his great spear. But that blow broke the iron shaft, and
as Hanuman fell stunned Kumbhakarna threw aside the piece
he still held and advanced on Rama unarmed.

No one remained except Lakshmana, but his arrows could
not penetrate the stiff coily hair that covered Kumbhakarna's
body wherever his armor did not. Kumbhakarna looked away
down at Lakshmana and said, "You also are dead, when
Rama dies!" Then he stepped over him and quickly advanced
on Rama.

Rama took three steps backwards and aimed an arrow with
bent knots like thunderbolts. He released it; it flew and struck
Kumbhakarna in the chest, right through his armor.
Kumbhakarna paused and stood still, and blood poured from
his wound.

That wound alone was fatal, but his hatred for Rama kept Kumbhakarna alive and his murderous heart did not fail. He cried out—*I am not Vali the monkey shot in the back; I am Kumbhakarna poised over you!*

Rama shot a straight-flying arrow with a broad razor head and cut off Kumbhakarna's right arm, which fell crushing trees and rocks. Still Kumbhakarna kept coming, he yelled—*I tear Earth apart and pull down stars; I fall on you like Doom!*

Rama cut off his left arm. It fell into the sea and bruised the whales, and Kumbhakarna shouted—*No one can slay me; no one can stop me!*

Again Rama twice drew back his bow, and with two thirsty arrows cut off Kumbhakarna's legs. The giant fell only a few bows'-lengths from Rama. Still he managed to move, something carried him on, and his mouth opened and closed—*Let all Creation see the might of Kumbhakarna awake, and tremble!*

Then with one final arrow Rama beheaded Kumbhakarna. The giant head rolled downhill into the sea and sank to the bottom. It was near the hour of dawn and Rama stood alone against the sky. For a few moments he kept shooting his gold-covered arrows up through the air and into Lanka, and the snap of his bowstring struck terror into the Demons' hearts. With golden arrows Rama was scattering the Night. The sky lightened behind Lanka. The stars faded, caught in the skies of heaven and defeated by the eastern Sun rising all in flames. Soon Rama stood in sunlight and unstrung his bow.

When he heard that Kumbhakarna's life was lost, the hot fumes of anger filled Ravana's heart. He stood on the wall and saw his brother's body and limbs blocking the fields outside Lanka. Smoke swirled out of his ten mouths and hung in the air round his heads like a dismal shroud.

The old Rakshasa Malyavan came and stood beside him at sunrise, and Ravana said—*Truly how has Rama done this?*

Malyavan answered, "He did it with glorious arrows lighting up all the directions of Earth, arrows washed first with gold and then with blood."

"Grandfather, as you look at me I am defeated although I seem alive. All is truly forever chance and change."

Malyavan said, "Like a mirror gleaming through from

within a black velvet bag, we may sometimes glimpse Reality shining here and there when it takes us unawares."

Ravana said, "Once when I was here at home, the cautious Wind blew cool from touching the waters; the waves of the surf stepped lightly; the careful warm sunlight was never burning hot; the Moon paled from dread when I went outside into my gardens. At my command trees blossomed and clouds poured rain and the sea-tide stopped." Ravana sighed. "But now, when talking the name Rama comes out in my speech. I see his face when I close my eyes. Monkeys have bridged the sea, and stones float for them unfairly, against the natural laws, and what never yet happened in the world has happened here! . . . This sad peril is all my fault. I have banished Vibhishana who was my conscience, and my young brother who loved me is dead. Where does Kumbhakarna go all alone?"

"He is in the bright heaven of warriors killed in war," said Malyavan. But he could not console the King, and he walked slowly away and left Ravana alone.

Ravana hung down his heads and wept for a long time. Then he said, "What have I to do with Empire? What shall I care now for Sita? I must avenge you, Kumbhakarna. *If I cannot kill Rama, then Death is my good fortune and this life is useless to me!*"

Then a voice behind Ravana said, "Oh King, banish sorrow!"

Ravana turned and looked into Indrajit's quiet eyes. "My son!"

Indrajit said, "I shall make my sacrifices to the Fire. Sire, be happy; drink your wines and sleep. Enjoy all pleasure, for your enemies are already dead and Sita is about to become yours!"

The Invisible Warrior

Do not complain about how heaven turns above,
For heaven will endure long enough without you.

I am all this,
All this Life;
I am all this.

That same fell Indrajit, able to assume shapes at will, stood there on Lanka's walls in the form of a golden young man. His hair was gold and his eyes were flecked with all the colors of gold. His skin was gold. He wore a golden war-robe and a golden belt and thin gold-leather shoes. He hid behind himself every enchantment and he was beautiful to see.

Ravana said, "I am in a deep and narrow pit, with steep walls, with no place to grasp them anywhere . . . and no way out. . . ."

"Father, I'm whoever I want to be." Indrajit knelt to Ravana on one knee, he touched together his hands and said—*I am Fire in the dry grass.*

"Now there's a thought!" Ravana was happy as a man high on a clear hill on a springtime morning, with his love beside him.

"Majesty!" Indrajit rose and pointed to Rama far away. "He does not know me, so he comes against us. Why does he stir the sweetly sleeping fire? What shall I do for you on my invisible chariot unswerving as the Truth?"

"Just kill Rama and Lakshmana, that's all."

"Yes!" said Indrajit. "Though my fire is an illusion, it will burn; the water will drown, it is no more false than Death itself."

Indrajit went outside Lanka to his hidden grove and built a smokeless fire on his altar. He raised a vessel of clear butter to his head. The fire burned in seven tongues of flame all playing about in the heat-waving air—one tongue black and one deep red and one starting to smoke; one swift tongue, one sparkling, one threatening, and one having all brilliant forms within it.

Indrajit took a sip from the bowl of butter. He poured it in the fire and quickly stepped back. The flame streamed up in golden splendor when he fed it. *Lord Brahma, I have won from you one hundred and eight kinds of illusion; I have won a quiver of arrows that never run out, and an invincible bow, and charms bringing darkness and ignorance, and the power of invisible flight, and an aerial chariot ever victorious. Give me my many prizes.*

Up out from the red flames rose Indrajit's dazzling fire-born chariot drawn by four tigers, a fire-hued war-car decorated with the golden faces of demons or of deer. It flew a red flag showing a lion of green with sapphire eyes, a banner hung with gold bell-bracelets all around. It bore a bow and a quiver of arrows of crooked ways, vaned with vulture feathers.

There were all Brahma's boons given Indrajit for freeing Indra. The cruel Indrajit smiled. *You shame me, Lord. Oh Brahma, your life endures while I exhale one breath!* Then Indrajit got onto his tiger chariot and dressed himself all in bows and arrows and swords and lashes and hammers, and tied back his hair, and whatever he touched turned all to gold. He wrapped himself in illusion and spread enchantment around himself with a wave of his arm, and vanished.

On the battlefield Vibhishana frowned. He shaded his blue eyes and looked up into the blue morning sky, where a few small white clouds had gathered. He told Rama, "Indrajit approaches us invisibly. I cannot see him unless I know just where to look; even Brahma cannot see him. For combat, he has called his chariot forth from the fire, and while he stays on that car he cannot lose a fight to anyone. To Indrajit now the thunder of heaven is but a whisper and Death's dread noose a bit of string. Your army are deer sent against a lion; there is nothing he cannot do."

Clouds spread over the sky. From within them Rama and the animals could hear the creaking of Indrajit's chariot-wheels and see the flashing of his gold weapons. They heard the flag-bells ringing and the four tigers growling—then there was a sharp noise from the sky like iron cracking and a flaming axe came from the clouds. It was falling fast aimed right for Rama. King Sugriva bravely jumped up to shield him, and that axe struck through his bold heart and killed him.

Indrajit stood firing down from the back of the beyond. Down came a rain of death. Thirty-three crescent arrows killed Prince Angada, and his blood made his gold fur red. An iron hook dashed in the chest of Nala the bridge-builder; he fell coughing and choking, and died strangled and frightened. Ten diamond-tipped arrows pierced the bear King Jambavan and he fell; a barbed bronze spear tore through Vibhishana's shoulder as he stood beside Rama and pinned him to the ground. The frightful cries of the dying filled the air.

Hanuman flew up into the clouds. He couldn't see Indrajit, but he saw a magic sword running at him like lightning, all by itself. Hanuman grabbed it, but that weapon became a fair young woman. She cried in fear, "Let me go! It's wrong to hold an unwilling woman!" So hearing that one word— *Wrong*—Hanuman released her. She became a sword again and cut him down from the sky.

Indrajit's assault covered the field with dead, and Rama stood among the rolling heads and broken bodies of his animal friends. He tried to aim by watching where Indrajit's arrows appeared to come from, but those arrows didn't fly straight, and their sources always shifted and changed. Rama shot his golden arrows out over the whole sky, and some few of them fell back from the clouds with their points covered with blood.

Then only Rama and Lakshmana remained standing, the two best men of all this world. Indrajit shot his arrows at them until there was not one fingertip's space left unpierced on their bodies. Their gold armor was no use. Those many wounds killed Rama first. He fell dead. Lakshmana couldn't believe what he saw and wept. He tried to blink the tears from his eyes, but more arrows came through his heart and killed him before he could see again.

And at mid-morning, Indrajit unbearable in war returned to his grove of trees outside Lanka. He became visible and got out of his chariot. The car and the tigers disappeared in a ball of flame. Indrajit said graciously to his servants, "Go through the underground passage into Beautiful Lanka. Tell my father—*Have no doubt, have no care. Rama is dead, I killed him.*"

When they left, Indrajit sat under his banyan tree, whose leaves were green, whose flowers were red as all the blood he'd spilled. Indrajit laughed. Then he said—*Om!* He leaned back and closed his eyes, and speaking no more he began to breathe slowly in and out, slowly and deeply, centering his mind only on his breathing. He made himself one with the breath of Life. The clouds left the sky, and Indrajit shut himself away from the world—*I breathe. I breathe.*

All that day the battlefield was like some slaughter yard in the sun. But when the ancient goddess Night came and increased the power of all Night-Wanderers, Vibhishana the Rakshasa stirred where he lay. He looked up at the stars, the open eyes of Night. He grasped the metal spear-shaft in both hands and twisted apart the tough bronze where it entered his shoulder, and pulled himself up leaving the spearhead in the ground. He sat bleeding and trembling in pain, but he joined his hands to honor the weapons Indrajit had used and spoke a secret mantra that healed his wound.

Vibhishana used his keen night vision and looked around for some friend alive. From the back of Rama's army all the way up to Lanka's walls were dead monkeys and apes and bears, many of their bodies cut into pieces. He remembered that Hanuman can never be killed and saw something white move a little in the gloom. Carefully Vibhishana got to his feet and went to see what it was. He found Hanuman sitting up, alive and covered with sword-cuts.

Vibhishana and Hanuman together searched among the dead, and there they found Jambavan near death and but faintly breathing, badly injured and burning with hot fever. Vibhishana bent over him and gave him water. "Riksharaja, King of Bears, are you alive? Have these sharp arrows yet spared your life?"

With great effort Jambavan replied, "Demon Prince, I cannot see. Tell me, does Hanuman the Son of the Wind still live?"

Vibhishana snapped his fangs. "You do not ask about Rama. You do not show such love for anyone else as you show for that white monkey Hanuman."

"Hear why I ask," said Jambavan. "While Hanuman lives, this army also lives; but if he is dead we are truly destroyed."

Hanuman held Jambavan's feet. "Here I am once more!"

"Life! Then we have narrowly escaped with life!" Jambavan's voice was weak but he smiled. He asked, "Indrajit?"

Vibhishana answered, "Now it is Night; this morning Indrajit killed Rama and Lakshmana and everyone else, except us three. He left and has not returned; he must be hidden in his grove of trees, in meditation. I have just revived, and I found Hanuman alive."

"Then this is not the time for grief and not the place," said Jambavan.

Hanuman asked, "Old bear, what do you mean?"

"Only from you have we any hope for our lives," said Jambavan. "My child, there is no one else. Instantly go back over the sea and north into the far high Himalya. At night from the air you will easily see the glowing Medicine Hill of Life, crowned with annuals and herbs, bright and luminous, long ago transplanted from the Moon. Those fragrant plants are potent to heal any hurt and restore life to the dead . . . bring them back . . . hurry—"

Hanuman bent his back, opened his mouth and jumped straight for the snowy lap of the Himalya Hills. He flew like a blazing comet, fast and generous, speedy and bright! He went over the dark sea and over the land. Soon he saw the River Ganga falling from heaven into Lord Shiva's hair; he saw Shiva, always visible to animal eyes, tall and fair and smiling, with a new moon in his hair, the new moon like Rama. . . .

Ahead on the horizon Hanuman saw high on a hill the flickering lights of many luminous plants shining with their own light like cold white flames of fire, shining in the clear night like silent lightning. On that Mountain of Life there is no difference between day and night. When the Sun departs, lights glitter and stream out from those medical herbs on the high summits and ridges; their new leaves sparkle and gleam, their stems glow like liquid silver, like moonlight on the waves as they bend in the wind, and the whole hill shines like a gem.

Hanuman looked down on the Himalyan rivers and mountain passes and caves, the icy cliffs and dark forests and the hidden retreats of holy saints. But the glowing plants felt him approach. They drew themselves down under the ground, their lights were hidden and they were lost in the dark night.

There was no time to dig them out. Hanuman said—*You foolish grasses with no compassion!*—and in three shakes of his shoulders he uprooted that whole entire mountain where they grew and held it over his head in his hands.

Hanuman flew back to Lanka, so fast that the Hill of Life grew very hot and all the herbs began to steam and bake. When he arrived outside Lanka, Hanuman could see nowhere to set the mountain down. As he stood on the air wondering what to do next, the scent of those herbs spread over the battlefield, and that fragrance alone was enough to restore the dead animals to life and heal all their wounds. But the dead Rakshasas were under the sea in other worlds, beyond the reach of any medicine of Earth.

Jambavan ran over and looked up. He saw Hanuman holding a huge hill bearing all its trees and stones and elephants and colored veins of ore and pockets of snow and falling rivers. Hanuman shouted, "Where do you want it?"

"—Oh Lord!" Jambavan laughed till he cried.

"What? Where?"

"Oh blessings, best of monkeys," said Jambavan. "We are saved! Turn away, put it back again where it belongs!"

The monkeys and bears formed into a guard around the battlefield. They held trees and stones; they looked calmly out in every direction. All night, when even a straw blew past them they struck it down lest it be Indrajit, or some Rakshasa magic.

Sugriva the Monkey King washed Rama's eyes with palmfuls of cold water and said, "We were all dead." He told him what Hanuman had done.

Hanuman returned again and landed with a thump beside Rama. "My Lord, you live!"

Rama embraced Hanuman and said, "Listen. So far by good fortune I see you all alive again, but were I to lose any of you, then without you my life would be empty and worthless. Never seeking in the world again could I find other friends so true. Why did I bring you here? Go home, King Sugriva. Take your people and no more of dying. Retrace your steps to Kishkindhya."

King Sugriva said, "After all we've gone through," and looked at Hanuman.

Hanuman answered, "Dear Rama, we are indeed your old good friends from long ago, and your companions of ancient days come here to help you. We are your forefathers. We are your ancestors the animals, and you are our child Man. As for our friendship, why we've known you a long long time, Rama, and the number of those days is lost in Silence. . . ."

That same evening just after nightfall the old Rakshasi Trijata hurried to Sita in the Asoka Grove and said, "Alas, all is destiny; in war victory and defeat are all uncertain!"

Sita asked, "What is it?"

"I don't know," said Trijata, "I'm not sure. Indrajit is supposed to have killed Rama and all his army. They say he has now destroyed the root of this war. But Ravana has been asleep all afternoon and no one has seen Indrajit since this morning."

"How dared they——"

"But wait," said Trijata. "Indrajit deals in illusion; don't be enthralled by his spells of doom. Daughter of Earth, I went over the wall and I saw Rama and Lakshmana and all their animals lying out there riddled with arrows; a strange sight, I cannot believe it's true."

Sita didn't cry. Her soft black eyes grew hard and there was a terrible anger in her face. Trijata said, "Lakshmi of the Lotus! Oh wait, my Lady—though covered with arrows, the light of Life still lingers in their skin; their muscles are not slack, nor their weapons dull. The dead do not look so. I speak to you from affection, I have never lied to you. Set aside your anger until you are sure. Throw it down . . . Sita, for the moment forbear . . . do not destroy us. . . ."

Sita sighed and was still. Then the other Rakshasis came and told her, "Come with us; get onto Pushpaka chariot. We've something to show you on the battlefield, you'll see!"

Trijata whispered, "It would be merciful to obey." Once on board the giant chariot the Rakshasis said, "Handsome Rama lying slain, and Lakshmana dead beside him!"

Then by thought they made Pushpaka start to rise into the air. But when that chariot was only a few hands' breadth above the ground Trijata cried, "I knew it! This is fine!" She smiled at Sita and stopped the flying car so he would rise no higher.

The other Rakshasis turned and screamed, "Welcome news! It's plain as day, they're dead!"

"No they're not," said Trijata. "This proves it's a lie. The flower chariot Pushpaka will carry no widow!"

"What? What?" they yelled.

"Stop it," said Trijata. "Be silent before I lose my temper. Why *me*, why must *I* suffer such fools all the time?"

Sita looked up at the northern sky and asked, "Trijata, what is that huge object glowing with heat and racing at us?"

"Hanuman and the Hill of Life," answered Trijata. "Dear

Sita, how can Hanuman do all these impossible deeds so easily?"

Sita smiled. They could smell the fragrant medicines. "It must be by the power of his wholehearted love for Rama."

Trijata brought the chariot down and said, "Sita, your sorrows are long and I wanted to comfort you. But instead, you have brought me happiness, and though I'm born in the demon race you have won your way into my heart."

Ravana slept all night, and when he awoke on the third morning of war his sentries from the walls told him how Rama was alive again. The Demon King went at sunrise to Indrajit's invisible grove and sat down by his son and softly said, "Help me once more."

Indrajit bowed his head a moment, then he said, "Majesty, for everyone there is the choice of two ways, right or wrong. Look at Rama. Regard his army. See his bridge! All this time millions of monkeys and bears have camped just outside your Lanka—and you could still not believe you were in any real danger—but even if Time and Death themselves overlook you when your life is full you can find no safety from Rama if you keep his wife. There is always a choice, Father—the Way of Life, or the path of Death."

"Kill him for me!"

"But I did that once," said Indrajit. "Think for a moment, remember the past. When you were young you grew strong by following Dharma and by sacrifice, and so you ruled the worlds. Yet once on the throne of power you slighted Dharma, you had no courtesy towards life. You drove out kindness, and denied freedom to the Universe, and made Creation suffer. The worlds are large, but your selfishness overmatched them. Now your wrongs devour us. In the far forests your intended victims drain our strength, and the smokes of their offerings spread over Earth's ten directions, and innocent holy men have promised we shall die."

"What of it?" said Ravana. "You are the best of warriors. You defeated the gods."

"Then bring on the gods!" answered Indrajit. "However great you may be, do not live hostile to every other soul. The fear and anger of the helpless has taken on the form of an army of animals. Death has led you on. You took Death on your lap the day you stole Sita, and Death have you courted all this time."

"Why, you captured Indra!"

"Now Dharma is on Rama's side," said Indrajit. "His army and his weapons are but the material instruments of Time. Now Rama rules Earth with all her creatures. All is Dharma, Majesty; there is no second thing in existence; there is Dharma alone in the world."

Ravana said, "My son, act now!"

"Then I will sacrifice to Fire—"

"No! If you love me, why offer more smoke to my slaves the gods?"

Indrajit laughed. "The gods are no one's property!" He got to his feet and put on a sword. "I won't use the fire offering unless I fail again."

Ravana arose. "Fight for me on Earth, as you did in heaven!"

"Yes, we seemed to have conquered heaven," said Indrajit. "But all we see is illusion. All is illusion, Demon King; loops and nooses of deception hold us. The gods of heaven—all they do is to obey the Dharma-Law, and all I do is tell the Truth to them . . . and I may sometimes use it for a controlling spell because it is so rarely heard."

Ravana embraced his son and smelled the crown of his hair. They went together through the tunnel to Ravana's palace in the city. Indrajit left his father there. "They will leave us in peace, don't worry."

Indrajit went outside and got a flying Rakshasa army chariot. He made a magic figure of Sita, lifelike and seeming to live, looking sad and thin and very beautiful. Then the chariot flew moving low over the Lanka wall, and in sight of Rama's army of monkeys he caught the false Sita roughly by her hair and drew his sharp sword.

Hanuman and many monkeys were near Lanka. Hanuman recognized Sita. The Sita on the chariot cried—*Oh Rama! Oh Lakshmana!*—and burst into heartbroken tears.

Hanuman yelled, "What are you doing?"

Indrajit said, "I would do anything to give you pain." He smiled and raised his sword. A scream cut the air and Indrajit cut Sita apart. He struck her left shoulder while he held her hair and cut down across her body, carving her in two along the line of the sacred thread lying across her breast, and half her body fell to the chariot floor.

The simple monkeys gasped in horror, and from their throats came a hopeless cry. Indrajit wiped his sword's blood on Sita's hair that he held; then he dropped the rest of her down into his car, turned in the air and descended once more into Lanka and out of sight.

The monkeys all ran. Hanuman tried to find Rama. He met Jambavan the bear and Lakshmana together, and rubbing tears from his eyes he said, "Indrajit killed Sita!"

Lakshmana was speechless. Jambavan said, "That ends the war; Rama will die."

Out of nowhere, Vibhishana the Rakshasa suddenly appeared beside them—*Hanuman, what is this?*

Hanuman told him and Vibhishana said, "That was an illusion."

"Oh no, I saw it, it was real!" said Hanuman.

"It was false!" Vibhishana grimaced and his face shattered and fell in pieces at his feet. His eyes broke like glass and were gone. He looked at Hanuman with empty eye-sockets in a horrible scar-covered skull. "Monkey, thus are you blind!"

Hanuman swallowed hard and stared at him. Vibhishana's eyes and face reformed and he said, "Take my word, it never happened. Do not grieve and please your enemies."

"What can we do?" asked Lakshmana.

Vibhishana replied, "We must hurry. Tie your armor and your hair; get your bow and arrows. Let Jambavan gather all his bears. It was foolish of Indrajit to touch Sita even in thought. He did not fight or remain before you because this time he did not have his tiger-chariot. Without it he has no divine protection in war, and cannot stay invisible if I reveal him. But now he hears us talking, he even knows what we think, and he will make the offering in his hidden grove unless. . . ."

Lakshmana asked, "What hidden grove?"

"It's not far from here, outside the walls," said Vibhishana. "I will make it visible." He knelt and bowed his head. *Queen of Dreamers, King of Dreams—*

> *Friends are impermanent,*
> *Wife and child are unreal;*
> *The world is untrue,*
> *And sorrow is a lie.*
> *Mother Night, we are shadows!*
> *Mother, show me my brother Indrajit!*

It got dark over that mountainside as though under some huge umbrella. They saw Indrajit near the southern wall, in a grove of ancient down-growing trees, in gloom and dark shadow. A flame burned on an altar of Earth and Indrajit knelt feeding it with butter from a double ladle of black iron. His back was to Lakshmana and Vibhishana. Tied to a stake, a black goat lay just killed in a pool of blood. Indrajit's hair was loose and he wore a crimson robe. By the altar were piled many armloads of javelins, each strung with a hundred little bells.

Lakshmana and Vibhishana watched with their blue eyes. Bears surrounded the grove at a distance. Still Indrajit didn't look up. He made a mark with ashes on his brow and spoke something. Cracks opened in the ground and up from the underworld Naga serpents came and bathed those javelins in their venom.

Indrajit's fire danced. He filled his ladle and stepped back. He was about to make the final offering; already Lakshmana could see the tigers beginning to emerge in the dark, pawing the air from within the fire; he could vaguely see the chariot, with its every golden face forming. . . .

Vibhishana said, "Ready?"

"Always have been." Quick as a lightning flash Lakshmana shot one arrow. He broke the iron ladle out of Indrajit's hand. His bow screamed like an eagle, and the Nagas dove underground in fear of their enemies, looking back up into the sky as they fled. Then Indrajit turned in a swirl of crimson. Then he knew he could be seen.

When Indrajit took his eyes off his fire, Agni the Fire Lord rose from the sacred flame and opened his mouth, and the seven tongues of flame came from his lips. He looked around for Indrajit. He saw Lakshmana, he saw the butter-ladle broken and Indrajit distracted. Then in surprise Agni turned away with a smile, and his form faded from the altar, and Indrajit's fire turned into a flaming madness. Burnt and gone were the tigers and their war-car.

Raven locks and red anger! Indrajit faced Vibhishana and Lakshmana. He looked at Ravana's brother. "Traitor, you have revealed me!"

Lights blazed in Vibhishana's dark-blue crystal eyes. "Why spear my shoulder?" He lay back his ears and snarled. "War was ever all you knew and all your skill."

Indrajit laughed happily. "May your new masters forsake you when all your old friends have died!"

"Say what you like," said Vibhishana. "How dare you defend the theft of Earth's daughter?"

Indrajit tightened his belt and gathered his hair. He drew in his power; he stood there now in silver armor and wearing a sword, firelight glanced from his silver helmet; he held a silver bow, and a quiver of silver arrows and a silver dagger hung at his side. He said, "Lakshmana, if you missed seeing my power before, see it now. *I ask you for the gift of single combat.*"

Lakshmana said—*I give.*

Indrajit narrowed his eyes and dropped down. He fell onto his left knee, held his great bow out flat before him and shot a thousand arrows at Lakshmana. Lakshmana cut them down as they flew and mocked Indrajit—*They're sharp and strong as lotus stems!* Lakshmana shot seven arrows and cut Indrajit's seven armor strings, and the silver mail fell down like a cluster of stars spilled out from heaven at night.

So fleet and swift were both warriors' hands that no one could see them notch an arrow or draw their bows, just as no one can see his soul behind his own senses; all you could see were the arrows flying. Arrows veiled the sky and made it even darker below; sparks and noise filled the air when they struck head-on. Indrajit seized a poison javelin and threw it; Lakshmana with arrows cut it down and left it in pieces no bigger than fingertips.

Indrajit again raised his bow, but this time Laksl.mana broke it with an arrow. Indrajit threw an Asura hand-arrow; it separated into a spray of flint darts, and like a swarm of needles they wounded Lakshmana a hundred times. The many darts that missed drummed on the trees and tore smoking holes through the leaves, as painful to meet as loud angry words from a friend. Lakshmana shot back. He hit Indrajit three times in the face, and pierced his body with five arrows that went right through the marrow of his bones and came out red, and flew on underground into the Earth covered with blood.

Indrajit drew his sword and whirled it over his head. That blade groaned and flamed at the cutting edge, but Lakshmana shattered it like glass with his arrows. Then Lakshmana slowed his hand, and carefully withdrew Agastya's arrow from its pocket in his quiver, a long grass arrow with a silver blade. He put it on his bowstring and pulled it back to his ear and said—*Kill him!* He released the bowstring and beheaded Indrajit.

For an instant Indrajit seemed to stand alone in light. Then forward fell his lifeless head, and backward fell his body. The altar and fire and weapons and offerings were gone and the grove was no longer dark. In death Indrajit's corpse and his head took on their true forms. Nothing beautiful remained. Seeing his look had long since made Indrajit abandon the desire for unreal and temporary illusions that depart and perish, and deal for himself in true reality and freedom.

Monkeys and bears fell into each other's arms, and Hanuman carried Lakshmana on his shoulders to Rama. Rama said, "That was a deed hard to do. We could never win this war while Indrajit lived; all Earth is grateful to you." He made Lakshmana lie down, and using herbs and moss Rama stopped his bleeding, and did not let his brother's life flow out.

It was a little past noon. The demons on the walls drew Indrajit's remains into the city by speaking mantras, by magic nets of words. They covered him and brought him along the streets and carried him to the King's palace, but no one dared tell Ravana. At last the minister Suka heard what had happened and quickly went to Ravana. He found him alone in his bedroom and said, "After delighting Lakshmana by the gift of many arrows, Indrajit is dead."

Ravana bowed his heads and wept burning tears that seared through the floor—*My son, my son. . . .*

Ravana sat for a long while in silence, then he said, "My loyal brother is dead and now you, my son! Now I begin to think much more of Yama, for he has brought you, Indrajit, under the law of Time!"

Suka said, "One lives while others remember him. Ravana, you might think people forget but they don't. They seem to worry over their petty cares, but they remember, they all remember the past and the dead, every Night. . . ."

Ravana didn't hear, but spoke as though he still could talk to Indrajit. "This realm is empty without you. Once you crushed the proud and empty gods for me. Now where have you gone, leaving your inheritance, leaving your father and your people? The old should die before the young—why am I left here all alone to make your funeral?"

Suka said, "Majesty, death is not life's end, and when the course of Time must bring something to pass, not wealth nor desire nor strength can make the smallest change. Ravana my King, this is still the way of warriors—*He who dies for his King wins heaven.*"

Ravana said aloud to himself, "Yama, Death Lord, come, tell me how this could be?" But Yama heard only that one word—*Come*—and stood by unseen and made no answer.

Suddenly Ravana grabbed a sword and ran for the open door to the Asoka Grove. But Suka stepped into the doorway first, held the walls and braced himself, and Ravana ran right into him and knocked him down.

The Demon King stopped, and with great care helped Suka to rise, and looking closely at him said, "Suka my friend, forgive me, at least I must kill her."

Suka held Ravana's arms. "Majesty, do not draw the sword of an Empire to kill a woman, or else you let anger lead you into shame!"

"Ah, Suka—" Ravana sighed. "Has Death destroyed my reason?"

"Tonight is just past the eve of the New Moon," said Suka, "and Night will be of her darkest. Fight Rama then."

Ravana sheathed his sword. "Yes. I accept your speech, those are good words. Let us quickly burn my son's body. And after, I will go out to war."

Ravana and Time

Valmiki the Poet held all the moving world inside a
water drop in his hand.
The gods and saints from heaven looked down on
Lanka,
And Valmiki looked down at the gods in the morning of
Time.

Oh Sita,
I sing this song.
Rama will untie your braid;
He will free you.

Remember his love for you.
My poem will outlast Time;
I sing this song,
Oh Sita.

When he had finished Indrajit's funeral, in the late afternoon Ravana commanded Suka the minister, "Let my armies attack now and kill the animals. At dark I will meet again with the nobles of Lanka, then I'll kill Rama. . . ."

Demon warriors crowded into the streets; their chariots and elephants and horses filled the high roads that led to the western gate of Lanka. Captains rounded up their bands of soldiers and called off all their names, and the battle-flags upon their tall staffs cast long black shadows, and banished all the lovely light of day around them.

The old Rakshasa Malyavan was dozing in an alley when the noise and dark shadows awoke him. The armies of the demons were marching again and shaking the Earth in rhythmic beats, as though somewhere nearby a giant or a great god was beginning to dance, jarring the ground with his feet as he took the first steps, starting the Dance of Destruction, timing his steps, the timing strong and sure—

Oh Shiva there before the waters were, never born, never destroyed—

And Malyavan remembered.

The shadows of Garuda's wings, the cry of Narayana's huge shell trumpet, the days of Malyavan's youth falling again over Beautiful Lanka of the Waves. There in the sky above, the dazzling red-and-gold Garuda, and on his back Lord Narayana tall and dark-blue, wearing saffron robes, a soft round jewel on his breast, his dark eyes smiling, murdering the brave Rakshasas. . . .

Malyavan ignored all the war-noise, he'd heard it all before. He went slowly by side-streets to a corner of Lanka's walls. He cast a dissolving spell and went through the stones, and walked through Rama's army unseen, and climbed by a narrow pathway up onto the highest summit of Trikuta Hill.

Standing in the air right above that very hilltop, long ago in his youth Malyavan with all his strength drove a black lance into Narayana's side and cried, "I swear I'll kill you!" And how easily the lance entered, it was not hard to wound Narayana, like wounding water. But the bird Garuda wheeled on the winds. He missed Malyavan, but his talons tore off the steel chain that the Rakshasa wore over his shoulders. Arrows flew like rushing comets, and Malyavan fell through the shrieks and screams, Mali was dead and Malyavan ran to the world Undersea.

Old Malyavan looked around. Trikuta Hill looked like the otherworldly landscape of Infinity . . . a place out of the past . . . .

> Through the floor of the Sea,
> Through the silent doors of Eternity;
> Blessed be you,
> Blessed be.

Shiva and the silence! Fortunate to see, gracious and auspicious the great Lord Shiva stood by Malyavan, and there was not a sound on the hilltop. Shiva the great ascetic seemed a tall fair-skinned man, with four arms, wearing deerskin and a snake, holding a trident, his throat a beautiful blue, and for a moment Shiva looked carefully at Malyavan, and saw his heart, and his eyes never blinked.

Shiva's two eyes were like honey, and his face was wrinkled with smiles. On his brow his terrible third eye was closed, and the new moon hung in his hair, low in the evening sky.

They stood there all alone. Malyavan looked down, and at his feet he saw the rusted links of his ancient shoulder-chain, long-lost and eaten by Time.

I saved your father. I found him newborn and abandoned and faintly crying on a lonesome barren hill. Shiva stood still and held out his hand.

Malyavan remembered his beautiful mother, the smiling daughter of a heavenly Gandharva. A little wind blew by his ears. A hundred thousand tiny silver bells were ringing and ringing, and all this beautiful world dissolved. . . .

Come, I will take you home again.

Late in the afternoon of the third day of war, the Grand Army of the Rakshasas gathered again by Lanka's west gate, an army of great honor and loyalty. Their fires flickered and threw off dark smoke and sparks, and their hair stood on end. Carrion birds wept on the housetops, facing south and biting their side-feathers; and by Ravana's palace gate jackals barked and howled with live flames on their breath. Clouds of ashes grated harshly in the sky and blew low down the city streets showering blood. In heaven there was a blue stain on the Sun, and the stars attacked him although it was still day.

Outside the golden walls there was a great explosion, and Indrajit's enchanted grove was destroyed and gone, leaving only a crater of smoke. Many omens appeared; the light was dim and wrong and the wind was dark; high things were low and the low were high.

The west gate opened and the movable bridge dropped like thunder. Then a pale headless corpse stood in the gateway, and with his wounded arms sadly tried to push back the Night-rangers of the Woods. On the hillsides by the city many trees fell, and birds flew over Lanka in left-turning circles. The Rakshasa warriors stumbled as though caught in snares; the whips fell from their charioteers' hands and their eyes watered.

The demon sentinels looked out from Beautiful Lanka's high golden walls, and out on the battlefield they saw the

bears watching them, staring at them, sleek and dark,
gathered round their King Jambavan like the sending of fate.
The bears' eyes were wide with wrath, and their mood was
murder. Behind them stood wild apes and monkeys from the
highlands who had already grown their thick winter's coats
hard for weapons to bite through, with many grey hairs that
made them look like long-murdered ghosts, or seem all silver
in the sun.

But the bold Rakshasas were not afraid. They drew their
glowing swords with a noise like a grindstone grinding iron,
and came outside the walls—warriors like hills, like living
flames, very strong and cruel. Then like the crest of a wave
the front lines of the Rakshasa army rose up into the air and
threw down spears and maces and fires on the animals. The
demons advanced through the sky in their wondrous waving
robes and the animals died by thousands, and backed away
from them as summer clouds will fly before the winds. And
all unnoticed in the havoc and ruin of war the many house-
gods of Lanka followed Ravana's armies out of their city,
now homeless, looking afraid and sad to leave, and not knowing where they would live now.

Only Jambavan the Bear King did not back off. All alone
he snarled and snapped and pulled down the demons; in a
terrible rage he ripped them apart, and left them there in
small pieces that a crow could swallow whole. He tore open
their throats; he bit and shook his head and broke them; he
clawed out their hearts. His mouth was wet and red, his
claws were red and his eyes were wild, and he reveled in
blood and bleeding demon flesh.

Tall and handsome, wearing the war-crown of the bear
kings, old Jambavan took on the whole army of demons. He
hugged them to death; he struck them with great round-
swinging blows that tore off their heads. Jambavan was unbelievably strong. Whichever weapons the Rakshasas tried to
use against him Jambavan destroyed; none could hurt him;
and he crushed their chariots with trees. With just a little animal courage he badly damaged them beyond repair. He was
Death on that field.

The demons thought—*We're outnumbered!*—and there was
no chance in that fight for their unreal illusions. When they
joined hands to cast a spell the monkeys broke their arms
with stones, and called out warnings in the ancient animal
tongues.

But there on the city wall were the two magicians, Light-

ning-Tongue and Thunder-Tooth. They had their heads together, talking and looking at Jambavan, rolling their eyes
and licking their ugly fangs. Their arms started to grow longer and longer, and razor blades appeared on their fingertips,
and they stretched out their hands for the Bear King.

Hanuman and Sugriva streaked through the air. The two
Rakshasa magicians drew back their arms, and they whispered to each other—*Just wish . . . I wish. . . .*

The monkeys were too quick. Hanuman cried—*No fear
and follow me*—and struck Lightning-Tongue from the side,
caught his throat in both hands, shifted his weight, threw him
down and twisted his head right off. He threw the head into
Lanka like a ball. It burst into a hundred and eight pieces
and the brains went flying out in fiery sparks.

Sugriva made his fingers into a fist and hit Thunder-Tooth
from above, so hard that he drove the magician's head down
into his belly and jammed his thighs up into his body. But
that didn't bother Thunder-Tooth a bit. He just stood there
grinning with his mouth at his waist and his eyes on his
breast, headless on stumpy legs. Then he winked one eye at
King Sugriva and touched his tooth. A staircase that seemed
to lead down to Hell rose out of the ground, and Thunder-
Tooth ran down it away out of sight and the whole thing disappeared before Sugriva could follow.

"Never mind," said Hanuman, "let's help Jambavan."

They flew back to the Bear King but there was no need.
Jambavan was humming war-songs, the Rakshasa attack had
failed, and it was nearly evening. Rama called back the animals and stood in their midst as though within an impenetrable forest. The light was fading away from the sky and the
animals carried their many dead up into the hillside forests.
King Jambavan drank some honey-wine and said, "Ah, it was
nothing. . . ."

The few remaining demons withdrew. The west bridge was
pulled up and the gate slowly closed. Then as before, from
within Lanka the Rakshasas removed their dead from the
battlefield and cast their corpses underwater into the sea, and
the tides were red.

So on that war-land outside the city there were left only a
few painted iron shields and brass clubs, some supple curving
swords like clear water, curious bows and arrows with glass
points, many trees and stones, torn banners and broken

wheels, and shiny gold bracelets winking like fireflies in the dusk fast approaching.

The day went by and was past, and the sunset quickly faded from the west. The new moon set and in Lanka's streets the demons lit their fiery torches made of burning bones.

Ravana sat on his throne in the royal courtroom, in the center of that long indoor altar of Earth where the grass had long grown green from the lights of the glorious lamps, and from the brilliance of the weapons hung round on the walls, and where two holy fires still burned at each end for the blessing and good fortune of the Night Demons. Ravana leaned back comfortably; he closed his twenty eyes and smiled ten smiles.

Then leaving their chariots and animals in the palace courtyards the nobles and elders of Lanka entered the room. Each one courteously bowed touching Ravana's feet with his head and took his place by rank. The greatest sat on raised cushions near the throne, the next ranks sat behind them on grass mats, and all the rest sat on the emerald floor. The smell of fine sandalwood and incense was mingled with patchouli perfume and the flower scent of colorful war-garlands.

They sat gazing up at the faces of the Demon King. Ravana folded his hands, ten by ten, and said, "I am Ravana. What do they say of me, out in the world?"

A herald rose from the ranks dressed in silver and black and answered, *"You are Ravana, King of the Night-Wanderers. You are Lord of Lanka on the Waves, the Protector of Heaven and the Guardian of Truth, the Defender of Love and Enemy of Evil. In anger you are a dark stormcloud threatening all that is wrong and moving if you will against the wind. You have jailed lies and you imprison all deceit— Majesty, rule right forever!"*

Ravana sighed. "Yet Earth fears me, I am her misfortune. I've never seen my armies lose a war, but now Rama has come, and our legions swiftly diminish like a water pond in summer. Rama defeats me by his mere presence, what to speak of his arrows? Tonight I am going out to fight him, and I ask you, leave Lanka now and hide somewhere to save your lives if you fear for my defeat."

No one moved, no one said anything for a long while. Ravana asked, "Will anyone wish to speak here in my council before I go?"

Then Suka the Minister of State arose from his corner seat holding a winecup. He said, "I drink to knowledge," and drank, and looked at the King.

"Come here," said Ravana.

Suka went before the throne and touched his hands together. He knelt and bowed his head. "Majesty!"

Ravana smiled. "Speak quickly, Suka."

Suka stood and said, "Soon or late, a King must hear his people, or he has no time to be a King."

"What do they say?"

"They say—*Why is Ravana blind? Why won't he hear?* They cry—*Where is my father? Where has my husband gone? Where is my son now?*"

"What else?"

"They ask, where are your wits? They ask why your fat and wrinkled sister had to see Rama in the greenwood, and why they must die for her belly's lust? They ask how can we fight Rama? It would be good to take the shelter of Rama."

"What do you think?" asked Ravana.

"Oh King," said Suka, "spare me from fame and the abuse that goes with it! How can you come to your senses when your senses are stolen by Love? What other person ever matched your sacrifices or received such boons as you got from Lord Brahma long ago, in those days long past? Now you've lost your way, and what is surprising in that?" Suka looked around him and shook his head. "It is wondrous and most marvelous, that now the people of such a King as you must face defeat. We can see no one in any world to dry away our tears."

"What would you do yourself?"

"I don't know," answered Suka. "Your brother Vibhishana did right to take Rama's protection; it was a good deed for him, well done at the right time."

"Then why did you not go with him?" softly asked the Demon King. "Why have you stayed by me?"

Suka said, "Once taking you for my King I think it wrong to leave you, Majesty."

"But you could live anywhere unknown; you could easily escape."

"Oh Ravana, this life is over in one instant, why spend it in shame?"

Ravana held out a long scarlet sash. "You always freely

chose to serve me, therefore I commission you my messenger. Wear this and carry a letter from me to Rama."

Suka slipped the sash over his shoulder. Ravana gave him a heavy Rakshasa letter written on a flat stone and sealed within a stone envelope. "Deliver this in the morning. Go to where Rama's bridge touches our shore and wait the night there, and then at sunrise take it to him in my name. Fear no one."

Suka took the stone letter. "Ravana, the like of this citadel and city of Beautiful Lanka as she was during your long reign was never seen before, nor will she ever be seen anywhere again."

Ravana dismissed his council and went walking through the halls of his palace swinging his arms, with garlands of flowers over his broad shoulders, and the jewels on his bracelet and armbands swung their all-colored lights over the shadowy walls.

Near the doorway to his bedroom he met Queen Mandodari. Ravana smiled at her, and held her gently in his twenty dark arms, and there was a dream in his eyes then. Ravana said, "It's nearly done, everything will be alright."

Mandodari the beautiful, the daughter of illusion dressed all in silks replied, "When I first saw you, you captured my heart. You have brought me delight, I love our life, I always approach you in joy."

"You must believe me," said Ravana. "Put your hope and faith in me once more, just one more time."

"Yes," said the Queen. "You are my Lord, and I will ever hold this thought, near to my heart, like a treasure. . . ."

Ravana embraced her. "Farewell my very love. . . ."

It was dark outside, and Ravana climbed alone onto the top of a watchtower that stood near the palace, and from there on its flat roof he could see the battlefield and his city below him, and above, all the stars in the black sky. Ravana laughed. How had Lord Brahma the Creator dared make so many stars!

Ravana saw the gods gathered in the sky to watch his war with Rama, and the Demon King looked back at them with his fiery red eyes, and spread wide his twenty arms.

At that moment all the bells of Lanka pealed, the great

gongs and brass drums rang out in the night, and kept ringing, and the little drums raced and sounded like thunders,
and Ravana lifted up his dancing foot and brought it down
and jarred all the worlds and shook them.

Ravana began to dance. His heart beat fast and he
breathed in deep the fresh clean air, and in the heavens the
charioteers of the gods tried to calm their animals. Ravana
felt he'd just broken an iron band tied round his chest for
years. The night air was cool and all the world was young
forever.

Stunning thunder and noise poured out of Lanka, and Ravana threw back his heads and waved his arms and spun
around. He called down the Wind, the Wind in the trees, the
long dry North Wind rising. From afar out at sea to the
north there was a little whisper, and the gods saw the air stir,
and saw the bright luminous wheel of the rays of the Wind
rolling towards them, violently arising and rushing aloud
away past them to the ends of the worlds and beyond, far
beyond.

Gales came in from the storm-wave ocean and tore up the
side of Trikuta Hill. Ravana heard the wild Winds running in
from the high Himalyas, booming through the black pines
and the dark deodars far away, blowing forever across the ice
and snow. Then the tiny wind-bells of Lanka sang, and the
great gold walls rocked and trembled.

The North Wind swept flat over the land and blew out every fire in the Universe and every light. Hanuman bent over
Rama to protect him and thought to speak to his father, but
that was impossible; they could hardly breathe; the air was
swifter than thoughts, and it was as if they were falling away
with a speed beyond knowing, and all the Earth was falling
with them.

Rama and the animals saw Ravana dance. Blue flames
shimmered round his form high above Lanka, electric thunders crackled bright in his long loose hair, and fiery sparks
streamed downwind from his arms as he turned and moved
in waving circles. In the wind and in the Night his twenty
dark arms opened and closed like the petals of a graceful
flower rising and falling. And Ravana looked out at Rama
and the animals as though to consume them, as though they
were already dead, as though he danced among charred
corpses in some horrible demon drinking-park set in a cremation ground.

Then Ravana clapped all his hands and stamped his feet

three times and ended his dance. It was full Night. He drove the storms away. The Wind fell like the sounds of waves growing softer and softer; at first still crying, then wailing by and weeping away, and at last only rustling through the leaves, and then gone.

There was sudden silence from the city and the worlds were clean empty of sound. Ravana disappeared from view and then, as he came down the winding stairway inside that tower the Demon King met Time waiting for him there, Time wearing a body so shriveled and old that he looked dead even when he moved. The way was too narrow to pass and Ravana had to stop.

"Oh welcome, Ravana." Time looked up and grinned happily. "Now at last your life is over, and you must pay me for the sins of a lifetime. You are about to die, and now for all Eternity Hell awaits you, and even your memory will be lost in endless years of silence. You will never again meet a friend or see any place that you love. Your glory and sweet memories will be lost like precious golden dust blown from your hand before your eyes, and the wonderful Earth will vanish from your sight for evermore. Go wear your best jewels, for who will wear them later? Look round at the beautiful world of life; see Lanka well, for now she is in my keeping. For your great wrongdoing I have fallen in beside you all unseen, moving where you move, waiting in your shadow for the moment—how have you eluded me so long?"

"Indeed," said Ravana, "I smile at your folly."

Time answered, "Oh do you think so, Ravana? Do you believe, Demon King, that I only control others, that Time will never rule you but only others. . . ." Then the face of Kala, the face of Time took on the cruel look of someone who has lied and pretended and waited his chance, and is at last in power over his enemy. "I'll have the last word; I'll humble you and kill your strength and spirit. The bright golden dawns of future lights won't be for you, I'll press loneliness into your heart and chill your bones, and there is no return. . . ."

Ravana laughed. "You little liar!"

"What? You stole Sita and you'll pay—"

Ravana threw out his arms like twenty bars across the narrow stair and looked down at Time. "Why I have all the time there is."

"What!"

"You are the thief and not I," said Ravana. "For a few

moments' pleasure you take whole lives in payment. And whatever you give you steal back, by fraud, from hiding, when you're not watched. Death and misery are your good friends—but you are yourself unreal; you do not exist; you cannot steal from me."

"Do you know who I am?" cried Kala.

Ravana answered, "A marketplace of sorrow, a well of lies."

"Never!"

"You're a fraud and you know it. Why . . . you're not looking so well." Ravana smiled. "May you feel worse tomorrow!"

"Oh take care!" said Time sharply. "Watch out, injustice angers me. . . ."

"That's a laugh! I'll faint from fear just as soon as I find someplace to fall down, alright?" Ravana twirled his moustaches. "Listen—

> *When my dancing footfalls stopped,*
> *I broke Time's small back*
> *With my last step.*"

Kala said, "Ravana, you are mad. There's no help for it, you are doomed . . . do what you will while you still can . . . your old home is empty, your friends have died, and all the good times are long gone by . . . things can never be still, nothing can remain the same, all must change and die and come apart . . . it will be as though you had never been. . . . Time will pass Ravana, time will pass . . . now be aware. . . ."

"We know better than that," said the Demon King, "Love is eternal and we are beyond your reach."

"Just a moment! Don't be absurd, you don't believe all those old stories, do you?"

"Oh, I believe them *just enough*—"

"There must be some mistake! No one is beyond my power."

"This time *you've* made a mistake—you have wrongly faced Ravana who has gambled his life for love . . . and always will, I guess."

"Never try to cheat your fate," said Time.

"When we sleep, where are you then?" asked Ravana.

"What?"

"And when we wake from a dream, you are pitifully slow to restore the scenery of the world around us."

"Nonsense!"

"All loss of love or life is a lie, old age is an illusion, and only bad things perish."

"Really, I fail to see what—"

"I'd forgotten you had that problem," smiled the Demon King. "But I must be on my way now, I can't be late, and my time is far too valuable to waste on anything but day-dreams. Be careful, turn and go, back away from Ravana who will fight and die for love—for Good Love never dies. . . ."

"How'd you find that out?!"

"Oh Kala stand aside. Pretend to rule styles and fashions if you will, but don't talk of being over me. You're but a poor slave yourself. You mean nothing to me. I command you to go."

"No! I won't!"

"*Aha!*" Ravana swiftly bent down and looked close into the wasted eyes of Time with that terrible demon look he had. The muscles on his arms stood out in knots and his hands moved round Kala like a cage. "Do you dare menace *me?*" The Demon King drew back his lips and his coppery eyes glittered, he made ready to seize Time and crush him with his steely strength—and Valmiki the Poet safely watching all this caught his breath in shock at that threat!

Then Ravana touched Kala but lightly with one hand and stood straight again. Time started to sweat. He sneezed and looked around; his face was worn and battered and his voice cracked when he spoke. "Why, it's all dusty . . . everything here, it's all covered over with fine dust. . . ."

Ravana stood with all his hands on his hips as he watched Time fade and vanish with a puzzled look, ever still trying in vain to say something more. Ravana stood on the empty stair.

Valmiki the Poet laughed with pleasure. *Oh Ravana, delightful, beautiful—Well done, Demon King!*

Ravana hurried to war. He put on his night-armor finely woven from dull black steel and ten dread dark helmets that hid his faces. Over his two-wheeled war-car he raised the battle-banner of Lanka, a cloth of gold shining bright, and said, "I send out many warriors and few return. Now I must go myself, let Earth take warning. . . ." And he thought to himself, "Death, now whirl your maces and rods and strike with your clubs—I am at chance this day. . . ."

On that chariot Ravana loaded a hundred tough horn-tipped bows as hard to stretch as the mind; and a thousand quivers of his own arrows, long and thick, vanes and shaft all made from one piece of blue iron; and a long straight sword; and an irresistible eight-sided mace. The chariot was armored by shields and plates cut from dark brass, and drawn by four white horses. Tied loose on the central flagstaff were the ten golden arrows for the ten directions of his Empire.

With his many hands Ravana needed no charioteer. He leapt like a lion into his car and drove out from his palace into the city streets. His horses broke into a run and the Rakshasa people along the way yelled and cheered, lining the wide streets, changing their shapes and colors from their emotions, and the chariot wheels crashed and clattered over the yellow bricks.

Then the Demon King left Lanka through the fifth gate, by the Gate of Illusion. The monkeys and bears were watching all the four city walls to see which one would open, when Ravana and his horse and chariot winked into view coming down through the air and hit the ground just west of Lanka with a smash like a mountain falling flat upon the world.

Ravana stopped a little way forward of the wall and looked out across the plain, where at a distance he saw the moving golden ends of Rama's bow like waving torchlights in the darkness, and saw Rama facing him on foot and un-afraid.

"Look, there he is." Rama pointed with his bow, and a lightning flash snapped across the sky though there were no clouds. "He's come before my eyes as though before a serpent who kills by looking."

The monkeys and bears all ran to Rama, and many of them were partly hard to see or all invisible from fright. With one hand Rama quickly strung his bow. He turned to Lakshmana and said, "Let my animal friends of the woods take cover, and you with them."

Hanuman was there and he said, "Don't worry about us, worry about fighting on foot against a deadly chariot."

Rama smiled. "Go back to the bridgehead. It's midnight, and from now on, the world is destined to grow light."

"He is a most glorious and magnificent king," said Lakshmana.

"His coming here is my good fortune," answered Rama,
"for now before me is the root of all evil, and the only one
left to die cut on the edge of battle."

Then they all left Rama standing there alone, his long
green hair no longer matted like a hermit wears but tied back
with a green silk war-band; but still he wore barkcloth over
his golden armor, still he walked barefoot without the sandals
he'd given Bharata—partly seeming a wanderer, partly a warrior, partly a King.

Still Ravana waited and did not move. Then suddenly a
starlight came down from heaven toward Rama. As it approached and drew near to Earth Rama saw that it was a
brilliant aerial chariot, a silver car with weapons hung in
racks that shone like lanterns, drawn by ten silvery-gray
horses flying abreast, coming closer and closer with many
fan-blades spinning and the silver wheels all flashing; then in
a cloud of dust, with a rumble of hooves and wheels, that
chariot landed not far away and drove full speed over the battlefield to Rama, and stopped before him. There was a
charioteer in the driver's box but the car held no warrior behind him.

"A friend wishes you well. I am Matali the heavenly charioteer." Matali stood beside Rama. "Lord of Men, this is Indra's celestial car. Best of Kings, these are his cloud-horses
shod in silver shoes; they are my rain-steeds—the sky-
climbers, the star-jumpers, the misty runners of the sky, and
our paths are everywhere."

"Welcome to you," said Rama.

"Solar King, we'll take you to Victory!" Matali looked at
Ravana. "Wherever I look, I seem to see Death, Death wearing many flowers waiting for him . . . ."

"I haven't forgotten," said Rama. "I still remember, we
saw you when Savari told us the tale of Hanuman—and I
had lost my Sita—"

"Oh this is a wide road for attack and no place for grief,"
said Matali. "Here I am in the dark in my cold bronze armor, and I've lost all my patience, and there's no escape for
him. I'll thread the paths and follow the roads to win! It's
hard to kill the Demon King! Get on!"

"The world will be without me, or without Ravana." Rama
put his arms on board the car. "Now drive straight against
him."

"Om!" The rain horses laid back their ears. Matali and Rama got in the chariot and Matali held the twenty long reins. He looked at his horses and glanced at the ground before them. Then his hands trembled slightly and were still, and the ten horses were walking. *"Go!"*

They went a little faster, at an easy gait. Then they quickened their step and they were half-running. *And I've been true*—whispered Matali—*I've been true, all this time, run!* And at last they went full running, silver shoes flashing, beautiful horses running abreast, beating down the ground—

Ravana's chariot leapt forward to intercept them. All at once the two cars were together, and the golden plates on the back of Rama's bow among the diamonds shone like fires out among the stars, all up close.

Ravana laughed in anger and lashed Matali with a whip. Matali struck back at him, but very fast Ravana backed and turned quickly and couldn't be reached.

Ravana shot eight bows at once. Thirty thousand dark arrows struck Rama. They tore away the bark he wore, and Rama's armor all of gold gleamed out in that night bright as the Sun.

The brilliant spires and towers of Lanka looked flaming and afire in that blazing light. The glare and the gold came reflected back from Lanka's wall and confused Ravana's aim, and Matali drove off a way and stopped.

Fierce and furious was that fight. Oh Rama! Waves were on the water in Valmiki's hand; storms swirled.

He saw Sita. In the clash and sting of war she loved you.

Now hear the melody of our sweet song, swiftly plunged into strife.

Majesty, it is Night, and people change at Night!

Swarming at Rama came a million arrows with iron arrowheads of sharp animal faces—the keen faces of wolves and eagles and sharks, iron teeth that closed and bit when they struck flesh. They tore down all over; but Rama answered them with flights of his Ayodhya arrows again all gold-covered, bearing his name, feathered with white and blue heron plumes; and he dropped them severed from the sky.

Then light-handed, Rama cut off Ravana's heads with arrow-blades, and the lifeless heads rolled away with their long earrings and shadowy helmets, dusty and bleeding dark. All

Fire-tempered, Rama's arrows with sharp heads and even knots flew howling like hurricanes.

But the heads grew back. Hundreds of heads rolled killed, but there was Ravana again, never turning back from war, bearing to Rama ill-will and weapons. There in his chariot stood once more the Demon King of many talents, many felonies, many evasions.

Rama squeezed his long green arms. First saying the Mantra, he called the Fire-weapon and shot an arrow straight up. Down upon Ravana fell arrows that burned. Their bright-burning points were windows of light; heaven through the dark was full of windows open to all the worlds above.

Ravana spoke the rain-mantra over an arrow and released it. Clouds came out of nowhere. Water drenched the world, the fire-arrows went out and blackness fell.

Rama used the wind-weapon. He shot an arrow into the clouds and his unbreakable bowstring rang out over the whole island of Lanka. The air sighed and the seven winds of heaven swept down their paths moaning and whirling, and by the bridgehead rolling breakers trailed white on the grey sea and the tall palms bent their heads and gave up their old leaves from the past. *Free,* sang the seven winds, *Free the world, Free!* They screamed through the high rocks on the summits above Rama's battlefield; the rainclouds fled before them, the sky was clear, the stars sparkled.

Ravana fired an arrow into the ground and from Earth arose steep walls of high mountains. Great solid rows of black stone, barren and lifeless, blocked the sky with jagged ridges and peaks and stopped the Wind. Those were the bare black hills of Hell, baking hot, and they creaked with the strain of the cool night air until, with a noise like a salvo of cannon, deep cracks broke through them and red canyons of heat glowed from deep within.

Rama fired Brahmastra, Brahma's weapon, and shot it arching up to fall on the line of hills. The arrow grew long and stout as a spear. The Wind entered its feathered wings; there were the Sun in its metal blade, skies and rainbows in its shaft, and all the worlds in its weight. It reached its height and began to curve down. In a burst of brilliance it scattered apart into 180,000 rocketing thunders. Bolts of light stabbed at the hills from above, and wherever they hit they turned the brittle stone to diamond. The Hills of Hell shuddered and dove back out of sight below ground.

"Enough of this," said Rama, "there's work to do! Now I take off my fancy rings!"

Matali looked over his shoulder. "But you aren't wearing. . . ."

"Charge!"

"Alright! And here he comes——"

From a standing start, in the wink of an eye Matali's horses were racing. Rama stood free, not holding any support, not swaying or even a little off-balance. The two war-chariots drove right at each other. At the last instant Matali turned. The cars tore past each on the other's left, throwing out clouds of dust and stones from their wheels. The horses seemed to touch, the axle hubs just missed, and Ravana wasn't fast enough. He had no time to shoot. Then they were by, traveling swiftly apart. But just as Rama passed he shot an arrow deep into Ravana's left shoulders and the Demon King had to hold onto his flagstaff with his right arms to keep from falling.

The chariots slowed and circled round facing again. Matali maneuvered for position and said, "Now I begin to see the end of Ravana's life."

And far north across the sea, the harmless woodsmen of Dandaka Forest walking in the silence of Night under the huge trees could see in the sky violet ribbons of light from the war of Lanka in the south, and they wondered—*Rama . . . Where is Rama-Chandra, the lovely Moon of Night?*

> *Only the sky will cover the sea;*
> *Only Rama can fight the Demon King.*

Rama and Ravana dueled with arrows. One after another, Rama broke the bows out of Ravana's hands until ninety-nine were gone and only one remained. The Demon King shot arrows long and short, thick and thin, quick and slow, from close range or far away; but Rama's armor was hard and impenetrable, he was unharmed and many arrows melted away when he saw them come.

Ravana seized his mace of iron set with lapis stones and embellished with gold, hung with iron-mouthed bells and entwined with red blossoms, for years daily washed with blood and now smoking and straining to strike, an eight-sided mace which would return from flight into the thrower's hands.

Ravana drove to attack. He gripped the iron handle with

four hands and swung as the chariots met. It was too soon and the blow fell on the charioteer and not Rama, but Matali knocked that mace hard aside with his bronze fist.

Then Ravana drew apart and stopped. He whirled his mace in a circle rising and dipping his heads; and the mace moaned—*Woe ... Woe ... Woe*—

The mace went faster and faster. Matali drove to deceive Ravana's aim and Rama reached for Indra's weapons-racks. He took a spear, held it in one hand, slapped it with the palm of his other hand and threw it. That great dart went at Ravana resonant and vibrating with sound, with a noise like the thunder of a rockslide, a loud falling noise like a cliff falling, the dark world falling, Ravana falling. . . .

And the Demon Lord let go his mace; it sped, and Rama stood in its way. Ravana's chariot turned to run.

Rama's spear broke Ravana's flagpole; the cloth-of-gold war-flag fell. Rama broke the ten arrows of the Rakshasa Empire, and when he did, the running demon car lost its rattle and clatter and its wheels turned on in mournful silence. The flag of Lanka lay in the dust.

Matali couldn't outdrive Ravana's mace, but he dropped his reins and stood up himself in its path; and it glanced off his broad chest and knocked him violently from the car, and went by Rama deflected just enough to miss him.

Rama wept and bit his lip. The mace turned to go back to Ravana, but Rama threw himself from the chariot and seized it. He knelt and broke it like a stick over his thigh—*Good Fortune to you!*—once, into two pieces—*Peace to you!*—and twice, into four. Deep red blood ran over his green skin.

The four pieces of the mace kept pulling back to Ravana, and Rama cried—*Would you?*—and hurled them at the Demon King. Ravana quickly turned aside; and as he had spurned them, the four angry chunks of iron tore into Earth and vanished noisily underground.

Matali lay on his back unconscious. His heavenly armor was torn, and his ten horses stood still, their faces near his, looking down at him. A flood of sorrow filled Rama's heart to see him hurt. Rama touched him and untied his breastplate, and said, "Here indeed your loyalty has had unjust reward!"

Matali revived from Rama's touch. He looked up and saw Rama bending over him, saw his horses raise their heads, and following their look saw Ravana's chariot coming again, but moving strangely slow. By some chance he yet lived, and he felt the life flow back into his body.

Rama brought water from Indra's chariot, and some cloth that he began to rip apart for binding Matali's wide wounds. The silver car was stricken and dented. The horses pawed at the ground with their front feet. "Majesty," said Matali, "I'll be well, there's time enough for that later."

Rama said, "Good. It's fast nearing dawn, but drink just a little." Then after Matali drank, Rama sipped water three times. "Lie still, I don't need the car now." Rama took up his every-colored bow, and there stood Rama the great archer, Rama the good bowman, the friend of every man.

He was all fiery to see. Wild little flames came from his skin, his green eyes gleamed, then swift as thought Rama shot his arrows. He broke off one wheel of Ravana's chariot and it tipped over and left the Demon King also standing on the ground, holding his last bow and a sword, facing him; and the white horses ran away with the broken car.

Rama opened a long bamboo case at his belt and took out the brass-bladed grass arrow given to him by Agastya, and notched it on his bowstring. That arrow could rend walls and gateways of stone; it breathed and sighed. Rama pulled his bow. He took three aiming steps backwards and held his breath.

Ravana took on the brilliant form of Indra the King of Heaven. He was glorious and gracious, all illumined; he could scarcely be looked at, and a halo of radiance and energy danced around him. Rama was dazed by Ravana's false figure. He could not bear to shoot at such a divine form, at such fair beauty.

Matali the Charioteer was watching. He could be enchanted by no beauty but a fair woman's. He raised himself painfully on one arm and called out to Rama—*Strike, Strike, That's not my Master.*

That was then the destined time and true setting of Ravana's death. Rama thought—*I must believe it! Oh kill him!*—

Rama shot. The bowstring rang out, all over the Universe. That arrow first broke the sword and bow Ravana raised to ward it, then it hit Ravana's breast and struck through his heart, stealing his life, and never stopped, but came out from his back and entered the Earth.

Down from Ravana's hands fell his broken bow and sword,

and the Demon King of Lanka fell dying in his own dark form.

At first Rama didn't move. Then he first unstrung his bow and put it aside. Then he lifted Matali into Indra's rain-chariot and the misty horses rose running through the sky and were gone.

At daybreak, at dawn Ravana died. He was a fire not burning, an ocean still with no tides. He could no longer speak. He could not know whatever might happen around him. He could not move; he grew cold; he had no thought; he did not breathe.

The Rakshasas who had watched the war turned away in fear from the walls and hid in Lanka. And darkly the Kings of the four quarters of the world glanced, but none saw what way Ravana went then.

That last night, Suka the Rakshasa Minister stood by Lord Rama's bridge, wrapped in his night cloak and holding Ravana's stone letter under his arm. All night he watched the garish lights and signs of war up on Trikuta Hill, and Lakshmana with the animals stood watching him.

Then at sunrise the first long rays of light reached the three summits over Lanka. Suka dropped his cape behind him, and wearing the scarlet sash of a messenger he walked slow and easy toward the city, and the animals made way for him. Only Prince Angada opened his mouth to speak, but Sugriva the Monkey King put his hand on the young prince's arm and pulled him back and Hanuman stepped in front of him.

Suka stepped into the air and flew back up the slopes to Lanka, and she was golden in the morning when he stepped on the ground. The sunshine, coppery and yellow and red and white, touched her like melted metals from a mountain. It was still, and silent, and Suka thought, "I remember this silence, the silence over all. . . ." Suka felt free. It was almost as though Ravana had sung again there on the battle-field the lilting songs that had won him his freedom from Shiva's prison, and Suka had also been released from somewhere.

Suka walked straight for Rama. Rama stood alone over the corpse of the Demon King. There was no one else about, nothing stirred. And where the wreckage of war was in his way, Suka by a look from his eyes blasted it silently aside and made his path clear.

He came to Rama and handed him the sealed letter. "For you from the Dead King."

And as he spoke of him, Suka looked down at Ravana. Suka's hooded eyes were half-closed, no expression crossed his face, yet for a moment Suka seemed to grow ominous and tragic; he seemed to darken even while standing there, in the sunlight.

Rama cracked open the stone envelope in his strong hands. He looked at the letter awhile, then turned to Suka. "Ah my friend," said Rama fondly. "Listen—"

Lord Narayana, you are the witness, you make the Moon walk in brightness and the stars vanish in the daylight.

Dear Rama, Lord of the Worlds—Think and remember, how you promised Indra to kill me forever. Nothing is forever except yourself. Except dying at your hand, how else could I make you take me into your own Self?

I was only a Rakshasa, and you were very hard to approach. Yet seeking wisdom I learned many things. You do not know who you are again. I knew it all along, but even still you do not know. Nothing you do ever fails, one glance of yours and people sing again the good old songs.

I took no protection against men. You go everywhere, and know every thing that ever has or ever will be done. How was I careless? I was nowhere careless! Oh Narayana, Lo, I looked, I marveled—Men are mines, Men are precious mines. Oh Rama, did you think that dark was bad?

You see whatever happens and you support all creatures. I saw that heaven was impermanent and Hell itself did not endure; I discovered that the time of every life is one day full; and I found how all creatures that are separate from you are ever and again reborn, over and over, always changing. I do not love things that come and go and slip away with Time, and Time himself I hate. I warned him when we first met that I took him for my enemy, I told him so.

Best of Men, there are many kinds of Love, and I never hurt her. I kept Lakshmi to lure you here. I offered you my life and you accepted it.

You are Narayana who moves on the waters. You flow

through us all. You are Rama and Sita born out of Earth and Ravana the Demon King, you are Hanuman like the wind, you are Lakshmana like a mirror, you are Indrajit and Indra, you are the Poet and the Players and the Play. And born as a man you forget this, you lose the memory, and take on man's ignorance again, as you will, every time.

Therefore welcome back your Sita. The war is done, and so we close our letter.

The two of them stood there by Ravana, still as statues in the new-risen sun. Then Suka took off his blood-red scarlet sash and folded it and laid it down on Ravana's breast.

Rama sighed and smiled. He broke the letter and threw it away. He said quietly, "Go, go, I do not care what all this means."

"I never dreamed of such a thing." Suka was smiling and smiling. "Oh, after all this long way around. . . ."

There was a soft whisper, and Suka became a rising wisp of smoke; he spread and dissolved in the air, in surrender. For many years he lived peacefully alone in the forests across the sea, and no one ever saw him sad.

This is an ancient tale.

> We choose the god-like splendor
> Of the best-loved Sun
> To inspire us;
> May the shining Sun
> Brighten your Life!

We sing Valmiki's song.

Oh King Rama, grand and glorious, the all-seeing Sun of a thousand rays lives in the sky. He is the Lord of Day and the eye of the world. He gives Life. Every morning he wakes people from sleep, and goes his way alone through the heavens above and through the heavens in the heart. Salutations and greetings to the Lord of the Sky and Maker of Days.

Praise and victory to the good and friendly King of Light who moves our thoughts and our blood within us and opens our senses by his beams. He is mighty strong. He is golden bright and his seed is golden. We can see no evil; we see no men who get no sunshine. Therefore shower gold, spend and be generous to those you love. For your sake spend your bright yellow gold, give gifts while you can and do good, choose your deeds well. You are wealthy, you have unlimited gold to draw on.

> *I don't respect the floating borders of Earth,*
> *I travel where I will,*
> *I love everyone.*
> *My friend the Moon has known this for long lifetimes,*
> *I am the Sun,*
> *All the same.*
> *Ancient stories.*
> *Ancient Sunpoems.*

Every morning you are new. My Lord Sun I am asleep, my body is like a corpse, until you come and raise me to Life. You reveal all things to me; you show me what they truly are. I look out on a happy world! I see you in your chariot behind your seven horses and you bring every kind of happiness. Dear Sun, behold me here below you, a Man, to myself the center of all these worlds.

You feed us all; every garden grows by your light. All our energy is yours. I bow to the Eastern Mountain where you rise, I bow to Sunset Hill in the west where you go down, setting low above the waters, in flame, all in gold.

You unfold the flowers of day. You are bright and beautiful. If there are clouds you are always behind them. You are the handsome ornament of all the heavens. Your heart is wide, it is immeasurably wide. How can I not speak of this? Why be silent about you? Take my song and give me light.

How can I be sad? Am I blind? The Sun shines on me. This very instant have I won brilliance for my wealth.

Oh Rama, it is Truth, we think, that moves the Sun across the sky. Oh Lord, look up at him, so joyful and fine!

Whoever sings this song or hears it sung, he comes by no misfortune. When he is in peril of his life, or is ill, or is in a lonely place, or in any fear, this bright tune will bring him victory. No thief can touch him, he will never dare. This song is named *Heart of the Sun.* It is warm and safe and strong. It makes troubles go. It is supremely good. If you are afraid in the long dark night, remember it.

Ayodhya King, our preceptor the Poet Valmiki saw all of this war gliding already into the past, becoming a wonderful tale, a beautiful story.

May all creatures be happy. We sing Valmiki's song.

> "Trust and be True:
> Serve Right as
> I serve You"
> —says the Sun.

PART THREE

THE DHARMA WHEEL

OM!
I bow to the great Lord Narayana,
And to the blessed Lady Sita;
I salute you, faithful Hanuman;
And Saraswati, Goddess take my gift:
JAYA!
Victory to you!

Here's Love!

And so the War of Lanka was ended on the morning of the fourth day, just past the first night of the New Moon, near to the solstice of Winter when Spring dares begin again, and the Sun turns in his sky to come back to us. Rama took off his armor and the day grew warm. Surya the Sun was pouring out bright silver and fine gold. He threw his beams down cordially over that morning world—a fine reliable figure of light, a handsome person, a happy sight—indeed a part of the world well-made, very well done, all of it.

Hanuman and the Rakshasa Vibhishana and his four demon knights came swiftly to Rama's side. Vibhishana held a bundle and said, "Dear Lord, wear these clothes Lakshmana sends to you now."

"They're not Rakshasa robes?"

"He carried and kept them somehow throughout all your wanderings." Vibhishana smiled. "They're from Ayodhya. I don't know how he did it."

"Fair Ayodhya!" Rama dressed, and saw that Hanuman also held something. "Monkey, what have you got there?"

"All the ornaments she let fall upon our hill." Hanuman looked at the dead Ravana. "Master, is he really dead? What did Suka say? What else happened? When can we—"

"Oh enough, Hanuman!" Rama looked round at the world. "Long love is now remembered. Be still. I've recovered her, we are reunited and all the old lovely colors return and come again into my view. Go to her, tell Sita we have won!"

"I'm gone!"

Vibhishana said, "We ask permission to make Ravana's funeral inside the city."

"Why is it so quiet?" asked Rama.

"Every soul's already left Lanka but for a few who will soon go."

"I had not wished harm to your beautiful city; now she is desolate."

Vibhishana laughed. "How many times, Lord? You know how we love to disappear, but I will stay here when I may."

"Is there any water?" One of the four knights gave Rama a waterjar. "Kneel, Vibhishana." Rama poured water over the Demon Prince's head. "Arise, Lanka King."

Vibhishana stood. "Our folk will return, but don't fear us. We Rakshasas are the guardians, we are the protectors; so were we created by Brahma. We'll guard the temples and not harm good men, and I'll hide Lanka's golden beauty and keep our home from others' eyes. All will be well with us always."

"What's keeping that fool Hanuman?"

Vibhishana answered, "It's been but a moment!" His four Rakshasa knights carried away Ravana's corpse. The west gate of Lanka opened for them and they entered. "They'll burn him quick. You'll soon meet Sita. I'm here; I'm going to be your wish-protector."

Rama asked, "What will happen to Queen Mandodari? What will she do?"

"Ah," said Vibhishana. "The Daughter of Illusion! Our people all have other lives beneath the Sea—but Mandodari's father is the Asura Maya, the great Artist. And if he still lives he will come to her here; he will take her home. *Maya! Maya! All is illusion . . . All is illusion . . . .* Maya the ancient architect, Maya the builder of young dreams might take her back to his Cave of Trees, and who will meet her next no one knows."

Vibhishana and Rama stood silent awhile, then the Good Demon Lord of Lanka said, "Queen Mandodari would have restored Sita's clear yellow robe for this day. It will take her time to dress for you as well."

"I don't care what she's wearing!"

"There's the smoke, that's Ravana's pyre burning behind the walls. I wonder—I would marry Mandodari myself if I only found her somewhere, someday—but even Time can't ever find out too soon what Maya the Asura wants concealed. Who knows?"

When she saw Ravana dead, the fair-skinned Queen Mandodari, dressed all in white, ran to him, and in the quiet city she held his hand in hers and bent over him silently weeping, shedding tears of sorrow, disconsolate with grief.

A Rakshasa priest approached her. "Faultless Queen, no

one must mourn a warrior slain fighting, so say all the ancient preceptors at arms. . . ." He put his arm round her
shoulder. "But I also am very sad this was his end."

Very swiftly some Rakshasas built a pyre of red and white
sandalwood logs, and laid a soft deerskin on top, and they
put Ravana's corpse on the deerskin. They washed the blood
from his body and put a new gold thread over his left shoulders and across his chest. They laid a new bow and sword by
him and put garlands of marigold flowers over him there, and
covered him with a golden cloth bordered with blue deer.
From brass ladles the priest poured butter and buttermilk
over Ravana, and then he lit the pyre from Ravana's birthfire
brought there in a burning jar.

All in a few moments the Rakshasas burned Ravana's
body. The few remaining Rakshasas of Lanka walked by,
throwing into his fire black aloes sticks and incense, handfuls
of pearls and broken sea-coral, and the fire burned fast. Ravana's earthly body returned again into the five elements it
had been made of.

Then Mandodari went alone to a mountain streamside in a
park and bathed in her wet white robes, and set down by the
waterside some seeds and sacred grass as offerings to the ancestors. She still had tears in her wide eyes. But so late in the
year the water-lotus stalks should not have flowers. She shut
her eyes and wiped her tears away, and looked again to see
more clearly.

"Father!"

There stood the Asura Maya, the Architect and Astrono-
mer of the Olden Gods, and he gently touched her. *Do not
cry. Do not cry.*

But Mandodari only wept anew. "Come," said Maya, "I
conjure you, speak to me."

"Oh," she said, "they may burn his body but never his
heart that he gave me years ago. What is now left to Ravana
of all his Empire? His body was happy and graceful in love;
he was hard to look at in anger. I loved all his brows and his
smooth skin with handsome scars—and now no more on
Earth, or any world!"

"Are you sure?" Maya sat down beside his daughter and
watched the water flow past. He said, "I liked it best when he
whirled his twenty eyes, when he came crunching down the
garden walks, when he drank and sang and wore all his flowers. . . ."

"They'll pay for this!" cried Mandodari.

"But—Why? What has happened?"

"What shall I do?" asked the Queen. "Which way is there to go? Where are all my people?"

Maya replied, "Why, what people did you own?"

"The people of this city! I am their Queen!"

"Who would believe it?" smiled Maya. "What city?"

"It's fading! Father, stop it, you can stop it. . . ."

"Come to our peaceful home; you are never alone and friendless."

Mandodari sighed. "Oh, let Lanka go, what good is she without my husband—" Tears filled her eyes. "A husband is most dear to a woman. With many sons and millions in gold, she cannot be happy without her husband. She is but a poor widow. . . ."

"I enchant you not to cry," said Maya. "Can you remember how to walk with me again, as when you were very young, as in those maiden days?"

I am the Asura Maya, a great Artist, the Master of Illusion. I will show you, my wonderful palace is still where it always was. I have food for all my family, and wine for you also.

"Father, tell me, why would my Lord forget our vows to always live together, and go apart along the unknown way, and leave me behind like a poor wayside beggar, and not comfort me?"

"Did he?" asked Maya.

"Oh Time destroys things so easily!"

"Does he?" Maya laughed and got to his feet. "Come on!" She stood by him. "Leave here everything that is Lanka's, and take away only your own deeds."

> *And besides that, only Love may go beyond, along*
> *   with us.*
> *See the world through my sight.*
> *See—*
> *All that magic!*
> *All yours!*

Then hand in hand they began to walk down a long hall of shady trees unfamiliar to the Queen, and Mandodari was like a little girl beside her father Maya. Her dress was blue and pink and silver; her shoes were gold and she smiled up at her father. Ahead of them there was an open door where sunshine entered.

Maya the Asura said, "Your mother has come back to us; our home is happy. Soon we will be like some story once heard as a child long ago, hard to remember, the bright shadow of what perhaps never was. . . ."

He led his beautiful daughter of illusion out through that garden door and far away.

Believe it and make it true. We are safe. Your love is here for you.

Thus Death's long evening shadows grew and reached to touch Ravana lying fallen in the dust. Life is very uncertain, and even royal fortune fails at last, and turns away from the greatest kingdom. Ravana was lordly and his dark arms were strong; he bound the worlds in ropes of illusion; so did he die.

What can one count on, except that whatever one has, it will soon be gone? Better to do right.

Ravana boasted and made good his boasts. He broke apart the sacrifices in the forests. He had a beautiful wife, but lust veiled his eyes so that he could not see, and he went falsely to steal Sita. He courted Death, or else what was he doing?

Ravana is gone, so forgive him. His flesh and bones were consumed by Fire, and his ashes were scattered by the winds. And yet men say that pyre still burns and that flame never perished, and long afterwards it sometimes can be seen at night high on a hill on Lanka Island, shimmering through the spells that hide a golden city somewhere there.

Hanuman flew like a flash to the Asoka Grove behind Ravana's palace, his white robes streaming out, his white fur ruffled with joy. He found Sita alone under the golden Sinsapa tree. But now she was dressed as a princess. Her dress was new; she wore a woven crown of fresh and fragrant wildflowers and new leaves, and her braid had a ribbon. There by her tree were a bronze comb and mirror, and sandalpaste and dark dust for brow and eye.

Oh blameless Sita, you are the fairest woman in all Creation, and no goddess can compare to you. Your face is bright as the Moon, you are more giving and forgiving than your mother Earth, more beautiful than Lakshmi, if that may have been. And Rama, what is the use our singing of her

charms when you and she have sung your two songs together?

"Well, this makes sense for a change!" Hanuman greeted
the doe-eyed Sita, so bold and beautiful. "This is the first nice
day there's been for a long time on Old Earth!"

"Oh, it's perfect!" Sita smiled, and her smiles were forever
warm and loving; they would carry anyone away, intoxicate
him more than any wine, and leave him floating on the
waves, in the air high above himself. "Now I leave all sorrow
behind me."

Hanuman hit his tail on the ground and tipped his head to
one side and laughed. "Mother, we are all well. Thanks to
you we have won. Ravana is killed and you must have no
fear, for you will soon be in your own house with Rama."

"Good betide you, Hanuman! My white monkey child
dearer to me than life, I am so proud of you! What have you
got there?"

The tip of Hanuman's tail curved up. "Look!"

"That's my yellow scarf!"

Hanuman said, "Guess what else," and opened his package.

"How heartwarming!" said Sita. "My ornaments from
Anasuya, and my pink shell necklace from Guha the Hunter
King." She put them on, earrings and anklets and bracelets
and necklace. "How do I look?"

Hanuman only smiled. Then he said, "Ask Rama."

Sita grew quieter. "How is he?"

"Come and find out!" Hanuman looked around with his
clear red eyes. "Where is everybody?"

Sita smiled, and drove out even the name of care from
Hanuman's monkey mind. "What have you to do with them
now?"

"Right, it's all finished and done."

"Thank you for your graciousness and true generosity,"
said Sita. "I have no fit reward for you—but Hanuman, Son
of the Wind, you will always know and remember the True.
You will always be strong and faithful, noble and wise and
daring! Always excellent powers will grace you and crown
you, and I give you my real love forever!"

"Oh," said Hanuman, "What else are treasures but your
good words and love? They are rare and precious jewels. It's
like finding a lost way, like lighting up a lamp in the dark,
like picking up what's fallen down or showing what's been
hidden."

"So promise me to pardon the race of demons now, and go tell Rama I'm ready, I await him. Where is he anyway?"

"Yes. The war's over. I promise," said Hanuman. "And I think he's waiting for *me!*" He leapt into the air and flew back to Rama's side.

Now we return to Rama, Lord of the World. Gradually the monkeys and bears came back to the field outside Lanka, friendly to each other but fearless in war, and Hanuman found Rama there among many friends, embracing the animal kings Sugriva and old Jambavan.

Hanuman said, "Go to her."

But Rama spoke to Vibhishana. "Lanka King, bring Sita here. Let her be seen."

Vibhishana obeyed. He went and told Sita, "I come from your own Lord Rama, with a glad heart."

One of Vibhishana's courtiers said, "My King and I myself . . . we bring our best and kindest wishes for you and all your friends, that is . . . for you and for the entire population of Earth. . . ."

Then Sita, whose waist could be clasped round by Rama's fingers, came out of Lanka. The monkeys and bears drew back to let her by, thinking—*Oh yes, this is from the old times back.*

Then as Sita walked to Rama, her gentle face aglow with love, King Vibhishana beside her, all the animals and Lakshmana also bowed to her. They were all kneeling in a circle around her, and they did not move.

Vibhishana the Rakshasa shaded his face with his dark hand and looked up at the sky with his blue crystal-clear eyes. There were two chariots in the air, gleaming bright, unwavering. Voices in the sky sang the praises of Rama firm in fight, and fragrant flower petals fell from heaven. The ravages of war all vanished and the last omens cleared away.

Agni the Fire God then appeared by Sita, and touched together his huge webbed hands shining with ornaments and rings. Agni said, "Rama's father Dasaratha is in that other chariot; he is very happy for you, my Lady." Then in his red robes, with his black curly hair and beard Agni took Sita's hand and led her to Rama.

The Fire Lord said, "Rama, from the portion of gentleness in you, people call you a part of the Moon. A king is the eye of his people, therefore Lord Narayana take back your Sita. Take her away with you; you have won her again."

Rama smiled. "Why call me by a great god's name?"

"But . . . . But my Lord—" Agni looked at him in amazement. "You mean you don't remember?"

"I am Rama, a mortal man."

Agni grinned, and shook sparks from his bare arms. His golden rings and hand-ornaments melted. "Have you any idea—?" Agni was all immersed in Fire there; he was a joyous furnace. "Oh Rama, I dwell within all life. I am the true witness never deceived. Again and again you have forgotten your secret. Sita has not the smallest fault, and she is innocent. Lakshmi of good fortune is your wife, and she loves you." Gold melted and fell from the Fire God in heavy smoking drops of metal, and his jewels shattered and crazed, his eyes were blazing.

Indra the Rain Lord came into view on the other side of Sita. He wore a thin cloak of fine-spun mist that was trimmed with dancing stars, and under that his old battle armor of worn leather hard as stone and unbreakable. He stood barefoot a finger's width above the ground. He was slender, and cast no shadow, and never blinked his deep black eyes. His straight hair was long and black; his skin was fair and white, and smooth as a girl's, except where his slim hands were covered with the old crossing lightning scars that were whiter still.

Indra King of Heaven said, "Narayana, Searcher of Hearts, what is this amusement, what is this play of yours? You have killed Ravana and freed people from fear."

Agni breathed out words from a furnace, like speech from an open burning hearth—*Remember her!*

Indra said, "The closing of your eyes is the Night of the World's End, and your awakening from sleep is Time's beginning. To favor men you are born as Rama, so let no one think men are weak and alone. It's heaven's own truth! It is you alone who gave to me the kingdom and rule of heaven."

Rama said, "That cannot be, how could I do that?"

"Oh forget it!" said Indra. "I mean—"

Agni said, "I am myself your anger; the universe is your whole body; the Moon is your delight." He pressed his hands together before his wide chest, so the fiery muscles stood out on his arms. "I can test the True. Only beside Truth, the lapping flames are dull and cool. Here is Sita. Here's Love."

Rama said in a happy voice, laughing as he spoke, "I've

won the war, what more do I need to know! Give me her hand."

Agni placed Sita's hand in Rama's, then drew back his own arm quick as a serpent's tongue. Rama had burned him!

Sita said, "With excellent joy, with delight cast looks on me. I am a fair free woman, I surrender to you of my own will, command me anything."

Rama tied Sita's wedding pearl-leaf back in her hair and unbound her braid. "Now you're mine again, with Fire for the witness."

The Fire God was happy. Indra shook his head. He had lived a long long time, but now he had come face to face with something older, some power immeasurably old, from before .... Indra looked helpless. He said to Sita, "We all serve you," and both gods vanished. And Vibhishana the demon also told Sita, "I too will always protect you wherever you are!"

Sita held Rama. *I am near to you.* She ran her fingers down his face and shut her eyes and slightly parted her lips. *Oh my love, my lover—Oh!*

Still all the kneeling figures on that plain did not look up or move or rise. Vibhishana looked away and the love of Sita washed over Rama. *I love you. Oh, it's all summer, and all roses—it's all gold and all you. . . .* She wept.

Vibhishana said, "Rama, Lakshmana made you a house downhill."

"Let's go," said Sita.

Rama smiled in a daze. "What? Oh!"

Sita put Rama's wide gold ring that Hanuman had brought her back on his finger. She whispered more words like honey in his ear, and at midmorning they walked away down the hill hand in hand, and Rama soon dropped Sita's hand and held her round her waist close to him as they went.

They reached a leafy cabin built by Lakshmana, and Sita sat and put Rama's head on her lap, and saw that he had hurt his leg fighting for her.

On what had been the battleground the animals and Lakshmana stirred at last, and got to their feet smiling. Hanuman asked Vibhishana the Demon King, "Why are the Rakshasas so quick to burn their dead or cast them undersea? Why do your weapons rust so soon?"

"Come, Hanuman," answered Vibhishana. "Come with me."

Vibhishana led Hanuman into Lanka, along the empty yellow brick streets to the royal palace where they entered. They went through a small side door in a plain room and descended many narrow stairs. For a way their path was lighted only by cut jewels set gleaming in the walls; then at the bottom of the stairs candles burned in branching silver trees, and they walked again along a level hall that widened and heightened and grew bright.

They stopped where the hallway ended at a storeroom door. There were locks holding it closed, locks strange and ornate and curious, and of those locks there were ten thousand and one. And though the keyholes were all of different shapes, Vibhishana opened them all with the same key, sweeping his hands to touch them and they opened to him. The demon pushed back the door and they came into a huge well-lit room with no other entrance to be seen.

On golden chains from the ceiling hung globes of glass that held lights within them. The air was fresh and sweet, and scented with musky perfumes. The whole room was cut out smoothly from the heartstone of Trikuta Hill. On the far wall Hanuman could read written in letters of gold inlaid on blue lapis stone—*Please yourself. Tell the truth and be tranquil.*

"Miraculous!" Hanuman saw shelves and racks all over holding cool fine linens of every color; beautiful patterned silks and folded skins of tigers and leopards and lions and silver wolves; rows of magical books and love potions and secret treasure maps and formulas and ore samples and delicious recipes; books of numbers and dictionaries of languages and stars.

There were perfumes and jewels and musical manuscripts and medicines to heal illness and sorrow and all wounds. On the walls were paintings in plaster and on hides; there were bins of irreplaceable wines and unknown scrolls, piles of gold and silver, and on the floor priceless musical instruments sat perfectly tuned in long rows; and over the vaults of the ceiling and on the upper walls were polished copper balls and silver stars, brass suns and bronze faces, golden leaves and moons of ivory and flowers of cold dark iron and blue steel.

Vibhishana pointed to the far wall. "That's the motto of Viswakarman the Architect of Heaven. who first gave beings their names and created them, who built Beautiful Lanka for the race of demons long ago. You are the only outside person who will ever see this room. These are the ancient timeless treasures of our race.

"Narayana drove us out of Lanka and Vaishravana the Lord of Wealth lived here but he never knew of this room. The bird Garuda watched sharp-eyed lest we return in those old days, but from here unseen doors lead down and down underground and we are ever careful of our possessions. We don't throw things away or lose them or forget. We Rakshasas protect many good things. We know a lot. We are strong." Vibhishana smiled with his long fangs. "Hanuman, by the good Dharma law, the Rakshasa knowledge may not perish. My friend, there are such powers of protection over this room that no thief would ever survive if he were but told all their names! These are the powers we draw on as guardians! But for you—if you need anything here, anytime, for anyone help yourself."

"Why will you do this for me?" asked Hanuman.

"You are my first and best friend of another race," replied Vibhishana. "You are faithful and very wise, when you stop to think. You put your whole heart into what you do; and you don't think twice when you've made up your mind, nor seek for any gain, so I call you my friend."

"I am."

"I know you are! In these vaults lies all the lore of old, gathered here since Time began again. People meet in this life and pass by each other like pieces of driftwood afloat on the wild and stormy sea, touching seldom, and once meeting, gone and parted again. Therefore a friend is also a treasure. Now you and Rama and all your armies will go from here. I am immortal; I will rule Lanka forever, and the Rakshasas will one day return who have now hidden themselves beyond your sight. I will cover Lanka and make her invisible from this time on, but you are always welcome here. For you I will reveal whatever you want to see, here on this island amid the great Ocean.

"And so," said Vibhishana, "if you find a friend hold him if you may. And giving gifts, giving to the poor and to others, that is always right; or else, what you save is spent to buy a homesite for you in Hell. So here's a present."

Vibhishana went to a shelf and took down a dusty book covered with the shastra marks of the Law, long shiny palm-leaves tied at the sides with faded string between wood covers. He opened it carefully. "By throwing them into the sea and by swift burning we have set our own war dead beyond the reach of life and death, of which they had grown weary. We long endure while we wish to, or we may sometimes escape life's wheel—and then our weapons rust! Here, learn this verse. Speak it correctly aloud on the hillsides where the dead animals lie, and they will again revive as they did before when you brought that Medicine Hill."

Hanuman learned those Mantras of Compassion and Vibhishana replaced the book where it had been. They locked the treasure room and retraced their steps. Hanuman stood on Earth outside Lanka and said the words, and brought back to life all the dead monkeys and apes and bears. And from then on, wherever any of those animals lived, no matter what the season the trees would flower and unveil before them and the land bear ripe fruit and all springs give water, full and clear.

Whoever was in Rama's army has all benefits and mercies. This is true because with Rama there is no fear, and no defeat, but instead great kindliness and victory.

However they had died, burnt or broken or cut or crushed to die, all the animals awoke from death unhurt, and they asked in great wonder, "What blessing is this? How are we restored?"

> *Once more!*
> *Live and grow, live and grow:*
> *Let me see my friends, my many friends,*
> *Let me look on you again.*
> *You left your homes behind for me,*
> *You cared nothing for Death,*
> *You lie pale and slain.*
> *I remember you,*
> *I remember all of you;*
> *I want you,*
> *I want you whole and strong!*
> *Once more!*

In the rainy summertime, the men and women of Fair Ayodhya light many candles outside the temple doors, big brass bowls filled with sand where a hundred candles may burn. And then the rain may fall and drench the Earth, and the wind may blow strongly. But the candle flames won't go out; they'll sputter and burn right on through the storm and the night. *Fill me and fulfill me, body and soul!*

The next morning there was Rama in the camp of his huge and famous army, and Sita was there, and he had unbound her braid, her sleek dark hair was combed out, free and scented, and her skin was again like warm gold.

Rama looked into the faces of all his animals, over and over. He said to Vibhishana, "Soon it will be springtime and the fourteen years of my exile will be full. If I am late my brother Bharata will enter a fire and die. Lanka King, have you any way for us to return to our homes that seem so far away and hard to reach?"

"Good fortune to you," said Vibhishana, "take the stolen chariot Pushpaka. But stay here as my guest for a few days."

"You must consider that already done. We will rest on-board that car, and go easily flying home."

"Then wait here," smiled Vibhishana. He entered Lanka and returned walking on foot with that vast and flowery car following along behind him; Pushpaka of a thousand wheels, like a small city, lightly riding just off the ground except when he rose all by himself to clear the golden wall.

Pushpaka came over the hill slopes. There he was, that grand and glorious chariot glittering with gold and silver, made by Viswakarman the heavenly builder, adorned with clear sapphires and golden rooms, with blue blossoms and red flowers and silver pavilions and nets of pink pearls, with his flags all flying and his wind-bells softly ringing. He was the immense mind-driven chariot taken from Vaishravana the Treasure King, easily able to carry any number of riders anywhere they would go. There were the great rainbows tied into beautiful colored knots and smoothed to make Pushpaka's frame, and bathing Vibhishana in colors and lights as he walked in the shadow below the car.

Pushpaka was painted in colors with trees and swarms of birds and stars and pictures of rivers; he had saffron canopies and lotus flowers strung over summerhouses of carved wood and wooden hills planted with grass and latticed windows; he had altars and upper rooms and dining halls and white flag-staffs, set in crystal bases; he had benches and beds and cov-erlets and good things to eat and drink.

Vibhishana arrived with that aerial chariot like a hill and said, "Climb on, it's here, what more shall I do?"

Hanuman flew onto the chariot and untied Pushpaka's many ladders and steps and let them down. Soon the animals were standing among the flowers and along the railings, lining the galleries and paths, running through the parks and cool fountains. With the sunlight pouring through his golden fur, Prince Angada leaned over and let down a big basket on a rope, and drew up Rama holding Sita. Then came Lakshmana carrying all Rama's weapons and his own.

Rama looked over the edge. "Vibhishana, give me your permission to go, Majesty."

Vibhishana replied, "There's lots of room on that thing. It's a fine large carriage. I want to see you made King of the Earth; take me along with my four ministers."

Rama heard something thumping next to him. He turned and saw Hanuman switching his tail against the wooden walkway floor, with his arm round Jambavan the bear. Hanuman smiled, "King Rama, we want to stop at Kishkindhya for our families, and then we all of us want to see all the people from the strange lands at the limits of the world, who will gather to see you made the Ayodhya King. We'll greet your mothers and bow to your friends and go through all your royal forests and gardens."

"Yes," said Rama. He looked back down. "Climb to Fair Ayodhya, Rakshasas."

When everyone was aboard, that huge chariot arose with a great noise like fireworks and waterfalls; then silently high in the sky he turned north in a wide climbing curve, carrying Sita who had been lost and found again, and two mortal men, and five demons and twenty-three million monkeys and bears sitting there at their pleasure in the free-flying gardens, facing the fresh morning wind as if they owned the world.

The Wonderful Return

On the hillside in the Sun,
The King is home, his war is done.
The fountains play and I can hear
The Master of the Revels cheer,
And singing soft and music clear.

The flowers in their colors there
Are falling down beside the stair,
And Fair Ayodhya at my feet,
And all along her silver street
My friends I find, my loves I meet.

And this is how my world shall be;
My days are bright, my ways are free.

Rama rode with Sita. He said, "Look down, there are the heavenly flowers marking where we fought and won you; there is the shore and our bridge thrown across the sea: there is Ocean, seeming endless with no farther shore, and that bridge seems to go off into the sky over the edge of Earth."

Vibhishana approached them. "Lord, free the sea as my gift." Rama smiled, and as they watched, the waters stopped holding up the bridge stones. The long bridge broke and sank; it was gone. The waves danced, leaping unbounded.

Pushpaka went on flying, and Rama continued, "There you can see gleams of gold far underwater, coming from Mainaka Hill who still has his wings, the golden-winged Friend of the Wind; now there is the northern seashore—see how far Hanuman can jump! Smell the sandalwood scent of the Malaya Hills; they look blue from here, and those lakes look green. There, through that spreading countryside below we marched from Kishkindhya; it will be an early spring this year. I think your mother Earth rejoices, and doesn't count the time."

Pushpaka started to descend. "There is the mouth of the cave city Kishkindhya, and there is Prasravana the Hill of Springs where I spent the rains, and I didn't even move out of the way when snakes crawled over me, I was so lost without you, and in that garden I killed Vali."

Sita said, "You are my Rama. Whatever you do is right."

Hanuman and Sugriva and King Jambavan were listening to Rama together. Hanuman sighed and said, "I wish I hadn't!"

"Hadn't what?" asked the Bear King.

"I wish *we* hadn't drunk up all Sugriva's wild honey wine."

The two Animal Lords smiled at each other. Pushpaka came in for a landing. Sugriva said, "Just get ready, monkey!"

"You mean? Where is it?"

Jambavan gave him a swat. "That monkey!! I don't see how we ever made it!"

"And it's not easy being a king," said Sugriva. "Remember that the next time you call me names."

Pushpaka caressed the Earth and was still and solid. All the monkey and bear children ran out of Kishkindhya cave as fast as they could. "What a car; can we ride?!"

Swiftly the animal wives and mothers and sisters dressed in all their best clothes and came to meet their men. Animal people were flying and running and jumping all over each other. Rama said, "We'll stay here overnight."

Hanuman was yelling, "You can ride tomorrow, all the way to Ayodhya!"

"There's Queen Ruma," said Jambavan. "Sugriva, go to her."

"Beautiful," said Sugriva. He turned to Rama. "Come inside with us until tomorrow."

Rama looked at Sita. Sugriva was turning his ears like an animal to hear where every sound came from. Down on the ground bears sat playing with their own children and holding baby monkeys. Kishkindhya monkey people were leaping and raising dust from the green forest trees. The whole world had gone out of its mind.

Jambavan gave a roar from deep in his throat and threw himself into the air. Hanuman plunged over the railing.

Sugriva started to twitch his tail but our Lady Sita buried her fingers in the thick golden winter's ruff round his neck.

Sita laughed like an angel. "We'd love to!"

Then on the next day they all flew to Ayodhya. Rama told Sita, "I'll show you; see, there is Rishyamukha Hill where we met that Hanuman; there is desolate Dandaka Forest, now free from harm, and there is where we burned the Vulture King Jatayu. Here come the Vindhya Hills and Agastya's hermitage. There is Chitrakuta—"

"Chitrakuta Hill in springtime!" Sita laid her head on Rama's shoulder. "Remember? And the birds all singing!"

"There flows the Yamuna river."

"From way up here the trees are like a carpet and the rivers are small as threads! How wonderful!"

Rama said, "By the grinding rapids of Yamuna and Ganga is Bharadwaja's retreat. Let me invite him to Fair Ayodhya to repay the feast he gave Bharata."

Pushpaka landed where Yamuna meets the Ganges. Rama met Bharadwaja and asked, "How is Bharata?"

Bharadwaja embraced Rama and smelled the crown of his head. "He is fine. But send him word you are safe."

"I will. Ride with us and be our guest; let us return the welcome, the feast that you gave."

"Oh Rama, a good dinner is as much a duty as fasting and not eating could ever be. Blessings, Majesty! I must be here where the two rivers change their colors and join—white Ganga and deep dark Yamuna! Blessed be you, Rama; blessed be!" Bharadwaja knelt before Rama. "I know all that has happened to you and all that you did. Now you must stay at home and live among your friends with Sita. Do as I say."

"Yes, I understand." Rama summoned Hanuman. "Go to Bharata and tell him we're coming home. I'll take the chariot to the Secret Forest of Guha the king of hunters for the night. Read Bharata's expression and his looks, and if he wants to keep Kosala as his own he may have her."

"He'll be the same," said Hanuman, and flew away.

Pushpaka chariot left Bharadwaja's hermitage and soon landed in a clearing in the Kingdom of the Far Forest, near the Ganges. Wherever he flew, there was always space there for Pushpaka to land when he arrived.

Rama and Sita and Lakshmana got down and walked through the forest trees. They heard whistling like a bird, then Guha came running at them. He fell on Rama and threw his arms around him. He looked as weird and outrageous as ever. He squeezed Lakshmana. He smiled his white smile at Sita. "Freedom! Freedom to you, my friends!" There he was again, the king of the wild, painted with yellow and green and red and blue all over his brown skin, wearing feathers long and waving in his curly hair.

"You'll stay for supper," said Guha. "Where did you get that flying city?"

"It's a magic chariot," said Sita. "Can the King of Lanka eat with us too? Our animal friends have their own food on the car, and. . . ."

"Yes, we're hunters, it's true. Vibhishana is welcome." Guha whistled and a forest man came bringing a new feather cloak for Sita, green and gold, just like the one he had given her fourteen years before. "Welcome to your tribe, princess. You are still my daughter, I'm glad you wear my necklace."

"It helped to save me," smiled Sita.

Guha said, "I sometimes take wild fruit to Bharadwaja the holy man. He often sent his students invisibly by air to the south, and from him I know most all you've done. Before, I didn't like to see you three enter the forest alone. But now the demons who ate unarmed men are gone from the woods as if they had never been. Oh, that was well done! Was that Hanuman we saw fly past?"

"Yes," answered Sita. "We have an army of monkeys and bears."

"An animal army. Yes, they're good fighters," said Guha. "Then that is the chariot stolen from the King of Wealth. It's all true!"

"Come to Ayodhya with us tomorrow," said Rama.

"No, I have the wild forest in me, I can't go into a walled-up city. I ran there once and came right back," said Guha. "Sumantra the Charioteer and the three Queens are well. Get Vibhishana, and come and eat now under that same big nut tree."

Vibhishana joined them and those five—the demon, and Rama and Lakshmana, and Sita holding Guha's hand—walked along the river to that old tree, and the silent dark hunters appeared to serve them.

It was evening. The running lamps on Pushpaka were lit, and he was like a city suddenly appearing complete amidst the forest. Shadows fell under the trees and Guha's men came out with torches. Rama and Lakshmana and Sita washed in the river. Then on blankets round a fire, under the ancient tree where they had been fourteen years before they ate with Guha, and with them Vibhishana first tasted the delicious wilderness cooking and ate a savage forest feast.

Hanuman flew over Kosala. He saw the roads coming to Ayodhya from many countries, the fields and farms, the flag-flying temples and holy bathing places along the rivers, the great white-walled city of Ayodhya seeming empty—and an earshot beyond, the little village of Nandigrama crowded with people.

Bharata sat there dressed in barkcloth at the foot of the red and gold Ayodhya throne, and on the throne were Rama's two wooden sandals painted with flowers. Every royal officer looked like a hermit all dressed in bark or skins, his hair matted into knots, his armor hidden as Rama's had been. Satrughna sat nearby on the grass. In all Kosala no man wore good clothes or any color, but the women dressed as they would, because Sita did not leave her robes and ornaments behind to go into the forest.

Hanuman dropped from the sky like a bouncing ball. He bowed first to Rama's sandals and then to Bharata. "Rama sends me to greet you. I am Hanuman the Son of the Wind. Is your kingdom well? Is there Dharma and Justice in Kosala? I hope lovers are not kept parted and young men respect the old, and do the rich not ignore the poor?"

Tears of happiness ran down Bharata's face. "Rama's land of Kosala is well; Fair Ayodhya is waiting. I give you a thousand cows and a hundred villages, and sixteen wives of noble birth, young and beautiful with skin like gold."

Hanuman laughed. "I touch them and give them back." He looked at Bharata with all the playful insanity of a cat. "What are you doing here like this? Rama and Lakshmana washed their hair out days ago! He'll meet you tomorrow by the city."

Bharata having truth for prowess said, "Set the signal fires to the villages and all the countryside." Satrughna set wine and fruit down by Hanuman. Everyone was smiling.

The priest Vasishtha approached and said, "The fourteen years are full. The trees are in blossom."

The Kosala men were changing clothes and bathing, lighting fires and trimming their hair and beards. Hanuman had a drink and ate three peaches. Bharata sent runners to Ayodhya to say—*Tomorrow,* and evening fell on the little village. In the reflecting firelight silver and gold, armor and rich silk were shining.

"Will you stay?" asked Bharata.

Hanuman said, "Surely."

Sumantra the old charioteer came, and many people sat circled round Hanuman and Bharata and Satrughna. Cooks brought fine food, a real dinner after fourteen years of eating hermit's food, fourteen centuries of grass and plain water it seemed.

Hanuman feasted on fruit and nuts, and Bharata said, "If we can hear it, unfold to us all that happened these many years to Rama."

"Well," said Hanuman, "Ravana stole Sita and—"

"What!" said Sumantra. "How did that happen?"

"We saved her. We fought a war and won."

"Ah," said Bharata. "The animals ... bless them all. ..."

"Now Ravana is dead," said Hanuman, "and Rama is tonight in Guha's kingdom."

Satrughna said, "Hanuman, we saw you fly over holding a red-hot mountain a few nights ago."

"We've heard this and that," said Bharata, "and we waited for Rama's call to aid him. You must tell us everything. After a long time our desires are fulfilled."

Hanuman settled back contentedly and the people grew still. "I will tell you Rama's story, filled with loneliness and love, romance and glamor. . . . Listen, Prince—I am Hanuman, the son of the far-going Wind, and one day on a hilltop. . . ."

> Let all cares be forgotten,
> Let your worries fly away:
> For the Master of the Revels
> Will rule the land this day!

It was early morning. The Revels Master stood up and slowly brushed fourteen years of dust and ashes and sand out of his old clothes. He found the wine-key he'd thrown away still on its chain; he found his vests and ribbons and his fur hat. The royal palace had been astir all night. He opened the king's wine-vaults and broke the seal on a tall dusty crock, and poured himself a cheerful cordial drink. The Master of the Revels smiled again.

In Ayodhya the gay silk pennons and streamers were unfurled. Musicians restrung their silent lutes; drivers put the wheels back on the Kosala chariots. They dressed and painted the royal white elephant, and Fair Ayodhya threw open her gates and waited for her Lord Rama.

Behold! Fair Ayodhya! the city of my dreams; Ayodhya of many dreams and gardens. No war was there; the war-songs were made into dances, and the marches were for parades for the children. In Ayodhya you could walk anywhere, anytime, free and unafraid. You could love openly, and couples embraced in daylight in the gardens.

She was in the low hills, the breathing hills of home, and she was the most beautiful city ever made by man, with her hanging stairway gardens and her sprays of flowers. Her homes were my dream houses; I knew that when I first saw them in the bright clear sunlight. Purple petals fell on the green barefoot grasses by the stairs outside, and vines of spicy sweet flowers seemed growing from her housetop roofs, and her flowering trees in blossom scented the air. The colored flower gardens fell down her slopes, holding ferns and green things and small tame wild animals. Her side streets were like long green tunnels overarched by old trees touching from each side. The leafy trees swayed in the gentle breeze of the Kosala hills, and I walked below through spotted sunlight and moving shade.

Hearts are young in Fair Ayodhya, and all's forgiven now. Her streets are sprinkled with sandalwood water. She has fish-ponds and splashing fountains lovely to hear, where flights of white birds play, graceful and happy. Bushes of ripe black-berries look like bees swarming. Her gardens are the flowery shelters of my childhood. Fair Ayodhya—won't you be mine, till the end of Time?

There's nothing I have to do, I've done it all. It's time to relax, time to have a good dinner, and to be peaceful. From peace in my own heart peace will go out to my courtyard, to my city, my kingdom, to all the world. . . .

> *The wine flows free, the music calls;*
> *I smile within the dancing halls. . . .*

I spend my days with my friends doing nothing. Sometimes the grey river mist comes in off the slow Sarayu river where I swim, and the tops of the tall trees are lost in the cool fog. It makes the trees like low clouds themselves; it is wet under them and nowhere else; and I hear the boatmen calling out on the river.

Fair Ayodhya, my old home; the city I love, my own free city; you are very dear to me. You are the home of friendship and alive, gleaming with lamps at night. You are where the great roads cross, and people traveling often stay here and go no farther. Fair Ayodhya, my love to you where the food is good and no man poor.

She was my city; I loved all of her, by day or night, and all her people. They were my family and my friends, where I belonged—good words and loving homes—cozy and warm, or easy and cool, just as I wanted. She was my Innocent City. Everything was all right there.

> Beyond the end of every Time
> You'll find Valmiki makes a rhyme;
> The blue Sarayu's flowing by,
> And butterflies like flying flowers
> Pass me by,
> I lie in bowers.
> Oh Rama!

Ayodhya was dancing, shining with decorations; and in the palace, men gathered the coronation supplies and women went in rustling dresses wearing gold. Shrill pipes and horns played in the street and shell-trumpets sounded from the temples. Royal musicians and courtiers smiled, and the dancing girls caught their breath.

People lined the wide streets and the rolling hills. Children were eating candy from gold-paper wrappings. The houses and doorways were all white and there were flowers in the streets. Rama had already spent a night awake in silence thinking of all those years before, and that when he came home now, he would be king without waiting.

Bharata and Satrughna and Hanuman, followed by the whole village of Nandigrama, went to a field outside the city with Rama's sandals on the white elephant's back beneath a white umbrella. Out from Ayodhya rode the Kosala warriors on a thousand horses with jingling rings and chains, carrying shining spears and long lances.

Then Pushpaka came, flying with colored banners in the sun. He landed in that field and his riders crowded to the rails high above. The ladders came down, and Bharata led the elephant over, and took the sandals from him. He was pulled up onto the chariot and fell into Rama's arms. And while all Ayodhya watched, Bharata knelt and swiftly tied the shoes back on Rama's feet.

Bharata stood and smiled, looking level into Rama's eyes. He ran his hand through his red hair and said, "Majesty! I return to you all your kingdom left in my care—how good to see you!" He faced Lakshmana. "Blessed is my birth since today I may see all of you safe at home."

Bharata told King Sugriva, "You are our brothers. Friendship grows from kindness and giving help, not from close ties of blood."

He told Jambavan, "Lord of Bears, I am your servant." He said to Vibhishana, "Lord, take the freedom of Fair Ayodhya as our guest forever; you have made this possible."

The animals and the five demons descending from Pushpaka were met by Kosala men and women and welcomed and led to houses and lodgings all over Ayodhya. The stories about a faraway animal city were true, Hanuman's story was true—it was all true!

Then Rama stood on the ground and the four brothers embraced, and Vasishtha led Sita to Sumantra's car to be driven to see her three mothers.

At arms' length Bharata put his hands on Rama's shoulders and said, "A child cannot easily pick up and carry the burden set down by a man. We have survived only by the power of your sandals. Take this land back, my king; take her back from me!"

"In a moment," smiled Rama. "Let's walk into town. I'm not used to all this."

At last Dasaratha's four sons were walking together, through Fair Ayodhya to the white royal palace on a hill, and the Kosalas stood quiet along the roads waiting to know what Rama would do. Rama and Lakshmana entered alone to see the Queens. They were combing Sita's hair with silver combs and Rama's mother Kausalya said—*We are well; by good fortune we see you again with all your enemies dead.* Then she hugged him.

Vasishtha came in. He said to Kaikeyi the youngest Queen, "By your doing were the worlds saved from tyranny."

He told Queen Sumitra, "Your son Lakshmana is the silent

support of Rama; Satrughna is Bharata's quiet companion; you are yourself the good friend of these two Queens."

He said to Kausalya, "We have lived to see this day!"

And he told Rama, "Rule as long as the world endures, as far as the world extends."

"Yes," said Rama.

Vasishtha said, "These hours and days are fortunate." He went to a window and shouted, "He will!"

A Kosala lion-roar came back from the street. The palace trembled with noise, incredibly loud. The first Ayodhya festival in fourteen years began, and the best celebration she had ever known. The people were dancing again, and men and monkeys and bears all jammed into the wineshops shoulder to shoulder, trading drinks and stories and lots of loose talk.

"I'll get ready," said Vasishtha, "and make you King tomorrow."

Sugriva found Hanuman wearing flower garlands piled round his shoulders up to his ears. The Monkey King gave Hanuman a golden jar and said, "For a present to Rama, fill this with water from each of Earth's five hundred rivers."

"Say no more!" said Hanuman.

"And don't try to fool me with well-water, because I know the taste of every sea and stream."

"Well, they won't let a monkey taste the Ayodhya King's waterjars!" laughed Hanuman.

"And if you see any fair or beautiful thing that may be brought, bring it."

The Kosalas gave the animals and demons new clothes and fine ornaments, and when Bharata served free food from the royal kitchens Ayodhya maidens carried tasty treats to monkeys and bears lying on soft beds or on grass in the parks. For Fair Ayodhya, all the sorrow in the world was used up. People poured into town from the countryside; they danced and heard music and gambled and watched tumblers and plays on the street corners.

The holy trees were hung with ribbons and brahmanas blessed everyone. In the early evening countless candles burned outdoors like blossoms of light and incense rose into the air. Lanterns glistened and torchlight burned. The night was warm and the stars were clear.

Then late at night Sita sat by a fountain in the palace while Rama slept on a bed in an open room nearby, and Manthara the hunchback came to her. Manthara knelt, "Forgive me for remembering those two wishes."

Sita was beautiful. She answered, "Not only men, but even the gods have been freed from fear of Ravana. Death had surrendered to the Demon King; the Moon and Sun were his subjects; and Indra King of heaven was a captive."

"Lord!" said Manthara.

Sita said, "Rama killed Ravana only because of what you did."

Manthara smiled, and sat beside Sita. "Queen Sita, I am always your faithful servant."

"Yes," said Sita.

After fourteen years awake and watching over Rama every night, Lakshmana slept, held fast in sleep beside his loving wife.

The night passed quickly by. Soon the sky grew light and the morning Sun rose red for Rama to see him. Bharata had brought the Ayodhya throne from Nandigrama village to the royal park by the palace so everyone could see Rama made king.

Rama came out, like a lion coming out of his cave, and girls tossed fragrant flowers from windows and rooftops. He walked to the park with Lakshmana holding a seven-tiered white parasol over him. White cows were tied all along the way. Bharata and Sugriva the monkey King stood behind the throne holding white yaktail fans. Rama sat on the throne facing east, and Sita sat on a lower chair beside him, on a deerskin cover trimmed in gold. The animals and demons and men gathered there sat down on the grass.

Virgin maids brought spotless white cattle with gold-plated horns, and unthreshed heads of grain for Rama to touch. Then Vasishtha entered the park holding a hollow horn wrapped in silver wire and a little dipper. First the priest stopped by Hanuman and dipped some of the river water of all the world into the horn. Four brahmanas unsealed four brimful stone jars of seawater. Four Ayodhya girls set before Rama a handful of jewels and one of seed, a handful of herbs and one of sea pearls.

Vasishtha put some of the waters of the Eastern Sea in his horn from the first stone jar. Four more girls came forward and put before Rama a jar of honey, parched grain dyed with saffron, a bowl of milk and some incense unlit.

Vasishtha dipped water out of the Western Sea, whose waters smell like camphor. Four more beautiful maidens brought Rama turquoise and blue water flowers, a lump of silver and a dish of curds.

Vasishtha added the black seawater of the cold North Sea; and the last four maidens set down by Rama's throne a fresh-loomed cloth unbordered, and corals, and beautiful seashells and white garlands. Then Vasishtha took water from the Southern Sea waterjar.

Finally at noon Vasishtha stood by Rama and emptied the water over his head, and made him King and Lord of Earth; the Solar King of Fair Ayodhya, the Kosala Lord, and Sita was his one Queen with him.

Rama gave many presents—horses and cows, earrings and bracelets, rings and bells and a silver crest for Sugriva, and round Sita's neck he fastened a smooth pearl necklace. Sita held the strands in her hand and looked at them, and looked at Rama, and looked at the animals.

Rama said, "Give those pearls to whom you please!"

Lotus-eyed Sita gave them to Hanuman. He knelt before her and she put the pearls around his neck and smiled at him. The necklace seemed to glow like little moons nestled in his white fur. "This gift is for your courage and strength, your valor and bravery and skill, and for your faithful service."

Rama said to all his people, "I am pleased that you have gathered here to welcome me."

They cheered back—*King Rama! Rule forever!*

The Ayodhya throne, all red and gold, was carried into the King's palace, and the coronation was over. All afternoon the animals and men ate their way through hills of food and drank up lakes of Rama's wines, and there was not one person without some gift. Evening came and the Sun set as Ayodhya sang her twilight prayers. Then Night veiled the worlds as Rama went into the inner rooms with Sita. So passed the first day of Rama's long reign of eleven thousand years. Rama could discover the truth of things, and men resorted to him from all over Earth, as the rivers of the world all flow to the sea. Rama was well-honored and well-loved. His presence filled the heart.

Rama was strong enough to support all men, and gentle as the new Moon's beams. Fame and Wealth never left him. When he was king men were long in life, and lived surrounded by their children and grandchildren and all their families.

The old never had to make funerals for the young. There was rain and fertile Earth; indeed, the Earth became bountiful.

Peace and Rama ruled as friends together, and bad things did not happen. Men grew kind and fearless. Everyone had about him a certain air and look of good fortune.

A King like Rama was never seen before and nowhere remembered from the past in any kingdom, nor did any like him ever follow in the later ages of this world.

THE END OF THE BOOK OF THE BATTLES.
HERE BEGINS THE SEVENTH AND FINAL BOOK,
THE UTTARA KANDA, THE LAST BOOK.

In What Dream?

At the end hear the first words. . . .

After a month in Ayodhya, early one morning before it was light, while the Kosalas still slept with closed eyes, Vibhishana and Sugriva met Rama in the palace gardens, and the Monkey King said, "Majesty, we have all seen you, now we shall go home to our deep forest and far countries."

"Blessed are friends like you," answered Rama.

"Farewell," said Vibhishana. He bowed his head, then with his four knights he flew to Lanka, going swiftly through the sky with a sound of thunders and gleam of lightnings.

Rama went outside the palace courtyard and looked out at the monkeys and the dark bears all gathered in the streets. He embraced Hanuman. "It seems you have been here but a moment."

"Farewell, Lord of Earth." And then with all desired things given them by Rama, the animals of the greenwood returned to dwell in their homes, blinking their eyes and half unwilling to leave Fair Ayodhya.

It was still very early, and as Rama walked alone back to his palace, through a grove of trees with fair new leaves in the morning, he heard a voice call from above him—*Rama, Rama, Rama*—and he found he stood in a long wide shadow.

Rama looked up. There were the giant rainbows over his head. "I am Pushpaka chariot, the spring flower car. By your leave I will return to Vaishravana the Treasure Lord. Give me permission to live on Kailasa Hill, and I will come back to you if ever you need me, whenever you want me."

Rama said, "Welcome to you, best of chariots. Go where you will. Be not sorry for our separation. May your ways be smooth and good forever." Then Pushpaka rose and flew north to the silver hill Kailasa from where Ravana had stolen him.

Indeed, when Rama was King many creatures and created things could speak to men sometimes. When deer ate the crops the Kosalas would speak with the deer kings in good-will, and those kings would withdraw their people to the wild grasslands. If one wished to hear stories of past times he could speak with an old sword about ancient battles, or hear the old tales told by the trees and stones.

Rama ruled from Fair Ayodhya and all the world saluted him, and time went by until his reign lacked only twelve years and a few months of being ten thousand years long, when one winter evening Rama met Sita wearing a beautiful robe, and saw that she was with child. Knowing of the strange longings of pregnant women he asked her, "Is there some wish of yours I may give?"

Sita smiled. "I want to go again to the retreats along the Ganges, just for a day or two, to eat the fresh wild food and sleep once more on grasses. And as we first went away from Ayodhya, thousands of years ago I promised Ganga to visit her . . . let me go now, my Lord. . . ."

Rama said, "Go tomorrow if you want to," and he embraced his Queen with great love and happiness.

And with those kind and innocent words sorrow again came into Rama's life.

We look at man's life and we cannot untangle this song.
Rings and knots of joy and grief, all interlaced and locking.

Later that night Rama met with some of his ministers and in passing he asked lightly, "What do my people say of me?"

"Majesty," answered the minister Bhadra, "they speak good of you as King, and in their homes tell stories of your war against Ravana long ago."

"The king is the refuge of those who have no shelter, so I must be without fault. People tread in their king's footsteps, so I must avoid even the report of any wrong. Hide nothing from me," said Rama.

Bhadra joined his hands. "They say—*today men stand at a ruined pier hung with colored rags on the far south shores and dream of a bridge a hundred leagues long across the dancing sea, where the ocean breaks in luminous waves. Rama*

*did a deed unheard of. Ravana was unconquerable. No man
ever brought the wild animals of the wood into his armies before*—and so they talk of many things."

"What else?"

"Majesty, Kings must hear good news and not think on
mistakes. Don't seek wisdom from coarse common people,
but forget their talk; pity them their ignorance and trust in
things to turn out right."

Rama said, "Those who live uneventfully at home with
their wives and families may alone really know life. No king
can ignore what his folk say of him . . . do not refuse to tell
me."

Bhadra said, "Rama, we must obey you. They also say—
*The King desires Sita although Ravana touched her. How
could he forget she lived with another? And the Queen must
also remember the Demon King*—so speak the lowest men."

And the other ministers of Kosala lowered their eyes and
sadly said, "Lately this is true."

Rama left them there without a word, and sent a message
to Lakshmana—*Come to me at once.*

Lakshmana and Rama met in a private room of the palace.
Rama stood alone by a window. His face was pale, his hands
trembled like leaves in a wind, the lights of his eyes were
gone as though clouded over.

Lakshmana frowned. He looked and saw no enemy; he felt
no threat. Lakshmana harshly threw the end of his robe back
over his shoulder, and knelt and asked, "Who dares?"

"Arise," said Rama. "Promise to obey me."

Lakshmana walked back and forth. "The threads of that
design! Who told you?"

"A king must be blameless."

"Such words pierce my heart," said Lakshmana. "Fire himself proved her innocent. She is fired gold, poured into golden
fire!"

Rama said, "Lakshmana, consider what is a king. Kings
cannot afford blame. Ill fame is evil to kings; they above all
men must be beyond reproach . . . see, into what a chasm of
sorrow a King may fall. . . ."

Lakshmana said, "Gradually everything seems to change
again, and even an Emperor must pay his way through life."

Rama faced his brother. "It must be! It's all the same,
can't you see? Where there is growth there is decay; where
there is prosperity there is ruin; and where there is birth there
is death."

Lakshmana sighed hopelessly. "Well, what will you do?"

"Sita expects to go to the forests tomorrow. Let Sumantra the Charioteer drive you both there, and when you arrive by the river Ganga abandon her."

"She will die. Your child will die!"

"No," said Rama. "I command you! Not a word to anyone."

Lakshmana said, "Surely a king is remote and lonely, and very far from reason. We cannot speak to you. . . ."

Rama said, "Each person can be told what he will understand of the nature of the world, and no more than that—for the rest, take my word."

"I'll take it," answered Lakshmana. "Just . . . leave her there, alone?"

"Yes."

Lakshmana looked around the room. "Rama, since we were young children I have followed you; now I will still serve you. For right and wrong are very subtle and hard to tell apart, and the Dharma Law is difficult to know—*and, it is inconceivable to me, that I should ever willingly disobey you, Rama.*"

The next morning Sita took some little presents for the hermits' wives of the forest, tied them in a silk cloth, and got on Sumantra's chariot with Lakshmana. Sumantra's four red horses went out of Fair Ayodhya and down along the Tamasa riverside, through plumes of morning fog.

They stayed that night in the woods meeting no one, and continued their way the next day. It was cloudy; the Sun had fled from having to see Sita betrayed. They came to the mouth of the dark Tamasa where she meets Ganga, and Sumantra found an ancient abandoned fisher-boat drawn up onshore and said, "Come across Ganga and we may meet someone."

At that instant, in the city of Lanka, Vibhishana the King felt danger to Sita. He went outside and looked far in every direction to see what was amiss. His far-seeing blue eyes gleamed and his black face darkened. He wrapped himself in a blue cloak and flew to heaven.

By the peaceful stream of the heavenly branch of the holy Ganga river he saw the sage Narada leaning back against a tree with his eyes closed. Vibhishana gently knelt on the ground of heaven and touched Narada's shoulder. "Wake up. Get moving!"

Narada opened his eyes, saw Vibhishana's face with his long fangs and decided he had a bad dream. He shut his eyes again. But King Vibhishana gripped Narada hard as steel and said— *For the protection of Sita, the Demon King calls on any power! Awake this instant, she is in danger! Get up! Do right!*

"Sita!" Narada was on his feet. "Where?"

Vibhishana said, "Down on Earth, oh Minstrel, across from where Tamasa flows into Ganga below, where inside an anthill sits the lone hermit Valmiki."

Sumantra and Lakshmana took Sita across Ganga in that old boat and helped her out on the other side. Then Lakshmana looked at her and wept.

"What's wrong?" asked Sita.

Lakshmana could not answer her, and Sumantra the Charioteer replied, "We see bad signs, Earth to us is sad, we are restless and empty of happiness."

Sita said, "You miss Rama, but when we see what hermits we will find and give them my gifts we may all go back home."

Sumantra sighed and bent low his head, and looking down he said, "This is the work of destiny that cannot be overcome. I was angry when Dasaratha banished Rama, but this time I made no protest, for this is fate. This was foretold, and I overheard it long ago."

"What?" asked Sita. "What are you talking about?"

Lakshmana replied, "In fear of scandal, like a coward Rama now uses this journey as the pretext to abandon you here in the woods." He turned to Sumantra. "This is clearly unjust. I cannot understand, what can we gain by doing wrong to please a fool?"

"Then suspend your reason and get a glimpse of Eternity." Sumantra looked at Ganga's waters flowing by. "This is in part ancient history beyond men's knowing, and in part what I have heard was to happen. Rama will live alone from now on, apart from you."

Sita wept, "Oh why?"

"My Lady," said Sumantra, "all the universe is but a sign to be read rightly; colors and forms are only put here to speak to us; and all is spirit, there is nothing else in existence. War and peace, love and separation are hidden gateways to other worlds and other times. Let us not grow old still believing that truth is what the most people see around them . . . Oh Lakshmi of the Lotus, Daughter of Videha, we are fit objects of blame for all men by leaving you. But banish your sorrow over what must be."

Sumantra silently spoke a spell that all forest creatures might protect Sita, and as he began to speak aloud again, the dark blue clouds settled lower on the hills around them.

Sumantra said, "Dasaratha and I knew part of our future, and I have never told this story. Now I am an old man, and I remember long times ago, and I break secrecy to tell you how it was, that Kaikeyi won her two wishes."

Listen, my children—

It was in the olden time, long before your births, when your father Dasaratha and I were young men . . . it seems now to have been in another age of this world. Little remembering your father as an old man, little looking at me now can you see the brave young prince and the lucky charioteer of those days, who fought on the side of the gods themselves against the Asuras of drought. With Indra and others, and helped by Jatayu the young vulture prince who made our friendship then, we tried to unlock the clouds where all the rain was imprisoned.

Then I fought alone as a warrior and did not drive Dasaratha's car that flew through the air by grace of Lord Indra's spell, pulled by the same four red horses I have used all these years since. There was a better driver than I to take your father against the demon strongholds in the black clouds—there was Princess Kaikeyi, nine years old and unafraid.

The demons armed the clouds with artillery and turned them into fortress cities. They shot many of our warriors from the sky. We never saw the Sun. It was hot and stifling. At night lights flashed overhead as gods and demons fought; by day we saw the shadowy giant warriors and heard the charge of horse and chariot and the clash of arms. Indra's white elephant called and trumpeted; he threw down the demon walls and many black stones fell on Earth. They broke our lands and the fields lay parched. That was dread fatal war: we faced famine.

Those days gone by seemed brighter and of more glory

than today, or darker with more sorrow. In the countryside our cattle shifted and lowed; the deer burst running through the forest like horses driven from a battlefield. The clouds were black, and dry, and rimmed with red; the world was dark; all daylight was gone. There was forever confusion in heaven, and our warriors who returned from flights above the clouds at night told us how the stars and planets swerved and could not hold their paths from fright, but went in fearful uncertainty blocking heaven's ways, striking against each other, a terror to mind and sight. Flames burst like blood from the stricken stars.

Your grandfather Aja was King. He helped Indra, and we fought back against the demons guided by our flares and fires high in the windy sky. We battled the drought demons with Indra's thunderbolts. I have myself thrown many brilliant thunders, made by Viswakarman for Indra, and for that we wore a thick glove of wet green leaves, and bits of fires scarred our arms.

Kaikeyi never failed Dasaratha. She could feel an enemy's shortcomings; she felt when to draw near, when to stay and when to turn away. She ran her four red horses through the celestial skies and ruled them by some miraculous power of friendship. Behind her was a seven-layered white umbrella with slender ribs of silver over the warrior's station on her chariot, and to each side of it a chowrie fan, gold on the right, silver on the left, and there stood your father fighting for rain.

One night high in the air, the demons attacked that car with conjurations on a hundred sides. Your father was sadly wounded. Part of a comet tore through his side, and a flying fragment of his shattered armor cut Kaikeyi's hand deeply. And at the same moment a demon arrow snapped the bolt-end off the right axle and the wheel started to slip off.

Dasaratha was unconscious and saved from falling to death by Kaikeyi. She drove the chariot so it did not overturn in the air, and kept that wheel on, and brought her horses and the car softly down to Earth.

Kaikeyi wore shimmering armor made from green silk threads and fine steel interwoven, a green cloak like winter's grass. It was strong, but she loved your father and tore away a strip of it to bandage Dasaratha's wounds, and her hand bled, their blood mingled. She nursed him for many days as he recovered slowly, and he told her—*You restored my life*

*that my enemies had taken from me . . . ask me twice for
anything in return.*

Then one night Indra came to Ayodhya. We met him as
comrades, we drank from the same cup. He healed Dasaratha
completely, and would have taken the scar from Kaikeyi's
hand but she refused him. We went to a field outside the city,
and there were all the gods of heaven, and they thanked us
for our help. The gods were cheerful; they had just received
the promise of aid from Lord Narayana.

We heard it. Out in the night, from far far away came the
call of Narayana's battle-shell. We felt the first winds of
Garuda's approaching flight. Our torches were blown out; the
shrill winds screamed around us. There was a great loud
sound as of many old trees straining and creaking in the
Wind, and that was the drawing back of Narayana's bow.
There was a hum and rattle and groan of metal, and that was
the razor-edged, diamond-naved discus whirling madly on its
pole. There was a terrific loud snap, and the bowstring of
Narayana was loosed and spoke death to the drought-demons.
We grown men shielded our eyes and covered our ears from
the wind and noise, but young Kaikeyi stood looking up into
heaven, standing beside Lord Indra, holding his hand and
smiling, a child fearless beside heaven's Lord.

The rain spilled down onto the land, and fell spraying into
our rivers. It came down on the mountains and fell into the
seas. And with the rain fell down demons covered with red
arrows and mangled.

Then through the night dark forms ran past us into
Ayodhya. They were demons and we followed armed, but
they were not invading; they sought refuge from Narayana.
They came to an old brahmana's house and his wife gave
them shelter. That old couple had never taken life, and always saved others when they could; and now they accepted
the demons' surrender in the name of King Aja, and sent
word to the royal palace.

Running to Ayodhya, we were thrown down and Garuda
swept past us screaming like a thousand eagles, flying low between the high towers of Ayodhya, shearing our city gates
and his claws tearing through our treetops. Riding on his
back we saw Narayana enraged. His dark blue skin gleamed
and his yellow robes flew. He killed that brahmana's wife
when she faced him, without letting her speak, and in terrible
anger he broke that sanctuary and beheaded the helpless
demons.

There was great turmoil. Down the street came King Aja, furious at the Lord's treason, that his protection and name had been ignored. The old brahmana wept over his wife's body. Then standing a little apart I overheard Vasishtha the priest speak an unbearable curse on Narayana the Lord. In hot anger Vasishtha threw down his staff and cursed Narayana to be born on Earth, in a royal family rich and wise, a family most honored and kind, and once born to be parted from his wife as he had broken that brahmana's marriage. Vasishtha said—*So will it be! He is a man of ours you harmed!*

King Aja drew the royal Ayodhya sword and spoke defiance and threats to Narayana and ordered him from our kingdom, but Narayana was departing as he spoke. Aja approached us, men and gods, and told us, "Can't you kill fairly, or must you enlist the aid of giant cowards? By heaven fight fair next time!"

We put away our lances and spears, our lightnings and swords. The Asuras that lock away rain were defeated; it rained for days, and then we saw the Sun again.

Vasishtha was appalled that he had cursed Narayana. But the words of a holy saint prove adamant—and we knew what must happen. All is destiny, all is change and what endures?

Vasishtha told me, "Be silent about this. But remember: Lord Narayana will never take man's life without accepting it all. He will have the adventure; he will take all the gain and all the loss."

For days Vasishtha sat alone in seclusion. When he left his meditation he said, *"Her large eyes are tearful and her ringlets are dark . . .* I can discover no more; we must wait."

"No one knew what that meant until now," said Sumantra. "Sita, I'm a chariot driver, a good guide, and you'll get back to Rama only by entering this forest now. Try to remember us well. This world's life is like vapor from breath blown on a mirror, it does not last, therefore summon patience. We'll tell no one where you are."

Sita said, "Goodbye, Sumantra. You have touched my heart."

Sumantra said, "Farewell, Sita. The light of our lives is gone, and this ends all that we've known. May I see you again."

"Goodbye, Lakshmana."

Lakshmana said, "I cannot go, this is a lonely wood and Rama is not here."

But even as he said that, Lakshmana was going. Sumantra led him back to their boat and they recrossed Ganga, and drove away in the chariot looking back many times.

It was noon. The Sun came out and Ganga flowed sparkling by. Sita stayed by the riverside, all alone with her small gifts of needles and thread and combs and mirrors and perfumes on the ground in a package beside her, and all the wood was silent but for the cries of peacocks far away.

Ganga the beautiful river goddess spoke softly from within her moving waters—*What price, what price? Let life go with love and not outlive it, cut the bonds when happiness goes. . . .*

Ganga whispered, "There is a home for you now. I am the curtain to pass through, beyond me golden rooms are yours forever. *Come home, come home, dive into me . . . .*"

Sita was entranced. She stared at the shimmering water. Then four hermit boys appeared from out of the forest, and saw her, and ran off. Then a wild shaggy man ran to her, covered with dust from an anthill, with hair and beard long as eternity.

"I am Valmiki. Make my hermitage your home."

Sita looked at him bewildered and Valmiki said again, "Make this your home, stay here." He smiled, and many hermit wives led Sita away. And so a hermit who became the first poet led the Queen of Ayodhya to safety.

The women took Sita to a quiet glen, into a new house of leaves in Valmiki's retreat that had just been created by one of Narada's songs. She stayed there, and when her time was come, there her twin sons were born. It was at night in the summer, and midwives awoke Valmiki and said, "Poet, protect the newborn."

Valmiki grabbed an armful of shiny fresh-cut kusa grass, the pale long grassblades used for sacrifice and ceremonies. He went to where Sita lay and rubbed her twin newborn sons with it. He rubbed the firstborn with the grass tips and named him Kusa. He rubbed his brother with the cut grass ends and named him Lava.

For twelve years Sita and her sons lived with Valmiki while he composed this *Ramayana*. He taught Kusa and Lava every verse over the years and they learned to sing this story to the music of a lute and drum.

When Kusa and Lava were twelve years old, Rama had ruled in Fair Ayodhya for ten thousand years, and once on a summer night that was neither hot nor cold he spoke with Lakshmana, and said, "I will declare a great public festival, a happy gathering somewhere in the countryside, a peaceful celebration that will be long remembered and a year's giving of gifts to all the world."

"A King's wife must be present," said Lakshmana.

"Happiness I want now," said Rama. "My heart must no longer hurt. I have made a golden statue of Sita that will stand beside me. We'll have food and music. We'll make it a thanksgiving for what good fortune we have, a long and excellent ceremony where all will be well-received, and let it begin next month. We will invite everyone. In Naimisha Forest, along the river."

Rama sent Kosala riders to Kekaya to invite Bharata's uncle and to Videha to invite King Janaka, and to all the kings of the world. Some went to Kishkindhya to invite the monkeys and bears, and from there Hanuman carried them to invisible Lanka, and Vibhishana was asked to come. And everyone that these horsemen met was told of Rama's festival.

Rama sent his brother Satrughna into the forests to invite the holy saints and hermits dwelling apart from men. Satrughna rode a black horse with a red mouth and the first person he met was Guha the hunter. He and his savage people accepted the invitation, for that yearlong festival would not be held inside any city.

Satrughna's last stop was at Valmiki's hermitage, and he knew nothing of Sita's living there or of her two sons.

Valmiki was all smiles. "Prince, welcome to you! By the Gods, that was a deed well done by Rama, when he killed Ravana! He freed all the worlds . . . ." Valmiki embraced Satrughna and smelled the crown of his head. "Rest here with your men, take whatever you want as some small gift from my love for all of you . . . ." And Valmiki in his old, holy hermitage talked with great gratitude of the battle of Lanka, as if it had happened just before his eyes, and not ten thousand years before.

"I invite you and all your people to Rama's festival," said Satrughna.

"I accept, we'll be there."

Late that evening Satrughna lay half asleep with his companions in one of the huts of Valmiki's retreat. And there in the night, from somewhere among the dark forest trees around him, he heard verses and parts of a musical song—

> . . . *Only the starbeams showed it then;*
> *Rama the refuge of the world,*
> *And all my hopes.* . . .

Satrughna heard Earth's first poetry, two high voices singing a true song telling everything just as it had been. Kusa and Lava were running through pieces of Rama's story in the dark wood, and Satrughna lay still and listened until they stopped.

> *In the land of King Janaka*
> *Is Shiva's bow no man can bend,*
> *Even in a dream.* . . .

Then they changed—

> *Out from the land, out from the land,*
> *There goes Hanuman swift as the Wind*
> *Racing to Lanka over the Sea,*
> *And Rama's ring gleams gold in his hand.*

Satrughna closed his eyes. The voices sang, and he saw Naga serpents with jewels shining in their heads at night, saw the Demon King and a golden deer, heard the screams of Jatayu the Vulture . . . was the past happening again before his eyes? Is this really Dandaka Forest again?

When silence returned the Kosalas were stunned and quiet a long time. They had tears in their eyes, they were breathing fast. Then they said, "We hear in song the past of long ago made alive again, as though happening right now. An excellent song, we see it all around us. It is a wonder, a precious treasure! Words like these were never heard before. Where are we, in what dream?"

They asked Satrughna, "Find Valmiki, discover whose song this is."

But Satrughna said, "After a long time the old memories return to my mind. It is wrong to pry into a saint's life. There are many mysteries here, and it is not for us to speak of them at all."

In the clear bright morning Satrughna departed. Once more returned to Fair Ayodhya he walked with Rama outside by the palace, under the falling blossom petals like white snow, and said, "I went far away and came back. Majesty, I will never more travel away from you."

Farewell Again,
My Lady and My King

*Rama, only you deserve the gift of this
first poem.*

Valmiki the Morning Star of Song!

And so it was, Saunaka, that in this very Naimisha Forest
where we are now, Rama gave a celebration and festival one
age of the world ago. The Kosalas cleared a great field by the
river, long and wide, and built guesthouses of brick. All work
was begun at the right hours on the right days, and in a
month a fairground stood complete.

It was less than a day from the city, but it was in the fair
countryside among the wild roses, among the flowering trees
of gold and red like smokeless fires, and the honeysuckle
vines, and lotus ponds of red and white and blue where weeping trees bent trailing their leaves.

Rama's guests arrived through welcome archways and gifts
were given. Brahmanas remembered the rules to make things
right in other worlds, and for this one, there were everywhere
hearty feasts and a wonderful hospitality. There were salons
for beautiful courtesans and homes for ascetics, taverns and
baths, stables and theatres. And at dawn, at the end of a
warm night under the stars, King Rama and Prince Lakshmana rode from Ayodhya to Naimisha Forest and opened
the festival park.

They found Vasishtha the brahmana and Rama said, "Let
it begin; let no barrier block my thanksgiving; let no flaw occur."

"Majesty, follow me." Vasishtha led Rama apart and the
King bathed at sunrise and spent the morning alone. He
bathed again at noon and all over the forest ground the fires
were lit and fed with butter, and brahmanas called the gods
to take their shares and offerings. Then Rama entered and

stood by his royal forest pavilion and rooms receiving people, and beside him as his partner in the merit of that feast and sacrifice was a golden image of Sita, dressed in gold cloth and wearing gold flowers.

Sita's father King Janaka came from Mithila; Viswamitra the brahmana came down from his hills; Guha the hunter king and his people came from the Secret Forest; Vibhishana and the old Rakshasi Trijata and many demons came from Lanka; King Aswapati with thundering running horses came from high Kekeya; Sugriva and Hanuman and Jambavan the bear and all the animals were there; the vulture king Sampati came from ruling Dandaka Forest; Sumantra and Bharata and Satrughna and the three Queen Mothers arrived; eighty thousand Kings came from every land in wonderful pomp and splendor, riding slowly through the smiling people; and the Poet Valmiki with his household also came, and in a solitary corner of Rama's clearing they all made little cottages of vines and boughs and lived in them, away from crowds and near the water.

Peace and good fortune be unto brahmanas and cows! First King Rama gave away all the world to the brahmanas, and Vasishtha spoke for them, "We cannot rule Earth's four quarters, Lord. We have no time away from our lonely thought and study." And Rama bought back the world from them and gave out her price in gold and cattle. King Janaka the husband of Earth looked on smiling to see land bought and sold by mortal men.

There in Naimisha everything good was gathered. Monkeys and demons gave out gifts. Everyone had a good time—the old, right, good-time ways! The world was all nice, for a change. Rama and the Kosalas—they were indeed great men.

At that celebration no one was judged and need was provided for and loud words softly answered. Men were transported by wine and carried away by women; the women were clothed in excitement and bright new robes. People sat by lovely easy stairways on the riverside, feasting under umbrellas and fans. Village girls danced with the dread royal warriors no longer grave and serious, and Hanuman and Jambavan chased animal children through the trees and streets, and they almost caught them eight hundred and thirty-seven times, and the celebration really started.

King Sugriva stood in the kitchens among the meats and

spices and steaming savory sauces along with Vibhishana and
many monkeys and bears and demons. The two kings said,
"Receive and serve our friends and please them. Be peaceful
and be generous. Cherish our guests. Don't be careless, don't
throw presents and shove food at people. You will be pouring
out the treasures of Ayodhya, and beware lest their mere
touch make you greedy."

When all had arrived Rama thanked them for coming and
housed them, and brahmanas blessed him by a three-sided
brick fire-altar. Then throughout the clearing priests set up
twenty-one ornamental stakes carved of fine woods, each taller than a man, with eight sides and hung with bright strips
of colored cloth and flowers and jewels like stars.

Among those stakes strutted the proud and powerful Kings
and Emperors of the world drinking from winejars and talking. They said, "Rama never came to us to fight Ravana, or
it would have been over just like that! Just right! That's the
whole truth—lucky for the demons!"

Hanuman was stuffed with apricots and apples and he
heard them from where he sat with Jambavan the bear
against a tree. He finished some wine and strolled grinning
into their midst, and bowed low to the Great King of the
East and to the Lord of the Western Tribes. Then he looked
up at them with a really silly smile and answered, "Oh Lords
don't think you're useless—we were but the blind instruments
of Ravana's death . . . he was really killed by your fatal
strength of tongue!" And Hanuman rolled laughing and
laughing in the dust, till the towering bear king came and
gently picked him up and carried him away in his furry arms
still laughing and kicking his feet in the air. And old Jambavan smiled and growled, "Why in the old days . . . ."

And also later on that first day of Rama's festival, we two
began to sing this song *Ramayana*, and everyone grew still
and quiet around us, and the King came to listen.

Now we have done this every day, for the year of this festival here in Naimisha Forest. And today is the last day of
your celebration, Majesty.

These will be the last verses of this song of our teacher
Valmiki.

Oh Rama, well done! We are delighted to see you and to
meet your courtesy. After walking over Earth of many fields
and ways we arrived here with some people of our hermitage,

and came along aisles of food and wines. Your demons scared us a little, for though we have often sung of them yet we had never seen one beside us.

Lion among Kings, we have spoken with the wise men of the forest who see all things as Brahma. They have seen the gods come here each day in the smoke of offerings and return much brightened to their heavens. You have given away a whole year's gifts and your treasury is still full. This is how things truly are, Rama. There is in you some grace that warms the hearts of all who know you, and without knowing why, men find that their lives and fortunes are good, when they are by you.

A year ago when we came here, Valmiki the first Poet in the world brought with us a basket of ripe mangoes from a hilltop by our hermitage. He poured them out on our small cottage floor and said, "Eat these right now, and your voices cannot fail, your memory cannot stray for the rest of your lives. Both of you, sing my *Ramayana* to the King. Today after bathing, go to an open place near Rama and start to sing. He will hear his name and come; sing well for him as you have done for me. Sing in parts, a little every day. Take no reward for it; of what use are riches to hermits living in the wild, eating roots and wearing skins? If Rama soon asks of you your names, say that you are my disciples. But each day before you start, first bow to the King as to a father, for he is the father of all the living people in his land."

"Indeed," said Kusa and Lava, "now the time is the present and we have finished all the sections of *Ramayana*."

Then, Saunaka, the two boys stopped singing, and Kusa held straight out his open hand and turned it over, saying— *This is all my story*.

Sauti the storyteller said, "But a thousand years later Valmiki composed the last part of *Ramayana*."

Saunaka who lived in the forest said, "Then there is more!"

Sauti smiled. "At Rama's festival this would have been a song of the future. Rama never heard these last verses, and they tell of the rest of his life."

Listen, my friend—

After Rama's great departure, and a thousand years after his festival here in Naimisha Forest, those after years of Rama's life were revealed to Valmiki as before. He taught his later verses to Kusa and Lava and they first sang them as grown men, there in Valmiki's hermitage to a forest audience.

Kusa and Lava welcomed the poem with great joy, and when they had learned it they tuned the lute and tightened the drum. Under the blue skies of many mornings they sang a little every day. Their voices were deep but they had lost no skill nor art. Kusa and Lava began to sing and many listeners gathered round them and Valmiki smiled. All the forest animals were hushed and still, and birds flew to hear.

They sang, "Be at your ease, free your mind from ill-will and all unkindness. Let go of anger and hear us ever without malice. Now hear the end—We sing a song of kingly fame, Oh Listen. . . ."

Now oh Father you begin to know who we were there singing to you, and why you have looked at us thinking to know us and wondering who we were . . . .

When Kusa and Lava sang Valmiki's song to King Rama every day for a year at his feast in the forest, people gathered round in a circle from every nation all over the world. The desert men and the people from beyond the hills, the silk-merchants and men from the Land of Gold all listened. Rakshasas and monkeys and bears listened, many figures, all still. At other times there was mirth and merry cheer, men were tired with elaborate pleasures, or did their jobs and followed their crafts. But when those two boys sang they stopped to hear.

There were gathered the King, old men of science and young mothers holding their children, actors and palm readers and fat cooks, grim philosophers who could answer every question but the one, and young warriors fearless of harm from all men's armies. Their hair stood on end, their hearts were ravished, each one was drawn into the music and story of Rama's Way as though it were the tale of his own life, unrolling there before him in great beauty and with great praise.

The audience were breathtaken and delighted with the charms of those verses of Valmiki; they were entranced and spellbound in rapture, surprised and wonderstruck; they laughed and cried aloud. Every day when Kusa and Lava

quit singing, ascetics snapped their fingers and waved their
upper garments in the air and shook their waterjars, and
noble kings threw their heavy bracelets into the circle. But
Kusa and Lava would let all such treasures lie and touched
none of them.

Ramayana is a fabulous and wonderful tale, an old well-
loved story of the younger age of the world. And now it ends
with this farthest last-following part. It will be the inspiration
and give themes to poets of the future, for this story of Rama
will endure forever in this world.

Ramayana will gain the hearer long life, health and
strength and a good and beautiful wife, every merit and
profit and success and skill. He will have children and riches
and good friends, and all his desires will be won. He will get
over every trouble and have good crops. The gods will be delighted with him.

This book frees a house from evil spirits. May good betide
you. In our bodies, there is inside the heart a spirit living quietly, and if a man will be victorious let him be tuned and at
one with this quiet person, and that brings happiness to the
gods and good to himself.

> *I am Valmiki's song;*
> *Valmiki made me:*
> *Ever true;*
> *Just for you.*

The greatest excellence, the one thing that made Rama's
festival so wonderful was the singing of Kusa and Lava, their
good music and fine words. Those two young boys sang
Ramayana to a silver-stringed lute and a two-headed drum.
They sang in unison or at intervals. The drum beat along
swift as rainfall or lingered in silence. The lute sang; it cried
and warned. It fought through perils, through chance and
sorrow; it triumphed and rejoiced.

On the last day of the festival Kusa and Lava ended all
Valmiki's verses of that time, and Vibhishana the demon said,
"Wonderful it is, after a long time the old recollections come
again to my mind. All you have said is true."

Sugriva the Monkey King told them, "Sunlight and glory,
song and wine! We must always feed the storytellers and give
them presents."

But Kusa and Lava took up their lute and drum and set

out for their cottage as they did after every day's singing.
And Rama looked after them and thought, "They are just
like me, boys just as I was then."

Rama told Lakshmana, "The longer I hear those two boys
sing the more I love to listen; the longer I look on them the
more I want to see them. Go follow them and give them
whatever they want."

Lakshmana caught up to Kusa and Lava and said, "We are
never satisfied hearing your song. Blessings and long life to
you. Blessed be you, blessed be! Beautiful is Valmiki's story,
beautifully have you sung and ended it. The King offers
you—"

"No, no," answered Kusa and Lava. "Thank the King, and
we must go to our master Valmiki."

Lakshmana returned to Rama, "They refuse all reward for
that tale whose words are touched by song."

"Those twin brothers are my two sons," said Rama. He
called Hanuman and said, "Son of the Wind, find Sita in Valmiki's house. Here and now this very day will I take her back
home with me before all my people."

Hanuman soon returned with the Poet Valmiki. Valmiki
said, "Majesty, good fortune to you. A husband is a wife's
lord, and Sita will come to you."

"She is here!"

"Rama, I will bring her to you. Those two boys are your
sons Kusa and Lava. They were born in my retreat."

"I know." Rama smiled and put his hand on Valmiki's
shoulder. "You have brought verse in to the world, and now
anyone can start a poem, but you have brought yours to a
blazing wonderful finish. You've brought it all together; you
did it right!"

Valmiki asked, "Did you like it, Rama?"

"It is excellent, Valmiki, I say it is excellent. I shall never
forget those verses."

"Oh Lord!"

"Poet, you have brought happiness to us all . . . I loved it
well. Surely you knew I liked it?"

"No, I didn't . . . if you don't tell me, how will I know?
You have to say." Valmiki smiled.

And Rama said, "See how the world flowers! All good
things have come to men."

Then Valmiki waved his arms. "Lord Rama like the Moon,
you are a mortal man. She loves you. The bounty of Earth is
not your doing, Majesty." Valmiki knelt down. "For ten

thousand years you lived with her, and for twelve she's been away. The ten thousand years were the rich ones. King, with your permission Sita will meet you this day."

Tears flowed down Rama's face from his green eyes. "Rise, Poet."

That afternoon everyone at the festival assembled outside, sitting motionless in a circle around the Ayodhya throne in the clearing where Rama's sons had sung his story, holding their breaths, not talking. Rama sat on his throne and the people left wide room around him. The golden statue of Sita had been carried away.

Then the crowd parted and Sita came there following Valmiki. She was beautiful; she walked looking down, but glancing up at Rama many times. Valmiki stopped, and Sita stood alone by Rama within that circle of people, dressed in bright gold and scarlet.

Then into that circle stepped King Janaka, Sita's father the Videha lord. Janaka had swift wide wisdom like a sharp keen blade; he opened locked doors, he found treasure and the True. In his youth Janaka fought a hundred battles. He took hard blows and gave harder. But then he changed. He was Earth's husband, and never more put his heart away behind armor.

Earth's forests and furrows confused his enemies and his kingdom was safe in the foothills. Janaka took all men for brothers; he ever watched for a stray life to save. Passing pleasures called him, in forms quite beautiful, but Janaka did what he knew was right and forgot the people who said he was wrong. And being free, having nothing to hide however small, he found the far sweetest pleasure of speaking out his mind to any man. He wed the Earth and loved her.

Janaka thought it all out for himself, and fought for Dharma. He warred on the loss of love through unkindness and the fetters of wrong desire; he fought for freedom by blasting off the chains of attachment; he killed deceptions with words that released the spirit. It was a hard fight, and Janaka told his warriors—*I give up owning the world's gear. I give up thirst for things to find true love, that never fades.* And his best guard of warriors answered—*We'll keep your word, we'll obey our King. We put down our swords and take the robes of harmless men. What?! Shall we have faced all our wars together and not go into this fight beside you?*

Janaka said to Rama, "There is no blame for this."

Rama answered, "Forgive me, and forgive us all." The people pressed forward around that circle.

Janaka raised his voice, "Ring this circle!" And his unarmed warriors stepped forward from the crowd, wayfarers to the True, and they joined their strong hands and arms like iron, and formed an inner wall that held everyone back.

Janaka said, "King Rama, I'll give you ten million pieces of gold if you will abandon your throne, and use your strength in my service."

Rama was startled. "I can't do that, Janaka."

"Then I offer you nine million pieces."

"But I cannot, it is wrong," said Rama.

"But I'll give you five million in gold."

"No."

"One million then," said Janaka.

"No."

"A thousand to serve me!"

"Janaka, what are you doing?" asked Rama. "In the world of men one offers more and more of money for what he cannot get at first, but you have swiftly lowered the price."

Janaka answered, "So quickly does your life pass by! Now men may live many thousand years, but what do you think? Is that long to put off what must be done?"

"It seems but a short while to me also."

"How long might it truly be then?"

Rama replied, "It is really but the time of one day. A whole lifetime may seem to have been very short as it closes, like a morning and an afternoon spent in the sunlight as Night comes."

"No," said Janaka.

"It is but an hour," said Rama.

"No, not even an hour."

"A lifetime, that is the time it takes to fill a waterjar at the riverside."

"You have not understood me."

Rama said, "All our life is but the blink of an eye."

"Yes," said Janaka, "now you understand. Make haste to follow the good Dharma law; hurry to do right while you can, before it's too late." Janaka embraced his daughter Sita. "I sowed seed in Earth and tended her, and she bore you to me from a plowed field. I've loved you all your life, though I let you marry and go."

Janaka left Sita alone with Rama, surrounded by specta-

tors. Sita looked at Rama and smiled. She looked out at the
people, and smiled at Sumantra the Charioteer, and at Trijata
the old Rakshasi, and at Lakshmana. Then her smile widened
bright; she saw Hanuman the monkey there in his best
clothes, wearing the pearls she had given him, his white hair
finely brushed like a halo round his head.

Hanuman smiled happily back at her, and when he did a
scented cool wind blew lightly through Naimisha Forest. That
was heaven's wind, come down to Earth as a witness. Vayu
the Wind Lord threw gladness and joy over all of them there,
like a wealthy king scattering jewels and flowers with abandon on all his friends. As when the world was newfound,
when Earth was young, a springtime wind blew again once
more through heaven and Earth and sky, all one.

Sita was forever beautiful. Wearing her ornaments she
turned slowly around and looked at every person there.
"Rama, let me prove my innocence, here before everyone."

"I give my permission," said Rama.

Then Sita stepped a little away from him and said,
"Mother Earth, if I have been faithful to Rama take me
home, hide me!"

Earth rolled and moved beneath our feet. With a great
rumbling noise the ground broke apart near Sita and a deep
chasm opened, lighted from below with bright lights like
lightning flashes, from the castles of the Naga serpent kings.

From underground rose four tall Nagas, like great cobras,
the treasure guardians of Earth's riches; their hoods were flat
out; they were hissing and weaving, swaying and spitting fire,
turning their red eyes at the people; they were all dressed in
jewels and rippling silver scales like moonlight on the ocean's
waves at night. That opening widened, the serpents were one
at each corner, and from below rose up a throne carved of
stones, and wrought of roots and set with diamonds.

On that throne sat Mother Earth. Earth was not old, she
was fair to look on, she was not sad but smiling. She wore
flowers and a girdle of seas. Earth supports all life, but she
feels no burden in all that. She is patient. She was patient
then, under the Sun and Moon and through the rainfalls of
countless years. She was patient with seasons and with kings
and farmers; she endured all things and bore no line of care
from it.

But this was the end of her long patience with Rama.
Earth looked at her husband Janaka and smiled. Then she
stretched out her arms and took her only child Sita on her

lap. She folded her beautiful arms around her daughter and laid Sita's head softly against her shoulder as a mother would. Earth stroked her hair with her fair hands, and Sita closed her eyes like a little girl.

The throne sank back underground and they all were gone; the Nagas dove beneath the ground and the crevice closed gently over them, forever.

The gods spoke, "Well done, Oh Sita. Praise to you." And every person watching Sita's descent into Earth, and all living creatures in the world were very happy. For a moment the whole Universe was everywhere equal. Happiness and great delight spread over the three worlds. Men cried aloud in joy; or were silent and held still by their happiness, unable to move. The wild animals of Naimisha Forest watched motionless from the trees as flowers fell from heaven above—yellow and red, blue and white and orange gold . . . .

Rama smiled. "I am King and Lord of Earth, but she has taken my wife away before my very eyes. I will never meet Sita again while I live as a man." Rama sighed, and still he was smiling. He turned to King Janaka. "Indeed, it is a brief life given to Man—but the Dream, the Dream!"

That festival and sacrifice was finished. It was excellent; it destroyed big and little sins, it brought heaven to everyone there. The guests departed, the foreign kings went home, and the ground shook with the tread of elephants and horses and the chariot wheels.

After the others had departed, Janaka and Rama, Lakshmana and Hanuman sat on the bare ground and drank wine in the afternoon. After one cup Lakshmana held his head and covered his eyes and fell over asleep. After a second round Hanuman dropped off. Janaka and Rama drank a third cup and Rama rubbed his eyes.

"What drink is this?"

"Varuni, the Goddess of Spirits, made this palm wine to bring sleep. Overcome her, drink her down."

Rama leaned back against a tree. "Janaka, why am I here? What am I doing here? Can you tell me why?"

"Whatever you have done, you did it to serve the good Dharma Law." Janaka filled the winecups and once more they both drank deep, sitting in the cool shade. "Rama, may you have love for us so we may find some place in your heart."

"I have."

"The honors you have given and the good words, these are natural to you. You are Rama, you are my safe refuge. We do not know what more to say to you. Lord, we have gone far, and we find you there still farther beyond us." Rama slept, and Janaka got to his feet and walked away.

Viswamitra, who had first taken Rama from Ayodhya as a boy, and King Janaka walked together back to Mithila city in the Videha land, just the two of them going by back roads and woodland trails. After a few days they began to climb into the foothills, and they could see Janaka's city.

They walked across the rich fields of Videha, through the new-plowed dirt, and Vishwamitra said, "Remember them? They were sixteen, and everyone loved Rama even then."

"See those trees?" asked Janaka. "They grow from fragments of Shiva's bow, thrown under Earth when Rama broke it."

"With one pull, after all the world had failed!" Viswamitra the friend of all stood leaning on his mendicant's staff. "Rama is a heart-winning man. He freed Ahalya the Beautiful, and she pressed beauty into him with her hand."

Janaka said, "There's no other person as brave as Rama."

Viswamitra answered, "There's Sita."

"There is no one else, only Rama! If you tell such lies get out of my ancestral kingdom."

Viswamitra smiled. "I obey. Where is your kingdom? Where do your lands end? What are the limits of your realm, and where is the dominion of another king?"

Janaka looked around, this way and that. "Well, my kingdom is not these fields, it might be the city."

"Where?"

"No, I see nothing of mine there. Surely then, my own body must be my kingdom, and I will look . . . ."

"What do you find?" asked Viswamitra.

"You may go or stay anywhere as long as you like," smiled Janaka. "Even this body is not mine, this I am not. It is no part of me. Or else—I rule all space, for I do not hold onto the sounds that enter these ears; I rule all land, for I desire no scents but let them come and go; I rule the waters for I do not grasp at any taste; my eye does not cling to lights and colors and so I rule all fire; I care not for any touch, nor do I avoid it, and so I rule the air and winds. . . ."

Viswamitra said, "Janaka, no craving nor thirst have you. You have found the everlasting Dharma wheel and truly set it turning, set it rolling out of the hills and past the reach of Death and beyond the rule of Time; beyond rebirth; beyond old age, beyond sickness, beyond death again—the glorious Wheel of the Good Law, the Dharma Law a man may win for himself as he wins a battle, with a lion-roar of victory and a shout of great joy!"

Janaka reached down and held the rich dark Earth in his hands. "Dissolution is the end of all things compounded out of the elements and each man fares according to his deeds." He crumbled the soil and let it fall through his fingers. "Sita has died to this world. May all beings everywhere be happy and safe! May all creatures born or seeking to be born have happy minds, may none wish another ill! May loving kindness wash over the worlds!"

Naimisha Forest was deserted and the jungle quickly grew back over Rama's clearing. Kusa and Lava and the poet Valmiki returned to their forest home. Rama ruled in Fair Ayodhya for a thousand years more, alone without Sita, keeping her golden statue by him in her palace rooms.

After a long time Queen Kausalya died looking on Rama's face. Then Sumitra and Kaikeyi followed her to the peaceful land of the dead, then to the Moon, and then wearing robes of light to heaven where they were all three united with King Dasaratha, and where no one is old.

Then one spring morning, after those thousand years were full, Time in the guise of a hermit came quietly to the Ayodhya palace door and told Lakshmana, "A powerful King sends me as an ambassador to Rama."

Lakshmana led the hermit inside to a private room and brought Rama. Rama asked, "Whose message do you bear?"

"Maharaja," said Time, "let us talk alone. Lion among Kings, good fortune to you. Oh King of the World and Lord of Men, Oh Rama order the door to this room closed while I am here with you, and promise me that anyone who shall see us together or overhear our words shall die."

"I promise. Lakshmana, shut the door and stand yourself outside, and prevent anyone from entering."

When they were alone Rama said, "Speak freely. Who sends you here to me?"

The hermit faced him. "Father, I am Kala, I am Time. I bring Brahma's words. But to speak first for myself, you stand always beyond me, you are forever older than I, and so

I call you Father. Whatever goes beyond me, you make it go. But even for you strength and youth pass away, and I flow as a river with no obstacle in her bed and nothing to hold her back, once gone by never to return. Spend me or waste me as you will, I can nevermore turn back to you."

Rama said, "Your end is your beginning, you start when you finish. Long since, my child, did the Sun and Moon and stars appear, and Time began to run again. You are my own dear son and my good true servant. You open the spring flowers and unite lovers. You forgive all; you hurt, then you heal. Time will always tell. Sooner or later you reveal all secrets, and you are wise, all the lore of all worlds knowing."

Time said, "I bring love, I marry men and women, I keep the little babies alive. I make the moon rise and I give food and wealth. Do you speak? . . . I let you. Do you do good? . . . My hand guides yours. When you meet a great new day . . . I made it come. It is all one, Rama, all the time that ever was or will be is all one . . . end and beginning are hard to see and they are one, Rama . . . ." Time smiled. "And oh, I lie a lot, Rama . . . I must admit . . . ."

Rama answered, "Time, you have taken dear parts of my life and put them beyond my reach. I have lived through so many cold winters and scented springtimes, so many days and nights that I cannot believe there will not always be more and more of them."

"Ah," said Time, "there you overreach me, I know nothing of poetry."

"What are Brahma's words?"

"Listen. The Grandfather of the worlds tells you—

You killed Ravana. Your promised time is full. Oh Nara-yana, Lakshmi awaits you, so have I heard. I send Time to re-mind you. Return to yourself, my friend, we have not seen you for a moment in heaven.

Rama replied, "Those are good words, I am pleased with your coming. I've not forgotten. I remember all of you. . . ."

And as Rama and Time were talking a while, the short-tempered brahmana Durvasas, a grim self-denying ascetic, a sky-clad hermit walked quickly up to Lakshmana at the door and said, "My time is passing! I need food, take me in there first to see the King."

"Great saint, Rama is busy," said Lakshmana. "Command me what to do and I will serve you."

Durvasas wiped some ashes from his brow. "I've just finished my fast and after many years the King must feed me! Admit me to him, I am impatient. Or I will curse all Kosala to burn if you do not announce me this instant."

"Those are dreadful words."

"Every soul will die. My anger is rising, I cannot restrain my growing wrath!"

"Forsake your ill will. My own death is better." Lakshmana pulled open the door. Time's iron staff fell from his hand and clanged on the stone floor, and that noise rang in Lakshmana's ears like the pealing of bells.

Lakshmana went in. "Durvasas needs to see you, Rama."

Rama said, "Lakshmana, you must die for entering here."

Time and Lakshmana looked at each other, and Lakshmana said, "Yes. Great halls are silent after Time has visited them, and dark and hidden is this person's course."

Time said, "Say not so, Lakshmana, say not so. I know the old deeds dimly remembered, the youthful deeds of past lives." Time looked into Lakshmana's blues eyes, blue as wildflowers, and backed away toward the door. "Oh people all like to abuse me, but I always politely wait my turn, I never crowd in. Rama's heart is boundless, above, below, and all around him. I take away, I take away all the things I've given, but no more than that. You four brothers have all the same nature. You will only go home first. Just as you are, you have won! Well, I must be moving on, Lakshmana, I can never stand still . . . ."

Rama said, "Kala, go, I dismiss you."

Oh, the Dharma Wheel, like a rolling golden Sun!

Then Rama fed the recluse Durvasas, until after a hundred dishes he was full, and without a word that brahmana turned his back on the king and went away into the forests somewhere.

Rama looked at Lakshmana. "Farewell, my brother."

Lakshmana made no answer. He walked three times around Rama, and left the palace. He went half a league to where the Sarayu river swiftly flowed.

Lakshmana sat by the running river. With open eyes he looked around him and saw all things as Rama, thought of them as Rama. He rinsed his mouth with the clear water and stopped his breathing. The luminous person within Lakshmana's heart, the soul no bigger than a thumb made ready to leave this world behind. The life-centers stopped spinning and went out, and Lakshmana's energy, the fourth part of Lord Narayana, rose step by step up along his backbone, seeking flight out the crown of his head where the skull bones join their seams.

Lakshmana shut his eyes and watched the lights of his life slowly die. The lights of war long ago, the lights of his first love and marriage . . . the lights of his childhood . . . . And he thought, ". . . it's like—something that I made once . . . all of us. . . ."

In heaven, Lord Indra heard empty stone vault doors closing one after another in echoes. Sight was closing, hearing closing, mind turning away. Spirit was rising and leaving empty rooms. The ether space within the heart was empty, fires and lamps turned off, locks and threads snapped and untied, and all released.

Indra swept across Kosala invisibly. He took Lakshmana's soul into his own heart and flew to heaven carrying him and bearing light. Indra the bright King of the Sky took him away. Lakshmana's body fell into the water and was gone.

Shiva the great god divided this romance into three parts, one for heaven, one for Earth, and one for the underworlds. He had one section left, and divided that into three. He had one verse left, and divided that as well. Shiva had one word left, that he kept for himself—the word *Rama*—as being the essence and heart of the whole thing.

One who sees Rama even for a moment gains heaven. He is Narayana, identical with the souls of all creatures. He is the Ocean and the forests and the air I breathe. He is more subtle than an atom. He goes everywhere by illusion, without beginning or end, unchangeable, unconquerable, holding a shell trumpet and a wheel, a mace and a lotus flower. So let us remember him when we are in any difficulty, from inside or out.

Tomorrow won't always be like today. Now, while there is time, today take this *Ramayana* to your home before the great world ends for you. Tune your senses to Dharma, say *Rama* while you have a chance, and make your heart a loving holy place, lighten it, clear it of good and evil, or high and low.

Very happy, or near to tears;
So keep this book, and live your years.
Oh Rama!

Thunders rolled over Ayodhya although the sky was clear. The white houses rocked and Earth shook. The brahmana Vasishtha was with Rama, and Rama said, "Where is my life and where am I? I'm going all the way on through to my own home now, I'm going back around by going forward, and I'll be again as I was before being born into this world. . . ."

Vasishtha said, "Look out at your city. The people kneel outside their homes; they lower their heads and do not move, or lie like corpses."

Goodbye, Rama; goodbye Father, goodbye, goodbye . . . .

Bharata and Satrughna entered, and Bharata said, "Fair Ayodhya is ended as we have known her."

Vasishtha said, "Majesty, I'll leave you now. I'll go alive to heaven for awhile, and rest and tend the cow of wishes in her peaceful pasture." And he left them there.

I think the Fair Ayodhya that Rama knew must now be sought for elsewhere than on this Earth. Those were other days. But though I must dream or die to do it—I've been to Fair Ayodhya and I'll go back there again.

Rama asked his brothers, "What can I do?"

"Don't forsake us, don't leave us behind," said Bharata.

"That's all we ask," said Satrughna. "Now all of us will follow the Well-Farer."

Rama asked, "Why will you go with me?"

"Near you is ever all my happiness."

"Whoever will, let them come. Then go and send the Kosalas who wish to stay behind on Earth to places far from here. Give them wealth and chariots and elephants; let them leave me and go into the woods or to the seas, or into the snowy hills."

Then learning somehow of Rama's great departure, that very day to Ayodhya came the monkeys and dark bears of the forest, and the Lanka king Vibhishana from over the sea. They spoke among themselves, "Now the waiting's done, now the day has come. Who would not be ready to follow you? . . ." The animals stood along the streets beside Kosala men and Gandharvas of heaven, beside Nagas from the underworld and hermits from the empty wood, all still and silent, waiting by the palace walls and gates, and along the roads to the Sarayu River.

The Kosalas told them, "Lakshmana is lost for a flawless promise. Dasaratha's four sons are dead. We follow Rama."

Vibhishana the dark demon said, "Set out the great brilliant umbrellas along the northern high road to the riverside."

Hanuman said, "That will look well, but if you want a high road to heaven, just say *Rama*."

Rama came walking on the streets. He wore thin green silk and held in his right fingers a sheaf of grass. He turned to the north, humming some of the song Kusa and Lava had sung a thousand years before. Our Lady Lakshmi of the Lotus walked on his right; Mother Earth went patiently on his left. And behind him walked many weapons in human forms, sharp spears and arrows and huge bows, merciless swords and heavy-set maces and the howling knives of war, and many tears of blood ran from their hard eyes.

First Vibhishana wearing gold approached Rama and said, "Let me also go through the open gates."

Rama replied, "Lanka King, you are immortal. Death will never touch you, while my memory lives. As long as the Moon and Sun and Earth shall exist, as long as the mountains and rivers continue on Earth's face, as long as the sea beats with his eternal waves against the solid land, so long shall my wonderful story of *Ramayana* remain in the world."

Then Sugriva the Monkey King came to Rama. "I give Kishkindhya to Angada. I will go with you."

Rama said, "Yes."

Jambavan the bear bowed to Rama. He did not speak, only a low growl came from his throat. Rama blessed the Bear King and said, "You will live while Valmika's *Ramayana* is heard on Earth." He bent close and gave Jambavan a charm, a present, something precious. "And Hanuman also will live so long, where is he now?"

Hanuman came bounding down from the sky. He hit the ground with a thud like a thunderstone. He was right close to Rama, smiling at him, laughing and gay.

"Oh Hanuman!"

"My King!" Hanuman knelt before Rama.

Rama said, "As long as men shall speak of you, you will live on Earth. No one can equal you. Your heart is true; your arms are strong; you have the energy to do anything. You have served me faithfully and done things for me that couldn't be done."

"It's nothing," said Hanuman. "I am your friend, that's all."

Rama wore a rare golden bracelet set with gemstones on his right arm, a costly irreplaceable ornament inherited from among the wealth of the Solar Kings from ancient days. He said, "Best of Monkeys, take this as my gift," and gave it to Hanuman.

Hanuman snatched the bracelet from Rama and started to turn it over and around in his white furry paws, looking closely at it. Then he bent and broke it; he twisted the gold and pulled out the jewels, and put them between his hard teeth. He bit down on the priceless gems and broke them like nuts, and carefully searched over the pieces, looking everywhere for something.

Rama asked him, "Monkey, at a time like this why are you still difficult?"

Hanuman answered, "Lord, though this bracelet looked expensive it was really worthless, for nowhere on it did it bear your name. I have no need of it, Rama. What do I want with anything plain?"

Vibhishana sniffed at that. "Then I can't see what value life has to you. Why don't you destroy your body as well?"

Then with his sharp fingernails Hanuman tore open his breast and pulled back the flesh. And see! There was written again and again on every bone, in fine little letters—*Rama Rama Rama Rama Rama* . . . .

Rama put down the grass he held, and with his two hands he pressed together Hanuman's parted flesh, and the wound over his beating heart came together leaving no scar at all, not even one big as a grain of dust, or the tip of a hair. Rama drew off his hand his broad gleaming gold ring that said *Rama*, the ring that Hanuman had carried to Sita. He put it into Hanuman's wet bloodstained paw and gently closed the monkey fingers over it.

Who is this monkey Hanuman? Rama has let him loose in the world. He knows Rama and Rama knows him. Hanuman can break in or break out of anywhere. He cannot be stopped, like the free wind in flight.

Hanuman can spot a tyrant, he looks at deeds not words, and he'll go and pull his beard. Disguises and words of talk cannot confuse a mere wild animal. Hanuman's rescue of brave poets in any peril may be had for their asking, and that monkey will break the handsome masks of evil kings.

Hanuman will take your sad tune and use it to make a

happy dance. We have seen that white monkey. Strong is his guard. Especially take warning, never harm a free Poet.

The Son of the Wind. The warm dry night wind, and all the trees swaying! I don't care for love or death or loneliness—here comes the high Wind, and what am I ... ?

Vibhishana and Hanuman and Jambavan the bear flew away. Rama stood speechless and bright and brilliant, like the lighted Sun.

Rama walked on to the Sarayu River, and whoever saw him pass followed him. Many stones wept that they had to stay behind, leaving streaks and marks one can still see. The tall trees swayed and bent creaking after him, and water ran along beside Rama's road. Some birds called out to him—*Stay right there, stay right there*—while others said—*go far, go fast! Go fast! We'll follow you, you.*

The deer came crashing noisily up through the brush and onto the road. Dumb beasts were walking along beside greatminded men. Little animals never seen in the city were going with Rama. Whoever breathed tried to follow him ... children skipped and ran, and women walked together, talking to monkeys and bears.

It was just afternoon, and they all passed between colored rows of Ayodhya umbrellas. Death was watching. Death wept with joy to see those beautiful colors, all like a glorious sunrise.

Oh Rama, nobody knows all of you. But here by Sarayu's water, we will step through, Lord.

By the river, in the saffron shade of the last umbrella stood Guha the hunter king, and Sumantra the old charioteer beaming in joy. Sumantra had freed the four royal red horses, but they followed him and stood there. Wild hunters wearing skins and feathers knelt barefoot and waited, resting their long bamboo spears pointing up to the sky.

Animal and human people touched and reached out to each other up and down that riverside then. A green hand and a red one, a bear paw, deer's hoof, little birds' wings, black skin and gold and brown, all touching, and the water flowing by like Time. Bharata gave Rama his birthfire and his brothers' all mixed, and Rama threw them into Sarayu. The fires stopped burning and were peaceful.

Trust the True! The King took a broad jump and went first

By J. A. Jance

J. P. Beaumont Mysteries

UNTIL PROVEN GUILTY • INJUSTICE FOR ALL
TRIAL BY FURY • TAKING THE FIFTH
IMPROBABLE CAUSE • A MORE PERFECT UNION
DISMISSED WITH PREJUDICE • MINOR IN POSSESSION
PAYMENT IN KIND • WITHOUT DUE PROCESS
FAILURE TO APPEAR • LYING IN WAIT
NAME WITHHELD • BREACH OF DUTY
BIRDS OF PREY • PARTNER IN CRIME
LONG TIME GONE • JUSTICE DENIED
FIRE AND ICE • BETRAYAL OF TRUST

Joanna Brady Mysteries

DESERT HEAT • TOMBSTONE COURAGE
SHOOT/DON'T SHOOT • DEAD TO RIGHTS
SKELETON CANYON • RATTLESNAKE CROSSING
OUTLAW MOUNTAIN • DEVIL'S CLAW
PARADISE LOST • PARTNER IN CRIME
EXIT WOUNDS • DEAD WRONG
DAMAGE CONTROL • FIRE AND ICE

Walker Family Thrillers

HOUR OF THE HUNTER • KISS OF THE BEES
DAY OF THE DEAD • QUEEN OF THE NIGHT

Ali Reynolds Mysteries

EDGE OF EVIL • WEB OF EVIL
HAND OF EVIL • CRUEL INTENT
TRIAL BY FIRE • FATAL ERROR

J.A. JANCE

A MORE PERFECT UNION

A J.P. BEAUMONT NOVEL

HARPER

An Imprint of HarperCollinsPublishers

HARPER

An Imprint of HarperCollins*Publishers*
10 East 53rd Street
New York, New York 10022-5299

Copyright © 1988 by J. A. Jance
ISBN 978-0-06-199929-1

First Harper premium printing: October 2011
First Avon Books mass market printing: November 1988

HarperCollins ® and Harper ® are registered trademarks of Harper-Collins Publishers.

Printed in the United States of America

Visit Harper paperbacks on the World Wide Web at
www.harpercollins.com

10 9 8 7 6 5 4

To J. L. and her quarter century
and
To Bill B. whose career as a technical advisor
was also short but brief

CHAPTER 1

"CASSIE, FOR GOD'S SAKE! WHAT THE HELL'S THE BODY doing out there already? I didn't call for the body. We're not set up yet."

Speaking through a megaphone from his perch on a raised boom, movie director Sam "The Movie Man" Goldfarb's voice echoed through the wooden maze of Lake Union Drydock like God himself speaking from the mount.

Cassie was Cassie Young, a punk-looking young woman who served as Goldfarb's right and left hands. She scurried toward the base of the director's boom as she raised a hand-held radio to her lips.

Because I'm a homicide cop, my ears pricked up when I heard the word "body." For the past two weeks I'd been trailing around Seattle, dutifully mother-henning a Hollywood film crew. Officially, I was on special assignment for Mayor Dawson's office, acting as technical advisor to His Honor's old Stanford roommate and buddy, Samuel Goldfarb. Unofficially,

I was doing less than nothing and felt as useless as tits on a boar.

My short venture into the moviemaking business had certainly stripped away the glamour. As far as I can tell, movies are made by crowds of people who mill around endlessly without actually doing anything. I mean nothing happens. They take hours to set up for a scene that takes less than a minute to shoot, or else spend hours shooting a scene that amounts to two seconds of film footage. The whole process was absolutely stultifying. I hated it.

My initial spurt of "body"-fueled adrenaline disappeared quickly. After all, movies are totally make-believe. On a film set, nothing is really what it seems. I naturally assumed that this was more of the same. Leaning back against a workbench in the pipe shop, I shifted my weight to one foot as I attempted to ease the throbbing complaints of the recently reactivated bone spur on my other heel.

I had been whiling away the time by chatting with a garrulous old duffer named Woody Carroll. Woody was a retired Lake Union Drydock employee on tap that day to keep a watchful eye on the cast and crew of *Death in Drydock*. His job was to make sure we didn't do any damage to company property in the course of our Saturday shoot.

Woody told me that he had worked as a carpenter for Lake Union Drydock both before and after World War II. He had been there steadily from the time he got home from a Japanese POW camp in the Philippines until he retired in 1980. He was full of countless stories, and his tales had kept my mind off the bone spur for most of the day. Hiding out from a blazing sun, we had retreated into the gloomy shade of the pipe shop. Seattle was sweltering through an unusually hot, dry August. People who live in the Northwest aren't accustomed to heat.

"I don't know what to think of these young 'uns today," Woody Carroll drawled, picking up his train of thought and resuming our conversation as though nothing had happened. He had been complaining bitterly about the quality of some of the younger employees around the drydock. "They'd rather buy and sell stuff to put up their noses than do an honest day's work. It just beats all."

Outside I could see Cassie Young returning her radio to her pocket. Now, shading her eyes with one hand, she called up to Goldfarb where he remained enthroned on the boom.

"The shop says they're still working on the body. It isn't ready yet."

"Well, what the hell do you call that? It's right in the way of the next shot. Get it out of there, for God's sake! What do you think I pay you for? And where's Derrick's stuntman? I need him. Now!"

Goldfarb had pointed toward a spot in the water near where steep wooden steps led up the wingwall of the drydock. They had been using the boom to shoot a fight scene on the narrow steps with the navy minesweeper *Pledge* looming in the background. Two of the movie's name-brand stars, Derrick Parker and Hannah Boyer, still clung to two-by-four handrails some twenty feet above the solid planking of the pier.

As the entire crew jumped in response to Gold-farb's barked commands, Cassie Young carefully picked her way across a snarled tangle of electrical cords toward the place Goldfarb had indicated.

I didn't much like Cassie. She was a scrawny, red-haired, postadolescent who went in big for the spiked, new-wave look. She wore a thick layer of white pancake makeup. Her eyelashes dripped with heavy, black mascara. She could easily have been mistaken for a refugee from a school for mimes. Looking at her made me grateful she wasn't my daughter, although she and Kelly were probably much the same age.

Cassie and I had crossed swords on numerous occasions during the course of my two-week stint of involuntary servitude on the set of *Death in Drydock*. I had a tough time taking her seriously. The feeling was mutual.

According to Captain Powell, my main assignment as technical advisor was to make sure Goldfarb didn't portray the Seattle Police Department as "a bunch of stupid jerks." I had quickly learned, however, that trying to tell Sam Goldfarb anything he didn't want to hear was like talking to a brick wall. Every time he had his pretend cops doing something unbelievably stupid, I squawked bloody murder. For all the good it did me. Cassie Young didn't mince any words in letting me know that I was to keep those opinions to myself. I was a technical advisor all right. In name only.

For the past week, I had called Captain Powell every morning at eight o'clock, begging him to let me off the hook and pull me from the assignment. No such luck. He kept telling me that the mayor wanted me on the set, and on the set I'd stay.

Still mildly interested in whatever had plucked Goldfarb's nerves, I watched as Cassie reached the edge of the dock and knelt down to peer over the side. Her knees had barely touched the wood when she sprang back as though she'd been burned. She covered her mouth with one hand, but still the muffled sound that escaped her lips was as bloodcurdling a scream as I'd heard in years. The wrenching sound echoed back and forth through the otherwise eerily silent wooden buildings.

For days I had lurked in the background of the process, staying out of the way of cameras and equipment. Now, the sound of Cassie's scream galvanized me to action. No matter what, I'm first and foremost a cop. In emergencies, we're trained to react. It's a conditioned response as natural as breathing. Without giving it a second thought, I started toward Cassie on a dead run, ignoring the quick stab of pain in my injured heel.

"Quiet on the set," someone boomed through a megaphone, but Cassie kept on screaming, pointing hysterically toward the water. I reached her and grabbed her by the shoulders just as the megaphone boomed again. "For God's sake, somebody catch Hannah! She's going to fall."

Cassie barfed then. I managed to swing her away from me just in time, then I held her by the waist while she heaved her guts out on the dock.

Between barfing and screaming, I prefer the latter.

At last Cassie straightened up and leaned heavily against me while her whole body quivered with terrible shudders. I held her, patting her gently on the back, soothing her as best I could, while I attempted to peer over her shoulder and see into the water, but we were too far from the edge of the dock. The angle was wrong.

"What is it?" I demanded finally, holding her at arm's length. "What's down there?"

Shaking her head from side to side, she seemed totally incapable of speech, but as soon as I took a step toward the edge of the dock, she came to life and fought me tooth and nail. Her ability to speak returned as well.

"No, no!" she protested, twisting her wrists to escape my grip. "I can't look again. Please don't make me look again, please."

By then, one of the electricians was standing beside us. I handed Cassie off to him, then went to the edge of the pier to see for myself.

As soon as I did, I understood why Cassie Young had fought my attempt to drag her back.

A corpse floated there in the water, or rather, what was left of a corpse. Although Lake Union has no natural currents to speak of, heavy boat traffic on the lake creates a lot of water movement. This movement, mimicking current, had left the body with its legs straddling a wooden piling.

I could tell the corpse was that of a man, but I could make out little else. The bloated body floated low in the water. What was visible could hardly be called a face. His features were distorted and out of focus where skin slippage and feeding fish had done their ugly work. His hair, slicked down against his scalp, was dark and shiny, matted with oil from the lake.

Horror movies manufacture phony death masks

all the time. Cassie Young was in the movie business. I found it surprising that she took it so hard, that she was so shocked and shaken, but of course horror-movie masks are done in the name of good clean fun. This wasn't fun or make-believe.

This was real—all too real.

I turned around to assess the situation. It was as though everyone on the set was frozen in place. Nobody moved. Nobody said a word. On the top surface of the wingwall stood a cluster of men, grouped in a tight circle around what I assumed to be a stricken Hannah Boyer. I was grateful someone had managed to catch her and drag her to safety. If a twenty-foot fall doesn't kill you, it cripples you up real good.

The first person to move was Woody Carroll, who hurried toward me as fast as his seventy-year-old legs would carry him. He stopped beside me and looked into the water.

"Call 911," I ordered. "Have 'em send an ambulance for Hannah and a squad car for him." Without a word of protest, Woody nodded, turned, and hurried away toward a phone which was visible near the base of the wingwall.

Lake Union Drydock consists of some 500,000-odd square feet, all of it sitting over thirty-five feet of water. Walking or driving, you have to cross a city-owned moat to get there. The various shops and docks are thrown together in a crazy-quilt, hodge-podge pattern. The company has been in continuous existence and use since 1919. Buildings and docks have been added whenever and wherever the spirit moved, giving the whole place a haphazard, thrown-together appearance.

Looking now at the maze of buildings and docks, I wondered how emergency vehicles would ever manage to find us. We were clear out near the base of the largest drydock.

Woody picked up the receiver of the phone. No sooner had he spoken into it than a shrill whistle sounded, sending five short sharp blasts into the air. Woody put the phone down and hurried back to me.

"You'd better go meet them and direct them here to us," I told him. "Otherwise they'll never be able to find us."

Woody laughed. "Those other guys I told you about are already on their way. That's what the whistle's for. Don't worry. They'll find us."

Woody had informed me earlier that a skeleton safety crew was playing cards upstairs in an employee locker room. I hadn't thought we'd need them. Now I was more than happy they were there.

Goldfarb, down from his overhead perch, stormed up behind me. "What's going on, Beaumont?" he demanded. "We've got a movie to shoot. We're losing the light."

In the days I had been on the set I had found Goldfarb to be an altogether disagreeable little man who put his bad temper on a pedestal and called it "Artistic License." I had watched over and over as the whole crew leaped to satisfy his slightest whim. But that was movie business. This was police business, my business—maybe homicide.

The crew suddenly came unstuck. They edged forward, trying to catch sight of whatever was under the dock. I shooed the nearest ones away.

"Get your people out of here, Mr. Goldfarb. We've got emergency vehicles on the way." Even as I spoke, I heard the thin wail of an approaching siren.

"Cops?" Goldfarb screeched, his voice becoming shrill. "You mean somebody's called the cops?"

"That's exactly what I mean, Mr. Goldfarb," I returned.

Goldfarb wasn't my boss, and I had developed a certain immunity to the director's ravings. He was a chronic complainer, always bitching and moaning, always at the top of his lungs.

"You can't do that, Detective Beaumont," he roared back. "You can't bring cops in here and order me to clear out my people."

"Watch me," I said. I turned to Woody. "Do it."

He did, quickly and effectively, leaving Sam "The Movie Man" Goldfarb hopping from foot to foot in total frustration.

"Cassie, can't you stop this?" he wailed. From bellowing one minute, Goldfarb was reduced to whining the next. "Robert Dawson's going to hear about this," he continued to me. "I'll see you fired before the day's over."

Hizzoner can stick it in his ear, I thought. I said, "Be my guest. You do that."

Seattle's Medic One has some of the best response times in the country. An aid car was the first emergency vehicle to appear on the scene. It rattled noisily over the wooden planks and jerked to a stop. I hurried to meet it and directed the medics to the stairs. "The woman's up there," I said, pointing. "On the wingwall."

"Great," the driver replied, shading his eyes and evaluating the perpendicular wall with its steep wooden staircase. "What's wrong with her?"

"Fainted probably."

He drove the aid car as close as he could to the bottom of the steps. He and his partner leaped from their vehicle just as a Seattle P.D. squad car pulled up on the dock behind me. Two uniformed officers got out, a man and a woman.

The man was a guy named Phil Baxter. I had seen him around the department before, although I had to check his name tag before I could remember his name. The woman was a young black with the name "Jackson" pinned to the breast pocket of her blue uniform. She was new to me.

"What's going on here?" Baxter demanded of no one in particular. "Who's in charge?"

"Looks like he is," Goldfarb said disgustedly, pointing at me.

I answered with no further prompting. "A body," I told Phil. "Over there. In the water."

Baxter walked to the edge of the dock and looked down. Sheer force of habit made me follow. It was still there, slapping against the wooden piling as the wake of a landing float plane rippled across the lake.

As the body rose and fell, a large decorative brass belt buckle glinted briefly in the sun, just under the water's surface. There was a design on it of some kind, and some printing as well. I squinted my best middle-aged squint. Try as I might I couldn't make out the letters.

"Can you read what it says on that buckle?" I asked Baxter.

He too squinted. "Not from here," he answered.

I hadn't noticed, but his partner, Officer Jackson, had followed us. "It says 'Ironworker,'" she remarked quietly.

I glanced back at her in some surprise. She was several feet farther away than I was, and she was able to read it when neither Baxter nor I could. "My vision's twenty-ten," she explained with a smile that made me feel ancient.

For the first time Officer Baxter looked me full in the face. "Why, excuse me, Detective Beaumont. I didn't recognize you. How'd homicide get here so fast? I was just getting ready to call you guys."

"Go ahead and call," I told him. "I'm not here representing homicide."

"You're not?"

I didn't want to go into all the gory details of why I was there. "Trust me on this one," I said. "Call Harbor Patrol and have them send somebody out."

Baxter turned to his partner. "Do that, would you, Merrilee?"

With a nod, Officer Jackson headed back toward the patrol car.

I felt a tap on my shoulder. When I turned, there was Derrick Parker. "Hey, Beau. What's going on?" he asked tentatively. "Hannah really got an eyeful. She fainted dead away."

"How is she?"

"Hyperventilating. She was coming around, but she had a relapse as soon the medics showed up. Hannah's got the hots for guys in uniform."

Derrick Parker wasn't the least bit fond of his female costar. He and I had chummed around together some while he had been in Seattle. We shared similar tastes, although his ran to Glenlivet rather than MacNaughton's. He seemed to enjoy slumming in some of my favorite watering holes. The waitresses at the Doghouse still hadn't tumbled to the fact that he was a genuine celebrity. Parker said he wanted to keep it that way.

"Who was he?" Parker asked, nodding toward the water.

"The dead man?" I shrugged. "That's up to the medical examiner and the detectives on the case."

"But you're a detective, aren't you?" Parker objected.

"This isn't my case. I'm doing a movie, remember?"

Officer Jackson came back to where we were standing. She gave Derrick Parker a small, tentative smile. I'm sure she recognized him, but when she spoke, Merrilee Jackson was strictly business. "They're all on their way."

"All?" I asked.

"Someone's coming from the medical examiner's office. So are two detectives. Davis and Kramer."

It wasn't exactly by the book, but Officer Jackson had taken a little initiative, and calling everybody at once would probably save time.

I nodded. "Good," I said. "By the way, we haven't been introduced. I'm Detective J. P. Beaumont, and this is Derrick Parker."

She held out her hand. "Merrilee Jackson," she said, shaking my hand, but flashing Parker a wide grin. "I'm glad to meet you."

Merrilee Jackson didn't comment aloud on Derrick Parker's star status, and neither did Baxter.

They had other things to worry about. A crowd of movie crew members was edging closer. "We'd better get these people moved back out of the way," Baxter said. "The M.E.'s van will need to pull up close to the water."

They had barely turned their attention to crowd control when another car with lights flashing and siren blaring pulled onto the dock. Detective Manny Davis got out on the rider's side and strode over to me while Detective Paul Kramer stopped to talk with Officers Jackson and Baxter.

"How's it going, Beau?" Manny asked with a chuckle. "How soon are we going to see your name in lights?"

"Cut the comedy, Manny."

"But I heard you were enjoying the movie business."

I glowered at him.

"Okay, okay," he said. "No big. What have we got, fish bait?"

"That's right. A floater."

Manny sauntered over to the edge of the dock and looked into the water. "He's been in the water awhile," Manny observed. As if to confirm his words, the wind shifted just then and the pungent odor of putrid flesh wafted over us like an ill-smelling cloud. Fortunately, Goldfarb had led Cassie away by then. Had she been within range, I'm sure she would have barfed again.

One whiff and Derrick Parker's engaging smile vanished completely.

"Jesus," he said with a grimace. "That's awful." He started to back away, but Manny stopped him.

"Hey, wait a minute. Aren't you . . . ." Manny paused, searching for the name, then broke off, embarrassed.

"Derrick Parker?" Parker finished for him. He sighed. "Yes, that's me," he said, and held out his hand.

Manny shook it wonderingly. "You know, my wife's crazy about you, your pictures, I mean," he said. "She was pissed as hell that Beau got this assignment and I didn't." Manny groped in his pocket for the small notebook he carried there. He found it at last and tore out a page which he handed to Derrick. "Could I have your autograph? For my wife, I mean. She'd be thrilled."

Obligingly, Derrick took the paper. Using the back of Manny's notebook as a writing surface, he scrawled his name. He was just giving the autographed sheet of paper back to Manny when Paul Kramer showed up.

Manny Davis has been around the department for years. The last time I had worked with him had been several years earlier on a bum-bashing case. Paul Kramer was the new kid on the block, and I use the word kid advisedly. He was thirty years old and had just moved up to homicide from robbery. His rise to detective had been meteoric, but word was out around the squad that working with Kramer was a royal pain in the ass.

Kramer arrived just in time to see Manny taking the piece of paper from Derrick and stuffing it in his pocket. He looked from Derrick to Manny and back again.

"Witness?" Kramer asked.

Manny glanced in my direction then shook his

head. "It's nothing," he said. "I was just lining Beau and his friend here up for a friendly game of golf."

Partnerships, like some marriages, aren't always made in heaven. Manny and Kramer's working relationship was evidently an uneasy one.

I understood the situation. So did Derrick. We both had sense enough to keep our mouths shut.

CHAPTER 2

CRIME-SCENE INVESTIGATION IS AN EXACT SCIENCE, complicated by the countervailing demands of accepted protocol and a need for swift, definitive action. What may seem absolutely straightforward in an artificial laboratory situation or in a case study at the police academy becomes less clear-cut in the real world. At crime scenes, hard-and-fast rules of evidentiary procedure often fall victim to jurisdictional disputes and personality conflicts. After all, cops are people too.

In this particular instance, the infighting started immediately after the arrival of an investigator from the Medical Examiner's office. Her name was Audrey Cummings, and she turned up almost on the heels of Detectives Kramer and Davis. As soon as Paul Kramer noticed her, he took offense and attacked.

"Who called you in?" he demanded. The question and the way he asked it were both only one step under rude.

Officer Merrilee Jackson had followed Kramer down the dock. Now she stepped forward, ready to accept full responsibility. "I did, Detective Kramer. It seemed like a good idea."

"That decision is supposed to be left up to the detectives," Kramer snapped, irritation sharp in his tone.

"Sorry," she answered.

"Don't worry about it," Manny put in quickly to Officer Jackson. "You were right. We do need her, and it's a good thing she's here. It'll save time." He turned to Kramer. "Don't get your bowels in an uproar, Paul," he said.

The admonition came too late. Detective Kramer is one of those intense, territorial individuals who can't stand having other people set foot on his private turf. As far as I'm concerned, he's in the wrong business. Murders seldom come posted with "No Trespassing" signs. In fact, at that very moment, Seattle's media clan, alerted by the sudden surge of mid-afternoon activity, was beginning to gather in a disorderly knot just outside Kramer's line of vision. Woody Carroll was doing his best to keep them herded together behind a blockade of police vehicles.

The lady from the medical examiner's office, a mid-fifties dame who had been around more than the barn, remained cool and collected in the face of all the wrangling. Audrey Cummings' studied disinterest made it clear that professional squabbles were old hat to her.

Waiting until the fireworks died down, she finally tapped one foot impatiently. "Well, do I get a look or not?" she asked.

Manny grinned and made a low bow, stepping aside with a gallant sweep of his arm. "Please be our guest, milady," he declared.

Smiling at Manny's courtly gesture, Audrey Cummings marched past us in a suitably regal manner. In the world of homicide, where death and disaster are daily companions, we tend to take our laughs wherever we can find them.

Audrey good-naturedly joined in Manny's joke, but only up to a point. The fun ended the moment she reached the edge of the dock. There she knelt down on one knee and took a long, careful look at the body in the water below her. At last she stood up and walked back to where we waited.

"I'll have to have one of the assistant medical examiners come take a look at this," she said. "I think Mike Wilson is on call."

"Any obvious wounds?" I asked, as she started to walk away.

She shrugged. "Possible homicidal violence."

The words "homicidal violence" constitute a catchall phrase that can mean anything or nothing.

Paul Kramer frowned, jerking his head in my direction. "Wait just a damn minute here. How come he's asking questions, Manny? I thought this was our case."

Manny made little effort to conceal his growing annoyance. "Professional courtesy," he answered curtly. "Beau was here when they found the body."

"Oh," Kramer replied. He didn't sound convinced.

I tried my best to give Detective Kramer the benefit of the doubt. After all, being a novice on the fifth floor of Seattle's Public Safety Building isn't any bed of roses. I thought maybe having a seasoned homicide veteran like me peering over his shoulder was making him nervous. Whatever was bugging him, Paul Kramer was creating a bad first impression as far as I was concerned.

Not wanting to escalate the situation further, I changed the subject. "That's one good thing about being called out on a Saturday," I said jokingly. "At least you won't be stuck with Doc Baker."

Manny snorted. "You got that right, Beaumont. Compared to Baker, Mike Wilson's a piece of cake."

On several different occasions in the past it had been my personal misfortune to summon Dr. Howard Baker, King County's chief medical examiner, away from a social engagement of one kind or another. Irascible under the best of circumstances, Baker could be a real pisser late at night or on weekends. Around homicide, a place where consensus on anything is virtually impossible, there seemed to be almost total agreement that Mike Wilson, Baker's newly appointed assistant, was a big improvement.

Wilson had a pleasant, easygoing way about him that was a breath of fresh air compared to his hard-assed boss. A recent transplant to Seattle, Wilson was an energetic man in his mid-thirties. Rumor has it that one of his undergraduate degrees is in philosophy, although that's probably something he wouldn't want advertised around in the law-enforcement community.

Mike Wilson arrived at Lake Union Drydock a few minutes later, still dressed in casual tennis togs. He went straight to Audrey Cummings. The two of them conferred briefly before going over to view the body, squatting together side by side on the edge of the dock. "How long do you think he's been in the water?" I heard Wilson ask.

Audrey cocked her head to one side as if giving the matter serious consideration. "A week, maybe?"

Wilson glanced up at the metallic blue sky above us and nodded in agreement. "Pretty good guess. Maybe longer than that, but in this kind of heat, a week is probably right on the money. That's about how long it would take for him to float to the surface."

Getting up, Wilson helped Audrey to her feet then ambled back to where the bunch of us still stood in a quiet circle—Manny Davis and Paul Kramer, Officers Baxter and Jackson, Derrick Parker and I. Mike glanced around the group, trying to figure who was in charge.

"We'll need a boat," he said finally to the whole group in general. "A boat and a body basket. Has anyone called Harbor Patrol?"

"They're supposedly on the way," Manny told him. He turned to Officer Jackson. "See what's holding them up, will you?" Merrilee Jackson nodded and left, slipping quickly through the assembled group of reporters, a few of whom had, despite Woody Carroll's best efforts, managed to work their way inside the perimeter of vehicles.

Meanwhile, Derrick Parker slipped away from us long enough to edge his way to the side of the dock and steal a curious glance at the body. He turned away, groaning. "I think I'll go check on Hannah and Cassie," he said, hurrying off without another word to anybody.

Manny watched him go. "Some hero, huh?" he said, shaking his head. "But my wife thinks he's the greatest thing since sliced bread."

"Come on, Manny," Kramer said shortly. "Quit stalling. Let's get this place cordoned off for a crime-scene search."

I couldn't believe what I was hearing. Crime scene? When a floater has been in the water as long as that one had, there's no way it would come to the surface the same place it went down. Not even someone as new to homicide as Kramer could be that stupid. It was a grandstand play, pure and simple, but I was in no position to call him on it. Mike Wilson did.

"Are you sure you want to bother, Detective Kramer? It looks to me as though the body's at least a week old. My guess is he died somewhere else and got carried here by the water. Not only that, we have no way of knowing whether or not it's homicide."

"But you can't say for sure one way or the other, can you?" Kramer insisted.

Wilson shrugged. "No," he agreed mildly. "I suppose not, but even if he went in the water on this very spot, look around. There's been a whole lot of activity on this dock. How can you expect to find any useful physical evidence in a place like this after that long a time?"

What Wilson was saying should have been clear to the most casual observer. Lake Union Drydock, already working overtime to get a series of naval minesweepers back in working order for duty in the Persian Gulf, was one busy place even before you factored in Goldfarb's moviemaking army. In fact, the naval repair contract schedule was so overloaded,

they had been forced to cut back our on-site shooting from two weekends to one. During the previous
week when I had stopped by the drydock with the
location manager, the place where we were now
standing had been a beehive of activity cloaked in a
cloud of sandblasting dust.

Wilson was right, of course. No physical evidence
could possibly have survived a week in that kind of
turmoil, but Detective Paul Kramer wasn't buying
any of it, and he was the one calling the shots.

"We're still going to look," he said shortly. He
motioned to Officer Baxter. "Go get some tape," he
ordered.

Baxter left, reluctantly, with Kramer right behind
him.

I turned to Manny. "That's one arrogant asshole,"
I told him. "What Mike said made all kinds of sense."

Manny gave a long-suffering sigh. "Just because
something makes sense to the rest of the world
doesn't mean it will to Paul Kramer. He marches to
a different drummer."

"But Goldfarb and his crew are going to need to
go back to work here. They've only got today and
tomorrow to finish filming this sequence."

Manny shrugged. "You're welcome to try to talk
some sense into him, Beau, but don't hold your breath.
Once Kramer gets a wild hair up his butt, you can't
change his mind for nothing."

I started after Detective Kramer. Sam Goldfarb
and Cassie Young intercepted me before I could
catch up.

"What's happening?" Goldfarb wanted to know.

"When are they going to clear out of here so we can get back to work?"

"I'm checking on that right now," I told them.

Kramer was removing a roll of Day-Glo crime-scene tape from the trunk of his unmarked patrol car when I caught up to him. He handed the tape to Baxter. "You and that partner of yours start roping off the area," Kramer directed. He pointed toward the minesweeper towering in the drydock. "Start from that boat over there and go all the way to the end of the dock."

"Come on, Kramer," I said. "Isn't this a little premature? Why rope off half of Lake Union when you still don't know whether or not you've got a homicide? You know as well as I do that you're not going to find anything. There've been dozens of people all over that dock today. There've been dozens of people on it all week long, and nobody saw anything."

I was stepping on toes, but Kramer needed to be taken down a notch.

"It's my case, Beaumont, and as far as I'm concerned, this is a crime scene," he insisted stubbornly. "If I say we do a search, we do a search." He slammed the trunk lid closed for emphasis.

"Are you aware they're trying to shoot a movie here this afternoon?"

"What of it?" he asked. "I'm a police officer."

"So am I, Detective Kramer. Like it or not, my current assignment is to help these folks get their movie finished."

He stared at me, his long look critical and appraising before he finally replied. "And my assignment is to find out how this dead bastard in the water got that way. That's just what I'm going to do. Get off my back, Beaumont. I'm not in the habit of taking advice from playboy cops."

With that, he stalked away. I stood there in a fury after he left, with explosions of light blurring my vision and blood pounding in my temples.

Playboy cop my ass! I was aware that there had been some idle comment around the department about my change in lifestyle. The red Porsche 928 and my penthouse condo in Belltown Terrace had been the subject of mostly congenial ribbing, especially on the fifth floor where some of the guys regularly asked me if I was still on the take. There may have been more serious gritching going on behind my back, but Kramer was the first one ever to tackle me about it head-on.

I wanted to wring his neck. Unfortunately, Kramer is built like a Marine, with a thick neck that goes straight from his chin to his broad shoulders with barely an indentation. Ripped as I was, though, I think I could have handled him.

Officer Jackson got out of the patrol car and came over to me while I was still fuming. "I've called Harbor Patrol," she said. "They say it'll be awhile. There's been an accident in the locks."

My legs still quivered as misdirected adrenaline burned off through my system. I had to really concentrate before Merrilee Jackson's spoken words penetrated the fog of anger and made any sense.

The Hiram Chittenden Locks form a narrow bottleneck between Lake Union and Shilshole Bay. The lake is freshwater and the bay is salt, a part of

Puget Sound. The locks raise and lower boats to allow access between the two bodies of water. On sunny summer days, mobs of amateur water-jockeys and serious drinkers simultaneously attempt to maneuver their boats through the locks. It can be tricky under the best of circumstances, because currents in the locks behave far more like those in rivers than they do those in lakes. Which is how Seattle ends up with weekend watercraft traffic jams that can rival any freeway.

If that was what this was, we could be in for a long wait. "Great," I muttered. "That's just great."

As Officer Jackson headed toward the dock once more, Cassie Young came up to me in a blind panic. "Why's that guy fastening tape to our boom?" she asked. "What's going on?"

"We've got a hotshot detective here who thinks the sun rises and sets in his ass."

"What's that supposed to mean?" Cassie demanded.

"That he needs to be taken down a peg or two." I left her standing there fuming and went looking for Woody Carroll. I found him in the midst of the bunch of milling reporters.

"Where's the nearest phone?" I asked.

"That one I used, down on the wingwall." He pointed, but that phone was already well inside Paul Kramer's barricade of Day-Glo tape.

"That one won't work. Are they any others?"

Woody shrugged. "Go on into the administration building. The girl in there will let you use one."

As I walked toward the office I remembered Ralph Ames, my attorney in Arizona, complaining that what I really needed was a car telephone in the 928.

Ames is a gadget nut, especially when it comes to telephones. For the first time, I thought maybe he might be right about a car phone.

The "girl" in the Lake Union Drydock office was probably pushing sixty-five. "It's not long distance, is it?" she asked in response to my request for a phone.

I shook my head and she pointed me toward a conference room where a high-tech push-button phone sat on a battered wooden desk. I went so far as to pick up the receiver and punch the first three digits of Sergeant Watkins' home phone number. Then, stopping in mid-dial, I stood there holding the phone.

The socialization of little boys includes very strong interdictions against carrying tales. My first lesson came when I was five. I've never forgotten it. My mother's alteration shop in Ballard was next door to a bakery owned by a friendly old man. One afternoon I overheard several older boys bragging about how a whole group of them would go into the store at once. One or two would occupy the baker's attention while others smuggled doughnuts out from under his nose.

Offended by their blatant dishonesty, I told my mother who in turn told the baker. He caught them in the act the very next day. Two days later, the older kids waylaid me in the alley behind the shops. I don't know how they found out, but they accused me of being a tattletale and a sissy. They dumped me out of my Radio Flyer wagon and proceeded to beat the holy crap out of me. When it was over, my shirt was so badly torn it had to be thrown away before my mother saw it. I cleaned myself up as best

I could, and when my mother asked what happened, I told her I tipped over in the wagon.

But I had learned my lesson. Permanently. And some forty years later, that lesson was still there, its taste as strong and bitter in my mouth as the dirt and blood from that long-ago alley.

I put down the phone without ever finishing dialing Watty's number. I'd take care of Paul Kramer myself, one way or the other.

"Nobody home?" the receptionist asked as I came back past her desk.

I shook my head. "Nope. I'll try again later," I said.

The aid car was just leaving as I walked back outside. I waved them down. "The lady's all right?" I asked.

The driver nodded. "Like you said, she just fainted. No big deal."

His partner leaned forward and grinned. "Yeah, we'll be happy to come back and administer first aid to her anytime."

Maybe Derrick Parker didn't like her much, but Hannah Boyer was obviously a hit with Seattle's Medic One.

By the time I collared Manny, my temper was fairly well back under control. "If that asshole Kramer wants a search, let's give him one, but let's get it over with now while we wait for Harbor Patrol to show up."

So for the next forty-five minutes, while we waited the arrival of the police boat, we diligently combed every inch of the area Kramer had cordoned off. It didn't take long, and it wasn't tough, either. The creosoted wooden planks yielded nothing useful. The whole dock was clean as a whistle. By the time Harbor Patrol got there, even Kramer was ready to admit defeat.

Harbor Patrol Three arrived along with two Seattle P.D. old-timers, Jim Harrison and Ken Lee, both of whom are contemporaries of mine. They brought their thirty-eight-foot Modu-Tech alongside the dock and gently eased in close enough to reach the corpse with a body hook.

That particular piece of police equipment is very much like a ten-foot-long question mark. The long handle has foam floats to help keep it on the surface of the water. Despite its name, the implement is neither pointed nor sharp. The curve at the end, formed by one continuous U-shaped piece of tubing, is about the size of a basketball hoop.

Harrison gently maneuvered the metal half-circle around the midsection of the corpse and pulled it toward the boat while Ken Lee untied the body basket from where it was stowed on top of the cabin. The basket, a man-sized frame of galvanized tubing lined with small-mesh chicken wire, was dropped into the water and positioned under the corpse. Once the body was tied in place, they hefted it into the boat.

All this was done with absolutely no discussion. Lee and Harrison worked together quickly and efficiently, the way good partners are supposed to.

Only when they were finished and had covered the body with a disposable paper blanket did Harrison look up. "Sorry it took so long for us to get here,

Manny," he said. "We were stuck in the locks. Do you want him here on the dock, or should we take him back to Harbor Station?"

Kramer answered before Manny had a chance. "Here," he said.

That's when I hit the end of my rope and bounced into the fray. "Wait a minute," I said, turning to Wilson. "Is it going to make any difference to you if you look at him here or there?"

"None whatsoever," Wilson replied. "Either place is fine with me, although I think the dock over at Harbor Station is a little easier to work from."

"Then how about doing it there?" I suggested. "That way these people can get back to work."

Kramer started to object, but for a change Manny beat him to the punch and backed me up. "Good deal," he said to Harrison. "Take him down to Harbor Station and off-load him onto your dock. We'll meet you there in a couple of minutes."

"Okay." Harrison nodded. "You're the boss."

Kramer's face turned beet-red. With a little help from his friends, J. P. Beaumont had won that round fair and square. I motioned for Officer Jackson. "Do you see those two people standing there with Derrick Parker?" Derrick was standing in a tight little threesome with Sam Goldfarb and Cassie Young.

Officer Jackson looked where I pointed and nodded. "I see them," she said.

"Go tell them to start getting their people lined up. Now that the body's leaving, we'll be able to get back to work."

Merrilee Jackson flashed me a smile. "I'll be more than happy to do that," she said.

Jim Harrison finished securing the body to the deck and straightened up. Catching sight of me, he gave me a half-assed salute. Naturally, he was wearing surgical gloves.

In the good old days at homicide, we wore gloves only when dealing with bloated and decaying flesh, bodies like this one. We wear them more often now. They're considered essential equipment, right along with our badges and our guns.

I wondered suddenly if the good old days really had been that good, or if I was just an antique.

The real answer was probably a little of both.

CHAPTER 3

BY THE TIME THEY RESUMED FILMING THAT AFTER-
noon, we had indeed lost the light. Goldfarb got in
a huge shouting match with several members of his
crew. As usual, the director carried the day. Over
strenuous objections, Sam "The Movie Man" decreed
they would reshoot the fight scene while somebody
rewrote the script so the body could be found at
night rather than in daylight. Meantime, techs scurried this way and that, bringing in more equipment,
including a tractor-trailer rig containing a huge
whispering generator to provide the juice to run the
carbon arc lamps required for a night shoot.

Screwed up and incomprehensible as it may seem
to a rank outsider, making a movie is a lot like living
life. You work with little bits and pieces without
ever getting a look at the big picture. It comes together gradually, in order or out of it, with no discernible pattern. No rhyme or reason, as my mother
used to say.

I was doing my best to follow the story, but it

wasn't easy. From scattered fragments, I had managed to determine that *Death in Drydock* was nothing more or less than an old-fashioned melodrama.

According to the story, Hannah Boyer, playing a somewhat less than virginal heroine, inherits a failing family business—the drydock company of the title. While attempting to turn the business back into a money-making proposition, she becomes romantically involved with a land-grabbing developer. The developer turns up dead in the water, and naturally the sweet young thing is a prime suspect. The lead detective on the case, played by Derrick Parker, is totally smitten once he encounters his gorgeous suspect.

The story itself was nothing short of ridiculous, and the idea of a cop falling for his suspect sounds like an overused cliché. It may be overused, but it does happen on occasion, even to the best of us. I should know.

The crew reshot the fight scene first, then they began working on the scene where make-believe cops pull the make-believe corpse out of the water. At least the water was real.

The retrieval scene was enough to make me want to turn in my technical advisor badge. Permanently. For one thing, Goldfarb couldn't be bothered with a boat. They dragged the body out of the water and dumped it directly onto the dock. For another, the dummy, fresh from the prop shop, had suffered none of the damage real corpses do. When they dropped it on the dock, the makeup was still totally in order, and all hair, fingers, and toes were still completely intact.

In addition, despite having seen a real body hook in action that very afternoon, Goldfarb insisted on using a sharply pointed metal hook to retrieve the body. All my pleas for realism fell on deaf ears. I tried to explain to Cassie Young that sharp hooks were used only for dragging the bottoms of rivers and lakes. I even offered to call Harbor Patrol and ask to borrow a real body hook to use in the scene. No dice. Cassie didn't pay any attention. She told me Goldfarb wanted a sharp point on the end of his body hook. That was what the script called for and that was the way it would be.

The reason Goldfarb wanted a sharp hook was soon obvious. Part of the retrieval scene included a special-effects sequence in which the sharp end of the hook is pulled free from the make-believe skin of the make-believe corpse. I took Cassie aside and attempted to explain that real human skin is amazingly tough, that body hooks catch on clothing, not on skin, but unrealistic or not, Goldfarb liked that ugly scene. He climbed down from the boom and crawled around on all fours to lovingly direct the cameras in capturing the sharp end of the hook as it came loose from the all too lifelike plastic skin.

For some reason, neither Cassie Young nor Hannah Boyer found any of this pretend gore the least bit distressing. So long as I live, I never will understand women.

In the end, the scene stayed as is. I didn't. I left the whole bunch of them to their own devices and went in search of Woody Carroll. If I had walked off the set completely, if I had pulled up my pants and gone home, there would have been hell to pay. I didn't need to have both Captain Powell and Mayor Dawson on my back. I was mad, but not that mad. Not yet.

After all, orders are orders. Instead, I hid out with Woody Carroll and some of the Lake Union Drydock employees. We settled down in the employee locker room and played several friendly hands of Crazy Eights on sickly green wooden lunchroom tables while Goldfarb went right on having his stupid cops do stupid things.

No matter what I did and no matter what Captain Powell wanted, the fictional Seattle cops in *Death in Drydock* were going to be a bunch of incredibly asinine jerks.

I stuck it out until almost midnight when Goldfarb finally called it a day. By then, even though I'd been off my feet for the last couple of hours, my heel was hurting like hell. The mobile canteen folks had brought dinner hours earlier, but it was that so-called nouvelle cuisine—the kind of food that looks real pretty on the plate but you're hungry again by the time you finish chewing the last bite. As I limped toward my Porsche parked five blocks away on Fairview Avenue East, I was craving a hamburger—a nice, greasy, juicy hamburger.

Derrick Parker hailed me from behind before I opened my car door. "Hey, Beau. Are you going straight home, or do you feel like stopping off for awhile?"

"What have you got in mind?" I answered. Parker waved away a limo driver who had been following, waiting for him to get in. "I guess you want a ride," I added.

Parker was already climbing into the car. He leaned back into the deep leather seat with a grateful sigh. "I've got to get away from these people. They're driving me crazy." As I started the car, he glanced slyly in my direction. "Let me guess," he said. "What you need is a chiliburger and a MacNaughton's from the Doghouse, right?"

I laughed. "Right, although I hadn't gotten to the chili part of it yet. If they run you out of the movies, Derrick, maybe you could get work as a mind reader."

"That's a thought with a whole lot of appeal," Derrick Parker replied. "This has been a hell of a day."

He didn't get any argument from me about that. We had put in a good, solid eighteen hours, and although I was tired, I wasn't the least bit sleepy. Neither was Derrick. I drove us straight to the Doghouse at Seventh and Bell.

In all of Seattle, it's my home away from home. The place has changed little over the years. The walls are still a dingy, faded yellow. Stray electrical cords still meander up the corners of the rooms. The duct-taped patch in the carpet has yet to be replaced. It's the kind of place where a guy can really relax. You can sit there and see what work needs to be done and revel in the fact that you personally don't have to do any of it.

Parker and I went directly into the bar. The only pleasant part of my moviemaking experience had resulted from Cassie Young asking me, half seriously and half in jest, to keep an eye on Derrick Parker. Her thought was that I would keep him out of trouble, make sure he showed up on the set on time, that sort of thing. The whole thing was a joke. Leaving J. P. Beaumont in charge of Derrick Parker was like the blind leading the blind. We were either very good for one another or very bad, depending on your point of view.

From a strictly business view, the Doghouse loved it. Not that many people in their lowbrow clientele of drinkers consume Glenlivet on the rocks, and certainly not in Derrick Parker's prodigious quantities.

The night waitress in the bar was a seasoned veteran named Donna. It was late in her shift and her feet hurt, so she was moderately surly. On that score, she had my heartfelt sympathy. When my feet hurt, it's hard for me to be civil, let alone cheerful.

Donna took our dinner order at the same time she delivered our drinks. Derrick blessed her with one of his engaging, boyish grins, but Donna wasn't impressed. Derrick Parker might be a household name all across America, but not in Donna's household, and not in the Doghouse, either.

Whenever that happened, whenever a waitress didn't recognize him or throw herself at his feet, Derrick acted both pleased and mystified. He liked to experience that rare sensation of anonymity, but it bothered him too, made him uneasy.

Derrick picked up his drink and took a long pull of Scotch. When he put down the glass and turned to look at me, the smile he had used on Donna was gone. "Do you know that's the first time I've ever seen a real dead body?"

"Is that so?" I responded. I was surprised. I think people hold the idea that movie stars have been everywhere, done everything. Derrick's comment was remarkably ingenuous.

He nodded. "I've just never been around when someone died. My grandmother passed away years ago, but my family's into cremation. We don't do funerals with open caskets and all that jazz." He shuddered. "Do they all look that way?"

"What way?"

"That . . ." he paused, looking for a word. ". . . gross," he added finally.

Gross did pretty much cover it.

"The floaters usually look like that," I told him. "Sometimes better, sometimes worse."

He seemed shocked. "And that's what you guys call them? Floaters?"

I nodded.

"That's terrible. I thought that was just in scripts." Derrick sat quietly for a few minutes letting that soak in. "How do you think he died?" he asked eventually. It was as though the dead man held a terrible fascination for Derrick Parker, as though he wanted to know all about him and yet, at the same time, he wanted to think about something else. I have a more than nodding acquaintance with that compulsion myself. It's what makes me a detective instead of a stockbroker.

"I can tell you one thing. He didn't jump," I said.

"He didn't? How do you know that?"

"The jumpers end up with their clothes all screwed up. Either they're torn to shreds or wrapped around their necks, depending on how they hit the water. If they go off one of the high bridges, the Freeway or Aurora, their clothes are usually torn to pieces on impact."

Derrick signaled Donna and ordered another round. With the drink in hand, he stared moodily into it, shaking his head. "Jesus. That's what you call them really, jumpers and floaters?"

"You got any better ideas?"

"No."

There was another pause when Donna brought our food. For late on a Saturday night, the place was practically deserted except for a few sing-along types gathered around the organ at the far end of the room. Derrick waited until Donna walked away.

"So what happens next when you find a body like that?"

"We try to determine how he died and get a positive identification. Then we notify the next of kin."

"You have to do that?"

I nodded.

"How old do you think he was?"

I shrugged. "I don't know. Thirtyish. Somewhere around there."

"And how do you go about finding next of kin?"

"What's with all the questions, Derrick? Have you decided you want to be a cop when you grow up?"

Derrick shook his head. "Nothing like that. I don't know what it is. I can't seem to get him out of my mind. It must be awful, having to talk to families like that, having to find them and tell them."

"It's no picnic," I said. "You're certainly right about that."

The conversation had set me to thinking about the

dead man too. I remembered the sunlight glinting off his brass belt buckle. "He was an ironworker," I remarked offhandedly.

Derrick looked thunderstruck. "One of those guys who builds tall buildings? The ones who walk out on those high beams? How in the hell did you figure that out—his build maybe?"

I laughed. "His belt buckle," I said. "He was wearing one that said 'Ironworker' on it."

"Oh." Derrick sounded disappointed, as though he had wanted my answer to be more exotic or complex, something brilliant out of Sherlock Holmes. It occurred to me then that Parker was getting his eyes opened about the reality of being a cop the same way I was learning about the reality of movies and movie stars. The lesson was clear: nobody has life completely sewed up. Not even Derrick Parker.

There was another lull in the conversation. I was thinking about Paul Kramer and about what an arrogant bastard he was, when Derrick interrupted my train of thought.

"You must really like it," he said.

"Like what?" I asked, puzzled. He had lost me.

"What you do. I mean, I've seen your place, your car. You're not stuck being a cop because you have to be. You must get a kick out of tracking things down, out of figuring out what really happened."

His comment made me laugh out loud. It was the other side of the coin, the same thing Kramer had said only turned around so it was a compliment instead of an insult. I had never given the matter much thought, but Derrick was right.

"I do like it," I told him. "When I finally break the code and know who did what to who, when I figure out how all the pieces fit together, I'm on top of the world. Not even a screw-up prosecutor losing the case later in court can take that away from me."

Derrick got up abruptly and signaled for the waitress. "I'm paying tonight," he said.

Donna brought the check and Derrick Parker paid for both our meals. He left a sizable tip on the table when we walked out. "It's nice to go someplace and not be hounded for autographs," he said.

The cast for *Death in Drydock* was staying in the Sheraton at Sixth and Pike. I dropped Derrick there and went home to Belltown Terrace. I was alone in the elevator all the way from P-4, the lowest level of the parking garage, to the twenty-fifth floor. Late at night, riding alone in the elevator is like being in a decompression chamber. I could feel the residue of the day's hassles dropping away from me. By the time I opened the door to my apartment, I was home. And glad to be there.

The red light on my answering machine showed there had been a number of messages while I was out, but it was after one in the morning, far too late to return any calls, so I didn't even bother to play them back. Instead, I poured myself a nightcap and settled into my recliner.

I was as bad as Derrick Parker. My mind was restless. No matter what, it kept coming back to the dead man in the water. The fact that he was none of my business didn't make any difference. It's not your case, Beaumont, I tried telling myself. He's not your problem. But the dead man wouldn't go away.

Ironworker. What was it about ironworkers? There was something about ironworkers that had been trying to nose its way into my consciousness ever since Merrilee Jackson had read the word to me off the glinting belt buckle. The thought had been there, poking around the edges of my mind, but with all the hubbub of the afternoon and evening, I hadn't been able to make any connections.

Now though, as I sat in the comfortable silence of my living room with the icy glass of MacNaughton's in my hand, it finally came to me.

Someone in my building. Someone from the ironworkers' local across the alley had rented a unit in Belltown Terrace. I knew it because, as one of the members of the real-estate syndicate which owns the building, I am apprised of comings and goings of tenants. I remembered the lady who handles rentals laughing and telling me that the new renter's vertical commute would be longer than his horizontal one since his office was in the Labor Temple across the alley at First and Broad. I tried to remember what else she had said about him. He was one of the union bigwigs, a business agent or something, not one of the regular working stiffs.

I felt better then, relieved somehow. It was a bit of information I could pass along to Manny and Kramer. Well, to Manny, anyway. Paul Kramer was a prick. I wasn't going to lift a finger to help him.

After two weeks it was good to know that no matter how long my exile in La-La Land might last, I was still a detective at heart. My mind would still work away at solving puzzles, even when it wasn't supposed to. With that knowledge, my body finally began to unwind.

I was going to have one more drink, but I never got around to it. I fell asleep in my chair without bothering to get up and pour that last MacNaughton's.

And without having anyone there to tell me it was time to wake up and go to bed.

CHAPTER 4

RON PETERS WOKE ME AT SEVEN O'CLOCK ON SUNDAY morning. It was a good thing, but not quite good enough. I was supposed to be on the set by six-thirty.

Peters and I were partners until a car accident broke his back and put him in Harborview Hospital on a semipermanent basis. By then he had been confined there for five long months and had finally worked his way onto the rehabilitation floor. The doctors said there was no way he'd ever be a detective again, but the department had cleared the way so that whenever he was ready to come back to work, on either a full- or part-time basis, a place would be waiting for him in the Public Information Office. Try as I might, I can't remember to call it Media Relations.

Despite his injury, things were starting to look up for Ron Peters. He had fallen hard for Amy Fitzgerald, his physical therapist. Fortunately, the feeling was mutual. The two of them were busy planning a late September wedding that would include Peters' two daughters, Tracie and Heather, as dual flower girls. They were all four counting the days.

While Ron was hospitalized, I had installed the girls along with their live-in baby-sitter, Mrs. Edwards, in an apartment on the eighteenth floor of my building. It was a lot easier for me to keep an eye on things with them seven floors down than it was to trundle back and forth across ten miles of bottle-necked Lake Washington bridge traffic.

"What are you up to?" Ron asked cheerfully. He is disgustingly bright-eyed and bushy-tailed early in the morning.

"Still asleep," I muttered. I'm not a rise-and-shiner, never have been, never will be. "What time is it?"

"Seven," he answered. "Aren't you working this morning? I thought they were scheduled to shoot all weekend long."

"Shit! You're right. I'm late." I struggled to sit up. The foot of the recliner dropped with a resounding thump.

"This won't take long," he said. "I need a favor."

"What's that?"

I paused long enough to let my head clear, more than half resenting the fact that Peters sounded bright as a new penny. That's one thing about hospitals that has always puzzled me. If patients in hospitals are supposed to be there to rest and get well, how come nurses wake everybody up at the crack of dawn, feed them, take their temperatures, and then leave them to spend the rest of the day doing nothing? At least they get an early start on it.

Peters had taken to this regimen like a duck to

water. He's been an early riser for as long as I've known him, and once the morning hospital routines were completed, he would invariably give me a call. I was his connection to an outside world of work and family that was otherwise closed to him. His calls were so regular that I had almost quit bothering to set my alarm clock.

"The girls have been bugging me about Bumbershoot," he said. "It's next weekend, you know. They're dying to go, but Amy's going to be out of town at a convention, and Mrs. Edwards just can't hack it by herself. Having the girls in a crowd like that would be too much for her."

Bumbershoot is an end-of-summer celebration, a four-day extravaganza that takes place in Seattle over Labor Day weekend. It's held at Seattle Center, the site of the 1962 World's Fair. Bumbershoot is like a gigantic medieval fair, complete with food booths, fortune-tellers, street musicians, jugglers, name-brand entertainment, and a crowd of approximately 250,000. I could well believe Mrs. Edwards couldn't hack going there with two little kids. I wondered if I could.

Peters continued. "I told the girls the only way they could go was if you'd agree to take them, but that I'd have to check with you first, for them not to get their hopes up."

"Sure, I'll take 'em." I couldn't believe I was saying it. Maybe it was guilt about my own kids that made me say yes. I remembered back when Kelly and Scott were little. I had worked event security at Bumbershoot for two of the three days. When I woke up Monday morning and Karen said that she wanted to take the kids and go Bumbershooting, she and I got in a hell of a fight. We ended up not going at all.

Did I say maybe it was guilt? Of course it was guilt. Who am I trying to kid?

"Thanks, Beau," Peters said. "I figured you would." I didn't tell him why I was such a pushover.

"They'll be thrilled," he continued. "I was afraid Heather would try to get to you before I had a chance."

"Nope," I said, glancing at the still-flashing light on my answering machine. There were at least five messages waiting to be replayed. "This is the first I've heard anything about it."

"Good. I'll tell Mrs. Edwards to get in touch with you to make arrangements.

"How's the movie going?" he asked, changing the subject. "Were you anywhere near where they pulled that body out of Lake Union yesterday?"

I glanced at the clock. I was already late. It didn't much matter if I got there later still. I took the time to tell Peters some of what had gone on the day before. As soon as I got to the part about the buckle, Peters stopped me short.

"Hey, wait a minute. Remember that guy whose boat blew up last week out in the middle of Lake Union? I seem to remember the papers saying the owner of the boat was an ironworker. He was missing afterwards. They had divers down and were dragging the lake, but they didn't find a body."

Peters' more than adequate memory had been honed even sharper by the months of hospital confinement. He would devour newspapers, remembering almost verbatim everything he read. His comment jarred my memory as well. I had heard about the case and the missing body. I had forgotten that the missing victim was an ironworker.

"I'll bet you're right, Peters. I wonder if Davis and Kramer have made the connection?"

"Kramer?" Peters asked. "Paul Kramer from robbery?"

Wanting to avoid going into detail about my hassle with Kramer, I had neglected to tell Peters the names of the homicide detectives assigned to the case. It was nobody's business but my own, one I didn't care to advertise.

"That's him all right," I said. "What about him?"

"He's a first-class son of a bitch," Peters growled. "When I was still in robbery, he almost caused me to quit the force. What's he doing working in homicide?"

Knowing I wasn't the only one bothered by Paul Kramer made me feel less like the Lone Ranger. "He transferred up just in the last couple of weeks. What's his problem?"

Peters paused for a moment. "Paul Kramer wants to be Chief of Police someday, Beau, and he doesn't give a shit who he has to step on to get there."

Suddenly, Detective Kramer's action made a hell of a lot more sense to me. "Thanks for the info, Peters," I said. "I'll bear that in mind."

"You want me to call Manny and tell him about that boat?"

I thought about that for a minute. And I thought about the guy in my building as well, the one who worked for the ironworkers' local. "No," I said finally. "I don't think so. If this Kramer character is so goddamned smart, let him figure it out for himself. If it looks like they're going to miss it altogether, then we can tell them. For all we know, somebody from Harbor Patrol has probably already passed the word."

"Just the same," Peters said. "I think I'll call the library and check out that story on the boat. I'd like to know more. For me."

I didn't try to stop him. I was still so delighted to see Peters showing an interest in the world outside the confines of his hospital room that I refused to discourage him in any way. Besides, I wanted to know myself. After all, I'm a detective. I've been one of those a helluva lot longer than I've been a technical advisor.

When I hung up the phone, I played back the messages on my machine. There was one message from Peters asking me to call him back, and four from Heather asking if I would please, please, please, please take them to Bumbershoot. The brat. She knows she has me wrapped around her little finger. I erased the messages and decided not to tell Peters that Heather had done her best to beat him to the punch.

I went slinking onto the set a little after eight. I thought I could sneak in unobtrusively. No way. Cassie Young caught sight of me and lit into me before I was within ten feet of her.

"Where the hell did you and Derrick go last night? He's late this morning, too. We're waiting to film the last fight sequence, the one between Derrick and the banker, and he shows up looking like something the cat dragged in."

"I didn't do it," I said. "I'm innocent. Parker was

in perfectly good shape when I dropped him off at the Sheraton last night."

She glared at me and sniffed. "As if you'd know good shape when you saw it." With that, Cassie Young turned on her heel and marched away. Woody Carroll eased up behind me. He was holding a styrofoam cup of steaming coffee.

"She's not having a very good day," he said. Woody Carroll had truly mastered the fine art of understatement.

I glanced enviously at his cup. "Where'd you get that?" I asked.

He nodded toward a table near the stairs leading up to the locker room. "They've got coffee and doughnuts over there. You look like you could use some."

"Thanks," I said, but I was getting tired of all the editorial comment, of everyone implying that I looked like I'd been run over by a truck. I did look like it, actually, but it had far more to do with working an eighteen-hour day than it did with anything I'd done after Goldfarb had finally closed up shop.

Woody followed me to the table where I helped myself to two fat doughnuts and a cup of thick, black coffee. "Is she always like that?" he asked.

"Who?" I returned.

"That woman—what's her name?"

"You mean Cassie Young?"

Woody nodded.

"As far as I can tell," I told him. "I've known her exactly two weeks, and she's been on a rampage the whole time."

"That reminds me," Woody said. "Speaking of

unreasonable people. Yesterday, when all those reporters were here, one of them wanted to talk to you. Insisted on it. Said he knew you, that you and he were old friends."

"Let me guess. His name was Maxwell Cole."

"So you do know him. I've read his column in the paper a couple of times. I guess I should have let him come to talk to you. I thought he was just giving me the business."

"He was. Max and I are old acquaintances. Fraternity brothers, not old friends. He was giving you that line so you'd let him on the set."

"You don't mind that I didn't let him through?" Woody asked, still unsure of my reaction.

"Not at all."

"He said he wanted you to introduce him to some of the movie people so he could do a story about a real murder showing up at the same time they're filming a fake one."

"If Maxwell Cole wants to be introduced to Cassie Young or Sam 'The Movie Man' Goldfarb, he'll have to get somebody else to do the honors."

Woody looked at me closely. "You don't like Cole much, do you."

"You could say that," I replied.

I couldn't believe that worthless asshole Cole would try to pass himself off as a bosom buddy of mine, but then, after all these years, nothing Max does should surprise me. Once an asshole, always an asshole.

The film crew had moved away from the wingwall area to another part of the drydock. They were out on a long, narrow wharf where a series of moored houseboats would provide the basis for a crashing climax in which Derrick Parker was supposed to track down the crooked banker, the real-estate developer's killer.

Houseboats had been collected from all over the city. There was to be a carefully orchestrated fight in which the stuntmen for both stars, Parker's and the movie's heavy, were to leap from boat to boat in a climactic chase scene.

Once more I had tried, unsuccessfully, to include a hint of realism in the process. The scene had been written to include two gun-toting characters, a good guy and a bad guy, crashing through groups of innocent bystanders. At one point in the script, they were to barge through a deckside family dinner, fatally wounding a child in a barrage of cross fire. In the real world that's called reckless endangerment. Cops who do it don't stay cops very long.

I had done battle over this segment when I first saw the script, and now I thought it worthy of one last-ditch effort.

I tracked Cassie Young down during a break in the filming. "Why does the little kid have to get shot?" I asked. "Police officers can't do that. They can't go shooting their way through groups of civilians that way. It's a joke."

"It's no joke, Mr. Beaumont," Cassie retorted, pointedly dropping the word "Detective." I had been summarily demoted. "We're making a movie here. We want people to care about what happens."

"And you don't give a shit if it's accurate or not."

She smiled sweetly. "That's right. Accuracy doesn't sell tickets. Emotions do."

Her remark made me wish that I *had* introduced Maxwell Cole to Cassie Young. They were two of a kind, a matched set, only he sold newspapers instead of movie tickets.

I made one final attempt. "But your cops look like jerks," I protested.

Cassie crossed her arms and looked up at me. "So?" she said.

The implication was absolutely clear. In Cassie Young's book, cops were jerks. At least the drydock cops would be generic. There was nothing whatever to connect them to Seattle P.D. Except me.

"I'm going home," I said.

"Can't stand the heat?" she asked demurely.

"Won't," I replied. "There's a big difference."

I left Lake Union Drydock, but I didn't go home. There wasn't a cat to kick, and in my frame of mind, I was mad enough to break up furniture. Instead, I made my way up Eastlake all the way around to the other side of Gasworks Park where I paced back and forth along the water until my blood pressure returned to normal. I started for home, but when I drove past the entrance to Harbor Station, something made me turn in. Force of habit, I suppose.

The City of Seattle covers an area of ninety-two square miles. What most people don't realize is that there's a whole lot more to the city than meets the eye—parts that are underwater. As a consequence the Harbor Patrol, based in Harbor Station, has jurisdiction over some ninety-three miles of shoreline, all within the city limits. Seattle operates a fleet of six boats and boasts the only twenty-four-hour municipal marine unit in the state. When King County's and Mercer Island's police boats aren't working, Seattle P.D.'s Harbor Patrol handles all of Lake Washington on an emergency basis.

Originally the unit was a separate police organization under the jurisdiction of the Port of Seattle, with a warden in charge. Later, it was part of the Seattle Fire Department. In the late fifties, Harbor Patrol became a branch of the Seattle Police Department. Some of the officers stayed with the fire department while others went through the police academy and became police officers.

Jim Harrison wasn't one of those originals, but he was close. I found him drinking coffee in the Harbor Station kitchen when I got there.

"Hey, Beau, how's it going?"

"Can't complain," I said. "How about you?"

He grinned. "I'm counting the days until I'm outta here," he said. "Then I'm going fishing."

I laughed. He sounded like a kid waiting impatiently for summer vacation to start. "After all these years, haven't you had enough of boats?" I asked.

"Working on boats, yes. Playing on boats, no."

I shook my head. Boats hold no fascination for me. I'm a believer in the old saw that boats are just holes in the water you pour money into.

"So what are you up to today?" Without asking, Harrison filled a cup with coffee and handed it to me. "From what Manny said yesterday, I was under the impression they were still going to be filming today and that J. P. Beaumont was stuck for the duration."

"I took a powder," I told him. "I'm playing hooky."

He shook his head and clicked his tongue. "Couldn't that have long-range repercussions? Isn't the director some kind of buddy-buddy with the mayor?"

I shrugged. "Let 'em fire me. I'm supposed to be there to give them technical advice, but they won't take it when I do, so what's the point?"

"Beats me," Harrison said, then, with a sly grin, he added, "Is that what you're here for, to cry on my shoulder?"

"Actually, I came by to ask you about that boat fire last week."

"Which one?"

"There was more than one?"

"Three by actual count. It was a bad week on the water."

"Peters told me it blew up."

Harrison nodded. "Oh, that one. It blew all right, to kingdom come. We're still not sure we've found the body. We had divers down for two days straight. They came up empty-handed."

"Where was it when it exploded?"

"Out in the middle of the lake. If the boat had been in a marina when it blew, we wouldn't have any trouble finding the body, but it wasn't. That's the way it goes."

"Any idea what caused it?"

Harrison paused thoughtfully. "Stupidity mostly. That's my guess. It was a gasoline-powered Chris-Craft. One of those old fiberglass jobs from the early seventies. We got there as fast as we could, but it burned all the way to the waterline. The boat's a total loss."

"What kind of stupidity?" I asked.

Harrison shrugged his shoulders. "We see it all the time. These goddamned landlubbers buy boats, keep them for less than two years, and then sell them again without ever learning a damn thing about the boat or how to use it. They don't bother to maintain their equipment properly. My guess is either his fume-sensor system wasn't working or his blowers weren't. The engine room filled up with gas fumes. You know all about low flash points."

"One spark?" I asked.

He nodded. "It must've popped him right out the top of the wheelhouse like a goddamned champagne cork."

"You're saying it's an accident?"

"That's right. It's a joint investigation, us and the Coast Guard. We're pretty much agreed on this one. The boat was called *Boomer*, incidentally, and it sure as hell did."

"How about the missing owner? Does he have a name?"

Harrison walked into the other room, plucked a file folder out of a drawer, and brought it back into the kitchen with him. "Tyree," he said. "His name's Logan Tyree. I told Manny and Kramer about him, just in case."

"And this Tyree character. Did he happen to be an ironworker?"

Harrison ran his finger down the file then peered at me over the top of his glasses. "As a matter of fact, he was. How'd you know that?" he asked.

"Just lucky," I told him. "What happened to the boat? What did you call it, the *Boomer*?"

"Like I told you, the fire was out there in the middle of the south end of the lake. We couldn't leave it there, what with float planes landing and taking off. We had it towed back to Tyree's moorage at Montlake Marina, over here by the bridge. The owner says the rent is paid through the end of the month." Harrison's eyes narrowed. "How come you're so interested in all this, Beau? You're not working this case, are you?"

"Curiosity more than anything else," I answered. I put down my cup, thanked Harrison for the coffee, and took off before he had a chance to ask me any more questions. I couldn't have given him a better answer, because there wasn't a better answer to give.

I got back in the Porsche and sat there for a moment without starting the engine, trying to sort out exactly what was going on. No, I wasn't working the case. Playing was more like it.

When I finally started the car and got going, I pulled up to the stop sign at North Northlake Way. I had two choices. I could go right and go back home, or I could turn left and drive past the Montlake Marina.

I turned left.

CHAPTER 5

ONCE YOU'VE SEEN A BURNED-OUT FIBERGLASS BOAT, you don't forget it in a hurry. It's a scary sight.

Just as Harrison had told me, Logan Tyree's Chris-Craft *Boomer* had burned right down to the water-line. Most of the wheelhouse had disappeared, melted into a gaping hole in the deck. What little was left of the superstructure was lined with an eerie fringe of blackened icicles which were actually melted fiberglass. It had obviously been one hell of a fire.

If Logan Tyree had been blown clear by the force of the explosion, he must have died instantly. On that score, I counted him among the lucky ones. To my way of thinking, instant death is preferable to enduring the well-meaning tortures of a burn unit's intensive care. If that ever happened to me, I'd want to go quick.

"Were you a friend of his?"

Startled by the sound of a voice, I turned from studying the charred wreckage to see a wizened old man limp onto the dock from a peeling junker of a boat that looked more like a derelict tug than any-thing else. The deck was cluttered with an odd as-sortment of mismatched patio furniture and the unassembled parts of several bicycles. Two lines of clean laundry hung lifeless from wires strung be-tween the cabin and the bow.

"I'm a police officer," I said, flipping open my identification wallet to show him my badge.

"Your friends have already come and gone if that's who you're looking for," he said. He was smoking a cigarette. He finished it and tossed the stub into the water between the two boats, where it disappeared with a minute sizzle. At first I thought the man was entirely bald, but closer inspection revealed his head was covered with a thin fuzz of iron-gray hair. The unshaven stubble on his jaws was much more plenti-ful. If he owned a set of dentures, he wasn't wearing them.

He ran one hand over the top of his head and then reached quickly for a baseball cap which stuck out of a frayed hip pocket. "Chemotherapy," he ex-plained self-consciously, covering his scraggly head. "The name's Red Corbett." He held out his hand in greeting. The jutting toothless chin evidently didn't bother him the way his bald head did. His hand-shake was firm and thorough enough to belong to an old-time politician.

"Those other guys told me to keep everyone away, but I suppose it's all right for you to be here. After all, you're one of them."

Not exactly, but I didn't disabuse him of the no-tion. "Who told you to keep an eye out? Detective Davis or maybe Detective Kramer?"

The old man nodded. "That last one. At least I think that was his name." He reached in his pocket, pulled out a bedraggled package of unfiltered Camels, and offered one to me.

"No thanks," I said. "I don't smoke."

He paused long enough to extract a cigarette and light it with a match from a book stored inside the cellophane wrapper. "I figure they can't hurt me any more than they already have. Why give 'em up?" He took a pensive drag on the cigarette. He seemed to have forgotten me completely.

I reminded him. "You were telling me about the detectives."

"That's right. They said it would only be for a day or two, until his family decides what to do with it. Logan's ex isn't going to be wild about payin' the moorage fees. I expect she'll get out from under 'em just as soon as ever she can."

"She'll get rid of the boat?"

Red Corbett nodded vigorously. "You'd better believe it. She'll take the insurance money and run. That broad's a lulu. Logan was right not to have nothin' to do with her after they split up. She's the jealous type, you know, one of them screamin' Mimis. And jealous of a boat besides. If that don't beat all. Anyone who hates boats the way she does has to have some kind of problem."

"Tyree and his wife were divorced?" My question was calculated to prime Red Corbett's pump. It worked like a charm.

"Separated," Corbett replied. "His wife gave him a choice between her and the boat, and he took *Boomer*. As far as I'm concerned, he made the right decision. That Katherine's nothin' but a ring-tailed bitch."

"Where does she live?"

Red Corbett shrugged. "Who knows? Down around Renton somewhere, I think, but I don't know for sure. Poor Logan was all broke up when Katy—he called her Katy—when she told him she was actually filing for a divorce. He come creeping onto that there boat of his with his clothes in a box and his tail tucked between his legs. I felt sorry for him. He acted like it was the end of the world. I told him not to worry, that there were plenty of other fish in the sea. It didn't take him no time at all to figure out I was right, neither."

"He found someone else?"

Corbett nodded. "That little Linda ain't no bigger 'an a minute, but she'd make two or three of those Katherine types easy. I'd pick Linda over Katy any day of the week."

"Linda's the girlfriend?"

He nodded.

"Do you know her last name?"

"Decker. Linda Decker. I told those other guys all about her just this morning. Don't you work together?"

For a change, a plausible lie came right to my lips. "One of the two detectives is pretty new on the job," I said casually.

Corbett gave me a sharp look then nodded sagely. "And you're backstoppin' him to make sure he don't miss nothin'?"

"That's right," I answered. My logical-sounding reply not only placated Red Corbett, it gave me some real pleasure. In actual fact, it wasn't that far from the truth, but Detective Paul Kramer would shit a brick if he ever got wind of it. "Tell me what you can about this Linda Decker," I urged.

Corbett eyed me uneasily. "She's a nice girl. Don't you go gettin' no funny ideas about her. The way I understand it, Logan met her in an apprenticeship class down at his union hall. He was teaching welding. She needed to be a certified welder in order to work as an ironworker." Corbett stopped short and looked at me with a puzzled expression on his face. "You got any idea why a cute little gal like that would want to work at a job like ironworking? I mean it's hard work, and dangerous too, walking them beams way up in the air and such."

"I can't imagine," I said, although I suspected that money had something to do with it.

"Anyways," Corbett continued. "They met there in that class. He came by here that night to have a beer and tell me all about this lady he had met. You'da thought it was love at first sight, I swear to God. He was grinnin' from ear to ear like the cat that swallowed the canary. And it went on from there. She was real nice to him, helped him work on his boat on weekends. And he idolized those two little kids of hers. He would have been a good father. Katy refused to have any kids, you know. Just out and out refused.

"So like I was sayin', Linda and Logan got along great. My wife and I looked after the kids a few times for them when they went out. You forget how hard it is to find a baby-sitter once you don't have to use 'em anymore. The wife and I figured they'd

wind up married sooner or later—I mean, as soon
as the divorce was final. I was real sorry when they
broke up."

"When did that happen?"

He shrugged. "Not long ago, I guess. Week before last maybe. Linda came over and they had a
hell of a row. I heard 'em yellin' back and forth. As
long as they'd been together, I'd never heard 'em
exchange so much as a cross word. When they left,
Linda's kids was both cryin' fit to kill."

"Did he say what the fight was about?"

"Not really. He was real upset about it. I figured
it had something to do with work, but he never said
what. All he told me was that sometimes a man has
to do what's right no matter what."

"And Linda Decker hasn't come back around?"

"No. Not even after the article about the fire was
in the paper. That kinda surprised me. I expected
to see her. I mean, they'd had a fight and all, but I
woulda swore she'd care about what happened to him.
Course, she mighta been out of town and just didn't
hear about it. That could be it."

"So you haven't seen her at all?"

"Nope. Not since the night they had that fight."

"Do you know if anyone from the department has
talked to her?"

Corbett shook his head and blew a cloud of smoke
into the air. "I doubt it. You know how it is. After
the fire some guys came around lookin' for the next
of kin, and Linda wasn't that. I gave 'em his wife's
name, and Linda's too, although I got the feeling that
there wasn't much chance anybody'd be interested
in talkin' to an ex-girlfriend. I was gonna give it to

your detective friends this morning, but they said the same thing, that the wife's name was enough. Said they'd get Katherine to identify the body."

"Kramer and Davis didn't bother to take Linda Decker's name?"

"Maybe they wrote it down. I don't recollect exactly, but they said that with an accident like this the wife would be all they'd need."

An accident. Jim Harrison at Harbor Station had called it that too, but that was a Coast Guard finding made in a vacuum with no knowledge of an ex-girlfriend and an ex-wife. A jealous ex-wife.

"Somebody already mentioned that to me," I said. "Something about the gas-fume sensor or the blowers being out of commission. What do you think?"

Red Corbett tossed the butt of the second cigarette into the water with a contemptuous shake of his head. "Well sir," he said finally. "It sure don't sound like the Logan Tyree I knew."

I had been chatting easily with Red Corbett, but that remark put me on point. He had my undivided attention. That kind of comment is a shot in the arm for homicide detectives. It's what makes them go combing through whole catalogs of victims' friends and acquaintances. Something in the circumstances surrounding the death that doesn't fit, something that isn't quite right.

"What do you mean?" I asked.

"Logan loved that boat. He worked on her and tinkered with her every spare minute. He kept her shipshape."

"You mean if something wasn't working right, he would have noticed right off and gotten it fixed."

"You're damn right!"

"Did you tell Detectives Davis and Kramer that?"

Corbett laughed. "Are you kiddin'? I didn't tell them two nothin'. They didn't ask."

I felt like I had stumbled into something important, and I didn't want to let it loose. "You wouldn't happen to have this Linda Decker's address and phone number, would you?" I asked.

Corbett gave me a wily toothless grin. "I sure do. Like I said, me and the wife looked after her kids a couple of times. Linda lived with her mother and she left us her mother's name, address, and phone number just in case there was an emergency. We never had any call to use it, but it's still written down inside the cover of the phone book. You want it?"

I nodded. Corbett turned and walked unsteadily back toward his boat. In a few minutes he reappeared on deck, trailed by a woman who appeared to be several years older than he was and in equally bad shape. She stopped on the deck long enough to gather up the laundry while Red tottered over to me with a ragged phone book clutched in his hand. "Leona Rising," he read, gasping for breath. The phone number and address he gave me were in Bellevue, a suburb across Lake Washington from Seattle.

As I finished jotting the information into my notebook, the woman stepped forward, stopping at her husband's side. She looked at me quizzically. "Red said you wanted Linda's number. Will you be seeing her?" she asked.

"Probably," I said.

"Well, you tell her Doris and Red are thinking

about her. Tell her we're real sorry about the way things worked out."

"I'll be sure to do that," I said. Turning, I walked away, leaving the two wizened old folks standing side by side. When I reached the car, I was still holding my open notebook with the scribbled name and address plainly visible. Looking down at them I knew I had stepped off the dock at the Montlake Marina and onto the horns of a dilemma.

What the hell was I going to do about that name and address? Look into them myself? Why? It wasn't my case. Turn them over to Manny and Kramer? Fat chance. They were already working on the assumption that Logan Tyree's death was an accident. I might be totally convinced that their assumption was wrong, but any contradictory suggestion from me was bound to cause trouble.

In the end, I decided to talk the whole situation over with Ron Peters. Young as he is, he's got a cool head on his shoulders. What's more, he has the ability to see several sides to any given argument.

I glanced up at the sky. It was almost afternoon. Over the past few months, I had made a habit of spending Sunday afternoons with Peters' two daughters, taking them to visit their father at the hospital and then messing around with them for the rest of the day. Our Sunday outings gave their baby-sitter, Maxine Edwards, a much-needed break. It was good for her, good for the girls, and good for me too.

I wondered briefly if I should go back to Lake Union Drydock and see how things were going, but even thinking about Cassie Young and her moviemaking cohorts filled me with a flood of resentment. It only took a moment to make up my mind. The day was an unauthorized day off, but it was still a day off, a jewel to be treasured. I hadn't had a break in over two weeks, and neither had Mrs. Edwards.

Maxine wasn't just relieved when I offered to take the girls off her hands. She was downright overjoyed. Less than forty minutes from the time I called downstairs to extend the invitation, the girls were at my door ringing the bell—freshly showered, shampooed, and dressed to go visit their father.

I looked them up and down and gave a low whistle. "Why so dressed up?" I asked.

Tracie's answer was serious. "Amy said she has our dresses ready to try on, so if we came over today we should wear our good shoes and stuff."

Amy Fitzgerald, Peters' fiancée, had been busy sewing wedding clothes for herself and for both of the girls as well. With the wedding less than a month away, activity was definitely switching into high gear. Women are like that. If men know what's good for them, they keep their heads low and go along with the program.

"So that's how it is. If Amy wants you dressed up, dressed up you'll be," I told them.

I traded my two-seat Porsche for Peters' rusty blue Toyota sedan. It was a considerable sacrifice on my part, but I believed in kids using seat belts long before the State of Washington made it a law. Once the girls were securely belted in, we headed for Harborview Hospital on First Hill—Pill Hill according to long-term Seattlites.

Peters' room was on the fourth floor, the reha-

Fitzgerald was a born mother, and both girls seemed to accept her without question or reservation.

"They're okay," Peters agreed quietly. He turned back to me. "So did you finish the movie then? From what you said this morning, I thought you'd be busy all day."

"The movie's not finished, but I am," I said.

"So that's the way it is." Of all the people around me, Peters was the only one who really understood my frustration and boredom with the moviemaking assignment. Neither one of us was any good at enforced idleness although Peters was learning to deal with it better than I was.

I nodded. "For today anyway." I changed the subject. "Amy tells me you've been tracking after the boat fire."

"The explosion happened last Tuesday, just before midnight. A forty-two-foot fiberglass cruiser named *Boomer*. The missing man's name is Logan Tyree."

"I know."

"How do you know that?" Peters demanded.

"I stopped by Harbor Station before I came over here."

"Has anybody besides us made the connection yet?"

"Jim Harrison said Kramer and Davis are tracking after it. They had already been to the marina by the time I stopped there this morning."

"Oh," Peters said. He sounded disappointed. "I thought maybe we'd beat them on this one."

"We may have," I said. "I talked to Tyree's neighbor, an old codger named Red Corbett. He says

Davis and Kramer are calling it an accident—faulty equipment. Corbett says that doesn't jibe with the Logan Tyree he knew."

"How's that?" Peters' curiosity was aroused the same as mine had been. I told him briefly everything Red Corbett had told me. He listened in silence. When I finished, he nodded slowly.

"It sounds like Kramer's up to his old tricks again."

"What do you mean?"

"Doesn't it seem a little odd to you that they've already decided it was an accident?"

"Corbett didn't tell them everything he told me."

"Because they didn't ask. Kramer's in the market for quick fixes, Beau. That's how he made such a name for himself in robbery, how he got on a fast track for promotion. He's left behind a trail of cases that got closed on paper, whether the close was for real or not."

"I thought maybe this was just a mistake."

"Mistake my ass!" Peters flared. "There's no mistake. Believe me, I've seen it before. You could wallpaper your house with his paper clears. They don't mean a goddamned thing but they look real good in the record books."

"But what about Manny?"

"You know Manny. He's easygoing. He'll take the line of least resistance, and that doesn't include standing up to Kramer's constant pushing."

"So what do you suggest we do?" I asked.

There was a long silence. Finally Peters looked over at me. "Would you consider checking this out on your own without anyone being the wiser?" he asked.

"I suppose so," I replied.

"Then do it," Peters said. "If there's anything to what that old man said and if Logan Tyree really was murdered, I'd love to see Paul Kramer take it in the shorts."

"Consider it done," I told him. "It'll be a pleasure."

Amy and the girls came back into the room just then. I was reluctantly drafted into the hem-pinning process. My job was to help the girls hold still while Amy measured the hem with a yardstick and stuck pins in the gauzy material.

"Did you know Amy made our dresses all by herself?" Heather asked.

"Yes, I did," I said, "and it doesn't surprise me. She's a pretty talented lady."

When we left the hospital, I took the girls to McDonald's for Big Macs. They promised they wouldn't tell their dad. Big Macs are not on his health-food list. Afterwards, Heather wanted to go down to Myrtle Edwards Park to feed the ducks. Myrtle Edwards is only about three blocks from Belltown Terrace. I knew from things the girls had said that they went there often with Maxine.

For me the problem with Myrtle Edwards Park was that I hadn't been back there since that unfor-gettable day when I had married Anne Corley in a simple sunrise wedding. I didn't want to think about it.

In the end, I caved in and went only because I didn't want to have to explain to Heather and Tracie why I couldn't go. I sat on a bench overlooking the water and tried not to think while the girls played tag and climbed up and down the rock sculpture.

When we got home to Belltown Terrace, it was time for dinner. I barbecued hot dogs outside on the recreation floor. I was standing over the grill, but my mind was still on Anne Corley. Heather came dashing up to me just in time to see me wiping my eyes on my sleeves.

"What's the matter, Unca Beau? Are you crying?"

She had me dead to rights, but I didn't admit it. "No," I told her. "It's nothing, just the smoke."

Satisfied with my answer, Heather went skipping off to the sport court where she and Tracie were playing badminton.

"Damn you, Anne Corley," I said aloud.

She broke my heart, goddamnit. In the process she made me a homeowner again and gave me back a barbecue grill.

CHAPTER 6

I DROPPED THE GIRLS OFF AT THEIR APARTMENT DOWN-stairs and dragged myself home. My foot was killing me. I noticed it the moment I was alone in the elevator. A bone spur is one of those nagging, ever-present ailments that slips into the background when you're busy but comes throbbing to the surface the moment you're not fully occupied. I figured a Jacuzzi and an early out would do me a world of good. That was not to be, however, at least not as early as I would have liked.

The phone started ringing as soon as I put my key in the lock. It was Captain Powell, boiling mad and ready to chew ass, mine in particular.

"Just who the hell do you think you are, Beaumont?" he demanded. "Ten minutes ago I had a call here at home from the Chief who had just spoken to the mayor. It seems the Dawsons had dinner guests tonight—Mr. Goldfarb and his assistant as well as some other friends of the mayor. It was supposed to be a small reception to celebrate finishing the location shooting."

I had some idea of what was coming, but I decided to play dumb. "What does that have to do with me?"

"They're not done, goddamnit. According to Goldfarb, you're the one who held them up."

"Me?" I couldn't believe I had heard him right. "I held them up?"

"That's what Dawson said. That you screwed them around all afternoon on Saturday and then walked off the set today. They're going to have to pay a king's ransom to rent Lake Union Drydock for a half-day tomorrow."

My first instinct was to fight back, to tell the captain to cram it, but something told me that maybe Powell wasn't playing with a full deck. "Wait just a damn minute here, Larry. Did anyone happen to mention the body?"

"Body?" Larry echoed, sounding surprised. "What body?"

"Nobody told you about the corpse we fished out of the lake Saturday afternoon?"

Powell exhaled a deep breath. "No, they didn't. I've been out of town, haven't had a chance to glance at the paper. Maybe you'd better fill me in, Beau."

By the time I finished telling Powell about Logan Tyree making an unscheduled appearance on the set of *Death in Drydock*, the captain was already apologizing.

"Sorry about that, Beau. Either His Honor failed to mention it, or the Chief neglected to pass the word. I don't know which. Excuse the fireworks. Who did you say is handling the case—Davis and

Kramer? I'd better get in touch with them and see if they can tell me anything more before I get back to the Chief. Thanks for letting me know."

He hung up the phone. I sat there looking at it, aware that I hadn't told Powell everything he ought to know. I hadn't mentioned my misgivings, that maybe Logan Tyree's accidental death wasn't. But then, aside from the vague ramblings of a talkative old man and my own gut-level hunch, I had nothing solid to tell him. Captain Powell has reamed me out more than once for what he calls my "off the wall" hunches.

I was still staring glumly at the phone when it rang again, making me jump. I picked it up. "Hello."

"Guess who?" There's a good deal of interference on the security phone in the lobby. I couldn't quite make out my male caller's voice.

"I give up," I said.

"It's me. Derrick. Guess who's with me?"

If I still owned a television set, I could have tuned to the building's closed-circuit channel and had a bird's-eye view of whoever was down in the lobby, but I didn't have one and I was far too tired to play games.

"I haven't the foggiest, Derrick. You tell me."

"Merrilee," he said. "Remember her? We're having a little party. BYOB. Can we come up?"

I could have said no. I didn't. When I opened the door it was clear neither one of them was feeling any pain. Out of uniform, Merrilee Jackson was more than moderately attractive. Her regulation shirt and trousers had concealed both her figure and her legs. The clingy knit dress she was wearing accentuated both.

Derrick made his way to the bar and poured three drinks, two from one bottle and one from another. "She offered to give me a little extra police protection," Derrick said with an exaggerated wink as he slopped an old-fashioned glass full of MacNaughton's in my direction. "Cutest little bodyguard I've ever had."

Merrilee had kicked off a pair of high heels at the door. Even without them, she was none too steady on her feet. She took the glass Derrick gave her and with a giggle the two of them toasted one another's health.

"How'd you two get here?" I asked dourly.

Merrilee grinned and toasted me as well. "A cab," she said. "I told him we're both too drunk to drive."

"You've got that right." It's hard to catch up when you come into a party that far behind the rest of the drinkers. I picked up the phone and dialed the doorman.

Pete Duvall is a full-time biology student at the University of Washington who works part-time as a doorman/limo driver for Belltown Terrace. It's a good job for a student. He can use the slack times to study.

Pete recognized my voice instantly. "Hello, Mr. Beaumont. What can I do for you?"

"What time do you get off, Pete?" I asked him.

"Eleven o'clock," he replied.

"How about making a limo run around ten-thirty. I've got some guests here who need to be hand-delivered."

"Sorry, Mr. Beaumont," he apologized cheerfully. "No can do. The Bentley threw a rod coming back from the airport tonight. We don't have a replacement vehicle until tomorrow afternoon at the earliest. Would you like me to call a cab?"

I turned around and looked at Derrick and Merrilee Jackson. They were sitting in my window seat, necking up a storm. I didn't much want to turn them loose in a cab in their current condition. Seattle still has enough of a small-town mentality to be scandalized by the comings and goings of movie people, stars especially. There had already been some unfortunate gossip about Derrick Parker's public antics, for which Cassie Young held me totally responsible. I had more faith in Pete's discretion than I did in some late-night cabbie's, but there wasn't much choice.

"You do that," I said. "Have the cab here just before you get off."

Parker was looking at me balefully over Merrilee's shoulder when I hung up the phone. "Some friend you turned out to be," he grumbled. "We just got here and already you're trying to throw us out."

"Look, Derrick, a few minutes ago I learned that I have to be back on the set at six tomorrow morning."

Parker poured himself another drink and offered one to Merrilee. She tossed down two fingers of Glenlivet as though she'd been weaned on it.

"Me, too," Parker sighed. "Isn't that a pisser! It was all scheduled to be over today. I mean, that's what the party's supposed to be for. Too bad." He dropped heavily back against the window. The drink in his hand sloshed precariously, but it didn't spill.

I glanced at the clock. It was only ten, but I picked

up the phone and dialed Pete again. "Go ahead and call that cab right now, Pete." I told him. "The party's over."

Ignoring Derrick's noisy protest that it was his very last one, I relieved him of the remaining half-bottle of Glenlivet and then escorted the two of them downstairs. Merrilee was a happy drunk, and leaving was fine with her. Derrick turned morose.

"Spoilsport," he grumbled. "We were just starting to have fun. Besides, those makeup people can work miracles."

"You'll thank me tomorrow when Cassie Young doesn't string you up by your thumbs," I told him.

As the elevator door opened into the lobby, we were greeted by the sound of a raised voice.

"If I wanted a goddamned cab to pick my mother up at the airport, I wouldn't be living in a luxury high rise! I made that limo reservation over a week ago. The concierge assured me it would be no problem."

Pete Duvall was doing his best to be polite. The man who was berating him was someone I had never seen before.

"I'm sorry, Mr. Green," Pete said. "As I was trying to explain, the Bentley was out of order with a fuel-pump problem last week. We got it out of the shop day before yesterday, but tonight it threw a rod. We should be able to have a substitute here by early afternoon, a Caddy probably, but your mother's plane reservation is too early for that."

Mr. Green bristled. "You know, when they rented me this place, they told me that the Bentley was one of the amenities. It was in all the ads, remember?

The property manager is going to hear about this. And so are the owners. Personally. I'll see to it."

Pete gave me a veiled look. "I'm sure they will," he said mildly.

In actual fact, I had already heard far more about the ancient Bentley than I wanted. It had been a pet project of one of the syndicate's five principals. The proposal had sounded fine when it was first suggested, but it had turned into a major headache once the Bentley actually arrived on the scene. The car spent far more time in the shop than it did on the road.

A cab pulled up out front and honked. Happy to be rescued from the irate Mr. Green, Pete hurried to the door. "Here's your cab, Mr. Beaumont."

He helped me shepherd Derrick and Merrilee into the cab. By the time we got back inside the lobby, Mr. Green had disappeared into the elevator. I watched the digits as the elevator monitor ticked off the floors of the building and stopped on seventeen.

"I take it Mr. Green is new to the building. I've never seen him before."

Pete nodded. "He's only been here a few weeks."

"He's not the one who works across the alley in the Labor Temple, is he?"

"I think so," Pete replied. "The concierge told me he's a big-time mucky-muck with one of the unions."

The elevator returned. With a good-night wave to Pete, I got inside. Once more I felt the aching throb in my foot. As soon as I was inside my apartment, I stripped off my clothes. Within minutes I was in my private Jacuzzi soaking away the day's problems. Not even early-bird Peters could be counted on to call at five A.M. I managed to fumble around and reset the alarm on my clock radio before I stretched out naked across my king-sized bed. I was asleep before my head hit the pillow.

When the alarm went off the next morning, the first thing I did was grope for the telephone and dial the Sheraton. I asked for Derrick Parker's room. The phone rang several times before anybody answered. Derrick sounded as though someone had pounded him into the ground.

"Up and at 'em," I told him, imitating Peters' brisk, early-morning manner.

"We . . . I just got to bed," Derrick croaked.

"Too bad," I said. "I'm picking you up in twenty minutes. You'd better roust your friend out of there. She's got to work today too, you know."

For an answer, Derrick slammed the phone down in my ear. Being the one making the wake-up calls for a change made me feel terribly self-righteous. I got to the Sheraton in time to see Derrick hustle Merrilee Jackson into a cab with a quick peck on the cheek. I wondered if she'd have time to get home and change into uniform before she had to report for duty.

Derrick was pretty hung over. He weaseled a couple of aspirin out of Wanda, the morning waitress at the Doghouse, and when the food came, he barely picked at it. He seemed unusually subdued.

"What's the matter?" I asked him finally.

He shook his head. "My conscience is bothering me. Groupies are one thing, but Merrilee's really a nice kid. I shouldn't have taken advantage of her that way."

I tried not to laugh aloud. The headlines on the *National Enquirer* never hint that movie stars might have attacks of conscience the morning after a romantic conquest, although AIDS has made old-fashioned one-night stands an endangered species.

"You don't strike me as the type for morning-after reservations," I said with a chuckle. "Besides, you're not that much older than she is. I'm sure Merrilee Jackson is perfectly capable of taking care of herself."

Parker brightened a little at that. He gave me a sardonic grin. "You know, you may be right. She was packing condoms in her purse."

I choked on a mouthful of coffee and spattered my clean tie. They don't seem to make women exactly the way they used to. For the most part, it's probably a good thing.

We got to Lake Union Drydock by a quarter to six. Unfortunately, someone hadn't negotiated an extension of the parking barricades for the last half-day of shooting.

Parking places are always at a premium in that Eastlake neighborhood. With both the weekday working people and the movie folks competing for space, it was almost impossible to park the car. We finally found a spot and walked back to the set at a respectable five after six.

The drydock was a whole lot more crowded than it had been on the weekend. The shipyard workers were all hanging around idle, swilling down free canteen coffee and doughnuts. I saw Woody Carroll just inside the gate with his own cup of coffee.

"What's going on?"

Woody shook his head in disbelief. "Nobody's working. Goldfarb's paying extra to keep the sand-blaster turned off until they finish up. Too much noise, he says."

Captain Powell had been right about the king's ransom, then. If Goldfarb was paying wages to keep unionized drydock workers standing around on the job with their hands in their pockets, then it was indeed costing money. Lots of it.

Cassie Young was waiting in ambush with both hands on her hips. She didn't appear to be overjoyed to see us. "If it isn't the gold-dust twins," she remarked sarcastically. "Makeup's waiting for you, Derrick." He took off without a word. "So you decided to come back after all?" she said to me.

"I didn't have a choice."

She shrugged. "It's a good thing. Mr. Goldfarb wants to talk to you. He's out on the houseboat dock."

So Goldfarb was going to chew me out, too. Some days are like that. He was sitting up in the director's boom overlooking the houseboats when I got there. I waited until they lowered him to the ground.

"I understand you wanted to see me, Mr. Goldfarb?"

Instead of climbing my frame, he clapped one arm around my shoulder. "I'm glad to see you, Detective Beaumont. You were absolutely right about that scene with the little kid. I saw the rushes late last night. It just didn't work. Too melodramatic. We're going to shoot it again today, the whole scene. Now tell me, just exactly how would you do it?"

Wonders will never cease. Sam "The Movie Man"

Goldfarb's sudden change of heart left me completely bewildered, but then I don't suffer from an overdose of artistic temperament. In fact, there isn't an artistic bone in my body.

Artistic or not, we did it my way, the whole scene, from beginning to end. Derrick Parker's gun stayed in its holster. When one stuntman finally tackled the other, it was a full body blow that sent them both crashing onto the deck of one of the houseboats. They rolled under the table where the unsuspecting family was eating a picnic dinner, but no one got hurt. The little kid didn't get shot and die.

Fight scenes are incredibly complicated and time-consuming to map out. Choreographing, they call it, and I can see why. It's very much like an elaborate dance. Everything has to come together in total synchronization. We worked on that scene all morning long, first one segment and then another. For the first time, I had some inkling of how the final product would look. Not only that, I finally felt as though I was making a contribution, doing what Captain Powell had asked me to do.

For a change, the cop didn't look stupid.

And I saved a little kid's life, even if it was only make-believe.

Protecting the lives of innocent people is what I get paid for, really. At least that's what it says in the manual.

CHAPTER 7

I LEFT THE HOUSEBOAT DOCK ABOUT NOON. AS FAR AS I could see, *Death in Drydock* was pretty much in the can, but I had still not been officially dismissed. I headed for the coffee station where I found Woody Carroll seated on a folding chair leaning back against the building. He was drinking coffee from a styrofoam cup and holding a newspaper in his lap. Several members of the Lake Union Drydock crew were gathered around and involved in a heated debate.

"I'd never let my wife work at a job like that. Never in a million years." The comment came from a long-haired type in grubby overalls.

Several of the group nodded in agreement while another hooted with laughter. "Come on, George, admit it. You couldn't stand it if your old lady made more money than you, that's all."

"It's not that," George insisted. "It's too damn dangerous for everyone else on the job. Women aren't strong enough. They got no business goin' where they're not wanted."

I edged my way over to where Woody was sitting. "What are they talking about?" I asked.

Wordlessly, he handed me the newspaper, opened to the front page. The picture that met my eyes was a real gut-wrencher. It was one of a construction worker tumbling head over heels past the face of an unfinished building. The headline across the page told it all: CONSTRUCTION WORKER PLUNGES 43 STORIES.

"It was a woman?" I asked.

Woody nodded. "Read it," he said.

I did.

"A 28-year-old Seattle-area construction worker fell to her death early yesterday during her fourth day on the job at Masters Plaza, a building under construction at Second and Union.

"Angie Dixon of Bothell, an apprentice ironworker, apparently became entangled in a welding lead and fell from the 43rd story of the new building, which is scheduled for completion late next year. Ms. Dixon was pronounced dead at the scene by King County's medical examiner, Dr. Howard Baker.

"One of the victim's fellow crew members, journeyman ironworker Harry Campbell, said he had sent Ms. Dixon to bring a welding lead. When she failed to return, he went looking for her in time to see her clinging to a welding hose outside the building. He was attempting to reach her when she fell.

"Mr. Raymond Dixon, the dead woman's father, said his daughter had only recently decided to break into the construction trade. He said she had previously worked in the union's bookkeeping department as a secretary and was frustrated by consistently low wages and boredom.

"Masters and Rogers, the Canadian developers of Masters Plaza, have been recording the emergence of the building with a series of time-lapse photographs. One of them, released exclusively to the *Seattle Times* today, happened to capture the woman's fatal plunge.

"Darren Gibson, local spokesperson for Masters and Rogers Developers, said a crew of ironworkers and operating engineers were working overtime both Saturday and Sunday in an effort to keep the building's completion deadline on schedule."

I didn't read any more. I threw the paper back in Woody Carroll's lap. "Those sorry bastards," I muttered. "They'll do anything to sell newspapers."

The debate was still swirling around me. "If she'da had more upper-body strength, she probably coulda hung onto that welding lead long enough for somebody to drag her back inside, know what I mean?" one man was saying.

"No way," the long-haired George responded. "He would have been killed, too."

Just then there was a sharp blast from the Lake Union Drydock whistle. To a man the workers got to their feet. "I guess that means we can get to work now," George said. He sauntered away, leading a group that headed in the direction of the drydocked minesweeper. There weren't any women in that particular crew. It didn't surprise me a bit.

Woody Carroll had pulled out a pencil and was

making a series of calculations in the margin of the newspaper. "How tall do you suppose forty-three stories are?" he asked me.

I shrugged. "I don't know. In a commercial building each story is probably ten feet or so, give or take. And the lobby level is often taller than that, say fifteen feet, somewhere around there. Why? What are you doing?"

For a moment Woody didn't answer me, but concentrated on what he was doing, his brows knit in deep furrows. Finally he glanced up at me. "She must have been doing about a hundred fourteen miles an hour when she hit the ground."

"A hundred and fourteen?" I asked. "That's pretty damn fast. I've been a cop for a long time, and I've pulled my share of pulverized automobile victims from wrecked cars. At fifty-five it's bad enough. I'm glad I wasn't there to scrape her off the sidewalk."

Woody nodded. "Me, too," he said.

I poured myself another cup of coffee. Math has never been my strong suit. It took me a minute or two to realize that Woody Carroll, without the benefit of so much as a pocket calculator, had just solved a fairly complicated mathematical problem.

"How'd you do that, by the way? You never struck me as a mathematician."

Woody grinned. "Snuck that one in on you, didn't I. It's simple. I thought I told you, I was a bombardier in the Pacific during World War II. I never got beyond geometry in high school, but the Air Force gave me a crash course after I enlisted. I cut my teeth on those Norden bomb sights. Did I ever tell you about that?"

"As a matter of fact, you didn't."

Woody was just getting ready to launch into one of his long-winded stories, when someone came looking for him. "Hey, Woody, they need you to help direct trucks in and out so they can load up and get out of our way."

Carroll got up and handed me the paper. "See you later," he said. "It's been a pleasure working with you, Detective Beaumont."

Left standing there alone, I didn't want to look at the newspaper in my hand, but I was drawn to it nevertheless. The picture repulsed me. The very idea repulsed me. I suspected that someone had made a nice piece of change, selling the developers' fortuitous snapshot of Angie Dixon's death to the newspapers. The editor who used it and the person who provided it were both scumbags in my book—but, inarguably, the picture would sell newspapers.

After all, look who was reading it. I was. Reluctantly. Furtively. As though hoping I wouldn't be caught. I usually make it a point not to read newspapers, especially in public.

The article went on to discuss Seattle's poor showing in the construction industry's accident statistics, how the city was tenth in the nation for number of construction deaths per billion dollars' worth of new construction. There was even a quote, attributed to Martin Green, Executive Director of Ironworkers Local 165, saying that part of the problem was due to a lack of building inspections by the state.

Martin Green. The name leaped out at me. I wondered if it wasn't the same irate Mr. Green from the lobby of Belltown Terrace. Probably.

I sat down and read the entire article again, and then, out of boredom, I read the whole paper. On the back of the front page of the last section, just before the want ads, was a much smaller article, a brief obituary about Logan Tyree, the victim of a boating accident, whose body had been pulled from Lake Union on Saturday afternoon. That one told me nothing I didn't already know.

I was almost finished with the crossword puzzle when Cassie Young came looking for me.

"There you are, Detective Beaumont. I couldn't find you anywhere." My work on the set that morning had evidently redeemed me in her eyes and she had restored me to the rank of detective. "Are you coming to dinner tonight?"

"I don't know. This is the first I've heard anything about it. What is it, a command performance?"

"Something like that," she replied dryly, ignoring the derision in my response. "Mr. Goldfarb said for you to meet us at Gooey's, the bar at the Sheraton. Seven o'clock. We'll all go together from there."

Derrick Parker came up behind her just as she finished speaking. "Go where?" he asked. The miracle-working makeup had been removed. He had looked fine during the filming, but now he was a wreck.

"Dinner tonight. You're invited too, Derrick. Are you coming?"

"That depends," Derrick waffled. "Can I bring a date?"

"Suit yourself." Cassie turned and started away.

"Hey, wait a minute," I called after her. "Does that mean we're dismissed? School's out for the summer?" She didn't dignify my question with a reply. I watched her walk away. "For someone her age, she doesn't have much of a sense of humor," I remarked to Derrick Parker.

He was watching her as well. Her punk red hair looked like a rooster's comb in the glaring sunlight. "Nobody in the movie business can afford to have a sense of humor," Derrick told me, "least of all if they're assistant to someone like Goldfarb."

Without further discussion, he and I started toward my car. On the way I handed him the newspaper section with the page containing the article on Logan Tyree folded out. "Thought you might be interested. That's the guy we pulled out of the water the other day," I said.

"So you found out who he was?"

"Somebody did," I answered.

Derrick scanned the article as we walked. "You were right about him not being a jumper. It says here his boat burned. That's funny. He didn't look burned to me."

"It exploded first," I explained. "He was probably blown clear by the force of the blast. I've seen people come through things like that with hardly a scratch. He must have hit his head on the cabin roof on the way out, or maybe he struck something in the water."

"The article said he was thirty-seven," Derrick continued. "That's only two years older than I am."

Derrick Parker must have been feeling twinges of his own mortality. I notice symptoms of that occasionally myself, especially the morning after, the night before, so I didn't have a whole lot of sympathy. "If you think that's bad, you should read what's on the front page," I told him. "She was only twenty-eight."

He read the construction accident article while we drove and, sure enough, he felt even worse. We went by my apartment so Derrick could retrieve his bottle of Glenlivet, then I took him back to the hotel. He said he was planning to take a nap. That seemed like a helluva good idea to me, too. As soon as I got home, I flopped across the bed fully clothed and fell asleep.

Peters called at six. "I gave you time enough to get home before I called," he said. "Did you see it?"

"Did I see what?"

"The article in the paper about the woman who fell off Masters Plaza yesterday morning."

"I saw it. What about her?"

"Don't you think it's a hell of a coincidence for two ironworkers to die in separate accidents in less than a week?"

Usually I'm the one who jumps to conclusions. I wondered briefly if Peters hadn't been in bed too long and his brain was going soft. "Wait a minute here," I cautioned. "Logan Tyree died in a boating accident. Angie Dixon fell off a building in front of God and everybody. How can the two be related?"

Peters didn't waste any time in throwing his best punch. "Tyree's ex-girlfriend left town."

"So what?"

Peters went right on, totally ignoring my question. "I was talking to Manny a little while ago, just passing the time of day. I asked how it was going. Manny said he and Kramer talked to Mrs. Tyree and then went to Bellevue looking for the girlfriend.

She's split. Gone. Moved out along with her two kids. They talked to the girlfriend's mother."

"When did she leave?"

"This morning, I guess, not long before Manny and Kramer got there."

"Where are you going with all this?" I asked. "Did the mother act as though there was any problem?"

"No, she says Linda always pulls stunts like this, like taking off without telling anyone where she's going."

"So what's the point? The mother's not worried, but you are?"

"That's right."

"How come, Peters? What's eating you?"

"Think about it for a minute, Beau. Didn't you tell me that Corbett guy said Tyree had a jealous wife?"

"That's what he said."

"And that the girlfriend, Linda Decker, met him while she was attending an ironworking apprentice-ship class?"

"That's right, too."

"And now this Angie Dixon. She's an apprentice, too. Maybe Logan Tyree made friends with more than one of his students."

It began to come together. I could see the pattern building in Peters' brain. It didn't take an overly ac-tive imagination. "You think maybe Linda Decker's scared that she's next? You think she's hiding out?"

"The thought crossed my mind."

"In that case, maybe somebody should check out Katherine Tyree."

Peters breathed a sigh of relief. "Bingo," he said.

"You're not a fast study, Beau. I thought you'd never pick up on it."

"Is this a subtle hint?" I asked. "And is the somebody doing the checking going to be me?"

"It sure as hell can't be me," Peters responded bleakly. "In the meantime, those other assholes are absolutely determined that the incidents aren't related in any way."

"Did you mention your suspicions to Manny?"

There was a slight pause before Peters answered. "No," he said reluctantly. "Not exactly."

I laughed. I couldn't help it. "All right, all right. I'll do it. I can't today because in a few minutes I have to be down at the Sheraton, but I told Watty I'd be taking a few days off once we finished up on the movie. I'll have some time to check into it and no one will be the wiser. You're still gunning for Kramer, aren't you."

When he answered, Peters' voice was hushed. "You'd better believe it," he breathed. "You'd by God better believe it."

CHAPTER 8

JUST WHEN I FIGURE I CAN COUNT ON PETERS TO WAKE me up, he lets me down. The next morning he didn't call, and I slept until after nine. Fortunately, I didn't have to be at work early that day. In fact, I didn't have to go to work at all.

My head was pounding. I lay there in bed trying not to move for fear I would shatter into a thousand pieces. Try as I might to remember, the end of the evening was a total blank.

From seven o'clock on, it had been one long wild party all over the Sheraton. Booze flowed like water. Vaguely I could recall closing down Gooey's in the wee small hours. There's an old country-western song that talks about how even ugly girls look good at closing time. I must have been thoroughly smashed. My last coherent thought was that maybe Cassie Young wasn't that bad-looking after all.

I finally dared open one eye. Glaring sunlight exploded in my head. Then, cautiously, I peered over at the other side of the bed. Thankfully, it was empty. I was all right so far. Hung over as hell, but otherwise all right.

Dragging my protesting body into the bathroom, I stood for a good twenty minutes under a steaming torrent of water. I should have felt guilty. Profligate even. It had been such a long, dry summer that the City of Seattle had limited yard-watering and was asking for voluntary cutbacks on indoor water usage. But I couldn't help it. It was either take the shower or stay in bed.

I ordered breakfast sent up from the deli down-stairs and was beginning to feel halfway human by the time I finished my third cup of coffee and a handful of aspirin. Mornings aren't good for me even under the best of circumstances. This was not the best of circumstances.

I was glad I had called in the day before to tell Sergeant Watkins we were done filming and to let him know I was on vacation until after Labor Day. Watty had suggested I go out and have fun, but the *Death in Drydock* party had been almost more fun than I could stand. By the fourth cup of coffee, I was ready to admit it was just as well my good drink-ing buddy Derrick Parker was on his way back home to Hollywood.

As the juices gradually began to flow I turned my mind over to the assignment Peters had given me the day before. After we had finished talking, there had been very little time to think about what he had said. On reflection, I could see that there was some merit in Peters' theory. Maybe Linda Decker was scared and hiding out. Despite what Red Corbett thought, it was possible Katherine Tyree had been jealous of more than just the boat.

Carrying Peters' conjecture one step further, I remembered something else Corbett had said, something about there being plenty more fish in the sea. If Logan Tyree had been mixed up with more than one woman in the apprenticeship program, nobody, including Katherine Tyree, had ever cornered the market on jealousy.

Both lines of reasoning were worth pursuing.

I already had Linda Decker's mother's name, address, and phone number jotted in my notebook. I didn't have a clue about Katherine Tyree. I turned to the detective's greatest ally—the telephone book. Logan Tyree wasn't listed there. K. A. Tyree was. The address given was on the Maple Valley Highway in Renton. That certainly squared with what Red Corbett had told me.

As I drove toward Renton, I wasn't looking forward to meeting Katherine Tyree. I'm not predisposed to like women who, deservedly or not, toss their husbands out of the house without much more than the clothes on their backs.

The house, a small, two-story bungalow, was on a wooded lot and set some distance back from the road. There were two cars parked out front, an older pickup and a late-model Honda. The man who answered the door was still buttoning his shirt. He told me his name was Fred McKinney, but he didn't say what he was doing there. When I showed him my badge, he invited me inside.

"Kate's upstairs taking a shower," he said. "She'll be down in a few minutes. The services are this afternoon, you know. Can I get you a cup of coffee?"

I followed Fred into the kitchen. He located two coffee mugs without having to look in more than one cupboard.

"Sugar? Cream?" he asked.

I shook my head. "Black."

He stirred several spoonfuls of sugar into his own cup and then offered me a place at the kitchen table. Fred, whoever he was, seemed to have an extensive working knowledge of Katherine Tyree's kitchen.

"Are you a relative?" I asked.

"Friend of the family," he said. "She's taking it pretty hard, you know," he added. "I mean the divorce wasn't final yet. It's like they weren't exactly married and they weren't exactly not. Know what I mean?"

"It's tough," I said, nodding. "It makes it difficult to know just how to act."

In another part of the house the sound of running water stopped. Katherine Tyree was evidently finished with her shower. Fred got up from the table. "I'll go tell her you're here."

I glanced around the kitchen. It was full of the kinds of decorative bric-a-brac popular with ceramic hobbyists—cutesy wall plaques complete with familiar Bible verses and age-old proverbs. To be honest, I suppose I had a preconceived notion of Katherine Tyree as some sort of femme fatale. Nothing would have been further from the truth.

The woman who followed Fred into the kitchen was a frumpy, overweight type wearing a frayed housecoat and floppy bedroom slippers. A damp bath towel was wrapped around her wet hair. She nodded silently in my direction when Fred introduced us, then went straight to the counter and poured herself a cup of coffee.

"Please accept my condolences, Mrs. Tyree," I said. She nodded again but then she turned away from me. Looking out the window over the sink, she quickly wiped her eyes. Fred had been right when he told me she was taking it hard. She seemed genuinely grief-stricken over Logan Tyree's death. It was a full minute before she turned back around and faced me.

"Fred tells me you're with the Seattle Police," she said, making a visible effort to control her emotions. "What can I do for you?"

She hadn't asked to see my identification, and I knew Fred hadn't examined my ID closely enough to remember my name. I decided to jump in with both feet. "I'm sorry to bring all this back up, especially since you've already been interviewed by a number of law-enforcement people, but I'd like to ask a few additional questions."

"What do you need to know?"

She came back over to the table and sat down between Fred and me. He reached over and patted the back of her hand. "Are you sure?" Fred asked solicitously.

"It's all right," she said wearily to Fred, and then to me. "Go ahead."

"A number of people seem to be operating under the assumption that your husband's death was an accident. I'm wondering if you have an opinion about that one way or another."

It was a back-handed way to start the conversation, but it struck a spark. The atmosphere in the room was suddenly charged with a surge of emotional electricity. Instantly Fred's hand closed shut around Katherine Tyree's fingers. His knuckles turned white. Fred's powerful grip must have hurt. Katherine Tyree winced but made no effort to pull away. The stricken look they exchanged told me I had unwittingly stumbled into volatile territory.

"You'd better tell him, Kate," Fred said grimly.

Katherine Tyree shook her head stubbornly. "No. I don't want to, not today, not like this."

"If you don't, I will." His words were weighted with gloomy determination.

Katherine stole a glance at me then dropped her gaze to her lap. "I can't," she murmured, her voice a strangled whisper.

Fred sat up, squared his shoulders, and looked me straight in the eye. "What she means to say is, we're engaged," he announced defiantly. He paused, waiting for a reply. When there was none, he continued, his voice somewhat more subdued. "We had planned to be married just as soon as her divorce was final. We had no reason to kill him. Logan and I were friends once—asshole buddies."

The fact that Fred assumed I was accusing them of murder led me to believe there was a whole lot more to the story than anyone had let on so far. I kept quiet, leaving an empty pool of silence between us. Fred rushed in to fill it up.

"You see," he said, "what you don't understand is that *Boomer* was my boat originally."

"You say you *were* friends? I take it that means you weren't any longer?"

Katherine Tyree started to say something then stopped.

"Nobody planned it this way. That's just how it worked out," Fred said. He shrugged. "Things sort of happened, got out of hand."

"Maybe you'd better tell me about it."

"Do you know what a boomer is?"

"Not really."

"In the trade it's a hand who knocks around the country, going from place to place, wherever there's work."

"What kind of work?"

"Construction. Working iron. That's how Logan and I met, on the raising gang down at Columbia Center. I came up here from California as a boomer and was living on the boat. Logan was interested in boats, had always wanted one. When he offered to buy mine, I took him up on it. I was tired of banging my head on the doorway every time I needed to take a leak.

"Logan and Kate here invited me out to dinner. Christmas, Thanksgiving, summer barbecues. That sort of thing. Kate and I just hit it off, didn't we."

Katherine Tyree gave a barely perceptible wordless nod.

"So that's how it started out, innocent like that. Once Logan had that boat, though, he wanted to spend every spare minute on it. He was gone a lot—on weekends, in the evening, after work. That's when things got out of hand with us, with Kate and me I mean. Like I said, we didn't intend for it to happen."

The last sentence lingered in the air for several seconds. I'm not exactly sure who Fred was trying to convince most—Katherine Tyree, me, or himself.

"Where were you two last Tuesday night?" I asked.

Fred didn't flinch or try to duck the question. "Right here," he declared resolutely. "Upstairs in the bedroom screwing our brains out."

"Fred!" Katherine Tyree wailed. "Don't!"

"Kate, honey, I've got to. Don't you see?" He let go of her hand and reached up and ran a finger tenderly along the full curve of her cheek. "We're better off telling him right up front, hon. It would be worse if he found out later. Lots worse. Besides, we had no reason to kill Logan. In another month the divorce would have been final and we could've been married, no questions asked. I'm sick and tired of sneaking around. With Logan gone, I don't care who knows about us. It's nobody's business but our own."

Fred's forthright narrative was pretty tough to counter. My gut reaction was that he was telling the truth, that his involvement with Katherine Tyree hadn't been planned or premeditated and that he was sincerely saddened by his former friend's death.

"Tell me about the boat," I said.

Fred shrugged. "There's not a lot to tell. It wasn't new. I bought it used for a song. Gasoline boats are a whole lot cheaper than diesel ones. I'd been living on it for a couple of years when I sold it to Logan."

"What did you think about it?" I asked, turning to Katherine. "About your husband's boat."

"I hated it," she said softly. "It was the last straw. I felt like he was using it to run away from me. It was a place for him to go, to hide out, instead of doing things around here."

"Was he hiding out?"

My question heaped salt on an open wound, but that's one way to get honest answers, to ask while people are still down for the count, before they have a chance to get up off their knees and reactivate their defenses.

"Yes," Katherine said softly.

"Why? What from?"

"I don't know. We were just too different, I guess. We sort of drifted apart. We got married way too young. Everybody said so—his family, my family. He wanted to have kids, I didn't. I wanted to travel, he didn't. When I met Fred, I could see how wrong it had been the whole time. We were only staying together because we didn't know what else to do."

"There are lots of marriages like that in this world," I observed. "Most of them end in divorce, not murder."

Fred leaped to his feet and slammed a fist onto the table in front of me so hard the three coffee cups went skittering in all directions. "Goddamnit! I already told you, we had nothing to do with it!"

I ignored him and once more directed my question to Katherine Tyree. "Does the name Linda Decker mean anything to you?"

There was a flicker of recognition in her eyes, but nothing else. No hurt, no animosity. "Yes," she answered quietly. "Linda was Logan's girlfriend."

"Did you ever meet her?"

Katherine shook her head. Satisfied that I was no longer on the attack, Fred sat back down.

me out to the gate. "Nice car you've got there. What are you, working undercover?"

I nodded.

"You don't think Logan was into something illegal, do you?"

"We're playing all the angles," I told him. My answer was vague enough that it would help keep me out of hot water as long as Manny Davis and Paul Kramer didn't tumble to the car. The red Porsche would be a dead giveaway.

Thoughtfully, I turned my key in the ignition. Old man Corbett had been right about some things and dead wrong about others. Katherine Tyree's screaming fits hadn't exactly been jealous rages—at least his interpretation of the boat being the root cause had been somewhat wide of the mark. And that little doubt made me begin to question his assessment of Linda Decker as well. I wanted to meet Linda Decker and decide for myself.

Ron Peters had already told me that Linda Decker had moved out of her mother's house, but that was the place to start if I wanted to learn anything about her. Of course, the sensible thing would have been to drop the whole program, to stay away, leave it alone.

But when have I ever done what's sensible? I pulled out of Katherine Tyree's driveway and headed for Interstate 405 and Linda Decker's former address in Bellevue.

I figured I could just as well be hung for a sheep as a lamb.

CHAPTER 9

BELLEVUE, A SUBURB WHICH STARTED OUT AS A BED-
room community due east of Seattle, has become a
city in its own right. The transformation from sleepy
suburb into a high-tech center has escaped the notice of confirmed cosmopolitan snobs who derisively
refer to the entire east side of Lake Washington as
the 'burbs.

To hear city dwellers tell it, Bellevue is a lily-
white, bigoted, upper-middle-class sanctuary. From
what I saw that day, the blush was off the rose. I
wouldn't call some of the areas slums, but they certainly qualified as pockets of poverty.

To begin with, I had a tough time finding Leona
Rising's address on S.E. 138th. It's always like that.
Bellevue's incomprehensible street system is a cop's
nightmare. While I drove around lost, wandering
in ever-narrowing circles, I saw a duke's mixture of
kids out skateboarding and biking their way through
the last full week of summer vacation. It didn't look
like a totally segregated bunch to me.

Then, when I finally did find the place, on a small dead-end street just off Newport Way, the address turned out to be in one of a series of battle-weary duplexes much older and much more worn than their single-family-dwelling neighbors.

On that particular block, a somewhat shoddy dead-end street, my red Porsche would have stuck out like a sore thumb. There was no point in advertising my presence. I drove back up Newport and parked a few blocks away in the lot of a nearby public library branch. I returned to the house on foot. The aspirin I had fed my hangover was also helping my foot. For a change, the initial stab of pain from the bone spur wasn't quite as acute as I expected.

Approaching the place, I noticed a young man sitting on the front porch. At least I thought he was young. He was dressed in a loud, orange plaid shirt. His Levis had been rolled up at the cuff to reveal a long length of white athletic sock. On the porch near his feet sat a large, old-fashioned black lunch pail as well as an expensive-looking stainless-steel thermos.

At first glance I thought maybe he was in his late teens or early twenties, but closer examination showed a slightly receding hairline with flecks of gray dotting the short brown hair. I revised my original estimate up to thirty-five or forty. He didn't look up as I neared the porch. Instead, he sat there unmoving, staring dejectedly at his feet. He was sucking his thumb.

"Hello," I said, stopping a few feet away. "Anybody home?"

Surprised by my unexpected intrusion, he started

guiltily, pulling his hand from his mouth and shoving it under his other arm. He held it there, pressed tightly between his arm and his chest, as though by imprisoning it he could conceal it from himself as well as from me. He stared up at me for a long time before he shook his head in answer to my question.

"I'm looking for Leona Rising."

"She's . . . not here." He spoke slowly, haltingly, in a deliberate monotone.

"What about her daughter, Linda Decker?"

His lower lip trembled. He began rocking back and forth, the repetitive motion slow and hypnotic. For some reason my question had brought him dangerously close to tears. "She's . . . not here either," he answered. "It's her fault I missed . . . the bus. It's all . . . her fault."

With that, he did burst into tears. He bent over double and sobbed while the comforting thumb crept out from under his restraining arm and back into his mouth. I stood there feeling like someone who has just unavoidably run over a headlight-blinded rabbit on the open highway. Whoever this guy was, he was no mental giant. My question had unleashed a storm of emotion I was helpless to stop. There was nothing to do but wait it out. Eventually, he quit crying.

When the thumb was once more concealed under his arm, he stole a sly glance up at my face. "What's . . . your name?" he asked ingenuously.

I stuck out my hand. "My name's Beaumont," I said. "What's yours?"

He stared at my extended hand for a long time as if trying to decide what he was supposed to do with it. As if remembering, he wiped his hand on a clean pant leg and shyly held it out to me. His grip was limp and sweaty, but he grinned at me suddenly, his tearful outburst of the moment before totally forgotten. "Beaumont . . . that's a . . . funny name," he said. "My name is . . . Jimmy."

There were no nuances or shadings in his voice, and the long pauses between words made it clear that he spoke only at tremendous effort.

"Do you live here?" I asked, deliberately keeping my question as simple as possible.

He nodded and pointed to a curtained window to the right of the front door. "That's my . . . room over there. Lindy . . . used to live here. She . . . left."

"Lindy?" I asked. "Who's that? Do you mean Linda Decker?"

He nodded again, once more becoming serious. "She's my sister. My . . . baby sister. She's lots . . . smarter. She's not like me. Not . . . retarded."

He spoke the words as casually as someone else might have said they were right- or left-handed or that they'd been sick with a cold. All the while he looked directly into my eyes with a disconcerting, unblinking gaze. I felt myself squirming under it.

"Do you know where your sister is?" I asked.

He went on, giving no evidence that he had heard my question. "Lindy's good . . . to me. Always. I don't want her . . . to go away. I want her here. With me. I . . . need her."

Once more his lower lip began to tremble and he fell silent, rocking slowly back and forth.

"Did she say why she had to leave?" I asked gently.

He shook his head slowly from side to side. "She said she had to . . . go. That's all. And then . . . those men came. I didn't like them."

"What men?"

"Big men, like on . . . TV. Detectives. They were asking Mama about . . . Lindy. They even . . . had guns. Real ones. Not toys. I tried to tell them. They wouldn't . . . listen. And Mama told me to . . . go sit down. To get out . . . of the way and be . . . quiet. I didn't want to. I knew the answer. That's why I . . . missed my bus."

His ragged, halting delivery made it difficult to extricate meaning from what he was saying. The story was lacking several key ingredients. I struggled in vain to sort out the connections, to see through to the pieces that were missing.

"I'm afraid I don't quite understand," I said finally.

Jimmy looked up at me determinedly. "I'm not a k-kid, you know. I'm a grown-up. Just like . . . you. When I cry, sometimes people make fun of me. Kids at the . . . bus stop. They . . . call me a baby. It makes me . . . mad!" The last was said so vehemently that two small streams of spittle slipped unnoticed out the corners of his mouth.

The missing pieces fell into place. "So you were crying and that's why you missed your bus?"

He nodded, no longer looking me in the eye, but relieved that he didn't have to go on explaining. His chin dropped until it disappeared into the collar of his shirt. Once more his thumb edged toward his mouth. "I lost my . . . paper," he mumbled in little more than a whimper.

"Paper? What paper?"

"With the . . . numbers on it. Bus numbers. So I can . . . find the right . . . bus. I never missed . . . work before. I go there every day."

Uninvited, I sat down on the porch next to him. "What kind of work do you do, Jimmy?" I asked.

He straightened his shoulders proudly. "Micrographics," he said. Surprisingly enough, the syllables of the long word rolled unimpeded off his tongue. "I take pictures. Important stuff. I put it on . . . fiche." He paused.

"You know about fiche?"

I nodded. "And where do you do this?"

"At the center."

"Is it far from here?"

"Too far to walk," he said glumly. He moved his foot slightly and bumped it against the lunch pail. He studied it for a long time as though he hadn't seen it before. "It isn't break," he said. "I'm hungry. Can I eat now?"

A golf-ball-sized lump bottled up my throat. Jimmy Rising was someone who was lost without his crib sheet to decode the bus system and without someone to tell him whether or not it was okay to eat his lunch. He needed permission from someone else. I swallowed hard before I could answer. "I'm sure it would be fine," I told him.

He quickly opened the lunch pail, pulled out a sandwich, unwrapped it, and ate it noisily with total self-absorption. When he finished the sandwich, he brought out an apple and poured some orange juice from the thermos. He bit off a huge hunk of apple.

"Lindy gave me this," he said proudly, patting the top of the thermos. "It keeps hot . . . things hot and cold things cold. Did you know that?" he asked.

"Yes," I answered.

He reached over and touched the lunch pail, running a finger lovingly across the folded metal handle. "I bought this all by myself. With my own . . . money." He was speaking less hesitantly now. The nervousness of being with a stranger was gradually wearing off.

"Money you earned from work?" I asked.

He nodded smugly. "It cost . . . ten dollars and forty-seven cents. I bought it at Kmart. It's got some . . . scratches now. Lindy says that . . . happens to lunch pails. Everybody's lunch pails. They get scratched."

"You must love Lindy very much," I suggested quietly.

He looked past me and stared off into the vacant blue sky. When he finally spoke, his voice was full of hurt. Again he was close to tears. "She was going . . . to take . . . me with her. She promised. But now she can't."

"Why not?"

"She lost her job. It was a . . . good job. Building great big buildings. She's got another one . . . now. Not as good."

"You told me you know where she is?"

He nodded, slyly, ducking his head.

"Would you tell me? I need to find her."

There was only the slightest pause before he began rummaging in his shirt pocket. Eventually he dragged out a rumpled wad of paper and handed it to me.

"Her . . . phone number's there," he said. "She told me I could call. Anytime I want to."

I unfolded the scrap of paper. It turned out to be two pieces, actually, one with a telephone number scrawled across it, and the other, neatly typed, saying "210 Downtown Seattle and 15 Ballard." Upset as he was, Jimmy had evidently crumpled his bus-schedule crib sheet in with his sister's telephone number.

I jotted the telephone number into my notebook then straightened the typed piece of paper on my knee and handed it back to him. "Is this the paper you lost?"

His eyes brightened when he saw it, then his shoulders slumped again. "This's it. But it's . . . too late to go now."

"I could give you a ride," I offered tentatively.

There was a sudden transformation on his face. Just as quickly, it was replaced with a kind of desperate wariness. "You're . . . making fun of me," he said accusingly. "I'm retarded. Not stupid. You don't . . . have a car. You can't give . . . me a ride. I'm too big to carry."

"My car's just up the street," I told him. "It's a red Porsche. We can walk up and get it and have you to work in half an hour."

Still he hesitated.

"What's wrong?" I asked.

"I'm not supposed to . . . ride with strangers. Lindy said."

Lindy had given him good advice, advice I wanted him to disregard. "Am I still a stranger, Jimmy?" I asked. "We've been talking a long time. And I really do have a red Porsche."

"Like on TV?" Jimmy asked.

I nodded. He struggled through a moment's hesitation before leaping off the porch like a gamboling puppy. "Really? You . . . mean it? You'd take . . . me all the way there?"

"I'd be happy to."

As quickly as it appeared, the animation went out of his face. "But I don't know . . . the way," he said hopelessly. "Do you? Have you been there?"

The bus directions had given me a clue. Dimly I remembered back in the sixties how the U.S. Navy had surplussed its Elliott Bay site, turning it over to a group of can-do mothers who had transformed it into a model center for the developmentally disabled.

I had gone to the center once on a mission to deliver a batch of free tickets for the Bacon Bowl, a Seattle-area police officer fund-raiser. It's an annual exhibition game between Seattle P.D. personnel and a team made up of police officers from Tacoma P.D. and the Pierce County Sheriff's Department. It gives a bunch of frustrated ex-jocks a once-a-year chance to get down on a football field and strut their stuff. Looking at Jimmy Rising, I wondered if he had been the recipient of one of those tickets, and if he had, did he like football.

Quickly, Jimmy Rising began gathering his belongings, his lunch pail and his thermos. "Can we go now?" he asked. His eagerness was almost pain-

ful to see. I don't think I've ever headed for work
with that degree of unbridled enthusiasm.

"Sure," I said. "Let's get going."

We set off walking at a pretty good clip, but I had
trouble keeping up. Jimmy kept bounding ahead,
then he'd rush back to hurry me along. Watching
him, I had an attack of guilty conscience, but I
pushed it out of my mind. He was such a guileless
innocent—it had been all too easy to con Linda
Decker's phone number out of him. Anybody could
have gotten it from him, if they'd only bothered
to ask.

Of course, my guilty conscience wasn't so serious
that I pulled the notation with Linda's phone number on it out of my notebook and threw it away.
After all, as long as I had the information, I could
just as well use it.

"Is Linda in . . . trouble?" he asked suddenly.

The question caught me off guard. I didn't know
if he was asking me if she was pregnant or if he
meant something else.

"What makes you say that?" I asked.

"Because those men were detectives. Just like on
'Miami Vice.' That's my favorite. What's yours?"

I don't watch television, but I didn't want to explain that to Jimmy Rising. "Mine, too," I answered.

"Who do you like the most?"

That was a stumper. He had me dead to rights. "I
like 'em all," I waffled.

"Oh," he said, and we continued walking in silence.

When I unlocked the car door and let him into the
Porsche, he was ecstatic. "I've . . . never been in a car

this . . . nice," he said. "Are you sure you don't . . . mind?"

"I don't mind," I said.

"But doesn't it . . . cost a lot of money? Mama's always . . . saying that. Cars cost . . . money." Reverently he touched the smooth leather seat. "Is this brand-new?" he asked.

"No," I answered.

We headed back down toward I-90. Jimmy was fascinated by the buttons and knobs. He turned the radio on full blast, moved the seat back and forth, rolled his window up and down. He had a great time.

It was well after two when we turned off 15th onto Armory Way and stopped in the parking lot of the Northwest Center for the Retarded. A woman walked out of one building and headed down a shaded walkway toward another. Jimmy leaped out of the car and bounded after her. "Miss Carson, Miss Carson. I'm here," he shouted.

Miss Carson stopped in mid-stride, turned, and came back toward us. Even from a distance I could see she was willowy blonde. I turned off the motor, telling myself that Jimmy Rising would probably need some help explaining why he was so late.

He came rushing headlong back to the car, dragging Miss Carson by one hand. "He's the one," he said, pointing at me. "He even knew how . . . to get here. I didn't have to . . . tell him."

Close up, Miss Carson was still blonde and still willowy. She had almond-shaped green eyes, a fair complexion, and a dazzling smile. She held out her hand. "Thank you so much for giving Jimmy a ride. That was very kind of you. He told me he missed the bus." She turned to Jimmy. "Did you tell him thank you?"

Suddenly shy, Jimmy Rising ducked his head and stepped back a step. "Thanks," he mumbled.

"I was glad to do it."

Miss Carson smiled at him. "You go on to work now, Jimmy. The others are just going on break. I want to talk to Mr. . . ."

"Beaumont," I supplied.

"To Mr. Beaumont," she added.

Jimmy hurried away without a backward glance, and Miss Carson turned to me. The smile had been replaced by a look of concern.

"I'm Sandy Carson," she said. "I run the micrographics department. Where did you find him? We called his mother, Leona, but she couldn't leave work to go look for him."

Briefly, I told Sandy Carson everything I knew about Jimmy Rising missing the bus, about his being upset because Linda Decker had left town without taking him with her.

"No wonder he got rattled," Miss Carson said when I finished. "His sister's really special to him. Are you a friend of the family? Do you happen to know his mother?"

I shook my head, not wanting to admit to Sandy that I was a total stranger who had wandered onto the Rising porch in the course of a police investigation.

"It's too bad Linda couldn't take him," Sandy said. "He'd be a lot better off with her. His mother's about at the end of her rope." She glanced down at her watch. "I'd better get going," she said. "They'll be tearing the place apart. Thanks again," she added. "Coming here is terribly important to people like Jimmy. It's more than just a job, you know. It's their whole life."

With that, she turned and walked away, still blonde and still willowy, disappearing behind the same door that had swallowed Jimmy Rising.

I couldn't help wondering if Jimmy Rising ever noticed that about her, or if to him she was simply Miss Carson from micrographics.

Either way, it was sad as hell for Jimmy Rising and not so sad for J. P. Beaumont.

CHAPTER 10

I'VE SAID IT BEFORE AND I'LL SAY IT AGAIN—THE TELE-
phone is a homicide detective's most valuable tool.
If we venture into areas where court orders are
required, telephone-company people can be hard-
nosed as hell. Outside those sticky areas, though,
they are worth their weight in gold.

Using the telephone over the years, I've established working relationships with any number of
people I never see, people I know by voice on a first-
name basis but wouldn't recognize if I ran into them
in the grocery store.

Gloria Hutchins is one of those people. I wouldn't
know her from Adam if I met her on the street,
but if I heard her speak, I'd know her anywhere.
Gloria is the gravelly-voiced lady in the security
department at Pacific Northwest Bell who handles
requests for information from law-enforcement
officers.

When I got back to Belltown Terrace late that
afternoon, I took out my notebook, opened it to the

page with Linda Decker's new phone number on it, and dialed Gloria Hutchins' number. I didn't have to look it up. That's one I know by heart.

"Hi, Gloria," I said casually. "Detective Beaumont here. How's it going?"

There was a warm greeting in her low voice when she answered. "Why, hello there, Beau. Long time no see. Where've you been, on vacation?"

"No such luck," I responded. "I've been locked up on a special assignment."

"What can I do for you?"

"I've got a telephone number, but I need an address."

"Case number?" Gloria asked.

I just happened to have one. I had jotted down the boat-fire case number from Jim Harrison's file folder at Harbor Station. I gave Gloria the case number and Linda Decker's phone number.

"Things are really popping around here right now," Gloria said. "It's going to be awhile before I can get to this. What's your number?"

The problem was, I was calling her from home. I didn't much want to give her that number for a call-back. That would look bad. Instead, I gave her my extension at work. "I'll be leaving here in a few minutes," I told her. "Just give the address to whoever answers. Tell them it's for me."

"Will do," Gloria said. "Anything else?"

"Nope. That's it for now. Thanks."

I hung up and turned to a stack of unopened mail that had accumulated on the table beside my chair. The first three envelopes were bills, but between the bills and the gaudy collection of junk mail addressed to "Resident" was a handwritten envelope with no return address. I slit it open and scanned down the scrawled page to the signature on the bottom—Martin Green.

Letting the letter drop back on the table, I went to pour myself a MacNaughton's. If I was going to be forced to endure a tirade about the Bentley, at least I could do it in comfort.

And tirade it was. Mr. Green informed that he was most unhappy with the lack of availability of the Bentley, especially since he had reserved it well in advance. He went on to say that the Bentley was one of the advertised amenities which had attracted him to the building in the first place. Since I was the only member of the real-estate syndicate who was readily available, he said he hoped we could get together to resolve the situation amicably. If not, he was prepared to take us to the Better Business Bureau.

I finished drinking the MacNaughton's and reading the letter at approximately the same time. I had wanted an excuse to talk to Martin Green. Now I had one, although it could hardly be called an engraved invitation. I retied my tie, grabbed my jacket off the dining-room chair, and retrieved my shoes from their place next to the front door. This felt like one of those situations where casual attire would be a distinct disadvantage. Somebody told me once that in winning by intimidation, you have to dress the part.

Secured-building etiquette requires that you call before you knock on someone's door. According to directory assistance, Martin Green had an unlisted telephone number. I went down to the garage and dialed his code on the security phone. A woman answered and I gave her my name. There was a good deal of background noise, and she evidently couldn't hear me very well.

"Who?" she demanded.

"My name is Beaumont," I repeated.

"There are too many people here. It's too noisy. Come on up. Apartment 1704."

The door to 1704 stood slightly ajar and the sound of voices told me a party of some kind was in progress. I'm not sure what I expected. For me the word "ironworker" conjures up a macho image of men in khaki work shirts and hard hats swilling beer and telling dirty jokes. Martin Green's party was nothing like that. The room was full of gray-suited bean-counter types and their female escorts who drank champagne from dainty crystal champagne flutes and nibbled bite-sized canapés.

A silver-haired lady in a pearl-gray dress met me at the door. "I'm Martin's mother." She beamed at me. "I'm playing hostess tonight. Won't you come in? What would you like to drink?"

"I just stopped by to see Martin for a few minutes," I told her. "Maybe it would be better if I came back another time."

She shook her head. "Oh, no. Don't do that. I'm sure he'd want to see you. He left just a moment ago to take some of his guests down to show them the recreation floor, you know, the pool and the Jacuzzi and all that. They'll be back in a few minutes if you don't mind waiting."

I allowed myself to be ushered inside. Almost instantly a glass of champagne appeared in my hand. The room was crowded and stuffy despite the fact that the heat-pump air-conditioning was going full blast. There were far too many people crammed in the relatively small living room. I made my way to the far side, hoping to escape the crush and also to gain a vantage point from which to watch the proceedings.

The 04 units in Belltown Terrace all have balconies which look out on the city. There was a lone man standing outside on the balcony peering out at the rank upon rank of downtown skyscrapers standing stiffly at attention against a pale blue August sky. Here and there hammerhead cranes served as lonely sentinels marking the emergence of yet more new buildings.

Another group of people came into the room, and those already inside pressed back. Feeling claustrophobic, I slid open the door and escaped onto the balcony. The lone man there glanced at me briefly, then continued to stare off into the distance. In his late thirties or early forties, he was reasonably well-built. The fabric of his jacket bunched tightly over muscular arms. He stood with one foot on the lower crossbar, his elbows resting on the upper railing. The drink in his hand wasn't champagne.

He said nothing, and I didn't either. Instead, I moved to the railing as well, and looked where he was looking—straight up Second Avenue toward the point where the raw skeleton of Masters Plaza climbed skyward. Swirling his drink, he gave me another sidelong glance as I stepped to the railing beside him, and then he drained his glass.

"It's bad luck to have a party like this the day after somebody went in the hole."

It was the first time I had ever heard that particular expression, but it wasn't hard to grasp the meaning. He was talking about Angie Dixon falling to her death. From the grim set of his mouth I could see it was gnawing at him. He assumed it was bothering me as well.

"Did you know her?" he asked.

"No," I said.

He shook his head balefully. "It always hurts to lose a hand," he added. "No matter how long a guy stays in this business it never gets any easier."

His fingers tightened around his empty glass. For a moment, I thought he was going to crush it barehanded. At last he opened his fist, letting the glass lay in his open palm. For the first time I noticed the callouses, the work-roughened texture of his skin. The rest of the men at Martin Green's party may have been bean-counting accountant types with Harvard MBAs, but the guy on the balcony seemed to be an ordinary Joe Blow, a regular working stiff. I wondered if, like me, he had wandered uninvited into the wrong party.

A waitress stepped out on the balcony carrying a tray of champagne glasses. I took one, but my companion ordered Scotch—neat. No rocks, no ice, no soda. As the waitress walked away, he reached up and yanked savagely on the knot of his tie, pulling it loose from the base of his Adam's apple.

"I hate these goddamned monkey suits," he complained, "but we have to wear 'em whenever the visiting dignitaries come to call."

"What visiting dignitaries?" I asked.

He glanced at me wearily. "You're not one of them, then?" he asked, nodding toward the roomful of bean-counters.

I shook my head in answer. "I'm a neighbor from the building," I explained. "I stopped by to talk to Martin. I didn't mean to crash his party."

He frowned. "But you know about . . ." He jerked his head in the direction of Masters Plaza.

"I read the papers," I said. The young woman returned with his Scotch. He accepted it gratefully and took a swift gulp. I waited until the woman had gone back inside and slid the door shut behind her before I spoke again. "You were saying about the accident . . ."

He turned away from me, once more leaning over the balcony. "Me and my big mouth," he said. "I was talking out of turn."

"My name's Beaumont. I didn't catch yours."

"Kaplan," he answered, offering me his hand. "Don Kaplan."

"What do you do?"

He laughed bitterly. "Me? I'm just a broken-down rod-buster who went bad."

"Rod-buster?" I asked.

"An ironworker," he explained. "Rebar—reinforcing steel—as opposed to structural. If my back hadn't given out on me, I'd probably still be tying rods on the I-90 bridge. As it is, they kicked me upstairs. I'm a business agent now."

A burst of laughter inside the room behind us. "And what's this all about?" I asked.

Lifting his glass to his lips, Don Kaplan paused

before he took a drink. "VIP's from International out pressing the flesh." There was an unmistakable trace of sarcasm in his voice.

Before he could say anything more, the door slid open behind us. "There you are, Don. I've been looking all over for you." Martin Green stepped onto the balcony behind us, leading a trio made up of two men and an accompanying sweet young thing. All three were laughing uproariously.

"Here's Don. You three will be riding with him. You know how to get into the parking garage at Columbia Center, don't you, Don?"

Don Kaplan nodded shortly, as though he didn't much relish the ride.

"And then if you'll drop them back off at the Sorrento after dinner."

"No problem," Don mumbled.

Green turned to me with a puzzled expression on his face. "I don't believe we've been introduced," he said, extending his hand.

"My name's Beaumont." I reached into my breast pocket and extracted the envelope. "I didn't mean to crash your party. I came by to talk to you about this. The lady at the door mistook me for one of your guests."

Martin Green laughed. "That's my mother all right, but this really isn't a very good time for me. We have a dinner reservation downtown in a little while. Could we make an appointment for tomorrow or the next day?"

The charming smile never left Green's face as he took me by the elbow and guided me unerringly through his guests to the front door where his mother was still holding court. It was one of the smoothest bum's rushes I've ever experienced. Smooth as glass and absolutely effective.

"What time tomorrow?" I asked.

"Nine? Nine-thirty? Whatever's good for you."

"Nine-thirty," I said. "Where?"

"Do you know where my office is next door in the Labor Temple?" he asked.

"I'm sure I can find it."

"Good," he said. "I'll see you then." With that he closed the door and left me standing in the hallway. Here's your hat; what's your hurry.

I had no more than gotten back to my apartment when the phone rang. The last person I expected to hear from was Marilyn Sykes, the Mercer Island Chief of Police. She and I had met several months earlier and had become friends. She was single and so was I. On occasion things came up where one of us needed to have an escort and we had called on each other to pinch-hit. We had good times when we were out together, with no pressure for our relationship to be either more or less than it was. We had only one hard-and-fast rule between us—no talking shop.

"How about a hot date?" she asked.

I laughed. "With you?" Our rare dates were fun but hardly hot.

"I know this is late notice. I was supposed to be out of town today and now I'm not. The Mercer Island Chamber of Commerce is doing its big benefit dinner tonight. Would you consider coming along and bailing me out of hot water? I really should put in an appearance."

"Sure," I said. "What time?"

"It's supposed to have started at six, but if we're a little late, it won't matter."

Had the Bentley been working, I would have had Pete drive me over to Mercer Island to pick her up—just to make a splash. As it was, I took the Porsche.

The first time I ever saw Marilyn Sykes she was a take-charge lady wearing a gray pinstriped suit and directing a SWAT team. When I picked her up at home that night, she had on a low-cut cream-colored evening gown. She's tall for a woman, five eleven or so, with hazel-colored eyes and naturally curly brown hair. I liked the dress a whole lot more than the suit.

I drove while she gave directions. It was a circuitous route that took us to the backside of the island and down a long hill to a magnificent house on the water. A parking attendant met us in the circular driveway to take care of the car while I went around to open the door for Marilyn.

"By the way, Beau," she said, taking my hand and letting me help her to her feet. "There's one thing I forgot to mention."

"What's that?"

"I told you it's a benefit dinner, but I didn't tell you what kind."

"Don't worry about it," I said. "As long as it's not my own cooking, I'll eat anything."

She smiled. "It's a murder mystery dinner."

I stopped in my tracks. "A what?"

"You know, one of those dinners where they hire

actors to do a fake murder and the guests try to figure out who did it. I was afraid if I told you, you might not want to come."

"You're right about that," I said. "But we're here now. We could just as well go on in."

The host and hostess met us at the door. Mercifully, when she introduced us, Marilyn kept quiet about my profession. When they ushered us inside, I could see we were more than a little late. The huge living room was already full of people. I guess it was a nice enough place, but I didn't have a whole lot of opportunity to check it out.

We had barely gotten inside the door when an elegant blonde made a move on me and started bending my ear about buying some real estate, something about the house next door. What did I think? Would it be a good investment or not? Totally without an opinion on the subject, I glanced around looking for Marilyn, hoping she'd rescue me. Instead, she made a beeline for the food and left me to handle the blonde on my own. I had about convinced myself the lady was a mental case when a man came striding up to us carrying two drinks, one of which he shoved in the woman's direction.

"You just can't do it, can you," he commented snidely to the woman. "You can't be trusted alone long enough for me to go order a drink."

"Wait a minute," I began, "we were just . . ."

"You stay out of this," he snarled at me. "This is between us. After all, she *is* my wife."

The blonde began twisting her wedding ring nervously. "Come on, Carl. It wasn't anything like that. I was only telling him about buying the house next door."

"Like hell you were! I saw the way you looked at him when he walked in the room. He's your type, isn't he. Tall—" He paused long enough to look at me. "Tall, gray, and handsome."

"Please, Carl, don't do this. Not here in front of all these people."

Carl shook his head. "I'd stay away from her if I were you. She collects men the way some people collect bowling trophies. They don't mean much afterwards, do they, my dear."

A deep flush began creeping up the back of my neck. Everyone in the room was staring at us, overhearing every word. On the far edge of the crowd, there was Marilyn holding a plate of hors d'oeuvres. She wasn't going to be any help at all.

Carl turned to me and gave me a companionable whack on one shoulder. "No hard feelings, of course, old boy!" he said. With that, he walked away.

At a loss for words, I turned back to the blonde just as she took a tentative sip of her drink. "I'm so sorry," she apologized. "He's been like that more and more lately, and the doctors can't tell me what's wrong."

"Try a shrink," I suggested. "I think he's off his rocker."

Suddenly, the blonde's eyes got big. She sputtered and choked.

"What's the matter?" I asked.

She looked at me helplessly, shook her head, and clutched at her throat. Staggering away from me, she fell facedown on the carpet and lay there without moving.

Carl raced to her side and turned her over. He placed his ear against her breast.

"Get an ambulance," someone shouted.

Carl sat up, gravely shaking his head. "It's too late for an ambulance," he said. "She's dead."

I glanced over at the spot where I had last seen Marilyn. She was almost doubled over with laughter. That's when I finally realized what was going on, that these were the actors and they had suckered me into their script as a reluctant leading man.

When I finally pushed my way through the crowd to Marilyn, she was still laughing.

"What's so funny? Did you know they were going to do that?" I demanded.

She shook her head. "I had no idea, but you were perfect. I didn't know you could act."

"I can't," I answered grimly.

Marilyn handed me a plate of food—smoked salmon, fruit and vegetables with dip. "Try this," she said. "After all that hard work, you should at least get something to eat."

Much as I hate to admit it, the evening turned out to be fun. The rest of the party was occupied with trying to figure out who had murdered the blonde. Some even suspected me which I found hilarious. Most suspected Carl. When all was said and done, though, the killer turned out to be Carl's gay lover.

It was late when I finally took Marilyn home, but she invited me up to her apartment for a nightcap.

We sat there for some time, laughing and comparing notes on the evening. I was about to get up and leave when she put her hand on my leg.

"You wouldn't be interested in spending the night, would you?" she asked casually.

I slid my hand over hers. "I could probably be persuaded," I replied.

And so she set about persuading me.

CHAPTER 11

MARILYN SYKES FIXED BREAKFAST FOR US THE NEXT morning. It was the kind of breakfast that made me think I'd died and gone to heaven—crisp bacon, over-easy eggs, toasted English muffins, black coffee, fresh orange juice. When she stopped beside me long enough to pour a second cup of coffee, I gave her a playful pat on the rump.

"You're my kind of woman," I said. "Your breakfast ranks right up there with the Doghouse."

She laughed. "Just don't let anybody around my department hear you say that. After all, I have a certain professional image to maintain, you know."

"You mean the chief's not supposed to cook great over-easy eggs."

She smiled. "Among other things."

"Don't worry. Your secret's safe with me."

When it was time to leave, Marilyn walked me to the door. By then she had put on her dress-for-success costume as well as her sensible shoes. The transformation seemed complete, but at the door she took hold of the two loose ends of my tie, pulled me close to her, and tied it for me. A perfect four-in-hand.

It was an awkward moment. I didn't know what to say, so I leaned over and kissed her. "I had a wonderful time," I said. "Thanks."

"Me too," she murmured. "We'll have to do it again sometime."

Marilyn's condominium complex has a guard shack with twenty-four-hour coverage. A young security guard had noted down my license number the night before when I brought Marilyn home, and now another beardless youth waved and checked off something on a clipboard as I drove past. I admit to feeling a little guilty, which was silly since Marilyn Sykes and I are both well past the age of consent. Nevertheless, it's one thing to do a sleep-over. It's something else to have a security guard taking down your vehicle license number while you do it.

I was soon too immersed in traffic to worry about the security guard. Living downtown, I seldom had occasion to drive from Mercer Island back into the city during morning rush-hour traffic. I hope I never have to again. It was a mess. Despite years of work, that section of I-90 still wasn't complete, and I soon discovered what Mercer Island commuters have been saying all along, that there aren't nearly enough on-ramps to allow island residents adequate access to the roadway.

I inched forward, one car length at a time. It wasn't as though there was a tangible reason for the problem on the bridge, not even so much as a flat tire or a fender-bender. I guess rush-hour traffic moves like that every day of the week. It would drive me crazy. It makes me glad I can walk to work.

Back home in Belltown Terrace finally, I had just time enough to change clothes before my scheduled interview with Martin Green. To reach his office, all I had to do was go downstairs and cut through the garage entrance on Clay. That's my idea of commuting. It was evidently Martin Green's as well.

The Labor Temple has been at First and Broad for as long as I can remember. It's a low-rise, two-story building that occupies the entire half-block. My only previous visits had been on election day when I went there to vote. The building directory told me Ironworkers Local 165 was located on the second floor.

There were a few men lingering in the gray marble hallway outside the ironworkers' office, burly men in plaid flannel shirts and work boots with telltale faded circles of tobacco cans marking their hip pockets. On the door was a typed notice announcing that the office would be closed the next day from 1 to 4 P.M. so office staff members could attend the funeral of deceased member Angie Dixon.

I stepped inside and announced myself to a female clerk who was seated behind a counter. She glanced uneasily over her shoulder in the direction of a closed door. "Is Mr. Green expecting you?" she asked.

"Yes," I said. "My name's Beaumont. I have an appointment at nine-thirty."

She looked slightly hesitant. "He has someone with him just now, if you don't mind waiting."

I sat down on a surly, swaybacked vinyl couch that squatted against the outside wall. Next to it sat a scarred end table with a few dog-eared magazines and a smelly, overflowing ashtray. If ironworkers had heard anything about the Surgeon General's warning on cigarettes, they weren't paying attention.

At the far end of the room, a second woman finished running an exceptionally noisy copy machine and returned to her desk. In the newly silent office, I became aware of the sound of raised voices coming from behind the closed door I assumed led to Martin Green's private office. I was looking at it when the door flew open and a man stormed out.

"I quit, goddamnit! If all I'm fit for is to sit in a tool shack and make up bolts, that's what I'll do, but I'll be goddamned if I'll do this son of a bitch of a job one more minute."

Saying that, he slammed the door to Green's office with such force that the frosted glass window shattered and slipped to the floor. As he rushed past, I realized it was Don Kaplan, the man I'd met on Martin Green's balcony the night before. He strode by me without any sign of recognition. I don't think he noticed anyone was there.

The two women working in the outer office exchanged guarded looks, then one of them rose and stepped gingerly toward the broken door. Instead of speaking to Martin Green through the jagged hole in the glass, she carefully opened the door.

"There's a Mr. Beaumont here to see you," she said. Green must have said something in return because she motioned to me. "You can come in now, Mr. Beaumont."

Martin Green came to the door to greet me. "You'll have to forgive the mess," he apologized. "We've had a little problem here this morning."

"I noticed."

He ushered me into the room. "We've got a hell of a union here, Mr. Beaumont, almost perfect. But it's like anything else. There are always people who don't like the way things are going."

"People who want it to be more perfect?" I asked.

Green nodded. "You could say that," he said with a laugh. "A more perfect union."

He directed me to one of the two chairs facing his desk. Perfect or not, Martin Green's union work space was a far cry from his private living quarters in Belltown Terrace. His apartment was definitely upscale, first-class cabin all the way and spare no expense. In contrast, Ironworkers Local 165 had him in lowbrow digs. The chair he offered me was one of the gray-metal/green-plastic variety. I recognized it instantly as a littermate of chairs we still use down at the department. You don't often see relics like that anywhere outside the confines of municipal police departments and old county courthouses.

Martin Green seated himself in a creaking chair behind a battered wooden desk and smiled cordially. "Now what can I do for you, Mr. Beaumont?" Under his outward show of easy congeniality, I sensed that he was still deeply disturbed by whatever had gone on between him and Don Kaplan.

"The Bentley, remember?" I reminded him.

"Oh, yes, that's right. In all the hubbub it slipped my mind. Is it going to be fixed soon?"

"Within a matter of days, we hope. In the meantime, we have the Cadillac. I know it's not quite in the same class . . ."

"Oh, the Cadillac's fine," he interrupted, waving aside my explanation. "As long as there's something available. Forgive me. I never should have gone ahead and mailed that letter to you. I was just so irritated. My mother would have been thrilled to be picked up at the airport in something as exotic as a Bentley. You know how mothers are."

I was a little taken aback by Green's total about-face, but I wasn't going to argue the point. If he was happy, I was happy.

"Does that mean you won't be taking us to the Better Business Bureau?"

"Of course not. There's no call to do that, none at all. As I said, I was upset at the time, but I'm not an unreasonable man, Mr. Beaumont. Surely you can see that."

"Indeed I can." I hadn't anticipated that the interview would go quite so smoothly. Martin Green was already getting ready to show me out of his office and I hadn't had time to mention my other reason for coming. "By the way, I noticed on the front door that one of your members passed away. That wasn't the woman who died in the accident at Masters Plaza on Sunday, was it?"

He rose and came around the desk, stopping in front of me with his arms crossed, nodding his head sadly. "I'm afraid it was. Angie Dixon was one of our newer apprentices. A most unfortunate circumstance, but then nobody ever said working iron wasn't dangerous."

Green motioned toward the broken window. "Actually, the guy who was in here just a few minutes ago, Don Kaplan, I think maybe you met him last night. He's the one who's in charge of our apprenticeship program. He's taking Angie's death real hard. Personally, I guess you could say."

Martin Green moved away from the desk and led me to the door. "Watch your step," he cautioned as I started across the jagged shards of glass. "I wouldn't want you to slip and fall. Kim, is someone going to clean this mess up?"

The woman who had let me into his office nodded. "I've called maintenance, Mr. Green," she answered. "A janitor is on the way." Something about the speed of her response, her quick retreat to the safety of her typewriter made me suspect Martin Green wasn't an altogether easy man to work for.

I stopped beside the counter and turned back to where he was still standing in the layer of broken glass. "By the way," I said. "Thanks for the champagne last night. I didn't mean to crash your party."

He waved. "Think nothing of it," he replied absently. With that, he turned and disappeared back into his office, closing the shattered door behind him while the two secretaries exchanged discreet looks of undisguised relief.

I left the Labor Temple with the feeling that my mission had been totally successful from a property management point of view. I had gotten Martin Green off the backs of the Belltown Terrace management group and made sure the Bentley wouldn't cause us any more adverse publicity. Green was willing to let bygones be bygones, and so were we.

In addition, I had discovered that Don Kaplan, someone I knew, if only slightly, was a person I could talk to in order to learn more about the ironworker apprenticeship program. How I'd go about it and under what pretext were details I hadn't quite handled yet, but at least I knew who to ask.

When I got back home there was a message on the answering machine from Margie, my clerk down at the department. The message said to give her a call.

"What are you doing, working on your vacation?" Margie asked.

"What makes you think that?"

She laughed. "Easy. I've got a message here for you from Gloria over at the phone company. She says the address you need is 24 Pe Ell Star Route. Where's that?"

"Beats me. Down around Raymond somewhere, I think."

"That's a little outside the city limits, isn't it?" Margie asked.

She was teasing me, and I knew what she was thinking. Cops do it all the time, use official channels to get the address or phone number of someone they've met and want to see again. It isn't legal, but it does happen.

"Leave me alone," I said. "Anything else?"

"As a matter of fact, there is one more message. It's from Big Al. He wants to know when you're going to stop farting around and come back to work."

"Tell him Tuesday, and not a minute before."

"Will do," she answered with a barely suppressed giggle. "He misses you."

Once I was off the phone, I dragged my worn *Rand McNally Road Atlas* off the bookshelf. It was several years out of date, but I suspected the only real difference would be in a few freeway interchanges. The rural roads, especially ones running through little burgs like Pe Ell, would be essentially unchanged.

The town was right where I thought it would be, about twenty-five miles off Interstate 5 between Chehalis and Raymond on Highway 6. I had never been there, had never wanted to go there, but I was going nevertheless.

By noon, I was on the freeway, headed south. Traffic was fairly heavy as out-of-state recreational vehicles lumbered home toward Oregon, California, and points south and east. There weren't any log trucks, though. The lack of rain had turned Washington's lush forests tinder-dry and shut down the woods to logging and camping both.

As I drove, I tried tuning in the radio. I heard a snippet of news reporting a fatal fire somewhere on the east side of Lake Washington. I switched the dial. I wanted music, not news. I was on vacation, out of town. Whatever was on the news wasn't my problem.

Highway 6 turned off at Chehalis and meandered west through wooded hills. Sometimes it ran under trees so thick they formed an impenetrable green canopy over the roadway. Other times it moved along near the bed of the shallow headwaters of the Chehalis River. I stopped at a wide spot in the road, a hamlet called Doty, to buy a soda and ask directions.

"Where does Pe Ell Star Route start?" I asked the woman clerk as she gave me my change.

"Just the other side of town," she answered, eyeing me suspiciously. "How come you wanna know? Lookin' for somebody in partic'lar?"

"A friend of mine from Seattle," I said. "She just moved down here."

"You must mean that crazy lady with the two little kids. Yeah, she's up the road here apiece—five, six miles or so. It's a blue house on the left. You can't miss it. Looks more like a jail than the real one does over in Chehalis."

I puzzled over that remark, but only until I saw the house. It was easy to find. The house, just across the road from the river, was nestled back against the bottom of a steep, timber-covered bluff. It was small, as two-story houses go. All the windows and doors on the lower floor had been covered with ornamental iron bars. It did indeed look like a jail.

A beat-up Datsun station wagon was parked near the house. On one side, two children were playing under a towering apple tree. A little girl sat in a swing with her hair flying behind her, while a boy, somewhat older, pushed her high enough to run underneath the swing when it reached its highest point.

I drove all the way past the house once, then made a U-turn and came back from the other direction. As I pulled into the driveway behind the Datsun, the little boy grabbed the rope and stopped the swing so abruptly the little girl almost pitched out on her face. He grabbed her by one arm to keep her from falling and pulled her down from the swing.

Stepping out of the car, I called across to them. "Hello there. Is your mother home?"

The little girl opened her mouth as if to answer, but the boy yanked on her arm and dragged her toward the house.

"Wait a minute," I said. "I just need to ask you a couple of questions."

Without a backward glance, the two of them scurried away from me like a pair of frightened wild animals, with the boy urgently tugging the girl along beside him. I paused long enough to look toward the house. An upstairs curtain fluttered as though someone behind it had been watching us.

I closed the car door and started after the children. When I rounded the end of the house, I expected to see them there, but they weren't. The back porch was empty. I stepped up onto the porch and tugged at the iron grillwork over the door. It was still securely fastened from the inside. That puzzled me. I didn't think the children would have had enough time to get inside the house and relock the door.

Just then I heard what sounded like a door slamming shut on the backside of the house, the side closest to the steep bluff behind it. I walked around the corner and looked, expecting to find an additional outside entrance. Instead, the only thing I could see was a rectangular box built next to the foundation of the house. The top of the box was a full-sized wooden door. The door itself was slightly ajar, resting on an empty metal padlock hasp that had been closed inside.

Was this the door I had heard slam, or was there another one, farther around toward the front of the house? I walked around to the front door. It too was protected by a formidable grill-work cover, the kind that give fire fighters nightmares. I tested the bars. They had been carefully welded and solidly set by someone who knew what he was doing.

There was a doorbell next to the door, so I rang it. I heard a multi-note chime ring in the bowels of the house, but no one came to the door—not the kids, and not whoever had been watching from the upstairs window, either.

I rang again, and again nothing happened. Linda Decker must have given her children absolute orders about not speaking to strangers. That's not such a crazy idea. I believe in that myself, but I was sure there was someone else in the house, some adult. That's the person I wanted to talk to. I needed some answers.

I rang the bell a third time.

"What do you want?" A woman's voice wafted down to me from an upstairs window. I stepped back far enough to see. Above the front door a window stood open, but the curtain was drawn. No one was visible.

"Are you Linda Decker?" I asked.

Instead of answering my question, she asked another of her own. "How did you find me?"

"Your brother," I said.

"What did you do, promise him a ride in that fancy car of yours if he'd tell you?" There was a hard, biting edge to her words. There was also a hint that the information wasn't news to her.

"It wasn't like that," I said. "He was upset. He had missed his bus. I gave him a ride to the center, that's all. I'm a police officer," I added.

"Right, and I'm the Tooth Fairy," she responded.

"Look," I said. "I've got my ID right here. Come to the window. I'll toss it up to you."

"Go ahead," she said.

I felt like an absolute idiot, standing out front of the little house, throwing my ID packet toward an open window. It took several tries, but finally I made it. My ID dropped inside the windowsill and fell between the window and the curtain. There was a slight movement behind the curtain as someone stepped forward to retrieve the wallet.

"See there?" I called. "That's me. That's my picture. Can I come in now?"

"Why are you here?"

"I'm investigating the death of Logan Tyree. I want to ask you a few questions."

"Just a minute," she said.

She was gone a long time, not one minute but several. I still couldn't see her, but eventually she returned to the window and tossed my ID back down to me. "You can come in now," she said, "but you'll have to use the kids' door."

"Where's that?"

"Out back along the side of the house."

"The side!" I echoed. "But there isn't any door there."

"The coal chute."

"That's how they get in and out?" She didn't answer. I was right then—the kids had gotten into the house some other way besides the back door. I couldn't help wondering what kind of mother would make her children come in and out of the house through a coal chute. Not your standard, garden variety, cookies-and-milk type mother, that's for damn sure.

"I'll meet you in the basement," Linda Decker called down to me. "I'll go switch on the light."

With a sigh I turned away from the front door of the house. The woman at the store in Doty was probably right. Linda Decker was crazy as a bedbug.

Regretting that I was wearing good clothes, I walked back to the coal chute and lifted the door. It was heavy but not so heavy that kids wouldn't be able to open and close it themselves. There was no squawk of protest from the hinges. Although there was still some rust showing, they had recently been thoroughly oiled.

I paused long enough to run my hand over the padlock hasp on the outside of the door. I wondered if sometimes Linda locked her children inside the house when she was away. If she did, she wouldn't be the first mother who made that sometimes fatal mistake in houses with barred doors and windows. They lock the doors to protect their children, and the children die of smoke inhalation or worse. The idea made me shudder.

I peered down into the coal chute. The top of a ladder was visible, coming up out of the darkened depths of the basement. It leaned against the inside of the box close enough that the top rung was within easy reach. A light switched on in the basement below me. I heard Linda Decker's voice again.

"Just step over the edge of the box and climb down the ladder."

Beneath me, the ladder seemed to be set firmly enough on a bare concrete floor. I put one hand on it and tested it for stability. It didn't wobble at all. If Linda Decker trusted the ladder enough to let her children climb up and down it, I supposed it was good enough for me. Not only that, the coal chute itself looked as though every trace of coal dust had been carefully scrubbed away. That must have taken some doing.

Swinging one leg up and over the side of the box, I found the top rung of the ladder with one foot and stepped onto it. Before starting down the ladder, I took one last look around outside. I was half afraid some neighbor would see me and think I was breaking into Linda Decker's house. There was no one in sight.

The ladder was solid and steady beneath my feet. I started down, one rung at a time. As my shoulders and head descended into the basement, I could see that the room was nearly empty, except for a scatter of boxes and a few odd pieces of discarded furniture. The room was lit by the glaring glow of one bare bulb dangling from an ancient cord in the middle of the raw plywood ceiling.

One foot was on the floor and the other was still on the bottom rung of the ladder when suddenly the heavy door to the coal chute slammed shut over my head. At the same instant the light went out, plunging me into total darkness.

Above me, I heard somebody struggling with the

hasp. The padlock! Someone was trying to fasten the padlock!

Scrambling hand over hand, I raced back up the ladder only to crash head-first into the door just as the lock clicked home.

"We got him, Mommie," a child's voice crowed in triumph. "We got him."

They sure as hell had.

CHAPTER 12

REELING FROM THE SELF-INFLICTED BLOW TO MY HEAD and afraid of falling, I clung desperately to the ladder as tiny pinpricks of light exploded around me. Unfortunately, the stars flashing before my eyes did nothing to lighten the inky blackness of Linda Decker's basement.

My legs shook uncontrollably. Fighting vertigo, I made my way back down to the floor. I counted the rungs on the ladder. Seven in all from the point where I'd banged my head.

I stood on the floor holding the side of the ladder for several minutes trying to get my bearings, waiting for the shaking and dizziness to stop, hoping that somehow my eyes would adjust to the darkness. Eventually the trembling diminished, but I still couldn't see my hand in front of my face when I tackled the ladder again. I didn't know what was going on, but one thing was clear: I had to try to get out.

Careful not to damage my head further, I counted the rungs as I climbed, inching my way up the ladder far enough to brace my back and shoulders against the door. I grunted with exertion, pushing against the resistant wood as hard as I could, but the pressure wasn't enough. The hasp, the hinges, and the wood all held firm.

Giving up, I stood for a moment hunched under the door, listening for any sound of voice or movement outside or inside. There was nothing—no footsteps in the room above me, no whispered deliberations outside—only the dull interior thud of my own pounding heartbeat.

I was over being surprised and scared. Now I was angry. Pissed. I was certain the childish cry of victory had come from the little boy as he slammed shut the coal chute door. What the hell were they up to? I could picture the three of them, Linda Decker and her two children, standing somewhere just out of earshot, gloating over my having fallen into their little trap.

They'd trapped me all right, but we'd see who had the last laugh on that score. Assaulting a police officer is no joke. Kidnapping one isn't either. Linda Decker hadn't figured that out yet, but I fully intended to show her, just as soon as I got the hell out of her goddamned basement.

Cautiously counting the rungs, I made my way back down to the floor. In the instant before the light had gone out, I could remember glimpsing a stairway on the other side of the basement. Now, with my eyes finally accustomed to the dark, I could see a faint glow that had to be daylight leaking into the basement through a crack under a door at the top of the stairs.

I attempted walking toward it, only to stumble over an invisible box on the floor and crash, nose-first, into a solid upright timber. A quick spurt of blood told me I'd done something to my nose—something bad, something that would add another lump to it and give my face more character. Just what I needed.

Maybe I'm not too bright at times, but at least I learn from my mistakes. I dropped to my hands and knees and began crawling toward that tiny sliver of light at the top of the stairs. The concrete floor was cold and damp beneath me as I groped my way across it, creeping along like an overgrown baby. The basement was musty and reeked with the smell of long-resident mice. The house had probably stood vacant for some time before Linda Decker and her children moved into it.

I made slow progress. The actual distance across the basement couldn't have been more than twenty feet or so, but in the dark it was one hell of an obstacle course. What had seemed like a relatively empty room with the light on was actually a jumble of wood and boxes, furniture and tools.

Along the way I jammed my knee down on something sharp, a piece of broken glass or a loose nail that my scouting hands had missed. There was a sudden telltale wetness on my knee and leg, unmistakably warm and slick. The texture of rough concrete on lacerated skin told me I'd torn the hell out of both my knee and my pants. The knee would heal; the pants wouldn't. And this was one pair I wouldn't be able to voucher. I'd never get Seattle P.D. to agree that tearing my pants in Linda Decker's treacherous basement ought to qualify as a line of duty mishap.

Had the lights been on, I'm sure I would have made quite a sight. The bloodied nose and the torn knee created a symmetry of sorts, the top and bottom halves of a matched set. An ugly matched set.

At last my fingers touched the far wall. I inched my way along it until I located the bottom of the stairs. They were made of rough-hewn cobweb-covered planks open at the back end. My hands searched in vain for a handrail on the outside. There wasn't any. Running my hands up and down the wall I located a two-inch pipe that had been bolted to the wall as a make-do banister. Clutching it gratefully, I eased my body up the stairs, feeling my way one step at a time, clinging to the pipe with one hand while sharp wooden splinters from the steps bit into the palm of my other hand.

Being blind must be hell, but real blind people have canes and seeing-eye dogs. I only knew things were in my way after I ran into them. That's a little late.

On step number twelve I barked a knuckle against something metal—something round and metal and cool. It was another grill, more of the ornamental iron bars I had seen on the outside of the house. Beyond the bars was the smooth finished surface of a wooden door.

Suddenly, I heard swift footsteps coming toward me. The light came on and the wooden door fell open beneath my hand. When the door gave way, it took me by surprise and I lost my balance. I had to grab hold of the metal bars to keep from pitching ass over teakettle back down the stairs.

When I righted myself and looked up, I found myself staring into the barrel of the biggest pistol I'd ever seen. From where I was, it looked a hell of a lot more like a cannon than a handgun. I was only dimly aware of the woman behind it, but her words came through loud and clear.

"Let go of the bars. Now!"

I let go and retreated down the stairs a step or two.

Her voice was steady even though the gun wasn't. "Mister, if you've got a gun on you, you'd better shove it under this rail right now before I blast you into a million pieces!"

There was no doubt in my mind that Linda Decker meant what she said. Even if she didn't, I couldn't afford to call her bluff, not with a gun pointed right between my eyes from some three feet away. A shaking gun at that.

"Okay, okay," I said. "Take it easy."

Cautiously I eased the Smith and Wesson out of my shoulder holster. I didn't want to do anything to alarm my captor. She was nervous enough already. Her finger was still poised on the trigger while the barrel of the gun trembled violently. It scared the holy crap out of me.

I slipped my gun, handle first, through a flat, clear space at the bottom of the metal bars. With a quick, deft movement she kicked it behind her, sending it spinning away across the linoleum floor until it came to rest against the bottom of a kitchen cupboard.

"Now take off your jacket and push it through here, too," she ordered.

"Look," I began. "You're making a terrible mistake."

"Shut up and take off the jacket."

I did. "What's going on? You already saw my ID. You know I'm a cop." I finished poking the jacket under the bars and glanced up at the gun. It was still pointing at me, still shaking.

"I don't know anything of the kind," Linda Decker answered. Without ever taking her eyes off me, she kicked my jacket away as well.

"Call my partner, Detective Lindstrom at Seattle P.D. He'll vouch for me."

"Cop or no cop, you're still working for them," she retorted.

I took a deep breath, summoned my most conciliatory tone, and tried again. After all, I'm supposed to be trained to talk my way out of tough situations. "Linda, I already told you, I'm investigating the death of Logan Tyree. I thought you'd want to help."

She winced when I mentioned his name, but she didn't back off. "Cut the bullshit. You tried that line already. I called Seattle P.D. just a few minutes ago. You're not assigned to Logan's case, so what the hell are you doing here?"

There was no point in trying to explain that I was on vacation and looking into Logan Tyree's death on my own because I felt like it, because I didn't like the way the official investigation was going. She wouldn't have believed that in a million years. Actually, I hardly believed it myself.

"I just wanted to talk to you, to ask you some questions."

"You went to a hell of a lot of trouble. I figured you'd show up today. I warned the kids to watch out for you, told them to come inside the minute they saw a strange red car."

She must have noticed the puzzled expression on my face. She answered my question without my ever asking it. "I talked to Jimmy last night. He told me all about you, about how you'd been so nice to him and given him a ride to the center. He told me you had asked about me, but he couldn't remember whether or not he'd given you my phone number. I guess we don't have to wonder about that anymore, do we. If you were on the up and up, you would have picked up a telephone and called."

She jerked the gun in my direction and my heart went to my throat. "Empty your pants pockets," she added. "Turn them inside out."

"Wait a minute . . ."

"Do it!" she commanded. "Now!"

I did. My car keys, change, and pocketknife ended up in a pitiful pile which I shoved under the grill.

The little girl appeared at her mother's side and clung to one leg, whining. "I'm scared, Mommie. What are we going to do with him? What's going to happen?"

"I don't know yet, Allison. Go on outside and play with Jason. I'll be out in a few minutes."

Allison backed away from the door, watching me warily through the bars as she did so.

"Now the ladder," Linda Decker ordered.

"The ladder!"

"Go get it, bring it over here, and shove it under the bars. It'll fit."

Linda Decker had evidently thought this whole scene through in some detail. She was leaving no stone unturned. I wouldn't get out of there until she was damned good and ready and not a moment before.

When the ladder had been shoved under the bars and moved safely out of reach across the kitchen, she sighed with relief.

"Now what?" I demanded. "I suppose the next thing you'll want me to take off my pants."

No matter how old I get, I'll never learn to keep my big mouth shut. I doubt she would have thought of it on her own if I hadn't been such a smart-ass and made the suggestion.

"That's a good idea."

And so the belt and pants came off, and my socks, and finally my dress shirt. I sat there in nothing but my shorts, feeling as naked as a plucked chicken. A trickle of blood was still running down my leg from the gash in my knee, but at least by then my nose had stopped bleeding.

"Now put your hands behind your head and keep them there."

I did as I was told, but I tried once more to talk some sense into her head. "Will you please listen to reason?" I asked. It's tough to sound reasonable when you're down to nothing but your skivvies, when you're talking to a total stranger who's packing a pistol.

I took a deep breath, searching for some scrap of

dignity. "I'm a sworn police officer, Linda. Are you aware you can go to jail for this?"

She waved the gun impatiently. She wasn't listening to me, hadn't heard a word I was saying. "Who sent you here?" she demanded.

"Nobody sent me."

"You tell me who sent you and then I'll figure out whether I should call the cops or plug you full of holes myself."

"I already told you, I came on my own," I insisted.

"You still expect me to believe that? Just how stupid do you think I am?"

When I didn't answer, she shrugged and turned away from me. She walked over to the counter long enough to pour herself a cup of coffee. Taking both the coffee and the gun with her, she sat down on a tall kitchen stool. She placed the gun on the counter beside her then sat there sipping coffee while she gazed at me speculatively. We had reached an impasse. Neither one of us said anything for some time.

Having the gun out of her hand made me feel a little better. Not a whole lot better, but a little. A loaded gun in the hands of a frightened person can be a deadly combination. There are plenty of dead cops out there to prove it's true. I didn't want to join them.

"Please listen to me. I'm a cop. A detective. I work for the Seattle P.D."

She laughed, but the sound was harsh and humorless. "Sure you are," she responded. "Can't you come up with something a little more original? We've been through that already and I'm not buying, remember?"

I didn't give up. "I came because I don't think Logan Tyree's death was an accident."

"Think?" she asked bitterly. "You *think* it wasn't an accident, or you *know*. Which is it?"

"You think I killed him?"

"Didn't you?" The countering question was quick and accompanied by a look of sheer hatred. "It doesn't matter," she added. "They're not here, either. You won't find them. They're in a safe place."

"What's not here?"

"After what happened to Logan, do you think I'm dumb enough to have those tapes with me?"

"What tapes?" I asked.

"And if anything happens to me . . ."

She was interrupted by a frantic pounding on the outside door leading into the kitchen. "Mommie, Mommie. Open the door quick. Somebody's coming."

Linda Decker leaped to her feet. She was wearing a loose-fitting sweatshirt and Levis. She stuffed the gun under her shirt and raced to the kitchen door, frantically unlocking a series of dead bolts and pushing open the grill to let the breathless children inside just as the doorbell rang at the front of the house.

"Who is it, Jason?" she hissed as she closed both the grill and the door and fastened all the locks.

"It's a policeman," Jason answered, his voice a high-pitched squeak. "With blue lights on top of the car and everything."

My first reaction was one of relief. A policeman. An ally. Someone who would make Linda Decker listen to me, someone who would help me out of my predicament.

The doorbell rang again, insistently. Wavering, Linda Decker glanced over her shoulder in the direction of the front door and then down at her two frightened children. Last of all she turned to me. Her face hardened. She reached under her shirt and tentatively touched the gun. For a moment I was afraid she was going to give it to Jason, but she evidently changed her mind. Quickly she retrieved my Smith and Wesson and shoved it under her shirt as well.

Then she came over to the barred basement door, close enough for me to hear her harsh whisper, but far enough away to remain safely out of reach.

"If you so much as make a sound, so help me God I'll kill you!"

With that, she slammed the door shut. The light went out. I was once more left in darkness, sitting almost naked on the wooden steps in Linda Decker's damp basement, smelling the mouse crap and feeling like a load of shit.

I didn't doubt for one minute that she'd do exactly what she said. I couldn't afford to doubt it. I was convinced she had balls enough and then some.

She also had the gun.

I waited. For a long time. I heard the sound of voices, and then the creak of footsteps as someone walked across a room, then the murmur of someone's voice, only one voice this time—Linda talking, but no one answering. She must have been on the phone. Again there was the creak of footsteps followed by voices again and then a whole flurry of footsteps, but no one came near the kitchen. No one opened the door to the basement for probably ten minutes or maybe longer. I'm not sure.

When the door did finally open, it was Linda Decker herself who flung it wide and hard, banging the doorknob into something metal, probably a stove.

She was different, totally different. Something had happened. Something had changed, and not for the better.

Before that, despite the trembling gun, she had been relatively calm, calculating, working a plan that she had laid out and rehearsed well in advance. Now as she stood staring at me through the barred door there was an icy fury behind her dangerously pale face. Her lips were pulled tight over clenched teeth.

Thankfully, she wasn't holding the gun. If she had been, I think she would have shot me on sight.

"You son of a bitch!" She barely whispered the words, her voice shaking with rage while ragged tremors raced through her whole body. "You goddamned son of a bitch!"

Jason hurried into the room, dragging the whimpering Allison with him. He stopped near his mother and looked up at her. What he saw must have frightened him. "Are you all right, Mommie?" he asked. The grave concern written on his face was far older than his years.

She tore her eyes from me and glanced down at her son. For a brief moment, her face softened. Her throat worked furiously as she tried three times to choke out an answer. Finally she nodded.

"I'm all right, Jason. Take Allison out to the car and fasten her seat belt. I'll be out in a minute."

"But the door is locked," he said.

Without a word, she walked to the door and unlocked the series of locks. I watched her hands. They were shaking so badly it was all she could do to control them. What had happened? What had made the difference? And where was the cop Jason had said was there?

When the outside door closed behind the children, she swung around to face me again. For a moment, she leaned heavily against the door as though every bit of strength had been drained from her body, as though she needed the door to hold her up.

"I'm sorry . . ." she began, then stopped as another violent tremor shook her body. By force of will she drew herself away from the door and started toward me.

She had begun with the words "I'm sorry," but there was no hint of apology in her body language. The gun was out of sight, but at that point she didn't need a gun. She was a menacing cat ready to spring at my face and claw me apart. For the first time, I was grateful for the bars that separated us.

"I'm sorry I didn't shoot you when I had a chance," she finished. She stopped only inches from the iron grill. Maybe I could have grabbed her through the bars, but I didn't try it. I don't believe in tackling wildcats with bare hands.

"It's up to them now," she added, "but if they don't take care of you, I will. That's a promise!"

With that she stepped back and slammed the wooden door shut. Once more Linda Decker's basement was plunged into total darkness. I didn't know I had been holding my breath until I let it out.

I felt a sudden rush of gratitude. I was the lucky man who is aware of seeing a rattlesnake only after he's already pulled his foot out of harm's way.

Linda Decker was gone, but in those last seconds before she turned away and slammed the door I looked into her eyes and knew what was different.

Before she left the kitchen to answer the doorbell, she had been undecided about what to do with me. Now she wasn't. Her mind was made up. And when I looked into her eyes, they were empty of everything but cold hatred. Hatred and a naked desire to kill me. I've seen it before. I know the danger.

In that moment, my life had hung in the balance, and yet, inexplicably, she had closed the door and walked away. Someone or something had stayed her hand, had kept her from killing me. I had been reprieved.

Almost sick with relief, I took a deep breath and settled down to wait.

I suppose my mother would have been proud of me. At least I was wearing clean shorts.

CHAPTER 13

I HAVE NO IDEA HOW LONG I WAITED. A HALF HOUR? Longer? It seemed forever, sitting there in the dark. There was no sound in the house. I knew Linda Decker had driven away. I had heard the door slam and the engine of a car turn over. What about the cop? Had he left along with them?

If I was really alone, I knew I should crawl back down the stairs and try to find some kind of tool that might help me break out of my prison, but I was understandably reluctant to search around in the dark. My knee still hurt. So did my nose.

I had started picking my way down the steps when I heard the distant wail of a siren. It was coming closer.

Cops don't believe in coincidences. They can't afford to. If there was a siren outside the house, it was because of me, because I was locked up in Linda Decker's basement.

The siren came almost to the house and then wound down to silence as I listened. Several car doors slammed shut and I heard a series of shouted commands. I should have felt relief. Here were the reinforcements I had wanted riding to the rescue, but now that they were outside, I didn't feel better. And I didn't call out to them. Some instinctive warning system told me that although they were cops and I was a cop, this time we weren't on the same side.

Heavy footsteps mounted the outside steps and entered the kitchen, accompanied by a series of barked commands. "She's got him locked up in the basement," someone said. "That's his car out there in the driveway. The red Porsche."

Whoever had come to the door hadn't left when Linda did, but he was cautious. He had called for a backup and then waited outside until they showed.

"Stay clear of that door," another voice ordered. It was a much deeper voice than the first one, that of an older man, someone in authority. "Is he armed?"

The first voice answered. "I don't think so. She said she took his gun away. It's right here."

Linda must have given him my Smith and Wesson. I listened as heavy footsteps creaked across the kitchen floor. There was a short silence, then the second voice, the older one, said:

"Beaumont?" The way he said it made my name sound ominous, threatening. "We've got this place surrounded. You can't get out."

"Surrounded?" I yelped the word. "Of course I can't get out. She locked the door. Who the hell do you think I am? I'm not armed. She took my gun."

"We *know* who you are, Beaumont. On the count of three, we're opening this door. I want to see you with both hands up behind your head or we'll shoot first and ask questions later. One. Two. Three."

Hands behind my head? What was going on? I sat down as the door flew open. There was no one there, only a doorway full of brilliant daylight from the kitchen window shining down the stairs, hurting my eyes, and casting long shadows of bars down the stairway. Then a lone man stepped into the light. He was a big sucker. His burly silhouette filled the entire doorway.

"Where the hell's the light switch?" he demanded. "I can't see a damn thing."

There was a quick shuffling of feet as someone searched for and found the switch to the basement light. It came on, leaving me exposed in all my bloody, nearly naked glory. The silence was so thick you could have cut it with a knife.

The heavyset man shook his head as though he couldn't quite believe his eyes. "I'll be damned," he said. "I been to three barn dances, a county fair, and a goat ropin', and I ain't never seen nothin' like this before. This what off-duty Seattle cops are wearing these days? On your feet, Beaumont. Come on up the stairs. Easy-like. No sudden moves."

I got to my feet and padded barefoot up the stairs with my hands behind my head.

"Stop right there," the man said, when I was almost at the top of the stairs. "Who has the key to this damn thing? Louis, did she give it to you?"

"Yessir."

A much younger, shorter man came into view and handed something over. A key. The big man fumbled with it briefly before inserting it into the lock and shoving the gate open. I had to dodge backward to keep from being pushed back down the stairs.

"Watch it, Beaumont. I said no sudden moves." He wasn't holding a weapon, but he spoke with the unquestioned authority of someone who doesn't think he needs one.

"What am I supposed to do, stand here while you knock me down the steps?"

I was close enough to see the badge on his khaki uniform, but there was no name tag.

"I'd keep a civil tongue in my mouth if I were you," he replied. Beyond him someone else in a uniform was sifting through my pile of belongings. He came up holding my car keys.

"Got 'em," he said. "They're right here. Want me to go search the car?"

"Right. Know what to look for?"

The younger man nodded.

"Hey, wait a minute. You can't search my car. You've gotta have a warrant."

"We've got one," the older man said, patting his breast pocket. He opened his jacket and drew out a long, slim envelope. "We've got ourselves one of those little hummers right here. It's all in order. Come on up here now. All the way into the kitchen. Keep your hands on your head."

I walked through the kitchen doorway into a crowded room. All told, there probably weren't that many people in the room—not more than six, me included—but it seemed like more. They were all cops, much younger ones except for the old guy who was in charge, all wearing versions of the same khaki uniform, all of them packing guns. If I'd made a break for it right then, they probably would have blown each other away, but I was in no mood for running.

And they were in no mood for laughing, either. Despite my lack of clothing, nobody cracked a smile. This was serious stuff. Dead serious.

Everyone waited on the older guy for direction. As soon as he spat out orders, they jumped to carry them out.

"What the hell is this all about?" I demanded. The older man didn't answer me. Instead, he turned to one of the younger ones.

"Cuff him, Jamie. Make sure there isn't a weapon concealed in his shorts. Shut up, Beaumont. You'll have plenty of time to talk later."

Jamie was a little shit with lifts in his shoes and a pencil-thin mustache. His search was enthusiastically thorough. "He's clean, Sheriff Harding," he reported.

I wanted to punch Jamie's lights out, but I didn't. He had given me one important bit of information, told me I was dealing with W. Reed Harding, Sheriff of Lewis County. Reed Harding wasn't a totally unknown quantity.

Like so many small-town sheriffs, he had cut his law-enforcement teeth in the big city, in this case Tacoma, and then moved into small-town police work when he tired of the rat race. I had never met Harding personally, but I knew officers who had worked with him and for him. Word of mouth said he was both tough and fair. I could have done a hell of a lot worse.

"Do you mind if I put my pants on?" I asked.

He shrugged. "Those them over there?" He pointed toward my pile of belongings still on the kitchen floor.

I nodded.

"Check 'em out, Jamie. If they're clean, let him put his pants back on. Then we'll find out what he's doing half-naked in this nice lady's basement in the middle of the afternoon."

Nice lady my ass! Linda Decker wasn't a nice lady in my book, but I didn't contradict him. Harding had gone to the door of the kitchen with his deputies, and the whole group was conferring with someone outside when Jamie brought my pants.

With my hands cuffed behind my back, there was no way I could manage them myself. Jamie held them out for me to step in. I knew the little bastard was suckering me, but I wanted clothes on so badly that I fell for it. As I raised my leg to step in, he brought the pants up and caught my foot, knocking me off balance.

I toppled over backwards. I knew what the metal handcuffs would do to my body if I rammed them into the small of my back. Twisting to one side in midair, I managed to land on one shoulder with a heavy, bone-jarring thud that knocked the wind out of my lungs. I almost blacked out.

Harding whirled and came back into the room, angrily looming over me. "What the hell happened?" he demanded of Jamie who was still standing there innocently holding my pants.

"I was helping him get these on. He tried to kick me," Jamie complained.

"Is that right!" Harding said. "Leave the son of a bitch naked, then." He glared down at me. "You try anything funny again, Beaumont, and you'll be wearing a straitjacket next, understand?"

I still hadn't gotten my breath back. "I understand," I croaked.

When Harding turned away, I caught Jamie's narrow-lipped smile of amusement. The asshole. He was probably five-six and a hundred and thirty pounds soaking wet—a little guy with a big chip on his shoulder. Sneaky, weasely, true to type. He wouldn't have lasted ten minutes at Seattle P.D., wouldn't have made it past the first physical, so he had to content himself with throwing his weight around in Lewis County.

I filed his face away in my memory banks. I'm no good with names, but I *do* remember faces. Maybe someday little Jamie would end up in Seattle and our paths would manage to cross. He'd best be looking over his shoulder if that ever happens.

Reed Harding returned to the outside door. "Come on, Jamie. Hustle on out there. They say the car's clean. He probably stashed the stuff somewhere nearby. Davis is organizing a search. You go help with that. I can handle this character. He won't give me any trouble."

"Yes, sir."

Jamie hotfooted it out of the house and Harding came back over to me. "Okay, Beaumont. On your feet."

He grabbed me under my arms and lifted me like I was a ten-pound-bag of potatoes. W. Reed Harding was strong as an ox. He dumped me unceremoniously on the kitchen stool where Linda Decker had sat earlier to drink her coffee. I didn't object. There wasn't an ounce of fight left in me.

"Is anybody ever going to tell me what the hell is going on?" I asked wearily.

"You bet, Beaumont," Harding answered. "I'll be glad to tell you. We're going to find where you stowed the stuff and then we're going to take you off the streets for awhile, lock you up, and throw away the key. I don't like it when cops take walks on the wrong side of the law. It gives all of us a bad name."

"Wrong side of the law? What are you talking about? What stuff?"

Harding bent down, holding his face only inches from mine. "The stuff you were going to use to burn down this house."

I was so dumbfounded I almost fell off the chair. "Burn the house down? You've got to be kidding. What makes you think that, for Christ's sake?"

"Because you already did it once."

"Did what?"

"Burned down a house," he answered grimly.

"Whose house?" I asked.

W. Reed Harding didn't answer me right away. His unblinking eyes bored into mine. I know how to do that too. It's a look calculated to make creeps squirm in their seats, to get them to spill their guts.

"Whose house?" I repeated.

"Linda Decker's mother's house," he said slowly. "Her mother's dead, and her brother isn't expected to make it."

His words hit me with the weight of a sledgehammer blow. Linda Decker's mother and her brother?

Jimmy Rising? The enthusiastic little guy with his stainless-steel thermos and Kmart lunch pail?

"No," I said.

Harding nodded. "And Bellevue P.D.'s got witnesses who say they saw you prowling around the house yesterday afternoon. Would you care to tell me where you were at midnight last night, Detective Beaumont? And you'd better make sure it's something that will hold up in a court of law, because you're going to need it."

Suddenly the snippet of news I had heard on the car radio, the one about the fatal eastside fire, resurfaced in my brain. Leona and Jimmy Rising. A cold chill passed over me. It had nothing whatever to do with the weather or my lack of clothes.

Somewhere outside myself I heard the words to the Miranda warning. Reed Harding was reading me my rights, as if I didn't know them already.

"So?" he asked when he finished. "Where were you?"

And that's when I remembered Marilyn Sykes. At midnight the night before, she and I had been getting it on in her Mercer Island bedroom. Dragging her into this for the sake of an alibi was out of the question.

"I want to talk to my attorney," I said. "His name's Ralph Ames. He lives in Phoenix."

Reed Harding looked at me gravely and shook his head. He seemed disappointed. "So that's the way you're going to play it?"

"Believe me," I answered, "I don't have any other choice."

CHAPTER 14

THAT GOSSIPY STORE CLERK IN DOTY HAD BEEN RIGHT. Linda Decker's house with its barred windows and doors looked a whole lot more like a jail than the new one did in Chehalis. Except for the discreet lockup and secured-entry system at one corner, the building we entered didn't remotely resemble a county courthouse.

Before they stuffed me in a patrol car somebody other than Jamie had finally helped me into my pants and put my shirt over my shoulders. Once inside the courthouse, Sheriff Harding told a deputy to take me into an unoccupied office to make my one phone call. That and removing my handcuffs were his only grudging concessions to professional courtesy. If I hadn't been a cop, I'd have been stuck out in the lobby using a pay phone along with all the rest of the scum. My escort removed the handcuffs but made sure I understood that an armed guard would be posted outside the door.

The advantage of having a high-priced attorney

like Ralph Ames on retainer is that he cuts through both bullshit and red tape with equal dispatch. As soon as I got him on the phone and told him what was going on, he let me have it with both barrels.

"Wake up, Beau. Get out from under your rock. That kind of chivalry went out with the Middle Ages. You tell that sheriff, Harwin . . ."

"Harding," I corrected.

"Whatever his name is, you tell him to get on the horn to Marilyn Sykes and straighten this mess out before it goes any further. Is there anyone else besides her who can say for certain you were there all night?"

Sheepishly I remembered the security guard and his all-knowing clipboard. "There was somebody else," I admitted reluctantly.

"Who for Chrissakes?" Ames demanded. He wanted this fixed, and he wanted it fixed now. He wasn't about to let me hide out under a blanket of genteel niceties.

"A security guard at her condominium complex. They keep track of all cars coming and going."

"Great. Have the sheriff talk to the guard as well. In the meantime, I'll catch the next plane out of Sky Harbor and be in Seattle sometime tonight. You take the cake, Beau. If it isn't one thing, it's three others. Try to get word to Peters if you still need me to come down to Chehalis. Otherwise, I'll meet you at your apartment."

"Do you think you need to come up?"

"Of course I'm coming up. If I leave right now I can catch the six-fifty. It's a direct flight."

There may be take-two-aspirin-get-plenty-of-rest

type attorneys in this world, but Ralph Ames isn't one of them.

"How come they picked you up, anyway?" he asked. "Didn't you tell them you're a cop?"

"I told them," I said, "but this woman was so totally convinced I was there to kill her, that she made the Lewis County Sheriff's Department believe it too."

"If she could convince them of that, she ought to be in sales," Ames suggested dryly. "Timeshare rowboats maybe, right here in Phoenix." With that, he hung up.

For several minutes, I sat alone in the office thinking about Linda Decker. I had been thinking about her all the while I was locked in the back of Reed Harding's patrol car with my hands cuffed firmly behind me. There hadn't been anything else to do *but* think.

I was sure now that I wasn't alone in thinking Logan Tyree's death was no accident. Linda Decker thought so too. Not only that, she was so sure she was the next target that she had barricaded her home and gone to some fairly dangerous lengths to entrap whoever might come looking for her.

Linda Decker was gutsy, I had to give her that, but she was also stupid. Her plan had worked, but only because I had come alone. If there had been anyone with me . . .

My old pal Jamie peered through the glass in the door and saw that I was off the phone. He entered without knocking. "Get going," he ordered curtly.

"I want to talk to Harding," I said.

"You already had your chance with Harding. You blew it."

"Look, you little jerk, my lawyer told me to confess, and I'm ready. Go get Harding and let's get this over with."

As soon as I saw the look on his face, I knew I had him by the short hairs. Jamie wanted to be a hero every bit as much as I had wanted my pants on earlier. He swallowed the bait whole. "I'll be right back," he said.

He took off at a dead run and was back in three minutes with Sheriff W. Reed Harding rumbling along behind him.

"Jamie here tells me you're ready to confess," Harding said to me. "Is that true?"

I grinned at Jamie. "I told him I wanted to talk to you, but he's blowing smoke about the rest of it. I don't know where he got the idea that I wanted to confess." My mother taught me not to lie. It's taken me a lifetime to overcome that training, but I'm learning.

Jamie flushed. I had gotten a little of my own back. Not enough, but it was a start. Harding bristled and turned away. "In that case, I'm going home to dinner. Lock this creep up."

Jamie started forward, but my next words caught Harding just as his hand closed on the doorknob. "Does the name Marilyn Sykes mean anything to you?"

Harding stopped and so did Jamie. The sheriff swung back around to face me. "I know Marilyn," he replied deliberately. "She's vice president of our state association. She's good people. Why? What about her?"

"Call her," I said. "Ask her what she was doing last night between midnight and one o'clock."

The sheriff's eyes narrowed. "Is this some kind of joke?"

"Believe me, it's no joke. I'm only following my attorney's orders."

"It's too late to call her," he objected. "She wouldn't still be at the office, and I doubt she'd have a listed number."

"I have the number," I said. "It's in my wallet. You've got that, don't you?"

Harding stood for a moment, looking at me, pondering, then he nodded to Jamie. "Go out and get me the envelope with his stuff in it. And don't open it." Once Jamie was outside, Harding closed the door, walked slowly back to the desk, and eased his heavy frame down into the chair behind it. "What's this all about, Beaumont? What are you up to?"

"Just call Marilyn and ask her what she was doing last night between midnight and one o'clock," I said again.

Jamie returned and handed over the envelope. While Harding fumbled with the flap, I was aware of Jamie's cold eyes drilling into me. Talking to Ames had buoyed my confidence. Now, for the first time, I wondered what would happen if Marilyn Sykes weren't home, or if for some reason she couldn't or wouldn't corroborate my alibi. After this latest setto with Jamie, if Harding left me alone again with that squirrelly little shit, I was in big, big trouble.

Marilyn, Marilyn, answer the phone.

Harding was still searching for the number. "It's on the back of one of her cards," I said helpfully. "Behind the money."

Harding located the card, turned it over, picked up the phone, and dialed. She must have answered on the first or second ring. I felt myself breathe a huge sigh of relief.

"Howdy there, Marilyn," he drawled. "This is Reed Harding, down in Chehalis. Oh sure, I'm fine. How's it going with you?"

I wondered if Reed Harding had always talked that way, or if he had affected the backwoods, good-old-boy style as a vote-getting technique. The accent wouldn't have played worth a damn in Tacoma or Seattle either one, but it sounded perfectly at home in Chehalis.

There was a short exchange of pleasantries, while Jamie and I stared at each other. I was gloating. There wasn't a goddamned thing he could do to me now, but suddenly I wanted him out of that room in the very worst way. Whatever Marilyn Sykes told Reed Harding was fine, but I'll be damned if I wanted Jamie to be privy to it.

"Well," Harding was explaining to Marilyn, "it's like this. We've got ourselves a sticky little situation down here. I hate to put you on the spot, Marilyn, but I need to know exactly what you were doing last night around midnight or so."

Jamie was bright enough to know that the tables had somehow turned, but he still hadn't figured out what to do about it. I stood up and stretched. Harding was so deeply embroiled in his conversation with Marilyn that he didn't pay the least bit of attention to me. With an armed deputy in the room and another stationed just outside the door, he didn't really need to worry.

I ambled over to the door where Jamie was still standing. "You'd better get out of here, you cocksucking little son of a bitch," I whispered, "before I crush your balls with a nutcracker and use 'em for chicken feed."

Jamie stiffened, paled, and left without a word. No guts. I turned back to Harding. He was still on the phone and shaking his head.

"So there was no way he could have gotten away between say midnight and one o'clock this morning without your noticing." There was a pause, and Harding chuckled. "No, I suppose not."

Chivalry be damned, Marilyn Sykes was coming through like a champ.

"And you say the security guard there keeps track of all vehicles after ten P.M.? Could you give me that number?" He jotted something on a sheet of paper. "Well thanks, Marilyn. You've been a big help. You want to talk to him? Sure. Hang on."

Shaking his head, he looked over at me and held out the phone. "She wants to speak to you," he said.

I can't say that I wanted to speak to her right then, but I took the phone anyway.

"I thought you told me you weren't the type to kiss and tell," Marilyn Sykes said accusingly.

"Marilyn, I'm sorry. It's just that . . ."

She laughed. "Don't apologize and don't give me any excuses, Beau. From what Reed tells me, it's a damn good thing we were at my place instead of yours. Your doorman goes off duty at midnight.

You need to live in a class-act place, Detective Beaumont, one with twenty-four-hour security."

Marilyn was sticking it to me and to Belltown Terrace as well, but I was in no position to object. I kept quiet.

"Anything else I can do to help?" she asked brightly.

"Not at the moment." I didn't want to say more, not with Reed Harding sitting there in the room. Marilyn was perceptive enough to figure it out.

"Call me when you get back home and let me know what's going on. It must be serious."

"It is that," I said. "I'll be in touch." I handed the phone back to Harding. He took it from me and sat there unmoving for several seconds with the receiver cupped in his hands. Finally, he tapped the phone on the desk a time or two.

"You'll bear with me while I go by the book and check out one more thing, won't you?"

I shrugged. "Be my guest."

He looked down at the notes he had taken during his call with Marilyn and punched a number into the phone. "Who am I speaking to?" he asked when somebody answered.

"My name's Harding, Sheriff W. Reed Harding down here in Chehalis. We've had a tip that one of our stolen vehicles was sighted in your complex last night. I understand that you keep track of license numbers of all vehicles entering and leaving the property, is that true?"

There was a pause. "I see, but you don't have last night's list there with you? Do you know where we could locate it? Yes, it is important. Fine, I'll hold."

Harding held his hand over the mouthpiece.

"He's transferring me to the security company's main office in Seattle," he said. "What's the license number on that Porsche of yours? I've got it in the file in my office, but I need it now."

I gave it to him. Harding went back to the phone. "Sure, just read me the whole list. That'll be fine." It took several minutes. Finally the list was completed. "Okay," Harding said. "Thanks for all your help. What's your name again?" He scribbled a name and number on the sheet of paper. "Sounds to me like we must have been mistaken."

He put down the phone and looked over at me. "In more ways than one, Beaumont," he added. "Just like you said. The number's there. In at eleven and out again this morning. I owe you an apology."

"It happens," I said. "We all make mistakes." I could afford to be magnanimous with Harding. He wasn't the one who had knocked me on my ass.

"But what the hell were you doing out there in Pe Ell anyway? And what's Linda Decker so scared of? It's a miracle she didn't shoot you on sight. She said you claimed to be working on her boyfriend's case, on his homicide, but that when she called to check, Seattle P.D. said no."

In less than a minute, Harding and I had gone from adversaries to allies. The shift was so sudden, it almost made me dizzy.

"There are two other detectives who are actually assigned to the case," I told him. "I've been working it anyway. I felt like it."

"Oh," Harding replied with a nod. "I got that much from Watkins."

"Watkins?" I asked.

"You know, Watkins, your sergeant up there in Seattle. I talked to him just a little while ago while we were still trying to check you out."

If Harding had talked to Sergeant Watkins, then my tail was already in a gate but good.

"Wonderful," I said. Watty would be ripped, ready to chew me to pieces. So would Detective Paul Kramer.

I changed the subject. "Is that when she called you for help, then, after they told her I wasn't assigned to the case?"

"She never called."

"She didn't? But what about the deputy who showed up at the house? How'd he get there?"

"We sent him out to notify her about what had happened to her mother and her brother. Someone from the brother's job had called us and asked us to let her know. As soon as she found out, she told the deputy about you. He radioed here for help while she loaded up her kids and headed for Seattle."

"To the hospital?" I asked.

Harding nodded. "Harborview. The burn unit." He cocked his head to one side and studied me. "I wonder what she would have done to you if my deputy hadn't turned up right then."

It was a sobering thought. "I don't want to think about it," I said. There was a pause. "Did she mention any tapes to you?"

Harding sat up straight, alert, interested. "Tapes? What kind of tapes?"

I shrugged. "Beats me. Videotapes. Cassettes

maybe. She let something slip about tapes, something about them being hidden in a safe place where
no one would be able to find them."

"So she thought you were after her or the tapes."

"Or maybe both. Somebody must want those
tapes real bad."

Harding pulled a small notebook from his pocket
and jotted something into it. "I'll call Watkins and
have him put a guard on her."

"Good idea. On her brother, too," I added.

"Tell me more about the tapes."

I shrugged. "I don't know anything else, except if
they were in her mother's house, they're gone now."

"Burned up?"

"That's right. I understand it's a total loss. Not so
much as a toothpick left standing."

I didn't want to think about the house or Leona
and Jimmy Rising, especially not Jimmy, but Harding had given me an opening.

"How'd the fire start?"

"Gas hot-water heater exploded. I guess initially
the fire investigators thought it was an accident, but
it didn't take long for them to figure out otherwise.
Not Linda, though. She knew right off."

"Knew what?"

"That it wasn't an accident. As soon as the deputy
told her, she said 'They did it again.' And she was
right. By then the arson guys in Bellevue had discovered that someone had messed around with the
water-heater controls."

"And since I had been seen in the neighborhood
the day before . . ."

Harding nodded. "You got it. Everybody jumped

to the wrong conclusion, including Linda Decker who figured you were after her even *before* she heard about the fire."

"If I'd been in her shoes, I probably would have thought the same thing," I said.

We were quiet for several moments and then Harding stood up. Slowly. Leaning against the desk for support like a man whose back hurts if he straightens up too fast.

"Come on," he said. "We'll go back over to my office and get your stuff. I had your car towed into a garage here in town. No charge, of course, but we'll have to bail it out of there before you'll be able to head home."

By eleven o'clock, I was back on I-5 heading north. It had taken time to get my car out of the impound lot and then hours more at the St. Helen's Hospital emergency room. They said my nose was broken but my shoulder wasn't. I could have told them that myself, but Harding insisted on doing it right.

As I drove, there was a dull ache in my shoulder where I'd fallen on the floor thanks to my friend Jamie. If it hurt this much already, by the next day it would be giving me fits. I was almost sorry I hadn't accepted the doc's offer of a painkiller, but I figured that and driving home to Seattle were contraindicated.

It was less than twelve hours from the time I had turned off the freeway onto Highway 6 going to Pe Ell. Twelve hours and a lifetime ago.

Those are the kind of hours that make a man old before his time. Driving home that night I was feeling downright ancient.

When the elevator door slipped open on the twenty-fifth floor of Belltown Terrace, an ocean of garlic washed over me. The garlic was thick enough that I could smell it despite my broken nose. Without opening the door I knew Ralph Ames was inside my apartment, cooking up a storm. My interior designer created a kitchen that unleashed Ames' culinary genius.

As I walked in the door, Ames glanced up from ladling a pot full of fettucini Alfredo into one of my best bowls. "How about a midnight snack," he grinned. "I'll bet you're starved."

Two places were set in the dining room. The middle of the table held a large wooden bowl of tossed salad as well as an uncorked bottle of wine.

I had kicked off my shoes and was shrugging out of my jacket when Ames came into the dining room and put the bowl of fettucini on the table. He gave me an appraising look.

"Other than a pair of shiners and a hole in your knee, how are you, Beau?"

I knew about the hole in my knee, but shiners? "You're shitting me."

Ames shook his head. "Go look for yourself," he said.

I did, he was right. I looked like hell.

"What did you do, walk into a door?"

"An eight-by-ten timber," I answered.

"Same difference. Are you hungry?"

"You bet." It had been some time since that long-ago breakfast Marilyn Sykes had fed me. I may not be the type to cook fettucini, but I certainly don't object to eating it. I dished up a mountain of salad and started on that while Ames poured two glasses of wine.

"By the way," he said. "Marilyn Sykes called here looking for you a couple of times. I told her you'd give her a call as soon as we finished eating. Hope you don't mind, but I filled her in on some of the details."

"Things would be a hell of a lot different if I had been home alone in my own little beddy-bye," I said. "Marilyn's alibi was what did the trick."

One of the things I appreciate most about Ames is that he's not above saying he told me so, but he doesn't usually rub my nose in it. He simply nodded. "I figured as much," he said.

"There are a few other messages as well," he added. "Two calls from Sergeant Watkins, and one from someone named Kramer. He sounded real upset. What's this all about?"

And so, during the course of our late-night dinner, I explained to Ralph Ames what I could about what was going on. I told him about finding Logan Tyree's body and about what I regarded as the erroneous determination of accidental death. I told him about Logan Tyree's womenfolk, his moderately grief-stricken widow and his grieving ex-fiancée. I told him about my meeting with Jimmy Rising and the subsequent fire. Sometime later, over wine, I even remembered to tell him about Angie Dixon and the news photo that had captured her fatal plunge from Masters Plaza.

Ralph Ames listened to it all, nodding from time to time, asking questions periodically. "There does seem to be a pattern," he observed when I finished.

"Certainly with Logan Tyree the killer or killers went to some length to make his death look like an accident. And the woman falling off the building sounds like an accident, too. Is there any connection between them?"

"Between Logan and Angie Dixon?" I shook my head. "Other than the fact that they were in the same union, there's no connection that I know of. Logan Tyree taught a certified welding class for apprentices. Presumably Angie Dixon was in Logan's class."

"The same one, you think?"

I shrugged. "Maybe, or maybe a later one."

"But you think they all knew each other?"

"Probably."

"What are you going to do about it?" Ames asked.

"Nothing. Not a goddamned thing. From now on, it's hands off as far as I'm concerned."

Ames smiled. "I'm glad you're being sensible for a change, Beau. From what he said on the phone, I'm afraid Sergeant Watkins will insist on it."

That turned out to be something of an understatement.

CHAPTER 15

I DIDN'T GO TO THE DEPARTMENT THE NEXT DAY. I DIDN'T have to. The mountain came to Mohammed. Sergeant Watkins turned up on the security phone downstairs at ten after eight. Once Watty was inside my apartment, Ralph Ames stayed around only long enough to say a polite hello and then made himself scarce while the sergeant and I retreated into the den.

"Coffee?" I asked.

Watty shook his head. "It's not a social visit. Just what the hell do you think you're pulling, Beau? Since when do homicide detectives go out and investigate any damn case they please? Since when did I stop making the assignments?"

"I didn't do it on purpose. It just happened. You know how that Tyree case started. He floated up right under my nose while I was working on the movie set. I know I wasn't assigned, but I was involved. I couldn't help it."

"That's bullshit, Beau, and you know it. 'I couldn't

help it' is an excuse a little kid uses on his mother after he wets his pants. You didn't *try* to help it. You got a wild hair up your ass that Kramer and Manny had it all wrong, and you set out hell-bent for leather to prove it."

"Maybe," I said.

"Maybe nothing! What's going on between you and Kramer anyway? He's been in my office twice this week complaining that you were messing around in his case. Bird-dogging him. I told him he was full of it, that you were working on the movie and later that you were on vacation. Obviously I was wrong. The shit is really going to hit the fan when he finds out about what happened yesterday."

"I think he already has. He called here last night before I got home."

"But you didn't talk to him?"

I shook my head. "Not yet."

"If I were you, Beau, I'd do some pretty serious thinking before I called him. He's pissed as hell, and he has every right to be. So's Manny. The homicide squad's based on teamwork, remember? We're supposed to work together, all of us. I don't need some loose cannon rolling around on deck screwing up the works for everybody."

There wasn't a damn thing I could say, because I knew Watty was right, and he was only warming up.

"We've worked together for a long time, Beau, been through the wars together, but you left me with my ass hanging out on this one. I spent all day yesterday dodging bullets in every direction. Calls from upstairs, calls from the press, and yes, goddamnit, calls from some of my own squad. All of 'em asking the same thing. All of 'em wanting to know what the hell was going on and how the hell you ended up in that woman's basement without any clothes on."

"Shorts," I put in lamely. "I still had my shorts on."

"Big fucking deal. Tell me about it. What happened?"

I took a deep breath. "I was convinced that Logan Tyree's death wasn't an accident."

"That's no answer," Watty interrupted. "Harbor Patrol disagrees with you. So does the Coast Guard. And the same goes for Manny Davis and Paul Kramer. Logan Tyree's their baby, and don't you forget it."

"But you asked me how it happened and I'm telling you. I was interested, so I talked to people—his friends, his ex-wife, people he worked with. They all said the same thing, that Tyree was careful, exceptionally careful, that he wouldn't have been out in a boat without the fume sensors and the blower working properly."

"That's it?" Watty demanded. "That's all you had?"

"Then there was the fight with his girlfriend. One of the neighbors said they had a serious quarrel and that they broke up a week or so before it happened."

"Breaking up with his girlfriend days before he died doesn't tell me Logan Tyree was murdered."

"There was something else as well. Tyree told his neighbor that he had to take some kind of action. I forget the words exactly, but something about a man doing what a man has to do."

"And this neighbor . . ."

"His name's Corbett, Red Corbett."

"What else did he tell you?"

"He gave me Linda Decker's name. Told me how to get in touch with her."

"How come, Beau? Why'd this Red Corbett character spill his guts to you and not to Manny and Paul? I've got their reports. I remember seeing Corbett's name. He told them some of this, but not all."

"Can I help it if Paul Kramer's an asshole?"

"Leave personalities out of this, Beau."

I went on. "Corbett offered to give Manny and Kramer Linda's name, but they said they didn't need it. That since the death was an accident, the ex-wife's name was enough."

Watty was shaking his head before I finished. "So they made a mistake. Kramer's new to homicide. He's entitled to some mistakes, but by the time they decided they did need to talk to her, Linda Decker was already gone. Not even her mother knew where she was. How'd you manage to find her when they couldn't?"

"I talked to her brother."

"The retard? The one who's in the hospital?"

"Is that what Kramer told you about Jimmy Rising, that he's a retard?"

"Developmentally disabled. You like that better?"

"Look, Watty, whatever's wrong with him, Jimmy Rising is one hell of a nice guy. He would have told Kramer and Manny just what he told me if they had bothered to listen. They ran right over him, ignored him, treated him like shit."

"And you didn't?"

"That's right."

Watty leaned back on the couch and looked at me, his arms folded over his chest. I had worked with Sergeant Watkins for a long time, but I had never seen him so thoroughly steamed.

"You're out to lunch on this one, Beau. This case, accident or not, is none of your goddamned business."

"So I'll leave it alone," I said.

"You'd by God better!"

"What about the woman who fell off the building?"

"What about her?"

"Is that classified as an accident, too?"

"Are you saying the two deaths are related?"

"Can you prove they're not?"

After this exchange we sat there for several long moments with neither one of us speaking. Finally, abruptly, Watty stood up to go.

"I came over here to tell you to mind your own business, Beau. It's not an official warning. Kramer hasn't filed a grievance yet. If he does, then it will have to be official, go across desks, through channels, and end up in your file. But just because it isn't official yet, don't get the idea that you're home free. You're not.

"I've known you for years, Beau. This isn't like you. I know you're a good cop. I can't believe you'd pull such a dumb-ass trick. With you down there by yourself, if that crazy broad in Pe Ell had blown you away, it wouldn't have done anybody a damn bit of good.

"I don't usually pay much attention to departmental gossip. Neither do you, but I think it's time you did. This is a hell of a nice place you have here. That 928 you drive is a sweet little piece of machinery. I happen to know where all of it came from, but you're getting a whole lot of notoriety both inside and outside the department. People are starting to talk about the playboy cop. When you go around pulling fool stunts like this, it sure as hell adds fuel to the fire."

I must have winced when he said it. The words "playboy cop" had hurt badly enough when I heard them from Paul Kramer. Coming from Watty, from someone I've worked with for years, someone I respect, they cut clear to the bone.

He didn't miss my reaction. "So you have heard it then," Watty said.

I nodded.

"Being a cop isn't something you do when you feel like it. It isn't something you do now and then just to keep your hand in. It's not a goddamned part-time job. It's something you do because you have to, because it's in your blood. But you do it by the rules. If you're tired of those rules, if you're tired of taking orders and being on the team, then quit. Get the hell out.

"Your net worth doesn't mean a damn thing to me, Beaumont. It doesn't make you sergeant. I'm still calling the shots. I assign the cases, and my people answer to me. I don't need any goddamned Lone Ranger on my squad. I won't tolerate it, and if you've got a problem with that, then maybe you'd better make this vacation permanent or put in for a transfer. You got that?"

"I've got it," I said.

I followed Watty to the door. He opened it and stepped into the hallway, then he turned back. "If I were you, I'd have someone take a look at that nose. It looks broken to me."

I watched him go. Watty had just climbed all over my frame, but he still worried about my goddamned broken nose. That hurt almost as much as the ass-chewing.

Ralph Ames came out of the guest room with an empty coffee cup in one hand and a fistful of papers in the other. He had told me that as long as he was in Seattle he could just as well do some work for the Belltown Terrace real-estate syndicate and save himself another trip later.

"How was it?" he asked, refilling his cup.

"Pretty rough," I said. "Watty told me to shape up or ship out. Either get back on the team or get the hell off it altogether. From the sound of it, he doesn't much care which way it goes."

"I see," Ames said and let it go at that. He took the fresh cup of coffee and disappeared into the guest room, leaving me to stew in my own juices.

There was plenty of stewing to do. Over the years, I've been in varying degrees of hot water on occasion, but that's not unusual among detectives. As a breed we're the ones who ask the questions, who ferret out information people often don't want us to have. It's a world that attracts pragmatists— self-starters with strong streaks of independence.

I had been reprimanded before, called on the carpet and brought back to heel, but never anything like this. Watty's words had gutted me, hit all my professional cop buttons, and left me empty, with nothing to say in my own defense because I knew damn good and well he was right. I had been out of line, off the charts.

Pouring myself a cup of coffee, I took it out on the balcony and stood looking down at the street far below, hoping the sound of morning commuter traffic hurrying down Second Avenue would help lessen the sting of Watty's departing words, but it didn't. Nothing could. Because for everything Watty had said, I could add three more burning indictments of my own.

Of course I should have gone to Manny Davis and Paul Kramer and told them what I had found out, what I suspected. Of course I shouldn't have driven to Pe Ell to question Linda Decker alone. Going without a backup was stupid. Inexcusable.

The personality conflict between Kramer and me was like a couple of little boys duking it out on a playground, fighting over who ruled a small square of gravel turf or who got the biggest swing. But I had let that little-boy game overshadow my professional judgment.

Professional? Who the hell was I to call myself a professional?

The phone rang, interrupting the self-flagellation. I was sure it was Kramer, and I started rehearsing my apology as I went to pick up the receiver. Instead it was Peters, calling from the hospital.

"So you made it back all right after all." He sounded relieved.

"Yeah," I said. "I should have called you last night, but it was too late. Sorry."

"Don't worry about that. How are things?"

"Watty was just here and reamed me out good. I deserved it."

"One thing to be thankful for, though. At least the papers didn't name names this morning. They called you an 'unidentified off-duty Seattle Police officer.'"

"So it's in the paper today?"

"Front and center."

"Great. Did the article say anything about Linda Decker's brother?"

"The one who got burned? Only that he's in the burn unit down here at Harborview. Critical condition. Intensive care. You know what that's like."

"One step away from the Spanish Inquisition."

Peters laughed ruefully. "Something like that," he said. "I assume Watty told you hands off?"

"In a manner of speaking," I allowed.

Peters knew me well enough to sense that what I said was only the tip of the iceberg, but he didn't press the issue. Instead, he went on to something else. "Has Maxine gotten hold of you to arrange a schedule for Bumbershoot?" he asked.

I had forgotten all about the outing I had promised Peters' girls. "No," I said guiltily. "She hasn't caught up with me. I've been a moving target."

"Maxine called here yesterday and said that she heard that kids get in free on Friday. She wondered if it would be possible for you to take them then. She's got a doctor's appointment in the early afternoon. Otherwise, she'll have to locate another sitter."

"Tell her that'll be fine. By tomorrow afternoon, I'm sure time will be hanging heavy on my hands.

Tell her to send them up here about eleven. We'll eat lunch over at Seattle Center."

"Okay," he said, "I'll let her know." He paused. "Don't kick yourself too much, Beau. You never would have done it if I hadn't been egging you on from the sidelines, remember?"

"Sure," I said, and we hung up.

I know Peters was trying to make me feel better, but it didn't work. When you've been flat on your back in bed for six months, you're allowed some lapses in judgment. When you're still supposedly dealing with a full deck, when you're still walking around upright, carrying a badge and packing a loaded .38, it's a whole different ball game.

Ames came out of the bedroom again. He was dressed in a suit and tie, briefcase in hand. He found me sitting in the chair by the telephone, staring off into space. He set the case down on the table for a moment and stood there looking at me.

"You could always quit, you know," he said.

"Quit?"

"The force. You don't need to work if you don't want to."

The realization that Watty might fire me had shaken me to my very core, but the idea of quitting had never crossed my mind.

"It's what I've always done," I said.

Ames shrugged. "Maybe that's reason enough to make a change. Lots of men your age do, you know," he added quietly. He picked up the briefcase again and started toward the door. "What are you going to do today?"

"I don't know yet," I said. "I'm going to have to think about it."

After Ames left, the silence in the room was oppressive. I felt restless, ill at ease. Unbidden, Jimmy Rising came to mind. I remembered how much he had wanted to go to work the day he missed the bus, how proud he had been of the thermos and the lunch pail. Well, he wasn't going to work now. The micrographics department at the Northwest Center would have to do without him for awhile. Maybe forever. The burn unit at Harborview is good, but they can't always work miracles.

I wasn't conscious of making the decision. Like an old war-horse that doesn't have sense enough to quit, I got up, put on my holster and my jacket. With my hand on the doorknob I paused. Would going to the hospital to see Jimmy Rising be considered meddling in Paul Kramer's case?

No, goddamnit. Sergeant Watkins could fire my ass if he wanted to, but I was going to go to the hospital and pay my respects to Jimmy Rising come hell or high water.

CHAPTER 16

WHEN I GOT ON THE ELEVATOR AT HARBORVIEW, FORCE of habit made me push the button to floor four where Peters is instead of nine for the burn unit ICU. A couple of uniformed nurses who were also in the elevator were openly contemptuous when I got off, looked around in confusion, and then got back on before the elevator continued up.

I've been in the burn unit before. I know the routine. Because recovering burn patients are so susceptible to infection, visitors are required to don sterile clothing before entering patients' rooms. The problem was, whenever I'd gone there before, it was always as a police officer on official business which gave me the secret password for admittance.

This time, I had no such magic wand. It was easy to tell which was Jimmy Rising's room. A uniformed officer, crossed arms resting on his chest, was seated on a folding chair outside a closed door just up from the nurses' station. When I asked about Jimmy Rising, the ward clerk, a scrawny man with an equally scrawny beard, eyeballed me thoroughly up and down. "Are you a member of the family?" he asked.

"No, just a friend."

"Mr. Rising is in no condition to have visitors," the ward clerk announced firmly. "Family members are allowed in for a few minutes each hour, but that's all."

I stood there flat-footed with no possible argument or comeback. The guard glanced in my direction, and I gave him a halfhearted wave. What the threat of losing my job had failed to accomplish, hospital bureaucracy did without a moment's hesitation.

I must have looked crestfallen enough that the ward clerk took pity on me. "If you'd care to leave something for him, I'll be sure it reaches him," he offered.

Nodding my thanks, I made my way back down the short hallway to the main corridor. Leave Jimmy Rising something? What? A note, a card, flowers? Before I knew it, I was standing in front of a gray-haired clerk in the gift shop on the main floor, and I still hadn't made up my mind.

"May I help you, sir?" she asked.

"Some flowers, I guess," I answered stupidly.

She pointed toward a refrigerated display. "What we have available is right there. Is this for an adult? A child?"

I looked at the display. It was an uninspiring batch of tired flowers in equally tired receptacles—the milk-white, lumpy-glass kind so popular in hospitals, with one or two ceramic teddy bears thrown in for good measure.

"An adult," I said.

"Man or woman? Does this person have any particular preferences?"

She was trying hard to be helpful. The problem was, I didn't know anything at all about Jimmy Rising's preference in flowers. All I knew about him was what I had learned during that brief afternoon interview on his porch and the equally short ride to the Northwest Center in Seattle. I could still see him sitting there on the top step, carefully pouring orange juice into the cup from his thermos.

And all at once it hit me. I knew exactly what Jimmy Rising needed. It had nothing at all to do with flowers.

"Never mind," I told the startled lady behind the counter. "I don't think he likes flowers."

With that, I beat it out the door and headed for the car. Smiling to myself, I made my way down to Jackson Street.

Welch Fuel and Hardware has been doing business on Jackson for as long as I can remember. I first saw the store years ago when I was a rookie. Back then it was a hole in the wall next to a Safeway store. Gradually the neighborhood changed, transforming into Seattle's less than malignant version of inner-city squalor. The grocery store had pulled out altogether, but not the hardware store. It had quietly expanded to include both buildings. While the neighborhood around it had slowly deteriorated, the store itself had unobtrusively prospered.

The displays seemed crowded and jumbled. Just because some item was no longer manufactured didn't mean it wasn't still available in some hidden nook or cranny of the store. The clerks, all of them old hands, knew what they had and where to find it. When asked, one of them pointed me to an aisle halfway down the long room. "The lunch pails are over there," he said. "You'll find the thermoses there, too."

I found what I wanted without any trouble on a crammed shelf bulging with housewares. There was a huge shiny black lunch pail for $10.88 and a stainless-steel thermos for three times that. I took them both off the shelf and went up to the cash register.

"You do gift-wrapping here?" I asked.

The clerk gave me an odd look. I don't know if it was because requests for gift-wrapping are that unusual or because my two black eyes, not black so much as deep purple, made me look like death warmed over.

"Not here, we don't," he said at last.

With no further comment, he rang up my two purchases and put them in a plain brown paper bag. They were still in the bag a few minutes later when I carried them up to the nurses' station in the burn unit at Harborview. The same ward clerk was still on duty.

"I see you found something," he said.

"Yes," I answered. I took the thermos and lunch pail out of the sack and put them on the counter in front of him. He seemed dismayed by my choice. He was expecting flowers. I didn't bother to explain. "Could I use a paper and pen to write a note?"

"Sure," he answered.

I was just signing my name to a brief note when a

woman's voice interrupted me. "What are you do-ing here?"

The voice was all too familiar. I had heard it be-fore. I looked up quickly and almost dropped the pen. Linda Decker was standing right beside me, loosening a surgical mask that covered the lower half of her face. Without the gun she was much smaller than I remembered, but every bit as scary.

"I brought him something," I said evenly, unsure how she would react to my presence, much less to what I had brought. I folded the note and stuck it under the latch on the lunch pail. Warily I glanced over at Linda Decker. She wasn't looking at me. She was staring at the lunch pail, tears welling up in her eyes.

Without a word, she reached out and stroked the shiny metal handle. It was almost a mirror image of what Jimmy Rising had done that day on the porch. "He may not live to see them," she managed.

"It's that bad?" I asked.

She nodded. "Less than fifty-fifty." She started crying in dead earnest then.

Quickly the ward clerk came around the counter and put a protective arm around her shoulder. "Come on, Mrs. Decker," he said quietly. "Let's get you in where you can sit down and rest for a few minutes. You've had a long day of it."

Worried about who I was and what I was up to, the guard hurried over as well, but Linda waved him away and allowed the ward clerk to lead her down the hall. As he did so, he glared at me over his shoulder as though he believed I was somehow personally re-sponsible. He didn't order me to leave, however, and

I followed them into a small waiting room around the corner. The room was windowless and crowded with furniture, the air thick with the smoke of a thousand despairing cigarettes. Still sobbing, Linda Decker sank onto one of the couches.

The clerk stepped away from her and saw me at the door. "I think maybe you'd better go," he said to me. "She needs to sit here and rest. She's had a rough night."

With a shrug, I started to leave. There was no sense in arguing. "No, it's all right," Linda Decker mumbled through her tears, as she groped for a tissue. "Let him stay."

I don't know who was more surprised, the ward clerk or J. P. Beaumont. The clerk shook his head dubiously. "All right. If you say so. What about the thermos and lunch pail?"

"Put them in Jimmy's room," Linda Decker said. "Put them somewhere so he'll be able to see them if he ever gets a chance."

The ward clerk gave me one last disparaging look and left. I stood there awkwardly, not knowing what to say or do, while Linda searched for another tissue and blew her nose. There was a coffee pot and a stack of styrofoam cups sitting on a table across the room. The light was on and the coffee smelled as though it had been there for hours.

"Would you like a cup of coffee?" I offered.

She nodded. "Please."

"Black?"

She nodded again. I poured two cups and brought them back to where she was sitting on the couch. Her hand shook as she took the cup from me. "Thank you," she said. The room was stuffy and hot, but she sat there shivering for several moments with both hands wrapped around the cup as though hoping to draw warmth out of the coffee and into her hands. She stared unseeing through a wavering column of steam.

"I'm sorry about what happened," she said, her voice almost a whisper. "Someone named Powell was here a little while ago. He said that you're a good cop, that you wouldn't be mixed up in anything crooked."

Under any other circumstance, a vote of confidence from Captain Larry Powell would have been welcome, but in this instance I was sorry to hear that he too had been dragged into the melee.

"It's all right," I answered. "You don't need to apologize. If I'd been in your shoes, I probably would have done the same thing."

She looked up at me, her face pained. "No, it's not all right. That was my fault, and so is this. Jimmy went back to get Patches." She broke off and put one hand over her mouth to stifle an involuntary sob.

"Patches?" I asked.

"A dog. A stupid stuffed dog that I gave him years ago. The firemen got him out of the house all right, but he broke away and went back after the dog. He was right in the doorway when the roof came down. He was completely engulfed in flames."

"Just because you gave him the dog doesn't make you responsible."

"You don't understand, do you." It was an accusation.

"I guess not."

"I used Jimmy as bait!" The last word was a cry of anguish torn from her body, one that left her doubled over and weeping. Unnoticed, the coffee spilled onto the floor beside her. I found a roll of paper towels and began to soak up the mess.

"Bait?" I asked, when she finally quieted. "What do you mean, bait?"

"Jimmy can't lie," she answered. "I knew if I told him where I was and if anyone asked him, he would tell them. After Logan and Angie, I figured I was next on the killer's list. And I was ready for him, ready and waiting. But you came instead."

I nodded. She closed her eyes and put one hand over them, shaking her head as if to deny the reality of what had happened. "I didn't think he'd hurt Jimmy and Mom. It never occurred to me."

My ears pricked up at the word "he." Not some nameless, faceless, sexless entity. Not some vague numberless they. But he. One person—a single, identifiable, male, he.

"Do you know who that person is?" I asked the question gently. I never considered not asking it. I'm a cop. They pay me to ask questions, but I was finally learning that for me asking questions is more than just a job. It's as necessary as breathing, a cornerstone of existence, and this time I was asking for free.

Slowly Linda Decker raised her head. Her eyes met mine and she nodded.

"Who?" I asked.

"Martin Green."

I tried to contain my reaction. Martin Green. The ironworker union executive director who was busy creating a "more perfect union." The same man who lived in my building and who had thrown a temper tantrum because his mother didn't get to ride home from the airport in the Bentley.

"Are you sure? Do you have any proof?"

"The night he was killed, Logan had an appointment with Green to tell him about the tapes. He called and told me so. I begged him not to go. I told him it was too dangerous, that they wouldn't tolerate someone messing up their little racket."

There were the tapes again, the tapes she had mentioned before.

"What tapes?"

"The accounting tapes. The ones Angie stole."

"Wait a minute. Angie Dixon? The woman who fell off Masters Plaza?" Linda Decker nodded. It was all coming together too fast. So there was a connection between Logan Tyree and Angie Dixon.

"Angie didn't fall," Linda said grimly. "I can't prove it, but I know she was pushed."

"One thing at a time. Tell me about the tapes."

"Angie used to work for a guy named Wayne Martinson. He kept the books for the local."

"More than one set?" I asked speculatively.

Linda looked at me quickly. "How did you know that?" she asked.

"It fits," I answered.

"Angie wanted to make more money. Martinson had her working part-time at minimum wage. Guys working iron make good money. Eventually, through her job, Angie figured out there was a lot of hanky-panky going on—people buying and selling union books, people bypassing the apprenticeship program, boomers paying to get put on the A-list. She started stealing the tapes. Not the journal entries, just the tapes. She took them at night as she left work."

"And then she blackmailed somebody to let her into the union?"

Linda shook her head. "That was what was funny. It ended up she didn't have to. They let her in anyway."

"But I thought you said . . ."

"Nobody knew anything about it, until this party thing came up. I think she was too scared to tell."

"What party thing?"

"International sent out an inspection team. Probably because of what happened to Wayne."

"Wayne?"

"Martinson, the bookkeeper."

"What did happen to him?"

"He went salmon fishing in Alaska last month and never came back. He's officially listed as missing. They haven't found his body."

"Another ironworker accident? How come nobody made the connection?"

"Wayne didn't just work for the ironworkers," she said. "He worked for several different unions."

"You mentioned something about a party."

"According to Don Kaplan, Martin Green expected some of us to show up and improve the scenery at his little get-together. A command performance. I figured he wanted to create enough of a smoke screen so no one would figure out what had really been going on. He's big on public relations."

Remembering the attractive young women scattered here and there around Martin Green's apartment the night I crashed his party, I suddenly saw that party in a far different and more ominous light. So that's what had been going on.

"And you were supposed to be part of the scenery?"

"Show up or else. That was the way Don Kaplan put it. We'd have drinks and dinner and guess who was supposed to be dessert."

"Angie Dixon too?"

Linda nodded. "That's when she went crying to Logan about the tapes."

"And what did you do?"

"I called Green on it. Told him I'd see him in hell before I'd do that. I turned in my union book and told him he could shove it up his ass."

"So you quit, but you said Angie went crying to Logan?"

Linda bit her lip and nodded.

"Logan didn't know about the tapes before?"

"Nobody did except Angie. He thought he could put a stop to it. I told him he was crazy, that he should mind his own business, but he was determined."

"Is that what you two broke up over, about his going after Green?"

She hesitated. "No," she said quietly.

"What then?"

"Angie. Logan was too naive, too big-hearted and honest to see that she was making a play for him. He asked me to copy the tapes. When I found out we had copied them for her, that was the last straw."

We were back to the tapes again. "But you did copy them."

"I didn't. Jimmy did."

"Jimmy!"

"I guess Sandy Carson over at the center is the one who actually did the copying. Logan had met her several times when we took Jimmy over to the center or went by to pick him up."

"Sandy Carson, the one who runs the micrographics department?"

"That's the one. And that's where the tapes still are, in a file in her office. Not the originals. I'm sure Logan had those with him on the boat. But the copies are there, on microfiche. After Logan died, I told Sandy that if anything happened to me, she should turn them over to the police. Angie knew about the copies, not where they were, but that they existed. I tried to warn her that she was in danger, but she didn't want to listen any more than Logan did. They both thought as long as the copies were safe, so were they."

"But she wasn't," I added. "And neither was Logan. Why didn't you come forward with this earlier, Linda? Why did you keep it quiet?"

"The cops insisted from the beginning that Logan's death was an accident. Martin Green has lots of money, lots of pull. I figured there was a payoff somewhere along the line."

Linda Decker stopped speaking. For several moments I couldn't think of anything else to ask. I didn't like her all too easy assumption that homicide cops were on the take. "Stupidity, maybe," I said finally. "Bullheadedness maybe, but not payoffs."

Linda Decker nodded. I wasn't sure whether or not she was convinced until she spoke. "I really was wrong about you, wasn't I," she said quietly.

"Yes."

"I'm sorry," she said again. "I know after what happened yesterday, I've got no right to ask, but you came here this morning because of . . ." She stopped and swallowed. "Because of Jimmy. You must care, or you wouldn't . . ." She paused again. "Will you help me, Detective Beaumont? I don't know where else to turn."

For the first time, in all the while we had been talking, Watty's words reverberated in my head. Keep your goddamned nose out of it. Mind your own business. And here I was, back in it up to my neck.

Linda Decker was looking at me, pleading, waiting for my answer.

"I don't know what I can do," I told her at last, "but I'll do what I can."

It wasn't much, but what the hell. I've always been a soft touch.

CHAPTER 17

As I went down in the elevator, I got off at four to see Peters. His bed was empty, and his roommate told me he was down the hall lifting weights in the gym.

"What's the matter with you?" Peters asked as soon as he saw my face. "Aside from the fact that you look like somebody beat you to a bloody pulp."

"It's a long story," I replied.

In a quiet corner of the small gym, Peters sat in his wheelchair and listened while I told him what Linda Decker had said.

When I finished, he nodded his head. "You don't have much of a choice, do you. Like it or not, you're going to have to talk to Manny and Kramer."

"That's the way it looks."

"Linda Decker doesn't have any solid proof?"

I shook my head. "Only the tapes."

"That's not much to go on. Purely circumstantial."

"Purely," I agreed. "The problem is, if somebody

doesn't start looking in the right places pretty damn soon, there's never going to be anything *but* circumstantial evidence."

Peters looked thoughtful. "What about this Martinson guy, the one who disappeared in Alaska? Is anyone down at the department following up on that case?"

"I don't know. Missing Persons, maybe. Without a body, it wouldn't have come to homicide."

"Did she say where in Alaska?"

"No."

"It's a big place. Maybe I can do some checking on that from here."

I got up.

"Where are you going?" Peters asked.

"To find Kramer and see if there's any way to eat crow and still keep my self-respect."

Peters looked at me, his eyes serious and steady. "Sounds to me like you'll have to find a way to do both," he said.

I nodded and started to leave, giving him an affectionate whack on the shoulder on my way past. "Thanks for the fatherly advice," I said.

He grinned. "Anytime. Advice is freely and cheerfully given."

Outside the hospital, the sky was a clear, unremitting blue. I was tired of summer, tired of blue skies, and tired of the sideways glances people gave me when they caught sight of my face. I needed to go somewhere to think. In the end I sought out the shady serenity of the Japanese garden in the Arboretum. There, beside a small, quiet pool, I sat for a full hour, trying to marshal my thoughts into some sort of reasonable order.

According to Linda Decker, we were dealing with union fraud perpetrated by thugs who didn't hesitate at murder. There were four victims dead already, if you counted Wayne Martinson, the guy missing in Alaska. Four and a half, if you counted Jimmy Rising in the burn unit at Harborview.

Martin Green and whoever else might be involved had to be stopped, one way or the other, and I sure as hell wanted to be part of the process, part of the solution. There was a major barrier to my doing just that—my bullheaded, bullnecked nemesis, Paul Kramer.

And I couldn't very well go to Kramer with nothing in hand but a lame apology and some far-fetched suppositions, wild-sounding accusations from Linda Decker, a lady who had lost big. Someone who has suffered that many losses is going to have a vested interest in seeing the situation resolved, in pinning the crimes on someone regardless of how remote.

I had to have something more solid than Linda Decker's unsubstantiated allegations. I had to come up with something powerful enough to jar Detective Kramer out of our juvenile rivalry and make him pay attention, take action, preferably some action other than going straight to Sergeant Watkins and having my wings clipped.

That brought me back to the question of what was actually solid. The tapes. The microfiche copy of the tapes. And what else? In my mind, I went back over everything Linda Decker had said. What was it about the union? What all had she claimed they were doing? Selling union books, taking pay-offs to let people bypass the apprenticeship program.

But those kinds of bribes only worked if the applicant had plenty of money available. For women, especially poor ones like Angie Dixon and Linda Decker, maybe the rats running the scam had been willing to take it out in trade, in services rendered, services that never made it onto Wayne Martinson's accounting tapes. Like being dessert at Martin Green's party for instance.

And what about Martinson's books, the journals themselves? Where were they? Despite what Angie and Linda had believed, the tapes themselves weren't that damning, not without the journal entries to go with them. But who had them? Had Martinson taken them with him on his ill-fated fishing trip, or were they still in his office somewhere? Or—and this was far more likely—had they been removed by person or persons unknown shortly after his disappearance?

I went back once more to what Linda had said about the union. Something was bothering me—something I couldn't quite put a finger on kept nagging at me, scratching at the door to my subconscious, demanding admittance. The union books, the apprenticeship program, and something else, a third item. At last it came to me. Boomers. That was it.

Boomers from out of town paying to get put on the A-list, that top work list of members who got called out first. Every union on earth has those kinds of lists, and every union comes equipped with a whole catalog of by-laws to say what you have to do to get on that list.

Well, I just happened to know a boomer—Fred McKinney, Katherine Tyree's fiancé. He had dropped into the Seattle union hall and landed on the iron-worker's A-list close enough to the top that he had worked on Columbia Center, Seattle's newest show-case high rise. Reason told me that work on that particular building would have been the private preserve of local hands no matter what trade union was involved.

Maybe, if Fred had paid bribe money, and maybe if he knew the same people had been involved in Logan Tyree's death, he would be willing to come forward and name names. Often, just knowing that we're nosing around in the right direction is enough to spook crooks into doing something stupid.

And there was Don Kaplan, the guy on the bal-cony at Martin Green's party. Unless I missed my guess, Angie Dixon's death had gotten him where he lived. He had seemed nice enough. If I tracked him down, it might be that he could shed some light on the subject.

About that time a busload of camera-carrying tourists came wandering through the Arboretum and interrupted my reverie. I turned toward the water, keeping my face and black eyes averted from the clicking cameras. I heard some whispered gritch-ing to the effect that I should have sense enough to move on so people could get a better shot of the pool. I refused to take the hint.

By the time they left, I found myself thinking about Angie Dixon. Linda Decker's comments were the first real link between Logan Tyree and Angie Dixon. I had theorized that there might be a connection, but now I knew for sure it existed. Logan and Angie had indeed known each other. Enough to make Linda jealous. Enough that Angie had confided in Logan about the tapes. Why did she find it necessary?

And if Linda was right, if Angie had been pushed, who had pushed her? Suddenly, the haunting picture from the paper came back to me as clearly as if I were holding it in my hand. In my mind's eye, I once more saw Angie Dixon plunging to her death. A comic-book light bulb clicked on over my head as I realized the picture might hold the key to the puzzle.

Adrenaline coursed through my body—adrenaline and questions. How many pictures were on that roll? How often were the pictures taken? And was there a chance, even a remote one, that another shot, taken earlier or later, might provide a clue as to what had gone on in the minutes before and after Angie's fatal plunge?

Getting a look at that film, prying it loose from whoever owned it was something only officialdom could accomplish, and officialdom would go to work on it only if I filled Manny Davis and Paul Kramer in on what was happening. It was time to straighten up and fly right, no matter how much I didn't want to do it.

I left the Arboretum and drove back downtown, conscious as I drove that it was after lunch and I had eaten nothing since Ralph Ames' midnight fettucini. The 928 headed for the Doghouse on automatic pilot.

The Doghouse is disreputable enough that no one raised an eyebrow at my purple bruises. It's the kind of place that says "Breakfast Anytime" and means it. That's what I had—bacon, eggs, toast, and coffee. Plenty of coffee. I didn't try calling the department until after I had finished eating. I believe it's called avoidance behavior. When I finally couldn't think of another plausible excuse to put it off any longer, I used the pay phone near the pinball machines.

I asked for Manny Davis. He wasn't in. I asked for Paul Kramer. He was. Too bad.

"Detective Kramer speaking."

"Hello, Paul. This is Beaumont."

Behind me some guy was racking up a huge score on the Doghouse's primo pinball machine. A group of enthusiastic buddies was cheering him on.

"Who?" Kramer demanded. "I can't hear you. There's too much noise in the background."

"Beaumont," I repeated, raising the volume. "I need to talk to you."

He paused. A long pause. "So talk. I'm listening."

At least he didn't hang up on me. I took a deep breath. "Not on the phone. I want to talk in person. To both you and Manny."

"Manny's busy. He's in court this afternoon."

"Well, to you then."

Behind me the pinball crowd cheered again.

"What's that? I can't hear you."

"To you then. Can you meet me?"

"Where?"

"Do you know where the Doghouse is at Seventh and Bell?"

"I know it," he answered. "What are you doing, out slumming, Beaumont?"

So that's how it was. He hadn't hung up on me, but we hadn't exactly kissed and made up, either. I didn't say anything.

"When?" Kramer demanded.

"As soon as you can get here."

He hung up and I went back to my table. My plate and dirty silverware had been cleared away. Left were a freshly poured cup of coffee and a newspaper with the unworked crossword puzzle folded out. The waitresses at the Doghouse take good care of me. That's one of the reasons I go there. It's got nothing to do with gourmet cuisine.

The crossword puzzle contained only three unfinished words by the time Detective Paul Kramer strode up to the table twenty minutes later.

"You wanted to see me?" he asked, easing his sizable frame into the booth across from me.

I set the nearly finished puzzle aside. "Wanting is probably overstating the case," I said. Kramer made as if to rise. "Sit," I ordered. He sat.

Jenny, the waitress, came to the table just then and offered him coffee which he accepted with a grudging nod. We sat without speaking until she finished pouring it and walked away, leaving us alone.

"What do you want? This ain't no pleasure trip for me, Beaumont, and I'm damned if I'm going to sit here while you dish out insults."

For some strange reason, the situation reminded me of the time years before when, at Karen's insistence, I had taken Scott to a local diner to administer the obligatory birds and bees talk. My son had been full of teenage resentment, angry and embarrassed both. In the end, the talk could in no way be called an unqualified success. We both went home frustrated and neither of us mentioned it again.

Now, with Detective Paul Kramer sitting across the table from me, I felt the air charged with the same kind of irritation and arrogance, the same counterproductive determination to miscommunicate. But that was where the similarity ended. With Scott and the birds and the bees, adult complacency had been on my side. I had known I was right and that time would bear me out. With Kramer I had no such delusions. He was right and I was wrong, and he didn't waste any time beating around the bush before he let me know it.

"Who the hell do you think you are that you can go messing around in my case?"

"I'm sorry," I said.

It wasn't what he expected. My two-word apology didn't derail him altogether, but it threw a real monkey wrench in his attack.

"Logan Tyree's our case," he went on. "Manny's and mine. You've got no business screwing with it."

"I know."

Kramer stopped and sat with his head cocked to one side, like someone who's afraid he's been suckered too far into enemy territory. "What did you want to see me for then?" he demanded.

Biding my time, I took a careful sip of my coffee. "Why'd you become a cop, Kramer?" I asked evenly.

"What is this, an occupational aptitude test?"

"Just tell me."

He shrugged. "It's something I have to do, that's all."

"You want to make the world a better place to live in?" I suggested.

"Something like that." He frowned. "What kind of deal is this, Beaumont? I'm here because I'm pissed as hell, and you sit there making fun of me."

"I'm not making fun of anybody, Kramer. I've never been more serious in my life."

Reluctantly, Kramer settled back in the booth, holding his cup while he studied me warily. He said nothing.

"And how long do you plan to be in homicide?" I asked.

"Me? As long as it takes."

"As long as it takes for what?"

"To be promoted out." At least we had cut through the bullshit. He was being honest.

"So you see homicide as a stepping-stone to bigger and better things?"

"There's nothing wrong with that," Kramer said defensively.

"I never said there was. What were you doing seventeen years ago?"

"Seventeen years ago?" He laughed. "I was thirteen and in the eighth grade down in Tumwater. What does that have to do with the price of peanuts?"

"Because seventeen years ago, I was just starting out in homicide. Fresh up from robbery, same as you are now."

"So?"

"It's my life's work, Kramer. I've never wanted to

do anything else. I never saw homicide as a spring-board. I do the job. I like it. I'm good at it.

"A few days ago, you called me a playboy cop. It hurt me real good, but I've been doing some think-ing. It's true. I've got more money right now than I'll ever know what to do with. I could quit the force tomorrow and never have to work another day in my life, but you know what? I don't know what the hell I'd do with myself if I quit. There isn't anything else I'd rather do except maybe drink too much and die young."

Kramer shifted in his seat. "Why are you telling me all this? What's the point?"

"The point is, we're on the same team, Kramer. Different motivations maybe, but we work the same side of the street. Logan Tyree's death is important, far more so than anyone's figured out. Solve it, and you'll be a hero. Screw it up, and your time in ho-micide gets that much longer."

"Does that mean you know something we don't know?"

"Maybe," I said.

"You can't do this, Beaumont," he protested. "You can't withhold information and you know it."

"I'm not withholding anything. That's why I called you here, to tell you what I know. But I want in on it."

Kramer looked astonished. "You're going to ask Watty to put you on the case?"

I shook my head. "No, Kramer. You are."

"Why would I? And why do you want on the case?"

"Because I give a shit about Jimmy Rising and Linda Decker and Logan Tyree and Angie Dixon.

Because I want to see the creeps who did this off the streets."

When I mentioned Angie Dixon's name, a spark of excitement came to life in Kramer's eyes. "The woman who fell. Did she have something to do with the others?"

I could see he needed to know the answer. As far as that was concerned, he was just like me, but I deliberately left him hanging without directly answering his question.

"I want in because I'm a good cop, Kramer. Because I've discovered things you need to know. I want this case solved. I want it every bit as much as you want to be Chief of Police."

I finished what I had to say and shut up. The cards were all on the table now. The question was, would he pick them up or not? There was a long silence. I was determined to wait him out. Selling Fuller Brush taught me that much. After you've made your pitch, keep quiet. The first one to open his mouth loses. I waited. The silence stretched out interminably.

"You want it that bad, do you?" Kramer said at last.

I nodded. "That bad."

"Then you'd better tell me what you know."

Eating crow was as simple as that.

CHAPTER 18

WHEN WE LEFT THE DOGHOUSE AN HOUR AND A HALF later, we had hammered out rough guidelines for an uneasy alliance. Kramer had called Watty, and Detective J. P. Beaumont was now officially part of the investigation into Logan Tyree's death. It was a big improvement over the other alternative of being flat-out fired.

We took Kramer's car and drove to the Northwest Center on Armory Way. The receptionist summoned Sandy Carson from the micrographics department. When she arrived, she was still blonde and still willowy, but she looked like hell. Her eyes were red. I'm sure she had been crying.

"I didn't want any visitors out in the shop today," she explained. "Everyone's still too upset about Jimmy. But Linda called and told me you'd be coming by. She said for me to give you this." She handed me a large brown interdepartmental envelope with its string fastener firmly tied.

"Who actually took the pictures?" I asked.

"Jimmy did. I supervised, of course."

"And do you have any idea what became of the originals?"

She shook her head. "I gave them to Logan when he came by and picked Jimmy up one day. He asked me to keep the copies here. He said he thought that would be safer."

"Do you remember when that was?"

"Several days before he died."

"And did you go to the police with it?"

"There wasn't any point. Everyone said it was an accident."

I glanced at Kramer, but I didn't say anything. There was no sense rubbing his nose in it.

"Any idea where we should go to take a look at these?" I asked.

Kramer nodded. "I know a place."

He drove us to the *Seattle Times* building on Fairview and pulled into the parking lot. "I know people here," he said. "They'll let us use their fiche reader. Not only that, maybe I can get a line on that Masters Plaza film."

One of my objections to the new breed of law enforcement officers is their total preoccupation with the media. These cops want to solve crimes, all right, but they also want the publicity. They want to be sure their names are spelled right in the papers, pronounced right on the eleven o'clock news. Old war-horses like Big Al Lindstrom and me don't give a damn what the media have to say one way or the other.

In this case, however, Detective Paul Kramer's

cozy friendship with the Third Estate paid off. Kramer's buddy in the news department hooked us up with someone from photography. He said the picture of Angie Dixon had come to the paper through a local free-lance film editor. The guy at the *Times* wasn't sure exactly how that had transpired, and the person who had handled the transaction wasn't in, but he was able to tell us that the company actually doing the filming was a small outfit called Camera Craft in the Denny Regrade.

Kramer's buddy also let us use a microfiche reader. It didn't do us any good. The fiche showed nothing but accountant's tapes, some with barely legible notations on them. Without the accompanying journals, they were worthless.

Kramer leaned away from the viewer long enough to let me take a look. "None of this makes sense," he said. "These aren't something worth killing for. Are you sure this is what Linda Decker thought they were after?"

"Positive."

"So what now? Go down to Camera Craft?"

"Seems like."

We were told that the owner of Camera Craft was grabbing a late lunch at the Rendezvous, a small restaurant just up the block. We followed him there. Like other places in the Regrade, the Rendezvous has a checkered past. In the old days it was a private screening house where local movie distributors could get a sneak preview of Hollywood's latest offerings. For years now, it has been a blue-collar hangout. The private dining area still boasts a minuscule stage and a battered projection screen, holdovers from days gone by. Occasionally some shoestring drama company will stage a production there.

The owner of Camera Craft, Jim Hadley, wasn't in the Rendezvous' old screening room. He was hunched over a hamburger and fries at a small table in the back of the dimly lit main dining room. He was evidently a regular. When we asked, the cashier had no difficulty pointing him out to us.

Kramer approached Hadley's table, flashed his ID, and introduced us both. Busy chewing, Hadley nodded us into chairs and swallowed a mouthful of hamburger. "What's this all about?" he asked.

"The picture in the paper."

"Oh," he said. "That one. It was a fluke, an absolute fluke. The odds of the camera going off just as she fell . . . It's like that guy taking pictures of Mount Saint Helens just as it exploded."

"I understand your company is in charge of doing the filming for the Masters Plaza folks?"

"That's right. We unload and load the cameras every morning, refocus, and reset the timers. After that they run all day and all night on their own. We've got a free-lance editor who supervises the film-to-tape transfer and then edits out all the night scenes and rough stuff."

"What kind of transfer?"

"You know, from film to videotape. That's where we do all the fine-tuning."

"You said cameras. Does that mean there's more than one?"

He nodded and swallowed another bite of his hamburger. "Two actually. Each of them is set to take one picture every four minutes—not at the same time, of course. One is set up right across the street in the Arcade building. The other's a block or so away. Now that they're up to the forty-second floor, the Arcade building isn't tall enough to show the whole building. The developer wants it for a corporate dog and pony production, a video to show what a hell of a good job they do."

"Which camera took the picture that was in the newspaper?" I asked.

"The one on the Arcade building. We keep that one focused on the raising gang. Putting up those beams is a lot more spectacular than most of the rest of it. It's certainly the most visual."

"And the most dangerous," I added.

Hadley shrugged. "That too, although it all looks pretty damn dangerous if you ask me."

Kramer shifted impatiently in his seat. "So how did the picture end up in the newspaper?"

"Our editor pulled a workprint that night. She's the one who noticed. She said she had some friends down at the *Times*, and she wondered if whether Darren Gibson would mind if she passed that one picture along. Of course he didn't mind. Publicity's publicity, especially if it's free."

"Who's Darren Gibson?"

"The local project manager for Masters Plaza. He said fine. Do it. Kath was way ahead of him."

"Kath?"

"Kath Naguchi. The editor I told you about. She figured he'd say yes. She was all set to pass it along to the *Times* as soon as he gave her the go-ahead. She was on her way down there within minutes. It was in the paper the next day."

"What about the rest of the film?"

Hadley shrugged. "Beats me. I suppose it's back at the shop where it belongs, along with the rest of the project."

"Could we see it?" I asked.

He shook his head. "Not without permission. The Masters and Rogers folks are paying us real good money to do this job. I'm not going to screw it up by showing you something I'm not supposed to."

"Has anyone else asked to see it?"

"No. Why would they?"

"So, the editor made a print of that one picture?"

Hadley shook his head. "She provided the film. I think the guys down at the paper did the actual blowup."

"Did anyone make prints of any of the other frames, either before or after the one in the paper?"

Hadley shook his head. "No. Not so far as I know. Like I said, she saw that one when she was doing the dailies."

"Dailies?" Kramer asked.

"It's a one-light print," I explained. "It tells what's on the previous day's shoot."

Kramer glowered at me. "Movie talk?" he asked disgustedly.

"You asked," I replied.

He turned back to Hadley. "We're helping the Department of Labor and Industries on this case. How do we get a look at that film?"

"I already told you. You've got to get permission from Masters and Rogers. They're the guys who write my checks. I wouldn't step on their toes on a bet."

"And Darren Gibson is the person we'd need to talk to?"

"Yes, but right now he's out of town. He was supposed to be in Toronto today. Back tomorrow most likely. I don't know if you'll be able to get hold of him or not."

"Do you have a phone number?"

Hadley leaned back in his chair and wiped his mouth with a paper napkin. "Back in the office," he answered.

He paid for his lunch. We followed him out the door of the Rendezvous and back down Second Avenue to his shop where he thumbed through a gigantic Rolodex on his receptionist's desk and read off two telephone numbers—one local and the other in Toronto.

Leaving Camera Craft we drove to the department. In our cubicle I found Big Al Lindstrom sitting in my chair with his feet on my desk. He was eating an apple and reading a newspaper.

"I didn't expect you in today," he said, scrambling out of my chair.

"That's obvious," I growled, sweeping stray bits of apple off the chair before I sat down.

"I thought you were on vacation until Tuesday." Big Al quieted suddenly when Paul Kramer appeared over my shoulder.

"I'll try reaching Gibson," Kramer announced, barely pausing on the way to his and Manny's cubicle. "You check with Missing Persons."

Big Al eyed me quizzically. "You taking orders from Kramer now? What's going on?"

"I *am* on vacation," I replied, dialing the number

for Missing Persons. "Doesn't it look like it? I'm taking a busman's holiday."

Big Al shook his head in disbelief. "To work with Kramer? No way."

"Hide and watch," I said.

"What happened to your face?"

"Walked into a post," I told him.

Big Al shook his head. He was unconvinced. "Like hell you did," he said. With that he picked up his cup and went in search of coffee.

That's the wonderful thing about telling the truth. People believe what they want to believe. It's a hell of a lot simpler than lying. There isn't the ever-present danger of getting caught.

It felt good to sit down at my desk again, to pick up my phone and dial a familiar number. It felt like I had been away from work, real work, for a long, long time. Naturally, Missing Persons put me on hold. While I waited, Margie popped her head in the door.

"I just wanted you to know that I never breathed a word about Gloria and the phone number."

"Thanks," I told her. "I owe you."

If Watty had heard about my tracking down Linda Decker's phone number under false pretenses, he would have fired my ass before I knew what hit me.

"What's this about a phone number?" Big Al asked, coming back with a cup of coffee.

"Never mind," I said.

The clerk in Missing Persons finally came back on the line. "This is Beaumont in homicide," I explained. "Do you have anything going on a guy by the name of Wayne Martinson?"

"Let me check." She put me on hold a second time, giving Big Al another crack at me.

"So what's it like to be in the movie business?" he demanded. "Are you ready to get yourself an agent and take the plunge?"

"Get off my back. The movie business sucks."

The clerk in Missing Persons returned once more, and I spent the next few minutes explaining that I hadn't said what she thought I said and that I certainly hadn't said it to her. Once her ruffled feathers were smoothed, she connected me with Detective Janie Jacobs who had Wayne Martinson's file in hand when she picked up the phone.

"Are you actively working the case?" I asked.

"Not so as you'd notice," Janie answered. "We took the report. His wife called it in, but since Martinson disappeared from a fishing resort in Alaska, it's outside our jurisdiction. The detectives there tell me they've got nothing to indicate foul play. He went fishing by himself in the morning and didn't come back. Most of his clothing was left in his room."

"Most?"

"That's right. Most but not all. Some of them weren't there. That's what makes the detectives at the scene think maybe he took a walk, a powder. He and his wife were evidently having problems. They think he decided to take off rather than hold still for a divorce."

"Sometimes running away has a whole lot of appeal," I said.

"It makes my life a hell of a lot tougher," Janie responded, adding with a half laugh, "but then, a job's a job I guess. Anything else, Detective Beaumont?

You want the wife's name and number? Let me give it to you. It's unlisted." I wrote down Gail Martinson's phone number.

"Thanks."

"So why's homicide interested in Wayne Martinson?" Janie asked.

"There may be a connection to a case we're working."

"Let me know if you put anything together. It would be nice if there were a connection for a change. Most of the time I feel like I'm working in a vacuum."

I hung up. "Who's Martinson?" Big Al asked.

"An accountant. The former bookkeeper for the ironworkers' local here in town."

"He's missing and you think there's some connection between him and that ironworker who got blown up down on Lake Union?"

"It's beginning to look that way."

"And that's why you're here working with Paul Kramer instead of taking vacation?" Big Al was incredulous. "You don't need a vacation, Beau. You should be on medical leave to have your head examined."

Big Al Lindstrom always says exactly what he's thinking. "You're not the first one to tell me that," I said just as Paul Kramer came back to the door of our cubicle.

"Tell you what?" Kramer asked, pausing there.

"That I'm a couple of bubbles out of plumb," I answered.

Kramer let it drop. "Gibson already left company headquarters in Toronto. He's catching the red-eye

back to Vancouver tonight. We'll have to try to locate him in the morning if we want a look at that
film. What did you find out from Missing Persons?"

I told him briefly what I had learned from Detective Jacobs. Paul Kramer shook his massive head. "It
still doesn't make sense. If Martinson ran off, I'd lay
odds it's got more to do with the ironworkers and
those goddamned tapes than it does with his wife."

It hurt like hell to admit Kramer might be right,
but his supposition certainly tallied with mine.

"Whoever the lady was on the phone in Toronto,"
Kramer continued, "she said Gibson is due back at
work here in Seattle tomorrow morning by seven.
Either at the job site or in their temporary headquarters in the Arcade Building. Want to meet there
about seven-fifteen?"

"In the office?"

Kramer shook his head. "Let's meet outside first.
By the fountain at Second and Union."

"All right, but I'll have to be back home by ten-
thirty. I've got a date for lunch."

I'm not sure why I said it that way instead of coming right out and telling him that taking Tracie and
Heather to Bumbershoot was a prior commitment.
By then we had been working together for several
hours with no recurrence of our ongoing feud.

A look of barely concealed contempt washed over
Kramer's face. "By all means, don't let this case
screw up your social life." With that, he turned on
his heel and stalked away.

Good riddance, I thought. If he's still looking for
playboy cop symptoms, I'll give him one every now
and then. Just for drill.

CHAPTER 19

RALPH AMES HAS BEEN ON AN ITALIAN FOOD KICK FOR as long as I've known him. By the time I got home that night, he had invited Heather and Tracie to dinner and had enlisted their help in making a gigantic batch of spaghetti. The three of them were already eating when I put my key in the lock.

My kitchen was a shambles. Some charred remains, vaguely recognizable as slices of French bread, sat on the counter giving mute testimony to at least one failed batch of garlic toast. A thin dusting of Parmesan cheese covered the floor. More dirty cooking pots than I could possibly own were scattered throughout. Whoever was volunteering for KP duty was in deep trouble.

I poured myself a MacNaughton's and water and carried it with me to the table. Heather beamed as Ames put a plate stacked high with spaghetti in front of me.

"We got to help, Unca Beau. He let us," she lisped happily. Her triumphant grin was missing two front teeth. "I got to stir, and Tracie fixed the bread."

With a slight warning shake of his head, Ralph Ames passed me a basket full of garlic bread which was only somewhat less charred than the discarded batch still in the kitchen.

I took a bite and nodded appreciatively at Tracie. "Delicious," I said.

She ducked her head and wrinkled her nose. "It's a little burned. I forgot to set the timer."

"It's fine," I told her.

The kids were excited and overflowing with news, babbling to Ames and me about their father's upcoming wedding, their new dresses, the foibles of poor Mrs. Edwards, and our planned outing to Bumbershoot the next day. I tried to stay with the flow of conversation, but my mind kept wandering back to Logan Tyree and Jimmy Rising and Angie Dixon. At least one of those three cases was now officially mine.

I must have been on my third or fourth Mac-Naughton's by the time the kitchen was mucked out and the girls had gone back downstairs. Finally, mercifully, the apartment was quiet. I leaned back in my ancient recliner, resting my head, closing my eyes. But as soon as I did, it all came back to me—Logan Tyree, Jimmy Rising, and Angie Dixon. Names with questions and no answers.

Sitting up, I wrestled the Seattle telephone book out of the drawer in the table next to my chair. I checked the K's and found there was only one Don Kaplan, a Donald B. Kaplan on N.E. 128th. I dialed the number. It rang and rang, and nobody answered.

Ralph Ames came into the living room from the kitchen just as I put the phone back in its cradle. He looked at me quizzically.

Instead of answering his unasked question, I got up and poured myself another drink, offering him one in the process. Ames shook his head.

"I was calling someone from Martin Green's party," I explained. "Remember me telling you about the man on the balcony, a guy named Don Kaplan? He's not home right now, but if he shows up there before it gets too late, I'll stop by and see him tonight."

I sat back down in my recliner. A little too hard. Some of the MacNaughton's slopped into my lap. I wiped it off.

"It's already too late, Beau," Ames said.

"What do you mean? It's just barely ten."

"It's too late for driving. Look at yourself. You're in no condition to drive, much less question a potential witness."

It wasn't the first nudge Ames had given me on the subject of drinking, not just counting drinks that night in particular, but drinking in general. He had mentioned my alcohol consumption on several earlier occasions, and I always resented it. I resented it now. Just because I had a drink or two or three in the evening after work didn't make me an alcoholic in my book. I thought he was overreacting and told him so.

"So what are you, my mother?"

"I'm your attorney, Beau. I'm concerned about you."

"Get off it, Ralph. If I want to drink too much, I'm not hurting anyone but myself."

Ames shrugged and dropped it for the moment. "What's bugging you tonight? All evening long when the girls tried to talk to you, it was like there was nobody home. You barely paid attention."

"This is beginning to sound a whole lot like a lecture," I countered. "I've been thinking about the case, that's all."

"The case," he echoed. "What case? And why do you want to talk to Don Kaplan? When I left this morning, I understood you were on vacation until Tuesday morning. Whatever happened to that?"

"I got Watty to put me on it after all," I said.

"The case he gave you strict orders to leave alone on pain of being fired."

I nodded. "That's the one."

Ames shook his head in disgust. "You drink too much and you work too hard. Definitely type-A behavior, Beau. Typical type A. Heart attack material. You'd best mend your ways, or you won't be around long enough to enjoy your money."

Our conversation probably would have deteriorated further into an all-out quarrel if the phone hadn't rung just then. It was Linda Decker.

"I talked to Sandy Carson," she said. "She told me she gave you the tapes. Did you look at them? Did they help?"

She sounded so eager it was hard to answer her. "We looked at them all right," I said slowly, playing for time, scrambling for the right thing to say.

I was hedging. I didn't want to have to tell Linda Decker that the information she had guarded with her life, the information that had cost her Logan Tyree, her mother, and maybe her brother, was essentially worthless. It's one thing to pay a price. It's something else to discover that the price was meaningless.

"We're still evaluating the information," I said at last.

She sighed. I could sense her disappointment. "What are you doing now?" she asked.

I glanced down at the drink in my hand and found myself wondering exactly how many MacNaughton's there had been in the course of the evening. I couldn't remember exactly, and now, suddenly it seemed important, not because of Ames but because of me. Maybe Ralph Ames was right to be worried.

"Just taking it easy," I said in answer to Linda's question.

"I don't mean right this minute," Linda Decker responded. "I mean what are you going to do next?"

"We're following up on the disappearance of Wayne Martinson."

"Wayne? Do you think he was involved?"

"Maybe, maybe not," I replied. "And then tomorrow we'll have a look at the pictures of Masters Plaza, to see if those tell us anything."

"That's all?"

"For right now." I heard Linda Decker's sharp intake of breath. For the loved ones, the ones left grieving and waiting, I'm sure the way cops have to work must seem incredibly cumbersome, agonizingly slow.

It's true. It is.

There was nothing more I could or would tell Linda Decker right then, so I changed the subject. "How's Jimmy?" I asked.

There was a long pause before she answered. "I don't know," she said softly. "He may not make it through the night, but at least the sons of bitches didn't get the tapes," she added fiercely. "Thank God for that."

"That's right," I agreed as consolingly as I could manage. "At least they didn't get the tapes."

I put down the phone and sat there looking at it. For a time I forgot I wasn't alone in the room.

"Who was that?" Ames asked.

The sound of his voice startled me, and I jumped. All the potential rancor in our previous discussion faded from mind. It never occurred to me to tell Ralph Ames to mind his own business.

"Linda," I answered. "Linda Decker, wondering how things are going."

"And the tapes?" he pressed.

I shook my head. "They're nothing really, just some accountant's tapes. Angie Dixon, the woman who fell off the building, insisted that they were part of a long-term swindle inside the union—bribes, kickbacks, that kind of thing. The problem is, we've only got the tapes, not the journal entries. Without those, we can't prove a thing."

"What are you going to do about it?" Ames asked.

Pointedly placing my empty glass on the table, I looked Ralph Ames in the eye. "Sleep on it," I said. "Go to bed and see if any bright ideas surface in my subconscious."

Of course, when I finally did manage to wrestle my nighttime demons into submission, I was too exhausted for any inspiration to pay me a nocturnal visit. There were dreams—disjointed, fragmented, ugly dreams in which I almost but not quite found something that didn't want to be found.

There were no flashes of psychic brilliance, no illuminating insights into the problem at hand. When the alarm went off at six the next morning I woke up with a throbbing hangover, no closer to solving the problem than I had been the night before when I fell into bed in a booze-induced stupor.

Hung over or not, I knew as soon as I opened my eyes that something was different. For the first time in weeks, the sky outside my bedroom window was gray instead of blue. Seattle's cool cloud cover was back, announcing that summer had just about run its course. I went out on the balcony. A cool freshening breeze was blowing in off Puget Sound. Sniffing it cleared my head and made me feel better.

Let it rain, I thought. Labor Day or not, Bumbershoot or not, let it rain. I'm ready.

Dressing quickly, I skipped out of the house without bothering to make coffee or waken Ames. I made my way down Second with the other early-morning pedestrian commuters. They were smiling and nodding at one another in greeting. The heat was leaving, the sun was going back where it belonged, and real Seattlites were happy to have their customary weather back.

It was only five to seven when I got to Second and Union, but Paul Kramer was already pacing anxiously back and forth by the empty, drought-dried fountain next to the Arcade Building. Manny Davis, more relaxed, lounged easily against one wall watching Paul Kramer's impatient antics with some amusement.

When he saw me at last, Kramer breathed an exaggerated sigh of relief, turned on his heel, and headed into the building. Manny waited until I reached him. "I figured you'd be on time. Kramer's got no faith."

"He's got all kinds of faith," I corrected, "in all the wrong things."

The temporary Seattle headquarters for Masters and Rogers Developers was on the third floor of the Arcade Building in two small but posh offices that had been sublet from someone else. The woman at the front desk would have made a terrific ice princess. Flawlessly made up. Coldly beautiful. No smile. No discernible sense of humor.

"Mr. Gibson has someone with him just now. May I ask what this is concerning?"

"It's police business, Miss," Manny offered. From the daggered look she gave him, Miss wasn't a term she found endearing.

She sat up straighter in her chair. "Mr. Gibson is meeting with some prospective tenants at the moment. He flew back from Toronto late last night especially for this meeting. I'm sure he'll be glad to talk to you once it's over, but I couldn't possibly interrupt him. It may take several hours. They're on a tour of the building right now."

"Several hours!" Kramer yelped as though he'd been shot. The probability was high that the Masters Plaza pictures would reveal nothing new, yield nothing we hadn't already learned from other sources, but Kramer was young and impatient. He needed to feel like he was doing something, getting somewhere. "We'll wait," he said stubbornly. "However long it takes, we'll wait."

He settled heavily into a chair next to a potted palm. Manny joined him and picked up a recent copy of *Forbes* that was sitting on an end table next to him.

The receptionist shrugged with studied disinterest and turned back to her computer keyboard. "Suit yourselves," she said.

I've seen this kind of corporate guardian angel all too often. They regard themselves as the keepers of all comings and goings. Over the years I've learned you have to get around women like that, because you sure as hell aren't going to get through them.

I made a point of looking at the clock on the receptionist's desk, turning the face toward me so I could see it. "You can wait if you want to," I said over my shoulder to Kramer and Manny. "I've got better things to do." Without saying anything more, I made my way out of the office. When I stopped at the elevator, I glanced back. Paul Kramer was glaring sourly at me through the glass, muttering something to Manny. Suspicions confirmed, probably. Smiling, I gave them a breezy wave and disappeared into the elevator.

I dashed across Second on a flashing DON'T WALK signal and ran all the way to the construction gate and elevator at the opposite end of Masters Plaza. I managed to squeeze on the elevator just as the door went shut, but the operator pointed at me and shook his head. "Where do you think you're going?"

"I'm with Mr. Gibson's party," I said. "I had to stop and take a leak."

The operator grinned. "Happens to the best of us, but you'll have to go back out to the tool shack and get a hard hat. I'll pick you up on the next trip."

I did as I was told, knowing that if the operator ran into Gibson on the way, the jig was up, but he didn't. He came back for me.

"I dropped Mr. Gibson off on the thirty-seventh floor a few minutes ago," the operator told me. "They said they'd work their way down from there. How about if I drop you at thirty-six?"

"That'll be fine," I said.

As soon as I stepped off the elevator, the wind rushing through the open spaces between the concrete beams caught me and almost blew the hard hat off my head. What was a freshening breeze at street level was a whistling gale on the thirty-sixth floor. Someone had hung a huge piece of heavy plastic along the side of the building, but it was flapping loose in the wind.

Since my suit and tie had been good enough to get me past the elevator operator, I figured I was looking for a suit and tie group. What I saw on the thirty-sixth floor were plumbers, electricians, and carpenters without a pinstripe or knotted silk tie in sight.

I took the unfinished metal stairway and clambered down to thirty-five. Still no luck. I finally caught up with them on thirty-three. There were six men in the group altogether. Quietly, I attached myself to the end of the procession. I figured the guests would think I was with Gibson, and Gibson would think I was one of the visitors.

And I didn't have any trouble picking Gibson out of the crowd. He was the one doing most of the talking, pointing out building features, gesturing this way and that. Periodically, one of the visitors would stop him long enough to ask a question.

Trailing at the end of the pack, it was far too noisy for me to hear much of what was said, but there was a good deal of nodding back and forth among the visitors. Gibson was evidently telling them what they wanted to hear.

At last we got back on the elevator for the return trip to ground level. The elevator operator recognized me and nodded, but he didn't say anything. Once we were back on the ground floor, Gibson stood to one side while the visitors headed for the tool shack to relinquish their hard hats.

I sidled up to him. "Mr. Gibson, could I have a word with you?"

He looked startled that I hadn't gone off with the others. "Sure," he said.

Pulling him aside, I discreetly showed him my identification. "My name is Detective Beaumont," I said. "I'm with the Seattle Police Department. We need your help."

Not nearly as cordial once he realized I wasn't a potential leasee, he glanced nervously toward the tool shack. "What do you want?"

"We need to get a look at that film of yours, the one with the lady who fell off the building."

Gibson swallowed. Clearly he didn't want his prospective tenants hearing about a police investigation into Angie Dixon's fatal fall.

Then he frowned. "Is there a problem?" he asked. "I thought that was all settled, that it had been ruled accidental."

"Maybe not," I answered. "How do we go about seeing the film?"

"I don't actually have it," Gibson said.

"I know you don't have it. Camera Craft does, but they won't show it to us unless you give them permission."

The first of the visitors was coming back from the tool shack. Gibson nodded hurriedly. "Okay, okay. I'll take care of it. Come along back to my office."

I did, trailing behind as before. When I sauntered into the Masters and Rogers office behind Darren Gibson and his guests, the look of absolute consternation on Paul Kramer's face made my day.

Gibson paused for only a moment beside the ice-lady's desk. "Call Camera Craft," he ordered brusquely. "Tell them to show this gentleman . . . What did you say your name was?"

"Beaumont. J. P. Beaumont."

"Tell them to give Mr. Beaumont here whatever help he needs." With that, Gibson swept into his private office with the entourage of potential customers following behind like so many trailing puppies.

"How'd you do that?" Kramer demanded in a startled whisper as he and Manny both stood up.

"Experience," I answered.

We started toward the door. "You're not going to wait then?" the receptionist asked.

"That won't be necessary now," I said, returning her chilly smile with a cool one of my own. "You just be sure to make that call to Camera Craft before we get there. It won't take us long."

CHAPTER 20

WE WERE THERE AT NINE, WAITING OUTSIDE ON THE street when Jim Hadley opened the doors to Camera Craft and let us in. "The secretary already called," he said, in answer to my question about Darren Gibson. "She said to show you whatever you need to see."

I was careful not to look at Paul Kramer. That was the only way to stifle a triumphant grin. Kramer was still dismayed by how easily I'd wrested permission out of Darren Gibson to see the film. I didn't want to shatter the fragile truce between us. My ability to keep my promise to Linda Decker depended totally on Kramer's grudging willingness to work together. One complaint from him, and Watty would have pulled me off the case in a minute.

"So when can we see the film?" I asked Hadley.

The owner of Camera Craft glanced at his watch and shook his head. "Not just yet, I'm afraid. Kath doesn't come in to work until almost three. The editing is one hundred percent her baby. If I go into that room and stir things up, she'll raise hell for weeks."

"Can't you call her at home then?" Kramer asked. "Ask her to come in early?"

Jim Hadley gave Kramer a derisive look and laughed aloud. "Are you kidding? No way. You've never worked with free-lance editors, have you? They're independent contractors, mostly a night-crawler variety, who won't answer telephones or show their faces before mid-afternoon. If I woke her up at this hour of the day, Kath Naguchi wouldn't ever work with me again, and she's damn good.

"Stop by around three," he added. "She'll be on her third cigarette and her second cup of coffee. By then she'll be about half civilized."

So there we were, stuck again. This job is like that. You get up early only to stand around and wait. Out on the street, Kramer was still in a hurry, still crabbing about finding Kath Naguchi early. His grousing was in direct opposition to Manny Davis' easygoing view of the world.

"Why'd you want to do a thing like that?" Manny asked, shutting off his partner's litany of complaint. "Sounds to me like we'd be better off tangling with a hibernating grizzly."

In the end, Manny's cooler head prevailed. I made arrangements to meet them back at Camera Craft at three.

"I suppose you're off on your hot date," Kramer noted sarcastically as I turned to make my way back home. I studied him for a long moment, wondering if I had been that ambitious in my youth, that ambitious and that obnoxious.

"Not hot," I corrected. "As a matter of fact, I'm taking two little girls to Bumbershoot. Care to join us?" Turning on my heel, I headed up the street just as the first real raindrops in more than a month began to fall on downtown Seattle.

It wasn't one of the Northwest's customary dry drizzles that you can walk for blocks in and not get wet. Instead of a light, gentle mist, this was a sidewalk-pounding, clothes-soaking downpour. I was completely drenched by the time I'd walked the six long blocks between Camera Craft and Belltown Terrace.

Annie, the building's concierge, was on duty in the lobby. She opened the door to let me in before I managed to get my key in the lock. Rivulets of water coursed down my face and dripped into my eyes. Looking for something dry, I wiped my forehead with the underside of my jacket sleeve.

"You're all wet," Annie observed unnecessarily.

I nodded, matching inanity for inanity. "It's raining out," I said.

"You're not really taking Heather and Tracie Bumbershooting in this weather, are you?"

I've long since learned that living in a high rise gives you about as much privacy as living in a small town. Which is to say, none. Everybody's business is everybody else's business.

"Who told you that?" I asked.

Annie laughed. "The girls did. They were down here just a few minutes ago looking up the street to see if you were coming. As far as I'm concerned, it's a rotten day for Bumbershooting."

"At least it won't be crowded," I replied.

She held the elevator door until I got on. "It won't be crowded because most people have sense enough to come in out of the rain." The door closed before I could manage to think of one more cliché and heave it in her direction.

While I was waiting for the girls to show up at the apartment, I reluctantly took Annie's hint and went searching for an umbrella to take along. Although the word "bumbershoot" means umbrella, it's usually not necessary to carry one the last weekend in August, even in Seattle. I scrounged around in the back reaches of my coat closet and resurrected a broken-ribbed relic that would have to suffice.

At exactly ten-thirty, the girls rang the bell. Mrs. Edwards had seen to it that they were properly dressed in matching yellow slickers that covered them from head to toe. When we stepped out onto the street and I cracked open the ancient umbrella, they both burst into giggles.

"Where'd you get that thing, Unca Beau?" Heather asked, pointing. "It's broken."

She was right. The umbrella, broken and not exactly waterproof either, was more a philosophical statement than it was protection from the weather. The plastic had torn loose from one of the ribs, and the resulting fold of material dripped a steady stream of water that ran down the back of my hand and up my sleeve.

"It'll be fine," I told the girls. "Let's get going."

The main gate to Seattle Center is only about three blocks from Belltown Terrace. The site of Seattle's 1962 World's Fair, it contains the Emerald City's signature landmark, the Space Needle, as well as eighteen or so acres of park that include exhibition halls, amusement rides, live theaters, a sports arena, an athletic field, fountains, and a building full of shops and fast-food vendors. On any given Labor Day weekend some 250,000 to 300,000 people find their way through the center to see live music and theater performances, hands-on exhibits, arts and crafts demonstrations, jugglers, magicians, and almost anything else you want to name. It's called Bumbershoot.

I've been there when that last bash of summer has been so crowded that it was all but impossible to move. You inched along, carried forward by the crowd, going whatever direction it was moving at the moment. But on this rainy, dreary Friday morning, that was certainly not the case. The place was almost deserted.

The Bumbershoot workers were delighted to see anybody who might be a potential customer. The girls raced ahead of me collecting a batch of goodies—free balloons and two totally unnecessary sun visors.

They darted past a jazz band playing halfheartedly on the steps of the semi-empty Flag Pavilion. I caught up with them just as they reached the edge of the International Fountain and before they could scramble over the low wall.

The fountain is a huge deep basin some two hundred feet across. The bottom is bordered with a matting of rough white rocks while the heart of the fountain is a slightly convex concrete mound studded with pipes and lights. A varied water show, programmed in concert with classical music, erupts periodically from the pipes. Despite the clearly posted DANGER signs, the interior of the fountain is regarded as a children's free-for-all playground on hot summer days.

"Can't we go in, please?" Heather begged. "Just for a little while. We won't get very wet."

"No way," I told her. "Mrs. Edwards would have a fit." Only a promise of immediate food kept them out of the fountain.

The area around the fountain was lined with wooden outdoor food booths. Every year crafts people, musicians, and food vendors bring samples of their ware to Bumbershoot in a gigantic outdoor festival. The food, with its wide variety of tastes and tantalizing aromas, is easily the most popular part of the weekend, and it's usually the most crowded. But not today. There were no lines, no jostling crowds. We were the only customers at a Mexican food place where the girls ordered bean burritos. I paused next door at a Thai booth for some beef *sate* with peanut sauce.

After lunch we sauntered through the arts and crafts display in the Exhibition Hall and on into the children's area in the Center House. While the girls listened to stories, touched the animals in the petting zoo, and posed briefly for a quick charcoal portrait, I watched from the sidelines with a cup of coffee in hand.

I watched, but my mind was elsewhere, restlessly sifting through the tangled web that led from Logan Tyree to Jimmy Rising. I kept one eye on the girls and the other on my watch, waiting for enough time to pass so I could go back to Camera Craft and see if Kath Naguchi's pictures held any answers to the questions circling in my mind.

At two-fifteen, when I announced it was time to leave, there was no argument. The girls were tired and more than ready to go back home. It was still sprinkling intermittently when we reached the main gate.

A ticket taker offered to stamp our hands. "That way you can get back in if you want to," he said.

Fat chance, I thought. I started to say no, but Heather pitched such a screaming fit that I gave in and we all three had our hands stamped.

On Denny Way Tracie walked briskly along beside me, chattering about all she had seen and done. Heather, tired and whiny, trailed along behind. Finally, despite my aching shoulder, I picked her up and carried her the last block and a half. She was sound asleep when I packed her into their apartment and deposited her on the couch.

Mrs. Edwards shook her head. "Looks like you wore her out."

"It works both ways," I told her, rubbing my shoulder while the difference in pressure again made me aware of the tender spot in my heel, the one my doctor jokingly refers to as my middle-aged bone spur.

"Thank you for taking us, Uncle Beau," Tracie said, as I bent down to give her a good-bye hug.

"You're welcome," I said.

I went upstairs and made myself a small pot of coffee. There was just time enough to gulp down one quick cup and to swallow one of my bone spur anti-inflammatories before I had to go meet Manny Davis and Paul Kramer.

Usually, I would have walked that far, but the hours in Bumbershoot had done their worst and my heel hurt more than it had for weeks. I opted for taking the Porsche, parking it at a meter across the street.

With a name like Kath Naguchi, I suppose I expected Jim Hadley's slugabed film editor to be a petite, dark-haired Asian. Wrong. When the owner of Camera Craft led us upstairs into the small, dimly lit editing room with its thick pall of cigarette smoke, Kath Naguchi turned out to be a behemoth of a woman, as tall as she was wide, with short, bright red hair, thick glasses, and the sickly-white skin of someone who shuns the light of day.

"These are the guys I was telling you about, Kath," Jim Hadley said without physically venturing any farther into the room than was absolutely necessary.

Kath Naguchi made a slight face but she didn't bother to look up. She was sitting in one corner of the room in front of a complicated-looking piece of machinery which I recognized from my *Death in Drydock* movie days as a flatbed editing table with a small viewing screen and numerous levers, knobs, and digital readouts. Three separate reels of film were loaded on the table. A long snarl of film rested in her lap and trailed across the floor under and behind her chair. The edge of the table was lined with a fringe of cut pieces of film. Trims, they call them in movie lingo.

"Watch where you step," she ordered sharply. "I'll be through here in a minute."

We waited patiently while she rewound the tangled film in her lap and hung the trims on clips over the trim bin at her elbow. She worked quickly and silently, with such total concentration that she could just as well have been alone. Only when she was completely finished did she light another cigarette, pick up her cup of coffee, and turn to face us.

"So you guys want to see the Masters Plaza film, do you?" she drawled.

"Yes, that's right." I answered for all of us. "The whole series of frames both before and after the one that was in the paper."

She shrugged. "Okay. No problem. Wait here."

Heaving her massive frame out of the chair, she huffed out of the room with the cigarette in hand. She was gone several minutes. When she returned, she was carrying another reel of film under her arm, a full coffee cup in one hand, and the cigarette in the other.

Effortlessly she cued up the film. "I think it's pretty close to the beginning of this one," she said. "I'll just run it."

We watched in fascination on the viewing screen while the building seemed to grow, floor by floor, before our eyes. The four-minute intervals between shots gave the movement of cranes and other machinery a jerky, fast-forward look, while shadows marching across the screen showed the rise and set of the sun. Five or six days must have flashed by like that before Kath Naguchi stopped the film.

"Here it is," she said.

At first all I could see was the building. Squinting, I moved forward until I was leaning directly over Kath Naguchi's ample shoulder. At that distance, I could see Angie Dixon—barely. She was hardly more than a pin-sized figure on the gray face of the building.

"Are you sure this is it?" Kramer asked. "The picture in the paper was lots closer than this."

"I can make it bigger," Kath Naguchi said. "But not here. This table is just for mixing. The blowup was done from a zoom shot we did down at Cine-tron."

"Where's that?" Kramer asked impatiently.

"Just up the street."

Kramer seemed to be antagonizing her, so I stepped in with the voice of sweet reason. "Could we go there? This might be very important."

"Maybe. It depends on whether or not the equipment is free. I don't usually schedule it until late at night."

"Would it be possible for you to check?" I asked.

"All right," Kath Naguchi agreed reluctantly. She wasn't going to offer anything on her own. We'd have to coax her every step of the way.

She picked up the phone and dialed a number. "This is Kath," she announced flatly into the phone. "Are you all booked up at the moment or could I come over and use the machine for a few minutes." She paused. "They're due at four o'clock? We should be done long before then. See you in a few minutes."

Without a word, she unwound the film and lurched out of the chair. She swept out of the room, down the stairs, and out of the building, leaving us to follow. She walked at a surprisingly rapid pace back up Second to Bell and then down to First Avenue where she led us into a derelict-looking building.

Derelict on the outside only. Inside, the reception area was comfortably if not lavishly furnished. Kath waved briefly at the receptionist then led us through an open door into another dimly lit room, one half of which was filled with a huge console complete with knobs, dials, buttons, and monitors, several showing wave forms only. The centerpiece was a massive television screen.

A man was seated on a high stool in front of the console. He turned as we entered. He too was holding a coffee cup in one hand and a cigarette in the other. They must be film-editor occupational hazards.

"Hi, Jack," Kath Naguchi said. "Thanks for working us in."

"What's up?" Jack asked. "It sounded pretty urgent on the phone."

Kath handed him a videotape. "These gentlemen are interested in seeing some of this. It's the Masters Plaza tape."

Jack looked at us questioningly, but Kath Naguchi offered no introductions, and we didn't volunteer any of our own.

He shrugged. "Okay. If you say so. It's not a free-bie, though. It's gonna cost you."

"You guys are paying?"

I nodded.

Jack got up and headed into another small room that opened off the one we were in. As the door swung open, I felt the cool rush of air-conditioning and glimpsed several stacks of humming electronic equipment that filled the room with a low-pitched semi-silence.

"Have a seat while we get set up," Kath ordered before she disappeared into the other room behind Jack.

Looking behind me I discovered a raised platform with two short love seats on it, love seats with ashtrays on or near all available flat surfaces. We sat waiting until Kath and Jack emerged from the other room.

For some reason I had expected Kath would be the one actually running the film, but Jack resumed his seat on the stool while Kath stood at his side. Paul Kramer had evidently been under the same impression.

"You mean you're not going to run it?" he asked.

Kath Naguchi laughed, a hoot that was half chuckle and half smoker's rattling cough. "Are you kidding? Nobody touches this baby but the master or one of his authorized disciples."

Jack laughed at that. "Where is it, Kath?" he asked.

"About six minutes in," she told him.

Jack twirled knobs this way and that, adjusting for light and color. At last he was satisfied. "This should be pretty close," he said.

Once more shadows raced across the screen, showing the passage of a day until the same frame was again frozen on the screen. Once more Angie Dixon, a tiny pin of a figure near the bottom right-hand corner of the picture, was an ungainly bird caught in a deadly free-fall toward the sidewalk far below. I tried not to think about that.

"Zoom in on the lower left-hand corner," Kath ordered.

"Like this?"

The figure of Angie Dixon grew larger. "Again," Kath said. Twice more the process was repeated. Each time Angie Dixon grew larger, and each time there was a pause while Jack adjusted the light and colors. As soon as he did it the third time, I recognized the picture that had been in the paper.

"Again?" Jack asked.

Kath nodded.

Once more the process was repeated. Now Angie Dixon filled the entire screen. At that level, there was some fuzzing of the picture, but not enough to disguise the look of horror on the woman's face as she plummeted to earth. Sickened, I turned away. I live with death far too much to want to see a detailed portrait of it in living color.

"Isn't that what you wanted?" Kath asked with as much emotion as a saleslady selling a pair of shoes. The picture was just that to her—a picture and nothing more.

"Can you do the same thing to some of the other frames just before and just after this?"

"Sure," she said. "No problem." She turned to Jack. "Let's try just before."

Jack nodded and called up another frame. "This is the one. See anything you want me to zoom in on?"

Kath moved closer to the large screen and scrutinized one corner of it intently. "Try up here near the top," she said.

He did. Once the adjustments had been made for light and color, it was possible to make out that there were two small figures standing close together.

"This one would have been taken four minutes before the other one?" I asked.

Kath nodded.

"Do it again," she said, pointing. "Right here."

Jack zoomed in again. Now there were clearly two figures showing on the screen.

I could feel the rush of excitement in my veins. "Again," I said, not waiting for Kath to give Jack his marching orders. I had abandoned the love seat and was standing next to Kath Naguchi. On the monitor two people were plainly visible, standing side by side near the edge of the building. There was some distortion in the lengthened faces, but they were both recognizable. One of the two was clearly Angie Dixon. The other was familiar as well.

"Hey, wait a minute. I know him."

Kramer bounded off the love seat to stand beside me. "Who is he?" he demanded.

"Martin Green."

"Martin Green?" Kramer echoed. "Who the hell is he?"

"The executive director of the ironworkers' local here."

"And you know him?" Kramer demanded.

"He lives in my building."

"What about him?" Manny asked, stepping forward so he too could see.

I tried to quell the rising excitement I felt but I didn't want to blurt out anything more in front of the two outsiders. "Let's take a look at the next frame," I said quickly.

"The one after the fall shot?" Jack asked.

I nodded.

With Kath Naguchi's help, we examined several more frames of film both before and after Angie Dixon's fall, as well as pictures taken at approximately the same time by the other camera.

There was nothing else unusual, only the unmistakable presence of Martin Green.

"Would you like a hard copy of this?" Jack asked when we finally told him we were finished.

"What do you mean, hard copy?" Kramer asked.

Kath Naguchi sighed. "Do you want a copy of the tape or not? It'll only take a few minutes."

"Yes, we do," I answered.

Once more Kath and Jack disappeared into the back room. Paul Kramer rounded on me. "Now tell me. Who the hell is Martin Green?"

"The guy Linda Decker suspects is responsible for Logan Tyree's death."

Manny whistled. "Hot damn! And maybe this one too?"

"Let's don't jump to conclusions," I cautioned, "but it could be. It just could be."

CHAPTER 21

WHEN YOU'RE FIGHTING IN THE DARK, ANY CONNECTION is better than no connection. And that was the way with this. If Martin Green had been on the iron with the doomed Angie Dixon only minutes before her fatal fall, then it was possible he had something to do with her death. However, we had all been cops too long for any of us to accept that premise at face value.

By the time we were back out on the street, we figured there was probably some perfectly legitimate reason for Green's presence on the Masters Plaza job site. Not only that, we'd made a joint decision to go ask him about it. With that in mind, we headed for the Labor Temple.

There was an election of officers going on in one of the union locals, and parking was at a premium. Kramer and Manny parked in a loading zone on Clay, while I pulled into the first floor of Belltown Terrace's garage and grabbed the first available spot. The weather had turned wet again and it was raining hard by the time I dashed across the alley that separates the Labor Temple from my building. Paul Kramer was just giving his card to the iron-workers' receptionist when I caught up with them. She gave me a funny look as though trying to place someone she vaguely knew.

"May I help you?" she asked.

"I'm with them," I told her.

She picked up her phone and spoke into an inter-com. "Someone's here to see you," she announced.

"Who is it?" he asked. "I'm busy."

"They're detectives," she answered.

Her quiet announcement brought Martin Green to the door of his office in a hurry. The broken glass had been replaced. The receptionist handed him Detective Kramer's card. Green glanced down at it and then up at us, his eyes traveling briefly from face to face until he stopped at mine. He frowned.

"Beaumont, isn't it? From Belltown Terrace?"

I nodded. "That's right."

"To what do I owe the pleasure?"

"We need to ask you a few questions."

"You're with these other gentlemen?" he asked, waving Kramer's card.

"Yes, I am."

"What kind of questions?"

"About Angie Dixon."

He frowned again and cocked his head to one side. "All right. Come in. Kim, hold all my calls, will you?"

Green ushered us into his office and then he had to step back outside to bring along an extra chair. "What about Angie Dixon?" he began, not waiting until he was seated before he asked the question. "I thought that was all settled, that her death had been ruled accidental. Has something changed?" Since we knew each other however briefly, his statements were addressed to me.

I took the ball. "When's the last time you saw her?"

"Minutes before she died."

Green answered evenly, without a moment's hesitation. His straightforward manner surprised me. There was no outward show of concern that our placing him at the scene of Angie Dixon's possibly non-accidental death might mean he was under suspicion.

"What were you doing there?"

"I needed to talk to her," he answered.

"You must have needed to real bad, to track her down at a job site on a Sunday morning."

Martin Green didn't respond, but he met my gaze with unblinking indifference.

"Why was it so important for you to see her?"

This time there was a pause, the kind of noticeable, momentary indecision that puts any detective worth his salt on red alert.

"She had something I needed," Green answered blandly.

"And what might that be?" Kramer asked, plowing into the process—the proverbial bull in a china shop.

Martin Green's eyes momentarily flicked from me to Kramer, as if assessing the weight of the interruption. By the time he answered, though, he was once more addressing me, closing out both Manny and Kramer. The two of us might have been alone in the room.

"Some tapes," he answered quietly. "I believed she had some accounting tapes. I wanted them."

The accounting tapes! Linda Decker's infernal tapes again. I tried not to let anything in my voice betray that we knew what tapes he was talking about, that we *did* have copies of them.

"And did she give them to you?"

"She was going to," Martin Green answered. "She said she wouldn't be able to get them until the next day."

"But instead, she died a few minutes later," I prompted.

Green nodded.

"Did it occur to you that there might be some connection between her death and her agreeing to give you those missing tapes?"

"No. The people I talked to said her death was an accident, and I believed them."

"And where were you the night Logan Tyree's boat blew up over on Lake Union?"

"The night Logan Tyree was killed? I was out of town."

The fact that he spat out that detail right off the top of his head alerted me further. Without careful reflection, people don't usually remember what they were doing on a certain day or at a certain time. Unless that time and date have some special significance.

"Where out of town?" I asked.

"Vancouver, B.C."

"Is there someone who can verify that?"

"No."

The abrupt certainty of his answer set more alarm bells clanging inside my head. "You're saying that you went to Vancouver that night, but no one saw you there."

"Why are you asking me about that night?"

"Because I have someone who claims Logan Tyree had an appointment to see you the night he died."

For the first time, Martin Green looked uncomfortable. "That's impossible. I wouldn't have scheduled an appointment with him. That's the night . . ." He broke off suddenly and didn't continue.

"That was the night what?" I prodded.

Green shook his head stubbornly. "I did see someone there, in Vancouver, but I won't bring her into it. She's married."

"To someone else?"

"That's right."

That struck me as ironic. Here was Martin Green claiming to be stuck with an unusable alibi. If the story was true, his reticence, for somewhat different reasons, was still the same as mine with Marilyn Sykes—confidentiality.

"But why would I want to kill Logan?"

"For the same motive you might have to kill Angie Dixon," I replied. "To get the tapes."

"Don't you understand?" Martin Green demanded. "I *wanted* the tapes. I didn't *have* to have them."

"Wait a minute. I thought you said you went to see Angie Dixon on the job because of the tapes."

Martin Green shrugged. "It would be fine to have them, sort of the capper on the jug, but they're not essential. We can nail Martinson without them."

So now the name Martinson had come up. He was the accountant, the erring husband, the iron-workers' bookkeeper who had disappeared on a fishing trip in the wilds of Alaska. Green seemed to be talking about the same puzzle pieces I already had in my possession, those Linda Decker had laid on me, yet there was a slightly different spin to them, a twist, that made them impossible to grasp and utilize.

"What do you mean, nail Martinson? I thought he was dead too. That's what I heard."

Green snorted. "He'd like us all to think he's dead, but I'm not buying it. He and his friends have been looting this local for years. He's got money stashed somewhere, in Canada we think. All of them do. I've got a private detective agency working on finding him right now."

"On finding Martinson? Why?"

Martin Green nodded. "As I said, we believe he's holed up somewhere in Canada. It was simpler for us to hire a private eye and send him after Martinson than it was to get you guys to go looking for him."

A piece of the puzzle finally slipped into place. "So what our witness told us about bribes and pay-offs in the union was true?"

"Unfortunately, yes. International received an anonymous tip about what was going on in Seattle. We put an independent auditing team on it, and they turned up all kinds of crap. International sent me out as a troubleshooter to try to get to the bottom of it, to find out who all was involved, that sort of thing. It's taken me months to even start scraping the surface. It's not just one or two guys, you know.

It's a whole clique. They got themselves elected and then made sure they stayed that way. They've been real cagey about it."

Cagey? Green was talking about the problem as though it was some kind of minor office scandal attributable to internal politics with no major consequences, no harm done. It was time for some shock therapy.

"They haven't been cagey at all, Mr. Green. They're killers, cold-blooded killers. Three people are dead so far. Another is in critical condition. Why didn't you call us in?"

Green's chin sank to his chest. He sighed. "International told me not to. They wanted to keep our investigation quiet, out of the media. Unions have enough of a black eye right now without this kind of scandal being blown all out of proportion. We're losing membership right and left as it is."

"Two of your members died here," I pointed out. "Logan Tyree and Angie Dixon. Didn't it cross your mind that the information you had at your disposal might have helped us solve their murders?"

"But the papers said both deaths were accidental."

A flashbulb of anger exploded in my head. "What the papers said!" I exclaimed. "For Chrissake, you mean you *believe* what you read in newspapers?"

He nodded. For the first time I wondered if Martin Green was as smart as I'd given him credit for being. He was our only solid lead. Suddenly I felt as though we were leaning on a bent reed.

"Wait a minute," Manny Davis put in. "Let me get this straight. You said a few minutes ago that these tapes aren't essential to nailing these guys. If they were so important once, why aren't they important now?"

Green got up and walked over to a file cabinet in the corner of the room. He pulled a key from his pocket and unlocked it. My body tensed, shifting into that keen wariness that warned of the possibility of danger. I wondered if maybe he had a weapon concealed in the drawer. Instead of a gun, he extracted two maroon, leather-bound accounting books from behind the files in the second drawer.

"Because we have these," he answered, casually tossing the two books in my direction. "The journal entries. Martinson's so dumb that he left them in his office. It's all right there. The top one is the one Martinson handed in, the legal one. The second one is real. It's the one he kept for everyone else, for the creeps he worked with. None of them are listed by name, only by number. Once we put the squeeze on him, we'll be able to put names on these numbers and nail those SOBs."

He was still standing up. Suddenly, he turned and rushed back to the file cabinet. "Wait a minute. I just thought of something."

Quickly he rummaged through the top drawer and pulled out a file folder. It was jammed full of receipts and copies of credit card transactions. He thumbed through a small stack of onionskin papers. "Here it is," he said triumphantly, handing me one of the receipts. "I have to keep all the receipts," he added. "It's a company car."

The receipt in my hand was from an Esso station in Langley, B.C. The gas had been sold by the liter, not by the gallon, and the date said August fourteenth, the day Logan Tyree's boat had blown sky-high. Martin Green's scribbled but legible signature was scrawled across the bottom of the receipt.

"You see, I got tied up here with a late meeting. By the time I finally headed north, I didn't think to check the gas tank. I almost ran out before I remembered. I realized it while I was waiting in line at the border crossing in Blaine. I got off at the first exit and found a gas station."

"What was the meeting about?"

"Meeting?"

"The one before you left town. The one that made you late."

"With Don Kaplan. I think you know him. He's in charge of our apprenticeship program. A number of women had either dropped out or were threatening to. If we lose very many more we'll be in a world of hurt with the EEOC and affirmative action. Federal and state contracts, that kind of thing. We had a meeting to see what could be done."

"I thought Don Kaplan quit."

Green laughed. "He quits every day at least once, but he's always back on the job the next morning."

"And was one of the women who quit Linda Decker?"

"How'd you know that?"

"I'm a detective, remember? It's my job."

"She was the first one to go. It's a shame, too. Hell of a little worker. She lifts weights, you know. Strong for her size. The guys didn't mind working with her. They figured she could take care of herself."

"So why did she quit then?"

"I don't know. She came storming in here one

day, threw her union book in my face, and told me I could shove it up my ass."

"That was it?"

"That's right. And that's why I was having the meeting with Don, to try to figure out exactly what was happening, to get a handle on it and fix it."

"Was he able to give you any answers?"

"Not really."

Green had said there was an entire clique involved. For the first time, I wondered about Don Kaplan.

"Is he in on it?" I asked.

Martin Green smiled and shook his head. "You've got to be kidding. Don in with Martinson? Never. He's absolutely straight-arrow."

"What makes you so sure?"

Before I could stop him, Green grabbed his phone, picked up the receiver, and punched the intercom. "Kim, is Don still here?" He waited impatiently for her answer, drumming his fingers on the surface of his desk. "Send him in, would you? I want to talk to him."

Martin Green settled back in his chair. "I've worked with Don Kaplan every single day for as long as I've been in Seattle. If he was mixed up in this business, believe me, I'd know it."

I was still holding the second accounting ledger in my hand. Opening it, I paged through it, noting the precise dollar amounts with single-digit numbers following.

"As near as we can tell, there are only nine people actively involved," Green explained. "At least, that's how many identifying numbers are in the book."

The phone rang and Green snatched it up. "Don?"

He stopped abruptly and frowned. "I thought I said to hold all my calls, that I didn't want to be disturbed." He hesitated. "All right. That's different. Put him through. Hello, Frank. How's it going? I'm having a meeting here, so make it quick."

There was another pause, a much longer one, but while Martin Green listened, his face broke into a wide grin. "I'll be damned," he said. "Good for you. I knew you could pull it off. Give me your number and I'll get back to you once the crowd thins out. I think I can make it up there tomorrow."

He jotted a number down on a piece of paper then hung up the phone and sat there looking smug. "We got him," he announced.

"Got who?"

"Martinson. Frank Daniels, my private eye, found him hiding out over in Victoria. He's willing to talk terms."

"Terms? What kind of terms?"

"Money terms, Detective Beaumont. If we had wanted him in jail, I could have turned you guys loose on him, but that's not the point. I want the names of everyone else who's involved. I want *them* in jail. And even if Martinson goes to prison too, he'll have a little nest egg waiting for him when he gets out. International will see to it."

"Wait just a goddamned minute here!" I interjected, not wanting to believe my ears. "You mean to tell me you're going to pay Martinson off in return for squealing on his buddies? You're going to let the ringleader off scot-free?"

"He's not the ringleader," Green assured me. "That's why we went after him in particular. He's the weak link in the chain. They needed him, and he needed money. One of his kids was sick, died eventually, to the tune of some fifty grand after the insurance had paid everything it would pay. That's how they suckered him in, I'm sure. He was up to his eyeballs in debt, his marriage was in trouble. They made him an offer he couldn't refuse.

"Unfortunately, he's a whole lot better at being an accountant than he is at being a crook. He couldn't stand not keeping meticulous records, even if it meant having two separate ledgers."

Green reached for the phone again. "Kim? Call Chrysler Air Service and see how soon I can get a charter plane to go from here to Victoria. And by the way, where's Don? I thought you said he was still here." Green paused. "What do you mean, he left? Just like that?"

Green slammed the phone into its cradle, shoved his chair against the wall getting out of it, and raced to the window where he stood looking down at Broad. "I'll be damned," he said.

I hurried to his side. "What is it? What's going on?"

"Don was on his way in here when Kim told him about Martinson, that Frank had caught up with him. Kim said he mumbled something about getting a briefcase from his car and left. Look, that's him now, getting in that white T-Bird over there. He didn't forget something; he's leaving."

I looked down across Broad through sheets of pouring rain where a dead gas station had been converted into a temporary parking lot. Don Kaplan was indeed climbing into a white T-Bird.

"You must be right about him," Green said grimly. "If he wasn't involved, he wouldn't take off like this."

"Let's go get him," I said, turning away from the window.

But I was too late. Nobody needed any urging from me. Kramer and Manny were already headed out the door, and I was left bringing up the rear.

CHAPTER 22

THE GOOD NEWS WAS IT WAS FIVE O'CLOCK. THAT WAS the bad news as well—rush hour, Friday. Seattle's rain-soaked pavements were slick as glass with the oily buildup that comes from more than a month without rain. The roar of traffic was punctuated by the sound of squealing tires as frustrated drivers tried to gain traction on steep, rain-glazed, hillside streets.

From Martin Green's window I had seen Don Kaplan's late-model white T-Bird turn right up First Avenue—a big mistake on his part. Instead of a free-moving thoroughfare, First Avenue between Broad and Denny had slowed to a commuter's-nightmare parking lot. Kaplan pulled into traffic, that was about all. He traveled only a few car lengths before he too was stopped cold. Nothing was moving.

Manny, Kramer, and I raced out of the union office, crashed down the stairs, and stopped on the sidewalk long enough to look up the street.

"That's him," I said, pointing. "The white T-Bird

in the left-hand lane." Unfortunately, the light on Denny changed. Kaplan's car inched forward.

"Come on," Kramer yelled, heading in the opposite direction. "Let's go get the car."

Manny took off after him, but I didn't. This was my neighborhood, my block. There are times when a car can be far more of a hindrance than a help. Wincing at the sharp pain in my heel, I headed up First on foot. In the snarl of traffic I figured I had a better chance of catching him that way than Manny and Kramer did in a vehicle.

And it almost worked. Kaplan's turbo coupe was stuck in a long line of idling vehicles waiting for the light to change on Denny a block and a half away. I was only three car lengths away and closing fast when Kaplan leaned over and caught sight of me in his rearview mirror. I doubt he recognized me. He was probably looking for any sign of pursuit. A man in a sports jacket jogging up First Avenue in the rain was a dead giveaway.

Laying on the horn, Kaplan muscled the T-Bird across the right-hand lane of vehicles and darted up the short half-block of Warren that reaches across Denny. At the corner of First and Warren I paused for a moment, undecided. Should I continue on foot or wait long enough to signal Kramer and Manny? The problem was, once Kaplan turned right on Denny, he'd have a clear shot at doubling back down Second, Third, or Fifth and eluding us completely.

Hearing the piercing screech of a siren, I turned and looked back. Kramer and Manny were just then turning off Clay onto First. They were on their way, but even with the help of sirens and lights, covering those two and a half blocks would take time—time we didn't have. They would be too late. Kaplan would be long gone.

I couldn't wait. With a burst of speed that surprised me, I sprinted up Warren after him. He was there, less than a tantalizing half-block away, his right-hand turn signal blinking steadily as he waited for a break in traffic.

I snorted and would have laughed aloud but I was running too hard. Driving habits are like that—so ingrained, so automatic, that even driving a getaway car a crook still uses his directional signals.

I was only thirty or forty feet away when he spotted me again and floorboarded it. He plunged into traffic on Denny while the rear of the T-Bird skidded crazily from side to side.

What happened next happened with blinding speed. A driver from the other direction, alarmed by Kaplan's skidding, stepped on his brakes and slid into somebody else. In the fender-crunching melee that followed, two more cars were caught and accordion-pleated. The fourth, an ancient Chrysler Imperial driven by a Mohawked teenager, successfully avoided hitting the other three only to slide sideways into the right-hand lane. The Imperial nailed Kaplan's left fender in a glancing blow that sent the T-Bird spinning up onto the sidewalk.

When the skidding stopped, the street was littered with wreckage and debris. There was a moment of stark silence and then, somewhere, a horn blared.

The Imperial, barely dented, had ended up closest to me, coming to rest with its nose against a fire hydrant which promptly spewed a geyser of water straight up into the air. The driver, unable to open the door, scrambled frantically through the broken window, cutting his hands in the process.

"I couldn't help it," he cried hysterically, running up to me. "My dad's going to kill me, but it wasn't my fault."

His mouth was bleeding, and there was a long jagged cut on one side of his head. I caught him by the shoulders and eased him down on the curb.

"Sit here," I ordered. "Don't move around until after the medics get a look at you."

He sat there, but he wouldn't let go of my hands. "It wasn't my fault," he insisted. "You saw it, didn't you? Will you tell my folks that I couldn't help it?"

"Yes, I will."

That seemed to satisfy him. He let go of my hand and I turned to look for Kaplan. He was gone. The crippled T-Bird, looking like it had been smashed in a garbage compactor, was still sitting half on, half off the sidewalk. Its left rear tire was flat and the driver's door gone. Kaplan was nowhere in sight.

I looked around for help, but it was hopeless. Denny was totally impassible. Kramer and Manny would never make it through the snarl of wrecks in time to be of much help. It was up to me. But at least now Kaplan and I were even. We were both on foot.

At the corner of Second Avenue, I paused to catch my breath and peer up the street. Second is a vast expanse of boulevard and sidewalk that seems to end abruptly in an elbow of skyscrapers a mile away. Through the rain I could see both sides of the street for blocks. There were people gathered here and there at bus stops, but no one was running. Don Kaplan was nowhere in sight.

I looked up Denny just in time to catch sight of him crossing Third in a crowd of pedestrians heading for Seattle Center. Once more I started after him. My breath was already coming in short gasps. The incline there seems benign enough when you're riding in a car, but on foot it's steep. And the blocks are long. And it was crowded.

Labor Day revelers had finally decided against letting the weather spoil Bumbershoot. Finished with work, they were coming out in force, milling up Broad and Denny in a slow-moving forest of open umbrellas that hampered both vision and speed.

Cops learn to think like crooks. I knew instinctively what Kaplan had in mind. Once he was safely inside the gates of Seattle Center, it would be all too easy for him to blend into the crowd and disappear. He was just leaving the ticket booth when I reached the main gate area. Here the crowd was denser, more so now that some people had turned away from the gate to watch the collection of emergency vehicles screaming in frustration as they attempted to reach the accident scene two blocks away.

I tried to force my way through the crowd. "What's the big hurry, Bud?" a man demanded as I pushed past him. "Where's the fire?"

Without answering, I kept on shoving, while fifteen feet and fifty people away, Don Kaplan handed over his ticket and slipped quickly through the gate.

Slowly the crowd gave way, letting me pass. I finally reached the gate and could see Kaplan inside the grounds. He was easy to spot. Except for me, he was the only person there without a raincoat or umbrella. I saw him dash past the fountain with its huge joke of ugly orange statuary near the bottom of the Space Needle.

A woman barred my way. "Ticket, please," she said.

Reaching for my ID, I was already launching into an explanation when she caught sight of the Bumbershoot stamp on my hand, the one Heather had insisted on getting as we left the grounds earlier that day.

"Oh," the woman said. "I didn't know you'd already been inside. Go ahead."

Grateful for small blessings, I darted past her and through the gate. The grounds of Seattle Center were far different from what they'd been earlier in the day. It was more crowded now, although still not as bad as it would have been in good weather. Kaplan had a good lead on me. Just as I cleared the gate, he disappeared around the bumper-car ride some fifty yards or so ahead.

I wanted to catch up, but I didn't want to alert him, to let him know I was still on his trail. I hurried up the outdoor corridor between the Science Center and the miniature golf course, using the golf concession to conceal my movements. I came out by an open-air stage where a noisy band was risking electrocution blasting heavily amplified rock music into the pouring rain.

If Kaplan had turned into the Center House, I would have lost him entirely. Instead, he turned up through the food concession area with its outdoor booths and grazing throngs. I followed as quickly as

I could. I figured he was heading for one of the other entrances where he'd be able to get back off the grounds and maybe call a taxi. I had to catch him before then.

I was closing the distance when suddenly he stopped and turned. Some sixth sense must have warned him. An electric arc of recognition passed between us. He broke and ran.

There was no longer any pretense of stalking him. I still couldn't draw my weapon, though, not in that crowd. My only hope was in actual physical contact. I ran, if you could call it that, pushing and jostling my way through resisting lines of people waiting outside the various booths.

Luckily for me, Kaplan wasn't thinking straight. Desperate to get away, he headed for the relatively open ground by the International Fountain with me in hot pursuit. He would have been better off sticking to the crowds. People around us were becoming aware that something was wrong. They moved aside and cleared a path, giving me the final edge I needed.

As he started by the fountain, I dove for him and caught him by the knees, bringing him down with the kind of flying tackle I hadn't attempted since high school football. He landed on top of me, smashing my face into the muddy grass. My nose started to bleed. Again.

He got up, kicking me in the head, and scrambling away across the rough paving brick that surrounds the fountain. When I got up, he was teetering on the fountain's concrete wall. With dogged determination I went after him again.

By now several uniformed security guards, alerted

by the crowd, were converging on the fountain. "Break it up," one of them shouted. I paused long enough to look at my reinforcements. When I did, Kaplan made a break for it and disappeared over the edge of the fountain. I dived in after him.

The fountain has steep sides that drop off abruptly above the border of rugged white rocks. The surface was wet and slick. I tried to stand up, but a sudden burst of water threw me off balance and sent me flying toward Kaplan. I crashed into him and caught him in a crushing bear hug. We both went down, rolling over and over down the incline as the symphonic music around us hit a crescendo. We landed on the rocks, with Kaplan on the bottom.

"Hands up," someone shouted over the music. "Get off him and get your hands up."

"It's all right," I said, standing up, dripping blood and gasping for breath. "It's okay, you guys. I'm a cop. Help me get him out of here."

One of the security guards had splashed down into the fountain beside me. I knew him. He was an off-duty patrolman from the David Sector in downtown Seattle. He recognized me as well. "Hey, Beaumont, what's going on?"

"Help me move him out of the fountain, then call dispatch. Have them tell Detectives Kramer and Davis where I am. Tell them I've got him. And get Medic One here too, on the double. This guy may be hurt."

Together the patrolman and I lifted Kaplan and carried him out of the fountain. We lay him flat on the grass. His eyes were open, but glazed with pain. He made no effort to move or get up. I knelt down beside him. "Are you all right?" I asked. "Can you move your fingers?"

He wiggled them and nodded.

"And your feet?"

He nodded again.

"It's over," I told him. "You guys are out of business."

"Damn," Kaplan murmured and closed his eyes.

The Medic One unit showed up minutes later and loaded Kaplan on a stretcher. They were just getting ready to haul him away when Paul Kramer and Manny Davis arrived on the scene. Someone had thrown a blanket over my shoulders, and I was standing there wet and shivering.

"Where is he?" Kramer asked.

"Kaplan?" I nodded toward the Medic One unit. "He's in there," I answered.

True to form, Kramer headed for the van. He didn't give a shit about whether or not I was hurt. He wanted to be sure Don Kaplan was locked up securely enough that he couldn't get loose.

Manny Davis came over to me then. "Are you all right, Beau?" he asked.

And that was the difference between them. Manny cared. Kramer didn't. It was as simple as that. The son of a bitch might very well end up as police chief some day. God knows he's ruthless enough.

I hope to hell I never have to work for him.

CHAPTER 23

I JERKED MY HEAD IN KRAMER'S DIRECTION. "TELL him I've gone home to change clothes. I'll meet you guys back down at the department and we'll finish sorting this out."

Manny at least made the effort to stop me. "Don't you want a ride, Beau? Our car's right over there, just behind the Coliseum."

I shook my head. "No thanks. I need to walk. It'll clear my head."

I limped back to Belltown Terrace. My heel was killing me, sending shooting pains across the top of my foot as I hobbled along. People steered clear of me. It wasn't until I saw myself reflected in the window glass of Belltown Terrace that I realized why. I was still wearing the soaking wet blanket. With two black eyes, my broken nose, and my freshly bloodied face, I'm sure I was mistaken for one of Seattle's more actively unfortunate street people. At least this set of torn and dripping clothing could go on a line-of-duty replacement voucher.

Annie, the concierge, was still on duty. "My God!" she exclaimed when I came into the lobby. "You're a mess, Detective Beaumont. What happened? I thought you were going to Bumbershoot." She must have been at lunch when I brought the girls home.

"I did," I told her. "It's really crowded."

Leaving a puddle of water on the marbled lobby floor, I stepped into the elevator and went upstairs. Within minutes I had stripped off my clothes and was lying in my Jacuzzi.

Good sense said I should have iced my foot, but the steaming water felt good on my chilled body and aching muscles. I should have felt victorious, triumphant. I didn't. I felt broken. Stiff. Old. And filled with a vague sense of discontent.

I guess it was professional pride. I had caught Kaplan, sure. And somebody else had nailed Martinson. But there were seven numbers besides theirs in that leather-bound ledger. That meant seven others still on the loose. Maybe we'd find out who they were if the private eye was right and Martinson was ready to talk, but he had been out of town when the murders started, when Logan Tyree's boat blew up and when Angie Dixon fell off Masters Plaza.

Murder is my bailiwick. Let somebody else deal with the union racketeering. It was the killer I wanted.

With a sudden sense of purpose, I scrambled out of the Jacuzzi, showered, and toweled off. I hurried to the bedroom phone, dialed Manny's number, and got Kramer instead.

"When are you going to question Kaplan?" I asked. "I can be there in ten minutes."

"We're not," Kramer answered shortly.

"What do you mean, you're not?"

"He's in surgery. Ruptured spleen. The doctors are taking it out. They don't know when we'll be able to talk to him."

"Damn. What about Martinson then?"

"Manny's working on it, but right this minute, Green is refusing to press charges."

"So do you want me to come back down or not?"

"I wouldn't bother if I were you. Stay home and take it easy. And keep this under wraps. We're not releasing any names until we see what information Green drags out of Wayne Martinson."

I wasn't dumb enough to believe I was talking to a transformed Paul Kramer, to somebody genuinely concerned about J. P. Beaumont's health and well-being. He was down at the department playing hero, letting the brass know how great he was and how he'd come up with all the answers, and he didn't want me down there gumming up the works.

Let him, I thought savagely as I slammed down the phone.

Pulling on a comfortable pair of sweats, I went on into the living room, poured myself a drink, and settled down in the recliner. Since I wasn't going back to the department, the situation called for a MacNaughton's or two. For medicinal purposes.

I tried to make my mind go blank, to blot the case and everything connected with it out of my head, but it wouldn't stay blotted. I kept coming back to those numbers, those seven people. And Martin Green.

For as long as I'd known him, I had thought of

Green as a problem, first in the building and then later, after I'd talked to Linda Decker, in the case. He was supposed to have been the villain of the piece, but now for the first time I began to think seriously about him as an ally, as someone who had come to Seattle to put a stop to the skullduggery in the union that had caused the deaths of Logan Tyree and the others.

What was it he had told us? Something to the effect that after months of work he was finally beginning to scratch the surface. Obviously Don Kaplan had blindsided him. Green hadn't expected Kaplan to be part of the conspiracy, but I wondered if maybe he had identified some of the other scumbags and was playing his cards close to his chest while he waited to bag Martinson and force a private deal.

I had picked up the phone to call him when I remembered that Martin Green had an unlisted phone number. Instead, I dialed the doorman in the lobby.

"I've lost Martin Green's number. Do you happen to have it?"

Pete Duvall sounded a little wary. "I do, but I'm not supposed to give it out. It's probably all right to give it to you, though. Oh, and by the way. When Mr. Ames went out earlier, he said to tell you not to bother to cook. He'll be home around eight, and he's bringing food back with him."

As if I would have cooked anyway. Ames must have been choking with laughter when he left that message. He knows I don't cook. His sense of humor and his self-sufficiency are two things that make Ralph Ames an enjoyable houseguest. He was being so goddamned self-sufficient that in my preoccupation with the case I had completely forgotten he was still in town.

When I got off the phone with Pete, I tried calling Martin Green. There was no answer. I found myself fuming that the man didn't have an answering machine on his phone. I've come a long way from the time when I didn't have one and wouldn't use one on a bet. I have Ralph Ames to thank for that, among other things.

He showed up right on schedule, bringing with him a selection of delectable carry-out Chinese food which he served with suitable ceremony. "So how did your day go?" he asked.

"Medium," I said, filling him in on the details as we worked our way through sweet-and-sour prawns, ginger beef, and pork-fried rice.

"And how's Jimmy Rising doing?" he asked, when I finished.

"I don't know," I said, "but it won't take long to find out." I went over to the phone and dialed Harborview's number from memory. When the switchboard answered, I asked to be connected to the burn unit.

"This is Detective Beaumont," I said. "I'm calling about Jimmy Rising."

"Are you a member of the family?" the woman asked.

"No," I replied. "I'm a detective. I'm working on the case."

"Hold the line. I'll see if I can put his sister on."

"This is Detective Beaumont. How's it going?" I asked Linda Decker a few moments later when she came on the line.

When she answered, her voice was strained and weary. "No change," she said. "He's no better and no worse."

"How are you doing?"

"I'm plugging," she answered, but it sounded like she was hanging by a thread.

I wanted to tell her about Don Kaplan. I knew how much she needed to hear some news, how much of a boost it would give her to know something was going on, but I kept my mouth shut. Kramer was right. We couldn't afford to let word leak out to any of the other conspirators before we were ready with our fistful of arrest warrants.

"I'll stop by and check on you tomorrow morning," I said.

She hung up. Long after I heard the dial tone I continued to stand there, holding the receiver in my hand, staring at it.

"What's the matter?" Ames called from the kitchen, where he was putting away leftovers.

Slowly I put down the phone. "I didn't tell her about Martinson, Kaplan, any of it."

"Of course not," Ames said. "Especially when you're operating under strict orders to act like a team player."

"But what if the team's screwing up?"

"That's not your problem," Ames said.

"The hell it isn't!"

Slamming my half-finished drink onto the table, I slipped on my holster and headed for the door to retrieve my shoes.

"What do you think you're doing now, Beau?" Ames demanded.

I stopped long enough to try dialing Martin

Green's number. There was still no answer. "I'm going to Renton," I said.

"Renton," he echoed. "Why Renton?"

"Because there's somebody down there who may know something about all this and I'm going to ask him."

"You shouldn't be driving," Ames said. "You've had too much to drink."

"You drive me then, because I'm going, and I'm going now!"

During the twenty-minute drive to Renton we spoke only when it was absolutely necessary. I gave Ames terse directions, telling him to turn here or turn there. I was steamed, but I knew Ames was right that night, the same as he had been the night before. I was in no condition to drive and was surprised by how quickly the booze had snuck up on me. My mind was fuzzy as we started out, but it cleared as we drove, as I concentrated all my physical and mental energies on what had to happen.

When we pulled into the yard of Katherine Tyree's house, the television set was going in the living room. Ames got out of the Porsche and followed me into the yard.

Fred McKinney answered the door and recognized me as soon as he opened it. He didn't seem startled to see me. "We heard," he said.

"Heard what?" I was almost afraid of his answer, afraid someone had leaked the Don Kaplan story to the press.

"About Linda's mother," he answered. "It's a crying shame."

I breathed a sigh of relief. "And did you hear

about her brother?" I asked. "He's in the hospital. Probably won't make it."

Fred nodded bleakly. "Will it ever stop?"

"That depends," I said.

"On what?"

"On whether or not someone finally has balls enough to come forward and say what's really going on."

"Who is it?" Katherine Tyree called from in front of the television set.

"It's one of those detectives," Fred answered. He looked at me, his eyes narrowing. "What do you want with us?"

"Do you have balls enough, Fred?"

"What do you mean?"

"You told me you came up here as a boomer. I want you to answer just one question. How did you manage to get to work on Columbia Center?"

McKinney dropped his gaze. As soon as I saw it, I knew I had him. "I bought my way on," he said quietly.

"How?"

"Five grand. Cash. I took out a second mortgage on my boat. I paid the second off when Logan bought *Boomer* from me."

"So you bribed your way onto that job?"

McKinney nodded.

"Who to?" I asked.

"You mean who'd I give the money to?"

"That's right."

"The guy who used to be in charge of book transfers."

"Who's that?"

"His name is Harry Campbell."

"Harry Campbell. Harry Campbell. The name sounded familiar, but I couldn't place it right off. "You say he used to be in charge?"

McKinney shrugged. "That's right. When Green came in he kicked him back in the gang."

"Do you know where I can find him?"

"The last I knew, he was working in the raising gang down on Masters Plaza."

And suddenly I realized why Harry Campbell's name was so familiar. I *had* seen it before. In the newspaper. He was Angie Dixon's partner. The one who had sent her after the welding lead.

Leaving a puzzled Fred McKinney standing in the doorway, I wheeled and charged back toward the car with Ames right behind me.

"Where to now?" Ames asked.

"Back home."

As soon as we were back in my apartment, I dialed Martin Green's number for the last time. His mother answered. "I think he's down on the jogging track," she told me. "He said he couldn't sleep and that he was going for a walk."

I found Martin Green smoking a cigarette on a bench at the far end of the building. It was almost eleven. The rain had stopped. The gardens next to the jogging track smelled fresh and moist. Green was sitting with his back to me, looking at the same cityscape Don Kaplan had been looking at when I first met him at Martin Green's party.

When he heard footsteps approaching, he turned and glanced at me over his shoulder. "Did you get him?" he asked.

"He's in the hospital. They're removing his spleen."

"I never thought about Kaplan being involved," Green said. "It irks me that he suckered me that badly." Then he was quiet, taking a long drag on his cigarette.

"When do you go to Victoria?" I asked.

"Chrysler Air was all booked up. I go first thing tomorrow morning."

There was another brief silence between us. "Aren't you going to hassle me about not pressing charges?" Green asked after a pause. "Your friends were ripped about it."

"I don't give a damn what you do with Martinson," I said.

"You don't?" Green sounded surprised.

"I'm a homicide detective," I told him.

"So?"

"So Kaplan and Martinson are only two of the nine. One or more of those other seven is a killer. That's who I want. Have you identified any of the others?"

"Only one. I caught him red-handed and fired his ass."

"Who was that? Harry Campbell?"

Martin Green looked at me, startled. "How'd you find that out?"

"How doesn't much matter. Think back to when you were up on the building with Angie Dixon," I continued. "Is there a chance that someone up there could have overheard her agree to give you the tapes?"

For a moment Green said nothing, then as the

realization dawned on him, he nodded, his mouth hardening into a grim line. "He was her partner, wasn't he?"

I nodded.

"Right off-hand, I'd say the chances are one hundred percent that he must have been listening."

"And is that crew working overtime again tomorrow?" I asked.

He nodded. "They start at six-thirty. If you want me to, I'll be only too happy to go along and point him out."

CHAPTER 24

I DIDN'T WANT TO GIVE WATTY ANY AMMUNITION
about my not being a team player. Martin Green and
I walked over to the Labor Temple and picked up
Harry Campbell's address. When we got back to my
apartment, I called Manny Davis at home, told him
what was up, and gave him Harry's address in Edmonds just north of Seattle proper. He said to hold
tight, that either he or Kramer would get back to me.

As soon as Ralph Ames caught wind of what was
going on, he went into the kitchen and started a pot
of coffee. He brought the pot and three cups on a
tray into the living room.

"Looks like it could be a long night," he said,
handing me a cup.

I accepted it gratefully, but I was watching the
phone, waiting for it to ring. Willing it to ring.

It did. Finally. Two cups of coffee later. But it
wasn't Manny or Kramer. "Sergeant Watkins here,
Beau. How's it going?"

"How the hell should I know how it's going? I've

been sitting here for forty-five minutes, cooling my heels, and waiting for someone to get back to me."

"There wasn't time."

"What do you mean, there wasn't time?"

"We had to get a warrant and negotiate a peace treaty with the Edmonds Police."

"Wait one fucking minute here! Do you mean to tell me Kramer and Davis have gone up to Edmonds to pick him up?"

"Kramer was still here working. He took off as soon as we had the warrant. Said he'd pick Manny up on his way north."

"What about me?"

"I already told you, Beau. There wasn't time. We were afraid Campbell might get wind of what had happened to Kaplan and take off. Besides, the doc says Kaplan should be coming out of sedation about now. I thought I'd send you up to Virginia Mason to talk to him."

"Talk to Kaplan!" I sputtered. "You mean . . ."

"Look," Watty interrupted. "I'm giving this one to Manny and Kramer. And if you know what's good for you, you will too. I had a chat with Kramer while we were waiting. You let them take credit for this and he won't file a grievance on the other."

"In other words, blackmail."

"Let's just say tit for tat," Watty responded. "Kaplan's up in Virginia Mason. Go see him, Beau. And let this be a lesson to you."

I flung down the phone. Ralph Ames and Martin Green had been chatting quietly on the window seat. They both looked up. "What's the matter?" Ames asked.

"I've just been screwed, blued, and tattooed. Without a kiss."

"What's that supposed to mean?"

"I'm on my way to Virginia Mason."

"Want me to drive?" he asked.

"No thanks. Believe me. I'm stone-cold sober!"

It was almost two o'clock in the morning when I walked up to the door of Don Kaplan's room in Virginia Mason Hospital. A police guard was standing by outside.

"He's awake," he told me. "One of the nurses was just in talking to him."

I pushed open the door. Don Kaplan lay in the bed, his eyes fixed on a flickering screen of a television set on the wall at his feet. He glanced over at me, and then turned back to the old movie.

"I want to see my lawyer," he said.

"You'll need one, you son of a bitch. By the time we finish talking to the prosecutor, we're going to nail you for murder every bit as hard as if you'd pulled the trigger yourself."

Kaplan turned and looked at me. "I want my lawyer."

Turning on my heel, I stalked out of the room. The threat had sounded good, but I wondered if we'd be able to make it stick.

There was an ambulance coming up Boren and I waited for it to pass. It was headed for Harborview. After a moment's hesitation, I followed it. There was no longer any reason not to tell Linda Decker what was happening.

The nurses' station was empty when I got to the ninth floor. I could see a flurry of activity down the hallway a door or two. The folding chair in the hall-way outside Jimmy Rising's room was empty. With an eerie sense of foreboding, I stepped to the door and pushed it open.

The room was dimly lit. The thermos and the lunch pail sat on a table near Jimmy Rising's head. He seemed to be asleep. I started toward the waiting room, thinking Linda might be there, when I ran into the guard. He was coming out of a rest room, zipping his fly.

"Where's Linda Decker?" I asked.

"Who are you?"

"Beaumont. Detective Beaumont from homicide."

"She left just a few minutes ago."

"Where'd she go?"

"The chaplain came and got her. I guess they were going to his office."

A nurse came bustling down the hall. She had to walk around us. "Excuse me," I said, "but where's the chaplain's office?"

"On the first floor. Why do you need to know?"

"I'm looking for Linda Decker. According to the guard here, she just left with the chaplain. They went down to his office."

"His?" the nurse asked, frowning.

"His," I repeated. Maybe she wasn't awake. "The chaplain's office."

"But the night duty chaplain is a woman," she said.

A hard knot of fear lumped in my gut. I turned on the guard. "What did this guy look like?"

The guard shrugged. "Fairly tall. Well-built for a minister, I thought."

"Did he say anything?"

"Something about her kids. I don't know exactly."

The nurse had gone on into the nurses' station and was studying a chart. "Can you call the chaplain's office?" I asked.

She looked annoyed, but she picked up the phone, dialed a number, and handed the receiver to me. A woman answered. "Lucille Kenmore. How may I help you?"

"You're the chaplain?" I asked.

"Yes, I am."

"Did you just send someone up for Linda Decker on the ninth floor?"

"No, I certainly didn't. I'm involved in a conference right now. If you could just leave your number . . ."

I handed the phone back to the nurse. My mind was racing. If the person who came for Linda Decker wasn't from the chaplain's office, then it was someone who had lied to the guard to gain access.

I turned to the guard. "How long ago did they leave?"

"Not that long ago. A few minutes maybe. I'm surprised you didn't run into them in the elevator."

The nurse was looking at me. "Is there a problem?"

"Do you have a phone number for Jimmy Rising's sister?"

"Yes, but . . ."

"No buts. Get it for me and get it fast. She may have been taken out of here against her will."

The guard shook his head, looking skeptical. "I doubt that. She knew the guy. She called him by name."

"What name?"

"Harry."

Harry Campbell. Shit! A wave of gooseflesh washed down my legs. My guess was that somehow Campbell had stumbled onto the fact that we were after him and he had decided to buy himself a little insurance. If one hostage was good, three would be better.

I wheeled on the nurse, who still hadn't moved. "Get me that number and get it *now!*" I barked.

"This is highly irregular."

"Look, lady, don't you understand? Lives are at stake!"

That finally jarred her loose. She took a metal-covered chart from its place on the counter and ran her finger down the first page. "Here it is," she said. "Would you like me to dial it for you?"

When she handed me the receiver I could hear a phone ringing at the other end. It was on its sixth ring when someone finally answered, a woman's voice still thick and groggy with sleep.

"Is Linda there?" I asked.

"No. Oh, wait. Maybe she came in and I didn't hear her."

"But this is where she's staying?"

"Yes, but she's been at the hospital most of the time."

"Are her kids there?"

"Yes, but . . ."

"Listen to me, and listen very carefully. My name's Beaumont, Detective J. P. Beaumont with the Seattle Police."

"Oh, I remember you, Detective Beaumont. I'm Sandy. Remember? From micrographics."

That was almost more than I could have hoped for—someone I knew. I wouldn't have to start the explanations from scratch. "Sandy," I said, "you've got to get those kids out of there."

"But they're asleep."

"Listen. I only have time to say this once. Wake them up. Get them out of the house. Where do you live?"

"On the back side of Queen Anne Hill just a few blocks from Northwest Center," she answered. "I usually walk to work."

"Load those kids into your car. You do have a car, don't you?"

"Yes."

"Take them somewhere, anywhere. My place. Do you know where Belltown Terrace is at Second and Broad?"

"I've driven past it."

"Take the kids there. Now. Call my apartment. A man named Ames will answer. Tell him I told you to come there and wait, understand?"

"But what's the rush?"

"I can't explain now, Sandy, but hurry. Please. Give me your address."

Sandy Carson's street address was on 13th. I took it down and then dropped both the phone and the note into the mystified guard's hand. "Call 911," I ordered. "Have them send a squad car to this address. No lights and no sirens, got that? Tell them to wait for me there." I headed for the elevator.

"Yes, but . . ."

"And get hold of Sergeant Watkins. Give him a message for me. Tell him that if Kramer and Davis are still in Edmonds, they're barking up the wrong goddamned tree. That's where they need to be. The address in your hand."

The elevator door slid shut behind me. The ride was surprisingly quick. It went all the way from the ninth floor to the bottom without stopping for anyone else. I couldn't believe my luck. As soon as I got on the street, though, I realized I'd screwed up. I had no idea what kind of car Harry Campbell might be driving, and I had no way of finding out. Once more I wished I had taken Ames' advice and installed a cellular phone in the 928.

The engine of the Porsche roared to life when I turned the key. Pulling a fast U-turn on Jefferson, I headed back toward Boren. The lights ahead of me turned green as I started down the hill. Fortunately, there weren't any stray pedestrians. And no traffic cops, either. I was doing sixty when I had to slow down for the Y at Stewart.

There was a car ahead of me, and I just made the yellow arrow onto Denny Way. The lights had been with me from the top of the hill. I knew I was making incredibly good time, but all the speed in the world would be meaningless unless Harry Campbell was going where I thought he was going.

On Denny Way my luck with the traffic came to an end. There was a car, an older-model Datsun, poking along in the left-hand lane ahead of me, and a Chevron gasoline tanker tooling along at my side. I flashed my high beams at the Datsun. Instead of moving to the right out of the way, it slowed, swerved toward the left, and straddled the yellow traffic divider in the middle of the roadway without leaving enough room between it and the tanker for me to pass.

Just then the driver's door flew open and a body fell out of the front seat of the Datsun, rolling over and over into the oncoming lane. My steel-belted radials smoked to a stop as I stood on the brakes, and the driver of the tanker blared his horn. Suddenly the body on the street rose to its feet and came scrambling toward me, arms waving frantically. I recognized Linda Decker's face as she grabbed desperately for my door.

"Please help me," she gasped, wrenching my door open. "Help me. He's got a gun."

"Get in, quick," I told her. "He won't get away."

She stopped and stared at me. "It's you!" she exclaimed. "How did you find me?"

"Never mind. Get in the car, goddamnit."

The truck driver had stopped half a block away and now he too came dashing up to the Porsche. "Lady, are you all right? Is something the matter?"

By then Linda was finally moving toward the rider's door. I leaned out the window and called to the truck driver. "Do you have a CB in that rig?"

He nodded. "Sure."

"Notify Seattle P.D. There's a fugitive in that Datsun up there. His name's Harry Campbell. He's armed and dangerous. What's your license number, Linda?"

She was crying, but she managed to choke out an answer. I started to relay it to the driver, but he waved me on. "Got it," he said and started back for his truck while I rammed the gas pedal to the floor and we shot forward. Ahead of us, the taillights from the

Datsun bounced back over the median and into traffic. Campbell was still heading west on Denny.

"He said he had my kids, that they were down in the car. That's why I went with him. He wanted me to drive him to Canada, using us as cover. He took me down the stairs," she added. "He was afraid we might meet somebody in the elevator."

"He was right," I said grimly. "You would have."

"I thought he'd done something to the kids, but when I found out they weren't in the car, that he wanted me to drive him to the house, I decided I'd try to get away from him before we got there."

"You did great," I told her. "And the kids are fine. I told Sandy Carson to take them to my place."

"Thank you," Linda murmured.

"Glad to be of service."

The Datsun was a few blocks ahead of us, but I didn't try to close the gap. Instead, I concentrated on maintaining visual contact. That was enough. No heroics. Not with Linda Decker in the car. Patrol cars were on their way. I'd let some Joe Blow patrol officer bring the guy to ground. At least it wouldn't be Detective Paul Kramer. Let him put that in his pipe and smoke it.

"But how did you know what was happening?" Linda Decker asked. "How did you know where he'd go?"

"I got lucky for a change," I told her. "For once in my life, I flat got lucky."

CHAPTER 25

A ROOKIE FRESH OUT OF THE ACADEMY ACTUALLY MADE the arrest. That was fine with me. As long as it wasn't Paul Kramer putting the cuffs on Harry Campbell's wrists, I didn't much care who did.

Ralph Ames had been far more right than he knew when he said it was going to be a long night. The sun was already up by the time Linda Decker and I left the department to go back to Belltown Terrace. And it was after five when she and Sandy Carson packed the two sleeping kids down to Sandy's car for the short ride home.

I was sound asleep at six when the phone rang. It was Linda Decker. The hospital had just called her. Jimmy Rising was dead.

He had been so badly burned, and the road back would have been so tough, that I couldn't help thinking he was better off, but I felt sick just the same. If there was anyone Upstairs keeping score, the good guys had lost big in this particular skirmish.

The next time I saw Linda Decker, it was the afternoon of Jimmy Rising's funeral at a cemetery somewhere in the wilds of Bellevue. She came over and stood beside me as they lowered Jimmy's simple casket into the ground.

"They're in there with him, you know," she said softly.

"Pardon me?"

"The thermos and the lunch pail you gave him. If heaven's perfect, Jimmy will have a job to go to every day. He'll need them."

Linda Decker walked away from me then. Her kids wanted her for something, and I was glad she left. I wouldn't have been able to talk for the lump in my throat.

As I started back toward where the cars were parked, Martin Green fell into step beside me. I had seen him in the funeral chapel, but we hadn't spoken.

"She's a gutsy little thing," he said, nodding toward Linda's retreating figure. "Did you know she's coming back to work at the hall?"

"No. I hadn't heard."

"It took some selling. I finally talked her into it. The union needs women like her," Green continued. "The good ones. The ones with some backbone."

"She's long on backbone all right," I said, remembering how Linda Decker had looked in Pe Ell when she'd been staring down at me over the barrel of a gun. "I wouldn't cross her if I were you."

Martin Green chuckled. "Don't worry," he said. "I already figured that out."

So maybe Ironworkers Local 165 will turn out to be a more perfect union after all. Good for Martin Green. Good for Linda Decker. I'm sure she'll do a

fine job of raising those kids no matter what kind of
work she does, but it'll be easier to do it by herself
on the kind of money she'll make working construction than it would be on what she'd earn tending bar in some backwater like Pe Ell.

About that time I caught sight of Linda's two kids
standing together next to the funeral parlor's lim-
ousine, waiting for their mother. Jason was holding
his little sister's hand protectively. As I got closer to
the children, I could hear they were arguing.

"Is too," Jason insisted.

"Is not," Allison responded. When I walked across
the parking lot to get in the Porsche, they followed
at a respectful distance.

"See there?" Jason announced archly as soon as I
opened the door to the 928. "It is too him. I told you."

When I turned on the ignition, the cellular phone
let me know I'd had a call. The readout didn't tell
me who had called, but I knew. Ralph Ames was the
only person so far who had the number. I called him
back and told him to meet me at the Doghouse for
lunch.

There wasn't much traffic on the bridge, and Lake
Washington was as still and blue as the sky above it.
I drove along and thought about Harry Campbell.
He had turned out to be a wormy shit. As soon as he
saw the writing on the wall, he spilled his guts, thinking that by naming names first and by agreeing to
turn state's evidence, he might be able to work himself some kind of deal. That remains to be seen. It's
up to the prosecutor's office. Once we turn creeps
over to them, it's out of our hands.

According to both Campbell and Martinson,

Don Kaplan had been the brains of the outfit, all the while seeming to be working the problem right along with Martin Green. Which just goes to show what a hell of a good judge of character I am. Martin Green wasn't the only one snowed by Don Kaplan. So was J. P. Beaumont.

It was Kaplan who had discovered the leak and sicced Harry Campbell on Logan Tyree and Angie Dixon in a futile attempt at damage control to cover up disclosure of those worthless tapes. In the state of Washington, conspiracy to commit murder is as good as doing the job yourself. In a year or so, maybe Don Kaplan and Harry Campbell will be occupying neighboring cells on Death Row in Walla Walla.

Ames was waiting when I got to the Doghouse. He had already ordered—for both of us. Wanda brought me my bacon and eggs, accompanied by a knowing smile. "I saw your friend's picture in the paper this morning," she said.

"What friend is that?" I asked.

"You know. The movie star."

"What about him?"

"He got married in Las Vegas yesterday to some woman he met while he was here in Seattle."

"Derrick Parker got married?" I asked incredulously, not quite trusting my ears. "You've got to be kidding!"

Wanda shook her head. "Hold on, I think I can find the picture."

Sure enough, when she brought it, there was Derrick Parker, grinning from ear to ear. Next to him stood a radiant Merrilee Jackson.

I didn't say a word. Who the hell am I to criticize whirlwind courtships?

When we got up to leave, there was a man waiting for a table. Somewhat oversized, he was wearing a black-and-white T-shirt, I'M FAT BUT YOU'RE UGLY, the shirt proclaimed. I CAN GO ON A DIET.

I'm sure Ralph Ames thought I was crazy when I burst out laughing.

"What's so funny?" he asked.

I nodded toward the shirt. "It reminds me of Detective Kramer and J. P. Beaumont."

"How's that?"

"Kramer's probably still down at the department sopping up every bit of glory he can muster."

"So?"

"So maybe I am a playboy cop, and maybe Kramer will turn out to be Chief some day when he grows up, but I'm like that fat man who can go on a diet. I can always quit. Anytime I want to."

Ralph Ames looked at me speculatively. "Anytime," he agreed, nodding. "It's up to you."

Don't miss a single one of *New York Times* bestselling author J. A. Jance's novels featuring Seattle private investigator J. P. Beaumont, whom *Booklist* calls "a star attraction."

UNTIL PROVEN GUILTY

The little girl was a treasure who should have been cherished, not murdered. She was only five—too young to die—and Homicide Detective J. P. Beaumont of the Seattle Police Department isn't going to rest until her killer pays dearly. But Beaumont's own obsessions and demons could prove dangerous companions in a murky world of blind faith and religious fanaticism. And he is about to find out that he himself is the target of a twisted passion . . . and a love that can kill.

INJUSTICE FOR ALL

It was a scene right out of a Hollywood "slasher" movie—a beautiful woman's terrified screams piercing the air, a dead body sprawled at her feet, blood staining the pristine sands of a Washington beach. But the blood is real, and the victim won't be rising when a director yells, "Cut!" In one horrific instant, a homicide detective's well-earned holiday has become a waking nightmare. Suddenly, a lethal brew of passion, madness, and politics threatens to do more than poison J. P. Beaumont's sleep—it's dragging the dedicated Seattle cop into the path of a killer whose dark hunger is rapidly becoming an obsession.

TRIAL BY FURY

"Jance delivers a devilish page-turner."
People

The dead body discovered in a Seattle Dumpster was shocking enough—but equally disturbing was the manner of death. The victim, a high-school coach, had been lynched, leaving behind a very pregnant wife to grieve over his passing, and to wonder what dark secrets he took to his grave. A Homicide detective with twenty years on the job, J. P. Beaumont knows this case is a powder keg and he fears where this investigation will lead him. Because the answers lie on the extreme lethal edge of passion and hate, where the wrong kind of love can breed the most terrible brand of justice.

TAKING THE FIFTH

There are many bizarre and terrible ways to die. Seattle Homicide Detective J.P. Beaumont thought he had seen them all—until he saw this body, its wounds, and the murder weapon: an elegant woman's shoe, its stiletto heel gruesomely caked with blood. The evidence is shocking and unsettling, even for a man who prowls the shadows for a living, for it suggests that savagery is not the exclusive domain of the predatory male. And the scent of a stylish killer is pulling Beaumont into a world of drugs, corruption, and murder to view close-up a cinematic dream at its most nightmarish . . . and lethal.

IMPROBABLE CAUSE

"Jance brings the reader along with suspense, wit, surprise, and intense feeling."
Huntsville Times

Perhaps it was fitting justice: a dentist who enjoyed inflicting pain was murdered in his own chair. The question is not who wanted Dr. Frederick Nielsen dead, but rather who of the many finally reached the breaking point. The sordid details of this case, with its shocking revelations of violence, cruelty, and horrific sexual abuse, would be tough for any investigator to stomach. But for Seattle Homicide Detective J. P. Beaumont, the most damning piece of the murderous puzzle will shake him to his very core—because what will be revealed to him is nothing less than the true meaning of unrepentant evil.

A MORE PERFECT UNION

"In the elite company of
Sue Grafton and Patricia Cornwell."
Flint Journal

A shocking photo screamed from the front pages
of the tabloids—the last moments of a life captured
for all the world to see. The look of sheer terror
eternally frozen on the face of the doomed woman
indicated that her fatal fall from an upper story of
an unfinished Seattle skyscraper was no desperate
suicide—and that look will forever haunt Homicide
Detective J. P. Beaumont. But his hunt for answers
and justice is leading to more death, and to dark
and terrible secrets scrupulously guarded by men of
steel behind the locked doors of a powerful union
that extracts its dues payments in blood.

DISMISSED WITH PREJUDICE

"She can move from an exciting,
dangerous scene on one page
to a sensitive, personal,
touching moment on the next."
Chicago Tribune

The blood at the scene belies any suggestion of an "honorable death." Yet, to the eyes of the Seattle police, a successful Japanese software magnate died exactly as he wished—and by his own hand, according to the ancient rite of *seppuku*. Homicide Detective J. P. Beaumont can't dismiss what he sees as an elaborate suicide, however, not when something about it makes his flesh crawl. Because small errors in the ritual suggest something darker: a killer who will go to extraordinary lengths to escape detection—a fiend with a less traditional passion . . . for cold-blooded murder.

MINOR IN POSSESSION

"One of the country's
most popular mystery writers."
Portland Oregonian

All manner of sinners and sufferers come to the rehab ranch in Arizona when they hit rock bottom. For Seattle Detective J. P. Beaumont, there is a deeper level of Hell here: being forced to room with teenage drug dealer Joey Rothman. An all-around punk, Joey deserves neither pity nor tears—until he is murdered by a bullet fired from Beaumont's gun. Someone has set Beau up brilliantly for a long and terrifying fall, dragging the alcoholic ex-cop into a conspiracy of blood and lies that could cost him his freedom . . . and his life.

PAYMENT IN KIND

"Any story by Jance is a joy."
Chattanooga Times

It looks like a classic crime of passion to Detective J. P. Beaumont: two corpses found lovingly entwined in a broom closet of the Seattle School District building. The prime suspect, Pete Kelsey, admits his slain spouse was no novice at adultery, yet he swears he had nothing to do with the brutal deaths of the errant school official and her clergyman-turned-security guard companion. Beau believes him, but there's something the much sinned-upon widower's not telling—and that spells serious trouble still to come. Because the secret that Pete's protecting is even hotter than extramarital sex . . . and it could prove more lethal than murder.

WITHOUT DUE PROCESS

> "Jance paints a vibrant picture,
> creating characters so real you want to
> reach out and hug—or strangle—them.
> Her dialogue always rings true, and the cases
> unravel in an interesting, yet never contrived way."
> *Cleveland Plain Dealer*

What kind of monster would break into a man's home at night, then slaughter him and his family? The fact that the dead man was a model cop who was loved and respected by all only intensifies the horror. But the killer missed someone: a five-year-old boy who was hiding in the closet. Now word is being leaked out that the victim was "dirty." But Seattle P. D. Homicide Detective J. P. Beaumont isn't about to let anyone drag a murdered friend's reputation through the muck. And he'll put his own life on the firing line on the gang-ruled streets to save a terrified child who knows too much to live.

FAILURE TO APPEAR

"Jance's artistry keeps the reader
guessing—and caring."
Publishers Weekly

A desperate father's search for his runaway daughter
has led him to the last place he ever expected to find
her: backstage at the Oregon Shakespeare Festival.
But the murders in this dazzling world of make-
believe are no longer mere stagecraft, and the blood
is all too real. The hunt for his child has plunged
former Seattle Homicide Detective J. P. Beaumont
into a bone-chilling drama of revenge, greed, and
butchery, where innocents are made to suffer in
perverse and terrible ways. And many more young
lives are at stake, unless he can uncover the villain
of the piece before the final, deadly curtain falls.

LYING IN WAIT

"[Jance] will keep the reader up nights."
Pittsburgh Post-Gazette

Else Didriksen is no longer the beautiful, troubled teenager who disappeared from Detective J. P. Beaumont's life thirty years earlier. Now she is a homicide victim's widow—frightened, desperate, and trapped in a web of murderous greed that reaches out from a time of unrelenting terror. And the dark, deadly secrets that hold Else prisoner threaten to ensnare Beau and new partner, Sue Danielson, as well—and to rock their world in ways they never dreamed possible.

NAME WITHHELD

"[Her work] can be compared to the work of
Tony Hillerman and Mary Higgins Clark.
J. A. Jance can stand tall
even in that fine company."
Washington Times

There are those who don't deserve to live—and the
corpse floating in Elliot Bay may have been one of
those people. Not surprisingly, many individuals—
too many, in fact—are eager to take responsibility
for the brutal slaying of the hated biotech executive whose alleged crimes ranged from the illegal
trading of industrial secrets to rape. For Seattle
Detective J. P. Beaumont—who's drowning in his
own life-shattering problems—a case of seemingly
justifiable homicide has sinister undertones, drawing the haunted policeman into a corporate nightmare of double deals, savage jealousies, and real
blood spilled far too easily, as it leads him closer to a
killer he's not sure he wants to find.

BREACH OF DUTY

"A thrill . . . One of Jance's best."
Milwaukee Journal-Sentinel

The Seattle that Beau knew as a young policeman is disappearing. The city is awash in the aromas emanating from a glut of coffee bars, the neighborhood outside his condo building has sprouted gallery upon gallery, and even his long cherished diner has evolved into a trendy eatery for local hipsters. But the glam is strictly surface, for the grit under the city's fingernails is caked with blood. Beau and his new partner, Sue Danielson, a struggling single parent, are assigned the murder of an elderly woman torched to death in her bed. As their investigation proceeds, Beau and Sue become embroiled in a perilous series of events that will leave them and their case shattered—and for Beau nothing will ever be the same again.

BIRDS OF PREY

"[A] fast-paced thriller . . . Vivid and well-drawn."
Tampa Tribune

The Starfire Breeze steams its way north toward the Gulf of Alaska, buffeted by crisp sea winds blowing down from the Arctic. Those on board are seeking peace, relaxation, adventure, escape. But there is no escape here in this place of unspoiled natural majesty. Because terror strolls the decks even in the brilliant light of day . . . and death is a conspicuous, unwelcome passenger. And a former Seattle policeman—a damaged Homicide detective who has come to heal from fresh, stinging wounds—will find that the grim ghosts pursuing him were not left behind . . . as a pleasure cruise gone horribly wrong carries him inexorably into lethal, ever-darkening waters.